THE BLUES

THE AUTHENTIC NARRATIVE OF
MY MUSIC AND CULTURE

CHRIS THOMAS KING

CHICAGO
REVIEW
PRESS

First edition

Published by Chicago Review Press Incorporated

814 North Franklin Street

Chicago, Illinois 60610

ISBN 978-1-64160-444-4

Library of Congress Control Number: 2021933190

Interior design: Jonathan Hahn

Printed in the United States of America

5 4 3 2 1

To my son, Dylan

CONTENTS

AUTHOR'S NOTE

MY MUSIC, THE BLUES, is the most influential and revolutionary music in the pantheon of Western culture. Yet those who originally introduced the blues to the world have been marginalized and exploited; recast as persons one should fear, loathe, or pity, with few exceptions. The blues was usurped the instant it could be monetized by the dominant culture. I decry their narrative of my music and culture therewith as subterfuge.

In 1928, Abbe Niles, a White cultural tastemaker of Negro music and the ghostwriter of W. C. Handy's 1941 biography, said, "In general, writers and speakers on [blues], friendly and unfriendly, don't know their subject, and the people who know it best, can't write."[1] Well, it is time the world read a narrative from someone who, as Abbe Niles said, "know it best," and dare I say, with great humility, can read and write.

My purpose for writing a Reformation of the blues, or *bleus*, is not to narrowly define it, but to broaden its understanding; to provide the greater context it has been denied since its conception. I will analyze and deconstruct popularly held beliefs about the blues' place of origin, its definition, indigenous meaning, and its cultural influences.

PROLOGUE

In the summer of 1999, a new millennium loomed. Tabby's Blues Box and Heritage Hall, my dad's famous ramshackle juke joint—which many deemed an immoral antediluvian relic—was targeted for demolition to make way for a road-widening project. Rumors predicting the demise of Tabby's Blues Box, one of the last real juke joints in America, had been commonplace since it opened in 1979. Yet, those rumors had always been greatly exaggerated—until now. Gentrification was knocking at the door. The proverbial fat lady was approaching the beer-scented microphone. The city's bulldozers were out front revving their engines. The obit of the Blues Box was written on the bathroom walls. Indeed, the time had come for the alleged "Devil's Music Hall" to face the executioner. Superstitious villagers, pitchforks in hand, gathered to witness its last rites read aloud. In hushed moral condemnation, they gawked, as the hangman readied his noose.

That summer, city officials went public with their devised plan to ease downtown traffic by razing Tabby's Blues Box and Heritage Hall. They proposed a bill to build an overpass over a nearby railroad track that would arch directly over my father's juke joint. "In case there's a train derailment, people would have another way out of downtown," said Fred Raiford, the public works director, to a reporter for the *Advocate*.

There hadn't been a train derailment in the area since the Blues Box opened twenty years ago. Many people in the Black community could not understand why the overpass required the loss of a major landmark and historical attraction—a loss that would further devastate the frail neighborhood.

"We cannot always put infrastructure improvements on the people who can least afford the improvements," said Cedric B. Glover, a state representative from the community, expressing his dissatisfaction with the plan on the evening news. "If the burden is placed on Rose and Thomas café"—a Black-owned mom-and-pop soul food joint next door—"and Tabby's Blues Box, we haven't gained as much as we think," he said into the camera.

Baton Rouge voters, after much consternation, approved a tax to pay for the road project. The road widening of North Boulevard, which many deemed an ominous harbinger of gentrification, was set to level every building remaining on the once burgeoning Negro thoroughfare, the conspicuous exception being the Masonic Temple Theater across the street. The project would cost about seven million dollars.

The development's main concern was the Kansas City Southern Railroad Line a block away from Tabby's Blues Box. The construction would also widen North Boulevard between North Tenth and North Nineteenth Streets into four lanes. The bridge would run above the Griffon building, built in the 1920s, which housed both Tabby's Blues Box and Rose and Thomas Café. Everyone understood that if the city bulldozed North Boulevard, supposedly to ease future traffic, the historic Black business district would be no more.

My family, along with other North Boulevard proprietors, received a letter from the director of the Department of Public Works. We were invited to a Metro Council meeting on the third floor of a governmental building at 222 St. Louis Street the following Tuesday, July 28.

When I arrived at the adjudication hearing with my father, every seat in the sweltering room was taken. The assembly was boisterous, the tension thick. The attendees were split down the middle. Some wanted to preserve our juke joint and the character of the neighborhood. Others urged demolition, demanding the officials' plans move forward.

When it was my turn to speak from the podium, using notes I'd prepared the night before, I talked about Tabby's contributions to the city's culture and economy. I argued that our juke joint had been undervalued. I had recently performed in Washington, DC, on a bill with Clarence "Gatemouth" Brown. In my hotel, I'd noticed a tourism ad for Baton Rouge. The ad featured a picture of a crawfish, a floating casino, and a picture of Tabby's Blues Box, "Home of the blues." I couldn't understand why our hall couldn't be interwoven into the city's plans for the future. I urged they consider the iconic juke joint as a potential key attraction in a redeveloped downtown.

I was unable to persuade the myopic officials to reconsider. I felt helpless. The diagnosis for my beloved Blues Box was terminal. My grief was the type reserved for the death of a family member.

"He's given so much over the years," I said of my dad to a local news reporter covering the event. "For the city to just bulldoze him down, I can't even believe that they would do that. I still can't believe it's gonna happen."

Wire services picked up the story. Articles of Tabby's demise ran in major newspapers across the country. In Europe—the most lucrative festival market for blues musicians—blues magazines covered the looming raze as though a Picasso or van Gogh was under threat from ignorant torch-wielding villagers. Rien Wisse, the editor of long-respected Dutch magazine *Block*, brought over a dozen European fans to Tabby's for a pilgrimage. He expressed to my family how it was a pity the city was razing our club. He said he didn't believe Louisiana knew or appreciated its rich legacy.

"It's one of the nicest clubs and one of the most original clubs in the South," Wisse said to *The Advocate* during his visit. "If it wasn't for Tabby, the blues in Baton Rouge would have been almost dead."

Many music aficionados shared his sentiment. There was the possibility of Tabby's moving to a new location; however, Rien Wisse believed, like many devoted fans, that the old, beautifully *weird* Americana Tabby's Blues Box represented would be lost in a brand-new location.

Later, word came to me at my New Orleans home—from my family in Baton Rouge—that Dad's eviction was near. He was planning a farewell jam and wanted me to attend. On the day of Tabby's last jam, I packed my guitar and went to visit him at the Blues Box to pay my respects. I wanted to catch up with my father during the calm hours before the throng of musicians and supporters arrived, knowing it would be our final chance to talk before eviction.

The narrow, rectangular-shaped building was nearly empty when I entered. Only a few regulars sat nursing drinks at the L-shaped bar. The familiar haze of cigarette smoke hung in the dimly lit room. The bar's tall antique wooden shelves, decorated with Christmas tree lights, were scarcely stocked with the usual juke joint commodities: near empty off-brand whiskey bottles, cartons of cigarettes, and jars of pickled pig's feet. The colorful old jukebox, the soundtrack to many fond memories over the years, was illuminated against the far wall. Like an open scrapbook, pictures of local blues legends taped to the plastered walls—including my dad, "Rockin'" Tabby—reminded me of the glory days of the Blues Box.

I found Dad sitting alone at a table near the bar and joined him. "Everything happens for the better," Dad said, wistfully. "This place has served its purpose. So many musicians learned to play here, went on to become band leaders, recording artists. It opened doors for all the old musicians to get a chance to come and be feted, be on festivals, and the young people, too."

As he spoke, I surveyed the rows of faded placards along the walls featuring guitar pickers who'd played the club over the years. Some had passed on, while others were still carrying on in the spirit of the Blues Box.

"The time has come to say farewell," Dad said.

While listening to him talk so calmly about the tragedy, I questioned, why am I so anguished? Was it because Tabby was from the old school, content to go along to get along? Was I some kind of agitator, using the Blues Box as a rallying cry for some larger grievance? No, I didn't have a hidden agenda. I had no ulterior motive. I simply believed it to be the end of something good.

For some, Tabby's had been a reminder of a crude past, best forgotten. The demolition would be a victory for moralists and old-time racists, who, from the start, never approved of our risqué interracial late-night Hoodoo Parties. I was sixteen when Dad founded the club in 1979 to reclaim Louisiana's blues heritage. Over the years, the Blues Box had become an iconic hall representing a slice of Americana. Through the power of music and dance, Tabby's helped to bring our segregated community from post–civil rights movement era race riots to the door of America's promise and Martin Luther King's dream.

Later that night, we held an unspoken jazz funeral for the Blues Box. I had expected a somewhat somber event, but spirits were high. Drinks flowed. The music was intoxicating.

"Ain't never gon' be another place like this," Dad said between songs from the bandstand to a cheerful audience. "This the first heritage hall, this the first real blues club, in the state of Louisiana," he proclaimed to loud applause.

With everyone on their feet he sang one of his most requested songs, "I Love Big Fat Women." The upbeat refrain was a tongue-in-cheek anthem serenading voluptuous women. It never failed to pack the dance floor. I even grabbed someone and danced—a rare gesture for me—knowing it would be my last opportunity.

At the end of the night, the music fell silent. For all those who loved the Hoodoo Parties Tabby hosted weekly, the serendipitous social experiment was over. Our guitars and amplifiers were packed away for the final time. The glowing rainbow of Christmas lights decorating the bar went dark, closing the curtain on the most crucial era of my life. As I drove away, Tabby's Blues Box and Heritage Hall disappeared in my rearview mirror. I bid farewell to my beloved sanctuary.

Back in New Orleans, in the days and weeks that followed, I became disillusioned and aloof. All the friction, as I came of age under the watchful eye of my dad; all the weight and responsibility of carrying on the family business, was now water under the bridge. I'd become a wayfarer, adrift. Resigned to carry on and let bygones be bygones. Forced to live out of a frayed suitcase, I found refuge in nonstop touring, faceless fans, indistinguishable hotels, clubs, and festivals. The road became my new asylum.

I have pondered over the years what the loss of the club meant to the Black community. If only those Blues Box walls could talk; I imagined the stories it would tell. The seventy-something-year-old building had seen the neighborhood prosper after World War II. It had witnessed boycotts in the '50s and civil rights marches in the '60s. It was boarded up and left for dead following riots in the '70s. In the '80s, it came alive again with ringing guitars and the shuffling of happy feet. Couples had met for the first time on its dance floor and later married. Somehow, during the '90s, it survived the crack epidemic and gang warfare. All along, Tabby's had been a beacon. Now, in its final act, it would return to dust to make way for twenty-first-century gentrification, packaged as "progress."

Sadly, the knowledge of Tabby's Blues Box would be recorded only in the memories of those who experienced it. But, I thought, what about future generations? What about my son, Dylan? How would he ever know the story? How his grandfather's love of the blues shaped his father. I became queasy in the pit of my stomach with an urgency like I'd never experienced; an urge to tell my story. Moreover, to tell the authentic Creole story of the blues to my son, and anyone who would hear it.

African Americans of my generation turned their backs on the blues after it was redefined by White usurpers in the 1960s and '70s. We survived, ironically, thanks to White supporters. Today, the blues is a White musical genre, dominated by Whites on and off stage, a conundrum I've grappled with over the years. Consequently, to make sense of the whitewashing of my music and culture, I developed an interest in literature on the subject. What I read astonished me. The dehumanizing characterizations, misinformation, and lies about the musical tribe from which I ascend were disturbing. Based on such sophistry, it's no wonder Black people abandoned the blues.

The historiography of the blues was built by White sociologists, folklorists, and record collectors. Their recordings and documents are indispensable. Indeed, I commend them for preserving and documenting noncommercial aspects of my culture that may have otherwise gone unnoticed. Despite that, I have a big problem with their pseudosociological conclusions that were formed, in large part, by their own privileged status during the Jim Crow era when deciphering such artifacts. A critical examination of their books, articles, and personal journals revealed that nearly all held an astonishing amount of condescension toward their Negro subjects, whom they recast as exotic primitives and noble savages. Moreover, this motley crew, motivated by greed, purposely obfuscated the truth, replacing it instead with myths, fairy tales, and half-truths. As a consequence, I have been alienated from my own culture.

The blues was invented in the 1890s, by Black Creoles in New Orleans, Louisiana. Whites rebranded New Orleans blues, which preceded blues from the Mississippi Delta by more than two decades, "Dixieland jazz" in the early 1900s. The word *Dixieland*, in the Black psyche, connotes Confederate romanticism. The early rebrand and whitewash of the blues (there would be many others, swing, rock and roll, etc.) was an attempt to crown the Original Dixieland Jass [*sic*] Band, Sicilians from New Orleans, "Kings of the Blues." The band was led by a racist trumpeter, Nick LaRocca, the son of poor Sicilian immigrants. Following the Original Dixieland Jazz Band's popular 1917 debut "Livery Stable Blues"—a minstrel rip-off, minus the blackface, of Black Creole artistry—ODJB fan clubs sprung up around the country. By the 1930s, all classic New Orleans blues innovations were rebranded "Dixieland Jazz," crowning LaRocca and dispossessing blues originators Buddy Bolden, Jelly Roll Morton, King Oliver, Bunk Johnson, Lonnie Johnson, and Louis Armstrong. Moreover, the Confederate rebranding of the blues acted as a repellent to Black musicians everywhere.

Erecting "Dixieland jazz" was similar to erecting Confederate monuments to Robert E. Lee or Jefferson Davis in the American psyche. Such maneuvers were designed to marginalize Black achievement and perpetuate White supremacy. Dropping the word Dixieland but retaining the mindless word *jazz*, which has no African or Creole meaning, was similar to my high school dropping Robert E. but retaining Lee, as in Lee High. It's just as offensive. According to pioneering blues clarinetist Sidney Bechet, "jazz" was what White folks called the blues. Trumpet legend Miles Davis would often scold critics for using the word jazz to describe his music. "It's a nigger word," Miles said of "jazz" to the *New York Times* in 1981.[1] Miles Davis believed the term *jazz* was used to diminish the important contribution blues made to the world of music because it was identified with Blacks.

It is extremely important formerly colonized peoples wrestle the power of definition away from postcolonizers.

To call my gumbo *soup* is an insult. It is neither chicken nor seafood soup. It's gumbo. The Anglicization of our gumbo would be devastating, culturally. Gumbo would lose its African Creole meaning and cultural significance. Gumbo is a Creolization of a Bantu word for okra, *tchingombo* or *ochingombo*. Bantu is a language spoken in at least twenty-seven African countries including Angola, Cameroon, Congo, and Nigeria. The beautiful okra flower, its green pods essential to gumbo, is a relative of both cotton and hibiscus. Like the trumpet and the blues guitar, okra can be traced to Ancient Kemet (Egypt), where, it is believed, its earliest cultivation began around 2000 BC. Okra was then introduced to medieval Spain by African Moors before appearing in Louisiana in the 1700s, likely imported to the Spanish-French colony by enslaved Africans.[2]

To be sure, gumbo was nurtured by African women who incorporated a chocolate-colored French roux with herbs, added shellfish from the rivers and Gulf, then served it up with love and care over a steaming bowl of rice (another essential African import). Although gumbo's main ingredient okra is African in origin, gumbo is a Creole invention, same as the blues.

Yet, our greatest invention, *the blues,* has been Anglicized and stripped of its Creole meaning and cultural significance. The Louisiana Creole term *blues* (or *bleus*), the name the originators gave their musical invention in songs such as "Jelly Roll Blues," "West End Blues," "Basin Street Blues," "Buddy Bolden's Blues," "2:19 Blues," etc., celebrated subversion, discordance, and freedom of expression among Louisiana Blacks whose preordained underclass status, constitutionally, liberated them socially and musically. Blues mocked Victorian prudishness. It was a humanizing force that threatened to normalize Black sensuality.

White superiority is a fragile Anglo-Saxon creation, to which Black achievement, or equality, is wildly suppressed as though it were kryptonite. Race is neither biological nor scientific. There is no such thing as a White or Black race. Therefore, I prefer to use micro cultural distinctions such as Anglo or Creole when appropriate.[3]

Greeks, Poles, Hungarians, Slavs, Italians, Sicilians, and other non-Anglo Europeans who immigrated to America in the late 1800s and early 1900s were not accepted as "White," initially. Summarily, however, after adopting White Anglo-Saxon Protestant mores, and adhering to a stringent social contract of White supremacy, non-Anglo Europeans, such as the Sicilian Dixieland Jazz Band, were allowed to become White and enjoy all the exclusive privileges of "Whiteness" in the racial hierarchy of America. As for Blacks, who had been fighting for first-class citizenship for nearly four hundred years, there was no such reward, only the cruelty of Jim Crow.

Indeed, blues was an enlightened expression that boldly challenged the authority of the church by refusing to conform to its draconian "blue laws" intended to punish non-Christian behavior. For this, in old Francophone New Orleans, the blues was deemed *sacré bleu,* the devil's music. The word *blues* is a Creolized abbreviation of the French blaspheme *sacré dieu.* The musical expression began in defiance of Anglo American encroachment and subsequent annexation in the late 1800s of the proud way of life of Black Creoles, also known as Free People of Color.

More dangerously, as the blues spread to Chicago, Harlem, and beyond, it became a threat to Jim Crow ideology. The rebellious music captured the imagination of White youth—inspiring White girls and boys to want to fraternize with Black girls and boys. To dissuade White youth from embracing the blues, a concerted effort was launched across America in the 1920s to demonize it. Hence, forcing Black practitioners to avoid being labeled blues so they could get good paying jobs in respectable venues.

This demonization scenario was rinsed and repeated for each new generation of White teens in an attempt to stop them from being seduced by the "Tambourine Man." (A mythical blues charmer who danced in front of second-line brass bands playing his tambourine. Bob Dylan loosely immortalized the figure in song after attending Mardi Gras in New Orleans in 1964.)[4]

Meanwhile, the Blues Mafia, art dealers who brokered in Black musical "authenticity"—that is to say, in Negro *primitivism*—were portrayed as benevolent saviors of Black culture. But in reality, the loose consortium of White record collectors and researchers were driven by egotism, power, and avarice.

By 1984, following the release of my first single, "Soon This Morn'nin Blues," the Blues Mafia became my greatest antagonist. I realized early on that their primitive fantasies of what my music ought to be would only reinforce the ostensible perception of my inferiority. How could I adhere to dictates of such gatekeepers, and thus, represent the blues as I knew it to be? How I overcame this conundrum is only half the story. How to undo the damage of cultural colonialism and establish the first historically authentic blues narrative is the other.

1

MY CULTURE

"ALL RIGHT, THEN, I'LL GO TO HELL," said Huckleberry Finn, when he finally made the decision to betray his upbringing and steal away his enslaved friend Jim, even if it meant eternal damnation for his soul.[1] Like unruly Huck Finn, the blues did not want to be "sivilized" by society's polite manners, social graces, and racist religion. Huck and Jim "lit out" on the Mississippi, where they could be "free and satisfied."[2] Indeed, not long after Mark Twain romanticized life on the Mississippi River in the late nineteenth century, the sound of New Orleans Delta blues began steaming upriver carrying liberating ideas, trumpeting new pathways to freedom, and ultimately reshaping the musical landscape of the entire world.

New Orleans, Louisiana, is a delta built up over ninety million years by the Mississippi River. In geological terms, "a 'delta' is a pile of gravel, sand, and mud that is being dumped at the continent's edge at the mouth of its major river."[3] Although New Orleans, that beguiling music city where the blues was born, *is* the Mississippi Delta scientifically, it has been erased as the Mississippi Delta from the conscious mind. Beginning in the twentieth century, folklorists and sociologists successfully hypnotized the public's conscious to render New Orleans out of sight and out of mind whenever they hear the phrase *Mississippi Delta*.

The Great River, as the Mississippi was known to Native Americans, is the largest river in North America when combined with its tributaries the Missouri and Ohio Rivers. In *Life on the Mississippi* Mark Twain said, "The belief of the scientific people is that the mouth used to be at Baton Rouge, where the hills cease, and that the two hundred miles of land between there and the Gulf was built by the river."[4]

Indeed, the New Orleans Mississippi Delta is literally built from a mixture of ancestral North America, continental drift, a volcanic hotspot, an asteroid collision with Earth, frigid Ice Ages, and earthquakes.[5] The eroding sediments, including silt, sand, and clay, drain into the river's basin forming fertile alluvial soil. Over thousands of years new land is created, often in the shape of a triangle. The New Orleans Delta, then, is imbued with everything from the Ozark Mountains to the hills of Tennessee, and even the cosmos no less. Thus, with all of America running through her veins, it's little wonder New Orleans is the heartbeat of the nation; an enthralling muse of poetry and song.

During the nineteenth century, riverboats were a critical mode of shipping. Many river towns were strategically built near large southern plantations for the convenience of loading commodities onto steamboats. Natchez, Mississippi, was a leader in commerce during the early nineteenth century. Steamboats carried people and goods, including lucrative bales of cotton, up and down the Mississippi River, traveling at what was then amazing speeds, about ten miles per hour.

In the mid-nineteenth century, a monumental railway boom took place across the United States, replacing canals as a more efficient way to move heavy cargo. By 1880, there were more than one hundred thousand miles of train tracks and a growing number of train lines taking much of the steamboat business. To compensate, steamboat companies begin adding entertainment, gambling, music, and fine dining for their elite passengers.

The earliest family story I can recall is the Mississippi River adventures of Dawson and Bill. Dawson McDowell, my great-grandfather on my mother's side, was born in 1864. He grew up on a plantation near Sicily Island, Louisiana, about thirty miles west of Natchez, Mississippi. Dawson was born half slave and half free, a paradox that wasn't resolved until the following year in Virginia at Appomattox Court House when Confederate Civil War general Robert E. Lee surrendered his troops. Dawson's younger brother, Bill, born free in 1866, was his best friend. They were both athletic swarthy boys who did everything together. But there weren't much doing they could do around Catahoula Parish.

During Reconstruction, which began in 1863, there were signs of progress. Freedmen earned the right to vote. Negroes were duly elected state legislators. Dozens more held local offices. Even had a Negro governor of Louisiana for a short while. But hope was dashed when federal troops, charged with protecting Black men and women from political violence, withdrew from the South, abandoning Blacks in their struggle for equality, thereby ending Reconstruction in 1877.

Around 1882 Dawson, eighteen, his brother Bill, sixteen, dissatisfied laboring in the cotton fields, got a notion to go down to the levee to seek jobs on a steamboat. Inspired perhaps by the tales of Tom Sawyer and Huckleberry Finn, they imagined life on the river would afford them a modicum of freedom and adventure. They wanted to visit river towns they'd only heard about, from New Orleans to St. Louis. They soon discovered, however, life on the river was nothing like they imagined.

The brothers earned meager wages from grueling exploitative itinerant work as firemen and deck hands, unloading and loading heavy freight and bales of cotton. When docked, they gathered weighty logs for the boiler. While steaming upriver, they fed those logs into the fiery pit of the blistering steamboat furnace.[6]

Riverboats would dock in towns all along the Mississippi from New Orleans to Baton Rouge, Natchez, Vicksburg, Greenville, Helena, Memphis, St. Louis, and Cincinnati, and down again. Whenever there was a layover along their route, Dawson and Bill would venture into town to find a barrelhouse where gambling and drink amused them through the night. Roustabouts loved to regale themselves with music. Dawson had an amateur interest in the banjo, but his rough fingers weren't very nimble. His younger brother Bill happened to be a pretty good singer. In each place they visited locals eagerly anticipated the latest news from various towns up and down the river.

Bill and Dawson would interact with amateur New Orleans musicians. These musicians didn't necessarily play in orchestras—the era of river orchestras would develop later—they worked on boats as roustabouts. Dawson and Bill, while partying with their fellow rousters, would delight whenever someone pulled out a rickety violin or guitar.

"They [roustabouts] weren't treated like other fellows. Had a captain over them with a whip or lash in their hands. I had never seen them whipped, but I had often heard they whipped them to keep them going,"[7] said Ferdinand Joseph LaMothe, famously known as Jelly Roll Morton. "They would carry on their backs all kinds of things, big boxes of lard. Carried this stuff up the gangplanks. Looked like a man couldn't carry so much. Singing and moving to rhythm of songs as much as they could." Morton worked for a short time as a dockworker but couldn't handle the backbreaking labor. These demanding jobs were performed exclusively by Negros with few exceptions.

For steamboat passengers who could afford to travel in luxury there were first-class cabins. Those who couldn't afford first class traveled in cramped conditions in the lower decks with the cows, pigs, and horses. My great-grandfather Dawson, and his brother Bill, along with other roustabouts and deck hands, traveled in the lowest deck and slept in the hold with the cargo or near the boiler room.

On November 17, 1883, the *S. H. Parison* steamboat left Yazoo City, Mississippi, and safely navigated the Yazoo channel carrying nearly seventy passengers and completed her load in Vicksburg. While docked, Dawson and Bill, along with the other Negro roustabouts and deck hands, loaded over three thousand bales of cotton, more than one thousand sacks of cottonseed oil cake, and five hundred barrels of cottonseed oil.[8] They had just departed down the Mississippi River for New Orleans when a haunting sequence of events began.

Soon in the morning, in the darkness before dawn, Dawson and Bill were awakened by the stench of smoke coming from the cargo area near the boiler room where they slept. Dawson and Bill, along with other firemen and deck hands, tried desperately to relay this information to the captain. But their warnings were ignored. The passengers in first class were drinking, gambling, and partying far above them on the top deck. They were either too engrossed in the goings-on to hear what the firemen were shouting, or they were simply ignoring the lowly workers. Under no circumstances were any Negro deck hand or roustabout ever to step foot on the upper deck.

Smoke began ascending from the stacked bales of cotton. The cotton began burning rapidly. There was a loud explosion! Everyone on board panicked. There were a few lifeboats but not enough for all the passengers. In the excitement, people jumped into the cold, dark river. A few who jumped drowned. Dawson and Bill, still in their long underwear, weren't good swimmers. They saw that only Whites were allowed on rafts. Fearing for their lives, they had no choice but to dive into the Mississippi to escape the sinking steamboat.

In the darkness of night, a fiery glow glistened on top the river. The steamboat burned and crackled like a huge log fire glowing brightly. Boxes, chairs, and any matter of thing that could float was thrown into the river by the crew so the White passengers could hold onto something; tread water until help arrived. Another large boat that happened to be a few miles away came for the desperate passengers and crew, passing up Bill and Dawson, who were struggling in the water begging for help. The steamboat, engulfed in flames, exploded again, quickly followed by a third explosion much greater than the two before. The blast tore out the boat's stern and submerged it. Dawson and Bill were forced to float ashore in the frigid waters clinging for dear life to pieces of charred wreckage. After barely making it to the muddy bank alive, both Dawson and Bill vowed never to work as roustabouts on the river again.

On November 19, 1883, the *New York Times* reported, "There were about fifty-eight surviving deck passengers. Many of them had insisted upon smoking their pipes and cigarettes during the night. It's unknown however if ashes from a pipe or cigarette found its way into the area where the cotton was stored."[9]

Indeed, Dawson and Bill's Mississippi River adventures didn't turn out like the escapades of Huckleberry Finn and Tom Sawyer. They found life on the river cruel and humiliating. More Jim than Huck. Without much opportunity around Sicily Island aside from going back to the cotton fields, Dawson and Bill thought it best they move on. By and by, Dawson married Mary Candy, my great-grand-mother, and along with his brother Bill they migrated south to work a plantation in Baton Rouge before finally settling in New Orleans.

———

The New Orleans Delta is the jewel of the Lower Mississippi Valley region that flows from Cairo, Illinois, and empties into the Gulf of Mexico. Cairo, Illinois, was named "Little Egypt" by settlers because they thought the low-lying area, prone to annual flooding, resembled the Nile in Egypt. The Mississippi River is 3,710 miles long and ranks fourth behind the Nile River, the longest in the world stretching 4,160 miles. Unlike the Mississippi, however, Africa's great river runs from south to north.

Ancient historian Herodotus (c. 484–c. 425 BCE) was in awe of the Nile River Delta and Egyptian civilization. The name *delta* derives from the fourth letter of the Greek alphabet, which resembles a triangle. "About why the Nile behaves precisely as it does, I could get no information from the [Egyptian] priests or anyone else," Herodotus said. "What I particularly wished to know was why the water begins to rise at the summer solstice, continues to do so for a hundred days, and then falls again at the end of that period, so that it remains low throughout the winter until the summer solstice comes round again the following year." While visiting Egypt, Herodotus was told by the Egyptian priests that most of Egypt had been built up by the silt from the river.[10]

There are many things New Orleans and ancient Egypt have in common. Both Louisiana and Egypt were built by great river deltas. More interesting, however, are the striking similarities between African Creole culture of Louisiana and that of North Africans in Ancient Egypt. Large numbers of enslaved Africans who shared regional African languages and cultural traditions, as was the case in Louisiana, retained their ethnic identities in the New World and organized social rituals, such as funerals and even revolts, along ethnic or national lines.[11] Our New Orleans funerary traditions are solemn processions before breaking out into joyous second-line parades as the departed passes into the afterlife. Similarly, ancient Egyptian funerals were ostentatious rituals attracting onlookers (second-liners) who would follow the procession of mourners to the burial with anticipation of partaking in festivities that were sure to follow. Close relatives would walk alongside the coffin, usually pulled slowly by oxen. Two women, either relatives or hired priestesses, would enact the mourning goddesses of Isis and Nephthys in the procession. Attendants would bring canopic jars or tomb gifts, "while others were hired dancers, musicians, and priests."[12]

Once at the edge of the Nile, they would sail their adorned boats across the Nile River to the West Bank—the usual burial location. Upon the procession's return, as the spirit of the dead gloriously journeyed into the afterlife, a musical celebration would break out. The ensemble, usually women, would strike up joyous rhythms for dancers, acrobats, and second-liners, as seen in ancient reliefs. The music would become jubilant as they all paraded back into town.

Spiritual worship dominated Ancient Egypt. Secular music, as we understand it today in New Orleans, was not known to Egyptians. Music seemed to exist solely for the sake of piety. It was integral to spiritual worship and stately ceremony, being that the early pharaohs such as Khufu, builder of the Great Pyramid at Giza, represented god in the flesh.

Black-skinned Nile Valley Nubians and Ethiopians were the founders of ancient Kemet (Egyptian) civilization.[13] In one of his most important observations, Herodotus, an eyewitness of Black Indigenous Egyptians, whose civilization lasted over three thousand years, said, "The people dwelling" in ancient Egypt "are of a black colour by reason of the burning heat" same as the "Ethiopians."[14] In ancient Greek, *Ethiopia* loosely translates into the phrase "burnt-face," meaning the skin of a people's face is the color black. Furthermore, Egyptians in their own words named their country Kemet meaning "land of the blacks."[15] In the ancient Greco-Roman world, black skin, as a descriptor of a person's physical appearance, was not a mark of inferiority. The racist idea that black skin stamps the African inferior has its "origins in fifteenth-century Europe, through colonial times when the early British settlers carried racist ideas to America."[16]

To justify the rise of barbarism toward Black human beings, a racist ideology began to coalesce among elite colonists in the New World in the sixteenth century during the Atlantic slave trade. In 1676, in Jamestown, Virginia, impoverished European colonists grew resentful of elite British planters and their cruel labor system. Landless, indentured, and with little hope of rising above colonial serfdom, armed Europeans joined with African bond laborers and those enslaved in a rebellion provoked by Nathaniel Bacon, an aggrieved elite planter. News of the violent European and African alliance echoed throughout the colonies, striking fear in the planter class. After Bacon's Rebellion, to appease European indentured laborers, a new "White" political class emerged, in part to divide unfree labor.

In Anglo-Saxon British colonies slaves were greatly outnumbered by Whites. Not so in the Caribbean, where uprisings or maroonage were more likely to succeed. In Spanish colonial America, language, culture, and religion were the dominant identifiers. Prior to the twentieth century, southern Europeans weren't accepted as White Anglo-Saxon Protestants. In the seventeenth century, the stark concept of "Whiteness" wasn't prevalent in Spanish colonies such as La Florida, which included present-day Louisiana. But that would soon change.

To quell the threat of uprisings racial distinctions were invented. Illusory concepts of "Whiteness" and "Blackness" denoting a superior racial hierarchy were contrived. White people were "deputized" by the elite Anglo planter class to police and oversee the enslavement of "Black" people. In exchange for patrolling an exploding importation of African humanity, impoverished and landless Europeans received entitlements and privileges under new laws classifying them as "White." In 1790, the United States Naturalization Law gave "free white person[s]" rights, privileges, and immunities that were withheld from all other "non-white" persons. New color laws dispossessed African descendants of personhood. Thenceforth, America would be built on chattel slavery. Abolitionist movements did persist, but multiracial rebellions were effectively divided and conquered.

By the nineteenth century slave owners were in high cotton. In the Deep South barbarism was a way of life. Desperate to elevate their social standing while continuing their medieval bloodlust against Black people, slave owners used their tremendous wealth and political influence to build what we've come to know as Ivy League schools. Colleges such as Harvard, Princeton, and Yale were charged with developing racial science to rationalize slavery. Their social pseudoscientific curriculums would recast Anglo planters as heroic and chivalrous, not the barbarians Africans knew them to be. What is more, the veneer of respectability would help feed their insatiable greed by prolonging their evil institution.

The planter class used sophism to appease Christians and abolitionists. Colonial reverend John Sharpe of the New York garrison lamented, "The Negroes have no immortal Souls but are a sort of speaking brute destined by God to a State of Servitude."[17] Planters tricked the poorly educated and willfully ignorant into seeing Black skin as a mark of inferiority, intellectually and otherwise. "As slave traders and planters came to power in colonial society, they took guardianship over education."[18] Founded in 1746, Princeton (the College of New Jersey) had a succession of eight slave owners preside over it during its first seventy-five years.[19] At Harvard, the wealthy West Indies slave trader John McLean created the McLean Professorship of Ancient and Modern History. In 1842, the Saint-Domingue slave trading business allowed James Perkins of Boston to fund the Perkins Professorship in Astronomy and Mathematics at Harvard.[20] To be sure, the residue of racial pseudoscience dominated Harvard textbooks in 1907, when folk song collector John Lomax arrived on campus from the University of Texas for graduate studies.

Pioneering folklorist John Lomax, born 1867, in Homes County, Mississippi, was best known for his discovery in 1933 of singer and twelve-string guitarist Huddie William Ledbetter, a charismatic Louisiana chain gang prisoner serving time in Louisiana's Angola State Prison. The Angola prison farm was notorious. It had been repurposed after the Civil War to sublease prisoners to former slave owners.

John Lomax was one of the first to propagate that blues originated in Africa. Though it is often repeated today by Blacks, it wasn't a compliment. Lomax believed the blues was *jungle music*, the howl of *savages*. Harvard-educated John Lomax's definition of authentic blues begins with the belief that Blacks were inferior. Consequently, he presumed, the blues, the folk music of the Negro, must be an expression of his inferiority.

Civilization relates to the Latin term *civitas*, meaning "city." "The use of letters," historians say, "is the principal circumstance that distinguishes a civilized people from a herd of savages incapable of knowledge or reflection."[21] In the twentieth century, among Anglo American scholars it was widely believed nomadic people without a system of writing or state-level organization were uncivilized and primitive. Ironically, during Egypt's Dynastic Period, it was the Anglo Americans' Germanic ancestors who fit that description. They were forest-dwelling barbarians barred from the Greco-Roman world.[22]

The ancient Egyptian script was established as early as circa 3100 BCE.[23] Ancient Africans made considerable progress in the abstract sciences including medicine, mathematics, and astronomy. Whereas "of these arts" the pre-Christian Anglo-Saxons, the Germanic tribes of northern Europe, "were wretchedly destitute. They passed their lives in a state of ignorance and poverty."[24] They were considered savages "without either cities, letters, arts, or money."[25]

In spite of that, Anglo Americans taught in their Indian and Negro schools, it was they who brought civilization. They filled in otherwise virgin pages of their history with abstractions, heroic legends, myths, and fairy tales. For centuries, Anglo Americans imposed such fairy tales on subjugated Native and African Americans. In books, movies, and media, they rewrote history, dispossessing Blacks and Native Americans of any claim to equality. They feared to do otherwise would shatter the fragile myth undergirding White supremacy.

Throughout the twentieth century folklorists and musicologists, guided by the myth Africans were primitives prior to contact with Europeans, searched the jungles of Africa for the roots of the blues, but to no avail. All the while, in Egypt, outside of their racist purview, primogenitors of the blues were abundant.

Beyond sharing common skin "colour," and shattering the inferiority deception, both New Orleans and ancient Egypt reserved a reverential place for musical
arts in their respective societies. Primogenitors of New Orleans blues instruments
such as Louis Armstrong's trumpet, Sidney Bechet's clarinet, Lonnie Johnson's
guitar, Warren "Baby" Dodds's drums, and Jelly Roll Morton's piano, and even
the second-line tambourine man's percussions, can all be traced back to ancient
Egypt.

I was taught in school the trumpet was invented by Europeans. To the contrary, only its valves and other mechanisms were added by Europeans in the nineteenth century. The oldest known trumpets are ancient Egyptian instruments
named the *sheneb*. In 1922, two metallic trumpets were found during the excavation of Pharaoh Tutankhamun's tomb by British Egyptologist Howard Carter. The silver and bronze trumpets lay buried in King Tutankhamun's tomb for
nearly 3,500 years (c. 1340 BCE).

The two shenebs (trumpets), the oldest on record according to the British
museum, are long and narrow with a protruding bell. One is 58 centimeters
long and made of silver, the other is sheet bronze and 94.4 centimeters in length.
African trumpets had no valves. The duo of trumpets were designed to be blown
together in harmony, as illustrated in many wall paintings and reliefs. A study by
historian Don L. Smithers revealed the longer trumpet is in the key of B flat and
the other is in the key of C.

By widening the sheneb's bell, which lowers the pitch to baritone and bass,
various brass instruments were developed, including the trombone and the tuba.
The French horn is basically a long angular African trumpet curled up like a
cinnamon roll. Professional string and woodwind musicians in Ancient Egypt
were usually high-status females, as depicted in many surviving reliefs. African
trumpets, however, were mainly played by men and used for royal pomp and military customs. The trumpet continued in this tradition until it was reintroduced
in sedate European orchestras. In New Orleans, in the early twentieth century,
the role of the trumpet was fundamentally transformed into an instrument that
expresses personal freedom as personified in Louis Armstrong's solos.

Similarly, Sidney Bechet's clarinet, the *memet*, is African in origin. It dates back
to Egypt circa 2700 BCE. There were single-reed instruments and double-reeds
"where two reed tubes were tied or glued together to form one instrument. Due
to fragility [few] instruments from antiquity were preserved."[26] However, icono-
graphic evidence dating back nearly forty-seven hundred years is depicted on
tomb reliefs at Saqqarra, Giza, and the pyramids of Queen Khentkaus.[27]

Likewise, Jelly Roll Morton's piano has Egyptian roots. The Ancient Egyptian harp is the primogenitor of the piano. It also dates back to Egypt, circa 3000

BCE. Open the lid of a modern grand piano and you will notice a large cast-iron frame resembling a harp. The cast-iron frame was developed in the mid-1800s. Earlier developments used a less resonant wooden frame. Tethering the strings to a cast-iron frame creates much higher tension, resulting in the big resonant sound of modern grand pianos. In other words, the grand piano is an African harp in a large box. Whereas the piano's strings are hit with hammers (keys), the harp strings are finger plucked.

By the same token, Egyptian cymbals and African hand drums are the primogenitors of the modern Akai drum machines. In fact, mechanization and mass production are the only innovations Europeans brought to early African American blues instruments.

The oldest primogenitor of Lonnie Johnson's blues guitar is the *tanbur* of "the singer Har-Mose," from about 1490 BCE. The remarkable guitar has three strings strung over a carved cedar sound box, a long narrow neck, and a rawhide soundboard. Attached to it was Har-mose's plectrum, or guitar pick, tied on a string. The plectrum is very important to the guitar. It's a major tool that distinguishes the guitar from the violin or viola—instruments that are strummed with a bow. Thirty-five hundred years later, I never go to a gig without my plectrum—thanks Har-Mose.

To put it briefly, African instruments were primogenitors of Louisiana blues instruments. But that doesn't mean the blues originated in Africa. On the contrary, blues thought—the artistic expression and philosophy behind the music— was new to the world when it was conceived in the late nineteenth century in the New Orleans Mississippi Delta.

THE GUITAR OF CONGO SQUARE: THE SPANISH TINGE

NORTH AFRICANS INTRODUCED THE GUITAR to Spain during the Moorish occupation (711 CE–1492 CE). The guitar was then brought to the New World beginning in the 1500s during the Age of Exploration. In the eighteenth and early nineteenth centuries, in Spanish colonial Louisiana, the guitar was played by free and enslaved Africans at an antebellum marketplace known today as Congo Square.

Jelly Roll Morton once said the "Spanish tinge" was an essential ingredient of New Orleans blues. Exactly what he meant by "Spanish tinge" is a bit mysterious because Jelly Roll was not asked by the interviewer who quoted him—folklorist Alan Lomax, son and protégé of John Lomax—to elaborate historically. Nevertheless, we can extrapolate it has something to do with the deeply rooted Spanish influence on Louisiana's African Creole culture and music.

Prior to France claiming Louisiana in 1682, the Lower Mississippi Valley territory was claimed by the Spanish Crown. Ponce de León claimed the territory for Spain and navigated up the Mississippi River around 1513. It is important to understand that free Black conquistadors and settlers accompanied Ponce de León and other Spanish explorers to the New World.

Despite this, 1619 erroneously marks the year in which the "first" Africans, bedraggled and chained, arrived in North America. In 1619, according to historians, about two dozen enslaved Africans arrived in Jamestown, Virginia, a British colony. But they weren't the first Africans to reach the shores of North America. Free *Negroes* lived in the Spanish colony, La Florida, which included what is now Louisiana, dating back to 1513, one hundred years prior to even English Puritans arriving on the *Mayflower*.[28] Therefore, the 1619 reference, without juxtaposition of free Negroes already residing in Spanish North America, is a glaring obfuscation of African American history.

America annually celebrates Christopher Columbus's 1492 "discovery" of America. Consequently, we were taught in our schools that not a single African sailed to, nor lived in, what is now North America between 1492 and 1619. Thus, African American history commenced when twelve enslaved Africans, captured from a Portuguese slave merchant, debarked in shackles from the hold of a ship at Point Comfort, Virginia, in 1619, to be sold as indentured servants. Indeed, it is a preposterous obfuscation of both African and American history to celebrate Spain's discovery of America and then virtually ignore Spanish colonial North American history. In truth, Africans played a significant role from the founding of La Florida, established 1513 and stretching to include what became Louisiana, the colony where Spain's greatest cultural influence on North America coalesced and still endures in New Orleans.

Furthermore, had the Dutch ship carrying those enslaved disembarked in La Florida in 1619, instead of Virginia, those enslaved Africans would have immediately been allowed to claim their freedom. Moreover, their freedom would have been protected by Black-led militias armed by the Spanish Crown.[29]

The guitar is the most iconic instrument of the blues, if not all of music. Yet the guitar of Congo Square, the forerunner of the blues guitar, is not part of the blues narrative. Dr. Freddi Evans, a graduate of Tougaloo College, Mississippi, in her book *Congo Square: African Roots in New Orleans*, adheres to the spurious Mississippi folkloric description that the stringed instrument was "a version of the banza (bania or banja)."[30] Dr. Evans went on to say, "The banza was the precursor to the banjo."

Europeans associate the guitar with the Renaissance, a cultural and intellectual movement. The banjo, on the other hand, they associate with slavery. The guitar, then, couldn't possibly have been introduced to Europe by Africans, they reason, because Africans contributed nothing to Europe's enlightenment. Such revisionist history only serves to hypnotize the public. They hid the cultural significance of the guitar of Congo Square in plain sight for two hundred years by calling it a banjo. But it was not a banjo.

While visiting New Orleans in 1819, British architect Benjamin Latrobe depicted a stringed African instrument at Congo Square with a large oval sound hole in the center of its body. A large sound hole is a major characteristic of an acoustic guitar. Indeed, a banjo does not have a sound hole in the center of its circular, drumlike body. Like a sailor trying to find his way through a storm with a faulty compass, such glaring errors obfuscate the genuine roots of the blues guitar. When retracing the guitar's route to Congo Square, we are directed to Spain and northern Africa. In contrast, the banjo was imported from West Africa.

The modern banjo most likely developed from the West African clawhammer style instrument the *akonting*. To further illustrate the historical inaccuracy, a late eighteenth-century watercolor painting, *The Old Plantation*—the name by which the unsigned painting is commonly known—depicts what are presumed to be enslaved Africans dancing in front of their plantation quarters accompanied by an African banjoist. *The Old Plantation* painting, however, neither represents nor should it be conflated with the urbane culture of free and enslaved New Orleans Creoles. The word *Creole* originally defined any African born in a Spanish colony. The term, after the Louisiana Purchase, would come to include all persons living in Louisiana prior to it becoming a state. Indeed, Creole Blacks had a distinctive language, culture, and religion—Catholicism infused with Voodoo—that was both foreign and shocking to their Black Anglicized counterparts in British colonies such as Virginia and the Carolinas.

Why is the guitar of Congo Square an important marker of Creole culture? Because its lineage can be traced from New Orleans to Moorish Spain, through North Africa, and to Ancient Egypt. The guitar is a symbol of Black civilization dating back to the epoch of Ancient Egyptian civilization.

Latrobe sketched the only eyewitness illustration of the "Guitar of Congo Square." It had a large round sound hole in the center of its calabash body. The guitar was played, according to Latrobe's diary, by a "very little old man, apparently 80 or 90 years old."[31] Based on historian Gwendolyn Midlo Hall's Louisiana Slave Database,[32] the "little old" guitarist most likely arrived in New Orleans in the 1720s or was Creole born in the 1740s. Thus we can conclude that from the beginning, the African guitar was central to the development of New Orleans music and culture. The roots of the Moorish guitar (lute) extend as far back as Ancient Egypt. Bas-reliefs from the eleventh and twelfth Egyptian dynasties depict clearly defined guitars played by female musicians.

Under Moorish Islamic occupation, between 711 and 1492 CE, Spain absorbed African culture and music traditions and blended them with local traditions. Flamenco music, for which Spain is universally known, is a synthesis of classic Spanish (African) guitar styles and the hand clapping and dance steps of North African nomadic tribes.[33]

Ziryab, a Black Moor, introduced the guitar to Europe during the Islamic dominion of medieval Spain. Ziryab was the most influential cultural figure in medieval Europe during the ninth century. *Ziryab* is an Arabic term that translates as "blackbird." According to historian Ibn Hayyan (c. 987–1075 CE), Ziryab was called Blackbird because of his extremely dark complexion. Ziryab was much more than a guitarist. He exerted enormous influence on medieval European society. Today you may not be aware, but how you dress, how and what you eat, how you groom, as well as how you enjoy the music of the ballet, were all influenced by Ziryab.

Ziryab, whose birth name was Abul-Hasan Ali Ibn Nafi (c. 789–857 AD), was a young music pupil in Baghdad. (He may have been born in Baghdad, but sources say he may have been born in Africa and journeyed to Bagdad with his African parents.) Blackbird's musical abilities far exceeded Ishaq Al-Mawsili, his musical master, causing a rift between the two. Although Baghdad was a cultural center, it wasn't ready to nurture a nonconformist innovator such as Ziryab. While exiled from Bagdad, Ziryab's fame grew from Egypt to Morocco. After settling in northern Africa, presumably among family, he was invited to Córdoba in southern Spain (then known as Al-Andalus) to join the royal court.

Upon his arrival to Córdoba in 822 CE in his early thirties, he learned that the prince who had invited him, Al-Hakam I, had died. The new prince, Abd ar-Rahman II, was a lover of music and art. Desperate to bring culture to primeval southern Spain, he eagerly extended the invitation and welcomed Blackbird into his court. Indeed, ninth century Al-Andalus was a provincial backwater; an outpost of Islamic Moorish occupation. The crude culture of medieval Spain was still heavily influenced by the Visigoths and Vandals—barbarians who in 410 invaded, and in 455 destroyed the last vestiges of, Rome. Ziryab was commissioned with the heavy task of introducing culture and refinement to the people of the Iberian Peninsula. Ziryab was named "chief of music and culture" and earned a hefty salary of two hundred gold dinars a month.

If Western historians mention Ziryab at all they allege he was a slave, most likely because Europeans equate black skin historically with slave by default. However, Arab historians dismiss such claims. Although it wasn't unusual for a court musician to be a servant of some kind, Ziryab's position was incomparable to other musicians of the era. Ziryab was a singular, highly influential, elite cultural arbiter who bestowed elegance on the court of Córdoba and brought refined Africanized culture to the people of Spain and southern France.

In the ninth century, Ziryab improved the African guitar by adding the fifth string and "using an eagle's beak or quill instead of a wooden pick."[34] Historians differ on whether his instrument was an early guitar, lute, or oud. It's important to note that the same string instrument can have numerous names depending on the language of the writer or whether the instrument is foreign to the observer. For example, the guitar of Congo Square has mistakenly been called a banjo for two hundred years even though an eyewitness drew an illustration of the instrument. Unfortunately, there are no contemporaneous drawings of Blackbird's instrument. Therefore, I surmise, regardless, if it was long or short neck, frets or no frets, it was a precursor to what became the modern guitar.

Ziryab composed hundreds of songs and was said to know thousands more. Moreover, he established the first music conservatory in Europe. Musicians across Europe studied his concepts. As a consequence, his musical innovations would influence Western classical music. His teachings continued for five hundred years, culminating during the Renaissance, which began in the fourteenth century.

One of Blackbird's greatest musical creations was the classical suite, originally known in northern Africa as nuba, a sequence of musical movements thematically connected. Ziryab developed twenty-four separate nubas—long vocal and instrumental symphonies—one for every hour of the day. The twenty-four nubas (suites) were instrumental in the development of medieval church music. Later, during the European Renaissance, Ziryab's suite concept would become the foundation of all "classical" suites. From the Baroque era into the Classical and Romantic periods, Europe's most celebrated composers—J. S. Bach, Handel, Beethoven, and Mozart—wrote numerous suites. One of the most enduring classical suites today is Tchaikovsky's *The Nutcracker* ballet.

Two notable suites of the Blues era are Duke Ellington's suite "Black, Brown, and Beige," first introduced at Carnegie Hall in 1943, and John Coltrane's masterful 1965 suite "A Love Supreme," which blurs the lines between the sacred and the secular.

What is more, Ziryab was far more than the greatest singer and guitarist in all of Spain. He, a Black man, almost single-handedly elevated European cuisine, table etiquette, hygiene, and fashion. In fact, prior to his arrival in what was then known as Al-Andalus, in 822 CE food was served crudely all at once on platters or on bare tables. Ziryab introduced the elegance of the tablecloth. He revolutionized the local cuisine. Ziryab is credited for introducing African fruit and vegetables to Spain, such as asparagus first cultivated in Ancient Egypt. In addition, Blackbird introduced the "three-course meal, insisting that meals should be served in three separate courses consisting of soup [first], the main course [second], and dessert [third]. He also introduced the use of crystal as a container for drinks, which was more effective than metal goblets."[35] Hence, the next time you sit down at a fine restaurant and order an appetizer, entrée, and dessert, you can thank Ziryab.

Moreover, Ziryab introduced an ancient West African toothpaste recipe, which he popularized throughout Islamic Spain.[36] "He opened a beauty parlor [cosmetology school] . . . near Alcázar," in Seville, "where he introduced under-arm deodorants" and "new short hairstyles leaving the neck, ears and eyebrows free,"[37] as well as perfumes and cosmetics, and shaving for men.[38]

Blackbird was also a fashion innovator. He introduced the change of clothing according to the season as well as the change of clothing for the day and for the night. Henry Terrace, a French historian, said Blackbird "shook the Muslim world." Though his wide-ranging innovations may sound like a myth, Ziryab is indeed a genuine historical figure.

While Ziryab was not alone in influencing high culture in his day, he was the most famous of his era. He was emulated by the masses. According to historian Robert Lebling, Ziryab was "very imaginative, very persuasive as a speaker and quite influential in royal circles." "Ziryab influenced nobles, with teachings that in turn trickled down to average citizens."[39] Historian Ibn Hayyan reported Ziryab had eight sons, five of whom became musicians, and two daughters who were also musicians.

Following their expulsion from Spain in 1492, Moorish Africans, such as Ziryab and his progeny, along with Spanish christened African conquistadors, common Negro settlers, and those enslaved under Catholic law, introduced the guitar during the sixteenth and seventeenth centuries to the "New World." By the eighteenth century, free and enslaved Moor, Wolof, and Bambara Africans were in Spanish colonial New Orleans[40] at Congo Square playing a similar African-Spanish style guitar made famous by Ziryab the Blackbird.

In Spain, by 1200 CE Ziryab's five-stringed African "guitar had evolved into two types: the guitarra morisca (Moorish guitar), which had a rounded back, wide fingerboard, and several sound holes, and the guitarra latina (Latin guitar), which resembled the modern [flamenco] guitar with one sound hole and a narrower neck."[41] It could be argued that Spaniards moved away from the African Moorish guitar and cultivated the Spanish guitar to make a break with their country's

Moorish past during the Reconquista of their homeland. Following centuries of political and religious struggle, undergirded by the Roman Church, Spaniards expelled the Moors and Islam from the Iberian Peninsula. Moors who remained after the end of the Reconquista in 1492 converted to Catholicism and took on Spanish names. That August, "a Genoese sailor named . . . Christopher Columbus . . . sailed westward under the Spanish flag and established a political, economic, and cultural presence for Spain in the Americas."[42]

In an open field near the French Quarter, now known as Congo Square, free and enslaved Negro Moors, along with Wolof (Senegal), Bambara (Mali), and other West Africans and Creole Blacks played African Moorish guitars and hand drums and danced in overtly Africanized expressions. Under Spanish colonial rule such rituals on the Sabbath were politically unremarkable and routine.

However, the Louisiana Territory was sold to the United States in 1803. Following the triumph of the Haitian revolt in 1804, large gatherings of unsupervised Creole Blacks playing their drums and guitars became a threat to antebellum Anglo American immigrants to New Orleans. By the 1830s, the music of Congo Square was suppressed further as racial and cultural tensions between Creoles and Americans rose.

To understand the enigmatic *Creole* culture of New Orleans, it is important to acknowledge free Blacks were among the earliest Spanish settlers in the New World. The crew of Christopher Columbus's first expedition included Negro conquistadors. *Negro*, the Spanish word for "black," had no pejorative connotation in the Spanish language. Negro was merely a descriptive term. Prior to 1492, there were as many Negro African Moors living in Seville, Spain, as there were Spanish Natives. Following their expulsion from Spain, many returned to Africa, while others took to the seas as conquistadors, such as Estéban de Dorantes. De Dorantes, a Negro conquistador, saved the explorer Álvar Núñez Cabeza de Vaca and his men from starving to death by persuading Native Americans to share their food with the shipwrecked crew. One of the earliest discoveries of the guitar in America was in Saint Augustine, Florida. Wiley L. Housewright wrote in *A History of Music and Dance in Florida, 1565–1865* that Juan García y Talvarea, an early settler to Spanish Florida, was buried in 1576 with his guitar.[43] Undeniably conquistadors set sail with their musical instruments, including the guitar.

Spanish christened Negroes, such as Juan Garrido (1480–1560), a Black conquistador who sailed alongside Juan Ponce de Leon in 1513 to claim Florida for the Spanish Crown, and later fought with Hernán Cortés in Mexico against the Aztec Empire, were far greater in number and significance in early Spanish settlements in the New World than many historians have acknowledged.[44] Juan Garrido is but one example. Following multiple conquests, Juan Garrido settled in St. Augustine, Florida, along with many other Negro conquistadors, artisans, and explorers who, records show, routinely reported their good deeds to the Spanish Crown to petition the king for land, status, and other financial rewards. In Juan Garrido's case, records show he was well rewarded. We know the names of Estéban de Dorantes and Juan Garrido because of their extraordinary accomplishments. Yet there were thousands of humbler Negro Spanish settlers, professional soldiers, and explorers who sailed across the Atlantic seeking fortune and adventure in the New World during the Age of Exploration.

Spanish names were common among Negro Spaniards. The tint of their skin was of little consequence in documents. By happenstance, their racial features went largely undocumented. This would change over time as race gradually became an important indicator of social standing in Spanish Louisiana in the years following the American Revolutionary War (1775–1783).

Africans and their Creole descendants were an integral part of the exploration and settlement of Spanish America, which extended over much of what is now the southeastern United States, including Alabama, Mississippi, and southeastern Louisiana—Baton Rouge, my place of birth, was West Florida from the fifteenth through the eighteenth centuries. It wasn't until April 30, 1812, Louisiana became the eighteenth state to join the United States of America. Indeed, the narrative of African American history should commence in the early Spanish frontier from Florida to what is now known as the state of Louisiana—including the entire southern border to California—more than two hundred years prior to Louisiana joining the Union.

British American colonies had strikingly different religious systems and legal systems compared to Spanish American colonies. Before 1782, the chattel British slave trade was illegal in Louisiana. Throughout Spanish colonial America the Black experience was similar to settlers of any other ethnicity. Spaniards were governed by Roman Catholic Castilian law, which dealt with slavery, more or less, as a legal form of indentured servitude. The color of one's skin was not a legal factor. "Castilian law considered slavery an unnatural condition and, therefore, provided many avenues out of bondage."[45] Thus, in Spanish colonial Louisiana, any person, regardless of race, could become a temporary slave or slaveholder.[46] More important, any slave could at any time seek manumission, in which slaves were granted or purchased their own freedom. For example, anyone enslaved could make a down payment on their manumission and be free to go and earn a living. However, if they missed a payment on their freedom, they could be returned to slavery.[47]

In stark contrast, in the dreadful British colonial institution of chattel slavery, the system was literally black and white. Any black-skinned person, including their progeny, could be claimed legally as the property of any White person, in perpetuity. Indeed, British colonial America dehumanized Africans. By law black-skinned persons were "the beasts of the people," property to be owned.[48]

Prior to the Underground Railroad that Harriet Tubman pioneered in the mid-nineteenth century, the enslaved only needed to get to the Spanish frontier of La Florida to reach freedom instead of journeying all the way to Canada. For example, if a free Creole African, a Negro born free in Spanish Florida or Louisiana, traveled into British colonial Carolina or Virginia, they could be abducted and claimed as the property of any White person and enslaved for life without due process. The captive's only recourse for liberty would be maroonage—to escape and live off the grid among fellow marooned Africans. To be sure, countless Africans lived invisibly as Maroons in the Americas throughout the colonial period. But if the captive could escape and return to Spanish Louisiana or Florida, she or he could legally reclaim their freedom.

According to historian Gerald Horne, by

> 1733, in St. Augustine, Spanish Florida, which had long since gained a justified reputation as a scourge of colonies to the North—notably, the Carolinas, from which the enslaved were fleeing in ever growing numbers southward, where they often wound up in [Spain's] military, eager to inflict mayhem on their former captors. . . . It did not take long before Carolinians began to condemn the reality of the steady stream of Africans fleeing southward, some committing murders "and other mischiefs" in their wake.[49]

The colony of Georgia was founded around 1732 as a pro-slavery buffer between Spanish America and British America to stem the tide, but the swamps and waterways of the South, in which Maroons could live in seclusion, encouraged "their determination to become runaways."[50]

In Louisiana, it was common for Maroons to stockpile guns and ammunition for hunting—and defense of their settlements from slaveholders and militias. Whites seldom ventured into the swamps to confront armed Maroons out of fear of armed battle. However, writes historian Gwendolyn Midlo Hall, "the greatest threat they posed was to the planters' [mental] control over slaves who had not run away."[51] Maroons didn't withdraw from New Orleans' economy altogether. "They cut and sold squared cypress logs to white sawmill owners and cypress troughs and tubs for processing indigo. They made and sold baskets and sifters from willow reeds. They fished, trapped birds, collected berries, and grew corn, sweet potatoes, and squash,"[52] and they traded at the marketplace now known as Congo Square and played their guitars and drums on Sundays.

Out of fear, Africanized musical expression, with drums in particular, was forbidden in the British colonies. The sound of African drums bedeviled Anglo settlers. The thunderous polyrhythmic music caused distress. Anglo Americans imagined, sometimes rightly so, that African drums were a clarion call to revolt. In contrast, drums were never banned in New Orleans. Africanized music, from the outset, was an important part of Spanish colonization in the Western hemisphere.[53] Indeed, liberal Spanish codes that eased racial attitudes in New Orleans would have a profound effect on African guitar and rhythmic expression.

In 1938, in an historic recording for the Library of Congress, Jelly Roll Morton said, "I'll give you my idea of what Spanish there is in the blues," then proceeded to demonstrate with a polyphonic rhythm of habanera (augmented to a tresillo feel in New Orleans) and the clave, which Africans developed in Hispaniola (Haiti, Dominican Republic) and Cuba. Add to this rhythm improvisational abandon and a touch of swing, and you've got classic New Orleans blues, which Jelly Roll Morton demonstrated on the Library of Congress's Steinway piano while playing his 1902 composition "New Orleans Blues" with the Spanish "Latin Afro" tinge. Proving, as only Morton could, culture is circular. It goes around the world and comes back around, sometimes unrecognizable by its original creators.

In the early colonial era of the 1600s, learning was mainly focused on biblical literacy. Preliterate Puritans and Pilgrims were extremely intolerant and hypocritical toward the Natives. These Christians believed their doctrines proved God was on their side. And furthermore, those who didn't submit to their brand of religion were heathens. The Natives and all other settlers entering New England were to be converted to Christianity or destroyed. Early settlements in the New World have been mythologized as religious freedom settlements, but they were obviously commissioned to expand the wealth and power of the British Empire.

Pilgrim and Puritan settlements in New England were capitalist enterprises. Both were backed by English investors whose substantial capital investments funded guns, ships, and the manpower to wage war, annihilating many Native peoples. Many Natives that survived the gun succumbed, eventually, to European diseases. Some who survived were enslaved, but the vast majority of Native survivors were embargoed on reservations or forced farther west.

To populate its new colonies Britain expunged itself of its prisoners and undesirables by sentencing them to indenture in the New World. "The colonists were a mixed lot. On the bottom of the heap were men and women of the poor and criminal classes." Among them "were roguish highwaymen, mean vagrants,

Irish rebels, known whores, and an assortment of convicts shipped to the colonies for grand larceny or other property crimes, as a reprieve of sorts, to escape the gallows."[54]

Orphaned children were no exception. "Labor shortages led some ship captains and agents to round up children from the streets of London and other towns to [sale into indenture] to planters across the ocean."[55] Indenturing someone into servitude, which could not exceed nine years, or purchasing someone's indebtedness should not be confused with African chattel slavery.

In contrast, colonial New Orleans, Louisiana, was an enigma. From the beginning, it was a Creole wonder with a vibrant alluring pulse like no other place in the British colonies. Louisiana's antebellum past does not fit neatly into the Anglicized black-and-white narrative of British colonial America. Moreover, New Orleans's kaleidoscopic history destroys White narratives of Black inferiority; thus, it was often removed from the Southern landscape as if it wasn't part of the South—especially in literature about the blues. New Orleans's rich African American history, originally written in French dating back to the 1700s, has been largely misunderstood, ignored, and exoticized. But from this little-known Creole culture came forth the blues.

In 1718, France founded the city of New Orleans and named it after France's ruling regent, the Duke of Orleans. Louisiana was named after King Louis XIV, also known as the "Sun King." In 1682, more than one hundred years after Spanish explorers first traversed the swampy Louisiana frontier, a group led by French explorer René-Robert Cavelier, Sieur de La Salle, reached the New Orleans Mississippi Delta. La Salle's chief motivation was to locate the source of New Spain's gold and silver and claim it for the French crown. To be sure, France and Spain were constantly jostling for each other's territory and wealth. Control of the Louisiana territory would pass between them more than once.

On his doomed treasure hunt in the loosely settled Spanish frontier that would become Louisiana, La Salle encountered both hostile and welcoming Native Americans along the Mississippi River. The Tangipahoa gave the French settlers a tour, showing them the ages-old byways connecting what is now Bayou St. John Portage to the Mississippi River. The Indigenous people knew the waterway as Bayouk Choupic. Parisian investors were optimistic because the location of the new portage colony was strategically placed where the Mississippi River meets the Gulf of Mexico. De La Salle promptly claimed the vast Mississippi River and all adjacent land for France. To put it mildly, French settlers in Louisiana had no respect for Native Americans' indigenous ownership of the so-called Newfound Land. The French only respected land agreements between fellow Europeans such as Britain or Spain.

For thousands of years, Native people had developed advanced systems of agriculture and spirituality. In their Indigenous history, there had been peace agreements among various nations. They lived in villages along the Mississippi River. The Choctaw dwelled in what is now Baton Rouge. The Houma and Natchez tribes lived in central Louisiana. The Chitimacha occupied what became New Orleans. Other tribes included the Tunica and Bayogoula. Although Native Americans had a spiritual symbiosis with their ecology, nothing could have prepared them for the European invasion of their sacred lands.

Well into the nineteenth century Native Americans fought valiantly to defend their homeland, but European settlers armed with advanced weapons defeated the Indigenous people and seized their ancestral homelands. The violent encroachment of Anglo Americans came to a head when President Andrew Jackson ordered the US militia to begin enforcement of the Removal Act signed into law in 1830. Native tribes were driven from their river villages and farms. They were removed from the most fertile acreages; lands they had cultivated for millennia. It must be understood that malnourishment weakens the immune system. Thus, genocide of Native Americans was not simply a matter of violent bloodshed and biological diseases brought on by Europeans, it was also the result of draconian American governmental policies. The ignoble Removal Act created a "Trail of Tears." Thousands of Native Americans—men, women, and children—died of starvation during the removal.

ENLIGHTENMENT CHOCOLATE AND WOMEN

MEANWHILE IN FRANCE OF THE MID-1700S, in what is referred to as the Age of Enlightenment, radical ideas of freedom that would later find their greatest musical expression via Louisiana blues first began percolating in the coffee houses and salons of Paris. For decades men of letters, such as Voltaire, Montesquieu, Rousseau, Diderot, and Condorcet, who questioned and debated every norm, especially that of absolute rule by the French monarchy, gathered outside of earshot of Versailles and the church to perfect their arguments of revolution. While the vast majority of France, as well as Europe, were still in the throes of medieval darkness, this small band of French thinkers had learned to read and write and solve math equations. Allegedly, the French secular movement was an expression of universal human rights and the radical ideal that all "men are born and remain free and equal in rights."[56] In practice, however, the privileged hegemonic group were only referring to elite men like themselves as free and equal—women weren't included in the all-male utopia.

To be sure, these gossipy and bitchy Frenchmen, in powdered wigs, stockings, and high-heeled shoes, thought themselves most clever. They rejected religious and supernatural explanations for the order of things, choosing instead to rely on science and reason. That is, except when it came to their ravenous justifications for chattel slavery. When it came to whether or not Africans were men, they were hysterically irrational. They disregarded science and instead coalesced around emotional desires and ignorance. What is more, they made fallacious arguments based on something as frivolous as appearances, as though the shape of one's nose or the texture of one's hair made him a man.

In contrast, enslaved West African men, many of whom were hardened teenage prisoners of war when sold and packed onto French slave ships headed for Hispaniola, believed such garrulous ridiculously attired neurotic Frenchmen to be less than men by African standards. Indeed, Enlightenment era philosophers, who seemingly pondered and questioned everything under the sun, lacked the self-awareness to question or be embarrassed by their masculine insufficiencies. They not only dressed like women (it's difficult to tell women from men in salon paintings from the period), they developed ideas and learned the art of conversation under the guidance of influential women. Unfortunately, however, the great women of the revolution remain in the shadows of history.

Salons, as such cultural gatherings in the homes of aristocratic women were known, created a safe space where prominent women, outside society's constraints, could express subversive new ideas in the company of men. Salon hosts would carefully plan the evening—what subjects would be discussed and which artists she would invite to entertain her guests. *Salonnières*, as the erudite hosts were known, regaled their guests with poetry, literature, art, and music, and they whispered revolution. The catalyst of the whole movement, no doubt, was a nouveau drug so exalted and euphoric inducing it would change the course of history and enslave the broad African diaspora: *sugar*.

Europe's crazed demand for sugar unleashed an evil upon Africans the world had never known. In the 1400s, the Portuguese captured the Canary Islands and enslaved the Native Canary Islanders off the western coast of Africa. By the same token, around 1460, the nearby island of Madeira was overtaken by the Portuguese. Portugal established extremely valuable sugar plantations on Madeira by enslaving West Africans. The rest of Europe took notice. Henceforth, the ruthless Atlantic sugar slave trade began.

By the eighteenth century, sugar was served in every salonnières' delectable cup of *chocolat*. Often mixed with coffee or wine, the newly wedded sugar and chocolate drink awakened the deepest desires of Parisian women. Chocolate became the supreme beverage of Enlightenment-era France. To be sure, *chocolat* literally and figuratively stimulated the French Revolution.

Around 1492, when Christopher Columbus and Spanish conquistadors began arriving in the New World searching for gold and silver, they discovered the highly valued cacao crops of the native Aztecs in present-day Veracruz, Mexico. Cacao beans, which chocolate is made from, derive from pods that grow on the tropical Theobroma cacao tree. Following Christopher Columbus's fourth quest, between 1502 and 1504, King Ferdinand and Queen Isabella of Spain received cocoa beans as a gift of conquest. However, the beans, a trifle among greater treasures, remained a curiosity.

Later, Spanish conquistador Hernan Cortés defeated the Aztecs in 1519. Upon his return he presented chocolate, the favorite drink of the great Tenochtitlán ruler Montezuma, whom he conquered, to the Spanish Crown. Gradually, sugar and spices were added to sweeten the cozy but bitter chocolate drink, making it delectable. Chocolate, "the food of the gods," became a luxurious secret indulgence so expensive only a queen could afford it.

Spain kept cacao and their production method for chocolate a secret from all of Europe for nearly one hundred years. Then, King Louis XIV married Queen Marie-Thérèse of Spain. Marie-Thérèse, a chocolate enthusiast, introduced chocolate to Versailles, France. The queen, whose chocolate indulgence was legendary, was even said to have given birth to a Black child because of her insatiable lust for chocolate.[57]

Sugar was rare and extremely expensive. Despite this, the subsequent queens of Versailles, including Marie Antoinette, who had a personal chocolate maker to the queen at the palace, customarily ordered artisans to make outlandishly opulent sculptures and artwork from sugar to show off her extreme wealth and power at taxpayers' expense. Outside of the palace, throughout the feudal kingdom and the rest of feudal Europe, the opulent taste of sweetened chocolate remained unknown to peasants and serfs.

Lowly milkmaids, having known only a cold and dreary existence of grueling menial chores and child-rearing throughout the middle ages, were taught a woman should be seen not heard. Obedience to her husband and the church were her saving grace and happiness. Then one day, she had the unimaginable pleasure to taste chocolate, that forbidden sweet. In an instant she knew, all her life she had been lied to. How could something so decadent be so delightful? She must have wondered is it sinful to crave such a guilty pleasure. Indeed, before the discovery of sugar and cacao beans, women of Europe hadn't known life could be so sweet. After one sip of chocolate, the earth was no longer flat.

Somewhere out there, beyond the evil haunted forests she had been warned since childhood never to venture beyond, was an exotic new tropical world where the sun showed year-round and chocolate grew on trees; an island where one could frolic carefree all day on white sandy beaches, then lay back and savor sweet chocolate while the sun set. Indeed, enlightened Parisian women came to realize that somewhere out there, in this lifetime, on this earth, was paradise. But she couldn't speak her innermost revolutionary thoughts in public. She would have to use her persuasive powers to plant enlightened ideas into the minds of men. Make him believe the ideas were his own, because only then would he act.

It was women like Émilie du Châtelet, a French mathematician and writer, who translated and wrote the commentary for Isaac Newton's *Principia Mathematica*, who were the true whisperers of the French Revolution. Émilie du Châtelet was married when she took Voltaire as a lover. While they were living together Châtelet inspired his writings. In 1740, he confided to a friend, "she dictates, and I write." Émilie "is a lady," Voltaire famously said, "whom I look upon as a man."[58] That was the highest of compliments, suggesting Voltaire saw her as an equal. Émilie du Châtelet and her lover Voltaire would frequently gather a select group of friends, whom they knew could tickle their intellects, to their home for chocolate and conversation.

In Voltaire's most popular novel, *Candide* (1759), the protagonist, in exile to escape the inquisition, is strolling along the streets of Paraguay when he "comes upon a Negro with one hand, one leg, and a rag for clothing." Candide briefly empathizes with the half-amputated man. Are you a slave? Yes, the man answered. The slave said he'd been mutilated by his master. "When we work at the sugar canes," the enslaved man said, "and the mill snatches hold of a finger, they cut off a hand; and when we try to run away, they cut off a leg. . . . This is the price at which you eat sugar in Europe."

Due to considerable pressure from the sugar-slave drivers, and due to extremely lethal working conditions, a slave catching his or her fingers in the vertical rollers was commonplace. "A hatchet was kept in readiness" by the driver "to sever the arm" so as to not impede production.[59] Such horrid inhuman butchery was routine.

The French colony of Hispaniola (Haiti) became the largest producer of sugar for Europe. Sugar was "white gold"; an addictive and unquenchable drug. Cultivated on Caribbean and Brazilian plantations, sugar ignited the Atlantic slave trade. Sugar slaves were the ultimate sacrifice to the merciless gods of capitalism. There is nothing patriotic or noble about sacrificing a person's limbs or life simply for a decadent pleasure commodity for royals and elites.

By the mid-1700s, Britain also looked to the West Indies for colonizing and selling of luxury goods. Elite Anglo colonial men of letters such as Thomas Paine, Benjamin Franklin, James Madison, John Adams, and Thomas Jefferson were close associates and confidants of French Enlightenment thinkers. French and English arguments for an egalitarian society, though fallacious at the time, gradually captured the imaginations of every man, woman, and child. It also enthralled the large sugar-enslaved population in the French colony of Hispaniola.

Since sugar gradually became one of the first luxuries consumed by the masses in Western societies (along with coffee, tobacco, rum, and chocolate, produced by the labor of enslaved people), it also became the principal incentive for transporting millions of Africans to the New World.[60] Some 95 percent of all African slaves brought to the New World went to the Caribbean and Brazil.[61] Only 3 to 5 percent were brought to what became the United States of America.

In the Caribbean a slave would be surrounded by his or her own people and thus would share in their developing culture, and might even have an opportunity to escape to a protected Maroon community. Whereas in North America the same African would be outnumbered by Whites and placed under their constant supervision, care, and control.[62]

In an extraordinary pamphlet of 1791, the campaigner William Fox wrote: "If we purchase the commodity we participate in the crime. The slave dealer, the slave holder, and the slave-driver, are virtually agents of the consumer, and may be considered as employed and hired by him to procure the commodity. . . . In every pound of sugar used . . . we may be considered as consuming two ounces of human flesh." In other words, Britons drank the blood of Africans in every cup of tea.

AFRICAN CREOLE ROOTS AND ORCHESTRAL CULTURE DURING SLAVERY

IN 1718, WHEN ENSLAVED WEST AFRICANS first began arriving in French cargo shipments to Louisiana, free Negroes were already settled in the former Spanish frontier—from St. Augustine, Florida, to West Florida in the Louisiana Florida parishes. Some Blacks had married into Native families.

During this time, West African kingdoms were embroiled in regional warfare. Their prisoners of war were often sold into sugar slavery. The most important kingdoms of Senegambia controlled which peoples could be enslaved and sold to the Europeans. It seems that during the 1720s, neither the Foul (Fulbe) nor the Mandingo sold their own people or allowed others to sell them. The Bambara (Bamana) enjoyed no such protection during the 1720s. "Those sent to Louisiana were mainly captives taken during the wars arising out of the founding and consolidation of the Segu Bambara [Bamana] Empire established by Marmari Kalubali."[63] In New Orleans, the Bambara far outnumbered enslaved Moors, Benin, and the Congolese. Subsequently, the Moroccan American Treaty of Friendship (Treaty of Marrakesh), signed in 1786–1787 by Thomas Jefferson and John Adams with Sultan Muhammad III, freed all African Moors in North America.

It is culturally significant that "almost all slaves brought to Louisiana under French rule came directly from Africa [not the Caribbean or West Indies] and arrived within a twelve-year period following the founding of New Orleans." Meaning they arrived with their African customs and languages intact. Very few slaves were brought to French Louisiana after 1731.[64]

French female settlers were in short supply. Intermarriage was forbidden under Code Noir laws. But that didn't preclude Frenchmen from raping enslaved and free Native and African women. Some took Africans and Natives as mistresses or common-law wives. A practice that was intolerable in Protestant southern states became commonplace in Francophone Louisiana from its inception.

In 1762, France transferred the Louisiana colony to Spain in the secret Treaty of Fontainebleau. In return, Spain fought alongside France in the war against the British. France and Spain lost the war, and consequently, Great Britain gained most of Louisiana along the Mississippi River. However, Spain kept control of New Orleans and parts of the vast eastern and western Louisiana territory. Upon seizing control of the fledgling colony, Spain promptly banned the trade of Native slaves in Louisiana. In addition, Spain eased some stringent French Code Noir laws by establishing *coartación* (a system of manumission), which allowed the enslaved to buy their freedom, and that of others.[65]

Like France, Spain was monarchic, her culture Latin, grounded in Roman law and Catholicism.[66] Despite the new sovereignty of Spain, Spanish did not become the official language. Instead, Louisianans continued to speak French and Creole, a dialect of the French language. Because France and Spain shared the Latin culture of Roman law and Catholicism, Creole declarations weren't as pronounced during the transition as they would be later, when Anglo Americans began immigrating to Louisiana following its statehood into the United States of America.

New Orleans blues is not rooted in slavery. The blues movement that began in the 1890s was a minimalist art movement where musicians such as Buddy Bolden, Jelly Roll Morton, and King Oliver led small minimalist Creole orchestras, breaking with New Orleans's long tradition of Black classical orchestras. Antebellum Blacks of New Orleans weren't limited to plantation songs, puritan hymns, and Congo Square folk rituals. Moreover, the music of free Negroes in New Orleans was also professional beyond ballroom dances. Beginning in the late eighteenth century residents and visitors to New Orleans attended French opera houses. Only blocks away from slave auction blocks during the height of slavery, New Orleans's Black population built their own opera theater. Indeed, Negro benevolent societies in New Orleans had a penchant for opera just like the rest of the Gallic population.

In 1792, a French theater, Le Spectacle de la Rue Saint Pierre, was established in New Orleans. The building was located at 732 St. Peter Street in what is now the French Quarter. There, a stringent code of conduct was enforced by police. Published in 1804, police orders stated: "The orchestra of the hall cannot be subject to fanciful demands to play this or that tune . . . no person shall disturb either the orchestra or the audience." There were a number of rules. If one were to misbehave "he will be brought before a competent magistrate to be punished by imprisonment or fine in accordance with the varying degree of trouble he may have occasioned."[67]

Furthermore, all orchestra musicians, as was customary, were under the tyrannical control of the conductor, who himself was chained to the written score. Contrary to myth, Black musicians in New Orleans *could* read and write music. The problem was the European system of musical notation was downright incapable of expressing the complexities and nuances of blues expression. Recognizing and rejecting such restraints enlightened blues orchestra leaders became minimalists. By the 1890s and early 1900s, seeking freedom of expression, on stage and for their boisterous fans, they developed scaled down, nimble orchestras led by musicians capable and flexible enough to compose on the fly.

For instance, the King Oliver Creole Orchestra, which featured a young Louis Armstrong, was a minimalist dance orchestra compared to its primogenitors, such as the one-hundred-musician-strong antebellum Black symphony orchestra established in New Orleans at the height of American slavery.

In 1830, the Negro Philharmonic Society was founded, establishing the Negro Philharmonic Orchestra. The orchestra had one hundred Black Creole performers at its largest. Black violinist Constantin Debergue was the director.

In 1840, the Negro Theatre de la Renaissance opened on Elysian Fields and Dauphine, featuring full plays, comic pieces, and variety shows. The dichotomy of free Negroes gaily enjoying the Negro Philharmonic Orchestra while nearby enslaved Blacks had no autonomy to develop such high art was striking, accentuating the fact that the Black antebellum experience in Louisiana was not monolithic.

By 1860, the number of free Negroes in New Orleans had grown to 18,647, the largest percentage of free Blacks in the southern United States.[68] Nevertheless, WASP antagonism led to the end of the Negro Philharmonic Society as racial tensions escalated because of Anglo American resentment. Planters feared the aspirational effects the large free and prosperous Black society of Louisiana were having on those enslaved. Two of its former members, violinist and composer Edmond Dédé (1827–1903) and Charles Lucien Lambert Sr. (1828–1896), fled New Orleans in the 1850s. Lambert exiled to France in 1853, where in Paris he published an original composition, "L'Angélus au monastère: Prière," for piano. While living in Paris, his most popular composition was "Variations et final sur l'air 'Au Clair de la Lune,' Op. 30," first published in 1859. Later, Charles Lucien Lambert Sr. moved his family to Rio de Janeiro, Brazil, and found similar success as a prominent composer and member of the Brazilian National Institute of Music.

Similarly, violinist and classical composer Edmond Dédé, a fourth-generation free Creole of dark hue, also exiled to Paris to continue his career, where he graduated from the Paris Conservatory. Dédé was a conductor in Bordeaux, France, for twenty-seven years.[69] Edmond Dédé and Charles Lambert were drawn to Paris following France's definitive decree on April 27, 1848, to end slavery in all its colonies, which included the West Indian Islands of Martinique and Guadeloupe, which had been colonized since the 1600s.

In fact, classical composers Dédé and Lambert weren't Creole Negro anomalies. One of the greatest French colonial classical composers, who laid the foundation for Dédé and Lambert, as well as all Black artists that would exile to Paris and find acceptance in the nineteenth and twentieth centuries, including me, was a gifted, multitalented Guadeloupian Negro slave; a Creole genius known speciously as the "Black Mozart."

CHEVALIER DE SAINT-GEORGES

IN THE LATE EIGHTEENTH CENTURY, Amadeus Mozart moved to Paris to challenge Chevalier de Saint-Georges, the most popular composer and violinist in all of France. Saint-Georges, a freed Creole man, is often characterized by historians as the "Black Mozart" because of the similarities in sound and feel of his and Mozart's compositions. But this moniker is misleading. To tell the truth, in 1778, Amadeus Mozart and Saint-Georges lived under the same roof in Paris for several months. Saint-Georges made an indelible impression on young Mozart, influencing the music he wrote while in France, and in the years that followed. To be sure, Saint-Georges wasn't the "Black Mozart," he was an original whose ideas and feel Mozart adapted into his compositions. A better moniker for the virtuosic violinist, though one isn't needed, would be the "Jimi Hendrix of Enlightenment Age France."

Joseph Bologne, Chevalier de Saint-Georges, was born a slave December 25, 1745, in the Americas on the French-ruled West Indian island of Guadeloupe. He was the son of planter George Bologne, de Saint-Georges, and an enslaved Senegalese beauty named Anne Nanon who was owned by Bolongne. Guadeloupe was originally claimed for the Spanish Crown by Christopher Columbus on his second voyage in 1493. The Native islanders, known as Caribs, defended their homeland against the Spanish invaders for more than a century before finally succumbing to violence, murder, and European diseases.

In 1626, French trader Pierre Bélain, sieur d'Esnambuc, expanded French colonization into the Caribbean by defeating the weakened Natives. Later, in 1635, he "established the first colony for the Compagnie des Îles d'Amérique on the island of Martinique, the first permanent French colony in the West Indies."[70] Guadeloupe, known as Karukera, the "Island of Beautiful Waters" to native Caribbeans, became a dependency of Martinique. France brought enslaved Africans to the islands in 1644 to established sugar plantations. In 1759, the English overtook and colonized Guadeloupe for four years, opening new lucrative trade routes into England and its American colonies. By 1763, the Guadeloupean sugarcane slave trade had become so profitable that in the first Treaty of Paris, France traded all of Canada to England for the island.[71]

In 1753, at age seven, Saint-Georges's father took him to France for his education.[72] In Paris, Saint-Georges grew to become a renaissance man. He was a great fencer, a virtuoso violinist, and Paris's most celebrated Enlightenment era composer. Furthermore, Saint-Georges pioneered the form symphony concertante; the new eighteenth-century classical style combined the symphony and concerto in a way that featured two or more soloists against an orchestra, instead of one single featured instrument.[73] The shared solo creativity his new form introduced wouldn't be surpassed until the early twentieth century with the advent of New Orleans blues and its improvised polyphonic approach to melody. Classic New Orleans blues featured three simultaneous solo instruments—trumpet, clarinet, and trombone—against the orchestra. Esteemed musicologist Lionel de La Laurencie observed, "Saint-Georges's concertos impress with their gracious thematic development, which has a tinge of characteristically Creole languor and melancholy sentimentality."[74] His compositions, Laurencie said, are "clear, flowing and airy."[75]

Chevalier de Saint-Georges was also admired for his stylish dress. "He never wore the same suit, the same jabot, the same boots two days running."[76] According to Alfred Marquiset, he was "a rooster receiving the adulation of a swarm of beauties, he was the star of all theatricals, suppers, and fétes."[77]

In 1773, Saint-Georges became director of Concert des Amateurs. Under his direction the orchestra, hosted at the Hôtel de Soubise, became "the best orchestra for symphonies that existed in Paris and perhaps in Europe."[78] In 1774, young Queen Marie-Antoinette, then nineteen years old, invited Saint-Georges, then twenty-nine, to come to Versailles and play music with her. Saint-Georges would become Marie-Antoinette's musical teacher and adviser, and even for some time her confidant.[79] The arrival of a Creole "colored" man into her immediate entourage, however, was a bombshell. Although Saint-Georges's immense talents and charisma proved too great to deny him an invitation into aristocratic social circles, bigotry kept him from reaching the highest positions—such as director of Concert Spirituel, to which he was appointed at the behest of Queen Marie-Antoinette but was denied because of racism. Three opera performers for the Concert Spirituel petitioned Marie-Antoinette stating they would not "be subject to the orders of a mulatto."[80] Even so, Saint-Georges's friendship with the queen continued right up to the Revolution. "Marie-Antoinette would regularly travel [from Versailles] to Paris to attend his concerts, even going to watch him skate on the frozen Seine in January 1789."[81]

In 1778, a frustrated Wolfgang Amadeus Mozart, age twenty-one, accompanied by his mother Maria Anna, arrived in Paris from Salzburg, Austria, his provincial hometown, to challenge Chevalier de Saint-Georges to become the most popular composer in all of France. When Amadeus arrived in the hope of establishing a career as a composer, Paris was the greatest city of the European continent, a leading musical center with many music-loving amateurs, a large music publishing industry, a busy operatic life, and a good deal of concert activity by the standards of the times.[82]

On March 14, 1778, Mozart and his mother, Maria Anna, left Mannheim, Germany, on a western-bound coach. When they arrived in Paris, Chevalier de Saint-Georges, now thirty-three, was conductor and violinist of Paris's leading symphony orchestra. After years spent on the road promoting Wolfgang's and his sister's music careers, Leopold Mozart, the ambitious family patriarch, was in near financial ruin. With few prospects in Salzburg, Leopold, a violinist and music teacher, sent young Wolfgang to seek a respectable musical post in Paris with the hope of paying their mounting debts.

While Amadeus sojourned in Paris, plotting his challenge to Saint-Georges, the preamble to the French Revolution was in full bloom. Whispers of revolution began in salons; Enlightenment sanctuaries where French literati and intellectuals could gather alongside poets, singers, and musicians to express radical ideas of a free society. Exclusive salon gatherings were held in the homes of aristocratic women, salonnières, patrons of the arts. In such circles Saint-Georges stood out. A former slave whose talent and intellect helped him gain social mobility and acceptance, Saint-Georges was the manifestation of Enlightenment's equalitarian ideals; the dream of a society where even a serf or former slave could rise to respectability based on his talents.

It's important to understand that Saint-Georges symbolized much more than musical achievement. He could be compared to baseball and civil rights pioneer Jackie Robinson, who broke the baseball color line by starting for the Brooklyn Dodgers in 1947. French and American Enlightenment thinkers, from Voltaire to Thomas Jefferson, who were questioning the cognitive and creative abilities of Africans, all knew or were aware of Saint-Georges's genius. He was the Black man as Enlightenment hero.[83] In other words, in real time, Saint-Georges fearlessly exposed fallacious arguments that Africans were inferior. John Adams, the future second president of the United States, took notice of the Creole Negro genius while visiting Paris in 1779. Adams wrote in his diary that Joseph Bologne, Chevalier de Saint-Georges was "the most accomplished man in Europe in riding, shooting, dancing, fencing, [and] music." A sentiment young Amadeus Mozart knew all too well.

By the time Mozart arrived in the city of light, Saint-Georges's music had been published around Europe for more than a decade. He was everything young Amadeus hoped to become. Mozart had performed at Versailles as a child wonder for the royals, but his child prodigy act was a novelty that had grown stale. Mozart had grown up to be a man-child. Though his musical abilities were undeniable, his naivete and immaturity were a hindrance. Mozart's unique childhood, driven by adulation, had left him petulant and conceited. On the other hand, Saint-Georges had to overcome being born a slave. Though he grew to become a respected gentleman, French Code Noir forbid him to marry into aristocratic circles. He never married. Perhaps such unfulfilled longing played a part in Saint-Georges's sentimental ballad "Adagio in F minor for piano," a quiet rumination on loneliness and isolation that hints at self-pity but, remarkably, doesn't succumb to it. In contrast, Mozart's music was charming and cheerful, the antithesis of his personality.

In Paris, however, Mozart's music wasn't well known outside of a small group of connoisseurs.

Amadeus's mother was often left cold and hungry in their small apartment as her son went out with Baron von Grimm, a fellow Saxon, and Mozart's link to Paris's cultural life, to salons to earn enough money to keep he and his mother afloat. Baron von Grimm, patron of the arts and diplomat and secretary to the Duke of Orleans, who lived in the same estate as Chevalier de Saint-Georges, paid Mozart's expenses while seeking paid commissions and sponsors for the young composer.

Whereas Saint-Georges arrived at salons and theaters on his one-horse chaise or by coach with a lovely lady on his arm, Mozart arrived muddied and disheveled after walking long distances. While Saint-Georges would need to be coaxed into performing, Mozart would leap at the chance to perform hoping to earn money or attract a wealthy patron. Mozart eagerly begged for introductions at these affairs from Baron von Grimm.

Frustrated, Mozart complained bitterly to his father in letters: "You say," Mozart tells his father,

> that I ought to pay a good many *visiten* in order to make new acquaintances and revive old ones. That, however, is out of the question. The distances are too great for walking—or the roads too muddy—for really the mud in Paris is beyond all description. To take a carriage means that you have the honor of spending four to five *livres* a day, and all for nothing. People pay plenty of compliments, it is true, but there it ends.[84]

Grimm introduced Mozart to salonnière the Duchesse de Bourbon. He was invited to her salon to perform for her and her guests. Mozart complained to Leopold,

> I had to wait for half an hour in a large, ice-cold, unheated room, which didn't even have a fireplace. Eventually the Duchesse de Cabot entered, with the greatest politeness, and asked me to do my best with the clavier in the room, as none of hers was in good order; would I try it? I said I would be happy to play something, but at the moment it was impossible, as I couldn't feel my fingers for the cold: could I at least be taken to a room where there was a fire?[85]

Mozart's request was politely ignored by the duchesse.

The duchesse and her invited gentlemen friends gathered around a large circular table, backs to Mozart, and began drawing. Mozart confessed to his father they were too enthralled in conversation to take an interest in him or his music. He was perturbed at being ignored. Nonetheless, Mozart played the clavier for more than an hour that evening to earn his pay.

Mozart's six-month stay in Paris was a disaster. Leopold, in a letter, had reminded Maria Anna that she should be bled, a tradition at this time of year. Although leeches were commonly used, it's more likely she cut open a vein with a sharp object and let her blood ooze out into a vase. After the backward medieval bloodletting procedure, on June 11, Mozart's mother was too ill to attend his debut at the Concert Spirituel. For days she suffered severe headaches, diarrhea, and loss of hearing. The Mozarts were reluctant to see a French doctor. Finally, when Grimm sent his doctor, a local German, she was delirious. Maria Anna, fifty-seven, died on June 30 in their cramped apartment on rue du Gros Chenet, leaving Wolfgang to fend for himself.[86]

A destitute Mozart was taken by Baron von Grimm (and Saint-Georges), at the urging of Grimm's well-connected companion Mme. D'Epinay, into the mansion D'Epiany, which Grimm, as the personal secretary to the Duke of Orléans, occupied. At the time, Saint-Georges also lived in the mansion. It is a matter of record that from July 5 to September 11, 1778, Mozart and Saint-Georges lived—and dined—under the same roof: that of Mme. de Montesson's mansion on the Chaussée d'Antin.[87] Amadeus wrote to his father, Leopold, from Paris, July 8, 1778: "I am writing this in the home of Mme. D'Epinay and of M. Grimm, where I now live, a pretty room with a very pleasant view—and [where] given my condition, I am content."[88]

Given Saint-Georges and Mozart lived under the same roof and broke bread together, one can presume the two had many opportunities to discuss music and compare notes. Perhaps they attended the same salons, operas, and parties. It is reasonable to assume this because musicians with similar musical interests often frequent the same circles. They certainly shared acquittances and a common liaison in Baron von Grimm. Unfortunately, we can only speculate what they might have discussed because neither man mentioned the other in their personal letters.

What is known, however, is that Mozart copied note for note a passage in his "Symphonie Concertante, K. 364," otherwise known as his "Paris Symphonie" from Saint-Georges's "Violin Concerto, Op. VII, No. 2."[89] American New York Philharmonic violinist Gabriel Banat, born 1926, in Transylvania, Romania, confirmed in his book *The Chevalier de Saint-Georges: Virtuoso of the Sword and the Bow*, that in "Mozart's symphony concertante K. 364 . . . a passage rising to the highest regions of the [violin's] fingerboard, only to plunge back to the lowest range of the instrument—may be compared with an identical passage (a half-step higher) in the rondeau movement of Saint-Georges' Violin concerto Op. VII,

No.1."[90] In other words, Mozart in his own handwritten score copied a unique passage of a Saint-Georges song note for note.

Chevalier de Saint-Georges, a celebrated composer, popular with the ladies, and confidant of Queen Marie-Antoinette, was everything Mozart had moved to Paris to become yet failed to achieve. Mozart confessed in letters to Leopold his resentment at having to adopt his music to Parisian tastes. "The few intelligent Frenchmen who are there will like it. As for the stupid ones," Mozart pouted, "I can't see that there is any great misfortune in displeasing them. Still, I have hopes that even the asses may find something in it to give them pleasure."

Another musical technique Saint-Georges made fashionable was the *coup d'archer*, which literally means the "first bowstroke," where all the instruments of a symphony boldly start together. Coup d'archer was all the rage at the Concert Spirituel. "I was careful not to forget the premier coup d'archer" Mozart moans to his father. "What a fuss these donkeys here make over it! . . . It's ridiculous."[91] Mozart resented the musical tastes of Paris, one can surmise, because he could not overcome Paris's entrancement with the musical genius of Chevalier de Saint-Georges.

After Mozart retreated back to Vienna, Saint-Georges continued to haunt him. In his post-Paris opera *The Magic Flute* Mozart based an evil villain "Monostatos" on Saint-Georges. Monostatos, a Moor servant of the prince, desires to rape the leading character, Pamina, the beautiful daughter of the queen. In the original libretto, Monostatos grieves because he is Black "and black is ugly." Paraphrasing, he sings, I must always live without a woman. I want to kiss Pamina, but I would burn in hell. Blatantly, the "original libretto by Emanuel Schikaneder," Mozart's collaborator, "is a thorough catalogue of the dark side of the Enlightenment, filled with racial hatred, misogyny and the supreme condescension of white-male power."[92] Monostatos is Mozart's vengeance upon his nemesis, the great Chevalier de Saint-Georges.

Saint-Georges's musical legacy is profound. Mozart's biographers often obfuscate Chevalier de Saint-Georges's influence on Mozart by substituting his name with the words "Paris" or "French." For example, Mozart's Paris influence is how they might describe the period. What is more, before the recent revival of interest in Saint-Georges's music, it was generally accepted that the influence of the French school on Beethoven began with Viotti, Rode, and Kreutzer. There is sufficient evidence, however, to suggest that it was Saint-Georges, ten years earlier, who stimulated this interest.[93] Moreover, Saint-Georges was largely responsible for the commissioning of Franz Joeseph Haydn's famous Paris Symphonies. Haydn would devote two years to writing his six Paris Symphonies. Saint-Georges organized rehearsals and directed their first performance in late

1787. Indeed, Chevalier de Saint-Georges has been denied not only his proper place in Mozart's otherwise meticulously documented biography, but his proper status as a supremely influential classical violinist and composer.

In 1789, the French Revolution began. The blood of thousands flooded the streets of Paris. The city of light was thrust into darkness while terror and pandemonium reigned. King Louis XVI was imprisoned and lost his head to the guillotine one cold and brutal day in 1793. Nine months later, his wife Marie-Antoinette, the queen of sugar, in an attempt to appease the starving pitchfork yielding peasants, is alleged to have said "let them eat cake" (I presume the cake in question was *chocolat*), before suffering the same fate of her husband. Saint-Georges fought for freedom and equality leading a Black French regiment on the side of the revolutionaries. Yet, after success on the battlefield amid the confusion he was imprisoned, but he was released after serving one year. A large amount of the Chevalier's music and personal letters were lost in the bloody chaos of revolution.

Meanwhile across the Atlantic in Spanish Louisiana, in 1788 an accidental New Orleans French Quarter fire spread quickly, reducing over eight hundred homes to ashes, including St. Louis Church and the town hall. The Spanish Crown managed to rebuild the French Quarter and the church, known today as St. Louis Cathedral. Subsequently, demoralizing hurricanes, floods, and another great fire in 1794 caused the Spanish government great consternation, hastening the desire to cut their losses and pull out of the unprofitable territory.

All the while, in Saint-Domingue, the sugar capital of the world, Napoleon Bonaparte, an ambitious French military leader who rose to power during the French Revolution, was on the warpath. Napoleon believed he was destined to conquer the world. His first mission was to take control of France's wealthiest colony in the Americas and secure its sugar slave industry. Napoleon must have been astonished to find himself locked in battle with his fiercest foe yet, Toussaint-Louverture, a poor, Black, formerly enslaved Saint-Domingue rebel general. Toussaint, along with fellow formerly enslaved Jean-Jacques Dessalines, his second-in-command, led a successful revolution beginning in 1791, with a militia of thousands of enslaved and free Blacks in France's richest overseas colony Saint-Domingue, as Haiti was then known.

On February 4, 1794, France abolished slavery in all its territories, the first European empire to do so.[94] Words of freedom as expressed in the Declaration of the Rights of Man spread throughout the French colonies—including Louisiana. Free and enslaved Blacks in Louisiana followed the breaking news of revolutionary battles in Haiti and in France. Whispers of freedom among the enslaved in Louisiana spread from plantation to plantation. A fearless enslaved group conspired to overtake Louisiana and make it a free republic. But something went horribly wrong.

In Louisiana, in the summer of 1795, along the banks of the Mississippi River, around Pointe Coupee Parish, thirty miles upriver from Baton Rouge, the stench of rotting flesh permeated from a gruesome display of colonial power. The severed heads of twenty-three African and Creole men were hung high on pikes as a dire warning against slave rebellions.

The Pointe Coupee Conspiracy, as the multiracial Louisiana revolt is known, "involved mulatto and black creole slaves born in Pointe Coupee, a creole of Jamaica, two creoles of New Orleans, one slave from New York, African slaves of eight different nations, free blacks and mulattoes, and white Jacobins[95] who hated slavery, including a [White abolitionist] schoolteacher" named Joseph Bouyavel, guilty of reading the French Revolution's Declaration of the Rights of Man to the slaves, and a "German tailor born in New York, and an indentured servant voyageur plowing the Mississippi River."[96] The planter class of Louisiana, horrified by the news of French blood being splattered across Saint-Domingue, understood the Pointe Coupee Conspiracy was more than a routine slave revolt. It had a philosophy. It was inspired by the doctrine of the French Revolution that sparked the Haitian Revolution. Could Louisiana be next?

After the trial, "fifty-seven slaves and three local whites were convicted. By June 2, [1795], twenty-three slaves were hung," their corpses mutilated, and "their heads cut off and nailed on posts at several places along the Mississippi River from New Orleans" to False River, an oxbow lake in Pointe Coupee.[97] When the *négre* Guillaume, slave of Widow Le Doux, "was asked before being sentenced why he lent himself to the crime of revolution to kill the whites, knowing that he deserved to be hanged. He replied, 'Because I was not afraid.'"[98]

Although slavery had been abolished by France in 1794, it was brutally reinstated by Napoleon Bonaparte as "fighting deepened in the Caribbean between slave rebels and French troops."[99] In 1799, Chevalier de Saint-Georges, fifty-three years old, died in Paris. Under Napoleon's reign, Chevalier de Saint-Georges's music was "removed from orchestra repertoires and essentially from the history books, not to be rediscovered for nearly 200 years."[100]

Little is known about the music of the enslaved because a scant amount of enslaved literature, high art, and music manuscripts have survived. Fortunately, a number of the Chevalier's groundbreaking compositions have resurfaced and are today performed by orchestras around the world.

Finally, after the French Revolution of 1789, when there were no more heads to sever and enough blood had been shed, a fledgling republic gradually emerged from the ashes. Spain, desperate to wash its hands with the hurricane-prone mosquito-infested bayou, was ready to make a deal with the French. In 1800, Spain ceded the Louisiana territory back to Napoleon and France.

By 1803, the heroic Black Haitian militia had overcome Napoleon's sixty-thousand-man army. After Napoleon withdrew in defeat, Haiti, one of the richest countries in the world, was declared an independent Black republic. Haitians could have continued its lucrative international sugar slave trade, but who would Haitians enslave to mine their labor-intensive white gold? Haiti chose to abolish slavery. Yet, somehow, without its most valuable cash crop, the impoverished Haitian government still managed to pay reparations to France, about 23 billion in today's American dollars.[101]

Napoleon's France, after overextending its empire and decades of war, was in chaos financially. Napoleon was forced, in 1803, to sell Louisiana to Thomas Jefferson, president of the United States. At the time of the Louisiana Purchase there were about five thousand Negros in New Orleans, half of them "free men of color" and half enslaved. Only three thousand of its eight thousand total population were considered "White." The "White" citizenry had been Latin Romance Spaniards and French, making New Orleans less Anglo than most American cities its size. The number of Blacks would increase greatly, however, when hundreds of free Haitians began arriving into Louisiana in the 1800s. In the state as a whole, by 1820, after "Louisiana entered the Union, the white and black population were about equal, both being under 80,000." By the 1860 census, there would be "350,373 Negroes and 357,456 whites." Among the Negro population, 18,647 in 1860 were free, many of them rich and educated.[102]

New Orleans's French officials had allowed French Saint-Domingue refugees to enter the city, but out of fear of revolt they attempted to stop the migration of free Black Haitian refugees. To the dismay of New Orleans city officials, the attempts to stop Black Haitians failed in Louisiana courts. Haitians spoke Louisiana's Francophone and Creole languages. They acculturated into the fabric of the city's free Negro culture, introducing red beans, Caribbean rhythms, and a passion for French opera. However, Voodoo religion, contrary to popular narrative, may not have been introduced to Louisiana by Haitian refugees, initially. There is evidence New Orleans Voodoo was merely strengthened by the newcomers' Vodou religion.[103]

For example, in 1758 French historian Le Page du Pratz wrote in *Histoire de la Louisiane,* African "slaves are very superstitious, and are much attached to their prejudices, and little toys which they call gris, gris. It would be improper therefore to take them from them, or even speak of them to them; for they would believe themselves undone, if they were stripped of those trinkets. The old negroes [will] soon make them lose conceit of them."[104]

Slaves from the Bight of Benin, Africa, probably account for the emergence of Voodoo in Louisiana, which was only reinforced by the massive immigration of Haitians. Moreover, the terms *ounga* and *gri-gri*, meaning harmful charm, have been widely used in New Orleans by speakers of English as well as by Creoles. Some elements of Voodoo no doubt originated in Haiti (Saint-Domingue) and were brought to Louisiana by immigrants from that former French colony, where Vodou is the primary popular religion, but the folk religion of New Orleans has its roots in the eighteenth century. For example, the term *gri-gri* appears in New Orleans court records as early as 1773. *Zinzin*, meaning amulet of support or power in Louisiana Creole, is a Bambara word with the same meaning.[105] It's likely, then, that eighteenth-century Voodoo from Africa and nineteenth-century Vodou from Saint-Domingue joined together in New Orleans.

Black Haitian immigrants, after 1803, along with free Creole Negroes purchased subdivided lots parceled out from the area once called Place de Congo, the African marketplace near the French Quarter where Africans had gathered for dance and music festivals since the early 1700s. They settled in the newly created faubourg Tremé, in which the town square was Place de Congo (Congo Square), known today as Louis Armstrong Park.

AMERICANIZATION OF CREOLE NEW ORLEANS

Originally, in the late 1700s in Spanish Louisiana, the term Creole was used to distinguish New Spain–born Africans from Blacks born in Africa. Consequently, "all first-generation slaves born in [Spanish] America and their descendants were" recorded as Creoles.[106] The word *Creole* (*criollo* in Spanish) "derives from the Portuguese word *crioulo,* meaning a slave of African descent born in the New World."[107] Therefore, *Creole* originally had nothing to do with skin color nor mixed-race heritage. Even the Blackest person born of African parentage in Louisiana was Creole by decree. In fact, at the time of the Louisiana Purchase, half the Negro population of Louisiana was free and likely descended from free Creole Negroes.

After Louisiana joined the United States of America in 1812, all Louisianans—Africans, Spaniards, and French—began identifying with the term *Creole* to distinguish themselves from Anglicized Black and White American newcomers. At the time of the American transition, wealthy and influential Black Creoles were vital to the economic and cultural life of Louisiana. It's important to understand that free Negro Creoles owned more land, were better educated, and wealthier than Anglo American migrants to New Orleans, initially. While the enslaved were deprived literacy, free Black Creoles were privately educating their families and passing on wealth and businesses to their children over generations. Free Blacks had the wealth to buy musical instruments for their children and the leisure necessary to appreciate and patronize high arts including the large Negro Philharmonic Orchestra at the Negro Theatre de La Renaissance.[108] Moreover, the patronage free Negroes provided to the one-hundred-member Antebellum Negro Philharmonic Society of classical musicians should dispel the more downtrodden theory of musicologists who focused on the banjo, one of the few instruments slaves had access to. Free Blacks had the leisure to purchase orchestral instruments and study music. Regarding the origin of orchestral instruments permeating the Black community of New Orleans, musicologists hypothesized that the proliferation of woodwind and brass instruments in nineteenth-century New Orleans was due to leftover Civil War instruments from military bands. Fact is, orchestral instruments were common in Black Creole New Orleans households as early as the 1830s.

The dark-skinned free Creole is often obfuscated from American history to dispossess Black Americans of antebellum agency and achievement. Violinist and classical composer Edmond Dédé, a free Negro Creole, swarthy as night, provides compelling evidence that the blackest of skin had no bearing on whether one was Creole or not. Edmond Dédé was born free into four generations of free Blacks on November 20, 1827, in New Orleans, Louisiana. The Dédé family exemplifies the numerous free dark-complexioned Creoles. While the wretched institution of Black slavery was well established in Louisiana, Edmond Dédé was born free and lived the life of a free man.

In 1785 in Spanish Louisiana, two years after the American colonies won their freedom from Britain, Edmond Dédé's great-grandfather, Francisco Dédé, purchased manumission of his thirty-four-year-old fiancée, Maria, from her master, Robert Montreuil, for what was then the handsome sum of eight hundred pesos.[109] When Edmond was around age ten, his father, Basile Dédé *fils*, had already started him on the clarinet. Edmond later switched to violin. And according to James Trotter, who wrote the first survey of African American musicians, Edmond Dédé studied with Ludovico Gabici, an Italian immigrant and music professor, and with Jacques Constantin Deburque (1800–1861), esteemed African American violinist and director of the Negro Philharmonic Orchestra. In 1852, Edmond Dédé composed what became the oldest surviving piece of sheet music by a New Orleans Negro Creole, "Mon Pauvre Coeur."

After 1840, however, there was a steady low-grade of White migration into Louisiana: slave traders, smugglers, gamblers, and desperadoes with little education. "Rich colored folk, even those who were well known, were often arrested and mistreated." In 1857, Louisiana governor Wickliffe

> informed the Legislature that the immigration of free Negroes . . . had been steadily increasing for years; that it was a source of great evil and demanded legislative action. Public policy dictates, the interest of the people requires, that immediate steps should be taken at this time to remove all free Negroes who are now in the State, when such removal can be affected without violation of law. Their example and associations have a most pernicious effect upon our slave population.[110]

It was under those racist circumstances in the 1850s that many free Blacks began taking their wealth and talents out of state or moving internationally. Edmond Dédé moved to Paris, where Enlightenment Age Creole violinist and composer Joseph Bologne, Chevalier de Saint-Georges, had left an enduring legacy for Black artists. France had abolished slavery in 1848. In Paris, Dédé continued his music education, becoming a student at the Paris Conservatoire of Music. He went on to Bordeaux to become the conductor for the ballet at the Grand Théâtre. As a composer in Bordeaux, Dédé wrote ballets, operettas, overtures, and more than 250 dances and songs. According to UC Davis professor of history Sally McKee, author of *The Exile's Song: Edmond Dédé and the Unfinished Revolutions of the Atlantic World*, his recently found (but never performed) opera, *Morgiane* (1888), is the earliest known full-length opera by an African American composer. He returned to New Orleans briefly in 1893, where he was honored by the Negro Creole community. In 1903, Edmond Dédé died in France.

———

From the American point of view, antebellum Louisiana was a place like no other. Northern American Protestant immigrants found the sweltering, swampy environs of New Orleans detestable. The perceived "decadence, ignorance, and moral deficiencies of creoles" both European and Negro, as observed by the Americans, both White and Black, created a deep chasm of indignation between Americans and Creoles. Americans made English the "legal language" of the state and attempted to replace civil with common law.[111]

From the Anglos' point of view, New Orleans was the most peculiarly exotic society in America. In fact, Louisiana had the largest number of Negro slave owners in the Union. Mind you, a slave in Spanish colonial Louisiana had manumission and other rights, unlike his British colonial counterpart. Free Negroes, many of whom were rich, educated, and respectable members of their communities, were met with suspicion and scorn by Anglo American immigrants settling into Louisiana.

Particularly offensive in the eyes of all Creoles were the American attacks on their traditional Creole habit of celebrating the Sabbath as a day of relaxed pleasure centered in bustling cafés, bull baiting, horse racing, theatrical performances, and the beloved dance. Shocked New England Puritans were forever posting signs beneath notices of Sunday balls admonishing the ungodly to "remember the Sabbath day to keep it holy!" while Protestant newspapers and ministers fulminated endlessly against a society capable of this "grossly sinful" rejection of established Christian morality.[112]

To be sure, Protestant Americans found the sensuality of New Orleans disturbingly exotic. The very public interracial sexuality, celebrated at Creole quadroon balls, was especially shocking. It is more myth than fact that free quadroon and octoroon girls eagerly became concubines of migrant Anglo men. It is more likely enslaved women were forced to attend the New Orleans tradition in which some of the more desirable enslaved girls in the city were summoned to ball with Anglo and Gallic males. On occasion, perhaps, free women of color may have attended, but it would have been odd, since the average Anglo migrants to Louisiana were dirt poor and likely illiterate. In contrast, free men of color were far more educated and, as a collective, were more prosperous than Anglo migrant men.

The clear majority of Protestant Anglo American immigrants were steeped in racial bigotry. They deemed quadroon balls an ungodly depravity. Quadroon balls should not be mistaken for genteel Victorian balls; they were lascivious affairs. Gallic females, especially the wives, weren't allowed. The practice of "protecting and flattering the virginity of a small class of women of their social clan, and keeping at their command poor women,"[113] White, Black, and Mulatto, was a confounding form of chivalry to say the least. It is a myth that young Creole ladies of color were customarily escorted by their mothers acting as agents seeking to catch a well-to-do protector for the young concubines. This may have been true for slave girls. However, Creoles of color dismiss such claims regarding Creole women.[114] Free Creole women weren't financially desperate.

Nonetheless, the music of choice at these scandalous—by puritan standards—affairs, were cotillions, schottisches, and quadrilles, usually performed by Negro orchestras. Despite all the ostensible shock and dismay of Protestant Anglo Americans, many of its gentries secretly desired, and certainly had, sexual relations with African women, often by force, but they kept such digressions hidden from polite society.

Most disturbing of all, perhaps, for the Anglo Americans new to Creole Louisiana, was the very public Africanized celebration of music, poetry, dance, creativity, Francophone literature, Voodoo spirituality, and wit of free and enslaved Creole Blacks. The Sunday marketplace at Congo Square where the free and enslaved celebrated, exercising free expression and cultural exchange, shocked the sensibilities of Anglo Americans and threatened social order. As a result, the gatherings were subsequently repressed. Thus, WASPs, repressive and racists edicts would become important antecedents of the blues as such.

From the Louisiana Creole point of view, the newly arrived Anglo Americans were condescending racists, hypocritical saints, and stringent "blue law" enforcers. Blue laws were forced upon Louisiana, where, unlike other areas of the South, Catholicism strongly affected the cultural beliefs and practices of the Creoles.

Beginning in the early nineteenth century, White Anglo-Saxon Protestant migrants took control of government and with due haste erected draconian moral codes, declaring a culture war on Creole decadence. The term *blue law* was not the name of the laws when they were first introduced by Puritans around 1610 in colonial Virginia. Crossing these stringent moral laws, in some instances for a repeat offender—such as failing to attend church three Sundays in a row—meant punishment by death.

The etymology of the term *blue laws* is unknown. However, the daily moral codes, and principally the Sunday codes, were unmistakably called *blue laws* by the time they reached Louisiana, because White Anglo-Saxon Protestants posted ordinances all over the city under that name. In Francophone Louisiana, the meaning of the Anglo word "blue" was easily conflated with the French word *bleu*, meaning off-color, subversive, or blaspheme. In Louisiana "blue laws" translated to the old French blaspheme *sacré bleu laws*. It was deemed sacré bleu, forbidden or greatly restricted, to enjoy sporting, horse racing, alcohol, dancing, and music on sacred religious days. Notwithstanding, such pastimes defined the Creole's way of life, especially on the Sabbath. As a result, tensions were heightened.

Creoles defiantly pushed back against the Americanization threat, forcing Anglo Americans to settle beyond the French Quarter in areas known today as the Garden District and Uptown. In effect, "it was the clash between original Louisianans [Creoles] and migrant Anglo-Americans after the Louisiana Purchase which for the first time made place of birth a critical issue and gave the Creole label its crucial significance."[115]

Recently, West Louisiana Cajuns, a unique culture unto itself, are now identified as provincial or country Creoles.[116] To understand the blues as a New Orleans Negro Creole invention, one must disregard the revisionist redefinition of "Creole" throughout the twentieth century that define it as mixed heritage and light skin. The large number of biracial families with lighter skin identifying as Creole aren't the rule but merely a vestige of the old days, prior to the annexation and the arrival of segregation. Anglo Americans forbade race mixing when they took control of the Louisiana government. Consequently, the Black descendants of original pre-American Creoles either darkened or whitened accordingly in the nineteenth and twentieth centuries.

Undeniably, African Americans in Louisiana have a history of agency and high culture even during slavery. It is important to appreciate how well prepared for leadership free Negro Creoles were during Reconstruction, which lasted from 1863 to 1877. Newly freed slaves, Freedmen, desired to become literate, to vote, and to own land. All three essentials had been denied the enslaved by law. During Reconstruction, Negro Creoles were best prepared to deliver a prescription for Black suffrage. The "Negro members of the [Louisiana] constitutional convention took a prominent and effective part."[117]

> Another factor was the numerous poor whites in the northern part of the State. Living close to the subsistence line on the thin soil of the pine hills back of the bottom lands, without schools, with but few churches, given to rude sports and crude methods of farming their ignorance and prejudice bred in them after the emancipation of the Negro, a dread of sinking to the social level of the blacks. The dread, in turn bred hatred, instigated very probably by the class above them.[118]

In the final constitution, a compromise provided "that the colored men's proposal for education," establishing the first publicly funded schools for both Blacks and Whites, "including no separation in schools, and a university, should prevail. The convention adopted the Constitution, March 19, 1868." This constitution gave Blacks the vote and denied the vote to former Confederates. It made Black men—not women—"equal to the whites and provided equal rights and privileges." Most important to Freedmen, "public schools were thrown open to both races."[119]

The new constitution of Louisiana was finally adopted and "signed by the black Lieutenant Governor of the state, Oscar J. Dunn," once a runaway slave who eventually bought his freedom, "and remain to this day the basic law of the state!" Dunn "was the only one of the seven colored men who sat in the State Senate in 1868 who had been a slave." [120]

In many ways, the failure of Reconstruction, along with the establishment of stringent Black Codes that affected the agency of all persons of color without distinction, brought on the strongest desire among Creole New Orleanians, those who remained in the state, to hold onto their agency, language, heritage, and culture.

2

THE AUTHENTIC NARRATIVE

IT MAY BE DIFFICULT TO POINT to one person as the father of the blues because it takes generations to accumulate the knowledge that inspires innovation. Be that as it may, the closest we have to an authentic "Father of Blues Thought" is pioneering civil rights activist, poet, journalist, author, and Louisiana Creole historian Rodolphe Lucien Desdunes, born November 15, 1849, in New Orleans, Louisiana.

Rodolphe Desdunes rose to prominence as a Creole leader during Reconstruction when as part of a Black militia supporting the New Orleans metropolitan police force he was wounded fending off an attempted coup by former Confederates known as the White Leaguers in the bloody "Battle of Liberty Place." Desdunes was the father of blues pianist Mamie Desdunes, born March 25, 1879, who, according to Jelly Roll Morton, was the earliest known blues composer. Jelly Roll Morton remembered hearing Mamie sing and play her composition "2:19 Blues" (aka "Mamie's Blues") when he was a child and learned to play it on piano. Morton said, "The one blues I never can forget out of those early days happened to be played by a woman that lived next door to my godmother in the Garden District. The name of this musician was Mamie Desdunes. Two middle fingers of her right hand had been cut off, so she played the blues with only three fingers on her right hand." Morton continued, "At that time, back in 1901 and 1902, we had a lot of great blues players that didn't know nothing but the blues. . . . Although I had heard it previously, I guess it was Mamie [who] first really sold me on the blues."[1]

Another contemporary of Jelly Roll Morton recalled playing the blues with Mamie: "I knew Mamie Desdunes real well," said New Orleans trumpeter Bunk

45

Johnson. "Played many a concert with her singing those same blues. She was pretty good looking—quite fair and with a nice head of hair. She was a hustlin' woman." Mamie was "a blues-singing poor gal. Used to play pretty passable piano around them dance halls on Perdido Street." Bunk continued, "When Hattie Rodgers or Lulu White would put it out that Mamie was going to be singing at their place, the white men would turn out in bunches and them whores would clean up."[2] "Mamie Desdunes died at 2414 Clara Street, New Orleans on December 4, 1911."[3] According to her Orleans Parish death certificate, the cause of death was pulmonary tuberculosis. She was only thirty-two years of age.

However, Rodolphe Desdunes, whom I have titled the Father of Blues Thought, deserves a place in blues history as much more than Mamie's father and the patriarch of one of New Orleans's most influential musical families. It was Rodolphe Desdunes who planned the first Supreme Court challenge to specious separate but equal Jim Crow laws, predating eventual Supreme Court justice and legendary civil rights attorney Thurgood Marshall by more than fifty years. Rodolphe Desdunes, having studied law at Straight University, utilized the judiciary to champion equality for all Black Americans, establishing the blueprint that Thurgood Marshall, the first African American Supreme Court judge, would follow in the landmark 1954 case *Brown v. Board of Education*. Moreover, Desdunes, along with Louis André Martinet, formed the Comité des Citoyens (Citizens' Committee), a precursor of the NAACP, to champion equality and civil rights for colored people.

A brilliant political strategist, Desdunes risked the arrest of his son, musician Dan Desdunes, by organizing a political action in which he refused to give up his seat on a segregated train sixty-three years before Rosa Parks followed his example and did the same in Montgomery, Alabama, in 1955.

Rodolphe Desdunes was from a relatively wealthy family. They owned a cigar business. Rodolphe, a part-time cigar maker, worked from 1879 until 1912 on and off "as a clerk for the U.S. Customs Service of New Orleans." In "1889, notary and attorney Louis André Martinet (1849–1917) started publishing a Republican"—the preferred political party of Black progressives at the time—Creole of color "newspaper, the *Crusader*; printed in French and English." The *Crusader* was the only Black daily newspaper in the country when it began publication. Its aim was "to inform and rally black and Creole leaders to challenge new segregation laws." Rodolphe Desdunes was a columnist for the Black-owned New Orleans newspaper and wrote several influential articles championing equality.[4]

In response to the Separate Car Act passed in 1890, which made legal "separate but equal" train car accommodations for Blacks and Whites, Rodolphe Desdunes "formed the Comité des Citoyens which enlisted [his] eldest son [musician]

Daniel Desdunes," a violinist and the coleader of the Coustaut-Desdunes band, to contest this act. Daniel, born in 1873, had attended local New Orleans public schools before attending Straight University. By 1892, he was a prominent local musician. He would eventually become a member of the influential Onward Brass Band.[5]

On February 24, 1892, Daniel Desdunes, the brother of the first blues composer young Jelly Roll Morton ever heard, pianist Mamie Desdunes, "boarded a white-only car on a train bound for Mobile, Alabama. The train was stopped at the corner of Elysian Fields and Claiborne, and Daniel was arrested and removed to the precinct." His father's Citizens' Committee had prearranged to pay his bail. "Shortly thereafter, Judge J. H. Ferguson ruled that enforcement of the Separate Car Act upon interstate travel was unconstitutional because only the federal government had the authority to regulate interstate commerce." Thus, the Citizens' Committee was encouraged to try again. This time they would challenge the law in federal court and focus on intrastate travel. For the federal challenge, they chose a neighbor with whom they had fellowship, shoemaker Homer Plessy (1863–1925).[6]

On June 7, 1892, Plessy purchased a first-class ticket and "boarded a first-class car of the East Louisiana Railroad to Covington."[7] When ordered to move to the car for Negroes, Plessy refused the order as planned. He was then forcibly dragged out of the first-class coach. Subsequently, as part of their grand strategy, Rodolphe Desdunes and the Comité litigated the White supremacist law until it reached the United States Supreme Court. The final ruling came "four years later, on May 18, 1896, that Plessy's constitutional rights had not been violated by Louisiana law." Years later, in his book *Our People and Our History* Rodolphe Desdunes wrote, "Our defeat sanctioned the odious principle of the segregation of the races."

It was during this great political and cultural battle led by the Desdunes family that the first discordant sounds of the blues began bellowing out of the music halls around New Orleans. It was a pushback from Louisiana's proud Creole culture against the Americanization and annexation of its way of life. The "Comité disbanded, and the Crusader ceased publication,"[8] but the writings and activism of Rodolphe Desdunes and his family had manifested in a unique musical expression that continued to Creolize everything Anglo Americans held sacred. Although this expression was deemed *sacré bleu*, and meant as a pejorative, the shortened Creolized term *blues* became a rebellious term of Creole pride among Black New Orleans youth.

The etymology of *the blues* derives from the New Orleans Creolization of the old French curse *sacré bleu*. Gradually, *the blues* became a term of enlightened Creole pride, an expression of humanity in defiance of a totalitarian government toward its Black citizens. The blues expressed rebelliousness, rejecting social control by the church and a racist Christian ethos in pursuit of equality and happiness. Consequently, in respectable theaters and among God-fearing Christians, the blues was deemed the music of the devil. In other words, We don't allow the blues in our respectable theatre, one might say. Granted, as the blues reached beyond South Louisiana and traveled north in the 1920s, its original Creole meaning was lost in translation. Ostensibly the blues was redefined as the downtrodden music of "happy slaves" and the cry of the "noble savage." In reality, it was a proud, defiant expression of freedom.

Many are familiar with the divergent philosophies toward equality of W. E. B. Du Bois and Booker T. Washington. Booker T. Washington and W. E. B. Du Bois were both dedicated to Black liberation. Washington thought southern Blacks should focus myopically on building agricultural skills in the pursuit of economic self-sufficiency. In turn, Blacks would refrain from politics, leaving the governmental sphere to Whites. Du Bois, one of the original founders of the NAACP, believed the way forward was to empower educated Blacks to fight in the political sphere for immediate equality. Over the years, Booker T. Washington has been greatly criticized for his "accommodating" approach to fighting racism. But there is a third philosophy, as defined by Rodolphe Desdunes, who excoriated the ignorance of W. E. B. Du Bois regarding his sweeping condescending generalities of the Southern Negro.

On February 17, 1907, W. E. B. Du Bois gave a speech at Carnegie Hall in New York City in which he discussed the "Negro Problem." A week later, on February 24, the *New Orleans Item-Tribune* reprinted parts of the speech: "After declaring that the negroes of the South are lacking in book knowledge, in industrial faculty and even unacquainted with the best traditions of family life, [Du Bois] charged that they were left without the protection even of life that the law affords the whites." In other words, Du Bois painted the entire Black South with the same broad brush.

Rodolphe Desdunes strongly objected to and challenged W. E. B. Du Bois's ignorance about Black Creoles of Louisiana. Desdunes responded by illuminating the duality of the Black community in Louisiana, one he called the "Latin Negro" (Creole) and the other the "Anglo-Saxon or American Negro." Desdunes felt that the two groups had evolved "different schools of politics [and differed] radically in . . . aspiration and method." He said the Creole Negro "hopes, while the [American Negro] doubts; . . . One aspires to equality, the other to identity. One will forget that he is a Negro in order to think that he is a man; the other will forget that he is a man to think that he is a Negro."[9]

In other words, Desdunes argued, as a man, the Negro should do what men do, go where men go, aspire to what men aspire to. He cautioned that if he identified first as a Negro, then he would only go where the Negro goes, do only as the Negro does, and aspire only as a Negro aspires. Indeed, Rodolphe Desdunes didn't fight for justice for a special class of descendants from free people of color, he fought for equal rights of all African Americans.

In 1908,

> while [Desdunes] was supervising the weighing of cargo on a ship for the Customhouse, granite dust blew in his eyes, leaving him legally blind. Fortunately, he had already completed the manuscript of *Nos Hommes et Notre Histoire*. After his retirement the following year, Rodolphe went to Omaha, Nebraska, where his son Daniel was living, and purchased a house. . . . While on tour around 1904, Dan Desdunes reached Omaha, Nebraska, and decided to settle there. . . . Rodolphe died on August 14, 1928, of cancer of the larynx.[10]

Desdunes, the authentic Father of Blues Thought, first published *Nos Hommes et Notre Histoire* (*Our People and Our History*), the first history of the Creole families of New Orleans, in French in 1911. *Fifty Creole Portraits* was translated to English posthumously in 1937.

By the 1890s, Creolization had become a way of life in South Louisiana, not only for original Negro Creoles, but all Blacks, including newly arrived Anglo Black immigrants from surrounding plantations who embraced the Crescent City and its Creole Catholic Voodoo culture, thus becoming proud Creoles themselves. The expression of pride in one's own culture manifested, as a discordant high-spirited musical expression called *the blues*.

BUDDY BOLDEN: THE BLACK ROSE

IN THE 1890s, the city of New Orleans became a hotbed of talented cornetists. The proliferation of brass musicians was due in part to fierce competition among numerous benevolent societies to book the hottest brass bands to attract dues-paying members. More than two hundred Negro benevolent societies and clubs were active in the city, including "lodges of the Odd Fellows, Masons, Knights Templar, and Eastern Star." There were "baseball clubs, rowing clubs, militia companies, religious societies, orphan aid societies," and so on.[11] Members pooled money to provide each other health care, banking, insurance, and general uplift.

There was an abundance of gigs for brass musicians, which helped to sharpen their skills. Music tastes had changed little over the years. High society balls required the obligatory waltzes, reels, schottisches, quadrilles, and marches. Parties of common folk required a ragged rhythm. The cakewalk became a national craze. The cakewalk was a common folk burlesque mocking formal Victorian elite. Competitions abounded, with first prize a large layered cake. Ragtime, an energetic, catchy new style with a strict classical aesthetic, was just starting to catch on.

Then, around 1893, nurtured by saliva and sweat from the horns of countless parade bands, something miraculously appeared on the scene: a black rose, Charles "Buddy" Bolden. The "black rose" sprouted up through a crack in the cobblestone streets of New Orleans. Seeds he planted are still in bloom. The echoes from his cornet still haunt the Crescent City. Though Buddy Bolden remains a ghostly figure to many, among his contemporaries—those that heard him play—he was undeniably the original soothsayer of the blues.

Buddy Bolden, born September 6, 1877, first began performing in public between 1893 and 1895 for parades and dances—many dances were held in uptown churches that also doubled as community centers. We can only imagine what Buddy Bolden's music sounded like because he left no written scores and made no audio recordings during his short career (1894–1907), when the recording business was in its infancy. There is only one known picture of the mysterious blues musician, circa 1895. Therefore, we must rely on the accounts of musicians who played in his band and fans who heard him perform to reconstruct his legacy.

What did Bolden look like? Well, according to trombonist Kid Ory, he was "brown-skinned, had brown hair and brown eyes, no beard. Hair wasn't black, was not exactly red, never combed it, always the way it was cut," Ory recalled years later.[12]

What songs were in Bolden's repertoire? Bolden's signature song was "Funky Butt," aka "Buddy Bolden's Blues," which had a vulgar lyric about the stench of a sweaty honky-tonk he happened to be playing one night.[13]

> I thought I heard Buddy Bolden say,
> Funky butt, funky butt, take it away.
> You're nasty, you're dirty, take it away.
> I thought I heard Buddy Bolden shout,
> Open up that window and let the bad air out.
>   "Buddy Bolden's Blues" (Jelly Roll Morton)

What effect did Bolden's music have on those who heard him? According to clarinetist George Baquet (1881–1949), who played with Buddy Bolden, he was a crowd pleaser. "One of his popular songs was 'Make Me a Pallet on the Floor,' said George, describing the first time he heard and played with Buddy Bolden at Odd Fellows Hall. "Everybody rose and yelled out, 'Oh, Mr. Bolden, play it for us, Buddy, play it!' I'd never heard anything like that before," said Baquet. "I'd played 'legitimate' stuff. But this, it was something that pulled me in. They got me up on the stand and I played with them. After that, I didn't play legitimate so much."[14]

"Legitimate" meant strict conformity to the written score. Buddy Bolden, in contrast, subverted the tyrannical written score, relying instead on improvisation. Even though Bolden could read music—he was regularly listed in the newspaper as a music instructor—he was not one to write his compositions down on paper.

At the turn of the century, legitimate musicians who could read and write music looked down on Bolden's new blues style initially. They believed blues music lacked proper technique, discipline, and social grace. Contrarily, from Bolden's point of view, legitimate musicians lacked the funky uninhibited feeling of the blues that his Back o' Town fans demanded.

During this period, playing by ear was a new idea for bands and orchestras. Fakers—as those who couldn't read music were called—weren't often invited to play high society gigs. Most legitimate players, such as drummer and violinist John Robichaux (1886–1939) were conventionally trained. Robichaux was often hired to play highbrow gigs for elite balls. The John Robichaux Orchestra, a rival of Bolden's Band, also specialized in quadrilles, waltzes, schottisches, and cotillions, but they didn't play them in the new bluesy style Buddy Bolden was developing. Moreover, the Robichaux Orchestra played neither slow-drags nor ribald tunes, both of which, due to their Victorian highbrow aspirations, were considered uncouth.

I would argue it was no coincidence that in 1896 a discordant sound, soon to be called the blues, began reverberating across New Orleans. The irony is not lost that the birth of the blues coincided with the landmark decision *Plessy v. Ferguson*. It was the same year the term Creole was stripped of its value. Following *Plessy v. Ferguson*, New Orleans became Americanized. Suddenly, Negro Creoles were forced to live under the same race-based American laws as other Black Americans.

Many jazz biographers tend to overemphasize the rift between Creoles of color and other Black Americans, creating a false dichotomy of hatred between the two communities based on their complexions: light skin versus dark skin. What caused the tension, however, was the encroachment of White Americanization on the Creole way of life. It wasn't taught in Black schools that one hundred years earlier, during the Louisiana Purchase, Negro Creoles were more educated than White Americans immigrating to Louisiana. They were more skilled, had more businesses, and were wealthier than White New Orleans immigrants. By 1896, many Negro Creole families, regardless of skin tone, had never been enslaved or denied education; it stands to reason that they were further ahead than their Black American neighbors, who were, after all, but one generation removed from slavery. Neither white skin nor light skin makes one more intelligent, yet colorism—a vestige of Anglo America's chattel slavery institution—was imposed on the Creole way of life. The "separate but equal" ruling outlawed marriage between Blacks and Whites, further alienating those Creoles who happened to be of mixed heritage.

To be clear, Creole was a term to identify descendants of Africans born in Spanish Louisiana or other Spanish territories. Therefore, nearly all musicians who gave birth to the blues were Creole in accordance with its original definition. Henceforth, for clarity, I will not continue to divide each musician by who is Creole and non-Creole. As I see it, from Buddy Bolden to Louis Armstrong, to Sidney Bechet to Jelly Roll Morton, they were all Negro, Creole, colored, African American, and Black.

It is common knowledge that America consistently broke treaties with Native Americans. Therefore, it should come as no surprise that the United States likewise rescinded its tolerance for Creole culture. Negro Creoles, in the aftermath of *Plessy v. Ferguson*, were forced to ride in the back of streetcars. They were forced into segregated schools, waiting rooms, railroad coaches, elevators, witness stands, and public restrooms. Consequently, it is no coincidence that, just as tyrannical race-based laws and the Puritan value system of the United States threatened to destroy their Creole way of life, the defiant blues rose up, and said, "Oh, hell no!"

In New Orleans's Lincoln Park, which opened in 1902, Buddy Bolden's new blues style inspired young musicians who went to hear him blow. Lincoln Park featured a pavilion and skating rink. It was operated by the Black community. Buddy Bolden's stentorian cornet echoed for miles. Lincoln Park's popular Sunday dances, sometimes billed as a "battle of the bands," showcased the best orchestras from around the city. Bolden's irresistible sound and flashy showmanship made him the crowd favorite. He won most of his battles, earning the legendary moniker "King Bolden." He also played at Union Sons of Honor Hall, aka Funky Butt Hall, squared by Perdido, South Liberty, Gravier, and South Franklin Streets, in the Back o' Town district. A tenement just down Perdido Street, at 1303, was where little Louis Armstrong would grow up.

Contrary to popular myth, Bolden's Band didn't play in the vice district of Storyville. He performed around the edges, in honky-tonks. Bolden was also known to hold court at Masonic Hall in Algiers. Moreover, according to several eyewitness accounts, Bolden's Band, between the years 1902 and 1905, performed on train excursions to Baton Rouge, from the baggage car.[15] At stops along the way, he entertained. Kid Ory said he saw Buddy perform at a stop on one of those excursions in Ory's hometown LaPlace, Louisiana.[16]

Bolden also performed regularly in West Baton Rouge in Plaquemines Parish for dances. Trumpeter Charlie Love, born in 1885 in Plaquemine, Louisiana, recalled a circa 1903 personal encounter with Bolden one night: Bolden had a busted valve on his horn. "'You wanta borry mine, I'll go get it,'" little Charlie said. "[Bolden] say, 'Yes, I can use it.' I jumped on my bicycle and I rode home down by the levee. Rushed back to the bandstand. Buddy held my cornet up and laughed at it and he say, 'Look what this boy done brought here. How in the world I'm gonna play this?' And he takes it out and made out with it and finished the job with it."

West Baton Rouge blues pianist and songwriter Clarence Williams, who would later become one of the greatest blues composers and a rival of W. C. Handy, said about his childhood encounter with Buddy Bolden: "I came to New Orleans in 1906, when I was 14 years old. It was after I heard Buddy Bolden; when he came through my hometown, Plaquemine, Louisiana, on an excursion, and his trumpet playin' excited me, so that I said, 'I'm goin' to New Orleans.' I had never heard anything like that before in my life."[17]

There is no evidence Bolden left the state of Louisiana, as many Louisiana musicians he inspired would do in the 1910s, for greater fame and fortune.[18] Buddy Bolden's distinctive musical approach was subsequently developed into a bluesy musical language by those who heard or played with him, such as Kid Ory, Bud Scott, Mutt Carey, and trombonist Bill Matthews. According to Matthews, "On those old, slow, low down blues, he had a moan in his cornet that went all through you, just like you were in church or something."

It's also reported that Buddy's band did not play extended solos, yet their music featured some improvisation. "Everybody was crazy about Bolden when he'd blow a waltz, schottische or old lowdown blues," Bill Matthews reminisced. "Louis Armstrong, King Oliver, none of 'em had a tone like Bolden."

Buddy Bolden didn't play in the upper registers of the trumpet as Armstrong would do later in the 1920s; Bolden's tone was mostly in the middle register. Bill Matthews went on to say, "Bunk Johnson got his style following Buddy with his sweetness, but could never play rough and loud like Bolden."[19] Regrettably, we will never have the pleasure of hearing him for ourselves. There were some whispers long ago that a recording was made of Buddy Bolden but subsequently lost. It's highly unlikely he would have had the opportunity to record *commercially* due to the rarity of orchestra recordings at that time.

By 1906, Buddy Bolden, then twenty-nine, was prone to erratic behavior. He had been living too fast, binge drinking, not sleeping for days at a time. "Fellas knew he was kinda losing his mind," recalled trumpeter Charles Love. "He had a way of calling his girl on his trumpet. He'd go outside and serenade her with a particular riff, and she'd usually answer to it. One night, he went out and called her on his horn, and she didn't come. And man, he went to pieces. Got to rubbing his head and carrying on. He got mad, threw his horn down. Bam! Jumped up. Kicked it! Took an' bent it all to pieces. Man, that's when it come out, that he'd gone crazy."[20]

Unfortunately, Charles Buddy Bolden, following bouts of depression due to an undiagnosed mental illness—reported to be caused by alcoholism—was arrested for a domestic disturbance and later committed to the insane asylum in Jackson, Louisiana, on June 5, 1907. He would spend the rest of his life there. On November 4, 1931, the last petal fell from the black rose. Buddy Bolden, the first man of blues, only a shell of his former self, quietly passed away.[21] He was fifty-four years old.

FREEDOM OF EXPRESSION

SYMBOLICALLY, ON SATURDAY NIGHTS in New Orleans, Blacks collectively celebrated their hard-won liberty. Saturday night became the freedmen's weekly Fourth of July festival, celebrated with "pomp and parade, shows and illuminations."[22] In the blues, we had found our freedom of expression, our unique "pursuit of Happiness." Until his last breath Louis Armstrong insisted the Fourth of July was his birthday. It should have been. His life, music, and broad smile epitomized the spirit of the young nation to-be.

The Fourth of July is the great day America has set aside to celebrate its independence from England's repression. The Revolutionary War happened at the height of what is known as Western music's classical period (1750–1820).

No composer of any note had been born in America prior to Francis Hopkinson, born in Philadelphia, Pennsylvania, in 1737. Hopkinson's "My Days Have Been So Wondrous Free," a secular song, is often cited as the first song published in America. Upon closer inspection, "My Days Have Been So Wondrous Free" was an English poem Hopkinson set to music in 1759. Therefore, how American the song was is questionable. Hopkinson went on to dedicate the song to his close friend, America's first president, General George Washington, in 1788. Hopkinson, a man of many talents, was also a signer of the Declaration of Independence as a New Jersey delegate.

America desperately wanted to establish its own cultural identity. Moreover, colonial America wanted the autonomy to seek its own destiny. The tyranny of a British aristocratic oligarchy was deemed intolerable. The young republic rebelled against "taxation without representation"—at least that's the story most Americans were taught. For planters, much more was at stake. England's chief justice, Lord Mansfield, had ruled in the Summerset Case of 1772 that enslaved people brought to England could legally claim their freedom and were no longer forced to return to its colonies. Following the landmark ruling, planters feared England would soon abolish the institution of slavery.[23]

Following the successful rebellion, the fledgling agrarian North American democracy was free to define itself and establish its own identity separate from England. Ironically, however, America would poach a quasi-English class system the Revolutionary War had been supposedly fought to resist. This tiered class system became a major part of American social life. English Anglo mores, fashions, prudishness, and etiquettes quickly became the ideals to which all other "respectable" Americans and immigrants would be measured.

On July 3, 1776, John Adams, the second president of the United States, wrote to his wife, Abigail, expressing his exciting vision for an annual Fourth of July party so grand even the biggest hip-hop mogul would be shocked and awed. John Adams wrote, "I am apt to believe that it will be celebrated, by succeeding Generations, as the great anniversary Festival . . . It ought to be solemnized with Pomp and Parade, with Shews [sic], Games, Sports, Guns, Bells, Bonfires and Illuminations from one End of this Continent to the other, from this Time forward forever more."[24]

Dancing to the melodious sounds of musicians performing tunes designed for dancing has been a great American pastime since its founding. Visitors, after receiving coveted invitations to the estates of rich tobacco gentry in Virginia, would travel many miles to partake in subscription balls. Fine food and wine were mere appetizers to a long evening of dancing.

In the parlor, young maidens of the host family, fresh from expensive music lessons from a local master, would exhibit their talents by performing piano or violin concertos for their guests. Servants and slaves would often provide dance music, quadrilles, and schottisches, while the master of ceremonies directed the night's program. Dance masters would have been employed months in advance to teach the latest dances, such as the waltz or the cotillion. Proper decorum would be taught to the young gentry. Social graces and a gentlemanly conversation were expected. Stylish dress, along with proper manners and restraint, were essential for entrance into these well-to-do affairs.

George Washington was known to have a voracious desire for dancing. As his fame grew, he was invited to countless balls, in which he eagerly partook. On one legendary occasion during the Revolutionary War the athletic inaugural president is said to have danced with an exhausted Kitty Greene, the wife of General Nathanael Greene, for three hours straight.

As a student, John Quincy Adams, our sixth president, while studying in Haverhill, Massachusetts, for his admittance into Harvard, enjoyed balls and dancing like most college-aged students even today. But also like most young people of any generation, the elders frowned upon young John and his friends' progressive culture and perceived lack of manners and decorum at their dance parties.

John Quincy Adams wrote in his diary of the anger and frustration he felt with a certain local Baptist minister who preached that dancing was as wicked a sin as murder and should be banished. Adams responded,

> Mr. Smith the minister of the Baptist society in this town, is violently opposed to dancing. It is in his mind. . . . heinous sin . . . and there are many people here so warped in prejudice that they are really persuaded they should incur the divine displeasure, as much by dancing as . . . perhaps committing murder . . . How one of the more innocent and rational amusements that was ever invented can find so many opposers [sic] is somewhat mysterious . . . There are many who are envious to others [dancing].[25]

Adams went on to say he and fellow members "wisely" ignored the elders and carried on with their "dirty" dancing parties. It sounds to me like John Quincy Adams could have been advocating for the blues or hip-hop.

Our founders—George Washington, John Adams, and John Quincy Adams—were great visionaries who enjoyed music, parties, dancing, and drinking very much. In fact, George Washington was an excellent moonshiner. They understood that music and dance were much more than mere amusement. They were also a way to find commonality and lift the spirit of a nation.

I presume, however, if they had the foresight to envision dances like the shimmy, the jitterbug, the slow-drag, or the twerk, they would have commandeered the next ship back to England and begged forgiveness. Maybe they would have loaded their muskets and formed militias to repress our revolutionary music and dances. Or maybe, just maybe, they would have stood with enlightened Black Americans and drunk a toast to our freedom of expression, no matter how bitter the cup of tea.[26]

In the eighteenth century, the United States was a fledgling agrarian republic built on the backs of the enslaved. By the end of the nineteenth century, it was well on its way to becoming a powerful industrial nation. Nevertheless, the quest to establish an "exceptional" national musical and cultural identity, worthy of an "exceptional" nation, remained elusive. The expectation was that a great White hope; an American-born composer from the elite class, would seize the moment. They never imagined the proverbial glass slipper would fit the progeny of the enslaved so perfectly.

Back in the early 1800s, Black plantation preachers, trained by their Puritan enslavers, helped to control the behaviors and thoughts of most enslaved Black men and women in British colonial America. Free Louisiana Creoles were an exception. The role the Black preacher played, delivering "slave sermons" of accommodation under the guardianship of White Protestant church leaders, was foreign to Black Creole New Orleanians.[27] Many Black Creoles were armed and had gained military training and experience in the official militias of Louisiana. By the 1830s, "free black Creoles of [Louisiana] had emerged from French and Spanish rule . . . with . . . rights and powers, . . .also with a peculiar assertiveness and self-confidence" confounding to Black immigrants from the former British colonies.[28] What's more, they had acquired wealth, artisan skills, and education beyond the reach—due to United States slave laws—of the average free Black in Anglo America.

Throughout the antebellum era, free and enslaved Black Creoles lived in nearly autonomous Creole municipal districts of New Orleans. Under American rule their tolerant culture of frequenting music festivities, bars, and dance halls— even on the Sabbath—continued despite the condemnation of Protestant American immigrants. Creoles conspicuously defied Puritan blue laws, which shocked Black Protestant religious leaders immigrating to the city. Black Americanized preachers had long urged their followers in the Old South not to revolt against the White power marshaled against them but rather to find shelter and solace in the church.[29] Black Creoles were dismayed by such docile sermonizing.

Mardi Gras was one of many cultural rituals in Louisiana where the sacred and the secular mingled freely. Tolerant Catholic attitudes toward alcohol consumption, prostitution, and gambling differed greatly from the temperance of Evangelical and Protestant southern states. Louisiana's *laissez les bons temps rouler* (Let the good times roll) attitude, along with a high regard for festivals, music, and dance, proved the perfect incubator for the blues.

Creole worship was a mixture of Catholic ritual and Voodoo expressionisms. Black Anglicized immigrants to New Orleans, uniformly to their White superiors, found Negro Creole worship exotic and impure. Notwithstanding, it was Creole bohemian defiance of such Anglicized superstition that allowed Black Creole musicians to eventually ascend from the margins and forge an alternative route to respectability via their so-called devil music.

To further illustrate the clash between Puritan blue laws and Creole blues, "in 1799 a Black Baptist preacher landed in a [New Orleans] Spanish jail for violating the colony's ban on all religious creeds except Catholicism."[30] It was the Baptists who attempted to establish the earliest foundations for the Black Protestant church in Louisiana. Creole Louisianans were more likely to burn the Baptist church down than attend it. "The First Baptist Church in New Orleans, which lasted from 1818 to 1820, began like those on the rural frontier—with both black and white members and a tolerance for black preachers. The First African Baptist Church with an all-black congregation, tried to set roots in New Orleans on October 31, 1826, but survived only until 1830, when its first pastor, Asa C. Goldsberry, died. Harassment [by Black Creoles] forced it to disband."[31]

By the end of the nineteenth century, descendants of Black Anglicized immigrants born in New Orleans had been acculturated. Although many were raised Baptist, they learned to love Creole bohemian culture, the blues, and even Mardi Gras, enthusiastically celebrating the Catholic holiday and tolerating all the vices that went along it.

In the 1890s, church buildings were very active in Black communities in the American section throughout the week. Churches were social hubs, used for secular traveling shows and plays, as well as the usual weddings and funeral functions. A Baptist church—sometimes called a holy roller church if boisterous music was allowed—could be found on every other corner in Back o' Town neighborhoods. Back o' Town, as the Back of Town area was known, was around South Rampart and Perdido Streets, where Louis Armstrong was born. At the time, it centered around the Black red-light district with a concentration of sporting houses, social halls, and vaudeville theaters ranging from honky-tonk dives to classy ballrooms. Sunday services could get rowdy, because holy roller church services were infused with the music of good-time neighborhood musicians.

A band, in support of the choir, would play spirituals with zeal and abandonment until churchgoers got the Holy Ghost. In Voodoo, this means possession or a trancelike state in which a great loa spirit enters the body, causing violent, seizure-like reactions, fevered dancing, and fainting. To the outsider, this ritual might look like great agony and suffering. On the contrary, it means the person is blessed and overwhelmingly happy because she's filled with the ancestral spirit. It was in the Baptist church that I, like my dad before me, first witnessed church ladies get the *spirit*. My family drifted away from St. Luke, Dad's family church, built by his stepfather, over the years. As a child, my family belonged to Greater

Beulah Baptist Church in South Baton Rouge. At Beulah, they would jump and shout, whoop and holler, dance and cry. They cried because they were happy. With everyone stomping, clapping, and singing, in a call and response, with the choir and the deacon leading the way, it was very easy for an impressionable music-smitten kid to get happily lost in the music.

JELLY ROLL MORTON

IN THE 1890S IN NORTHERN STATES, in order to assimilate into "Whiteness," meaning first-class citizenship, many Blacks practiced assimilationism, similar to Sicilians, Greeks, and other non–Anglo European immigrants, who were moving up America's racial hierarchy into "Whiteness." Accommodationists Blacks argued privately, and publicly, that if the Black race were conspicuously "dignified" in the eyes, ears, and minds of Anglo Victorian–era Americans—denouncing the blues and its rebel culture of sensuality and vice—they too could achieve equality.

What's more, the Anglicized curriculum of European history, philosophy, and Christianity imposed on Black universities was consequential in shaping the aspirations of educated Blacks—often referred to as the Black bourgeoisie. This was especially true for many disillusioned Creoles of Louisiana—now renamed Creoles of color—who had no desire to deny their African heritage prior to the *Plessy v. Ferguson* ruling in 1896 legalizing Jim Crow segregation.

To be sure, the Creole way of life became tenuous due to the rise of post-Reconstruction Black Code laws. During the antebellum years, many free Creoles had routinely married and lived among the enslaved yet retained their freedom. However, by the 1890s, intermarrying and social mixing with formerly enslaved people, which had been common among free Creoles prior to emancipation, could now, under Black Code laws and the rise of Jim Crow, put the social privileges of Creoles of color at risk. To distinguish their Creole children from the children of the formerly enslaved, a faction of Creoles of color attempted to protect their children by prohibiting them from socializing with downtrodden Blacks.

Nevertheless, any words leaving the tongues of Creole of color parents to dissuade their mulish son Ferdinand Joseph LaMothe to stay away from the allure of a tempting horn summoning him to a funky dancehall, imbued with the seductive scent of perfume and sweat from incandescent young people stomping and slow-grinding their bodies, would fall impotently on ears engrossed with a music exuding bawdiness, ribaldry, and naughtiness, in an atmosphere known to be low-down, dirty, hot, erotic, prurient, sensual, and raunchy, or as his Creole-speaking community would *préciser, sacré bleu* or *les bleus*. The call of *les bleus* proved irresistible to young Ferdinand LaMothe, soon to be known as "Winin' Boy" and later as piano genius Jelly Roll Morton.

Jelly Roll Morton, born Ferdinand Joseph LaMothe in New Orleans between 1885 and 1890, was playing music in Storyville brothels at a tender age.[32] His conservative Creole family were outraged to learn he was crazy for the blues. They wanted him, as most parents would, to take up a respectable vocation. However, young Ferdinand was infatuated with the blues and its free-spirited culture. Moreover, he was enthralled with the money he could earn as a professional musician. Ferdinand LaMothe didn't have many options. Only menial jobs were available to Negroes and Italian immigrants. By 1900, *Plessy v. Ferguson*, brought by New Orleans Black Creoles, had become constitutional law throughout the former Confederate states. Racial segregation under the separate but equal doctrine brought an end to the Creole way of life around the Vieux Carré that had lasted for nearly two hundred years.

Ferdinand LaMothe was of slight build; his skin tone was lighter than a brown paper bag. His light complexion may have allowed him a picayune amount of social status within the Black community. But in general, his light skin was inconsequential. To White people, he was just another Negro.

In his remarkable 1938 Library of Congress recordings, conducted by folklorist Alan Lomax, Ferdinand "Jelly Roll" LaMothe recalled his earliest recollection of hearing the blues as a young child. "I was quite small," Jelly Roll said, but he was "always hanging out with older men, I'd be with [them] when they all get together—a whole lot of sweet mamas and their sweet papas—to have a little bit of a ball off to their self." Morton continued, "Josky Adams," a local pianist and singer, "would sing and play the blues."[33]

> I got a woman lives right back of the jail,
> She got a sign on her window—Pussy for Sale.

When Jelly Roll spoke of blues during the historic interview, he defined it for the most part as it had been defined in old French-speaking New Orleans: *bleu* meaning risqué, or blue as in blue entertainment. In other words, not exactly the type of songs a nice Catholic boy from a respectable Creole of color family should perform, neither at home nor in public.

The LaMothe family, trying desperately to hold on to their tenuous Creole respectability, gave young Ferdinand, who first adopted the Storyville Bordello name "Winin' Boy," an ultimatum. Winin' Boy chose the blues and was kicked out on the streets. After hustling around Storyville, young Winin' Boy was taken in by his godmother, Laura Hunter, aka Eulalie Echo, a prosperous Voodoo priestess. (Eulalie is perhaps a misspelling of Erzulie, which means Loa or Goddess.) Laura Hunter had a home in the Garden District and another in Biloxi, Mississippi. As a child, Winin' Boy had an insatiable interest in the music he heard echoing out of sporting houses in Storyville. His godmother, recognizing he had a gift for music, paid for young Winin' Boy's first guitar lessons. Ever since he was knee-high and wearing short pants, his godmother had treated him special.

The greatest influence on young Winin' Boy was Storyville piano master Tony Jackson. Jelly Roll Morton said Tony Jackson was "the world's greatest single-handed entertainer, could play & sing from Opera to Blues in its correct formation, knew everything that probably was ever printed."[34]

Tony Jackson, born by most estimates in 1876 in New Orleans, was according to witnesses openly queer. "Tony happened to be one of those gentlemen that a lot of people call them lady or sissy," Morton recalled.[35] As a young man, Morton was very conscious of the fact that his instrument of choice, the piano, in many rough and tumble Back o' Town circles (those barrelhouses of vice in which Jelly Roll liked to hang out) was seen as a "sissy's instrument." The piano, in the Black community, had long been an upper-class parlor instrument associated with debutantes—young polite society girls. Most Black and poor people didn't own pianos. Jelly Roll Morton may have developed an over-the-top macho persona to mask his insecurity about the perceived femininity of the piano.

Moreover, pianos had not been part of the brass band tradition. Therefore, you didn't hear Jelly Roll Morton talk much about local parade bands having a heavy influence on him, as you would a horn player. Nonetheless, Morton famously adopted and transposed many brass orchestra arrangements for piano.

Jelly Roll Morton raved about his mentor: "Tony was real dark and not a bit good-looking, but he had a beautiful disposition."[36] Tony Jackson, although he specialized in the blues, played whatever music the people in the room wanted to hear. That's how a piano professor made good tips in Storyville. Judging from Morton's diamond-studded smile, like Tony, Jelly too learned to entertain the high-rollers. Morton said Tony Jackson "had a beautiful voice and a marvelous range. His voice on an opera song was exactly as an opera singer. His range on a blues would be just exactly like a blues singer."[37]

Tony Jackson moved to Chicago around 1912. He was a popular attraction at the Elite Cafe. While working there, Tony hired and mentored Alberta Hunter, a young singer fresh up from Memphis. Alberta Hunter would go on to become one of the most popular female blues singers in the 1920s. Born in 1895, she remained active until 1983 and helped popularize many of Tony Jackson's songs, including his most famous composition, "Pretty Baby."

"Tony was instrumental in my going to Chicago the first time," Morton said. But Morton didn't stay long. In fact, he stayed no place for very long. Jelly Roll was restless. He neither settled down nor ever became a family man. He was a creative pioneer in perpetual motion.

In his historic nine-hour Library of Congress recordings from 1938, Morton said of his mentor Tony Jackson, "We were very, very good friends and whenever he spotted me coming in the door, he would sing a song he knew I liked 'Pretty Baby,' one of Tony's great tunes." It is not known when Tony first wrote "Pretty Baby" but it was published in 1916.

Strangely, two Tin Pan Alley writers appeared as cowriters of Tony's tune: Gus Kahn and Egbert Van Alstyne. It was a harbinger of things to come for Black blues composers like Jelly Roll Morton, Clarence Williams, Spencer Williams, and others to follow. Taking credit for a song meant taking a share of Tony's royalties. In the publishing business, it would soon become a lucrative practice to swindle copyrights from Black songwriters. In the case of "Pretty Baby," Kahn and Alstyne may have added a trifle of new words to clean up Tony's original blue risqué lyrics about his male lover.[38] Yet, I would argue, neither censorship nor editing is authoring.[39]

There is no way of knowing how Tony Jackson originally performed the song in Storyville; there is no known recording. However, we can be certain it was nothing like the sterilized Tin Pan Alley version that became a major hit for numerous artists including Frank Sinatra, Al Jolson, Judy Garland, Doris Day, Dean Martin, and Brenda Lee. The song also inspired the 1978 movie *Pretty Baby* starring actress Brooke Shields, who played a twelve-year-old working in a New Orleans brothel. Johnny St. Cyr said, "[Tony] was known as the man of a thousand songs. . . . Really the best pianist we had was Tony Jackson, but, with the exception of Tony Jackson, Jelly Roll was the man."

Bunk Johnson compared Jackson's to Morton's popularity. Jelly was "noted more so than Tony Jackson and Albert Cahill because he played the music the whores liked," said Bunk. "Tony was dicty. But Jelly would sit there and play that barrelhouse music all night—blues and such as that. I know, because I played with him in Hattie Rodgers's sporting house in 1903." Bunk continued, Morton "play and sang the blues till way up in the day and all them gals would holler, 'listen at Winding Boy!' He was really a ladies' man, really stylish. But, even when he dress up, he still look like a kid."[40] Jelly Roll Morton's age, like many Blacks of the era, was not well documented. Even so, Bunk said the conspicuously successful Jelly Roll, all dressed up and working in Storyville brothels, looked "like a kid."

I too was at a tender age when I began playing in juke joints. I tried to grow facial hair; I lied that I was older when I was clearly a boy. But my talent was my ticket into the adult world of what was considered blue entertainment, similar to that of Winin' Boy.

Jelly Roll said of Tony Jackson's demise, "The poor fellow drank himself to death."[41] Tony Jackson died in 1921 in Chicago, reportedly of liver disease just as the phonograph business was taking off. Unfortunately, he made no phonograph recordings.

Young "Winin' Boy" was surrounded by blues and Voodoo. On many occasions he watched his godmother prepare gris-gris, potions, and elixirs for customers. He recalled hearing voices that seemed to emanate from jars of water she placed all around her home. Although Morton was Catholic, he respected the power of his godmother's Voodoo religion.

On one occasion, during one of her rituals, Winin' Boy felt weird and outside of himself for days. The frightening experience would haunt him during the course of his life. He often wondered if he'd been hexed. Whenever he ran out of luck, he harkened back to that strange, confusing experience.

Winin' Boy, now going by his new moniker Jelly Roll (a sexual connotation), lived in Biloxi, Mississippi, off and on, between 1907 and 1908. During his stay in Biloxi, Morton introduced his New Orleans blues to Mississippians who hadn't heard the blues before. He had already written a number of piano blues tunes including "New Orleans Blues" and "King Porter Stomp." Indeed, Morton planted blues seeds and affected local musicians everywhere he held court. Everyone who heard Morton tried to add a little bit of his style to their own playing. Morton recalled hearing a few piano players in Alabama and Mississippi around 1907, but he said he wasn't impressed. They hadn't yet caught onto what Morton, Buddy Bolden, Tony Jackson, and others had long been developing in New Orleans.

Jelly Roll Morton played at a dive called Flat Top, a hole-in-the-wall honky-tonk on Reynoir Street in the small but vibrant tenderloin district. He became a big hit in Biloxi. While in Mississippi, he also sharpened his skills as a pool and card shark to support his taste for finer things—including women. Morton wore the sharpest clothes. He even had a diamond in one of his gold-encrusted front teeth. Morton was good looking, an intellectual, and a musical genius. He could get a patron sugar momma in any town he rambled into.

While in Biloxi, he courted Bessie Johnson, the sister of notable Creole bass player Bill Johnson and his brother, piano player Ollie "Dink" Johnson. Bessie was light skinned with long straight hair. She could easily pass as a non-Black. "I didn't know at the time" they were in Biloxi, Bessie said, that "he had any family because he said he was a foundling from a Catholic home." Bessie later recalled, "Jelly used to come over and see me, making like it was to visit my brothers. I never gave him a second look because he wasn't decent. Used to play piano in a sporting house."[42]

Indeed, Morton played sporting houses, barrelhouses, and juke joints in New Orleans. He played all around Mississippi between 1907 and 1908. Morton said, "I worked McHenry, Hattiesburg, Jackson, Vicksburg, Greenwood, and Greenville, but I spent the biggest part of my time in Gulfport."[43] Morton revealed that on one gig in Meridian, Mississippi, he "came down with typhoid fever and returned to Biloxi on a stretcher."[44]

Trumpeter Bunk Johnson corroborated Morton's account in the book *Mister Jelly Roll* published in 1950 by folklorist Alan Lomax. Bunk Johnson said that in 1907 he ran into Jelly Roll in Gulfport, Mississippi, and played with him at Busy Bee Park on Labor Day.

To be clear, these are some of the earliest documented accounts of the blues making its way into Mississippi for a sustained period of time. In 1907, blues was neither on record nor radio. One had to be in the room to hear the music played by a practitioner such as Jelly Roll. Earlier that summer, following reports of erratic behavior, the great Buddy Bolden had been institutionalized, leaving piano professor Tony Jackson and Jelly Roll Morton as the greatest blues protagonists on the road.

To put Jelly Roll Morton's Delta influence in context, Robert Johnson hadn't been born yet. Charlie Patton, an early Delta guitarist on the Dockery plantation near Greenville, Mississippi, would have been about fourteen and just starting to learn the guitar in church—his father was a lay preacher. Whereas Buddy Bolden and others in New Orleans had been playing the blues since at least 1895. Jelly Roll Morton didn't stay in Mississippi long. He made a short sojourn to Chicago, then made his way to New York City.

In 1911, the great stride pianist James P. Johnson—later to become the father figure of Harlem pianists, influencing piano titans such as Duke Ellington, Fats Waller, and Thelonious Monk—was an eyewitness to Jelly Roll Morton's historic performance as he planted his blues seeds in Harlem. Johnson recalled the striking display; a kind of music he had never heard before. Jelly Roll's blues left an indelible mark on young Johnson.

"In 1911, when I was still going to school in short pants, I was taken uptown to Baron Wilkins' place in Harlem," remembered James P. Johnson, and "who was playing the piano but, Jelly Roll Morton . . . He was red hot. The place was on fire! We heard him play his 'Jelly Roll Blues.' Blues had not come into popularity at that time, they weren't known or sung by New York entertainers."[45] Another budding piano titan, Willie "the Lion" Smith, was also there that night to gain ideas and inspiration from Jelly Roll Morton. Indeed, after Jelly Roll planted his blues seeds, Harlem music was changed forever.

James P. Johnson, best known for his 1923 hit "The Charleston," became one of the best piano players on the East Coast. He recorded some of the first blues piano rolls from 1916 on. Johnson accompanied many of the early female songstresses such as Bessie Smith, Ethel Waters, and Ida Cox. It should be noted, however, that West Baton Rouge–born New Orleans blues pianist and composer Clarence Williams was the first to train, produce, and accompany Bessie Smith on records. Williams was crucial in shaping Smith's sound. He hired his New Orleans pals such as Louis Armstrong to back her. Smith would become the first queen of the blues in the 1920s. Subsequently, Johnson accompanied her on occasion.

Like Jelly Roll Morton, James P. Johnson (1894–1955) painted his adaptation of the blues in broad strokes. In 1940, he composed and produced an ambitious blues opera called *De Organizer* with lyrics by famed Harlem poet Langston Hughes. The *New York Times* in 2002 reported that "as far as is known, *De Organizer* was performed just three times, all in New York in 1940 under the auspices of the International Ladies Garment Workers Union. Efforts to stage it more widely or to have it played on radio were unsuccessful."[46]

Indeed, even today, a successful blues opera seems unimaginable. Not because blues musicians are incapable, but because blues, by Black performers, is still constrained by cultural brokers who romanticize the blues as a primitive expression from a primitive people; a mere artifact, not high art. The truth, however, is that from its inception blues was the highest form of musical art.

In 1912, Jelly Roll Morton made his way back to Chicago and reconnected with his mentor Tony Jackson, the first musician to establish Louisiana blues roots in Chicago. Morton, an incessant rambler, soon made his way out to California, following Bessie Johnson and her brothers who had moved to Los Angeles and founded the Creole Band featuring Freddie Keppard on trumpet. The Creole Band was the first blues-inspired band from New Orleans to tour nationally. Bessie Johnson changed her name to Anita Gonzales and passed as Hispanic in her new life on the West Coast. She eventually gave Jelly Roll Morton a second look and they became a serious couple, living together in California from 1917 to 1923.

Anita Gonzales was an astute businesswoman. She purchased a small hotel in South Central Los Angeles and for a time Morton helped her run it when he wasn't on the road. Yet whenever she accompanied Morton on gigs, he made her sit by his piano all night. She was neither allowed to dance nor fraternize with her friends. Jelly Roll Morton's jealousy could be overbearing, especially for a strong enterprising woman such as Anita. Yet, Anita put up with him because she loved Morton. Although a marriage certificate has never surfaced, she claimed to be the one serious love of his life. Morton is said to have later married New Orleans–born showgirl and dancer Mabel Bertrand. Mabel lived with Morton on and off during a fourteen-year period. Even though Morton frequently referred to her as "my wife" in his letters, she, like Anita before her, could not produce a marriage certificate.[47]

While in Los Angeles Jelly Roll Morton played in various configurations, solo and with accompaniment. He performed for a time with the Creole Band led by Anita's brother, bassist Bill Johnson. However, it wasn't until after he moved back to Chicago in 1923, leaving Anita in Los Angeles, that he made his first recordings. Upon his return to the Midwest, Jelly Roll recorded "Big Foot Ham" and "Muddy Water Blues" for Paramount.

It's an interesting aside that around this time, a little ten-year-old boy back in Mississippi got the nickname Muddy Water. Perhaps McKinley Morganfield, aka Muddy Waters—he added the *s* after moving to Chicago in 1943—got the nickname from Morton's phonograph of the same name. Sure, this anecdote may be a minor coincidence, but it does illustrate how the phonograph record spread New Orleans blues vernacular far and wide. New Orleans blues had a transformative cultural effect, not only on Mississippi sharecroppers but on all of American music. Moreover, many of Muddy Waters's most popular tunes, such as "Hootchie Coochie Man" and "Got My Mojo Working" were filled with Louisiana Voodoo imagery.

Jelly Roll Morton, a perfectionist, was extremely demanding of his musicians. He was most comfortable when accompanied by Louisiana musicians such as Kid Ory, Barney Bigard, Johnny Dodds, Johnny St. Cyr, and Baby Dodds because they all spoke the same musical language. In 1926, Morton formed the Red Hot Peppers and recorded for the Victor record label. Morton composed and recorded such standards as "Wolverine Blues," "Dead Man Blues," "Shoe Shiner's Drag," "Black Bottom Stomp," "Buddy Bolden's Blues," and "King Porter Stomp."

In 1929, national phonograph sales had surpassed one hundred million. But the Great Depression brought on a near collapse of the booming music industry. By 1932, phonograph sales had plunged to less than six million. Near-bankrupt record companies sold the original metal masters of their blues catalogs for scrap—without those masters, there could be no future pressings of original recordings. The collector's market was created.

By 1938, Jelly Roll Morton was out of sight and out of mind. He had gone nearly eight years without a recording contract. The New Orleans blues had evolved into a 4/4 dance band medium dominated by big swing bands on major labels. *Swing* was the new term used to separate White appropriators in the marketplace from Negro or "race" artists.

In 1938, Jelly Roll Morton and other New Orleans blues musicians were seen by a new generation of musicians as moldy figs; antiquated artists. In the aftermath of the Depression, Louis Armstrong was one of the few New Orleans bluesmen who continued to make high profile recordings. Exacerbating the problem was the fact that his classic blues style, developed under his mentor Joe "King" Oliver, had been recast as "Dixieland jazz"—a corny rebranding that zapped the soul and indigenous meaning of classic New Orleans blues.

Moreover, White Dixieland purists and fanatics were stringent about how it should be performed, limiting its freedom of expression and improvisation. White appropriators such as Bix Beiderbecke and the Original Dixieland Jass Band—hence the name Dixieland—were the real heroes of Dixieland purists. Furthermore, the word *Dixieland* acted as a repellent for Black musicians and audiences alike. Emerging progressive-minded Black musicians during the bebop movement—*bebop* was another mindless Anglicized name for a subgenre of blues that its Black practitioners hated—saw Jelly Roll Morton and Louis Armstrong as Dixieland jazz pacifists, not the enlightened trailblazing blues artists they really were.

Morton, at the low point of his career, moved to Washington, DC, where he managed the Jungle Inn on U Street in the bustling Black club district. He performed occasionally, singing and telling stories alone at the upright piano. Spare crowds of admirers kept the semiretired Jelly Roll musically engaged.

Morton was in fine form in 1938 when he was asked to give a series of oral interviews to Alan Lomax for the Library of Congress. The landmark session turned out to be the most informative oral history ever of America's greatest art from—the blues. Jelly Roll's knowledge and talent was staggering in those immortal nine hours of audio. The Library of Congress recordings sparked renewed interest in Morton. However, his revived recording career was brief, as his health took a sudden turn for the worse. Morton confided in friends that he believed his misfortunes were due to a possible Voodoo curse.

Anita Gonzales told Alan Lomax, "Laura Hunter, who raised Jelly Roll, was a Voodoo witch. She made money at Voodoo. People were always coming to her for some help and she was giving them beads and pieces of leather and all that." Anita continued, "Well, everybody knows that before you can become a witch you have to sell the person you love the best to Satan as a sacrifice. Laura loved Jelly best. She loved Jelly better than Ed, her own husband. Jelly always knew she'd sold him to Satan and that, when she died, he'd die, too—she would take him down with her."[48] Morton died July 10, 1941, in Los Angeles, California, within months of the death of his godmother Laura "Eulalie Echo" Hunter.

Even in death, Jelly Roll continued to dominate blues folklore. According to Anita Gonzales, Eulalie Echo sold young Morton's soul to the devil decades before the legend was fixed to Robert Johnson. Now, I don't wish to create an impression that Jelly Roll got his talent from Voodoo, because he didn't. Neither do I agree that Voodoo is evil. Those outside the religion may demonize it. But those who follow Voodoo see their spirits as angelic and loving just like any religion. Whether one is Jewish, Catholic, Christian, Mormon, Islamic, Buddhist, or other, at some time, each religion has been demonized. Voodoo is not evil to those who practice it. What we know for sure is Robert Johnson's crossroad legend is a myth; most likely culled from Jelly Roll's legend. Eulalie Echo and her Voodoo religion were real.

In the posthumous Alan Lomax book *Mister Jelly Roll: The Fortunes of Jelly Roll Morton*, released in 1950, Morton unapologetically called out those who usurped his ideas as well as the publishing cartel that marginalized and exploited him. Ferdinand Jelly Roll Morton's remarkable life was later immortalized in the acclaimed musical *Jelly's Last Jam*, a successful play that was performed on Broadway in 1992, with tap dancer Gregory Hines in the title role. Regrettably, Jelly Roll Morton was portrayed in the script as arrogant and cruel, a mischaracterization considering the times in which he lived.

Contrarily, however, it was the world around him that was arrogant and cruel. If Morton had come of age in the 1960s, during the era of Malcolm X and Muhammad Ali, or even today among rappers with outsized egos, his conspicuous self-confidence may have been celebrated. The cruel reality was that there was no comfortable place in American society during Jim Crow for an assertive Black man as brilliant as Jelly Roll Morton. Morton was a blues genius far ahead of his times and he knew it.

In the 1910s, minstrelsy and vaudeville dominated Black entertainment. The arrival of the blues, an authentic African American expression, signaled an end to Blacks in blackface perpetuating demeaning grotesque caricatures of themselves. The assertive Creolized aesthetic, central to Louisiana blues, inspired Negroes everywhere to straighten their spines and assert self-confidence. Moreover, the blues represented social mobility. In the blues, one needn't come from an elite family nor have an elite education. Even a former pimp or prostitute could attain dignity, class, and respect via the blues.

New Orleans blues musicians defiantly shrugged off the harsh condemnations of both Anglicized Black and White critics alike. They refused to acquiesce to prudish Victorian ethos. Instead, they invented a music to celebrate their humanistic character. Indeed, the blues were a prophetic cultural expression that trumpeted the collective genius and unlimited potential of the Negro to the world.

New Orleans trumpeter Willie Gary "Bunk" Johnson (1879–1941), according to the landmark book *Jazzmen* (1939), played in Buddy Bolden's band between 1895 and 1900.[49] An important blues pioneer, Bunk Johnson, after leaving the Buddy Bolden Band, joined the Superior Orchestra and later starred in Frankie Dusen's Eagle Band. The Eagle Band became the most popular blues band in the city. Bunk Johnson's most powerful playing days predated the blues recording business. Nevertheless, he was a strong influence on younger musicians like Louis Armstrong, who, in his youth, studied Bunk in person. Bunk Johnson was a very important link in the historiography of the blues from Buddy Bolden's rise and fall to a gifted boy named Louis Armstrong. Armstrong dramatically expanded the possibilities of the blues for soloists by building on the foundation laid by his predecessors, Bolden, Bunk, and Oliver.

When Bunk was holding court in New Orleans honky-tonks, Louis Armstrong and trailblazing clarinetist Sidney Bechet were kids in the crowd, just learning what the blues were all about. In 1950, in the July/August issue of *Record Changer,* a jazz magazine, Louis Armstrong said, "Bunk didn't actually teach me anything; he didn't show me one thing. . . . I was about 17—and I'd hang around this honky-tonk where Bunk was playing. . . . I would sit in front of that horn and the port wine was coming out of that bell. But I'd stay there and them notes were prettier than that wine." Some jazz and blues critics took this to mean Louis was being dismissive of Bunk Johnson, but he wasn't. "You don't need to give the credit" for my style "to Bunk, other than the tone," Armstrong said. "I mean, there could be similarity of tone, but that's all."[50] I take this to mean Louis studied how Bunk got such a sweet tone.

Perhaps what critics of Bunk Johnson failed to understand was that blues was a spiritual mystery and an unspoken philosophy, not simply notes on a written page. Bunk Johnson's influence on Armstrong, then, was philosophical; how the air from that horn filled the room with good vibrations inspiring his audience. It went beyond conventional music lessons. Only soul-searching improvisational music possesses such power. By no means was Louis impeaching Bunk's influence, he was only setting the record straight. Armstrong said many times the cornet/trumpet man who really taught and mentored him was Joe "King" Oliver.

In his 1961 autobiography, *Treat It Gentle*, Sidney Bechet said of Bunk Johnson, "He was a great blues player. . . . I was about 17 when I first started playing with Eagle Orchestra. I was living at home, and Bunk Johnson came and promised my mother he would watch out for me; he'd come by for me when we was to play, and he'd take me back [home]. . . . Somehow ragtime had a way of being easy for the Creoles, but when it came to the blues you couldn't beat Bunk or The Eagle Orchestra."

In his 1971 book *Autobiography of a New Orleans Jazzman*, bassist Pops Foster recalled the early days of blues—already an established form in New Orleans by 1914—and Louis Armstrong's first big boy gig. Foster said:

> About 1914 I was playing with [Kid] Ory's band doing advertising for an affair the Turtles were putting on at National Park. . . . So, then we needed a trumpet player very bad. After we went a few blocks, I saw Louis Armstrong standing on a corner watching, and said, "Hey, there's little Louis over there!" We got him in the wagon, and he went on to play the advertising with us, and then we carried him out to the park to play. The only thing Louis could play then was blues, so we played them all day long. Louis played them good too. As far as I know, that was the first time Louis played with a big-time band. Before that Louis just played with kid bands.

When people hear the names Bunk Johnson, Louis Armstrong, Sidney Bechet, or King Oliver, they immediately think of a style of music called "Dixieland jazz." However, these musicians weren't "Dixieland jazz" musicians. I'm sure they found the name "Dixieland" insulting. Dixie, really? What a tomfoolery name for the blues. Early New Orleans musicians saw themselves as blues musicians.

Casual observers may also believe these men were jazz musicians. However, in his autobiography, *Treat It Gentle*, Sidney Bechet said with contempt, "Let me tell you one thing, jazz, that's a name the white people have given to the music . . . but jazz, jazz could mean any damn thing. . . . It used to be spelled jass."

New Orleans has always been indifferent, to say the least, about promoting itself as the "Birthplace of Blues." The city was ashamed of the discordant blues from its inception. In the 1960s, local White Dixieland jazz revival musicians, such as the Italian Dukes of Dixieland Band led by Frank Assunto on trumpet and his brother Fred Assunto on trombone, along with trumpeter Al Hirt (1922–1999) and clarinetist Pete Fountain (1930–2016), began gaining popularity through national TV appearances. Their successes awakened city leaders to the financial possibilities of a permanent Dixieland presence in the French Quarter's nightlife—both Al Hirt and Pete Fountain established popular music clubs on Bourbon Street. City leaders foresaw Dixieland jazz, led by nonthreatening White faces, as a positive national and international image to attract New Orleans tourists. Civic leaders realized "we might have something salable here."[51]

At that time, the 1960s, the streets of America were on fire. Both the militant Black Panther Party and the nonviolent civil rights movement were making good trouble. For White southerners, the new Dixieland branding promoted warm nostalgic images of the gay Old South, where festive riverboats sailed gamblers down the lazy Mississippi and happy Blacks knew their place. New Orleans leaders branded Bourbon Street in the French Quarter "Dixieland," the "Birthplace of Jazz," effectively orphaning the blues.

Steeped in the classic New Orleans tradition, having played as a youngster with many of the aging Black pioneers in the 1970s and '80s, clarinetist Dr. Michael White, born 1954, said,

> The post–Civil Rights climate of the mid '70s was a time when some older musicians and younger ones, like myself, openly expressed resentment at the term "Dixieland" in reference to black traditional jazz. In addition to its negative historical racial implications, "Dixieland" implied a White imitation of jazz. It was commonly understood and defined as such in early jazz history. It also conjured up images of plastic hats, garter belts worn on the sleeve, striped vests, corny behavior, funny band names, and a fast, loud, bland sound that was a far cry from the more socially driven and spiritually powerful original black jazz of the brass and dance bands that evolved from the days of Buddy Bolden and King Oliver.[52]

The crass commercialization of Bourbon Street *jazz* no doubt boosted tourism. However, popular memory of original New Orleans blues was lost. Indeed, the original musicians referred to their most personalized music as the blues. Relabeling these blues pioneers' music as *jazz* or *Dixieland* neither captured the essence of their music nor its cultural significance.

Moreover, private letters sent from Chicago in 1930 by Joe "King" Oliver, Louis Armstrong's mentor, cornetist, and bandleader, provide evidence that he and his friend trumpeter Bunk Johnson referred to their own music as blues, not jazz or Dixieland:

> Now Bunk you must keep in touch with me because I can't tell just when something good will turn up. If I know how and where to reach you it will mean a wonderful break for you. In the meantime I will send you a few numbers to arrange. I can give you some extra change as a side line. Have you got any good blues? If so send them to me and I will make them and bring you some real money. When making my arrangements, always write the cornet a real low down solo a la Bunk, remember how you use to drive the blues down? Oh boy.[53]

King Oliver's letters from Chicago mailed back home to Louisiana refer to the music he had been playing for decades as the *blues*. Oliver clearly defines the new compositions he wished to receive for recording purposes from his friends as blues. "Driving the blues down" does not mean Oliver is seeking sad and depressing music, it means Bunk Johnson was in rare form, really playing the blues with a spirit that made the place go wild. "Oh boy!"

Also around this time King Oliver wrote a letter to cornetist Buddie Petit seeking new compositions:

> If you've got a real good blues, have someone to write it just as you play them and send them to me, we can make some jack on them. . . . Now, have the blues wrote down just as you can play them, it's the originality that counts.[54]

In those letters, we have three blues musicians corresponding without any coaxing or leading questions from a journalist or folklorist. King Oliver never expected these two letters to be read by anyone other than Bunk Johnson and Buddie Petit. There is no hidden agenda. He was genuinely seeking fresh blues tunes—he didn't write the words *jazz* or *Dixieland* to reference his music. Because the letter was written in early 1930, the good old days to which Oliver is referring are the Storyville years (1897–1917), because Oliver had left New Orleans for Chicago by 1919.

Also, it's important to note, King Oliver, Bunk Johnson, and Buddie Petit were "legit." In other words, they were musically literate musicians. Judging from personal correspondence and interviews of the most successful New Orleans musicians, it is safe to assume most of them could read music and did compose blues.

In the early days, as the blues emerged from Louisiana and took Chicago and Harlem by storm, the definition of *blues* was Anglicized and redefined as a pejorative by those who hated it for what they believed were discordant sounds emanating from the Negro. Paradoxically, the average Negro heard concordant sounds from those same musicians. From the average Negro's prism, the blues spoke to him with respect and empathy, instilling a sense of great pride. Culturally, Negroes wanted freedom from repression. The genius philosophy of the blues is that it broke free from the repressive major scale system of Europe that had been so stringently adopted by America. Louisiana blues pioneers created a new Creolized tonality that augmented diatonic scales and tones.

Louisiana musicians had mastered European dance music such as the schottische and quadrille. They went beyond the limitations of placid Victorian dance music and created a new flexible scale system to better express the emotional energy of bawdy Creole dance culture to accompany sensual downtempo dances like the slow-drag. The new scale would become known as the blues scale. The new feel would come to be called swing.

Jazz critics had a real conundrum in trying to separate New Orleans jazz from blues. The 1980 book *101 Best Jazz Albums* said it this way: "New Orleans musicians mastered the blues tonality, absorbing it so thoroughly that there is occasionally no demarcation possible between the blues and early jazz."

When Bunk Johnson was reigning in the 1910s with the Eagle Band, they played the blues. The word jazz wasn't even part of the vernacular. Many musicians who knew Bunk Johnson believed he reached his prime as a player in the Eagle Band. Unfortunately, however, Louisiana Negro musicians didn't begin to make records until the 1920s. Fledgling record companies believed, with good reason, that White families, their target audience, would recoil at the thought of inviting Negroes' music into their homes.

Although Bunk Johnson hit the road in 1915, he didn't relocate like most expatriate Louisiana musicians. Bunk retired from the road around 1931 and settled in New Iberia, Louisiana. Bunk gave up the music business. Over time he lost his teeth. Without money to have major dental work done, he couldn't play his horn. Instead, Bunk became a truck driver and laborer. He focused on raising his large family but found time to teach music to children. His career was revived by two young, White record collectors and researchers, Bill Russell and Frederic Ramsey. Bunk featured prominently in the collected essays in Ramsey and Charles Edward Smith's seminal book, *Jazzmen*, published in 1939—the first extensive book published on blues. Russell and Ramsey helped to raise money for Bunk to have the necessary dental work done so he could resume his career. The dental work was performed by the brother of clarinetist Sidney Bechet, who happened to be a dentist.

Thereafter, Bunk revived his music career and became a major attraction in the 1940s. He made numerous recordings and performed in concert halls from San Francisco to New York City. In 1947, at the height of his career, he co-headlined Town Hall in New York City with Lead Belly. The two Louisiana pioneers shared the stage, performing their original brand of blues. It must be noted that even though the music they played was blues, it was now relabeled Dixieland in honor of Nick LaRocca and his Original Dixieland Jazz Band by nostalgic White enthusiasts and record collectors.

The Dixieland jazz revival, which began on the West Coast in the late 1930s, soon spread from coast to coast. One of the most famous revival bands was Lu Watters and the Yerba Buena Jazz Band, who created a sensation in the 1940s in Oakland, California. Soon, White Dixieland jazz revival bands were a dime a dozen from the Midwest to New York City. The revival was supported by the growing popularity of record collecting clubs such as the United Hot Clubs of America.

Although the Dixieland revival movement brought belated international fame to New Orleans musicians such as Bunk Johnson, it muddled the authenticity and meaning of New Orleans blues. A new school of Black musicians wanted no part of Dixieland or jazz. They had disdain for both words. Musicians such as Miles Davis, Charlie Parker, and others created a new way to express the blues, which came to be known as bebop.

For a young musician, "being in Doc Paulin's band was like going to school," Dr. Michael White said of his mentor trumpeter Ernest "Doc" Paulin (1907–2007). "It was a unique way of gaining authentic, hands-on experience that could only happen in New Orleans." White came along after the civil rights movement. He despised the Dixieland jazz branding.

Dr. White said, "Many (at least publicly) remained silent, noting, 'Well, they call us worse things than that. Why create problems for yourself and not get work?' Doc Paulin didn't worry about labels or sometimes being called an 'Uncle Tom.' I heard him debate one musician and say, 'What do I care about what they call it? Dem people say 'Dixieland.' De point is, I'm tryin' to make some money and go 'bout my business. I got thirteen churin to feed. Ain't dat right?'"[55]

KING OLIVER

IN APRIL 1923, blues took a quantum leap forward when King Oliver and his protégé Louis Armstrong entered an Indiana recording studio for the first time. Cornetist Joe "King" Oliver is one of the most important blues musicians in history. If he were the Socrates of the blues, then Louis Armstrong would have been his Aristotle. Louis Armstrong idolized his mentor and friend, whom he called affectionately "Papa" Joe. It was King Oliver who gave young Louis his first cornet. King Oliver's early recordings featuring Louis Armstrong on the second trumpet set the 1920s ablaze in hot blues.

Joseph Nathan Oliver was born May 11, 1885, on a plantation in the small town of Aben, near Donaldsonville, in metropolitan Baton Rouge, Louisiana. He moved to New Orleans as a boy, and by 1908 he was immersed in its brass band scene. He lost a semblance of sight in one eye but downplayed the impediment. He refused to cover his bad eye with a patch.

After spending his formative years in various youth orchestras, Joe Oliver grew to become a member, at various times, of the finest orchestras in the city, including the Olympia, the Onward Brass Band, the Original Superior, and the Eagle Band, which included Buddy Bolden's former players. By the late 1910s, while playing with Kid Ory's band, he had earned the moniker "King"—he was the new cornet king of the New Orleans blues dynasty that had begun with King Bolden.

King Oliver was distinguished by his cornet/trumpet innovations. In his desire to emulate the expressiveness of the Negro voice on his horn, Oliver used mutes, bottles, and plungers, creating his signature wah-wah vibrato that slid from one note to the other. It could be argued Kid Ory's expressive slide trombone style had an influence on Oliver. Because after all, the slide technique is natural for the trombone. Indeed, the trombone is said to have been Oliver's first instrument. Regardless of where Oliver got the original idea, the purpose was to sing through his horn. Ultimately the slide vibrato became a defining feature of the blues because it emulated the Negro voice.

It could also be argued Oliver's innovation was later adopted by blues guitarists who used a bottleneck slide, and later a wah-wah pedal, to emulate the technique of exultation first introduced by King Oliver. The slide guitar technique exploded once the wah-wah sound was heard on newly accessible 78 phonographs. Over the years, there has been much conjecture that the slide technique in blues was influenced by Hawaiian music. But I'm not convinced. Today, when I hear the slide and wah-wah pedal sound, I'm reminded of King Oliver's trumpet plunger.

King Oliver was a broad-shouldered, dark-skinned man. He was assertive onstage, but offstage Oliver had a quiet demeanor. He wasn't a rabble-rouser. He didn't have issues with alcohol like his predecessors King Bolden and King Keppard. He was an organized, dependable band leader. Oliver possessed a quiet dignity and a disdain for Jim Crow, which, in the South, was harshest for those with darker skin such as his.

One night a fight broke out on a gig King Oliver was playing in New Orleans. Police arrested the fighters, Oliver, and his band. Joe Oliver was roughed up by the cops. Stella Oliver, King Oliver's widow, later recalled the arrest was what made Oliver finally leave the South.

In 1919, Joe Oliver went to Chicago to join Bill Johnson's Original Creole Band, replacing the unreliable Freddie Keppard, for a stint at the Dreamland Ballroom. He returned to New Orleans briefly, then moved to Chicago for good in 1922. King Oliver eventually became the leader of the Original Creole Band and added the new buzzword jazz to its moniker. His newly christened Creole Jazz Band became the hottest band in Chicago. Oliver was the star of the Chicago scene, packing them in at Lincoln Gardens. Though he referred to his music as blues in his private letters, in public he adopted trendy marketing monikers such as jazz and Dixie, as in King Oliver and the Dixie Syncopators (1926–1928).

Such gimmicky and trendy names may have helped African American New Orleans bands cash in on the popularity of New Orleans blues, which first came to national attention by way of the White Italian Original Dixieland Jazz Band in 1917, but names like Dixie and jazz did long-term damage to their legacies as blues pioneers. Moreover, the word Creole, an exotic and meaningless word to Whites outside of Louisiana, was also retired. Creole, by the 1920s, was a pejorative word in Black communities. Because of the color line, many mixed-raced Creoles disassociated themselves with Blacks to gain social mobility and respectable jobs. Consequently, the complex authentic history behind the birth of Creole blues was lost in translation. Besides, record labels and promoters were only interested in cashing in on the latest fads, not elevating the consciousness of music consumers.

After Oliver left New Orleans, Louis Armstrong replaced him in the Big Easy as the up-and-coming prince of the cornet. In 1922, King Oliver sent for Armstrong to join him in Chicago. In his 1936 biography *Swing That Music* Louis Armstrong said, "In April 1923, when our winter engagement at the Lincoln Gardens was over King Oliver took us on a road trip down through Illinois and Ohio and Indiana, playing one-night stands in ballrooms. . . . We stopped at Richmond, Indiana, to make some phonograph recordings for the Gennett Company. It was my first experience making records."

THE KING OLIVER–LOUIS ARMSTRONG SESSIONS

ON APRIL 5, 1923, in Richmond, Indiana, King Oliver's Creole Jazz Band gathered around an acoustic horn for the first take. The studio was located in an adjacent building in the rear of the Starr Piano Company's manufacturing plant. The session was for Gennett Records, a subsidiary of the Starr Piano Company.

A wax disc turned at 78 revolutions per minute (rpm), anticipating the pulsing beat that would cut a smooth groove into the wax from the outer edge toward the center. As the band swung into the opening number, the powerful blare of Oliver's and Armstrong's cornets overwhelmed the recording device. The wax cylinder's needle went haywire. The session was abruptly halted.

The engineer, Ezra Wickemeyer, the son of German immigrants, reassembled Oliver and Armstrong. They were placed nearly twenty feet away from the horn so the blast of their cornets wouldn't destroy the sensitive recording machine.

When Wickemeyer resumed the session, King Oliver's Creole Jazz Band with Louis Armstrong on second cornet recorded ten landmark blues sides over two days: "Mandy Blues," "I'm Going Away to Wear You Off My Mind," "Just Gone," "Canal Street Blues," and "Chimes Blues." On the second day, April 6, they recorded "Snake Rag," "Froggie Moore," "Weather Bird Rag," and what would become the band's signature song, "Dipper Mouth Blues."

King Oliver's Creole Jazz Band, like all hot New Orleans blues orchestras during this time, was steeped in collective improvisation. Lead cornet would play the melody while simultaneously riffing around it. The clarinet and trombone would simultaneously perform counterpoint improvisations above and below the cornet. It was a trinity of call-and-response; each instrument in a harmonious spirited conversation with the other two. Polyphonic improvisation was the cornerstone of early blues. No one across the country had ever heard anything on a record like King Oliver and his hot blues band.

The members of the Creole Jazz Band on this date were Louis Armstrong on second cornet, his soon-to-be wife and manager Lillian Beatrice "Lil" Hardin on piano, John M. "Johnny" Dodds on clarinet, Warren "Baby" Dodds on drums (percussion) including woodblocks, Honoré Dutrey on trombone, Arthur "Bud" Scott Jr. on banjo, William Manuel "Bill" Johnson on double bass—and of course, Joseph Nathan "King" Oliver on first cornet.

"Dipper Mouth Blues" is easily the finest recording of the entire session. It sold briskly upon its release. From its introduction the song was instantly infectious. The woodblock percussion and banjo laid a rollicking foundation to the catchy tune. "Dipper Mouth Blues" was a twelve-bar blues done in 2/4 meter, which was the typical dance meter of the early twentieth century. The introduction was cleverly conceived without a beat, like a fanfare, a call to the dance floor; announcing the hot tune to follow.

The second movement was a twenty-four-bar break featuring Johnny Dodds on clarinet. Dodds made the clarinet sing. He was expressive. Nevertheless, because of the crude recording conditions of the time, his clarinet didn't soar above the powerful breaks played by the orchestra. His phrasing is all there but wasn't felt by the listener as I believe it would have been if Dodds had been positioned more intimately to the horn.

Following the breaks, the band returned to the A section with Armstrong adding cornet riffs under his mentor, setting up King Oliver's feverish crescendo. Oliver's cornet improvisation, which featured his clever economic note choices, is all blues. He used a toilet plunger to mute his cornet to better emulate the cry of a singer. His cry is one of pure ecstasy, not a cry of woe.

I've often witnessed this same selective note choice when performing on stage with B. B. King, Buddy Guy, and so many other great guitar soloists. Astute note selection is an indelible signature of the blues. There are rare exceptional musicians, such as Charlie Parker, who can turn density into soulful expression; however, I have always chosen to perform my music with an artful measure. Just three or four notes expressed with various bends, pulls, and sustained vibrato can better express my essence to the listener—penetrating emotionally in my opinion—than a dense, less-discerning solo. It's the same philosophy that was instilled in young Armstrong by King Oliver. Likewise, a muted trumpet and astute note selection are what distinguished Miles Davis's late 1950s albums from the density of early bebop recordings.

Judging from these sides, however, Oliver was still the master and Armstrong the apprentice. A somewhat shy Louis Armstrong was not yet ready to lead his own orchestra and had yet to find his voice on the cornet. Yet, Armstrong did record his first solo on record during the session on "Chimes Blues," another twelve-bar blues done in 2/4 meter. Although his tone is instantly recognizable, his phrasing is understandably uncertain because he was an inexperienced singular soloist. Orchestras from New Orleans rarely featured individually extended soloists; polyphonic improvisation had always been the signature of the Creole band. "Chimes Blues" would, subsequently, become a precursor to what was to come in only a few short years from the rapidly evolving Louis Armstrong.

The great irony of King Oliver's historic blues session was that it was produced courtesy of the Ku Klux Klan. As it turned out, the engineer, Ezra Wickemeyer, was a longtime member of the Indiana Ku Klux Klan. But more than that, he produced all of the Klan's propaganda recordings. In fact, only a few weeks after Oliver and the gang packed up their instruments, the Ku Klux Klan entered the same recording studio with Wickemeyer, as they often did, to record the infamous 78 rpm "The Bright Fiery Cross."

In the 1920s, Indiana had the largest Klan membership in the United States, boasting more than three hundred thousand statewide (of the nearly two million members nationally). Xenophobia was widespread during the 1920s. The toxic atmosphere allowed the Klan to go mainstream. Influential White Anglo-Saxon Protestants, paranoid of Jewish and southern European immigration and resentful of northern migration by the Negro, sought to maintain White social and political supremacy. The Klan, a terrorist organization that grew out of the resentment of the former Confederacy, was recast as heroes, protectors of WASP purity. The success of the racist 1915 movie *Birth of a Nation*, based on the fictional 1905 book *The Clansman*, along with 78 rpm propaganda recordings, helped to drive up Klan membership to an all-time high by the 1920s.

The irony that the Gennett Company, with its questionable Ku Klux Klan ties, recorded the first great blues records is difficult to reconcile. One would assume they recorded Negroes not because of artistic merit but strictly to raise money. What is known, however, is artistic merit and profits from its race series far exceeded that of their Klan recordings.

As a blues artist, I've experienced glass ceilings, bigotry, and exploitation, but the dangers, inequities, and indignities Joe "King" Oliver had to overcome make his artistic achievements even more remarkable. I can only imagine what it must have been like for King Oliver and Armstrong, who were managed by Chicago mobsters, and ordered, sometimes by gunpoint, to perform at fellow mobster-owned speakeasies; and moreover, to have their records produced by the Ku Klux Klan, all while forced to endure the affronts of day-to-day Jim Crow travel. What Oliver accomplished in the face of such depravity surely taught his protégé, Louis Armstrong, how to compartmentalize such obstacles and soar over them with dignity.

It is reported that when King Oliver was later invited to become the star attraction in New York's City's "Whites-only" Cotton Club, which presented racist stereotypes, portraying Negroes as wild primitive savages on a utopian southern cotton plantation, he turned the gig down, choosing pride over profit.

Many thought it was the worst business move of Oliver's career. The bandleader who accepted the demeaning but high-profile gig in his place was none other than Edward "Duke" Ellington. Duke Ellington would go on to parlay the Cotton Club gig into a major success while King Oliver, whose cornet prowess rapidly declined due to gum disease, spent his last years away from music, indigent and working as a janitor in Savannah, Georgia.

The great Joe "King" Oliver died April 10, 1938, in Savannah, Georgia. His body was transported to New York City for funeral services attended by Louis Armstrong and Clarence Williams, among others. King Oliver, like many great blues musicians before and after him, was buried in an unmarked grave.

I GOT THE BLUES

THE SHOCKING 1890 MURDER of beloved New Orleans police chief David Hennessy was blamed on Sicilian immigrants. In an area known then as Little Italy, hundreds of Sicilians were rounded up and arrested. In 1891, following acquittals for some, a White mob stormed the jail and lynched eleven Italians. It was one of the largest mass lynchings in American history. The lead instigator of the mob, John M. Parker Jr., who later became governor, said Italians were "just a little worse than the Negro, being if anything filthier in habits, lawless, and treacherous."[56]

Italian immigrants arriving in New Orleans during the latter part of the nineteenth century settled in decaying apartments in the poorest part of the French Quarter. Sicilians were under constant suspicion and marginalized because they were not yet assimilated into "Whiteness." Whiteness meant mainstream: privileged status, first-class citizenship. There were tensions between Irish, Italian, and some mixed-race Creoles of color, all jockeying to be accepted as "White." Ethnic groups that remained the "other," like the dark Negro, would continue to be marginalized and discriminated against.

Italians, often referred to pejoratively as wops ("without papers"), had to hustle menial jobs alongside Blacks, which created cultural proximity and, therefore, opportunity. Louisiana's Black Creole musicians, even though they invented the blues, would neither be first to publish, copyright, nor record their new creative expression. Italians would be the first to officially publish and record the blues of New Orleans.

Antonio Maggio, born in 1876, in Cefalu, Sicily, became the first to publish a twelve-bar song with blues in its title when he published "I Got the Blues" in 1908. Maggio, a classically trained Italian violinist, immigrated to Louisiana in 1892. He worked as a barber in Plaquemine, Louisiana, and played music on the side before settling in New Orleans in 1896.

In the summer of 1901, while traveling with a musical troupe in New Mexico, Maggio reportedly told his fellow musicians he knew of a plot to kill President William McKinley. Shockingly, on September 6, 1901, President McKinley was assassinated by Leon Czolgosz. Antonio Maggio was immediately arrested by US Marshals as an accomplice in the conspiracy and held on $10,000 bail in Albuquerque, New Mexico. Maggio admitted he was an anarchist but denied involvement in the plot. After several months in detainment, the case against him fell apart and he was released.[57]

Back in New Orleans, Antonio Maggio worked odd jobs and played music on the side. In 1908, Maggio published "I Got the Blues," which became a local favorite. Maggio's "I Got the Blues" was the first blues published in what would later become its Anglicized mode; a twelve-bar pattern using the word *blues* for a melancholy state of mind. But how did an Italian come to publish the first blues? Actually, he learned the song from a Black guitarist while visiting Algiers—a district across the river from the French Quarter.

In 1955 Maggio admitted, "I heard an elderly negro with a guitar playing three notes [chords]. He kept repeating the notes for a long time. I didn't think anything with only three notes could have a title, so to satisfy my curiosity I asked what was the name of the piece. He replied, 'I got the blues.'"[58]

The name of the Black guitarist is unknown. But Maggio's appropriation, recording of, and profit from a song by an "elderly negro with a guitar" was an omen of things to come. Jelly Roll Morton said in 1938, "Music is such a tremendous proposition that it probably needs government supervision." Morton added, "I also advocate much more rigid laws so thieves may get their just deserts. There are many who enjoy glory plus financial gain's abundance, even in the millions, who should be digging ditches or sweeping the streets. Lack of proper protection causes this."

There was nothing original about the Original Dixieland Jass Band (ODJB), except that they were an Italian New Orleans orchestra playing Black Creole blues arrangements. Nonetheless, the Original Dixieland Jass Band—forerunners to Elvis Presley and the Rolling Stones—were very important in spreading the blues invention to mainstream America. They were the first New Orleans blues band to enter a recording studio. In 1917 their recording of "Livery Stable Blues" opened the commercial door for the new Louisiana sound.

Earlier, in New Orleans, prior to leaving for Chicago, members of the ODJB had all played at one time or another in Papa Jack Laine's Reliance Brass Band. Dominick "Nick" LaRocca (1889–1961), son of impoverished Sicilian immigrants, the leader of the band, was drawn to Back o' Town orchestras led by King Oliver and Kid Ory. Like LaRocca, the upstart musicians wanted to play the blues, so they left Papa Jack's society band and formed Original Dixieland Jass Band.

LaRocca, a cornetist, studied the playing style of local Black Creole cornet masters. LaRocca and the boys, according to Kid Ory, would often show up at their gigs to absorb their style.[59] "Oh sure," Ory said, "LaRocca and those boys, used to stand on the walkways out at Lake Pontchartrain and pick up everything we [Kid Ory and King Oliver] were doing. I saw them."

By 1916 the demand for New Orleans blues was high in the Windy City thanks to Tony Jackson, Jelly Roll Morton, and a slew of migrant Creole brass orchestras from Louisiana—many of which had been playing on excursions upriver and in vaudeville houses for years.

In 1916 while visiting New Orleans to see a prize fight, Harry James, an enterprising owner of a Chicago café, heard a trio led by drummer Johnny Stein and enticed him to put together a dance band and come to Chicago to work in his café. Stein's Dixie Jass Band, as they were initially billed, moved from New

Orleans to Chicago to catch the wave. After some members shuffled in and out the name was changed to Original Dixieland Jass Band to distinguish themselves from competitors, including the White Tom Brown's Band from Dixieland (later renamed the Louisiana Five).

Al Jolson, a schmaltzy blackface singer whose shameless signature song "My Mammy" helped to make him a major star, heard the ODJB in Chicago and wired Max Hart, his New York City agent.[60] Max Hart had a knack for promoting Whites that could imitate Negro music in blackface for mainstream audiences. However, in a move that showed great foresight, he would allow the Original Dixieland Jass Band to continue performing without blackface. Max Hart arranged a residency in New York City in the Paradise Ballroom at the Reisenweber Building, a venue just off Columbus Circle in Manhattan.[61] Original Dixieland Jass Band caused a sensation, attracting major recording offers from Columbia and Victor.

An Italian American band with a Black sound was attractive financially. Blackface entertainment had been a pre-phonograph phenomenon, in part because everyone went to the theater for entertainment. However, the new portable gramophone would allow the sound of blues to be portable for the first time in history. One could virtually invite the band into their home.

A conundrum for aspiring Black recording artists was the fact that White record buyers in 1917 weren't accepting of Black music in their homes. Unlike going to the theater, playing records in the home was personal. The White faces of the ODJB would make the blues somewhat palatable in the living rooms of bigoted White gramophone owners. Due to pervasive racism, the thinking was that a genuine natural-faced White orchestra would be less threatening on a record cover than a blackfaced White orchestra. In other words, the marketers wanted there to be no mistake. The sound was Black, but these were wholesome, safe, White musicians.

In New York City on February 26, 1917, the Original Dixieland Jass Band arrived at the Victor Talking Machine Company Studio on West Thirty-Eighth Street to record two songs, "Dixieland Jazz Band One-Step," the A-side, and "Livery Stable Blues," the B-side. The arrangement of "Livery Stable Blues" was in the same hot style Black Creole New Orleans orchestras had been developing back home and subsequently in Chicago. One of the identifying features of a New Orleans blues progression was how a quick sixth chord was added to the turnaround followed by the second chord in the scale. "Livery Stable Blues" was a twelve-bar tune in 2/4 time. Blues in 4/4 time had not yet arrived for popular dancing.

There were catchy breaks in the song where the band would break for two bars while one of the instruments filled the space with improvised notes. Jelly Roll

Morton said he was the first to start breaks in the music around 1902, but we can't verify this because he didn't begin recording until the 1920s.

Some of the instruments on "Livery Stable Blues" sound as if they're trying to imitate barn animals. The animal-like sound effects gave ODJB's music a satirical blackface tone instead of an emotionally complex blues feeling.

At the end of the recording session, Victor engineers asked LaRocca what the name of the blues song was. LaRocca said, "Livery Stable Blues." After the band left the building the Victor engineers renamed the song "Barnyard Blues" and the bands' agent Max Hart filed the "Barnyard Blues" copyright in his own name. However, when the song was pressed, LaRocca's original title, "Livery Stable Blues," was on the label.

The 78-rpm phonograph was released a few weeks later, and unexpectedly, the B-side became an instant novelty hit. "Livery Stable Blues" sold in the tens of thousands—a major commercial success for 1917. The Dixieland Jass Band helped to usher in the roaring Blues Age of the 1920s.

Following the success of "Livery Stable Blues"—as royalties began to accumulate—a high profile copyright dispute arose. In Chicago, clarinetist Alcide "Yellow" Nunez, who in 1916 had exited the ODJB due to a disagreement with Nick LaRocca, purchased sheet music of the song for his new band and discovered the song wasn't copyrighted. Nunez filed a copyright for the song naming himself as the sole writer via a Chicago music publisher.

When sheet music began appearing under Alcide Nunez's name, Nick LaRocca filed an injunction to stop the sale. LaRocca followed with a lawsuit of his own to recover the copyright and lost royalties. The case to determine the composer of "Livery Stable Blues" was tried October 1917 in Chicago. The case was closely followed in New York City on Tin Pan Alley where the fledgling recorded music publishing industry, still in its infancy, was centered.

Alcide Nunez testified under oath, "Nobody wrote the 'Livery Stable Blues.' Naw, nobody writes any of that stuff. I invented the pony cry in the 'Blues,' and LaRocca, he puts in the horse neigh. We were in the Schiller Café, rehearsin', see? And I suggests that we take the 'More Power Blues' and hash 'em up a bit."[62]

One of the expert witnesses, a Black piano player, Professor James "Slap" White, provided expert testimony from the witness stand.[63] He was quoted as saying, "The two pieces of sheet music are different, but they were both blues songs, and all blues is blues."[64] His statement "blues is blues" made headlines in newspapers in Chicago. (Notice White did not say jazz is jazz.)

After several days of testimony, Judge Carpenter threw the case out stating, "I am inclined to take the view of Professor 'Slap' White in this case, that it is an old Negro melody, that it has been known for a great many years. The finding of the Court is therefore that neither Mr. LaRocca and his associates nor Mr. Nunez and his associates conceived the idea of this melody."[65] To the frustration of all concerned, the song was placed in the public domain.

The question that must come to mind is why the Original Dixieland Jass Band is not mentioned in today's history books on blues, even though all involved with the song swore under oath "Livery Stable Blues" was a blues song. The fallacy that is perpetrated today is that ODJB was a jazz band and "Livery Stable Blues" was a jazz song. Yet, under oath, the word jazz was never uttered. Jazz is a misnomer of the blues. The blues was subsequently suppressed, but it reemerged under different guises like jazz and swing.

Moreover, high art, White institutions believed, could not emanate from the Black underclass. The belief that the Black race was inferior was supported by pseudoscientists to justify the enslavement and subjugation of African Americans. Even when Black genius was undeniable, it had to be labeled "evil" or the "work of the devil" to protect the colonial and Jim Crow narratives that Blacks were less than human, all in order to dissuade young Whites from becoming attracted to and seeing Negros as their equals. In other words, as blues became a pejorative description for the music and culture, jazz became one of its more acceptable euphemisms. Nevertheless, Original Dixieland Jass Band's "Livery Stable Blues" success opened a Pandora's box that would change American popular culture forever.

THE CONTROVERSIAL LEGACY OF NICK LAROCCA

As TASTES FOR THE BLUES SPREAD, young White record collectors began to demand "authenticity" over novelty. However, the record companies and the vast majority of record buyers still were not ready to fully accept the blues when recorded by its originators, no matter how excellent. They preferred to have it delivered by someone who looked like them. This racial dichotomy created a lucrative market for White musicians such as Paul Whiteman, Bix Beiderbecke, and later Benny Goodman, to name only a few.

The legacy of the Original Dixieland Jass Band is one of controversy because Nick LaRocca "was a self-aggrandizing, reality-denying bigot, desperate to legitimize himself—and delegitimize his black predecessors. 'Our music is strictly white man's music,' LaRocca wrote to *Tempo* magazine in 1936. 'My contention is that the Negroes learned to play this rhythm and music from the whites. . . . The Negro did not play any kind of music equal to white men at any time.'"[66]

LaRocca and many other White musicians who would appropriate Negro music in the decades to come should have humbly acknowledged that their privileged White skin was their most precious asset—a few did, but even so, financial acknowledgment in the form of royalties rarely made it back to the originators. White privilege allowed advantages and opportunities that Negro musicians couldn't even dream about, no matter how talented.

To be fair, King Oliver and Louis Armstrong were indeed influenced by ODJB's mainstream success. They did buy LaRocca's records and absorbed aspects of his presentation, such as dropping the fiddle from their lineups. In fact, every popular Black musician in America has incorporated some influence from White musicians into their own compositions and performances. It's unavoidable when sharing the same milieu. But sometimes it's done for commercial reasons.

When a White band has a hit record appropriating our original music, it forces us, whether we want to or not, to adopt certain aspects the public found exciting in order to stay relevant in an ever-shifting marketplace. I would also agree with LaRocca that Negroes from New York, in 1917, could not syncopate like his band. W. C. Handy's stiff New York recordings are an example of a Negro orchestra struggling to adopt an unwritten Louisiana blues language. Still, LaRocca loses all credibility when he argues Buddy Bolden, Louis Armstrong, Jelly Roll Morton, King Oliver, Sidney Bechet, Bunk Johnson, Kid Ory, Freddie Keppard, and others were not able to play the blues or syncopate before he did it. In other words, that we as African Americans owe our rhythm, our groove, our swing, our shuffle, our funk, our hip-hop, and soul, to Nick LaRocca. I imagine that even David Duke would disagree with LaRocca's racists boasts.

Indeed, Black Louisiana musicians were spreading the blues in live performances long before Nick LaRocca left New Orleans. Piano professor Tony Jackson and Jelly Roll Morton established the blues in Chicago and beyond a decade before the Original Dixieland Jass Band arrived in the Windy City. Sidney Bechet and Manuel Perez were in Chicago as early as 1915. Supreme clarinetist Sidney Bechet also played the blues in Europe in 1919 prior to ODJB touring abroad. In addition, the Original Creole Band, led by cornetist Freddie Keppard, was one of the first to introduce audiences from California to New York to the revolutionary sounds of New Orleans as one of the traveling bands in a vaudeville show.[67] In fact, Keppard's Original Creole Band was in New York City around the time of ODJB's first "Livery Stable Blues" recording session, performing a two-week engagement at the Monmartre, a late-night supper club at Broadway and Fiftieth Street. At the same time LaRocca's ODJB was playing an extended booking at the Reisenweber's Restaurant nearby. Legend has it the Original Creole Band was offered to record first but Keppard inexplicably got cold feet and turned down the opportunity.[68]

LaRocca's disdain for Negro culture, while at the same time attempting to usurp and profit from it, is highly disturbing. Unlike Antonio Maggio, who at least gave credit to an unnamed Negro guitarist for his song "I Got the Blues," Nick LaRocca grew more bitter and resentful with age. He clung to his racist justifications into the 1950s. Dominic "Nick" LaRocca died in New Orleans in 1961.

Of course, the first orchestras allowed to record would be non-Black. But in later years, once the public finally got a chance to hear the likes of King Oliver, Jelly Roll Morton, Louis Armstrong, and Lonnie Johnson, the public's ear became more astute. To distinguish the authentic blues from its usurpers, record aficionados and collectors dubbed it "hot blues" or "hot jazz." The boom years for what we can now call "Classic Creole Blues" were 1919 through the 1920s.[69]

It will offend many jazz musicians and devotees to hear me say that jazz is a misnomer for blues. However, if they follow the contemporaneous primary evidence provided by the pioneers themselves, not the distortions of their critics, they will be forced to accept the truthfulness of my assertion.

This assertion is not meant as a polemic on working jazz musicians nor their fans. To put it simply, I'd rather defer to Ice Cube and Dr. Dre, not their mainstream critics, including Tipper Gore, when it comes to properly defining and contextualizing their music.

Throughout the 1920s, the New Orleans Creole blues dominated the music business. Indeed, by only a few degrees of separation, nearly every hit recording of the era, including the inspiration of the singers and musicians of those recordings, could be traced directly to a New Orleans musician or a New Orleans blues influence. The following examples are only a selected few.

First, the phonographic blues era truly began with Dope Andrews's trombone solo on Mamie Smith's seminal 1920 hit "Crazy Blues." Dope Andrews was influenced by the long-established stylings of trombonist Kid Ory. Andrews's horn played counterpoint, weaving around Mamie's vocal exuberantly, creating tension and release. Creolized instrumental counterpoint would go on to become a defining aesthetic of the blues.

Second, Lucille Hegamin's "The Jazz Me Blues" is another example of New Orleans influence—by degrees. Hegamin's early recording was notable because she was the second Negro singer to record the blues following Mamie Smith.[70] Hegamin recorded "The Jazz Me Blues" and "Everybody's Blues" in 1920. The record was released the following year, in 1921.

Hegamin had been trained by incomparable New Orleans piano professor Tony Jackson in Chicago. Hegamin was born 1894 as Lucille Nelson in Macon, Georgia. She was on the road around 1909 with the Leonard Harper's entertainment company when they were stranded near Chicago. Hegamin decided to remain in Chicago and pursue a recording career. Tony Jackson introduced her to the blues and featured her as a vocalist from 1914 to 1917. During that time, Jelly Roll Morton, a protégé of Jackson's, also featured Hegamin on occasion.

Third, the first recording to feature a Negro blues band (without a vocalist) was Kid Ory's Sunshine Orchestra. They recorded two instrumentals "Ory's Creole Trombone" and "Society Blues," but in the same 1922 session they were the backing band for Roberta Dudley on "Krooked Blues" and "When You're Alone Blues." Moreover, during the same session, another female, Ruth Lee, sung "Maybe Some Day" and "That Sweet Something Dear."[71]

Finally, Bessie Smith (no relation to Mamie), born 1895, came to define the female blues style of the 1920s. In 1923, Smith was produced and accompanied by pioneering New Orleans blues pianist, songwriter, producer, and publisher Clarence Williams on her first ever recording. The duo recorded "Down Hearted Blues" and "Gulf Coast Blues" for Columbia Records.

What's more, Bessie Smith's 1925 cover of W. C. Handy's "St. Louis Blues" featured the great Louis Armstrong on trumpet. The recording defined the classic blues counterpoint between vocal and instrumental soloist for the rest of the twentieth century. Armstrong's brilliant melodic counterpoint influenced all twentieth-century soloists.

As an aside, another notable early blues recording was "Sobbin' Blues," believed to be one of the first mixed-race blues sessions. It was recorded in 1923 by the New Orleans Rhythm Kings, an all-White orchestra, with Jelly Roll Morton on piano.

All the preceding examples prove two important things. The first being, New Orleans musicians had a hand in all the earliest blues sessions and phonographs. Second, these early blues recordings should no longer be defined as jazz. New Orleans musicians continued to defiantly name and define their songs as blues, years after the word jazz had emerged.

On June 20, 1918, the *New Orleans Times-Picayune* denounced the blues in an editorial that began, "Rhythm is not necessarily music, and he who loves to keep time to the pulse of the orchestral performance by patting his foot upon the theatre floor is not necessarily a music lover." What snobs found vulgar, Black audiences found beautiful and liberating.

In 1918, New Orleans desperately wanted to distance itself from the blues craze infecting America. New Orleans's polite society denied responsibility for what it deemed a musical atrocity. The *Times-Picayune* editorial board declared the syncopated noise emanating from its Negro citizenry illegitimate. The diatribe continued, "In the matter [of the blues craze] New Orleans is particularly interested since it had been widely suggested that this particular form of musical vice had its birth in this city—that it came, in fact, from doubtful surroundings in our slums. We do not recognize the honor of parenthood [of the blues],[72] but with such a story in circulation, it behooves us to be last to accept the atrocity in polite society, and where it has crept in, we should make it a point of civic honor to suppress it. Its musical value is nil, and its possibilities of harm are great."

The 1918 editorial literally closed and padlocked the city's wrought iron gates to its blues musicians. Astonishingly, one hundred years later, New Orleans still can't bring itself to fully embrace its greatest export. It is no wonder blues musicians had to leave New Orleans in the 1910s and '20s to find gainful employment and respectability. Despite its sophistication and cosmopolitanism, New Orleans was still located "way down south, in Dixie."

During the 1910s and '20s, White Tin Pan Alley songwriters appropriated and stole blues tunes and fed them to White singers and orchestras. In 1915, the Columbia Orchestra, later named Prince's Band and Orchestra, cut the first known recording of W. C. Handy's "Saint Louis Blues." White flapper girl Marion Harris became a popular female blues singer following her 1917 recording "When I Hear That Jazz Band Play."

In the 1910s, White appropriators strained to "shimmy like my sister Kate."[73] They were not yet capable of inspiring foot tapping and slow dragging among African Americans.

Black music lovers, having migrated in large numbers to northern industrial cities such as Chicago, New York City, and Detroit, were accumulating discretionary income for entertainment. However, they were neither going to spend their hard-earned dollars on Marion Harris's records nor Prince's Orchestra. Yet, Negroes were eager to buy phonographs, if only the fledgling phonograph companies would produce something worthy of their hard-earned dollars. In 1920, Mamie Smith's recording of Perry Bradford's "Crazy Blues," one of the first vocal blues recordings by an African American, fed that demand, reportedly selling an astounding seventy-five thousand copies in its first month of release.

PERRY BRADFORD'S CRAZY BLUES

SONGWRITER AND RECORD PRODUCER Perry Bradford, born in 1893, was not from Louisiana, but like fellow Alabamian W. C. Handy, he was one of the first Black songwriters outside of Louisiana to capitalize on the blues craze. In his 1965 autobiography *Born with the Blues: The True Story of the Pioneering Blues Singers and Musicians in the Early Days of Jazz*, he confessed to spending time in New Orleans seeking out its blues scene. "I joined Allen's New Orleans Minstrels in my hometown, Atlanta, Georgia, in the fall of 1907," Bradford said. "We played a two week stand in New Orleans at the fairgrounds during the Mardi Gras in 1908." Bradford would have been about fifteen years old if the date is correct. "Every night some of our boys and girls would go slumming aroun' to all the saloons, honky-tonks, and dives, and to what the natives called the top sporting houses, where no coloreds were allowed. . . . This classy love-joint is where I first met Tony Jackson, whom the Creoles were acclaiming as the king piano man."

Perry Bradford's sojourn to New Orleans conflicts with an assertion he once made—in order to promote himself as "Father of the Blues"—that neither blues nor jazz began in New Orleans. In fact, to the contrary, the only way to have heard the blues played in America between 1900 and 1908 was to visit Louisiana's honky-tonks, Lincoln Park, or Storyville, or catch a Louisiana musician performing outside the state, because the music was yet to be recorded on portable 78s. Ironically, by placing himself in New Orleans just as the blues was enrapturing the city, Bradford impeaches his earlier claim that neither blues nor jazz began in New Orleans. Instead, he makes himself a witness to the fact that there was indeed a thriving blues scene in New Orleans during his visit in 1908.

Buddy Bolden, the cornetist credited with starting it all, had been removed from the scene—institutionalized—a year prior. Nevertheless, in 1908, while a teenaged impressionable Perry Bradford was taking notes, Tony Jackson, Bunk Johnson, Kid Ory, King Oliver, and Jelly Roll Morton were all spreading the blues in New Orleans and beyond.

We know that before Bradford wrote "Crazy Blues" he was part of a short-lived act with Creole blues genius Jelly Roll Morton. Therefore, Perry Bradford had ample opportunity to learn New Orleans blues from the great pianist and arranger himself. In 1913, while both were based in Chicago, Jelly Roll Morton and Perry Bradford met and became fast friends, putting together a "big act"

Bradford later recalled: "We tried it out in South Chicago" but "the act laid an omelette, it was so terrible." Bradford also wisecracked on Morton's ham acting but acknowledged Morton "could really play a mean piano."[74]

In later years, both Perry Bradford and W. C. Handy—in order to brand themselves the "Fathers of the Blues"—attempted to obfuscate New Orleans as its birthplace in their respective autobiographies. Notwithstanding, Perry Bradford and W. C. Handy both deserve credit as pioneering Negro entrepreneurs. They had the ingenuity to recognize the genius and marketability of New Orleans Creole blues and they possessed the tenacity to capitalize on its commercial appeal.

Perry Bradford realized early on that nothing could be more culturally inspiring for the Black community (with the exception, perhaps, of heavyweight champion Jack Johnson knocking out another White contender) than to hear musicians who looked like them expressing the blues on record.

In 1919, in the hope of getting a green light for his vision of a Negro phonograph industry, Bradford went door knocking around Manhattan with his idea to produce blues songs that would appeal to an untapped Negro market. After being rejected by every established phonograph company in New York City, Bradford met with Fred Hager, recording director of upstart label OKeh. Hager was impressed with Bradford's pitch, but he wanted Sophie Tucker, a White singer, to record Bradford's blues songs. Bradford insisted Hager give Mamie Smith, a veteran Negro singer, dancer, and actress, a chance. Hager, though hesitant, gave Perry Bradford a green light to produce the first blues record in the Negro aesthetic with a Black female singer.

Backed by a White house band with no feel for the blues, Mamie Smith's first session produced "You Can't Keep a Good Man Down" and "That Thing Called Love." Although the songs are written as blues per se, and Mamie was doing her best to emotionally phrase the melodies as such, the band was pallid. The all-White orchestra lacked the necessary funkiness and feeling of the blues. Moreover, the record sounded uninspired because the musicians were neither enthralled with the material nor with having to back a Negro singer. Nevertheless, the 78-rpm sold modestly well, prompting Hager to order a follow-up session to build on its momentum.

For the next session, Perry Bradford was allowed to assemble a Negro band, the Jazz Hounds, which included Johnny Dunn on cornet and Dope Andrews on trombone. "Crazy Blues" (formally "Harlem Blues") was recorded under Bradford's direction and aimed not at the polite Victorian parlor crowd but patrons of Harlem speakeasies and rent parties. "As we hit the introduction and Mamie started singing," Bradford recalled, it gave me a lifetime thrill to hear Johnny Dunn's cornet moaning those dreaming blues and Dope Andrews making some down-home slides on his trombone, while Ernest Elliott was echoing some clarinet jive along with Leroy Parker sawing his fiddle in the groove. Man, it was too much for me.

Some would like to give Columbia record man Ralph Peer credit as the mastermind behind the landmark recording "Crazy Blues," but they would be greatly mistaken. Ralph Peer was a salesman and market researcher at the time of the session, not a record producer. Later, he would become famous for coining the derogatory marketing term "race records," which effectively established the Jim Crow sphere of the record business. However, in 1920, Ralph Peer had no idea what kind of music Negroes wanted to buy. Indeed, it was Blacks like Perry Bradford and Clarence Williams, pioneering A&R producers and publishers, who paved the way to the Negro record buyer. Ralph Peer and other White record executives followed.

Ralph Peer was a shrewd early record man who would go on to dominate the market for hot blues recordings by signing Louis Armstrong's Hot Five and Hot Seven; the king of blues guitarists, Lonnie Johnson; Jelly Roll Morton; and hundreds of others. Peer ultimately established OKeh Records as the number-one "race label" in America during the blues craze of the 1920s.

Perhaps Ralph Peer's most famous sessions are the Bristol Sessions he recorded for Victor Records, which was a defining moment in country music. Peer came up with the marketing term "hillbilly." To make it plain, early hillbilly, the foundation of country music, was basically rural White performers performing Negro blues.

In August 1927, in a makeshift studio in Bristol, Tennessee, Peer made field recordings of the legendary Jimmie Rodgers and the Carter Family. Rodgers was an outstanding White yodeling blues singer and guitarist. Peer said of Jimmie Rodgers, "He was singing nigger blues" and his backing band was "doing old-time fiddle music; its oil and water, and they don't mix." Therefore, Peer decided to record them separately. "I recorded the string band, gave them four selections. . . . I got Jimmie back alone and recorded him."[75] Later, in 1959, Ralph Peer, reflecting on his pioneering and lucrative career as a producer and publisher, said proudly, "I invented the Hillbilly and the Nigger stuff." Peer's condescending statement revealed the disdain he held for many of his artists, both White and Black.

Indeed, modern country music, whose song structure and rhythmic foundation draw from blues and hip-hop, began with artists such as Jimmie Rodgers, Bob Wills, Roy Acuff, and Clarence Ashley in blackface singing Negro blues at medicine and tent shows. In fact, blues was the foundation of country music.

Marketing terms like hillbilly, Dixie, bluegrass, country, rockabilly, and later, rock and roll, were all initially devised to assuage the racial prejudice of Whites. The early forms of these Jim Crow genres (genres of segregation) were performed by Whites who sounded too Black for comfort. Therefore, their Whiteness had to be accentuated with various marketing terms.

The White forerunners and heroes of each of these genres, everyone from Hank Williams to Uncle Dave Macon, Roy Acuff, Buddy Holly, Elvis Presley, the Beatles, and the Rolling Stones, all adopted their styles from the hottest Black blues musicians of their day. Over time, casual observers have forgotten the role blackface minstrelsy and Jim Crow segregation played in the creation of such marketing terms. To be sure, White appropriation has always proved lucrative for the best Negro imitators.

As for copyright thieves, Ralph Peer made millions by demanding his unsophisticated artists record original material and sign their copyrights over to his personal publishing company.

Perry Bradford, though a shrewd music publisher himself, was not rewarded for his role in pioneering the race market. Instead, he was trampled in the gold rush and discarded. Bradford said—and it remains true today—the reason some artists were promoted over others more talented was because they had signed the rights of their music over to powerful exploiters such as Ralph Peer for perpetuity—something he refused to do.

In his 1965 autobiography Bradford argued that White critics and unscrupulous publishers and their publicists concocted a fictionalized blues narrative designed to enrich themselves at their artists' expense. Bradford said he would not sell the rights to his "1400 song catalog" for mere crumbs, therefore, he was literally starved out of the business. Yet in his biography he insisted he wasn't bitter, only that he wanted to tell the truth; set the record straight so generations to come would know his cautionary tale.

Perry Bradford had envisioned a Negro music market that would benefit Black song publishers and writers; a market where he and others alike would get their fair share of the profits in the booming billion-dollar record and publishing industry they had built. However, his dream of independent wealth, by the end of the blues craze, became a sharecropping nightmare.

As for Mamie Smith, Bradford's protégé, after gaining early success recording for OKeh throughout the 1920s, and subsequently opening the door for talented Black female blues singers such as Gertrude "Ma" Rainey, Bessie Smith, and Billie Holiday, she died in 1946, destitute at age sixty-three in Staten Island, New York. Perry Bradford was certain he would suffer a similar fate. He too died unsung in 1970.

LONNIE JOHNSON: TRUE KING OF DELTA BLUES

IT IS A LONG-STANDING FALLACY, the notion that the blues began on antebellum Mississippi Delta cotton plantations, and then mysteriously made its way to New Orleans. The authentic narrative is the reverse: the blues was indigenous to cosmopolitan New Orleans, and then subsequently made its way to rural tenant farmers in the Mississippi Delta by way of the phonograph.

The guitar, my chosen instrument, is today the most recognized emblem of the blues. But during the first half of the twentieth century the cornet-trumpet, its first lead instrument, was its ubiquitous emblem. Cornet-trumpeters Buddy Bolden, King Oliver, and Louis Armstrong laid the foundation. Jelly Roll Morton expanded its philosophy, and guitarist Lonnie Johnson's remarkable acoustic guitar innovations made the cosmopolitan blues accessible to impoverished remote tenant farmers and sharecroppers across the rural South.

Lonnie Johnson, born February 8, 1894, in New Orleans, was the first guitar virtuoso in all of American music. Part of his genius was how he melodically transposed the improvisation and phrasing of blues trumpeters such as King Oliver and Louis Armstrong to the guitar. In addition, he reinvented the all-encompassing hot piano style of Jelly Roll Morton for the guitar.

Lonnie Johnson, the authentic forerunner of what became known as Delta blues, reigned during the Acoustical era. The casual observer might wonder what is meant by the term *Acoustical era.* The technical evolution of music regarding the guitar and the recording process can be broken up into periods. For example, America experienced the Agrarian era, the Industrial era, and now we're in the present-day Digital era of Automation. Similarly, in music, we've had the Acoustical era (1877–1928), Electrical era (1928–1945), the Magnetic Tape era (1945–1980), and the Digital Recording era (1980–present day). During the Acoustical era, the recording process and all musical instruments were acoustic.

Dirt-poor tenant farmers and sharecroppers were unlikely to purchase a trumpet, trombone, or clarinet. An expensive piano was out of the question. However, once they heard the acoustic guitar recordings of Lonnie Johnson, a way was shown into the exotic, magnetic world of blues. Moreover, an acoustic guitar was portable, perfect for a day laborer or a rambling itinerant worker. A select few tenant farmers and sharecroppers could afford to order cheap guitars from the Sears catalog and pay on time.

The roaring 1920s were a time of great contrast between life in urban industrial cities and life on archaic tenant farms. The difference between an amateur guitarist on a cotton farm and a worldly professional like Lonnie Johnson was stark. Lonnie Johnson represented modernity and Blues Age glamour. He was playing music all night and sleeping half the day, while tenant farmers in rural Tennessee, Mississippi, Oklahoma, and Arkansas were toiling from sunup to sundown. While most tenant farmers were living in squalor, Lonnie Johnson was fraternizing with newly liberated flappers in New York City. Lonnie Johnson wore dapper cotton suits and picked a guitar for a living. Sharecroppers picked cotton. When Mississippi Delta sharecroppers heard Lonnie Johnson's guitar and heard about the lifestyle his music afforded him, they all wanted to move to Chicago and become Lonnie Johnson.

Thomas Edison introduced the phonograph recorder in 1887. For the first time in history, a music performance could be frozen in time and made portable. By 1920, the production of the windup Victrola phonograph player had risen to six hundred thousand. With new models being introduced each year at increasing prices, outdated models became affordable. A tenant farmer could purchase a used windup Victrola for about two dollars a month from a peddler. The salesman would return on his route every other week to collect payments and peddle the latest blues 78 rpms. The spread of early New Orleans blues on phonograph records transformed musical culture in all of America, but in the newly developing Mississippi Delta, it had the most striking effect.

When the blues was first invented in New Orleans in the 1890s, there was no musical culture in the Delta because there were virtually no people in the Delta to form a musical culture. Prior to it being drained and cleared, well into the 1910s, the Mississippi Delta was a safari populated by black bears, Florida panthers, and wild wolves. Delta musicians Charlie Patton, Mississippi John Hurt, Robert Johnson, and Muddy Waters were all first introduced to the blues primarily by phonograph recordings. In their own words—in letters and interviews—they each acknowledge phonograph records were their greatest influence. They all, without exception, either recorded Lonnie Johnson songs or copied lyrics and riffs from his phonograph records to create derivative songs. Patton, Hurt, Johnson, and Muddy were neither pioneers nor originators. In regard to blues origins, they were secondary sources.

To put it another way, Lonnie Johnson was the figurative "Tambourine Man" of blues guitar for downtrodden aspiring tenant farm guitarists desperately in need of a muse. Bob Dylan said in his biography *Chronicles, Volume One* that Lonnie Johnson changed the way he approached the blues. In 1964, in the wee hours following a long night of Mardi Gras, as "vague traces" of blues Bohemia echoed down cobblestone streets, Bob Dylan sketched the first draft of his expressionistic song "Tambourine Man" in the French Quarter. Metaphorically speaking, restless Delta musicians were "ready for to fade" into their "own parade." Lonnie Johnson cast his "dancing spell" on phonograph records and they all fell "under it."

By the 1920s, about 12 percent of Black families owned a Victrola.[76] Tenant farmers who couldn't afford a Victrola would gather to listen at a fellow tenant's shack. "I began to listen to Lonnie Johnson's records in the late 1920s," blues guitarist Brownie McGhee recalled. "I had never thought that kind of music could be made with voice and guitar, and I just kept listening." McGhee added, "His musical works may" one day be, "and should be, the first book of the blues bible."[77]

Blues legend Robert L. Johnson (no relation), a mythical Delta guitarist who, according to legend, sold his soul to the devil for mastery of the guitar, was a Lonnie Johnson impersonator, according to his closest friend Johnny Shines. In fact, Robert Johnson learned to play the blues by studying Lonnie Johnson's records, not because of a Faustian pact. In a *Living Blues* interview Johnny Shines, the Mississippi guitarist who rambled with Robert Johnson, said, "Robert often talked about Lonnie Johnson. He admired his music so much, that, he would tell people . . . he was related to Lonnie Johnson."

Robert Johnson was born 1911, in Hazlehurst, Mississippi. Hazlehurst is not in the Delta. It is located south of Jackson. Young Robert's formative years were spent in Memphis. He was a second-generation Delta guitarist. He was a virtuoso in his own right. But he borrowed heavily from his idol Lonnie Johnson. Young Robert even passed himself off at times as Lonnie Johnson. He told people his middle initial, L, was for Lonnie, instead of Leroy, his birth name. Robert Johnson's "Malted Milk" and "Me and the Devil" are both rearrangements of Lonnie's "Blue Ghost Blues." Robert Johnson borrowed the majority of his themes and narratives from Lonnie Johnson. He also vocalized in Lonnie's vocal style and timbre, borrowing from Lonnie recordings such as "She's Making Whoopee in Hell Tonight" and "Blues for Murder Only."

Undeniably, aspiring tenant farm guitarists in the South put down the plow, got a hold of a Lonnie Jonson phonograph, then studied and played it over and over again until his unique style became standardized in the Delta. Countless aspiring tenant farm guitarists studied Lonnie's lyrics and guitar licks, then created derivatives of his songs.

In the early 1900s, Delta tenant farmers were tethered to the land. They had neither electricity nor indoor plumbing. They were often on the brink of starvation. Yet, there was a makeshift theater in every nearby town, and later a nickel video jukebox called the Nickelodian. Tenant farmers were awed by what they saw and heard coming from Chicago and New York City in short films and "soundies." While the blues' decadence threatened rural Protestant Christian values, the liberating spirit of the music captured the imaginations of young musically oriented sharecroppers like Robert Johnson. It wasn't long before every dilettante plantation guitar picker in the rural South began dreaming of putting down that old plow and hopping the next northbound train to Chicago, New York City, or Wisconsin, the home of Paramount Records. They all wanted to be like their guitar hero Lonnie Johnson. Indeed, even though he was born in New Orleans and spent no time on a Delta plantation, Louisianan Lonnie Johnson is the rightful king of Delta blues guitar.

Alonzo "Lonnie" Johnson had five sisters and six brothers. Bassist George "Pops" Foster, in his book *The Autobiography of Pops Foster*, said, "Lonnie Johnson and his daddy and brother, whose moniker was, 'Steady Ramblin' Johnson, used to go all over town playing on the streets." In his youth, Lonnie was proficient on violin, piano, and guitar. He purchased his first quality guitar in 1917. Lonnie once said he played "nothing but the blues."

Lonnie joined a theater company as a musical act singing and playing guitar in between routines. In 1917, during World War I, he went to England for two years to perform for the troops. It is believed his service was in the role of entertainer, not as a military soldier. Consequently, Lonnie Johnson was the first American blues guitarist to perform in Europe. Lonnie and company entertained American troops from a base in London from 1917 to 1919.

In the fall of 1919, when Lonnie Johnson returned home, he learned that a flu epidemic had swept the United States. More than 25 percent of the population had been infected. While Lonnie had been away in Britain, the influenza epidemic killed all five of his sisters and four of his brothers. His brother James "Steady Ramblin'" Johnson was the only surviving sibling. In all, between 1917 and 1919, some 675,000 Americans died in the pandemic. Though little is known regarding birth and death records of the Johnson family, Lonnie Johnson biographer Dean Alger, in his book *Lonnie Johnson: The Original Guitar Hero and the Power of Music,* suggested his mother and father may have survived the epidemic.

Lonnie Johnson had little choice but to strike out on his own. He toured with pianist Fate Marable's highly respected band on riverboats up and down the Mississippi River between St. Louis and New Orleans. Subsequently, he and his brother relocated to St. Louis, determined to make a living playing the blues. Soon after arriving in the Midwest Johnson was in high demand because no one there had ever witnessed a blues guitarist so extraordinary.

In 1922, Johnson became an accompanist for the popular vaudeville act Glen and Jenkins. They played New York City; Winnipeg, Canada; and crisscrossed the Midwest. The tour received notable reviews in *Variety* magazine. From 1923 to 1924 Lonnie performed on his own or with his brother Steady Ramblin' Johnson as a duo. He also teamed up with blues singer Mary Smith, and later married her. Finding gigs was never a problem for the multitalented guitar master. He was booked to play with a St. Louis group led by trumpeter Charlie Creath and the Jazz-O-Maniacs, whose pianist John Arnold would subsequently accompany Lonnie on his first recordings. Lonnie also worked as a duo with vocalist Mary Hicks.

Lonnie Johnson, like many New Orleans blues musicians before him, was a road warrior. He toured constantly, spreading his brand of blues throughout Illinois, Florida, Texas, and Oklahoma. In 1924, Lonnie Johnson was encouraged to enter a big music contest at the Booker T. Washington Theater in St. Louis sponsored by talent scouts of OKeh records. The fledgling OKeh company was seeking artists for its new "race" series. The contest lasted for eighteen weeks. It was no surprise to anyone competing when Lonnie Johnson won first prize: an eleven-year recording contract with OKeh/Columbia Records.

On November 4, 1925, accompanied by John Arnold of the Jazz-O-Maniacs on piano, Lonnie Johnson entered a recording studio for OKeh. He gathered his guitar and sat right in front of the large protruding acoustic horn. The piano was positioned in the background accordingly. Mind you, in the early 1920s recordings weren't electric. An acoustic guitar was rarely heard over a loud brass section. Because of the frequency limitations of Acoustical era direct-to-disk recording devices—anything below two hundred hertz would have damaged the phonograph—bass and drums were usually omitted. Later, during the Electrical era, the sonic range was expanded to handle the full range of a big band. Therefore, the setup for the OKeh session was virtually a solo performance. It was all about focusing the listener on Lonnie's singing and playing. Lonnie smartly chose to record with only a piano accompaniment, ensuring every note he played would be heard. Lonnie counted it off. He fired into the intro with a quick-fingered obbligato announcing something of significance was about to go down. The song was called "Mr. Johnson's Blues." It should be noted that Negro men at that time were called boys, never Mister.

Between 1917 and 1925, Lonnie Johnson developed a singular style no one had heard on record before. Lonnie's singing voice was also revolutionary because up until this session, only Negro women had recorded blues, with few exceptions. Today, a casual observer may find Lonnie's singing and playing very familiar, even formulaic. That's because everyone plays and sings the blues today in accordance with his original style. Lonnie's opening stanza drew the listener in:

I want all you people to listen to my song
I want all you people to listen to my song
Remember me after the days I'm gone.

Everything about the performance was dignified. Mr. Johnson confidently exclaimed he had something important to say. The remaining verses showed off Johnson's original guitar style. His single-note guitar phrasing answered his vocal lines in counterpoint, adding another layer of interest to the words of his song. With each new vocal and guitar riff, Lonnie Johnson constructed a perfect edifice of musical style that could stand for all time.

Lonnie Johnson made the acoustic guitar an iconic solo instrument. By the late 1920s, the introduction of amplifiers and microphones would change how music was recorded. Record companies began using electromagnetic discs broadening the dynamic range of vinyl records. The development of the microphone allowed singers to croon (sing just above a whisper) whereas the earlier singers had to shout to be heard over the power of a big brass band. The advent of the microphone allowed the acoustic guitar, if positioned properly in the studio, to be heard over the band, too. Consequently, by the late 1920s aspiring guitarists could hear every intricate detail of Lonnie Johnson's guitar with the backing of full bands, further establishing a blueprint for aspiring blues guitarists to follow.

In 1927, Lonnie Johnson joined Louis Armstrong's Hot Five and Seven blues bands at the peak of Armstrong's legendary power. Two standout sides he recorded with Armstrong and Kid Ory were "Savoy Blues" and "Hotter Than That," composed by Lil Hardin, Armstrong's wife, pianist, and promotor. Lonnie Johnson also recorded with pianist-composer Duke Ellington.

In the early 1920s, Duke Ellington realized his band, the Washingtonians, lacked the nimble vibrato and spirit of the swinging New Orleans blues sound. Consequently, he hired one of the best blues musicians Louisiana ever produced, Creole clarinet virtuoso Sidney Bechet. Sidney taught Ellington the blues idiom during his short stint with the band. Duke, an astute composer and arranger, absorbed the profound depth and improvisational spirt of New Orleans blues. Afterward, Ellington's orchestra swung away from their previously stiff high-brow arrangements. Duke subsequently expanded upon the foundation of blues composing established by genius blues arranger, composer, and pianist, Jelly Roll Morton.

By 1928, when Lonnie Johnson joined Ellington for several recordings, including the classic "The Mooche" recorded in 1928 for OKeh, Duke Ellington had begun composing and arranging his orchestrated version of New Orleans blues. Duke Ellington would also back Lonnie Johnson on piano under a pseudonym on some of Lonnie's recordings. In his autobiography, Duke Ellington said of Lonnie Johnson, "I have always felt indebted to him because his guitar added a new luster to my adolescent orchestral attempts on records we made in 1928."

In 1929, Lonnie Johnson made a series of groundbreaking recordings with White guitarist Eddie Lang. Lang was heavily influenced by Lonnie Johnson and hot New Orleans trumpeters. Lang was an improviser who held his own beside Lonnie Johnson on their duo recordings. Eddie Lang recorded with Lonnie Johnson under the pseudonym "Blind Willie Dunn" to get around stringent Jim Crow practices. Their series of recordings are celebrated for their musical merit, but also because they defied the color line. The interracial instrumental guitar duo's blistering improvisations anticipated guitar virtuosos Django Reinhardt, Charlie Christian, and Wes Montgomery.

Between 1925 and 1929 the prolific Lonnie Johnson recorded over two hundred sides on his own and dozens more with the leading artists of the era. Once Lonnie Johnson's phonographs were distributed around the country every aspiring guitar picker from Texas, Oklahoma, Mississippi, Illinois, Missouri, and beyond perked up their ears and studied his landmark licks.

Radio reception in many rural areas was unreliable. Besides, radios were costly. Therefore, more Black sharecroppers owned phonograph players than radios. On Delta plantations such as Dockery Farm, phonographs and Victrolas could be purchased at the plantation commissary. Lonnie's records were distributed from New York City down to plantations unconventionally. Because record distribution to African Americans was in its infancy, Negro Pullman porters made extra money by selling Lonnie's records to Negroes along their train routes from New York to Chicago, Memphis to Mississippi and New Orleans.[78]

The phonograph was, therefore, the primary way New Orleans blues eventually made it to tenant farmers on the Dockery plantation in the Mississippi Delta.

Nevertheless, folklorists, musicologists, and academics still cling to the notion blues began in the Mississippi Delta on the Dockery plantation without any evidence to support the hypothesis. When Buddy Bolden and Bunk Johnson were playing the "low-down" blues in New Orleans as early as 1895, there was no Dockery plantation. The only sounds haunting the Delta were the roar of bears and the howl of wild wolves.

BLACK FRONTIERSMEN IN THE MISSISSIPPI DELTA

NEW ORLEANS, IN REALITY, is the Mississippi Delta and birthplace of the blues. What, then, is the universally mythologized Mississippi Delta of blues lore? According to the U.S. Department of Agriculture and the geography and map division of the Library of Congress, the Mississippi Delta begins at the foot of Louisiana, in Lafourche, Jefferson, Plaquemines, St. Bernard, and Orleans Parishes. It extends north along the Mississippi River into parts of Arkansas, Mississippi, Tennessee, Kentucky, Missouri, and Illinois. Of all the states in the Lower Mississippi River Valley, because its name is one with the river, Mississippi is the only state colloquially referred to as *the* Mississippi Delta.

On a contemporary map, the mythologized Mississippi Delta of blues lore is located to the north of Interstate 20 that runs east and west across central Mississippi. Interstate 20, which connects Vicksburg to Jackson, marks the original antebellum northern border of the state. When Mississippi joined the union in 1817, everything above what is now Interstate 20 was owned and occupied by the Chickasaw and Choctaw nations.

Andrew Jackson, as president, signed the Indian Removal Act of 1830. Even so, it took several more years to uproot the holdout Chickasaw warriors from their sacred lands. Prior to the Jacksonian genocide of the Delta Natives, which culminated in a Trail of Tears, no White planters or enslaved Black people lived in the Indigenous Mississippi Delta. To be clear, neither Jackson nor Vicksburg is located in the Delta of blues mythology.

Around 1840, a small group of planters from the hills of Tennessee and nearby Kentucky moved south into the newly opened southern frontier. Two prominent families, the Alcorn family and the Worthington brothers of Virginia, established plantations near the Mississippi River, "but these had not been fully developed."[79] Inland, in the mythologized Delta proper, only a small number of poor and uneducated Whites and a handful of yeoman farmers proved desperate enough to attempt settling in the dense undeveloped hardwood forests, cane breaks, and swamps.

By 1860, a year before seceding from the Union, in the entire state of Mississippi there were 353,899 White people and 437,404 enslaved Negroes.[80] Of the total number of enslaved Black people, less than 1 percent inhabited Panola County, "the land where the blues began," in what would become the Mississippi Delta of popular blues lore. That's because before the Civil War all plantations were small settlements along the banks of the Mississippi and its tributary the Sunflower.[81] The river location was beneficial for cotton exports.

At the time of the Civil War, about 90 percent of the state of Mississippi was unpopulated wilderness. Agricultural activity in the Yazoo Basin had been impossible because of unpredictable flooding.[82] In the aftermath of the Civil War, many wealthy antebellum plantations along the river were financially devastated and abandoned. There had been some attempt at levee building, but these inadequate earth barriers to the floods had fallen into disrepair during the war. The oldest Black generation in Coahoma County were people who migrated there in the 1870s and 1880s. These Freedmen and women came from outside the Delta, from Alabama, and a few from Georgia.[83]

In 1880, along the river, "there were 170,000 people living in the Delta. For all this population, there were but two towns between Memphis and Vicksburg that contained more than 1,000 people within their limits. There was but 30 miles of railroad track in the Delta, and that was narrow gauge."[84] Without levees, annual flooding kept the Delta undeveloped and uninhabitable.

Near the close of the nineteenth century, however, dams were finally built to alter the river's course and drain the rich alluvial bottomland. Yet, by the early twentieth century, the Mississippi Delta remained a barren wilderness. It is correct, then, to conclude that African Americans had virtually no history in the Mississippi Delta during slavery.

The first Black frontiersmen to establish themselves in the Delta didn't play the blues. They had never heard of such a thing. Even if they had, they would have banned the subversive music from their ultra-conservative community. They were hardworking small farmers, family oriented God-fearing people with a strict moral code.

In 1887, two former slaves, Benjamin Green and his cousin Isaiah Montgomery, the latter born in 1847, purchased 840 acres near an Indian mound and incorporated it as Mound Bayou, establishing the first all-Black town in Mississippi and one of the few in America. The uncleared wilderness in Bolivar County was purchased from the Yazoo-Mississippi Valley Railroad Company. At the time of the purchase, that part of Bolivar County was impenetrable forest through which the railroad had blazed its right of way.[85] Isaiah Montgomery sold subdivided lots to Negro farmers who cleared the land, sold the timber, built a town, and grew their own crops.

In 1890, Isaiah Montgomery, the leader of Mound Bayou, was the only Negro delegate invited to the Mississippi constitutional convention. Isaiah Montgomery's "speech" at the convention "expressed his willingness" to appease White supremacy by disenfranchising Blacks of the vote in the delusion they would be left alone to live in peace. "This event preceded Booker T. Washington's [infamous] capitulation during the Atlanta Exposition by five years."[86] White attendees demanded a White supremacist state constitution. Editor for the *Greenwood Enterprise* James K. Vardaman, who in 1903 became governor of Mississippi, "was unambiguous as to the meaning of the constitution":[87] "I am just as opposed to Booker T. Washington as a voter, with all his Anglo-Saxon reinforcements . . . as I am to coconut headed, chocolate-colored typical little coon, Andy Dotson, who blacks my shoes every morning. Neither is fit to perform the supreme function of citizenship."[88] Nevertheless, Isaiah Montgomery's politics of appeasement would suffice for the fledgling Mound Bayou for a time.

In 1902, the self-governing, self-sustaining, all-Black, mostly literate population of Mound Bayou numbered six thousand, including the surrounding frontier. The citizenry was a mix of planters, business owners, local government officials, small farmers, and service workers. National Negro leader Booker T. Washington "took part in some of its economic development, which included" a Black-owned bank, railroad station, telephone exchange, newspaper, churches, schools, "and other Black-owned businesses and industries."[89]

In addition, a Black-owned cottonseed mill—one of the only Black-owned cottonseed mills in the nation—was Mound Bayou's main economic engine and one of the most profitable mills in the region. By the 1910s, Mound Bayou was a respected boomtown praised as a model of Black achievement by President Theodore "Teddy" Roosevelt, who made a train stop there to greet the locals during one of his hunting safaris in the Delta.

One evening, two White travelers got off the train at Mound Bayou's railroad station needing a room for the night. One of the travelers, a reporter, wrote in a Memphis newspaper about his overnight stay. "When I realized," the reporter said,

> that we would be compelled to remain overnight in Mound Bayou I began to wonder what treatment we, the only two white people in the place would receive. I asked [Isaiah] Montgomery about someplace to eat and sleep, and he replied that there was a room at his [twenty-one room] home that had never been occupied excepting [*sic*] by white people. To his house, my companion and myself were taken. We were met in the hall by Montgomery's wife and two daughters, neatly dressed and with a manner and refinement that were a revelation. They had prepared for us a savory supper, which we ate with much relish in the regular dining room all by ourselves.
>
> Our bedroom was neat, clean, and as nicely furnished as you will find in the average hotel. After some conversation with Montgomery concerning his colony and the general condition of the negro farmers of Mississippi, we retired to our room. The thought occurred to us, while the storm was raging outside, what a difference between our position and the position of two negroes who might have strayed into a town populated entirely by whites, and in which negroes were not permitted to live. Here we were at Mound Bayou—two white men—among 7,000 negroes, and our treatment had been irreproachable.[90]

Booker T. Washington praised Mound Bayou as a model Negro town. Washington and Montgomery shared an accommodating vision toward Jim Crow. They offered up Black disenfranchisement in the South as a means to solve the "race problem." It's reasonable to discern that Isaiah Montgomery's bargain with

White resentment protected his community from fiery White mob violence similar to that which destroyed the extraordinary Black town in Tulsa, Oklahoma, in 1921, known as "Black Wall Street." But to voluntarily withdraw from politics altogether—although Mound Bayou often held symbolic mock votes—proved to be too high a price for many Blacks who decided to migrate North with hopes of better social and working conditions in urban industrial factories.

Mound Bayou began its decline when cotton prices collapsed following World War I. The town's workforce was further devastated by the advent of agricultural mechanization. What's more, the boll weevil infestation bankrupted the town's cottonseed mill and its bank. In the aftermath of the Great Depression of 1929, Mound Bayou's economy further collapsed along with the entire southern cotton industry. Worst still, capital from federal government farm programs such as the Agriculture Adjustment Act of 1933, to support farm prices and restrict production, were denied to Black farmers. Bankrupt and without political influence, small Black farmers in Mound Bayou lost their land to prospectors. As a result, the population became tenant farmers and sharecroppers—along with thousands of small Black farmers across Mississippi—on newly cleared White-owned Delta plantations such as the Dockery plantation in Sunflower County.

Still all was not lost in Mound Bayou. Its independent-minded citizens, the few that remained, forged ahead through the Great Depression. In the 1950s, residents helped spearhead a Mississippi civil rights movement. Medgar Evers, a budding civil rights leader, moved his family to Mound Bayou in 1952 to sell insurance for the prominent Dr. T. M. Howard, a notable civil rights activist. While residing in Mound Bayou Evers became a leading organizer for voting rights. Medgar Evers was assassinated on June 12, 1963.

Mound Bayou also played a protective role in the Emmett Till murder trial at a tipping point in the civil rights movement. Dr. Howard hosted Negro reporters and witnesses in his Mound Bayou home, providing them a safe place to stay during the infamous trial.

The Black population of Mississippi has always been extraordinary. They have made great achievements in every field imaginable: science, medicine, education, and literature. The music of the Mississippi Delta is without question one of America's great cultural exports. Nonetheless, prior to Negro tenant farmers migrating there after the turn of the century, the Delta, from Yazoo to Sunflower County, remained a frontier densely inhabited by black bears, panthers, and wolves. Therefore, it is impossible that Delta blues could have predated New Orleans blues.

What's more, Will Dockery didn't purchase his vast acreages of wilderness and bottomland in the Delta near Cleveland, Mississippi, until 1895. It then took the Dockery family another year or two to clear the cheaply purchased wilderness and cultivate it. It took a few more seasons before Will Dockery could entice Negro tenant farmers and sharecroppers to migrate to his plantation. It is imperative, when discussing blues origins, to understand the Dockery plantation, long proclaimed to be the "birthplace of blues," was not an antebellum plantation but a twentieth-century tenant farm.

In 1901, Charles Peabody from Harvard's Peabody Museum of American Archaeology and Ethnology arrived in Coahoma County to begin archaeological excavations of Native American mounds located near Clarksdale, discovered during the draining and clearing of the Delta. Charles Peabody—a great-nephew of the Peabody Museum's founder, George Peabody—was an archaeologist (not a folklorist) studying Native American earth mounds when he hired a group of Black men to carry his equipment and provisions to the first mound about twenty miles north of Clarksdale. It was a difficult journey because the mound was in the thick of the safari. During the excavation, Peabody became enchanted with the singing he heard among the Negro excavators he had hired. Charles Peabody observed the men singing songs to keep rhythm while they worked, similarly to a team of loggers or railroad workers in order to pull together. Peabody described in his journal as best he could—he was not a trained musician—the sounds he witnessed. Between 1901 and 1902, Charles Peabody documented the earliest academic reports of Blacks singing in the Delta.

What Peabody described was said to be, by later academics, a primogenitor of the blues. I find upon closer examination, however, that what he documented was not representative of blues, except for a few lyrics the itinerant workers may have picked up. Mind you, any type of lyric can be transposed into a blues. Furthermore, the men Peabody used for excavation in the Delta didn't live in its deep wilderness; just like Charles Peabody, they ventured into the Delta for the excavation missions or to build levees and clear the forests. It's important to understand, there was no Delta musical culture as we think of it today.

Therefore, it strains credulity to expect one to believe the blues originated in the Delta wilderness before 1903 as W. C. Handy once suggested in an aggrandizing tale. Delta blues devotees and researchers often cite Handy's recollection of his chance encounter with a wayfaring guitarist as proof the blues originated in the Mississippi Delta. In his 1926 book, *Blues: An Anthology*, Handy claimed that in 1903 at a train stop in Tutwiler, Mississippi, while he and his Delta orchestra waited for a train, he overheard a drifter playing a "weird" tune on a guitar. He later recalled it was his first encounter with the blues.

However, upon closer examination, Handy's anecdote begs the question: if blues was indigenous to the Delta, why would it sound strange to him or his

Mississippi orchestra? Meanwhile, in 1903, blues pioneers Jelly Roll Morton and Buddy Bolden—the former in Storyville, the latter, "calling 'em home" in Lincoln Park—were already earning a living performing blues indigenous to New Orleans for enthusiastic crowds. There are ample newspaper reports, photographs, and eyewitness accounts verifying that by 1903 blues was already a ubiquitous part of New Orleans culture and had been for some years. Meanwhile, the Mississippi Delta, which stretched from Yazoo City as far north as Tunica, just south of Memphis, was still a scarcely inhabited frontier. The area was still in the process of being cleared, drained, subdivided, and sold to twentieth-century planters. This understanding may be a rude revelation to Delta blues fans whose romanticism about its genesis are based on myth and folklore, not primary evidence.

HOLT COLLIER AND THE DELTA TEDDY BEAR

To ILLUSTRATE FURTHER that until the twentieth century the Delta was a wilderness with no musical culture, there's a little-known Delta story about a legendary Negro bear hunter named Holt Collier, who happened to be the best bear hunter in all of America. Holt Collier was the protagonist in the original story of how there came to be a "teddy bear."

In 1902, Holt Collier was personally chosen by President Theodore Roosevelt, an avid sportsman, to guide him on a ten-day safari in the Mississippi Delta to hunt black bear. There were more wild bears, panthers, and wolves, in the Delta wilderness than there were people at the time. Born in 1846, Holt Collier, a former slave, was the best bear hunter in the nation. Collier was known to have killed over three thousand bears, more than Davy Crockett and Daniel Boone combined.[91]

President Roosevelt placed full responsibility of planning his hunt upon the rugged, dependable shoulders of the illiterate Collier. The former Confederate sharpshooter knew the heavily wooded Delta like a second home. During the Civil War, in which he served as one of Nathan Bedford Forrest's most trusted cavalry scouts, he led the ambushed 9th Texas Brigade out of the wilderness to safety.

Holt Collier scouted a hunting site for the president on the muddy banks of the Little Sunflower River.[92] The safari campsites were said to have been near what is now Cleveland, Tunica, Clarksdale, Bobo, and Rolling Fork. "One day Major Helm came to me," said Holt,

and said, "If you can get things ready in a month and not let anybody know
what you're doing, President Roosevelt will go hunting with us." So, I got things
ready. Found a beautiful campin' place. I was boss of the hunt. Along came the
President with a car-load of guards, but he left all but one of 'em in the car.
Anyway, he was safer with me than with all the policemen in Washington. The
President was a pleasant man; when he was talking he'd stop every little while to
ask other people's opinion. Sometimes he asked my opinion about something,
and he talked to me about as much as he did to anybody else; he had a thousand
questions to ask. We sat on a log to talk and in ten minutes, thirty-five people
were sitting on the log. It was going to be a ten-day hunt, but the President was
impatient, "I must see a live bear the first day," he said. I told him he would if
I had to tie one and bring it to him. Mr. Foote made fun of me. The President
looked doubtful, but Mr. Percy and Major Helm said I could do it.[93]

The next day, just before dawn, Holt Collier, on horseback, set out from the
camp with his prized pack of dogs numbering about fifty. It was a few hours before
Holt's dogs finally caught the scent of a large black bear. Holt tracked, then caught
up to the bear, trapping it in the canebrake. The bear, ferociously fending off the
dogs, snatched one of Holt's prized canines into his powerful jaws, forcing Holt,
who was blocking the bear's escape, to leap from his horse to save his dogs. Rifle
in hand, Holt would've already killed the bear, but he had promised the shot to
the president. He leaped toward the bear, clubbing it across the skull to subdue
it. With his rifle bent beyond use, the bear still aggressive, Holt wrestled the large
brawny animal to submission before finally roping it to a tree. He blew his hunting
horn for the president and his party, who were about a mile back, to join him.[94]

After lagging about a mile behind, President Teddy Roosevelt arrived primed
to take his deadly shot. He jumped from his horse into the muddy swamp water,
waded his way to the bank, aimed his rifle, saw the large bloodied bear tied to
a tree, then curiously, he froze. The hunters, having arrived with the president,
urged Roosevelt to take his shot. But Teddy Roosevelt couldn't bring himself to
shoot the pitiful suffering animal. He lowered his rifle, turned his back, and pardoned the tethered bear.

On November 16, 1902, within days after the incident, a *Washington Post*
political cartoonist, Clifford Berryman, took a light-hearted jab at the president.
Roosevelt was known as a fierce macho hunter. But Berryman's illustration in
support of the article "Drawing the Line in Mississippi" characterized Teddy
Roosevelt holding his rifle with his back turned to a frightened cute little bear
that sat helplessly tied to a tree. The illustration revealed a sensitive side of Roosevelt. The warm Teddy's bear story proved an enduring novelty across the nation.

Brooklyn candy store operators Morris Michtom and his wife, Rose, inspired by the story, created and sold little stuffed bears from their store window. It caught on. Morris Michtom named the popular toy "Teddy Bear" after Teddy Roosevelt. The Michtoms, with the blessing of Teddy Roosevelt, mass produced the cuddly stuffed bear, which sold in the hundreds of thousands annually. The teddy bear has become a family heirloom throughout the world. Obfuscated from this cute bedtime story was formerly enslaved Holt Collier, the brave sportsman and bear hunter who won the respect and admiration of President Roosevelt.

The point is, the 1902 teddy bear adventure of Holt Collier and the president took place around Coahoma and Sunflower Counties where the blues is supposed to have originated. The story further illustrates that the Delta, where the teddy bear hunt took place, the area where they say the blues was born, was overrun with black bears not Black people. The vast majority of the Delta was still an undrained virgin frontier devoid of Black churches, schools, and people. Most of Mississippi's large Black population still lived in the southern part of the state, between Jackson and the Gulf Coast. They didn't migrate into the Delta until after it was cleared and drained in the early 1900s.

Furthermore, in 1902, Charlie Patton, one of the first Delta guitarists to record, was only nine years old. Tommy Johnson was only seven. Son House was a newborn baby. As for Muddy Waters and Robert Johnson, they were not yet born. By contrast, in 1902, Tony Jackson, Jelly Roll Morton, Bunk Johnson, Buddy Bolden, and numerous others had already established the blues from New Orleans to Baton Rouge.

THE SOULS OF "PRIMITIVE" BLACK FOLK

THE LAND WHERE THE BLUES supposedly began has a long history of investigations by social scientists and folklorists. Yet evidence of the blues originating in the Mississippi Delta is unfounded. What we have instead is folklore rooted in *eugenics*. The twisted fantasies of eugenicists, their fairy tales and folklore imposed upon the Delta folk, was rooted in scientific racism. Eugenic data collectors with nefarious agendas, under the guises of sociologists and folklorists, roamed the South in the early twentieth century recording prisoners, chain-gangers, and peonage slaves. Their collection methodologies were designed to demonize, for the general public, the *Souls of Black Folk*.

If the Negro was proven to be inferior biologically and mentally, racist governmental policies of social control would have scientific and academic cover. There would be no moral obligation, then, to invest in equalitarian programs and policies. If the Negro problem was innate, it would then be prudent to protect the superior race by investing in segregation, policing, and prison warehouses.

In 1903, W. E. B. Du Bois wrote, "The problem of the twentieth century is the problem of the color line." With Thomas Edison's new graphophone cylinder recorder, eugenicists set out to prove that the problem of the twentieth century was the problem of the "colored mind."

Was the blues the ravings of the feebleminded? Was it proof of Negro genius? The stakes to control the public's perception of the blues in the early twentieth century could not have been higher.

Eugenics was the "practice or advocacy of improving the human species" by selective breeding of "people with specific desirable hereditary traits." It aimed to breed out disease and disabilities. "Early supporters of eugenics believed people inherited mental illness, criminal tendencies," and sexual perversion. They believed strongly in a poverty gene. In other words, poverty was a biological condition that couldn't be solved unless it was "bred out of the gene pool." All of these "degenerate" traits were evidence of *feeblemindedness*.[95]

The hierarchy of intelligence was rooted in the philosophy of social Darwinism and its assumptions about race. In other words, superior human abilities began with well-born White Anglo-Saxon Protestant men on top, and eastern and southern European immigrants beneath. Africans were presumed to be the lowest of the primitive races. Among the elite, poetic and musical talents were held in high regard. Musical talent was thought to be an expression of intelligence, something the Negro race, it was theorized, with a few exceptions, did not possess.

One sphere of the movement was musical eugenics. Phycological experiments and tests were developed by eugenic psychologist Carl E. Seashore under the guidance of Charles Davenport and Madison Grant, thought leaders to wealthy and powerful industrialists. Seashore, with the backing of George Eastman, Kodak millionaire and the founder of the Eastman School, was developing a program to perform psychometric tests to detect musical ability and measure *inherited* musical talents. His goal was to breed into being superior Anglo musicians. These supermen with Nordic features would compose the finest high-art music, thus imbuing America's exceptional culture with elite eugenicists ethos.

This may sound nuts today, but eugenic beliefs were mainstream in the United States for much of the first half of the twentieth century.[96] It remains an unspoken influence on public policy debates over how much funding is provided for policing and prisons verses schools and health care in majority Black communities. Eugenics didn't earn its evil reputation until Adolf Hitler adopted the program and took it to its ultimate conclusion with his obsession to create a superior Aryan race.

Another sphere of musical eugenics—that grew to become the matrix of folk-blues—encouraged field recordings of the "feebleminded" Negro in its natural habitat for eugenicists' laboratories under the veil of folk. It was believed the field recorder could make photophonograpic recordings of the Negro's mind for scientific analysis, thus proving once and for all, scientifically, the race's intellectual inferiority was innate.

In 1907, Howard W. Odum took up his wax cylinder recorder, saddled up his mare, and rode out from Oxford, Mississippi, into the edge of the Delta frontier not to document Negro folk songs, but to collect data for eugenic laboratories. The 1840 census had found that only two thousand enslaved Blacks were held in Panola County. Bearing in mind that when they weren't tied to whipping posts they were preoccupied battling malaria, typhoid, and yellow fever, the question becomes: did those enslaved Africans create an original musical culture or give birth to the blues?

Odum's field trip to study the Negro in its habitat and record its songs wasn't intended to answer such questions. Besides, he had never heard of a music called blues. Odum wasn't a talent scout and had no musical training when he sought out informants among the descendants of Panola and the adjacent Lafayette County.[97]

Odum recorded the sound waves of the Negro cranium in the same spirit that Third Reich eugenicists took up calipers—to provide hard and "objective" proof of Black inferiority.[98] The songs he captured were beside the point of his mission. The carefully selected Panola and Lafayette County descendants, those who fit his eugenic criteria, sung either a cappella or with amateur accompaniment into his tin-horned graphophone cylinder recorder. What twenty-three-year-old Howard W. Odum recorded shocked his WASP sensibilities. "[Their] songs tell of every phase of immorality and filth," he wrote, "sung by individuals who revel in their suggestiveness."

Odum published his data as *Social and Mental Traits of the Negro* in 1910, under the tutelage of professor Franklin H. Giddings of Columbia, the well-known sociologist and eugenicist. Odum earned a doctoral degree from Columbia University in sociology under Giddings, who became a charter member of the advisory council for the American Eugenics Society.

Odum described what he thought he heard: "a putrid bed of rottenness [that] intensifies his [the Negro's] already depraved nature." The songs Odum collected confirmed his, and Giddings, racist "belief in the innate inferiority" and feeblemindedness of the Negro. "The vivid imagination of the Negro," he continued, is "openly descriptive of the grossest immorality, and susceptible of unspeakable thoughts and actions, rotten with filth, they are yet sung to the time-honored melodies."[99]

Some of the informants' *bleu* lyrics, sung to the melodies of recognizable sacred WASP hymns shocked—as enlightenment expression was designed to do. "It is a marvel of the Negro's mental tendency that he can keep together such a vast heap of moral refuse and filth," Odum said, not knowing some of the bawdy verses were the repertoire of King Buddy Bolden, who had reigned from New Orleans to Baton Rouge for a decade with songs such as "Careless Love" and "Make Me a Pallet on Your Floor." "Nor are the religious songs free from the invasion; parodies as vulgar as the accumulations of indecent thought can contrive, are sung to standard tunes and stately measures. It is the saddest side of the Negro's nature."

Although the music on the cylinders Odum recorded was incidental, the scientific data of the Negro's neurology, physiology, and psychology was meticulously preserved, measured, and analyzed. Two years later, on September 26, 1912, in an article in the *New York Times* Giddings warned, "'Race War Coming." Dr. Franklin H. Giddings *"Declares enfranchisement of negro was a great mistake."*

What eugenicists feared most was a mass of well-informed Black voters: "Giddings concluded 'that political rights had been a hindrance rather than a help to the negro.' He predicted that a great race conflict would come in this country when the negro reached a plane where he could back up his demand for equality. 'Washington and Dr. Du Bois, and the property owners and men of achievement' he conceded 'are the exception.'"

It is clear that Giddings viewed Booker T. Washington, founder of Tuskegee Institute in Alabama, a willing avatar through which he and Charles Davenport, and their industrial backers including steel industrial magnate Andrew Carnegie, could impose their experimental program of passive political socialization upon the Negro. "The [Black] mass," Giddings said, "has not yet reached the level where it may be trusted with political power where it may control a voting majority."

Booker T. Washington did not endorse a liberal arts education for the Negro race as did W. E. B. Du Bois, his philosophical rival and perhaps the most brilliant historian, sociologist, and political thinker of his time. The expectation for Du Bois, educated in Germany and the first Black graduate of Harvard, was that he too would be an avatar for the elite, but Du Bois had gone rogue.

"I am also certain that the problem of the future will be even greater than that of the present," Giddings continued in his *New York Times* piece. "The white man considers the black man so inferior to himself that he does not oppose him or give him much consideration as a rival. But with the improved opportunities of the negro, with a better education and extended privileges, he must inevitably claim a place alongside of the white man as his equal. If he should be able to back up his claim on the strength of educational and economic equality, then we may prepare to witness a race conflict compared to which the present situation is a love feast."

The accommodation philosophy of Booker T. Washington and Giddings and their patrons was largely rejected by southern Negroes who had begun to migrate to the North soon after Washington implored them in 1895 to "cast down your bucket where you are." Indeed, many Black leaders, out of fear of retribution from Washington's powerful "Tuskegee Machine," quietly murmured among themselves that Washington was an Uncle Tom. In contrast, Du Bois's skilled polemics, without resulting to such petty personal disparagement of his powerful rival, resonated most with activists.

Du Bois's counterargument to the philosophy of Booker T. Washington, which he expressed in his 1903 master work, *The Souls of Black Folk,* was the push for "civic equality and the education of [Black] youth according to ability." Du Bois said of Washington: "He insists on thrift and self-respect, but at the same time counsels a silent submission to civic inferiority."

During the blues craze of the 1920s, to counter his rivals in shaping public opinion toward the blues, W. E. B. Du Bois ventured into the record business. He joined former W. C. Handy publishing partner Harry Pace to create the Black Swan record corporation. Black Swan Records, founded in 1921, was the most widely distributed Black-owned record label of its day. Du Bois was a stockholder and board member.

Black Swan's mission was to produce highbrow music of uplift. Du Bois's noble mission, however, turned out to be a bad business plan for a blues label. Blues practitioners and fans were challenging social and cultural constructs and having too much bawdy fun in the process. Black Swan went out of business two years later but not before launching the careers of Ethel Waters, Fletcher Henderson, and James P. Johnson.

Indeed, Howard W. Odum's sociological study, *Social and Mental Traits of the Negro,* pales in comparison to Du Bois's landmark study *The Philadelphia Negro* (1899). "Du Bois conducted door-to-door empirical research in Philadelphia's Seventh Ward, to capture, in both *The Philadelphia Negro* and his later Atlanta University Studies [*Of the Sorrow Songs*], the extraordinary experiences of a vast group of human beings moving from slavery to freedom. He studied their education, their churches, their work opportunities, their families, even their involvement in crime."[100]

On the other hand Odum, and folklorists such as John and Alan Lomax, began with a predetermination of Black inferiority, and then proceeded to screen out any talent or persons that would "taint" their "scientific" data of primitiveness.

Astonishingly, the long-debunked early twentieth-century eugenic criteria used to measure the Negro's primitiveness remains the defining criteria for *authenticity* of today's Black blues festival performers. White blues musicians, to be sure, are not measured with the same calipers.

The mystery of New Orleans legend King Buddy Bolden's lost cylinder recording, believed to have been made around the turn of the century, was always thought to be a lost *commercial* recording. What if it wasn't? What if it was a psychological eugenic experiment to get inside Bolden's head? What if he was recorded and tests were done that shocked and frightened the scientists—who would have had no idea how to decipher his extraordinary sound waves?

It's reasonable to conclude, then, Bolden would have been diagnosed a degenerate, a dangerous influence on his followers. Bolden's wild sensual approach to music and life fit every eugenicist's definition of *feeblemindedness*. Sometimes a person can be convinced that their idiosyncrasies are insanity. To be sure, no White sociologist would have considered a "primitive" Black man a genius. It wasn't long after the mystery cylinder recording, in 1907, that Buddy Bolden, the first man of blues, was committed and spent the rest of his life in the insane asylum at Jackson, Louisiana.

As a consequence, when cornetist Freddie Keppard, crowned in Bolden's absence, was offered a chance to become the first from New Orleans to make a commercial blues phonograph, he turned down the opportunity. Perhaps Bolden's strange and sudden demise had spooked him. Maybe Keppard believed the mysterious wax cylinder recording, now lost to time, was a burning effigy of the soul of Buddy Bolden.

CHARLIE PATTON: TENANT FARM BLUES

INDIGENOUS BLUES WAS CITY MUSIC. Only later did it make its way to rural tenant farmers by way of the phonograph, not the other way around. Charlie Patton was Dockery plantation's premier guitarist. But there is no evidence that Charlie Patton was playing the blues before he heard it on phonograph records. Charlie Patton's repertoire was steeped in conventional plantation frolic tunes, likely played with fiddle and guitar to accompany buck dancing and two steps. He may not have played many formal quadrilles or schottisches; formal dances were rare on tenant farms. There was no professional musical culture in the Delta that could rival New Orleans. What Patton most certainly played were Baptist gospel tunes like "I Shall Not Be Moved."

Like most rural Negro musicians of the period, including Blind Lemon Jefferson of Texas and others, Patton's father was a lay preacher. Hence, half of Patton's recordings were straight gospel. It is within the old-time gospel style that Charlie Patton was most comfortable.

When Charlie Patton heard Lonnie Johnson's phonographs for the first time—most likely at the Dockery plantation's commissary—he wanted in on the fun. He had never imagined a Black guitar player could be celebrated like Lonnie Johnson. Charlie Patton was prideful. He reckoned himself a worthy picker. He began reworking his gospel material to fit the secularized blues as best he could. Blues improvisation was foreign to Charlie and others in the Delta, which might explain why their music and improvisations sounded crude compared to Lonnie Johnson and other New Orleans musicians.

When Charlie Patton learned Henry C. Speir of Jackson, a White victrola and furniture store owner, was also a regional scout for Lonnie Johnson's label OKeh and had connections to Victor, Paramount, and Gennett Records of Indiana, Charlie wrote Speir a letter asking to be recorded.

H. C. Speir was born in Mississippi in 1895. At the start of the Creole blues boom in the early 1920s, he lived in New Orleans and worked at the Victrola plant there assembling phonographs. The cabinets were made up north and shipped to New Orleans where the motor and other parts were assembled. While living in New Orleans, Speir became familiar with the sound of Creole New Orleans blues emanating from every dance hall, honky-tonk, and park pavilion. He relocated to Jackson, Mississippi, around 1925 to open a furniture and phonograph store downtown. Speir had music industry contacts from his time at the Victrola plant in New Orleans. He was the only record business purveyor in Mississippi with connections to the blues phonograph craze that was sweeping the nation. H. C. Speir's store sold lots of phonographs. Lonnie Johnson's records sold particularly well.

Speir auditioned thirty-eight-year-old Charlie Patton and sent him off to make his first sides for Paramount on June 14, 1929, in Richmond, Indiana. Charlie Patton made his debut in the same studio owned by Gennett Piano Company where King Oliver and Louis Armstrong had laid down the landmark classic "Dippermouth Blues" seven years earlier, in 1923. Lonnie Johnson and Jelly Roll Morton had also recorded the blues there years earlier, prior to Charlie Patton's first session. By 1929, the time of Charlie's first recordings, blues was at its commercial peak. Blues records were selling in the tens of millions. Henry C. Speir's store was in high cotton. The latest releases were flying off his shelves.

Moreover, by 1929, Lonnie Johnson had released more than one hundred recordings, many of them accessible to Charlie Patton and everyone else in the Delta. Charlie Patton borrowed parts of his repertoire directly from Johnson's records. In his most popular recording, "Pony Blues," Charlie mashes up a Lonnie Johnson lyric, "blues, fallin' like showers of rain," from Lonnie Johnson's 1925 recording "Falling Rain Blues," a song in which Lonnie played blues obbligato on the violin.

Frankly, neither Charlie Patton nor his violin accompanist, Henry Sims, also a Lonnie Johnson devotee via the violin (Sims accompanied Patton on a follow-up recording session in Grafton, Wisconsin), possessed the talent nor the nimbleness to match the multi-instrumental proficiency of Lonnie Johnson.

Such was the case for most dilettante tenant farm musicians in the 1920s. They all sounded unpolished compared to Lonnie Johnson. It stands to reason because Lonnie Johnson had been playing blues on violin, piano, and guitar for some twenty years around New Orleans and in England before recording his first record. In "Pony Blues" Charlie Patton sang about what he knew best: mules, plowing, milk cows, and such, the hard life of a tenant farmer. These images, however, shouldn't be confused with slavery, even though the day-to-day lifestyle of a sharecropper had not changed much since then.

In 1929, Charlie Patton recorded an arrangement of "Some of These Days," a popular song recorded by Louis Armstrong that same year. It had been previously recorded by the New Orleans Original Dixieland Jazz Band in 1923. "Some of These Days" was originally associated with White pop star Sophie Tucker, who first recorded it in 1911.

So, where did Charlie hear that Tin Pan Alley tune? I assure you Sophie Tucker didn't take off her pearls, lay down her mink coat, and hop a freight train down to Dockery's farm to give Patton oral musical lessons. Thus, Charlie Patton's repertoire was inspired by New Orleans blues recordings and other popular tunes he heard at the plantation store. It is ludicrous to say Louis Armstrong learned the blues from Charlie Patton. Nevertheless, that's what many jazz historians would have you believe.

BLUES LITERATURE: A CLOSER LOOK

"I AM A MAN OF SUBSTANCE, of flesh and bone, fiber and liquids—and I might even be said to possess a mind. I am invisible understand, simply because people refuse to see me." In Ralph Ellison's 1952 novel, *Invisible Man*, the protagonist found a home in a hole in the ground. His hole was cozy, full of light, and filled with the sounds of New Orleans blues. "There is a certain acoustical deadness in my hole," the Invisible Man said, "and when I have music I want to *feel* its vibration, not only with my ear but with my whole body." He longed to hear "five recordings of Louis Armstrong playing and singing 'What Did I Do to Be So Black and Blue'—all at the same time."[101]

Ralph Ellison, born 1914 in Oklahoma City, Oklahoma, won the National Book Award in 1953 for *Invisible Man*, his debut novel. A trumpeter in high school, Ellison earned a music scholarship to the Tuskegee Institute in Alabama where, inspired by poet T. S. Eliot, he decided to become a writer. Ellison's name-less invisible protagonist marveled, "Louis bends that military instrument into a beam of lyrical sound." He admitted, "I like Louis Armstrong because he's made poetry out of being invisible." Indeed, while smoking reefer, the Invisible Man "discovered a new analytical way" of listening to the blues. "I not only entered the music but descended, like Dante, into its depths." Rarely has anyone writ-ten about my music, the blues, so eloquently. Ellison's fictional blues was *real*, whereas White nonfiction on blues was fiction.

Mentored by groundbreaking author Richard Wright (1908–1960), Ralph Ellison began his literary career later in life. The success of Richard Wright's debut novel, *Native Son* (1940), opened the door for a new generation of Black writers including Ellison, James Baldwin (1924–1987), and Lorraine Hansberry (1930–1965). Ralph Ellison wrote many essays on music in which his main interest was the blues aesthetic. A collection of his essays on blues are compiled in the book *Living with Music* (2002), including his review of Richard Wright's memoir *Black Boy* (1945).[102] "*Black Boy* is filled with blues-tempered echoes," Ellison wrote at the beginning of his career in 1945 for the *Antioch Review*. "And like a blues sung by such an artist as Bessie Smith, its lyrical prose evokes the paradoxical, almost surreal image of a black boy singing lustily as he probes his own grievous wound." No one elevated the blues with such eloquence during the period.

To be sure, during the first half of the twentieth century Whites across Amer-ica routinely created grotesque caricatures of Blacks in books, films, theatricals, and advertisements. Even acclaimed White writers Ellison admired—Faulkner, Dickens—depicted Black characters as one-dimensional. The refusal of White writers to see the Negro as fully human rendered him *invisible*. For this reason, Ellison's three-dimensional way of presenting his subjects set a new standard in blues literature.

Ellison's definition of the blues was elastic, similar to a musician bending a note to fit his emotional state. Sometimes his prose was in the key of B flat, the popularly held Anglo definition: downtrodden, sad, melancholic. Other times his writings were in the key of B major seven, when he wished to express energy, assertiveness, and intellectual creativity of bluesmen and women. But most often Ellison, in the key of B natural, swung words with his typewriter like a master trumpeter in a smoky afterhours joint, revealing vulnerability, triumph, and everything in between. In other words, he depicted blues men and women as *natural* human beings with a range of emotions and complexities—a rarity in literature during the first half of the twentieth century.

Another great writer and thinker on blues music and culture was Albert Murray (1916–2013), Ralph Ellison's trusted confident. The two shared a passion for both great literature and the blues aesthetic as expressed in numerous correspondence with one another over their long friendship. Albert Murray's *Stomping the Blues* (1976) exemplified his profound depth of knowledge about my music and culture.[103] He was one of the last great writers on the subject that didn't submit to specious class and anthropological distinctions. In *Stomping the Blues* Murray makes no distinction between Robert Johnson and Count Basie, Lead Belly and Duke Ellington, Lonnie Johnson and Charlie Parker or Bessie Smith and Billie Holiday. There's no such thing as a "jazz" artist in Albert Murray's book—all were blues artists.

Murray's prose isn't as fluid as Ellison's, perhaps, but Murray's writings are fundamental for anyone seeking a deeper understanding on the subject. What's more, Murray's carefully arranged photo-essay in *Stomping the Blues* serves as an important gallery, illustrating how blues was understood by its creators and fans alike prior to the 1960s.

In the 1960s, blues musicians were split into tiny superficial tribes. Between country and urban. Free jazz and folk-blues. The potency of the blues was diluted further by artificially partitioned commercial genres such as rock and roll (meaning blues for Whites by Whites only). To be sure, in the rock industry segregation was stringently practiced, decades after Jim Crow was abolished. Built on the Black creativity, rock became the most dominant and lucrative music market of the twentieth century by exploiting blues and its creators.

In anticipation of rock's invasion, a radical young poet and activist declared war on White music critics and their self-appointed authority to define and control the public's perception of blues authenticity. LeRoi Jones, born in 1934 in Newark, New Jersey, published *Blues People* in 1963, a year before the Beatles—John, Paul, George, and Ringo, the four Elvises—invaded America and awakened the suppressed desires of White teenagers with their British-honed version of Black American blues.

Blues People is rare in blues literature. It stood as the only history of the blues written by a Black author for nearly sixty years. Moreover, it is one of the few blues books to delve deep into the bayou and argue Congo Square in Old Louisiana was prologue. I must point out, however, that LeRoi Jones was convinced, at the time, that neither blues nor jazz originated in New Orleans. Nevertheless, *Blues People* remains one of the few books to credit both Louis Armstrong and Jelly Roll Morton for teaching the world how to sing. "The first great soloist of jazz, Louis Armstrong, was a formidable blues singer, as was the great jazz pianist Jelly Roll Morton," Jones wrote. "Both men sang blues almost as beautifully as they played their instruments." And that's saying a lot.

Understand, the terms jazz and blues were still interchangeable in 1963. However, the signification of the words was in flux. Descriptions such as "Negro" and "blues" were fast becoming pejoratives in progressive Black communities. We find Jones, who later changed his name to Amiri Baraka, on the cutting edge of a Black is beautiful art movement. New terms such as *Afro-American* and *rhythm-and-blues* and *soul* were in vogue—replacing *Negro* and *blues* respectively, muddying the discourse.

Blues People was reactionary to White encroachment. It was an attempt by Jones to reaffirm that America's most lucrative and influential art form was Black. Jones wrote, "The idea of a white blues singer seems an even more violent contradiction of terms than the idea of middle-class blues singer."[104] Where Ralph Ellison sought mainstream affirmation, LeRoi Jones sought affirmation from the streets.

In a review of *Blues People* Ralph Ellison wrote "[Jones's] assertions—which are fine as personal statement—are not in keeping with the facts." To be fair to Jones, while researching his book in the late 1950s and early '60s, serious scholarship on the blues was fledgling. According to Jones, his professor at Howard University, notable poet Sterling A. Brown, wasn't allowed to teach about blues or jazz in the classroom. Brown held court with Jones and other students in the dormitory or at his home, using his personal record collection. There were no Afro-studies programs nor Black professors in segregated White colleges. Off-campus intellectualism filled the void. Ellison continued, "Read as a record of an earnest young man's attempt to come to grips with his predicament as Negro American during a most turbulent period of our history, *Blues People* may be worth the reader's time." But, Ellison cautioned, Jones stumbled by ignoring intricate details of Negro culture as if attempting "delicate brain surgery with a switchblade." There were many conclusions drawn by the twenty-nine-year-old Jones that relied on conjecture. This is understandable due to the circumstances. Scholarship on the blues was still in its infancy. "To make his ideological point," wrote Ellison, Jones "might have come much closer had he considered the blues not as politics but as art." Clearly Ralph Ellison was uncomfortable with Jones's militancy. The generational divide between the two was striking. Amiri Baraka chose guerrilla war tactics to fight

White supremacy's takeover of the blues; ambushes, sabotage, raids, by any means necessary, as opposed to traditional rules of engagement defined by the enemy.

Regarding the music, Ralph Ellison clearly agreed in his review of *Blues People* that "Armstrong, Hawkins, Basie and Ellington, all Negroes, [were] all masters of the blues and jazz tradition." Here, even Ellison is caught grappling with the new vernacular. The specious separation of blues and jazz was shifting under his feet.

Finally, Ellison suggests LeRoi Jones "could learn much from the Cambridge School's . . . poetry, drama and ritual as a means of analyzing how the blues function" in their anthropological and sociological environment. Here is where I get off the Ralph Ellison train because the "Cambridge School" was what LeRoi Jones prophetically warned against.

It's incredulous that blues history books romantically recall an old melodious South where the city of New Orleans miraculously disappears. Is it because New Orleans's intricate high culture would complicate or destroy their revisionist thesis of primitivism?

As a blues artist from Louisiana, with a lineage to its early developments, I have found literature on blues origins embarrassingly deficient. If White blues and jazz historians are not intellectually dishonest but merely ignorant of the facts, I hope they will welcome further wisdom, as opposed to clinging to their flawed antiquated academic understanding of my music and its culture therewith.

Dennis McNally, in his 471-page book *On Highway 61: Music, Race, and the Evolution of Cultural Freedom* (2014), stated, "It is quite true that no one can say for certain where the blues began. . . . My assumption that they began in the Mississippi Delta is, I freely acknowledge, based on post hoc logic, although the weight of evidence is considerable."[105] McNally makes such a lazy attempt of blues origin explanation that it's difficult for me to take anything else he had to say seriously. Which leads one to believe that if the evidence is considerable, then McNally should have stated unequivocally where and how the blues originated; instead, he relies on an assumption.

McNally referenced recordings, but his references were merely straw man arguments for his theory. The problem McNally grappled with is the same problem all music historians encounter when they try to force the blues to have originated in the Mississippi Delta. There has never been any firsthand evidence to support such a premise. Interstate Highway 61 leads directly into the Big Easy near Perdido Street. Perdido Street is in the old neighborhood that once housed the "Funky Butt Hall." McNally, an American history doctoral graduate from the University of Massachusetts Amherst, seemed to have run out of gas along Highway 61 before he reached New Orleans.

McNally continued, "It is also true that the first recorded rural blues was by a Texan (Blind Lemon Jefferson)." If by "rural" he meant an acoustic blues solo performance, then Papa Charlie Jackson of New Orleans predated Blind Lemon Jefferson. Jackson's success soon opened the door for Blind Lemon Jefferson and others. McNally states, "The first hits came from Piedmont pickers who'd moved to Chicago." This is also untrue; Papa Charlie Jackson's big hit "Salty Dog Blues" was the first "rural" blues hit. McNally goes on to say, "Mamie Smith had the first hit with a pop tune that contained some coloration, but so what?"

"So what?" he asked. That's what Miles Davis asked his critics on the opening thirty-two-bar blues song "So What" from his landmark album *Kind of Blue*, but I digress.

He was technically correct. I acknowledge that Mamie Smith had the first Negro vocal blues hit phonograph with "Crazy Blues" in 1920, which McNally strangely labels a pop tune. Calling that recording a pop tune is another way of saying it is somehow too sophisticated or too commercial to truly be a blues.

In his lists of firsts, McNally avoids mentioning anyone from New Orleans. Moreover, his evidence does nothing to support his original argument that blues began in Mississippi. In frustration, McNally throws up his hands and says, "So what?"

Finally, he tries to cover all angles by stating, "The formation of the blues didn't happen all at once or with any one person, and if it did not happen on the Delta's plantations, it surely found its most favorable reception there." I will only concede that a derivative of New Orleans blues was developed in the Mississippi Delta. That derivative eventually, during the folk movement of the 1960s, became known as Delta Blues, of which Louisiana's Leadbelly sociologically, if not musically, was the archetype.

Historian Ted Gioia said of the Mississippi Delta: "We cannot prove that the blues began here—the assertions of tourism brochures notwithstanding—although the Delta's claim as its birthplace is as strong as any other regions."[106] Gioia admits that "one cannot prove that the blues began" in Mississippi, but his statement is contradicted in the same sentence—"the Delta's claim . . . is as strong as any other regions."

Prior to the 1960s folk movement, New Orleans had made many claims as the birthplace of the blues. There were Hollywood movies such as *Birth of the Blues* in 1941 and *New Orleans (The Movie)* released in 1947 starring Louis Armstrong and Billie Holliday. Louis Armstrong performed his tune "Where the Blues Was Born, in New Orleans" in the movie. Ted Gioia must have known that Louis Armstrong made such claims, but like fellow musicologists and historians, to force the narrative of primitivism he chose to ignore those claims. A most conspicuous example of intellectual dishonesty can be found when comparing Ted Gioia's books *Delta Blues* (2009) and *The History of Jazz* (2011). In the *History of Jazz* Gioia goes on and on about Buddy Bolden, King Oliver, and Jelly Roll Morton playing the blues in New Orleans beginning in the 1890s. However, in his book *Delta Blues* he does not mention any of this. Why? I conclude it is because it would spoil his narrative that the Delta was the great incubator of the blues. In my reading of blues and jazz literature, I have seen such obfuscations over and over again. These are not casual omissions. It reveals something duplicitous.

Elijah Wald, a refreshingly cynical music historian, also fails to follow the evidence that would prove Louisiana as the birthplace of the blues. In his book *Escaping the Delta* (2001) Wald said, "Blues has come to be generally understood as the range of music found in the blues section when we go shopping for CDs."[107] Wald presents the term *blues* merely as a commodity in the marketplace. But this definition does little to add substance to an origin argument. Based on the information I've found in his books, Elijah Wald has attempted to demystify Robert Johnson—something I began doing in the 1990s by pointing out Johnson's crossroads myth as racist long before Wald highlighted the flaws of such superstition in *Escaping the Delta*.

Too often, historians ignore evidence that would counter their preconceived conclusions about my music and its culture therewith. I find the glaring omission of New Orleans from the blues origin narrative similar to that of the nineteenth-century pseudohistorians who, with their magic quills, attempted to disappear Egypt from Africa because Ancient Egypt complicated their savage primitive African mythos. Similarly, the high Creole culture of New Orleans confounded blues historians.

A refreshing book, *In Search of the Blues* (2008), by Marybeth Hamilton, asked the right questions. Instead of focusing on the usual Mississippi sharecroppers, Hamilton, a White scholar and one of only a few female authors on the subject, pulled back the curtain on the folklorists, record collectors, and myth makers. The *New York Times* said, "*In Search of the Blues* is not about the blues, or the people who made the blues. It's about people who made the dark side of blues music into what popular mythology calls 'the Delta blues.' Those people aren't singers or players but folk song scholars and record collectors."[108]

Hamilton went in search of the blues in its "birthplace," the Mississippi Delta, but found no facts to support the popular story. What she discovered instead were the misshapen primitive and racist fantasies of John Lomax, Dorothy Scarborough, and an obsessive broker of Negro primitivism, James McKune. Hamilton claimed the little-known McKune was a highly influential figure among Blues Mafiosos.[109]

The *New York Times* reviewer found the book "frustrating and sometimes infuriating," dismissing Hamilton for focusing only on Whites: "Virtually no black voice is heard." Blues fans I spoke to dismissed her as an interloper. But I found *In Search of the Blues* fascinating. I saw it as an exposé, an unmasking of the big lie. Marybeth Hamilton makes "the music invisible" the reviewer quibbled. But I would argue, in her search, Hamilton made the blues *visible* for many, perhaps for the first time.

THE ANTHOLOGY OF AMERICAN FOLK MUSIC

ANOTHER INFLUENTIAL DELTA GUITAR PLAYER who greatly admired Lonnie Johnson was Mississippi John Hurt. In 1928, John Hurt became one of the first Delta guitar players to record. Hurt recorded for OKeh Records, the same label Lonnie Johnson helped to establish. However, following the crash of 1929, and consequently the near collapse of the music business, John Hurt, like many other Delta guitarists during the Great Depression, drifted back into obscurity. Over the next thirty years, John Hurt quietly sharecropped and raised a family in Avalon, Mississippi.

Hurt's fleeting brush with the music business was all but forgotten until two of his recordings, "Frankie" and "Spike Driver Blues," were featured in 1952 on Harry Smith's compiled *Anthology of American Folk Music*. The anthology was massive: three separate boxed sets, containing eighty-four obscure folk and blues performances, on six LPs; two LPs in each box, with extensive liner notes. The *Anthology*, released by Moses Asch's Folkways Records label, was priced at a whopping $25—$220 in today's money. Asch and Smith didn't pay for licenses, and no royalties made their way to Mississippi John Hurt. It is likely Mississippi John Hurt was not aware of the anthology's release. Besides, as an impoverished sharecropper who likely earned what amounted to a dollar a day, he wouldn't have been able to afford a copy. Greil Marcus said Harry Smith's *Anthology* captured "old weird America."

The *Anthology of American Folk Music* was mythologized by middle-class White kids interested in authentic music expression in the style of the Carter Family—acoustic guitar and tightly harmonized melodies. The problem was, the *Anthology* conflated acoustic African American blues with that of genuine Anglo folk music. Consequently, this sphere of rural acoustic Negro blues was recontextualized cut off from its origin. It was presented as if it were a continuum or relative to sixteenth-century Elizabethan folk, an Anglo folk aesthetic established by impoverished and illiterate English milkmaids and plowmen. The aesthetic was first documented in America in the Appalachian region of the United States by nineteenth-century Harvard English professor and folklorist Francis James Child.

In the 1950s, the Negro blues songs included on the *Anthology* by Mississippi John Hurt, Furry Lewis, Charlie Patton, Blind Lemon Jefferson, and others, in the young minds of White middle-class teens such as Bob Dylan, Joan Baez, John Cohen, and Dave Van Ronk, were believed to be ancient; the raw beginnings of African American blues. In fact, the country blues was merely an offshoot; a derivative of the original blues that exploded out of Creole New Orleans with Jelly Roll Morton, King Oliver, and Lonnie Johnson. Nevertheless, according to Dave Van Ronk, Harry Smith's *Anthology* became the sacred doctrine of folk-blues purists. "The *Anthology* was our bible," Dave Van Ronk wrote in 1991. "We all knew the words to every song on it."[110] In 1959 and 1960, at the University of Minnesota, in Dinkytown coffeehouses, the "*Anthology of American Folk Music* was Bob Dylan's first true map of a republic that was still a hunch to him."[111]

In 1963, following his unlikely "discovery"—a colonizer's term for possession—by northeasterners Tom Hoskins and Nick Perls, John Hurt was whisked off by his new handlers to Washington, DC, a city that would become Hurt's new home. There, soon after his arrival, at Ontario Place, on October 13, 1963, Tom Hoskins recorded an interview with the shy, reluctant sharecropper as part of a plan to launch his new recording career.

The plan the cultural brokers mapped out worked like a charm. They booked Hurt on the prestigious Newport Folk Festival. As fate would have it, Hurt became the seminal "rediscovered" folk-blues guitarist from the Mississippi Delta. Pseudo–blues aficionados recast the soft-spoken, functionally illiterate seventy-one-year-old sharecropper as the prototypical "authentic" folk-bluesman. Tom Hoskins later said, "I know how Howard Carter felt when he opened Tutankhamun's tomb and looked in." Only John Hurt was "alive and he still had it."

Mississippi John Hurt's meteoric rise on the East Coast coffeehouse circuit led to appearances at college campus theaters and even a *Tonight Show* appearance with Johnny Carson. Hurt's reemergence officially marked the beginning of the revisionist folk-blues era.

Yet, the landmark interview revealed something his new handlers preferred to keep hidden. The marketing materials they presented to buyers accentuated the "primitive," the "exotic." Whereas when we listen to the interview in its entirety, we learn that the high cultured New Orleans blues was his inspiration and Lonnie Johnson his guitar hero.

During the interview, Mississippi John Hurt said his mother, when he was a boy, bought him a "second-hand guitar for $1.50 from a white gentleman," who Hurt recalled "lived right up the road." For impoverished farmers, a hand-me-down guitar was relatively affordable.

During the course of the interview, Mississippi John Hurt remembered little about his early influences, except for his hero Lonnie Johnson. Hurt shared a story about his very first recording session, which took place in Memphis around 1928. Hurt encountered a guitarist hanging around the studio who claimed to be the great Lonnie Johnson. "He said he was Lonnie Johnson," Hurt said of the young guitar man, "but he wasn't." Hurt confessed, "I don't know who he was." (I wonder, could that have been a young Robert Johnson, who was not yet ready for prime time, attempting to talk his way into a Memphis recording audition for OKeh?)

Lonnie Johnson did attend the February 1928 session in Memphis, but he wasn't scheduled to record until the day after John Hurt. They didn't cross paths. It seems Lonnie traveled with Okeh field producers across the South that year as an accompanists and arranger. Keenly aware of the type of material Okeh was seeking, his responsibility was to play guitar, violin, or piano to support the local inexperienced musicians Okeh had invited to record. "Playing with the Strings," one of Lonnie's most amazing virtuosic recordings, concluded the Memphis sessions.[112] Later that year, Mississippi John Hurt was invited up to New York City for a follow-up OKeh session. At this recording session Hurt actually met his idol, the *real* Lonnie Johnson, who had just finished recording when Hurt arrived for his appointment. "Me and Lonnie," Hurt said excitedly, "we was in the recordin' room there and I had just written this 'Candy Man.' I forget some of the verses, so they typed them on the chart . . . so I was singin' . . . I was practicin' on it while they were gone. And Lonnie says, 'Ain't [that] a little too high.' I say yeah, he says, 'gotta be low. Gotta let it down son.' . . . I'll never forget the manager, T. J. Rockland come in he says, 'Who's been messin' with that chart.' Lonnie says, 'I did. And what are you? I didn't think it would do any harm, it was too high.' Ah well, [Rockland] looked at me and says, 'Is it too high for you,' I says, yeah, it was a little too high."

Lonnie Johnson helped to get Mississippi John Hurt comfortable in front of the recording horn so that his guitar playing and singing could be heard properly. The song "Candy Man" turned out to be one of Mississippi John Hurt's most popular recordings. Hurt, a timid lifelong tenant farmer, would have never questioned a White man's authority. His observation of a confident Black musician commanding respect from an important White OKeh executive was impressive. Hurt said, "That's how I know it was for sure Lonnie Johnson, but that other guy in Memphis, he was black, I didn't know [him]" but this, "yeah, this was [the real Lonnie Johnson]." When Hurt said, "that other guy in Memphis, he was black," what he meant was the guy was of dark complexion, again leading me to wonder if it could have been dark-skinned Robert Johnson impersonating Lonnie that day.[113]

After the recording session, Mississippi John Hurt spent a memorable evening balling with Lonnie Johnson. At an after party in Harlem, Hurt said he played guitar while Lonnie, to the delight of everyone in attendance, played the piano. Mississippi John Hurt's trip to New York City had been the highlight of his recording career until he was rediscovered in the 1960s.

The overarching point here is: the Delta blues of Charlie Patton, Robert Johnson, Mississippi John Hurt, and their Delta contemporaries were all rural derivatives of Lonnie Johnson's cosmopolitan blues. Charlie Patton's supposed pure folk bonafides were "tainted" by folk snob standards, because folk is generally passed down as an oral tradition, not in a conservatory or classroom nor by the written score or phonograph recording. In contrast, guitarist Lonnie Johnson, whose blues was indigenous, had learned orally by playing in a family band on the streets of New Orleans long before blues made its way to phonograph records. So, why wasn't Lonnie Johnson the darling of folk-blues revivalists such as Tom Hoskins and Nick Perls?

Indeed, Lonnie Johnson is the rightful forerunner of Delta blues. Lonnie Johnson inspired tenant farmers and sharecroppers such as Robert Johnson to write songs about moving north such as "Sweet Home Chicago," the city New Orleans musicians had made a Blues mecca.

Later, in 1934, Charlie Patton traveled to New York City to record, but again, New Orleans musicians had been there, too, and gone. Mind you, in 1911, Jelly Roll Morton first turned Harlem onto the blues, inspiring pianists Johnny P. Johnson and Willie "the Lion" Smith to follow in his wake.

BLUES ON RECORD

BORN 1915, BLUES LEGEND Muddy Waters admitted his first introduction to the blues was listening to phonograph records as a child. "Our little house was way back in the country," Muddy said. "We had one house close to us, and hell, the next one would've been a mile. If you got sick, you could holler, and wouldn't nobody hear you. . . . The lady that lived across the field from us had a phonograph when I was a little bitty boy. She used to let us go over there all the time, and I played it night and day."[114] Between 1925 and 1926, when Muddy was "a little bitty boy" (about nine or ten years old), Lonnie Johnson's records were popular in Mississippi.

The times I spent personally with B. B. King, who was born in 1925, were always interesting because he enjoyed talking about his developmental days. He was always quick to credit Lonnie Johnson as his inspiration. King said to me, "Lonnie Johnson was my biggest influence." B. B. King perfected Johnson's single note guitar solos and added to it his own signature vibrato. As guitarists began to copy B. B. King, they were basically copying Lonnie Johnson by degrees. B. B. King once stated to a guitar magazine, "I was able to go and see one of my idols, Lonnie Johnson, and I was able to shake his hand and thank him. Because he was one of the people that made me want to play."[115] I too owe a great deal of homage to Mr. Lonnie Johnson for my own career and guitar stylings. I hear references to Johnson in the playing of thousands of guitarists. Everyone from T-Bone Walker and Buddy Guy, to Eric Clapton and Stevie Ray Vaughan have absorbed Lonnie Johnson's blues guitar philosophy into their respective styles.

In the 1930s, following the Great Depression of 1929, the record industry went bankrupt. Sales had sunk from ninety million to just four million by 1934. Effectively, it was the end of the commercial blues boom. The independent labels, such as Paramount and Gennett, liquidated their original master disk inventories of important blues recordings for scrap. Thousands of master recordings were destroyed or discarded. Consequently, the scarcity of hot blues recordings created a collector's market. Record collectors, by default, became custodians of early recorded blues history.

Eventually, record collectors would rewrite the story of blues from a myopic collector's perspective. If it was not on record, did it really take place? We are now in the post-phonograph era. Blues is performed and recorded all over the world. Its narrative no longer is told by matrix numbers of an obsolete medium such as phonograph records. The blues was established in New Orleans at least twenty-five years before it made it onto Victrolas. Fact is, Lonnie Johnson mastered the blues guitar long before the music appeared on records in the 1920s. The academic narrative of the blues the world has come to rely on, then, was created post-Depression by record collectors who started with recordings that began in the middle of actual blues history.

LONNIE JOHNSON ENLIGHTENS BOB DYLAN

In the postwar era, Lonnie Johnson's career was sporadic. He took odd jobs to make ends meet. By the early 1960s, a new generation of folk idealists romanticized a bygone era of blues—that never existed in reality—and set out to revive it. It seemed Lonnie Johnson, who had started it all, was destined to ride off into the sunset on the shoulders of folk-blues purists. As it turned out, the great Lonnie Johnson was left scratching his head by the side of a metaphorical crossroad.

Bob Dylan, at the start of his career in Greenwich Village, received a personal guitar lesson from Lonnie Johnson that profoundly changed his approach to music. In his autobiography, *Chronicles: Volume One*, Bob Dylan said, "I played in the casual Carter Family flat-picking style and the playing was more or less out of habit and routine," but he wanted to "replace it with something more active with more definition of presence. I didn't invent the style. It had been shown to me in the early '60s by Lonnie Johnson."[116]

Dylan elaborated, "Lonnie took me aside one night and showed me a style of playing based on an odd instead of even-number system. He had me play chords and he demonstrated how to do it." Dylan said Lonnie told him, "This might help you," and indeed it did. A door was unlocked that night for Bob Dylan; a door he hadn't known existed.

Bob Dylan adapted Lonnie's special guitar technique as best he could, but more important, he was awakened by Lonnie's enlightened blues philosophy. Later, a newly converted Bob Dylan, the darling of the folk movement, was exiled from the scene by folk-blues purists for having betrayed their aesthetics.

Throughout the 1960s, condescending folk snobs were busy elevating dilettante guitar-playing tenant farmers—sometimes to the surprise of the tenant farmers themselves—above their biggest influence and the father of blues guitar, Lonnie Johnson. They made Johnson's devotees his superiors. Johnson was metaphorically sentenced to Siberia by communist folk purists even though he was the authentic and rightful "King of the Blues Guitar."

Folk guitarist Dave Van Ronk, the subject of the Coen Brothers film *Inside Llewyn Davis*, was disillusioned by the cold reception Lonnie Johnson received from the revivalists. In his memoir, *Mayor of MacDougal Street*, Van Ronk said Lonnie "would get onstage with a flat-pick and play jazz [*sic*] standards, improvising lovely, long choruses on things like 'Red Sails in the Sunset.' All the hard-core folkies and blues buffs would be sitting in the audience, going 'Arghhhh! Sing "Mean Old Bed Bug Blues!" What's the matter with you?'" Van Ronk sighed, "They were really disappointed and upset, they were a bunch of tone-deaf snobs. If they had just listened with an open mind to what the guy was putting down, they would have loved it, but they could not bring themselves to do that. . . . I felt bad for [Lonnie] because as far as I was concerned, he was playing as well as he ever had. But, like any scene, the revival had its own aesthetic, and he did not fit it."

Two additional folk protagonists who redefined my music and its culture therewith as something that originated on an isolated tenant farm instead of New Orleans were Pete Seeger and Alan Lomax, both second-generation folklorists. To be sure, in 1925 when Lonnie Johnson released his groundbreaking phonograph,

"Mr. Johnson's Blues," Pete Seeger was only six years old. While Lonnie Johnson's phonographs were selling like hotcakes at plantation supply stores, Pete Seeger—born in Manhattan, his father a Harvard professor and folklorist—was still wet behind the ears. Alan Lomax, also the son of a Harvard graduate and folklorist, John Lomax, was only ten years old at the time. Yet, they would become the leading arbiters of Negro blues.

Neither boy had any idea in 1925 that Jelly Roll Morton, Buddy Bolden, King Oliver, Louis Armstrong, and Lonnie Johnson had already established an indigenous blues dynasty in New Orleans going back some thirty years. Lonnie Johnson had grown up in the culture, playing the music on the streets of New Orleans with his father and brother. He was playing the blues in London in 1917 before Pete Seeger was even a gleam in his father's eye. Nevertheless, by the 1960s neither Lonnie Johnson nor any of his New Orleans contemporaries fit into the neo-folk-blues aesthetic of the revisionists.

During the so-called "revival," in order to be accepted as an authentic blues guitar picker one needed to be a *cotton* picker. The image folkies wanted was that of a tenant farmer, preferably a malleable geezer with a beat-up acoustic guitar. The folk movement desired a Negro guitar player that could be the embodiment or the poster boy of their quasi-communist labor movement. Pete Seeger, Alan Lomax, and the like usurped the blues, in large part, for their cause.

The seminal American communist movement of the 1930s attempted to organize sharecroppers and tenant farmers into unions. Their goal was to force landlords to give sharecroppers and tenant farmers a fair share. I can sympathize with that, but don't seize my music and culture therewith in the process, and then deny its indigenous creators their due. New Orleans blues musicians had grown up just as poor as tenant farmers but didn't live off the land. They lived, instead, off the blues and its subversive culture. They were bohemian urbanites. A family was very important to them but not necessarily as important as their music. They were spiritual, but they wouldn't allow some backwoods preacher's brimstone and damnation slave sermonizing to suppress their liberating Creole music philosophy.

Lonnie Johnson was neither a cotton picker nor a tenant farmer, and the folk communists held it against him. Moreover, the fact that he was a sophisticated professional musician who had earned commercial success was doubly held against him. The great Lonnie Johnson, like all classical New Orleans blues musicians, was born into an ingenious musical culture. It was impossible for him to acquiesce to neo-blues paternalism.

Lonnie Johnson resettled in Toronto, Canada, in 1965, and started a business. He opened up the Home of the Blues Club. In between tours throughout

Canada he primarily performed at his club. In 1969, while taking a daily walk in Toronto, he was hit by an out of control car and was severely injured. Despite his ailing health, he performed in front of a live audience for the last time at Massey Hall with fellow Louisiana guitar great Buddy Guy. Lonnie Johnson was beloved by Toronto's music fans, who gave the aging legend a standing ovation. Following a prolonged battle with the injuries suffered in the accident, along with other medical complications, Lonnie Johnson died of a stroke in Toronto, June 16, 1970.

The idea that blues is dying out simply because the agrarian folkways of Black tenant farmers were replaced by mechanization and automation is ridiculous. Some ostensibly benevolent blues societies—though they won't admit it—believe that because the vast majority of Blacks have become literate, streaming their music on smartphones, thus, the blues they make today isn't authentic. Such thinking is a primitivist stereotype. African Americans are a diverse bunch, just like every other ethnicity.

The idea that the Delta is the genesis of the blues is an antediluvian fallacy that must be debunked to make way for an authentic reformation of the blues. Many hardcore Delta blues devotees who came to this music by way of misguided folklorists, collectors, and academics are still in denial. I know my assertion that New Orleans is the origin of the blues is a revelation for fans of usurpers such as Elvis Presley, the Rolling Stones, Eric Clapton, et cetera. Nonetheless, it is my hope that both fans and academics alike will finally do away with the residue of cultural colonialism and embrace the true father of the blues guitar, Lonnie Johnson, along with his Louisiana contemporaries as the authentic blues pioneers.

In 1912, a White man, Leroy "Lasses" White, wrote and published a twelve-bar, lyrically sad, depressed, and melancholy song titled "Nigger Blues." It was recorded in 1916 by George O'Connor for Columbia Records. On the flip side was a song by blackface performer Al Jolson singing "I'm Saving Up the Means to Get to New Orleans." One side of the record was a song called "Nigger Blues," and the other side told a story about a poor boy missing his home in *N'awlins*. The producers of this offensive recording were no doubt exploiting the popular New Orleans blues trend. At the time, Louisiana Blacks weren't allowed to record in their authentic voice.

"Nigger Blues," one of the vilest song titles ever, was a big seller for the fledgling Columbia record company that produced it. Columbia and other record companies formularized the successful arrangement to have it duplicated by upcoming artists in an attempt at an assembly line approach to hit making.

One listen to "Nigger Blues" and you immediately recognize the lyrical A A B stanza, the twelve-bar form, and the lamentable lyric. The absurd exploitative appropriation of indigenous New Orleans blues became a prototype to be used time and again, codifying the form, and ultimately changing the meaning of the blues for those outside its indigenous culture. It is arguable that this song, "Nigger Blues" is the foundational formula of White blues appropriation, even though many are too ashamed to acknowledge its influence.

In contrast, Jelly Roll Morton's first published song, "Jelly Roll Blues" (1915), was snappy feel-good blues. New Orleans blues arrangements had creative catchy musical introductions. Morton's expression of the form danced around the twelve-bar formula instead of becoming a slave to it. After all, the whole idea of blues was freedom of expression.

Unfortunately, it's the "Nigger Blues" form and Anglo definition that White record label executives pushed on their Negro artists. The style was solicited from the first female Negro blues singers such as Bessie Smith, Gertrude "Ma" Rainey, Bessie Brown, and Alberta Hunter. In turn, the melancholic style of these classic female artists became standardized further by subsequent Negro artists. The rigid blueprint was used over and over again as if the production of commercial blues were overseen by Henry Ford himself.

I've been known to perform a lonesome twelve-bar song of lament every now and then, but we New Orleans musicians did not invent the sad song; it's ancient. Hell, our music at funerals isn't sad. Why would our Saturday night music be? Nonetheless, Louisiana culture steadfastly maintained the indigenous bohemian French meaning of *les bleus*, an enlightened, subversive musical philosophy that celebrates freedom of expression and the pursuit of happiness. Over the years my indigenous music has been culturally colonized and redefined by White cultural brokers. I find it increasingly difficult to remain true to the indigenous expression of my culture in the current marketplace. I often feel shunned, or alienated, relatively speaking, from participating in what is supposed to be my own culture.

GENESIS OF THE FOLK-BLUES DYSTOPIA

VOLKSGEIST REFERS TO THE "SPIRIT" of the Germanic people. It is a term first popularized by German philosopher Johann Gottfried Herder (1744–1803). In 1778, Herder published a collection of songs he gathered from preliterate Saxon peasants. He dubbed the collection Volkslieder—folk song. Herder's goal was to use the music of "the volk," which he extolled as "the spirit" of the Saxon people, to construct a national German identity. Herder was part of a movement known today as the German romantic movement that was based on a preoccupation with the oral prerational culture of Saxon peasantry.

Jacob and Wilhelm Grimm, known as the Brothers Grimm, were inspired by Herder during the German romantic movement. They collected folktales depicting Saxon peasants as brave, ethnically pure, and of exceptional character to inspire intense nationalism. "Snow White," whose title alone invokes the ethnic purity motif found in many of the Grimms' tales, was included in their first book, *Nursery and Household Tales*, first published in 1812.

Brothers Jacob Grimm (b. 1785) and Wilhelm Grimm (b. 1786), went on to publish hundreds of folktales over the next fifty years including "Cinderella," "Little Red Riding Hood," and "Briar Rose," best known as "Sleeping Beauty." The Grimms' tales shaped Anglo-Saxon identity not only in Germany but in all of Europe, including England and the United States.

Indeed, folklore and folk music shape the character of a nation. The spirit and virtue of a nation is often illuminated in its folksongs and folklore. If a nation is to be "governed by the people"—the folk—it is essential, then, to identify who "the people" truly are. Nothing wrong with a fledgling nation forming a national identity around folklore and fairy tales. However, a problem arises when a nation uses that fiction as propaganda and pseudo-history, obfuscating facts and science that would otherwise counter such falsehoods. When folklore and fairy tales are forced upon "the people" as reality, when it is no longer an innocent bedtime story but a form of psychological control, it can have a dangerous effect on the psyche of a nation pitting tribe against tribe.

Fairy tales and folklore have been used as propaganda to enslave, subjugate, imprison, and discriminate against particular groups. Such was the case in Nazi Germany when the Nazis, in the run-up to World War II, used ostensibly innocent Grimm fairy tales such as "Snow White" and "Little Red Riding Hood" as propaganda to promote a romanticized Anglo-Saxon notion of superiority and ethnic purity.

American Anglo-Saxon folklore, fairy tales, and folk music, adopted from England and Germany, on the surface are harmless Disneyesque entertainment. But their effect has been an affirmation of White identity. In other words, in America "we the people" or "the folk" have always been categorically Anglo-Saxon or White. But America is neither homogeneous nor has it ever been ethnically pure. In order for America, a diverse nation, to be truly representative, all of "the folk" must see themselves in the nation's folklore as pure, exceptional, and of high character.

The blues was America's foundational music. Regrettably, however, America hid its truth. In the early twentieth century the United States had no cultural identity of its own except what had been borrowed from Europe. The time had come for America, emerging as a world power during the Industrial Revolution, to seek and define a unique cultural identity of its own. The problem was, White nationalists didn't want the blues nor the swarthy people who invented it to be protagonists in the nation's identity. Indeed, the blues and its practitioners were a threat to the fragility of White nationalists' romanticized sense of supremacy. Therefore, the blues was obfuscated and marginalized until it could be Anglicized and recast as a White phenomenon, a fairy tale that has become our reality.

THE CHILD BALLADS

ONCE UPON A TIME, music was fleeting; it lasted only as long as the musicians played, then wafted away, disappearing forever, except in the collective memories of those in close enough proximity to witness and hear the music in person.

The ballad, as folk music was once known, had no known authors. It was a nonprofessional oral tradition without musical notation. Popular in England and Scotland during the Dark Ages, the ballad, sung by milkmaids and ploughmen, was the music of preliterate communities. Ballads were sung a cappella, but on occasion singers were accompanied by string instruments. Subjects included romantic riddles, heroism, and tragedies. Considering medieval Europe was illiterate, the first popular ballad collections weren't recorded in writing until the eighteenth century.

British universities of the nineteenth century did not consider music from the lower classes worthy of study, so Harvard University English professor Francis James Child (1825–1896), encouraged by his British colleagues, took on the challenge of documenting and publishing in 1882 what became America's seminal folk song collection, *The English and Scottish Popular Ballads.*

Francis James Child, a pioneering folklorist who defined the American folk ballad as songs deriving anonymously in the oral tradition from preliterate British Isles peoples, established that the medieval ballads and folkways from the Lowlands of England and Scotland had crossed the Atlantic to America. Moreover, those traditions had continued largely in isolation by illiterate Anglo settlers in pastoral Appalachian communities, among whom a dialect of sixteenth-century Elizabethan English was still spoken.

"Barbara Allen," one of the more enduring ballads Child collected, had been orally passed down for generations in Appalachia. Likewise, "Lord Randall,"

"Thomas the Rhymer," and "Sir Patrick Spens," along with dozens of variations on the adventures of "Robin Hood," were also widely performed. By the 1960s, "The Elfin Knight" became the most popular ballad in the Child canon when it was recorded in 1966 by Simon and Garfunkel as "Scarborough Fair" for their album *Parsley, Sage, Rosemary, and Thyme*. Paul Simon had learned the song while in England in 1965 from folk singer Martin Carthy. In 1967, "Scarborough Fair" was featured prominently in the groundbreaking movie *The Graduate*. It peaked at number eleven on the Billboard singles chart in 1968.

Francis Child's folk song collection was published between 1882 and 1898 in ten parts forming five large volumes. It contained 305 English and Scottish popular ballads. Naturally, in the oral tradition with each reciting words were often changed, omitted, or added. For that reason, Child included extensive notes and numerous versions of songs, grouping each variant with a numbering system. For example, "Scarborough Fair" was based on "The Elfin Knight" (Child 2; Roud 12).

Similarly, during the early 1900s some folklorists, inspired by Child's *The English and Scottish Popular Ballads,* started collecting secular songs from aging Negro informants, witnesses to a fading slave plantation culture, out of the fear such songs could be lost forever. The problem was, however, early twentieth century Anglo folklorists were unequipped to define an authentic African folk criterion. As a consequence, they created an absurd false equivalence between European folk music and that of Africa, and in particular, that of Negroes in America.

It was tragically ironic, though not surprising—given the widely held belief of White scholars that Negroes were innately inferior—that neither Negro nor African scholars were consulted during the formation of what became a Eurocentric criterion for African and Negro folk music authenticity. Nevertheless, the Texas Folklore Society, led by folklorist John Lomax, pioneered the study of "authentic" Negro music. John Lomax ignored popular musical expressions within the Negro community for a more obscure primitive expression.

Strikingly, the major requirement in John Lomax's flawed criterion for Negro authenticity was a dilettante Black bard he could gauge to be illiterate and savage. In other words, his idea of authentic Negro folk music was music made only by Negroes whom, for whatever unfortunate reason, hadn't progressed from the "folkways" that slavery had wrought. Indeed, the culture of the enslaved was peculiar. Slavery was, no doubt, a part of African American history. It's crucial to understand, however, the culture of the enslaved was not authentic African American culture. Indeed, a people must have agency to form a truly authentic culture. Moreover, folk music, as defined by European and Anglo American folklorists, never existed in Africa. The root of the problem began when early folklorists created a disturbing false equivalence that distorted the understanding of African American musical expression.

The American Folklore Society, founded in Cambridge, Massachusetts, in 1888, around Francis James Child's pioneering research, became the first folklore society in the United States. Naturally, Francis James Child became its first president. In 1904, Professor Child was succeeded as president by his former student George L. Kittredge, born 1860, in Boston, Massachusetts. Like Child, Kittredge was an English professor at Harvard University. It was Kittredge who subsequently urged his forty-two-year-old student, John Lomax—who was returning home to Texas in 1907 after one year of Harvard graduate studies—to form a folklore society back home.

John A. Lomax (1867–1948) and Dr. Leonidas Payne (1873–1945) founded the Texas Folklore Society in 1909. The society's initial mission was to collect cowboy songs and to preserve Texas folklore. Soon, however, Lomax's interest spread to Negro folk songs in Louisiana. Lomax romanticized the singing of formerly enslaved tenant farmers he heard as a boy on his family's farm in Bosque County, Texas. With such slave era melodies as a reference, Lomax, assisted by his apprenticing teenaged son, Alan, set out in 1933 to record Negro ballads with his new cutting-edge but clunky portable disk recorder. His plan was to cajole bygone "darkie" melodies from downtrodden Negro informants for his benefactor the Library of Congress.

His most famous field recordings were made from 1933 to 1934, when he captured the songs of then-prisoner Huddie William Ledbetter in metropolitan Baton Rouge at the notorious Angola Prison Farm. John Lomax saw Ledbetter as a "savage" who could sing like a bird. He didn't recognize Ledbetter, a troubled man of many gifts, as the descendant of great African civilizations, whose ancestors were wrought primal and illiterate by depraved colonialists during the Atlantic slave trade.

To put it bluntly, Lomax was a White supremacist; a conservative sympathizer of "The Lost Cause." For example, in the 1920s, while the "New Negro" was in the throes of a belated Renaissance, he wrote, after attending a concert at a Black university, it is "pitiful," now, that "blacks are civilized." Indeed, Lomax, based on his personal correspondence letters, believed such progress to be counterproductive. Furthermore, in 1932, he fondly remembered a Negro house party he encountered while on a field trip. He imagined being "carried across to Africa" he reminisced, "as if I were listening to the tom-toms of savage blacks." *Savage* being his favorite word to describe "authentic" Negroes.[117]

Without a doubt, John Lomax's theories and analysis regarding "Negro folk authenticity" reinforced pseudoscientific racism and should be isolated and detached from his Library of Congress collections. Regrettably, Lomax's mis-guided procurement techniques, analysis, and conclusions weren't uncommon. Folklorist Dorothy Scarborough, a colleague of John Lomax's, expressed similar condescension and bigotry toward her Negro informants.

The year 1925 marked an important turning point for the blues. In 1925, Dorothy Scarborough usurped the blues by conflating it with slave songs, tether-ing it to a culture wrought by slavery. By the 1960s, John Lomax's and Dorothy Scarborough's misguided ideas about Negro authenticity would inspire the Blues Mafia's Negro folk-blues primitivist movement.

ON THE TRAIL OF NEGRO FOLK SONGS

IN 1925, folklorist Emily Dorothy Scarborough, born 1878, together with Negro appeaser William Christopher Handy, composer of "St. Louis Blues," conflated the complex countermelodic, polyrhythmic, Creolized blues of New Orleans with dilettante "primitive," "savage," Negro slave music. And, by doing so, they rede-fined a renaissance music of free expression as music of slavery and appeasement.

To execute this grand deception; to make the blues fit ostensibly into the pseudoscientific racist ideas of the early twentieth century, the blues origins had to first be relocated from its cosmopolitan birthplace, New Orleans—a city whose exceptional cultural achievements were largely defined by educated free Negro Creoles, free Haitian immigrants who fought a successful revolution-ary war, and by those enslaved under Spanish rule—to the primitive environs of the Mississippi Delta and it's unfortunate, uneducated sharecroppers who, subjugated by plantation owners, picked cotton under similar conditions to antebellum slaves.

Second, Black musicians from New Orleans, bohemian urban dwellers, had to be removed from the narrative because they didn't fit the plantation mode. Even if their literary skills were crude, their musical skills were of the highest sophistication. High artistic achievement, to be sure, is a defining attribute of high civilization. Finally, to suppress the blues and make it conform to pseudo-scientific assumptions about White intellectual supremacy, New Orleans was a problem that had to be obfuscated from the blues origin narrative—except for the occasional Voodoo curiosity—because New Orleans wasn't "primitive" enough.

In 1910, Dorothy Scarborough, aka "the Song-catcher," became a dues-paying member of the Texas Folklore Society. By 1914 she was its first female president.

Her father, John Scarborough, a Confederate veteran from Louisiana, moved his family from Sweetwater, Texas, to Waco, in 1887, so that his children could continue their educations at Baylor University.[118] Scarborough left her post as president of the Texas Folklore Society after a few years and moved to New York City in 1916 to teach literature at Columbia University.

Dorothy Scarborough was no flapper girl. She never embraced the Roaring Twenties. Although Scarborough claimed to be fascinated with Negro music and culture, she wasn't one of the throngs of young White women who—liberated by the private mobility of the automobile—went on "slumming dates" to Harlem. Slumming dates were a new phenomenon that broke with Victorian traditions such as "coming to call," in which a young man would have been received in the family parlor and expected to make polite chitchat over tea with his date and her mother. Perhaps on subsequent house calls the girl would showcase her piano skills while the young man and her family listened politely. Indeed, social mores during the Roaring Twenties were changing rapidly. Dorothy Scarborough was, however, an antebellum romanticist. Although the New Orleans Creole blues had reached an apex in Harlem, slumming was not her cup of tea. Scarborough quickly grew weary of the hustle and bustle of cosmopolitan New York City life. Blues modernity in Harlem only heightened her longing for the placidity of a bygone South.

Dorothy Scarborough wrote novels and essays depicting her interest in mid-ninetieth century Negro songs at a time when the study of Negro folklore by the dominant culture was in its infancy. "Both of my grandfathers owned large plantations with many slaves, and so my parents grew up amid a wealth of Negro folklore and song, which they passed on to us children," she wrote in her book *On the Trail of Negro Folk-songs* published by Harvard Press in 1925.

Scarborough fondly recalled an infamous slavery-time song about a slightly crippled runaway slave who wobbled clumsily when he walked. The runaway was easily caught, then mocked by the slave patrol. "'Run, Nigger, Run'" is a song, she continued, "which I had heard mother sing, it is one of the oldest of the plantation songs."

> Run, nigger run; de patter-roller catch you.
> Run, nigger run, it's almost day.
> Run, nigger run, de patter-roller catch you.
> Run, nigger run, and try to get away.

What I find more disturbing than her mother singing this wretched plantation melody to her as a child is her inability as an adult—residing in cosmopolitan

New York City, just outside of Harlem—to contextualize "Run, Nigger, Run" as the vile racist song it was.

Scarborough continued sentimentalizing: "How many memories of my childhood and youth are associated with loved black faces!" In her youth, emancipated slaves were still fettered to her family's plantations, but not once does she acknowledge what slavery had wrought upon those "loved black faces."

She sojourned to Texas, Louisiana, and Mississippi several times between 1921 and 1925 to "catch" songs from surviving former slaves. Some of her informants, she claimed, were more than one hundred years of age. Scarborough published two major folklore collections during this period, the novel *In the Land of Cotton* (1923) and the highly influential *On the Trail of Negro Folk-songs* (1925). The latter was based on an article she first published in 1923 titled "The 'Blues' as Folk-Songs," a disturbing pseudo-anthropological study of Negro music and culture that included her dystopian thoughts regarding the blues.

I found it very revealing that in the mist of Black Harlem a self-described "song-catcher" of Negro songs would leave New York in search of a "primitive" Negro, which she believed still existed, with any luck, somewhere deep down south. She imagined she'd find Black musicians in the South who were unaffected by phonograph records, city lights, and the ambitions of migrant Harlemites.

Many Negro authors, such as Alain Locke, Zora Neale Hurston, Langston Hughes, and Jean Toomer (born Nathan Pinchback Toomer, the grandson of P. S. Pinchback, the first African American to become governor of a US state when he became governor of Louisiana in 1872) began publishing their literature in magazines, journals, newspapers, and as novels during this time. The era became known as the Harlem Renaissance, a literary movement in which Negro authors proclaimed their humanity through poetry and prose.

Alain Locke wrote in his essay "The New Negro," also published in 1925, "The American mind must reckon with a fundamentally changed Negro." Nevertheless, Dorothy Scarborough and her fellow *song-catchers* were only interested in the "Old Negro." White folklorists preferred to seek their own "authentic" representatives of the Negro race—beyond Harlem.

Negro Folksongs chapters were divided by various idioms: Negro Ballads, Reels, Children's Game-Songs, Lullabies, Songs About Animals, Work Songs, Railroad Songs, and Blues.[119] Several familiar plantation spirituals were also included in the collection such as "Swing Low, Sweet Chariot" and "Roll Jordan Roll."

Scarborough shared a story told to her about a remarkable Negro inmate who played guitar. Dorothy Scarborough recalled she once spent three nights as the guest of Texas governor Pat Neff in the governor's mansion. One evening, Governor Neff shared a memory of a song that had made a strong impression on him while visiting a state prison farm. It was sung by a charismatic Negro prisoner believed to be "Walter Boyd." Scarborough printed a verse of the mysterious prisoner's song:

> If I had the gov'ner Where the gov'ner has me, before daylight I'd set the gov'ner free. I begs you, gov'ner, upon my soul: If you won't gimme a pardon, Won't you gimme a parole?[120]

The talented prisoner was actually Huddie Ledbetter, anonymous at the time, going by the assumed name Walter Boyd. Ledbetter had been convicted of homicide on June 7, 1918, and was serving out his sentence at the penitentiary in Sugar Land, Texas. Ledbetter's plea must have made a great impression on Governor Neff, because "Walter Boyd" was pardoned on January 15, 1925, as one of Governor Neff's last acts in office. Later, in 1934, it was publicly revealed and acknowledged—after Ledbetter had been famously released from Angola State Prison Farm in Louisiana—that the obscure songster Governor Neff had pardoned was none other than Huddie "Lead Belly" Ledbetter.

It was reported by John Lomax that Lead Belly was pardoned from Angola after one of his recordings reached the Louisiana governor. However, there was no evidence to support Lomax's claim. In spite of that, Lomax sold the pardon myth to exploit Lead Belly's prison record. Like an unscrupulous carnival barker, John Lomax cashed in on Lead Belly's concert tours by promoting his discovery as a "savage Negro murderer from the swamps," not a singer of ballads worthy of the public's attention, as would have been expected from a serious musicologist. In April 1937, an article in *Life* magazine was titled, "Lead Belly—Bad Nigger Makes Good Minstrel." Indeed, long after Lead Belly had parted ways with Lomax, the "savage" narrative continued to define him. Furthermore, Lomax's archetypical image of Negro authenticity has endured into the twenty-first century. Modern hip-hop "authenticity" is largely based on Lomax's "savage" criterion.

Like John Lomax, Dorothy Scarborough was haunted by plantation melodies she had grown up with—melodies that indulged her nostalgia of a fading genteel agrarian world where Negro men stepped off sidewalks, bowed their heads, and wouldn't dare make eye contact with a White woman. It was a time when an "old darkie," wrinkled and gray, happily answered "yes ma'am" to a child who gaily wanted the bent old man, for the hundredth time, to sing and dance a jig for her amusement.

Scarborough's temperament toward Harlem's New Orleans–derived blues culture is that of a young southern belle frightened by a strange new world, as though she were Alice in Wonderland. Dorothy preferred the reassuring lullabies sung by her Black nanny rather than the sassy bellowings of Bessie Smith.

Granted, in 1925, aspects of blues were similar to European folk music because it originated from poor Louisiana musicians and not from the elite classes. But the blues was neither antebellum slave music nor part of an African continuum, it was an entirely new Creole invention. Illiteracy of the slave was by decree; therefore, it was atypical. Scarborough wondered, "Why has nobody ever discussed the puritanism among negroes?" Perhaps because the blues challenged the church in ways unthinkable for a devout Puritan. To be sure, the blues was not imbued with Puritan aesthetics found in the plantation-era melodies and spirituals Dorothy Scarborough had been collecting. "I hope that I may sometime spend a sabbatical year," she yearned, "on the trail of more Negro folk-songs, before the material vanishes forever, killed by the Victrola, the radio, the lure of cheap printed music."

She comes across here as a typical antiquarian. Her exploits of door-knocking and song-catching seemed to be a labor of love. Yet I find her paternalism unsettling. My suspicion that Scarborough's procurement techniques were tainted by her deeply held racist beliefs are confirmed when she concludes that "the colored mind is not essentially logical."

Scarborough was undoubtedly one of the first Negro primitivist romantics of folk music. *Primitivism* was an early twentieth-century art movement that subsequently inspired "primitive" (hot) record collecting. During the folk movement of the 1960s, Scarborough's Negro primitivist song collecting criterium was adopted by the Blues Mafia, a loose consortium of "primitive Negro" record collectors who became powerful brokers of Negro culture.

In spite of their many shortcomings, Dorothy Scarborough, John Lomax, and his son Alan Lomax, along with the Blues Mafia, should be acknowledged for contributing to a rich musical archive we can all enjoy for years to come. They collected songs from people like Lead Belly whose stories and songs may have otherwise been lost. Although we are pleased to have such historical recordings and documents for posterity, the dangerous narrative they constructed around my culture is in dire need of reformation.

To put it another way, at one time Europeans believed the world was flat. Christopher Columbus thought he was in India. Likewise, the mistaken belief that the blues was a continuum of slave "songs of sorrow" that originated in antebellum cotton fields of the Mississippi Delta shall, too, one day pass into debunked posterity.

Scarborough, in her final chapter of *The Blues,* contradicts all that she had written in previous chapters regarding the social function of "happy-faced" former slaves. The racist folk music she had been collecting was not thought to be obscene in her Confederate-sympathizing home. Her dear mother, after all, had gaily sung "Run, Nigger, Run" to her on many occasions as a bedtime lullaby. Scarborough's idea of folk-blues grew out of music she heard her mother and servants sing; melodies sanctioned by slave masters, missionaries, overseers, and more recently, chain gang wardens.

In contrast, blues, an enlightened music, had been incubated in and around a bohemian district tolerating prostitution, gambling, alcohol, reefer (Louis Armstrong's preferred recreational drug), interracial dating, ribald poetry, and, most horrible of all, dirty dancing. Yet, Scarborough's myopic idea of folk-blues was imbrued with Victorian prudishness.

In spite of this, she commences the first known attempt at establishing a blues historiography. She pondered the question: "Blues, being widely published as sheet music in the North as well as the South, and sung in vaudeville everywhere, would seem to have little relation to authentic folk-music of the Negroes."

I concur with this sentiment. It was the most profound thought I found in her entire book regarding the blues. She should have stopped right there, stood up, and backed away from the typewriter. She was finally on the right track, because the blues, in 1925, was something entirely new and exciting. But she continued. "In studying the question," Scarborough wrote, "I had a feeling that it was more or less connected with Negro folk-song, and I tried to trace it back to its origin." Her notion of blues origin as rustic and primitive has led to mind-numbing frustrations for nearly all musicologists because they cannot find facts to support this romanticized origin theory. Second, blues and folk, during this time, were the antithesis of one another. "Negroes and white people in the South," Scarborough continued, "referred me to W. C. Handy."

What Dorothy Scarborough found when she entered Handy's handsomely furnished Manhattan publishing office for the interview in the Gaiety Theater Building, 1547 Broadway at Forty-Seventh Street—known as the Black Tin Pan Alley, because several Black publishers had offices there, including Handy rival blues composer Clarence Williams from New Orleans—certainly did not fit her preconceived notions of what the blues should be, nor what image should represent it.

While the primitive stereotype of the Mississippi Delta bluesman had yet to be created, W. C. Handy, the usurping protagonist at the center of blues' illegitimate historiography, was prepared to lay the blueprint for Scarborough. Just a few years earlier, in 1919, the former minstrel trumpeter and popular composer had described slave songs and blues songs as separate idioms:

BLUES music moves our feet and we know not why. We feel no tears . . . The songs of the slaves represented their sorrows rather than their joys. Like tears, they were a relief to an aching heart. The sorrow songs of the slaves we call jubilee melodies. The happy-go-lucky songs of the Southern Negro we call "Blues."[121]

I agree with Handy's 1919 assertion that "BLUES music moves our feet" and had no connection to the "sorrow songs" of the slaves. Blues, as invented by Lonnie Johnson, King Oliver, Louis Armstrong, Tony Jackson, and Jelly Roll Morton, was, in fact, a separate idiom from the "sorrow songs" of slaves. Astonishingly, and most regrettably, however, Handy changed his tune in 1925 to appease racist eugenicist ideas held by Dorothy Scarborough and her colleagues.

During the interview, Scarborough asked Handy, "Have blues any relation to Negro folksong?" Handy could have repeated his definition of the blues from 1919, but instead he chose not to challenge her primitive Negro fantasies. Handy had been anticipating this very question since publishing "Memphis Blues" more than a decade before. Moreover, the erudite trumpeter had been carefully cultivating an image as "Father of the Blues." Handy couldn't wait to spring forward and answer her unequivocally, "Yes, they are folk-music."

Dorothy Scarborough eagerly created an alternative history for the blues with her willing accomplice, forcing a marriage between a subversive music of free expression with the melodies of bondage. The conflation created a confounding paradigm shift. Up until then, the blues was seen as discordant. It had challenged the authority of Jim Crow institutions. Afterward, it was thought to be submissive antebellum "sorrow songs." Consequently, the pressure that was on America to accept the blues as a genius idea trumpeting the arrival of the "New Negro" was stalled.

Shortly after *On the Trail of Negro Folk-songs* was published, W. C. Handy was rewarded by White primitivists. Handy relished his new role as drum major of the blues. He was skipped to the front of the New Orleans blues parade in subsequent articles and books written by White elites and academics. Ultimately, W. C. Handy was crowned "Father of the Blues"—a title Creole piano genius Jelly Roll Morton challenged as belonging to him in a letter published in *Downbeat Magazine* in 1938 and, later, expounded upon with astounding veracity at the Library of Congress during Morton's momentous recording sessions produced by folklorist Alan Lomax.

Not surprisingly, however, Jelly Roll Morton's counternarrative of the origins of the blues was suppressed by Alan Lomax. Morton passed away on July 10, 1941, and his most important recordings—which could have changed the course and history of blues—were buried by the Library of Congress; hidden away for the next sixty years. Following the death of Alan Lomax on July 19, 2002, *The Complete Library of Congress Recordings*, all nine uncensored hours, finally came out on a lengthy boxed set of eight CDs in 2005, vindicating Jelly Roll Morton's claim that blues originated in Creole New Orleans, and he was an eyewitness and one of its greatest protagonists. The *Complete Recordings* won him two posthumous Grammy Awards and cast serious aspersions on Alan Lomax's claim that the Mississippi Delta was "the Land Where the Blues Began."

Dorothy Scarborough and W. C. Handy, along with John and Alan Lomax, hijacked America's most vibrant commercial and revolutionary music by constructing a false equivalence between the blues and Anglican folk aesthetics. Their fallacious construct has deluded the public for nearly one hundred years.

Celebrated playwright and author Tennessee Williams once said of his beloved muse New Orleans, "It's the last frontier of Bohemia." Indeed, Handy and Scarborough's invention of "folk-blues" shackled a revolutionary bohemian music that threatened to Creolize and define American culture. The blues of the 1920s artfully mocked specious Victorian respectability, but more important, it struck fear in segregationists because it posed a threat to the Jim Crow social order.

But what of Black intellectuals? What did they have to say on the matter? Couldn't they have seized the narrative and shaped the public's conscious regarding the blues? To highlight how even the brightest Negro scholars, writers, and artists were often cajoled into propagating the same narrative as White primitivists and passing it off as authentic blues and African American history, we must pull back the curtains on the Harlem Renaissance.

FOLKLORIST ZORA NEALE HURSTON AND THE HARLEM RENAISSANCE

In the early twentieth century, primitivism permeated all liberal arts and sciences in America. The Black literary movement of Harlem was not immune. In fact, the Harlem Renaissance was financed and controlled by White primitivist Charlotte Osgood Mason (1854–1946). Hidden in the shadows behind the smart Black faces of the Harlem literati, like the Wizard of Oz or, rather, the "Godmother"—as she demanded her Negroes address her (and they did)—was primitivist Charlotte Mason, born Charlotte van der Veer.

To be sure, Black novelists who loved the blues such as Langston Hughes and Zora Neale Hurston—and knew it to be an enlightened music that could uplift the Negro—were controlled by the patronage of a wealthy White primitivist.

Mason, an eccentric widower, resided at 399 Park Avenue in a splendid high-rise penthouse filled with primitive art. She once moonlighted as an anthropologist among Native Americans. However, by the 1920s, during the height of the blues craze, she, like Dorothy Scarborough, became enthralled with the "savage" "primitive" Negro.

Charlotte Mason was around seventy when she attended an African art lecture by Alain Locke in 1927. Locke, born in Philadelphia, Pennsylvania, on September 13, 1886, was celebrated as the first African American Rhodes scholar. A leading intellectual, Locke was a graduate of Oxford University in England and earned a PhD in philosophy from Harvard University.

Carefully mannered in the ways of an Anglo Oxford gentleman, Alain Locke was well versed in Anglo thought. He was taught and accepted the criteria first established by Francis James Child and Harvard's American Folklore Society, which measured and defined African American folklore by Anglo standards. He was taught at Oxford and Harvard that Western culture was the beginning of civilization and African Americans were an innately primitive people. As a result, to solve the "Negro Problem" he strove to produce an Anglicized Negro, which he coined the "New Negro." But Locke was a conflicted man, as many highly educated African Americans of his era were, when it came to the "Negro Problem." He thought by making the Creolized blues more Anglicized, it would become more respectable, and thus more civilized. However, Charlotte Osgood Mason was the hand that fed his movement. She had her own thoughts on how to shape Negro thought. Indeed, while proclaiming herself "a better Negro" than most Blacks she knew (this revealing statement was made with Alain Locke in mind) she was not interested in making her "primitive people" more Anglicized.[122] Nevertheless, Alain Locke was useful to his "Godmother" as a conduit through which she could vicariously influence and collect "primitive" Negro culture.

Locke was a professor of philosophy at historically Black Howard University when he met and became Charlotte Mason's trusted advisor in all things Negro. Charlotte Mason paid Alain Locke, the "dean" of the Harlem Renaissance, handsomely over the years to supply her with talented Negro writers and artists who would depict her fantasies of Negro primitivism. He brought to her painter Aaron Douglas, sculptor Richmond Barthe, musician and composer Hall Johnson, and writers Claude McKay, Langston Hughes, and Zora Neale Hurston. Mason required all those who benefited from her benevolence, including Locke, to call her "Godmother" and she insisted they keep her identity a secret.[123]

Poet and novelist Langston Hughes became one of Mason's favorites. Mason took good care of Hughes's every financial need. She bought him "fine bond writing paper and even finer suits from the best shops on Fifth Avenue. Mason even footed the bill for Langston's recalcitrant stepbrother, Gwyn Clark, to attend a New England Preparatory School."[124] In return, Hughes was obligated to submit all of his work to his Godmother for screening. Mason regarded the young poet "a golden star in the Firmament of Primitive Peoples."[125]

Based on estimates, in the late 1920s and Depression-era '30s, Mason gave roughly $100,000 to her Black "godchildren," writers and artists like Locke, Hughes, and Hurston. In 2017, the relative value of her patronage was about $1,470,000.00. Indeed, Negro writers are impoverished in boom times, yet this was during the Great Depression. Therefore, the value of Mason's patronage was even more crucial to the survival of her Negro protégées.

Zora Neale Hurston, an extraordinary novelist, folklorist, and anthropologist, grew up in the rustic all-Black town of Eatonville, Florida. She was the most qualified of all Harlem Renaissance writers to fulfill Mason's primitivists desires. Born in 1891, Hurston, at age twenty-six, represented that she was only sixteen in order to re-attend high school. She earned her diploma in 1918. She attended Howard University, where her creative writing skills caught the attention of professor Alain Locke. After two years at Howard, she relocated to Harlem with a dream to make her mark as a novelist.

Zora's flamboyant but folksy persona, derided by Black critics as minstrelsy, created opportunities for her in elite White circles. In 1925, while mingling at a banquet for *Opportunity*, the leading magazine of "New Negro" writing, Hurston made an impression on Annie Nathan Meyer, founder of Barnard College in Manhattan. Meyer offered Hurston a scholarship to attend the private women's liberal arts college as a transfer student from Howard University.[126] When Hurston graduated in 1928, she became Barnard's first Black graduate.[127]

While at Barnard, Hurston studied anthropology under one of the world's great anthropologists, Franz Uri Boas. A German Jewish American immigrant, Boas had founded the anthropology department at Columbia University.[128] (Barnard was the women's wing of the all-male Columbia University.) Professor Franz Boas's thoughts on the importance of Southern Black culture and its connection to exceptional African cultures had already impacted W. E. B. Du Bois by the time Zora Hurston came under his tutelage. Importantly, Boas was not a primitivist—he was an exception.

Although she was thoroughly learned, Zora was unlike Locke and other carefully mannered Negroes of Mason's acquaintance in that her negritude seemed undiminished by her education. "Alan Lomax, who worked with Hurston on a seminal 1935 Library of Congress folk-music-recording expedition, wrote of her unique ability to win over the locals since she 'talks their language and can out-nigger any of them.'"[129]

Field recordings of Zora Neale Hurston singing work songs such as "Mule on the Mount" recorded in her hometown of Eatonville, Florida, in 1939 created a complex dichotomy for folklorists. To document a folk song from a bright intelligent person such as Zora Hurston was not satisfactory for the Lomaxes; they wanted it from their idea of an "authentic" Negro, preferably a downtrodden illiterate person whose disposition was similar to a slave, not someone as polished as Zora Neale Hurston.

This raises the question, When it came to African Americans, were folklorists collecting songs or a snapshot of the primitive? If they were purely collecting songs, it shouldn't have mattered if the informant was well read. It should have been a plus, as long as the poetry, melody, and sourcing were reliable. Many illiterate Negro chain-gang workers would often sing commercial songs they heard in honky-tonks such as "Careless Love" or "Buddy Bolden's Blues," but because their disposition fit the primitive stereotype, they were documented as authentic folk informants. Besides, it was unthinkable for an illiterate, downtrodden Negro to argue about the authentic representation of his culture to a White man from *Harvard*.

I would argue the work song can be just as authentic, and sometimes more so, when produced commercially either on Broadway, such as "Ol' Man River," which was sung so beautifully by the incomparable Paul Robeson, or the "Banana Boat Song (Day O)," a million-selling studio recording sung by gifted folk-singer and civil rights activist Harry Belafonte. Later, in 1960, Sam Cooke's "Chain Gang" became a popular hit, capturing the essence of the work song perfectly. These commercial work songs were sung and produced by professional artists and cited and credited accordingly. They didn't pretend to be anything more than what they were—which made them authentic in their own right.

Therefore, when I analyze the antebellum work songs, it is with the understanding that the planter found comfort in the slaves' unison singing. Moreover, he benefited financially from it, earning 100 percent of the profits work songs—as a tool—helped to produce. In fact, the work song became a necessary tool for tempering uprisings on plantations. Granted, the enslaved may have gotten some picayune amount of relief from the daily grind of forced labor by singing a sanctioned work song, but only because this type of enforced synchronized singing could provide a fleeting umbrella from the white heat of slavery.

Zora Hurston's idiosyncrasies were often misread by both her White and Black colleagues. Though married briefly twice, she lived most of her life as a single woman and had no children. She was a pioneering Renaissance woman often at odds with fellow Harlem literatis as well as her patron Godmother, Mason. Hurston signed a stringent contract that gave her Godmother full control of all material and stories she collected on her southern folkloric and anthropologic expeditions. Additionally, she gave Mason the authority to shape her information. Mason paid Hurston a hefty sum of $200 monthly and bought her a new automobile and a motion picture camera.

To be sure, Mason's coveted financial support obligated Hurston to her primitivist fantasies. "In letters, she signed off as 'Godmother's pickaninny' and addressed Mason as 'Dearest, little mother of the primitive world' and 'Darling Godmother, the Guard-Mother who sits in the Twelfth Heaven and shapes the destinies of the primitives.'"[130] Hurston was a complicated folklorist. The "degree to which Hurston bought into her patron's primitivist ideology is difficult to ascertain."[131]

Hurston was often torn between the ideologies of fellow folklorists John and Alan Lomax, who wished to preserve and accentuate the "primitive" aspects of the "Old Negro," and the Harlem literary movement of Alain Locke who wanted to modernize the "Old Negro" or shun him altogether. This dichotomy played out in her books and essays.

For instance, in "How It Feels to Be Colored Me," a controversial essay published in 1928, Hurston said, "Slavery is the price I paid for civilization and that is worth all that I have paid through my ancestors for it." Hurston left the impression in "Colored Me" that she believed her ancestors were savages who were lucky to be plucked from the jungles of Africa and enslaved by civilized Whites. The inference being, due to the institution of slavery, she, as a descendant of slaves, had an opportunity to finally become civilized. This strikingly misguided sentiment was shared by many college-educated Blacks in the early nineteenth century. It was the sentiment of Booker T. Washington's 1901 *Up from Slavery* biography.

This idea of Negro inferiority permeated the libraries of historically Black colleges. In fact, Alain Locke was miseducated at Oxford and Harvard to accept the false equivalencies between Anglo "folk" and African American "folk" first established by Francis James Child then taught by Harvard's American Folk Society to Harvard graduates such as John Lomax.

Alain Locke taught this false equivalency idea at Howard and helped to canonize it as the authentic African American origins of the blues. Harvard published Dorothy Scarborough's *On the Trail of Negro Folk-Songs* and similar books that have filled libraries the world over with pseudo-blues history. It's no coincidence the Blues Mafia's primitive folk-blues movement was reignited in Cambridge coffee houses within earshot of Harvard University in the 1960s. It is this idea that must be eradicated as the authentic history of the blues and its culture therewith.

If we as Black Creole Louisianans don't reclaim the blues and its authentic cultural narrative, we will be remembered as happy downtrodden people. A feeble-minded people who, even at funerals, couldn't wait to dance and get drunk to music. History will remember us on rooftops during Katrina begging for help because our culture lacked the fortitude of more Americanized communities.

Every year, during Black History Month, a supposed blues musician or historian is trotted out in front of classrooms all over America to reinforce the idea that music wrought by slavery is authentic African American culture. The inference being that, for the African American, slavery was a natural (authentic) state of being. They stand in front of impressionable youth and equate the blues with pre-literate Appalachian culture, with no mention of Creole New Orleans. Instead, they pretend its origins derived from one of the most impoverished regions in America, the Mississippi Delta—the supposed Black equivalent to Appalachia.

Just one problem: there were never any antebellum slave plantations in the heart of the Delta. It was a safari until the twentieth century. However, they don't teach that to students because it is counter to the Anglicized narrative. This self-loathing view of blues and its culture therewith was indoctrinated into the curricula of predominantly Black schools. It was this type of miseducation that caused Southern University in 1983, following our second inaugural Baton Rouge Blues Festival (established by my father's Blues Society), to expel us from the campus. We weren't allowed to have any further blues festivals on the Bluff because what we represented, we were told by administrators, was "unbecoming of an institution of higher learning."

The self-loathing problem was elucidated by Carter G. Woodson, the founder of Black History Month, and one of the first African Americans to graduate from Harvard. Like his fellow alumnus Alain Locke, Woodson earned a PhD of philosophy from America's most celebrated college.

In his book *The Mis-Education of the Negro*, published in 1933, Woodson said, "The educated Negroes have the attitude of contempt toward their own people because in their own as well as in their mixed schools, Negroes are taught to admire the Hebrew, the Greek, the Latin and the Teuton (a Germanic tribe), and to despise the African." I envision Woodson was speaking of himself and Alain Locke. Woodson continued, "When a Negro has finished his education in our schools, then, he has been equipped to begin the life of an Americanized or Euro-peanized white man." Indeed, the Creolized African American culture of Louisiana was thought to be too exotic and of no consequence in Black classrooms.

Unapologetically subversive, the blues was a high art form in which the Cre-olized African in Louisiana proudly expressed his uniqueness on his own terms. Creoles of New Orleans built a metaphoric wall to protect their culture from Anglo Puritan encroachment. Contrarily, many educated Blacks in other regions of America attempted to out-European Europeans as a means to equality. In other words, to enculturate and measure themselves by Anglo aesthetics. By attempting to perfect their diction, and by worshiping an Anglo Jesus with a fanatical zeal that the average White person would have trouble matching. All in an attempt to erase their Blackness and be accepted as Whites. Whereas, Creoles and blues musicians of Louisiana attempted to gain equality on their own terms. They chose instead to Creolize or Africanize European language, social customs, and religion.

For W. C. Handy and Zora Neale Hurston, primitivism represented the beginning of a civilizing journey for former slaves. Or in the words of Booker T. Washington, if Negroes only "pulled themselves up by their own bootstraps" they could aspire to become civilized and, thus, equal—someday.

On the other hand, White folklorists John Lomax and Dorothy Scarborough, along with White Harlem Renaissance benefactors such as Charlotte Osgood Mason, were out to *preserve* the Negroes' "authenticity" from "corrupting forces," such as assimilation and modernity. To be clear, founding folklorists and anthropologists believed Negro primitivism was innate, not what centuries of bondage had wrought. They studied their subjects through the prism of White supremacy. The folklorists and the informants were talking past each other when they concocted the fallacy of folk-blues.

Meanwhile, by 1925, New Orleans musicians had exported their Creole blues to Chicago and Harlem. It brought the Negro into vogue and ushered in the Harlem Renaissance. But at the crucial moment when the Creole blues was threatening to Creolize American culture and expose the pretense of White cultural supremacy, W. C. Handy used his celebrity as the de facto spokesman for the blues to assuage White fears. He accommodated White America's need to deny the blues was a genius high art form and America's greatest cultural achievement.

It just happened to be a bonus for the accommodationist that his "Great Harlem Compromise," as I have dubbed it, conveniently suppressed his rivals; trumpet geniuses such as King Oliver and Louis Armstrong, as well as rival composers Jelly Roll Morton, Spencer Williams, and Clarence Williams. To be sure, W. C. Handy's "Great Harlem Compromise" made him the "accommodationist" of the blues, not its father.

The idea that music wrought by slavery is authentic African American culture infers that slavery is the authentic culture of the African American. It is not. But in the twentieth century, this dangerous idea had no real counterweight. The Harlem literati could have provided a challenge to this notion, but they were compromised by White primitivists and miseducated by Harvard folklorists and anthropologists.

LEAD BELLY: THE "SAVAGE" FOLK-BLUES ARCHETYPE

MY QUANDARY WITH THE BLUES MAFIA for taking folk-blues digital was similar to Bob Dylan going electric at Newport. By the 1990s the Blues Mafia and their disciples had permeated the music industry. They were threatening to banish me for sampling and digitizing folk-blues and embracing hip-hop aesthetics. I was confused; I didn't understand why modernism was forbidden for a folk-blues artist. Later, I would learn the Blues Mafia's rubric. During the 1920s and 1930s, pioneering folklorists John Lomax and Dorothy Scarborough possessed unwarranted and paternalistic fears about the Negro. They believed the emergent phonograph record industry and urbanization were corrupting the purity of idyllic Negroes, the likes of which they had grown up with on their families' plantations. In their youth, they became enchanted with the voices of former slaves whose singing and music was untainted by edification and modernity.

With this in mind, John Lomax and Dorothy Scarborough developed a methodology that was greatly influenced by scientific racism. Although race has no basis in scientific validity, eugenicists believed the "White race" was on top because they were scientifically superior to the less evolved Negro. Such racial hierarchy propaganda was popularly upheld as scientific fact in the early twentieth century. It was preached in pulpits and taught in classrooms as the "natural order."

John Lomax applied this inferiority rationale when collecting "authentic" Negro folk songs. He believed modernism and high art could not be genuine expressions of an inferior race. Lomax thought barbarousness was the true expression of the Negro—the more primitive and grotesque, the more "authentic." Thus, in order to collect and record "authentic" Negro folk songs unaffected by modernity, John Lomax decided to forgo recording the precursory musical influences of the great Lonnie Johnson, a highly influential Louisiana guitarist, who was well known in the Northeast, and instead, sojourn south to the most notorious prison in America, Louisiana's Angola prison farm. There, Lomax believed, he could find a "darkie" songster, still caged and chained; a savage locked in an antebellum time capsule.

In 1933, John Lomax pitched the Library of Congress on the idea of collecting Negro folk and work songs in the Deep South. To accomplish this, he told them, he needed a portable recorder that could play back the disks immediately after a recording, one that would fit into the trunk of his car and could hold up to the rigors of field recording. The Library of Congress delivered such a machine a few weeks into his journey. In July 1933, John Lomax picked up a delivery of one of the first portable recorders in Baton Rouge. It was a heavy cutting-edge quarter-ton aluminum phonograph disk recorder. John Lomax and his son, Alan, put it in the trunk of his Ford sedan and headed straight for Angola, the infamous Louisiana State Penitentiary, to record the music of its prisoners. The Farm, as Angola was known because of its fertile fields worked by shackled prisoners when they weren't being leased out as indentured laborers, was located in metropolitan Baton Rouge, about fifty miles northeast of downtown in agriculturally rich West Feliciana Parish, formerly home to numerous wealthy slave owners and planters.

During his Angola sojourn, John Lomax recorded several prisoners, many of whom were unremarkable. Some of them had not played an instrument for years or had forgotten lyrics and songs altogether. Later in the session Lomax doubted himself, wondering if his assumptions were misguided. Then a dark-skinned, ruggedly built prisoner was brought into the session carrying a twelve-string acoustic guitar. He was dressed in the infamous black-and-white striped uniform of the chain gang, like the other prisoners. A stylish bandanna he wore around his neck distinguished him. He looked the part of the prisoner-prodigy Lomax was seeking, but could he play and sing?

The inmate started singing the blues. He sang field hollers, he sang spirituals, cowboy tunes, and novelties. John and Alan Lomax, still learning the limitations of their new recorder, did all they could just to keep up with the prisoner, frenetically trying to record everything he had to offer. John Lomax stopped the session briefly to play back a disk, testing to make sure there weren't any recording problems. The prisoner listened in wonder. Hearing his voice for the very first time, he was inspired to sing and play guitar with even greater passion when the session resumed.

It seemed the prisoner could recall every song he'd ever heard since childhood. They were gratified to learn he had original material, too. Among the many songs recorded that day were a few he'd written: "Angola Blues" and a lonesome ballad he called "Irene." The lyrics of "Irene" tell the tale of the singer's troubled past and his longing to see his true love again. After recording seven disks in a variety of styles, the charismatic prisoner sat down his guitar and wiped his brow with his bandana, revealing a wicked scar on his neck he had received in a knife fight. He seemed proud and satisfied with his performance. John Lomax was satisfied too. He was overwhelmed by the prisoner's talent and vast knowledge of bygone plantation songs. A contented John Lomax had found his boy. His name was Huddie William Ledbetter, better known as Lead Belly.

Lead Belly was born January 20, 1885, to Wesley and Sallie Ledbetter near Mooringsport, Louisiana. By 1903, he "was already a singer and guitarist of some note. He performed" regularly in Shreveport, Louisiana, in a notorious red-light district in the city, St. Paul's Bottoms. At around seventeen, Lead Belly began to develop a guitar style based on the rhythms he heard from New Orleans blues musicians gigging in Shreveport on Fannin Street, which featured "a row of saloons, brothels, and dance halls."[132] Lead Belly adapted, for twelve-string guitar, the boogie-woogie baselines he heard from a barrelhouse piano player called Pine Top, a man who had played in New Orleans and in barrelhouses from town to town in Louisiana.[133] However, Lead Belly's volatile temper led to numerous confrontations, sometimes deadly. To avoid the law, he moved to New Orleans briefly before settling in Texas under the pseudonym Walter Boyd. While in Texas, Lead Belly befriended and performed around Dallas with then-unknown guitar player Blind Lemon Jefferson. When John Lomax visited Angola in 1933, Lead Belly had already served nearly four years of a mandatory ten-year sentence for attempted homicide.

In 1934, the following summer, John Lomax returned to Angola to record more of Lead Belly for the Library of Congress. Lead Belly believed John Lomax to be a big man that could help him launch a music career, but first, he'd have to be unshackled. John Lomax took a song Lead Belly recorded as a plea to "Louisiana Governor O.K. Allen at Lead Belly's urgent request. The petition was on the other side of a recording of his signature song, 'Goodnight Irene.'"[134] A month later, on August 1, 1934, Lead Belly was released.

Legend has it that he sang his way out of Angola, charming the governor with his songs. For a time, Lomax promoted the myth that the phonograph he'd taken to the governor had hastened Lead Belly's release. Whether or not Lomax believed this at the time is difficult for us to know. But it did create a legend around Lead Belly's music that got people to stop and listen. In later years, Angola prison officials in Louisiana repeatedly denied Lead Belly had been pardoned.

There were several conflicting stories about how Ledbetter acquired his "famous nickname. Some say his fellow inmates dubbed him 'Lead Belly' as a play on his last name and reference to his physical toughness; others say he earned the name after being shot in the stomach with shotgun buckshot. Another theory has it that the name refers to his ability to drink homemade liquor. Whatever its origin," the name served to create a dangerous persona.[135]

John Lomax took his "primitive" songster north to show him off. The transformation of the one-time convict into a pop culture icon was rapid and extraordinary. Just months after being released, his schedule included performances in Philadelphia and a performance for an informal gathering of professors from

Columbia and New York Universities in New York City. Lead Belly was filled with great consternation when he realized that he was being paraded around New York as if he were the great ape King Kong—a spectacle, not a musical artist. The *New York Herald Tribune* described him as "a sweet singer of the Swamplands, here to do a few tunes between homicides." Moreover, he was made to perform in striped prison clothes. Lead Belly desperately wanted to be presented in a dignified manner, yet Lomax presented him as some type of savage captured deep in the swamps of Louisiana.

Indeed, the way Lomax handled Lead Belly resonated with a current of primitivism that ran through early twentieth-century modernism.[136] The terms "savage" and "primitive" were often used to describe entertainer Josephine Baker. Picasso and the Cubists incorporated the stark geometries of African sculptures in their work. Art collectors and intellectuals sought out these sculptures for galleries and studies.[137] Even the music of a sophisticate such as Duke Ellington was promoted as "jungle music." "The Primitive" became "a symbol that could encompass violence, sex, irrationality, and, at the same time noble innocence [the noble savage] and childlike naiveté."[138]

Three months later, Lead Belly decided to dump Lomax and strike out on his own. After unleashing his singing jail bird on genteel music halls and causing a sensation among music critics, John Lomax and Lead Belly parted ways, never to be reunited.

Lead Belly settled down in New York City, and over the next decade he recorded hundreds of songs. It was a constant struggle to earn a living with his guitar, even though he performed concerts at music halls and colleges nationwide. It didn't help that John and Alan Lomax owned the rights to his most popular songs and received the royalties they generated. Even so, by the 1940s, Lead Belly was the most influential folk-blues singer in America. On December 6, 1949, Lead Belly died penniless in his adopted hometown, New York City. Within six months of his death, his song "Goodnight, Irene" became a million seller for the White folk group the Weavers. Posthumously, dozens of Lead Belly's songs became standards, including "The Midnight Special" and "Rock Island Line."[139] Over time, John Lomax, the first self-appointed "arbiter and chief" of Negro authenticity, made Lead Belly the archetypical folk-bluesman. Novelist Richard Wright characterized John Lomax's handling of Lead Belly as "one of the most amazing cultural swindles in American history."

THE FALLACY OF THE WORK SONG

INDIGENOUS NORTH AMERICANS, or as Christopher Columbus named them, "Indians," lived in what would become North America before Europeans began their invasion of the "New World." Puritan and Pilgrim invaders seeking freedom of religion—along with ruthless secular invaders seeking land expansion and gold—sailed for what would subsequently become New England.

In the early colonial era of the seventeenth century, an emphasis on literacy was mainly focused on biblical literacy. Hypocritically, however, Puritans and Pilgrims were themselves intolerant. According to them, their doctrines proved God was on their side. And furthermore, those who didn't submit to their brand of religion were heathens. In colonial Jamestown, for a time, skipping church was a high crime. If a citizen of Jamestown skipped church three times they were executed. The Natives and all other settlers entering the New World were to be converted to Christianity or destroyed. Early settlements in the New World have been mythologized as religious freedom settlements, but they were obviously commissioned to expand the wealth of the British Empire.

Indeed, Pilgrim and Puritan settlements in New England were capitalist enterprises. Both were backed by English investors whose substantial capital investments funded guns, ships, and the manpower to wage war, annihilating many Native peoples. Many Native Americans who survived the gun succumbed, eventually, to Europeans' diseases. Some who survived were enslaved, but the vast majority of Native survivors were embargoed on reservations or forced further west.

Summarily, Black Africans were enslaved to work the harsh tobacco, sugarcane, indigo, and cotton plantations. Planters could more easily deny legal rights to Africans because unlike escaped White indentured servants, Africans' black skin and wooly hair serendipitously made it difficult for them to blend into an Anglo population. Unlike the rights of fellow European indentured servants, enslaved Blacks had no redress in colonial courts in the New World.

At the height of the Atlantic slave trade, the number of Africans arriving in the New World far outnumbered Europeans. According to historian David Brion Davis, "By 1820 nearly 8.7 million [enslaved] had departed from Africa for the New World, as opposed to only 2.7 million whites."[140] Of the millions of enslaved Africans who survived the horrific Atlantic voyages, only a small percentage were taken to North America. Which raises the question, if the blues are synonymous with work songs, if they were the inherent music of enslaved people. why would the blues only develop in North America? Why not the Caribbean, Cuba, or Brazil?

With mortality rates during the Middle Passage astonishingly high, captains of slave ships, out of fear of losing their human cargo packed tightly in chains beneath the ship, forced the captives to dance on deck. Initially, White bagpipers and fiddlers were hired on voyages to perform dance music for enslaved Africans. But these dance parties weren't benevolent. Neither were they antecedents to today's blues cruises. They were joyless, cruel, and unusual exercises.

In 1693, Captain Thomas Phillips wrote in his journal how he'd forced his slaves on deck during a voyage to "jump and dance for an hour or two to our bagpipes, harp, and fiddle, by which [they] exercise to preserve them in health."[141] To the captain's dismay, most of the Africans refused to dance. Those who refused were brutally beaten and whipped, further damaging the captain's valuable human cargo.

I imagine, from the enslaved purview, the sound of that bagpipe must have been excruciating, bedeviling the poor souls. I presume a few, driven to madness by the bagpipe, jumped overboard to escape the evil emanating from the screeching contraption.

In due time, the shrewd captain, out of barbarous greed, realized Africans were more willing to dance if they heard a familiar instrument. Thus the bagpipe was replaced with the African banjo. The captain, on ensuing voyages, forced the enslaved to perform the music themselves for his vile dance parties.

The banjo, because of its usefulness to the captain, became an invaluable instrument during the Middle Passage. Mind you, there was no checked luggage of the enslaved. The banjo (akonting) only made it on board because the captain demanded it.

Captain Phillips's musical manipulation technique was summarily adopted by plantation owners and slave drivers as an invaluable tool for productivity and profits. Therefore, Middle Passage music and so-called dances weren't precursors to Don Cornelius's *Soul Train* line, neither was its accompanying music a precursor to the blues. It was, however, a harbinger of the "work song."

Slave masters were "fearful of the silence of the slaves," Duke Ellington said. "Their masters commanded them to raise their voices in song so that all opportunity for discontented reflection or plans for talkathon and salvation would be eliminated."[142]

Solomon Northup, the primary author of the seminal 1853 slave narrative *Twelve Years a Slave*, is perhaps the most reliable witness in history to whether or not the work song was a forerunner of the blues. Born a free man of color in New York around 1808, Solomon was a literate man of many skills, most notably a professional violinist.

In 1841, at about the age of twenty-six, Solomon was married with a young family. He owned land in Hebron, New York. Incredibly, Solomon would spend the next twelve years of his life enslaved on Louisiana cotton and sugar plantations struggling to retain his humanity and regain his freedom.

Two men, small-time hustlers Joseph Russell and Alexander Merrill, booked Solomon to perform with them on a road trip. While playing a gig in Washington, DC, he was drugged and kidnapped by the two hucksters and sold into slavery. Solomon was shipped down to New Orleans and sold to planter William Ford in Red River, Louisiana, near Bayou Boeuf. Solomon called Ford a "model master."

Regrettably for Solomon, following a fight with an overseer he was sold to a new master, sadist and miserable drunkard Edwin Epps. "His chief delight," according to Solomon, "was in dancing with his 'niggers,' or lashing them about the yard with his long whip" just for the sadistic pleasure of "hearing them screech and scream." Make no mistake, those screams and hollers weren't precursors to the blues. Those hollers, according to Solomon, were produced by the "great welts" and painful cuts "painted on their backs"[143] by Epps's bloody cow whip.

For twelve horrendous years, Solomon toiled in Louisiana sugarcane fields, picked cotton, and cleared levees. He was leased out to surrounding plantations for similar harsh labor. Forced to serve the whims of his barbaric owner, Solomon spent many nights performing Scottish reels and schottisches for his drunken master's dance parties in the master's home. Solomon was forced to perform while fellow slaves were forced to dance for the master's amusement, even into the wee hours of the morning. At which time, when the rooster crowed, they were expected to hit the fields bright and early or they would be tied to Epps's bloody whipping post. The aesthetic in which Solomon performed, akin to the enforced music of human cargo during the Middle Passage, was not in his true artistic voice. Solomon's music as a slave was that which slavery had wrought.

Subsequently, as Solomon's reputation as a violinist grew, he was leased out and forced to perform for nearby balls and festivals. According to Solomon, the repertoire of enslaved musicians was most commonly derived from their master's tastes. It was common for slaves to learn the cotillion, the quadrille, the schottische, and Scottish reels. Solomon derived no pleasure from the music he performed while enslaved—although, at times, he did earn a few picayune and a reprieve from fieldwork.

Most important, Solomon, a sharp observer of enslaved culture and music, included in his book the score to "Roaring River," a song that is an invaluable artifact illustrating the general repertoire of the enslaved. If one were to play Solomon's "Roaring River" on fiddle, they would hear something resembling a Scottish reel, confirming the music of those enslaved was not the roots of blues. Solomon, in his well-documented memoir, didn't describe any music that can be mistaken as the roots of the blues. Music historians who eschewed Solomon's eyewitness account of the slaves' musical repertoire did a great disservice to our understanding of what is and isn't the roots of blues.

Solomon said nothing directly of cotton field hollers and chain gang chants, thought by some to be precursors to the blues. Yet indirectly, one can surmise, because Solomon had a trained ear, he understood that field hollers were merely the ambient sound of toil. The plantation singing and humming, which came to be known as the field holler of a single slave, acted as a locator, reassuring his master he hadn't run off. In other words, a field holler was an invisible leash or cowbell tethered to a slave while laboring way out yonder, perhaps behind a mule, beyond the comfortable sight of his overseer.

Work songs couldn't have been a genuine expression of the enslaved because the enslaved had no agency. Work songs were mechanisms of efficiency; a means to quell a potential rebellion and maximize profits. According to Solomon, a slave could not have expressed their innermost thoughts and honest emotions through music any more than they could have in a journal or letter. If Solomon's master had discovered he could read and write (he was literate) or that his music was subversive (it was not), he risked torture or death by lynching.

Solomon is obviously the foremost authority on the musical culture of the enslaved, especially in Louisiana. Isn't it peculiar then, that he is not referenced in blues and jazz histories concerning field hollers and work songs? Is it because Solomon could read music? The sheet music he included in his memoir would certainly have been disqualifying for most anthropologists and folklorists because they were myopically focused on the primitive, the savage, the illiterate.

In 1853, following his release from bondage, Solomon published his harrowing narrative. It was an "as told to" narrative ghostwritten by David Wilson, a White attorney who convincingly wrote the memoir in the first person. In the first few years of its release his book rivaled Frederick Douglass's slave narrative in popularity and sales. *Twelve Years a Slave* is the only known slave narrative of a free professional musician.

In the aftermath, Solomon Northup became a celebrated speaker for the abolition movement. Solomon's cultural experience, those twelve years he spent enslaved in Louisiana, was the norm, not an outlier. The veracity of Solomon's story has been verified by public records and countless historians. Indeed, Union soldiers who encountered his notorious former master Edwin Epps as they marched through Louisiana during the Civil War said Edwin Epps himself cor-roborated the story. Solomon Northup shined a flicker of light on a dark period of Black American music and culture.[144]

FEDERAL MUSIC WORKS PROJECT

BETWEEN 1938 AND 1939 folklorist Herbert Halpert traveled through the south-eastern states recording regular folks singing traditional songs from as early as they could remember. The mission was funded in part by the Works Progress Admin-istration (WPA) and Columbia University. Halpert set up his tape recorder and recorded Zora Neale Hurston, a brilliant novelist and folklorist in her own right, singing the work song "Mule on the Mount" among others at the Federal Music Project Office in Jacksonville, Florida, in 1939. Hurston eloquently told the backstory of the song and how there are endless verses, thirty or more that she knew of, that loosely made up the song.

Hurston delivered for the record all that is needed in the documentation of a work song. Mind you, it was not meant to be a commercial recording but a doc-ument. Hurston's voice was both sweet and sour. Sweet in the sense that it rode effortlessly atop the scenic melody, but sour because she was interpreting a work song sung under an overseer's duress. It was the type of song many song seekers believed were a precursor of the blues, but this is a false association. What it rep-resented was a romanticized notion of blues. According to Anglo historians, if blues is defined as sad, down in the dumps, they reasoned, then the poor workers singing such a miserable song must have really had the blues.

Negro subjects like Zora Neale Hurston created a complex dichotomy for subsequent folklorists such as Alan Lomax. Recordings such as Hurston's were not deemed to be authentically representative. One could easily conclude that folklorists viewed their Negro informants as inferior specimens.

Documenting traditional songs was commendable. However, folklorists and sociologists overstepped their mission when they held up those from the Negro community most wrought by the deprived vestiges of slavery as the authentic representative of the Negro race, and, conversely, tagged educated Negros as tar-nished by modernity and thus inauthentic. This is why the conflation of folk and blues was so harmful to the indigenous meaning of the blues, which was commer-cial popular music. If a blues song gained commercial radio play, it was tainted in the eyes of folk purists. One old-time hillbilly said to Herbert Halpert during a recording, "This younger generation, they want something quick and devilish." In the 1930s, blue entertainment—subversive music such as blues—was commonly associated with the devil. The old-timer continued, "Where we useta make these amusements for ourselves, now they pay somebody else to do it for 'em."

W. C. HANDY'S DECEPTIVE BLUES ANTHOLOGY

FOLLOWING THE 1925 PUBLICATION of Dorothy Scarborough's *On the Trail of Negro Folk-Songs,* and in particular the last chapter, "The 'Blues,'" W. C. Handy was seen by the academic community as the most prominent blues informant in America. Edward "Abbe" Niles, a White lawyer who wrote about Negro music as an avocation, became intrigued with the historiography of the blues. Abbe Niles had studied classical piano while in school in Connecticut before subsequently entering Harvard Law School. He had recently moved to New York City to join the Wall Street law firm of Cadwalader, Wickersham, and Taft in 1925. Niles, after reading Dorothy Scarborough's *On the Trail of Negro Folk-Songs,* contacted W. C. Handy to satisfy his growing curiosity about the blues idiom. He and Handy hit it off. In short order, a series of meetings and interviews took place between the two, resulting in the first attempt at a blues canon. The collection was titled *Blues: An Anthology* and published in 1926. In the forward of the book, Niles wrote:

> One evening in the spring of 1925 I set out to satisfy an old curiosity about the blues by calling on W. C. Handy at his publishing office on Broadway and harassing him with questions. . . . I hope that herein I have salvaged for Mr. Handy some of the time he obligingly lavished on my education. (The blues) is a subject as to which Handy remains the source and fountainhead of information, as he is of the larger part of the solid material of what follows.

Abbe Niles's forward of the collection all but acknowledged the *Anthology* was merely a veiled biography and songbook designed to promote W. C. Handy—its sole contributor and editor. Abbe Niles would later become Handy's attorney, and later, in 1941, his official biographer.

A notable difference between Handy's *Blues: An Anthology* published in 1926, and Handy's biography *Father of the Blues* published in 1941, was the former placed the birth of the blues in Memphis, seemingly to give significance to

Handy's "Memphis Blues," which he promoted erroneously as the first published blues song. The latter book claimed the Mississippi Delta as the origin.

The problem with Handy's claim was that by 1926 no Mississippi Delta blues musician had been recorded. Moreover, no blues songs from the Mississippi Delta appeared in Handy's *Anthology*. If Mississippi were the birthplace of the blues, as Handy claimed, shouldn't the first blues anthology have included Delta-derived songs by Delta blues musicians? No, because what we now call Mississippi Delta blues, that is, blues songs derived from Black sharecroppers and guitar pickers during the Depression era in the Mississippi Delta, didn't come into being until after those Delta musicians learned how to play the blues on guitar from studying phonograph recordings of New Orleans blues. According to the testimony of one of the first Delta blues guitarists to record, Mississippi John Hurt, guitar pioneer Alonzo "Lonnie" Johnson was his biggest influence.

Ironically, a song by New Orleans–born songwriter Spencer Williams (1889–1965) titled "Mississippi Delta Blues" was indeed included in W. C. Handy's blues anthology. Imagine that, even the first song titled "Mississippi Delta Blues" was actually written by a New Orleanian.

Spencer Williams was the composer of many classic blues recordings during the music's formative years. He was a nephew of popular bordello owner Lulu White, in whose Mahogany Hall he lived after the death of his mother.[145] Williams wrote the song "Mahogany Hall Stomp" about his auntie's place. It was later recorded by Louis Armstrong in 1929.

Other hit compositions by Spencer Williams included "I Ain't Got Nobody," "Royal Garden Blues," "Everybody Loves My Baby," and "Tishomingo Blues." His most enduring song, "Basin Street Blues," is one that I along with so many others have recorded, including Bing Crosby, Dean Martin, Sam Cooke, Miles Davis, Ella Fitzgerald, Dr. John, and of course, Louis Armstrong.

Williams's song "Mississippi Delta Blues" was first recorded by Bessie Brown on August 19, 1924, in New York City for Columbia Records. Bessie Brown was accompanied by Fletcher Henderson on piano and the great Coleman Hawkins on tenor saxophone.

If Abbe Niles truly wished to create an anthology on the blues or any subject with credibility, the first rule would have been to consult multiple informants and primary sources. Handy's *Anthology* was hardly comprehensive. Niles acknowledged in the introduction that Handy, who was also the editor, was "the larger part of the solid material of what follows."

References included in the book were *Slave Songs of the United States* (1867); *Introduction to St. Helena Island Spirituals* (1925); *Twenty-Four Negro Melodies* by Samuel Coleridge-Taylor (1904); *Famous Negro Spirituals* (1924); *The Book of American Negro Spirituals*, by James Weldon Johnson (1926); and last but not least *On the Trail of Negro Folk-Songs* (1925) by Dorothy Scarborough, the book in which Handy had recently affixed modern blues to "sorrow songs" of the enslaved.

It must have been blatantly obvious to New Orleans blues practitioners of the 1920s that the main purpose of the book was to exploit Handy's song catalog, which included his most popular hit, "St. Louis Blues." Many Louisiana blues pioneers openly questioned Handy's knowledge and musical talent. W. C. Handy could not improvise or play the blues as it was supposed to be played according to Jelly Roll Morton, who publicly challenged Handy's claim as the author of "St. Louis Blues." Another famous Louisiana musician questioned Handy's authorship of "St. Louis Blues": William Huddie "Lead Belly" Leadbetter. Lead Belly once said to recordist Alan Lomax in the introduction of one of his recordings of "Careless Love" that "St. Louis Blues" had been popular in Louisiana back when he was a little boy. Lead Belly was born in 1888 in Mooringsport, Louisiana. Lead Belly's claim is plausible because Handy didn't copyright "St. Louis Blues" until 1912. Lead Belly went on to say, with great skepticism and more than a hint of sarcasm, "When I moved up here to New York, I heard that Handy had written it."

Indeed, Handy added words to dozens of unclaimed songs, melodies, and couplets, and then copyrighted them as his own during a time when few Negro composers copyrighted their music. Yet he boldly claimed to have invented the blues. It is important to note here that to be influenced by the music of others is quite common. We are all influenced by the music we've heard. The main problem with W. C. Handy's claim is that he was the *inventor*; the "Father of the Blues." Therefore, if the songs were well established in the public domain around New Orleans before Handy copyrighted them, it makes his "Father of the Blues" claim fraudulent.

Nonetheless, the anthology was a compendium of fifty songs, including lead sheets arranged for piano and voice. In addition to Abbe Niles's contribution of extensive notes and a short biography of Handy, a third collaborator, Miguel Covarrubias, a bright young artist, drew illustrations.

Miguel Covarrubias was a twenty-two-year-old artist who had moved to Harlem less than two years earlier, in 1924, with a grant from the Mexican government. Born in Mexico City, Covarrubias was not fluent in English; nonetheless, the blues spoke to him. It wasn't long before he connected with Harlem scene makers Langston Hughes, Zora Neale Hurston, and socialite Carl Van Vechten, an influential White photographer and writer whose provocatively titled novel *Nigger Heaven* (1926) was said to be his love letter to Harlem. Miguel Covarrubias specialized in modern, smart, distinguished caricature. He contributed eight illustrations to Handy's book. His hand-drawn illustrations were a notable break from the grotesque "coon" caricatures Blacks often endured in popular advertisements in the 1920s. Miguel Covarrubias's art in *Blues Anthology* illuminated the optimistic spirit of blues with depictions of elegantly dressed Negro women and men dancing the night away in swanky Harlem nightclubs. His depictions of sharply dressed musicians playing drums, banjo, and trombone gave the impression blues was a modern cosmopolitan party, not a rustic plantation frolic.

Miguel Covarrubias's sophisticated subjects didn't jive with the down-home, rural, folksy, historiography Abbe Niles and Handy tried so desperately to weave. One is not convinced that the characters in Covarrubias's illustrations, emanating their cool pleasure, were swinging to rural plaintive songs of woe and want. Of the three contributors, Miguel Covarrubias's highly regarded illustrations best captured the glamor of the "Blues Age." Today, when one thinks of the "Blues Age," the idea of flappers, speakeasies, gaiety, and swinging music should come to mind. However, author F. Scott Fitzgerald, in his 1925 novel *The Great Gatsby*, coined the era the "Jazz Age" and it stuck.

There's no mention of Lonnie Johnson or King Oliver in Handy's *Blues Anthology*. Moreover, it's unforgivable that a cornet player such as Handy would produce an anthology in 1926 on the blues, then fail to devote a page or two to Louis Armstrong. There is also a glaring omission of rival composer Jelly Roll Morton's compositions such as "Jelly Roll Blues." Could it be the New Orleans blues was too wild and bawdy for the Victorian parlor market Handy's book was after? It's more likely, however, that Handy didn't want to share the spotlight with his rivals. There are brief mentions of Louisiana blues composer Spencer Williams. But Clarence Williams, a renowned blues composer, producer, pianist, and publisher, whose publishing offices were located in the same building as Handy's, does not have a single song in the so-called anthology.

Ironically, Handy and Niles included "The Schoolhouse Blues" by White Tin Pan Alley songwriter Irving Berlin, as well as "The Half of It, Dearie, Blues" by Ira Gershwin. And most conspicuously of all, Handy featured two symphonic blues songs by George Gershwin: "Concerto in F" and his masterful classic "Rhapsody in Blue."

To be clear, I have no issue with Handy's inclusion of George Gershwin's "Rhapsody in Blue." Gershwin's ambitious symphonic composition should be included in any blues anthology. Gershwin expertly adapted the rhythm and phrasing of the blues and added orchestrations and artful musical restraint. His restraint went against the blues' original idea of unique Creole expression, which discarded outdated tyrannical Anglo American aesthetics of musical art. Still, Gershwin was talented enough and sincere enough to not come off corny. He seemed to approach his subject, the blues, asking the question "what can I bring to you?" instead of "what can I steal from you?"

Indeed, Gershwin helped to expand the language and possibilities of the blues for Anglo audiences. "Rhapsody in Blue" is, for lack of a better term, "symphonic blues," so Handy and I agree, the blues can be sweetened for highbrow consumption while maintaining its emotional spirit.

What's more, I have always admired Gershwin's boldness and musical adventurism. However, I would argue, the blues didn't need Gershwin nor Paul Whiteman to become a civilizing force and America's classical music. The blues was an enlightened force from its inception. It was destined to become America's music regardless of White appropriation. Our music and its culture therewith was an unstoppable force in spite of segregation laws and subterfuge propagated by officials as a means to quarantine our subversive enlightened music before it could infect White youth.

"Rhapsody" helped set the stage for Duke Ellington, who was just as ambitious as Gershwin, to compose and record his own long-form blues orchestrations. George Gershwin's success also helped to open the door for numerous White practitioners, such as clarinetists and big band leaders Benny Goodman and Artie Shaw, who would swing the blues into the 1930s and 1940s.

Gershwin subsequently created a brilliant, albeit controversial, 1934 blues opera, *Porgy and Bess,* a Black Broadway musical with a libretto of Porgy, a disabled Black beggar living in the slums of Catfish Row in Charleston, South Carolina.[146] The most popular song in the opera, "Summertime," became a standard. It has been covered by hundreds of notable artists over the years. Perhaps the greatest testimony to Gershwin's sincerity is the fact that posthumously, per his wishes, his estate has never allowed his opus, *Porgy and Bess*, to be performed unless it featured a Black leading cast.

The *Anthology* was released in the midst of the Blues Craze and the burning debate surrounding it. Can or should Negro music become America's music? To make the blues more palatable for mainstream Victorian society, while at the same time attempting to reclaim it from White interloper Paul Whiteman (the self-proclaimed "King of Jazz"), Handy and Niles packaged the book in the guise of earnest rural Negro folk music stripped of all lewdness and Storyville New Orleans decadence. Handy envisioned the book—essentially his publishing catalog and biography—sitting atop pianos in middle-brow homes everywhere. The 1926 dust cover read:

Ever since the enormous vogue of the "St. Louis Blues," and the "Memphis Blues," still the most popular jazz pieces today, W. C. Handy, their composer, has taken his place as the Father of the Blues. His selection of over forty pieces, ranging from the early blues to the most popular jazz today, will necessarily find its place on the rack of every piano this year.

(The words *blues* and *jazz* were interchangeable in the 1920s, just as *rap* and *hip-hop* are today).

Except for a few mentions in the notes, New Orleans—where the blues had been verifiably ubiquitous for more than twenty-five years—was written out of Handy's blues narrative altogether.

The legacy of Handy's *Anthology* is problematic for folklorists and Blues Mafia brokers. "Rhapsody in Blue" tainted the collection for folklorists. It was omitted in subsequent revisions. As for Delta blues birthers, the fact that no Delta blues artist or composition was featured in the *Anthology* hurts their argument. The omission of Mississippi Delta compositions and performers was not due to any obfuscation. It was due to the fact that the anthology, published in 1926, was compiled and published before Mississippi Delta musicians had even begun to record the blues. It is comically ironic then, that W. C. Handy's seminal blues anthology, considered to be an important primary source for the theory that blues developed first in the Mississippi Delta, does the opposite. It provides us with further proof that the Mississippi Delta origination story was a fairy tale.

IT'S ALL ACADEMIC

THE DECEPTION OF W. C. HANDY'S 1926 *Blues Anthology* must be examined against the backdrop of his academic experiences. What in his educational background aligned his views of blues with that of sociologists and folklorists whose fascination with Negro primitivism dominated fieldwork? Where did W. C. Handy get such an ill-conceived notion to conflate cosmopolitan blues with downtrodden plantation songs? To uncover the motivation behind such brazen fairy tales, one must examine closely the early twentieth-century era of blues thought.

William Christopher Handy was born in Florence, Alabama, on November 16, 1873. He grew up in a middle-class home. His father and mother were educated. Handy said, "My mother admitted a fondness for the guitar, but she could not play it because the church put a taboo on such instruments."[147] His father, Charles Handy, was a minister of the AME chapel in Florence. Charles Handy didn't approve when W. C. bought his first cornet. When young Handy began lessons from its former owner, the reverend was dismayed. Handy's father believed, like many Anglo Americanized Negroes, that the instrument was a tool of the devil. Reverend Charles Handy expected his son to become a minister, a schoolteacher, or both. He didn't expect that after earning a teaching degree his son, who had a flair of sophistication about him, would become the trumpeter of a traveling minstrel troupe. Handy saw minstrelsy as the only way he could become a professional musician, but his father, along with many in the Negro community, saw the blackface minstrels as undignified "coon" entertainment. Indeed, it was the lowest epoch of American popular entertainment.

In 1896, W. C. Handy, who had been formally trained in religious a cappella choral music—singing without the accompaniment of instruments—during his eleven years at the Florence District School for Negroes, joined the Mahara Minstrels as a first cornetist. Before long, "he was appointed the director of the troupe's forty-two musicians. Minstrel shows were held in the evenings."[148] Mahara Minstrels were known to stage elaborate parades in their colorful uniforms through the center of small rural towns in which they were to perform in order to promote upcoming engagements. They would perform patriotic march tunes as they strutted down main street.

In 1900, Handy took a break from the minstrel tours in an attempt to earn a respectable living teaching. Shortly after returning home to his wife and young kids in Florence, Alabama, Handy was offered a low-wage teaching job at his alma mater, Teachers Agricultural and Mechanical University (now Alabama A&M). Teachers A&M president and founder, William Hooper Councill, who served as president from 1890 to 1909, had been born a slave in 1848. Councill was a conservative Democrat. The Democratic Party was home to Confederate veterans and the notorious Ku Klux Klan. The fact that Councill had to align himself with such racists politically is telling. Many other former slaves who became leaders and educators in the South after the failure of Reconstruction who were trying to fund and protect their Negro colleges in the late nineteenth century became staunch Democrats.

President Councill had hired Handy with the hope that he would help him emulate the success of Fisk University's Jubilee Singers. The songs of the Fisk Jubilee Singers—antebellum melodies of Negroes in bondage—were seen by Councill as music of edification for the race. The Fisk's choirs' national tours had raised thousands of dollars for Fisk University. However, the slave songs of sorrow, which may have nourished the soul and provided a flicker of light during a period when there was only darkness, should not be conflated with blues thought and music. Whereas blues was born out of humanistic agency and freedom of expression, enslaved human beings, to the contrary, could not freely express critical thought for fear of horrid retribution.

Handy was hired to teach choir. He was also expected to assist in weekly prayer services and lead Sunday school lessons along with other more menial tasks. Councill envisioned that Handy would develop a choir that could raise money for his university. In his 1941 biography, *Father of the Blues*, Handy said, "Councill's strategy was to show Southerners that the aim was not so much to lift the Negroes socially but to make better cooks, nursemaids, mechanics and share[cropping] farmers of them." Councill, like Booker T. Washington, a fellow Alabama educator, was not interested in liberal arts education for his students. Yet Councill and Washington were mentors of Handy and gave him encouragement to edify melodies of the enslaved.

There was a popular notion, which Councill shared with the powerful Booker T. Washington, that music was a tool through which formerly enslaved men and women had transcended what Councill and Washington supposed was their inferior moral and intellectual evolutionary state. Ironically, neither Booker T. Washington nor William Councill overtly expressed a similar thought about the evolutionary state of many post-Reconstruction Anglo-Saxon Protestant Democrats, whose violence, savagery, backwardness, and intellectual deficiencies were rampant.

Handy held ambitions to become a "cultivated musician of his race," but he had yet to find his musical calling. He had been inspired by Washington's desire to raise up a Negro composer, as Washington said, "To give permanence to the folk-songs of his people by giving them a new interpretation and an added dignity."[149] Handy dreamed of becoming that composer.

In 1903, William Christopher Handy, not contented with teaching school, moved to Clarksdale, Mississippi, to take a job as bandleader of the Knights of Pythias. During this time his orchestra was said to be the most popular Black orchestra in Mississippi. Handy's nine-member orchestra played schottisches, waltzes, and quadrilles for White audiences in a manner not much different from violinist Solomon Northup's description of his performances of schottisches and quadrilles as a slave musician in his popular antebellum narrative. In other words, Handy still played conventionally White dance tunes by the book without improvisation or bluing of notes, just as the Anglo audiences desired. In contrast, by the early nineteenth century popular New Orleans musicians had moved on from the restraints of schottisches and quadrilles as well as Anglicized songbooks for a funkier Creolized expression.

Handy and his orchestra often traveled the Yazoo on the Mississippi Valley Railroad, a newly completed railroad line known as the Yellow Dog. The line would transport Handy's orchestra to engagements throughout Mississippi. Handy recalled his first accidental encounter with what he later dubbed folk-blues in his 1926 *Blues: An Anthology*. Handy claimed the first time he heard a musician play in such a "weird" style was around 1903, while he waited in a Tutwiler train station for a train ride back to Clarksdale:

> A lean, loose-jointed Negro had commenced plunking a guitar beside me while I slept. His clothes were rags, his feet peeked out of his shoes. His face had on it some of the sadness of the ages. As he played, he pressed a knife on the strings of the guitar in a manner popularized by Hawaiian guitarists who used steel bars. The effect was unforgettable. His song, too, struck me instantly. Goin' where the Southern cross' the Dog, The singer repeated the line three times, accompanying himself on the guitar with the weirdest music I had ever heard.

W. C. Handy, who is said to have fancied himself the Black John Sousa, had highly trained ears and was an astute practitioner of march music. If the blues was popular in the Delta during his extended stay in Clarksdale as band director of the Knights of Pythias Fraternal Society—which took him and his nonet orchestra all around central Mississippi for performances—he should have heard the blues many places. It shouldn't have sounded "weird."

Furthermore, one would think that a few of the musicians in his nine-member orchestra—who were from the area—surely would have been familiar with the blues, perhaps playing the blues at sound checks if only to pass the time while warming up for a show. Moreover, they would've known someone who played blues on occasion in the area and shared that information with Handy. But no, to hear this stranger at the train station playing what Handy later deemed "the blues," was an epiphany—as if an angel was sent down to Handy with a guitar and a switchblade for a slide, to show him the way.

W. C. Handy's anecdote about the "loose-jointed Negro," and how rare it was for him to hear that sound in the Delta, if true, gives reliable witness to the fact that the blues did not exist in the Mississippi Delta frontier at the time, except for the occasional drifter or roustabout playing for coins at a random train station.

What is more, Handy didn't ask the musician if he was from Mississippi, Louisiana, or Arkansas. Neither did he inquire where he picked up the style. Who's to say the street performer wasn't from Louisiana or had visited South Louisiana, where he surely would've heard blues played around the clock? My best guess is the guitarist, if he existed at all, could have been a levee roustabout or day laborer from Louisiana who came into town to earn a few extra dollars busking. Because there were no phonographs of blues, the drifter would have to have had personal contact with a performing blues practitioner to pick up the new style.

Thus, the only place that could have happened was in Louisiana, or on the road, from a traveling New Orleans musician.

Enthusiasts have long romanticized that the "loose-jointed Negro" in Tutwiler was proof blues began in the Delta, with only dubious evidence and magical fairy tales for support. In contrast, there are hundreds of photographs of blues orchestras, along with living oral testimony, court records, and real-time newspaper accounts that prove the blues not only existed but was thriving in Louisiana during this period. Handy's serendipitous encounter, if true, only confirms blues did not exist in the Mississippi Delta in 1903 apart from the rare visit from an itinerant day laborer who happened to be a musician—if one believes Handy's Tutwiler antidote at all. In other words, Handy is a primary witness that in the Mississippi Delta there was no culture of blues, just a single unknown drifter with a guitar.

A clue to Handy's earliest brush with New Orleans musicians came around 1896 just as the blues was beginning to take shape in Louisiana. In 1957, in an interview about his career, he was asked, "'Mr. Handy, when you were a young man, did you hear anything about the New Orleans musicians that jazz historians are writing about today, such as Bunk Johnson and Buddy Bolden?' 'No,' Handy said, 'I didn't hear about them, but I had associations with others; my best trombone player was from there, and I carried New Orleans musicians with me when I had a band in 1896 and '97 all over the United States.'"[150] According to this interview, Handy could have first heard New Orleans style blue notes from his trombonist or other New Orleans musicians he played with.

Later, not long after that famous night in Tutwiler, W. C. Handy witnessed another performance that he claimed convinced him of the crossover commercial appeal of the blues. Handy and his orchestra shared the stage one night with a ragged rustic Negro string band consisting of mandolin, guitar, and bass. The string band led "by a long-legged chocolate boy," as Handy described him, began playing and shouting their lyrics with more vigor and rhythm than the train station guitar player he'd heard before. Handy was amazed to see the excited White folks throw money at the stage. "A rain of silver dollars began to fall around the outlandish, stomping feet" of the string band, Handy said in his autobiography. This convinced Handy of the crossover potential of adding similar elements to his repertoire.

After his brief stay in the Delta, he was recommended by Booker T. Washington for an orchestra director's gig in Memphis. Handy was hired in Memphis, Tennessee, as the music teacher for the Memphis fraternal chapter of Knights of Pythias marching band. Handy moved his family to Memphis to begin a new chapter on his musical journey. "In 1909, W. C. Handy wrote 'Mr. Crump' as a campaign song for political machine leader E. H. Crump. The song was later renamed 'The Memphis Blues.'"[151]

In 1912, three years after he composed it, W. C. Handy self-published "The Memphis Blues." Handy shrewdly advertised "The Memphis Blues" as the first blues published, but it wasn't. In 1908, four years earlier, a little-known Italian musician in New Orleans, Antonio Maggio, published a song he had copied from a local Black guitarist, "I Got the Blues."

In addition, Baby Seals, a Black vaudeville musician, wrote and published "Baby Seals Blues" in New Orleans in 1912 while living in the French Quarter and playing regularly at the local Iroquois Theater. According to digitized historical Black newspapers, blues songs were heard in southern vaudeville as early as 1910. More impetus was provided in 1912 when the repertoire was modestly expanded by the first burst of blues sheet music.[152]

Nevertheless, Handy's publication sold well in Memphis, introducing "blue notes" to piano-owning households in Tennessee and beyond. In 1914, Handy published "St. Louis Blues," which subsequently became one of the most recorded songs in popular music. Handy relocated to New York City and became an astute music publisher and self-promoter. W. C. Handy was not a blues musician per se—as a trumpeter he could not improvise like King Oliver and Louis Armstrong. Handy's greatest attribute was as a pioneering African American music publisher.

Until recently, researchers didn't know who the musicians were that night in Cleveland, Mississippi, who inspired the White audience to throw coins on stage. Moreover, what song they were playing that inspired W. C. Handy to want to become a blues composer was unknown.

A few years ago, a remarkable discovery of an early manuscript from Handy's 1941 autobiography exposed the real origin of his blues ideas. In it, Handy identified the leader of the trio—the "long-legged chocolate boy"—as Prince McCoy (1882–1968). Prince McCoy was originally from St. Joseph, Louisiana, but had been based in Greenville, Mississippi, at the time of Handy's enlightenment. The song McCoy was playing was "Winin' Boy Blues" by Jelly Roll Morton. Prince McCoy "later moved to Winston-Salem, North Carolina, where he died in 1968."[153]

In one draft of the manuscript, Handy wrote, "McCoy used to play a piece called I'm a Winding Ball [sic] and I Don't Deny My Name." "Windin' Ball" (aka "Winin' Boy Blues") was a well-known Jelly Roll Morton composition. Moreover, Winin' Boy was Jelly Roll Morton's nickname prior to his adopting Jelly Roll. By the time Handy's biography was published in 1941, the editors had removed McCoy's name along with the name of the song and the identity of Jelly Roll Morton, the song's composer, in order to protect Handy's carefully cultivated and profitable brand as "Father of the Blues." Furthermore, Stack Mangham, a clarinetist and one of Handy's musicians that night, "recalled that Handy's 'Memphis Blues,' also known as 'Mister Crump,' was the same thing we heard that night in Cleveland" from Prince McCoy.[154]

If this information had been known early in Handy's career, it would have elevated Jelly Roll Morton as the rightful Father of the Blues, or at least Handy's main inspiration. Moreover, it would have been an antidote pointing the way to Louisiana as the birthplace of the blues. Instead, Handy's self-aggrandizing obfuscation misdirected many researchers away from New Orleans to the Mississippi Delta on wild goose chases, seeking the "Holy Grail" of blues when all the while New Orleans was its birthplace.

Critics of Jelly Roll Morton's claim that he invented the music in 1902 argue he would've been twelve years old; therefore, he was too young to have conceived the blues. But many of those same critics have no problem accepting Mozart's musical genius as a child. Someone as profoundly gifted as Jelly Roll Morton would likely have expressed such genius at an early age. "A baptismal certificate issued in 1894 lists his date of birth as October 20, 1890"; however, Morton and his half sister said that September 20, 1885, was the correct date. Morton's "World War I draft registration card showed September 13, 1884," and finally, to confuse the matter further, "his California death certificate listed his birth as September 20, 1889."[155]

Regardless, at either twelve or seventeen, in the rich musical milieu of New Orleans in 1902, it's easy to believe he could have been that special one to first recognize and bring together the disparate elements that later became formularized as the blues. Both men were intellectuals, but unlike Handy, Morton had the talent at an early age to bring it all together musically by 1902.

My theory is that Jelly Roll Morton wrote his 1938 polemic in *Downbeat Magazine* calling out W. C. Handy as a fraud and choose 1902 as the year he invented the blues (the word jazz would come into being about fifteen years later) only to predate W. C. Handy's 1903 train station anecdote from his 1926 *Blues: An Anthology* so that he, Jelly Roll Morton, could reclaim what he believed was his rightful place in music history. Jelly Roll Morton once lamented, "Copyright doesn't always prove the rightful owner to a piece of music."[156]

At long last, over one hundred years later, the Mississippi Blues Trail Foundation erected a marker in Cleveland, Mississippi, to primarily commemorate Jelly Roll Morton's influence on W. C. Handy. It also credits Louisiana musician Prince McCoy as inspiration for W. C. Handy's "enlightenment." So, there you have it, William Christopher Handy appropriated Jelly Roll Morton's "Winin' Boy Blues" and denied his name.

Handy aspired to become one of the "talented tenths"; conversely, White society was more infatuated with the exotic, primitive, and thrillingly savage "submerged tenth." This dichotomy reveals Handy's true motivation and thought, which was to conflate folk with blues in his *Anthology*. Handy knew he could not convince Dorothy Scarborough nor Abbe Niles that he was anything other than a bourgeois middle-brow Negro. So, it is my conclusion that Handy developed the myth of the "loose-jointed Negro" to insert himself into the narrative to give himself "dirt road" primitive credibility. A closer examination of W. C. Handy's academic influences, far less dramatic or exotic, wouldn't have interested White folklorists and primitivists.

When Handy discovered New Orleans blues and its commercial appeal to White audiences, he attempted to tether the enlightened twentieth-century music to plantation melodies. He only knew the blues as a schoolteacher would know it—academically. Handy had not performed in honky-tonks and sporting houses in and around New Orleans or elsewhere. He was a polite society man. Nothing wrong with that, but Handy was beyond his depth. He had no real understanding of the complexities of Louisiana's long musical history. To be fair, there were no books for him to study on the subject during this time. There were plenty of Black New Orleans poems and music to study, but the history of Black Creole New Orleans had been written in French.

Nevertheless, Handy's biggest crime was the role he played as an accomplice in shackling New Orleans's liberating blues to Negro melodies of bondage. Booker T. Washington said, "One reason for publishing this slave music is, that it is rapidly passing away. It may be that this people which has developed such a wonderful musical sense in its degradation will, in its maturity, produce a composer who could bring a music of the future out of this music of the past."[157] Haunted by those words, Handy aspired to become that composer by usurping Jelly Roll Morton and New Orleans blues.

DR. HARRY OSTER AND THE LOUISIANA FOLKLIFE SOCIETY

By the 1960s, the rewriting of blues history was a cottage industry. White musicologists, folklorists, and academics rewrote blues history to advantage White imitators. Elvis Presley, Bob Dylan, Eric Clapton, and Mick Jagger, to name a few, could conspicuously flaunt their wealth yet retain their "authentic" credibility. In contrast, Black blues practitioners were expected to dress down and play up their early cotton plantation experiences in order to meet Anglo expectations and acceptance. The original New Orleans blues pioneers, poor bohemian urban dwellers from one of the most civilized cultures in the United States, were deliberately banished from the blues narrative.

In the 1950s, in this new revisionist reality with Louisiana's rich blues history scrubbed from popular memory, folklorist Dr. Harry Oster, an English professor at Louisiana State University from 1953 to 1964, and Richard Allen of Tulane University, created the Louisiana Folklore Society in 1956.

The continuum that should have linked the emerging 1950s commercial Baton Rouge blues scene to blues pioneers such as King Oliver, Jelly Roll Morton, Lonnie Johnson, Lead Belly, Papa Charlie Jackson, Clarence Williams, Louis Armstrong, Richard "Rabbit" Brown, Guitar Slim, William "Champion Jack" Dupree, Smiley Lewis, James Booker, Earl King, Fats Domino, and Professor Longhair was broken. Suddenly, according to musicologists and academics, Louisiana didn't have a blues history. Harry Oster decided to record what he deemed the founding roots of Louisiana blues using eugenic criteria and methods he had learned while at Harvard.

Born in Cambridge, Massachusetts, the epicenter of folk-blues primitivism, Oster first became interested in Yiddish folk songs before turning his attention to the blues. His Louisiana Folklore Society followed the pattern of John Lomax's Texas Folklore Society. He began collecting music of Acadians producing LPs of Cajun music, then got the notion to record "authentic" Negro blues similarly to John Lomax, whom he seemingly modeled his methodology after. Oster went on a quest to find and record a most "primitive" "savage" Negro songster. Where else could he find such a downtrodden Negro—shackled, chained, and caged like an antebellum slave—but in Metro Baton Rouge's notoriously harsh Angola Prison Farm.

In 1958, Dr. Harry Oster went to Angola to collect Negro "work songs"— songs that are vestiges of slavery. There, he discovered previously unrecorded guitarist Robert Pete Williams, a convicted murderer serving a life sentence.

Robert Pete Williams was born in 1914 just north of East Baton Rouge Parish in Zachary, Louisiana, to sharecropping parents on a plantation called Mr. Anderson's Place. Around 1928, young Robert Williams moved with his family to Scotlandville, Louisiana, a predominantly Negro community located in North Baton Rouge and home to Southern University. Pete Williams worked in the fields with his tenant farming parents as a young child. His first instrument was said to be a homemade cigar-box guitar he obtained in 1934. Pete played for parties around Zachary and Baton Rouge. But men like Pete didn't develop callused fingers from picking guitars; they had rough sandpaper callused hands from a life of hard labor.

In one of his last known interviews, Robert Pete Williams recalled the circumstances surrounding his murder conviction in 1956. Williams said he had to commit the act in self-defense, to defend his honor:

This wife I got here is my third wife. But all those others I had, they wanted that good time. I had this fall and I got in trouble and they send me up to Angola State Prison April 6, 1956. But I got out in three and a half years? Well, how did I get in this trouble? I used to take my family to the picture show. I let them see the show and I come back up to this place in Scotlandville, at Rally's, and sat down and drank a beer. But that night when I walked in there, there was two mens leaning upon the bar and one man was standing by the side of them. And when I walked in there, he said, "Hello Pete, how you doing." Well I know him, his name was Lee James. I said, "Well, hello Lee." But this big guy he raised up off the couch asked me, he said, "Where'd you come from?" Now I got to give you the story like it went. He said, "You a son-of-a-bitch!" Excuse me, na'. He put his finger on my nose. He says, "You better go back to Zachary and pick some mo' got damn cotton, 'cause you hang around here I will fuck you up!" Excuse me y'all, but that's what he said. You asked me for the story ain'tcha. And I looked up at him, I said, "Well I don't have that to do." And I walked off from him and I got me a table and I ordered me a quart of beer and they brought it. When I got up and started t'orward the door this guy seen me finna to get away from there and he made it to me, and he grabbed me! When he grabbed me with his left hand and come out his pocket with that knife. I got close to the door, but ah, the peoples blocked the door and I couldn't get out! When I saw that knife in his hand and I couldn't get out—'cause I look like this both sides—I shot this man above his navel. In that time, where I was living, you had to carry a gun or a cannon because the people would mess over you. Understand? And he didn't fall, he throwed his left hand upon the table and he grabbed here with the knife and all in his belly. When he went down, he straightened up but he still tried to get to me, and he fell on his face and I walked out the door.[158]

Dr. Harry Oster made Pete's first-ever recordings, including his most poignant song, "Talking Prison Blues," in Angola's tool room. The session was originally released on Oster's Louisiana Folklore Society label. The "Angola Prisoners Blues" album was later released in 1970, by Arhoolie Records.

When you hear "Talking Prison Blues" for the first time, you can just hear the first few seconds of Pete's earthy speaking voice, the sound of an open-tuned acoustic guitar, and think you are about to hear something similar to John Lomax's Angola recordings of Lead Belly: a conventional blues folk song that has been whipped into shape in front of crowds in sporting houses, honky-tonks, and on street corners. But after about thirty seconds in, as Pete starts talking about his late mother, you realize this is a man just speaking his aching soul, letting the words flow from his subconscious mind as he strums his guitar. And then, you begin to ache because the story and his voice are so real, too real in fact. You begin to understand the deep pain and torment he's in as he sings "sometimes, I feels like committing suicide."

You know this is a music that he feels deeply. This recording has nothing to do with radio or commercial recording. This is a musical document of a caged man who sees no way out. It brought tears to my eyes the first time I heard it because one's own humanity hates to see or hear someone suffer so. It doesn't have aspiration of bright lights in the big city. It's not the music of a rambling restless troubadour. It's not about all the women he's had or dreams of having. It's a lonesome isolated lament that has accepted the fact that he's doomed with one foot in the grave. His hurt is so deep, his voice tails at the end of a phrase, barely able to muster enough spirit to get the words out of his soul and into being. The mere fact that he can get the words out into the ether is a testament to the endurance of the Negro spirit in America since slavery. This is the kind of deep sorrowful song Frederick Douglass wrote about in his life story. It's truly the sound of the caged bird singing. "Talking Prison Blues" is a landmark recording of the Louisiana prison blues era. Robert Pete Williams fit the blues revival's primitivist fantasies perfectly.

Dr. Harry Oster sent Pete's recordings to Governor Earl Long and the parole board, accompanied by letters he had written, pleading for the governor to pardon Robert Pete Williams. The campaign was successful. Governor Earl Long pardoned Williams from a life sentence at Angola in 1958, but with a catch. Williams was required to complete a seven-year sentence of "indenture" on a nearby plantation. Consequently, upon Robert Pete Williams's release he was condemned to "servitude parole," a mandatory eighty long hours of difficult neo-slave labor per week to be served on a plantation in Denham Springs, Louisiana, without pay. Worst still, just like a slave, it was forbidden for him to leave the plantation. Pete was a twentieth-century slave, a seventeenth-century indentured servant, a serf.

His parole prevented him from travel, earning a living wage, or being hired to play his music. Williams did slip away occasionally to play with guitarist Willie B. Thomas, born 1894, and guitarist and fiddler Butch Cage, born 1912. They would gather at the home of Thomas in Zachary, Louisiana, on occasion. Folklorists recorded the sessions and released them on the Folk-Lyric label. Subsequently, the recordings were reissued on Arhoolie Records as *Country Negro Jam Session*. The sessions were lively Louisiana country blues performed in a relaxed setting. As a child, I attended similar jam sessions with my father and elder rustic blues musicians. And like Robert Pete Williams, I too would be recorded and introduced to the world by folk label Arhoolie Records.

Robert Pete Williams spent the next five years as a neo-slave in Denham Springs. Meanwhile, his prison recordings caught on with the Cambridge blues revival scene. Promoted by Dr. Harry Oster, Robert Pete Williams's music spread across the country and achieved favorable word-of-mouth reviews while he had been indentured and couldn't leave Louisiana.

Eventually, in 1964, Robert Pete Williams received a full pardon. Later that year, Williams performed outside Louisiana for the first time at the prestigious Newport Folk Festival sharing the bill with Bob Dylan and Johnny Cash, as well as Mississippi rediscoveries Skip James, Son House, and Mississippi John Hurt.

Williams went on to tour the United States and Europe. He remained active into the late 1970s. "Prisoner's Talking Blues" and "Pardon Denied Again" were his most requested songs. Williams's hypnotic blues sound gained devotees in West Africa, influencing Mali guitarist Ali Farka Toure among others. Robert Pete Williams died of heart disease in Rosedale, Louisiana, in 1980, at the age of sixty-six.

Dr. Harry Oster and Richard Allen's Louisiana Folklore Society went on to record and archive what they deemed the primitive origins of south Louisiana blues. They recorded blind guitarist Snooks Eaglin of New Orleans, Smoky Babe, Butch Cage, Clarence Edwards (one of my big influences), Hogman Maxey, Willie Thomas, and Guitar Welch for the Folk-Lyric label. Later, albums appeared on Prestige-Bluesville and Arhoolie, among others. Dr. Harry Oster left Louisiana State in the fall of 1964 to join the English department at the University of Iowa. There, he taught courses in bluegrass, jazz, blues, and folk tales until 1993. He died in 2001.

The problematic legacy of Dr. Harry Oster and the Louisiana Folklore Society is that it reimagined the blues of Louisiana as an offshoot of Mississippi Delta blues. The Baton Rouge region was effectively rebranded "Swamp Blues," a label none of us liked. Even though my dad, Tabby, wrote many songs featuring New Orleans Hoodoo imagery, played piano with the classic New Orleans triplet blues feel, and was influenced by Fats Domino and Professor Longhair—his guitar playing was styled on Lightnin' Slim. Dad and his Louisiana peers were cut-off, in the public psyche, dispossessed from the blues origins. During the folk revival, Louisiana blues practitioners were decontextualized and recast as virtual Mississippi Delta blues hacks.

For folk and blues revivalists, it was a deliberate pattern, the eschewing of New Orleans, a metropolis with a history of high art and culture, from the blues origin narrative. The implication being that sophistication, high civilization, and high art are exclusive European characteristics. Fact is the primogenitors of every instrument in the European classical orchestra originated in Africa. Thus, it was devastating for Black blues men and women when eugenics became the criteria for blues authenticity: slavery, chain gangs, downtroddeness, illiteracy, and Mississippi sharecropping. Reducing blues authenticity to "primitive" and "savage" allowed a White supremacist fairy tale to become reality.

Ostensibly incapable of intellectualism, our guitar licks, rhythm patterns, melodies, and poetry could be claimed as the intellectual property of others for perpetuity. Indeed, from the 1950s onward, the blues, my music and culture, was colonized, mined for gold and platinum records. Bluesmen were reduced to miners for the segregated multi-billion-dollar rock industry.

TOM WILSON REIMAGINES BOB DYLAN AND FOLK MUSIC

I WANTED TO BE AN ARTIST, not an artifact. I wanted to make albums that illuminated my full humanity. However, to do so I would have to battle my existential nemesis, the Blues Mafia, cultural brokers of "authentic" folk blues. But what is "authentic" folk blues? Dave Van Ronk, a key figure of the 1960s Greenwich Village folk scene, in his memoir *The Mayor of MacDougal Street*, defined it this way. "Folk [blues] songs are the musical expression of preliterate or illiterate communities and necessarily pass directly from singer to singer." Ronk's well-articulated definition of folk-blues as a crude primitivist ethos was a perception I wanted to shatter by exposing it as a cultural conspiracy that was destroying the true meaning of my music and culture therewith.

What would be authentic about my embracing the Blues Mafia and folk revivalists' eugenic criteria of illiteracy, poverty, and primitiveness as proof of authenticity? The whole reason I wanted a major record deal was aspirational. I wanted to transcend such deprivation. After the release of my major label debut, *Cry of the Prophets*, in 1990, I vowed my next album would embrace modernity, be a game changer. The problem remained: if I broke with tradition by dragging the blues kicking and screaming into the digital twenty-first century, I would be in the crosshairs of primitivists. Absolutely, I would be made to disappear, blackballed and banished from my own culture.

If there is any doubt about the dichotomy I faced; if one believes I was only paranoid or being pretentious; if one does not believe there was a primitivist folk doctrine that permeated popular culture and threatened my humanity, then I give you Bob Dylan at Newport 1965. Dylan's ostentatious choice to go electric was an earthshaking event. There should be no doubt, then, that as a favored folk-blues man, my iconoclastic philosophy was even more dangerous.

In 1963, Bob Dylan was on the cusp of becoming the folk movement's biggest star following the release of his sophomore album, *The Freewheelin' Bob Dylan*. He made his debut at the prestigious Newport Folk Festival organized by George Wein. Alan Lomax and folk legend Pete Seeger curated the Rhode Island festival. Dylan's debut engagement was greatly anticipated. He shared the stage with popular folk darling Joan Baez, and together they delivered.

"Blowing in the Wind," the opening track of *The Freewheelin' Bob Dylan*, quickly became one of the great anthems for the civil rights movement. The song is based on the slave song "No More Auction Block for Me, Many Thousands Gone," which had previously been recorded and performed by another rising folk star, Odetta, and prior to her, the great Paul Robeson.

Pete Seeger, a mentor to Dylan and many others in the folk movement, was a humble messenger and preservationist of the songs he sang. Seeger respectfully rewrote a line or two in a song if the line was crude or outdated. But Dylan rewrote such songs entirely, which was distasteful to the folkies who believed the song belonged to the village, not the individual. Writing new folk songs set to established melodies was virtually taboo at the time.

In 1961, after arriving in Greenwich Village, the center of the folk scene, Bob Dylan, born in Duluth, Minnesota, in 1941, quickly distinguished himself singing blues songs, slave songs, and ballads. His heroes were Lead Belly and Woody Guthrie. His early presentation was humble and conventional. In 1963, at the March on Washington, he'd sung on stage as an opening act for Martin Luther King Jr., where King gave his historic speech, "I Have a Dream." Dylan had been to the mountaintop and seemed to have a direct line to an enlightened source. The leaders of the folk movement put their faith in his apparent authenticity. Dylan espoused their virtues. His lyrics unambiguously rejected commercialism and the exploitation of the downtrodden.

However, an important person was tragically eschewed from Bob Dylan's story and folk music altogether. Behind Bob Dylan's meteoric rise was a producer extraordinaire, a visionary whose genius transformed music as we know it. "Without this producer, Bob Dylan would not have broken through like he did—effectively bringing on the swinging sixties and changing music forever."[159]

No, I'm not alluding to John Hammond, the legendary talent scout who signed Bob Dylan to Columbia Records. Indeed, the visionary producer behind Bob Dylan's success was Tom Wilson, a Black man.

Tom Wilson, born March 25, 1931, in Waco, Texas, ignited what became alternative or indie rock—but that was only one of Wilson's visionary feats. He guided Bob Dylan from an unplugged Woody Guthrie impersonator to become an impressionist poet for a generation, a rock star. Wilson also made stars out of Simon and Garfunkel, signed and championed Frank Zappa and the Mothers of Invention, and started an indie jazz label that launched the careers of Cecil Taylor, Sun Ra, and Odetta. If you've heard Dylan's "Like a Rolling Stone" and "Subterranean Homesick Blues," the Velvets' "Sunday Morning," Simon and Garfunkel's "The Sound of Silence," or visionary albums like the Mothers' kaleidoscopic head trip *Freak Out!* or Nico's gothic-cabaret jewel *Chelsea Girl*, you've heard just a sample of Wilson's work.

Tom Wilson, while attending Harvard, studied political science and economics. The handsome six-foot-four Wilson was into jazz. He joined the Harvard New Jazz Society. After graduating from Harvard cum laude in 1954, Wilson borrowed $900 and started his own label, Transition Records. His first investment was in an unknown folk singer, Odetta. Her first album, which Transition helped finance, was released on another label. He signed Donald Byrd, whom he recorded with pianist Horace Silver and drummer Art Blakey. He signed Sun Ra and recorded Sun Ra's first LP. Wilson also recorded free jazz pianist Cecil Taylor, and in 1956, he recorded a young John Coltrane. Tom Wilson joined the staff of United Artists before signing on as a producer for Columbia Records in 1962.

John Hammond had signed Bob Dylan in 1961 and had produced his first album, *Bob Dylan*. The album was a commercial flop. When the album failed to connect, Columbia executives began doubting Hammond's vision. Inside Columbia's corporate offices, the oddball new signee Bob Dylan became known as Hammond's "folly." Columbia didn't know what to do with the scruffy young troubadour who was trying to pass himself off as a hard-living, train-hopping hobo, essentially an itinerant Black bluesman from the South. Columbia assigned Tom Wilson to take the reins away from John Hammond Sr. and complete Dylan's second album, *The Freewheelin' Bob Dylan*. Though Tom Wilson was not credited as producer for *Freewheelin'*, it was well received, setting higher expectations for Dylan's follow-up.

Wilson, an intellectual who saw through the primitivist dogma of the folk revivalists, was the perfect producer for Bob Dylan in 1963. Wilson encouraged Dylan—to the chagrin of the folkies—to break with convention and broaden his prose. On their second album together, *The Times They Are A-Changin'*, the duo

Chris Thomas, as he was known then, performing for his mentor Uncle Don and his grandmother Mama Willie in her home in Baton Rouge, LA, December 1967. © *Chris Thomas King Tours, LLC*

Don Washington, the youngest brother of Tabby and uncle to Chris Thomas. Don Washington mentored Chris from the age of seven to become a cornetist and trumpeter. Photo taken while Don was stationed in Japan while serving in the Vietnam War, 1969. © *Chris Thomas King Tours, LLC*

Chris's older brother Tammy with his uncle Don Washington, youngest brother of Tabby. Don had just returned from the war, circa 1970. He gave Chris and Tammy horn lessons every weekend. *Courtesy Chris Thomas King Tours, LLC*

After Tabby's debut recording for Hollywood Records in San Francisco, CA, Tabby relocated home to Baton Rouge, LA, in the mid 1950s. *Photo by John H. Williams, © Chris Thomas King Tours, LLC*

Tabby Thomas back in Baton Rouge shortly after his California recording debut. The newspaper this ad ran in originally is unknown. The rare ad was found in the archive of Southern University. *Courtesy Chris Thomas King Tours, LLC*

The Arts and Humanities Council of Greater Baton Rouge

presents

A SATURDAY MORNING OF BLUES

with

HENRY GRAY	GUITAR KELLY
TABBY THOMAS	SILAS HOGAN
MOSES "WHISPERING" SMITH	

SATURDAY, JUNE 14TH
9 A.M. — 12 NOON

Lawn of the East Feliciana Parish Courthouse in Clinton

FREE ADMISSION

From Baton Rouge, take Plank Road to Clinton. Turn left on Hwy. 10 to the Courthouse.

Co-sponsored by the Louisiana Division
of the Arts and the Clinton Bank and
Trust Company.

June 14, 1977, flyer for the Arts and Humanities Council of Greater Baton Rouge's "A Saturday Morning of Blues" with Henry Gray, Tabby Thomas, Moses "Whispering" Smith, Guitar Kelly, and Silas Hogan. Photo shows Silas Hogan and Arthur "Guitar" Kelly. *Courtesy Chris Thomas King Tours, LLC*

June 14, 1977, (left to right) Moses "Whispering" Smith (harp), young Chris Thomas (sitting), Rockin' Tabby Thomas (piano). Standing behind Tabby in a hat is Arthur "Guitar" Kelly. Cameraman Jimmy Beyer was also the festival organizer for the Arts Council at the East Feliciana Parish courthouse in Clinton, LA. © *Chris Thomas King Tours, LLC*

Family trio onstage rehearsal circa 1979 at Tabby's Blues Box Baton Rouge, LA. Chris Thomas (bass), Tammy (drums), Rockin' Tabby Thomas (guitar). © *Chris Thomas King Tours, LLC*

Chris Thomas proves blues art form alive

By SONNY ALBARADO
Advocate staff writer

The tightly packed crowd around the stage caught the spark that leaped from Chris Thomas' searing guitar strings and ignited in a shout of affirmation.

Thomas, the young son of Baton Rouge blues guitarist Tabby Thomas, cranked up the volume on his solid body guitar and sang-spoke the opening words to "Mannish Boy" into the microphone.

The pounding bass line had the young/old, black/white audience at the Third Annual River City Blues Festival undulating like a pit full of vipers and feeling just as mean.

"I'm a man. You spell it M . . . A . . . N," Thomas growled as his father shouted encouragement to him from across the riser stage underneath the massive oak on the Old State Capitol grounds.

The crowd, which festival officials estimated at 2,000 to 3,000 at a time and 10,000 to 12,000 throughout the six-hour blues celebration, reacted as if Thomas' appearance was one of the more electrifying moments of the festival.

There were other bright moments — such as Silas Hogan's appearance with Tabby Thomas and Flo Lollis' vocals with Bo Melvin and the Nightshawks — but Chris Thomas forcefully demonstrated that the blues as an art form lives on as long as there are children who listen and learn.

"The blues is live, and it'll be here long after I'm gone," Tabby Thomas shouted to the appreciative audience when he took the stage after Henry Gray's houserockin' set with Moses 'Whisperin'' Smith and Arthur "Guitar" Kelly.

Smith, tall and sharply dressed in black pin-stripe suit and white open-necked

(See **BLUES**, Page 3-B)

After the festival was barred from the Bluff on HBCU Southern University's campus it drew more than twelve thousand integrated fans circa 1984 in downtown Baton Rouge at the Old State Capitol Grounds. It was "Mannish Boy" Chris Thomas's coming out party. Thomas "had the young/old, black/white audience . . . undulating like a pit full of vipers and feeling just as mean." *Courtesy Chris Thomas King Tours, LLC*

Group photo. circa 1980, Tampa Bay, Florida. (Left to right) Moses "Whispering" Smith (harp), Chris Thomas (guitar), Henry Gray (piano), Tammy Thomas (drums), Rockin' Tabby Thomas (guitar), Joe Hunter (bass), Lowell Folson (guitar). Chris would later play Folson in the movie *Ray*. Also pictured are the promoter and his family. © *Chris Thomas King Tours, LLC*

First solo release of Chris Thomas King, aka Chris Thomas: "Soon This Morn'nin Blues," recorded November 1984 at Reel to Reel Studio Baton Rouge, LA. Features Tammy (electric drums), Joe Hunter (bass), and Chris Thomas (guitar, vocal). The song was first released on Tabby's label, Blue Beat Records. *Courtesy Chris Thomas King Tours, LLC*

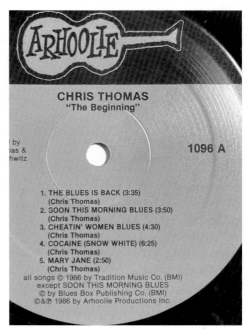

(Left to right) Joe Hunter (bass), Tammy Thomas (drums), and Chris Thomas standing in front of the original Tabby's Blues Box in 1984. We had put away our horns and band uniforms to embrace modern blues, electric guitars, and drums. © *Chris Thomas King Tours, LLC*

The A side of Chris Thomas's debut album on Arhoolie Records in 1986. Chris's original 1984 composition "Soon This Morn'nin Blues" is retitled "Soon This Morning Blues." The album was produced by young Chris Thomas and all instruments were performed by Chris except on two songs—rare for any recording artist, especially in blues. © *Chris Thomas King Tours, LLC*

Clifford Antone, Chris Thomas King, and Clifford's friend (name unknown). At Antone's Blues Club on Guadalupe Street, Austin, Texas, circa 1989. © *Chris Thomas King Tours, LLC*

Chris Thomas King at Lounge Ax in Chicago, IL, July 12, 1990, during the *Cry of the Prophets* tour. *Photo by Paul Natkin/Getty Images © 2019 Paul Natkin*

After returning from exile in Europe, Chris Thomas King in Los Angeles for a recording session. The long dreads show this is before filming *O Brother, Where Art Thou?* © *Chris Thomas King Tours, LLC*

Chris Thomas King on guitar, Graylon Neal drums. © *Chris Thomas King Tours, LLC*

Chris onstage a New Orleans's legendary Tipitina's live music club, 1990s. © *Chris Thomas King Tours, LLC*

Tabby Thomas, seated in his North Boulevard blues bar. The Blues Box played a large role in the Baton Rouge music scene. *Advocate*, March 13, 1994. *Photo by Philip Barr.* © *The Advocate*

Tabby's Blues Box Last Days, by *Advocate* staff photographer Jeff Adkins, on July 16, 1998. *Photo by Jeff Adkins 7/16/98 © The Advocate*

Chris Thomas King in New Orleans's French Quarter in front of Reverend Zombie's Voodoo Shop, with guitar, 2003. *Photo by Bob Compton, courtesy of Chris Thomas King Tours, LLC*

Chris Thomas King on the red carpet for the *Ray* premiere in Hollywood, October 19, 2004. © *Chris Thomas King Tours, LLC*

Chris Thomas King and Darryl White in New Orleans, LA. © *Chris Thomas King Tours, LLC*

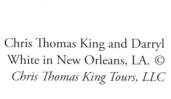

"A NEW ORLEANS LEGEND"

CHRIS THOMAS KING

"HIP-HOP BLUES" (STAR OF "O BROTHER, WHERE ART THOU?") "HIP-HOP BLUES"

PERFORMS LIVE @
VIRGIN MEGASTORE IN TIMES SQUARE
THURSDAY 6PM JUNE 24, 2004
With DJ SPIN

WEDNESDAY, JUNE 23 ROCKERFELLER PARK 7PM
THURSDAY, JUNE 24 BAM RHYTHM AND BLUES FESTIVAL - BROOKLYN 12:00 (NOON)

Down from the Mountain tour passes assigned to Chris Thomas King and Mariann Thomas. *Courtesy Chris Thomas King Tours, LLC*

21st Century Blues Records advertisement for King's *Dirty South Hip-Hop Blues* release. *Courtesy Chris Thomas King Tours, LLC*

Chris Thomas King as Blind Willie Johnson on the set of the movie *Soul of a Man*. Actress in the background is Monique Moss. *Courtesy Chris Thomas King Tours, LLC*

Chris Thomas King composing with guitar and piano at home. In the background are platinum records awarded to him. *O Brother* went on to sell more than ten million units in the United States alone. *Photo by Greg Miles, courtesy of Chris Thomas King Tours, LLC*

Chris Thomas King composing at his piano at home in Prairieville, LA, September 4, 2006. *Photo by Greg Miles, courtesy of Chris Thomas King Tours, LLC*

After his workshop on Delta blues, King discuss the origins of the blues with university students in West Africa, February 18, 2009. © *Chris Thomas King Tours, LLC*

King performs with Abuja student during a workshop on Delta blues Nigeria, West Africa. © *Chris Thomas King Tours, LLC*

Rockin' Tabby Thomas, recent stroke survivor, holds onto his son, Grammy-winner Chris Thomas King, as he takes his last stand on the stage of Blues Box (number two) on a Sunday morning, thanking musicians and patrons before playing his final song. *Advocate staff photo by Kerry Maloney 11/20/2004* © *The Advocate*

Rockin' Tabby Thomas waves good-bye for the last time to his devoted fans while leaving the stage of Blues Box (number two), thanking musicians and patrons before closing the door on an era. *Advocate staff photo by Kerry Maloney 11/20/2004 © The Advocate*

Buddy Guy, B. B. King, and Chris Thomas King during B. B. and Friends: An Intimate Concert and Dinner celebrating B. B. King's eightieth birthday in Los Angeles. *© 2005 John Heller/WireImage.com*

Chris with his longtime drummer, Jeff Mills, in concert in Greenville, SC, at the Handlebar, September 14, 2011. © *Gene Taylor*

struck gold. Building on their success Tom Wilson produced *Another Side of Bob Dylan* and *Bringing It All Back Home*, each album more popular than the last.

In two short years, Tom Wilson had helped Dylan find his voice and shed his beguiling hokum act that bordered on minstrelsy. As a Harvard educated Black man from the South, Tom Wilson could see through Dylan's bullshit tenant farm Black bluesman act, and in turn, Bob Dylan could bounce ideas off an unconventional Black intellectual. It can't be overstated: had Dylan been produced by Alan Lomax or any other folk purist, he wouldn't have broken the mold. His career may have traversed more conventionally like his contemporaries Dave Van Ronk, Jack Elliott, Erik Darling, Rolf Cahn, Eric Von Schmidt, and John Hammond Jr.

Yet, Bob Dylan wasn't the only artist Tom Wilson helped to find their voice and reach heights no one thought possible. In 1964 alone, Wilson not only produced two Bob Dylan albums, but also somehow found the time to produce the Clancy Brothers and folk legend Pete Seeger. Moreover, around this time, he produced Simon and Garfunkel's Columbia debut *Wednesday Morning, 3 A.M.*, a near a cappella album except for Paul Simon's soft accompanying acoustic guitar. The album included an acoustic version originally titled "The Sounds of Silence." The song and album found little success outside the small folk market. Having failed to find commercial success, Simon and Garfunkel went their separate ways. Garfunkel went back to school and Simon became an expatriate in England working the coffee house circuit around London.

Meanwhile, back in New York City, Tom Wilson, having never given up on "The Sounds of Silence," decided, on his own accord, to rearrange and record the song with a rhythm section of his choosing. Part of Wilson's genius was the foresight to add backing tracks to his original acoustic production of "The Sounds of Silence." By 1966, the "Sound of Silence," retitled without the *s*, was number one on the *Billboard* charts. The following year, in 1967, director Mike Nichols made the song the central theme of his groundbreaking 1967 film *The Graduate*. Simon and Garfunkel reconvened and became one of the biggest acts of the '60s.

Tom Wilson had a similar vision for Bob Dylan's next session; a bold vision that would be a game changer. Wilson hired musicians, reserved the studio, and prepared to record Dylan's next single, "Like a Rolling Stone." The accompaniment for "Like a Rolling Stone" also featured Tom Wilson's protege Al Kooper of the Blues Project on organ and Michael Bloomfield, a hotshot from the Paul Butterfield Blues Band, on electric guitar. In the summer of 1965, the snarling refrain "Like a Rolling Stone" was unleashed on the public. It became Tom Wilson and Bob Dylan's greatest recording, reaching number two on the *Billboard* chart—once a feat unthinkable for John Hammond's folly—making Bob Dylan an international star.

Indeed, Tom Wilson was a transformative figure during the folk revival. Why, then, has he been so conspicuously absent from its narrative? One must conclude that Tom Wilson, the Ivy League intellectual, didn't fit the primitive narrative reserved for Black folk and blues people during the revival. He never dumbed down his artistic vision or pretended to a claim of "authenticity"; he didn't have to. He was the producer, the executive behind the board of the most important folk hits of the era. He produced not only Dylan, Pete Seeger, the Clancy Brothers, and Simon and Garfunkel, but also Dion, Eric Burdon and the Animals, Nico, the Velvet Underground, Frank Zappa and the Mothers of Invention, Connie Francis, Soft Machine, Country Joe and the Fish, Al Kooper and the Blues Project, and Hugh Masekela, among others.

In an article in *Texas Monthly* published in 2014, Michael Hall wrote, "Tom Wilson made history. Modern music wouldn't be the same without him, and, a word to the Rock & Roll Hall of Fame, he deserves to be honored for that." But what was Tom Wilson's reward? He was made to disappear. He was eschewed from the Bob Dylan narrative and the narrative of folk music altogether. When Tom Wilson died on September 6, 1978, in Los Angeles, California, he was only forty-seven years old.

THE AUDACITY OF BOB DYLAN

Upon his arrival in Greenwich Village, Dylan realized that as Robert Zimmerman, an upper-middle class Jewish kid from Duluth, Minnesota, he would not be embraced as an authentic folk-bluesman. So, he lied about his past. He was astute enough to know that merely sounding folk was not enough: one had to *be* "folk."

Dylan became a convincing performance artist. He developed a minstrelsy act, on stage and off. "My son is a corporation and his public image is strictly an act," said his father, Abe Zimmerman, to a hometown reporter in 1963. That same year *Newsweek*, in an expository feature by reporter Andrea Svedburg, completely shattered his ruse of folk-blues authenticity:

> He has suffered; he has been hung up, man, without bread, without a chick, with twisted wires growing inside him. His audiences share his pain, and seem jealous because they grew up in conventional homes and conventional schools. The ironic thing is that Bob Dylan, too, grew up in a conventional home, and

went to conventional schools. He shrouds his past in contradictions, but he is the elder son of a Hibbing, Minn, appliance dealer named Abe Zimmerman. He attended Hibbing high school, and briefly the University of Minnesota.[160]

In fact, the artifice of Dylan's identity had been copied in part from Woody Guthrie's fictional 1943 autobiography, *Bound for Glory*, in which, ironically, Guthrie had largely expropriated his persona from John Steinbeck's 1939 Dust Bowl novel *The Grapes of Wrath*. Woody Guthrie's Okie hobo veneer as an agrarian troubadour of the folk was, to a large degree, a romanticized myth created by Guthrie to make himself an authentic folk hero.

Moreover, just as Dylan's big hit "Blowing in the Wind" had been lifted from the sentiment and melody of the slave song, "No More Auction Block for Me," so had Guthrie's biggest hit "This Land Is Your Land," which was copied from the Negro hymn "When the World's on Fire (Rock of Ages)."

The folkies had learned their rambling young freight train hopping hobo's backstory was pure fiction. For an embarrassed and cornered Bob Dylan, the jig was up. His brief authentic relationship with the folkies as a hard-living "Black" bluesman was nigh; he desperately needed to cross over to a less discerning listener, and he went for it. Dylan reinvented himself once again for a pop audience.

Bob Dylan was part of a new wave of White American musicians who, for the first time, had the audacity to promote themselves as blues musicians within the new folk aesthetic as blues was redefined by the Blues Mafia. They ostensibly rejected the over-commercialized genre of rock and roll, claiming it an exploitative and bastardization of "real" blues.

White musicians such as Dave Van Ronk, Bob Dylan, John Hammond Jr. (son of legendary Columbia producer John Hammond Sr.), Michael Bloomfield, Charlie Musselwhite, Elvin Bishop, Al Kooper of the Blues Project, and Paul Butterfield, who fronted the Paul Butterfield Blues Band, were all baby boomers looking for an outlet to express rejection of their parents' conventional "plastic" culture. Both John Hammond Jr. and Michael Bloomfield had grown up in wealthy homes, which should have made their "real" blues appropriations conspicuously suspect to folk-blues purists. Which proves, from the beginning, the Blues Mafia forced their most stringent primitive eugenic criteria for blues authenticity upon Black bluesmen, giving White blues appropriators room to become "serious artists."

Granted, in the early '60s, most White-led American blues bands were integrated. The Paul Butterfield Blues Band, who formed in Chicago in 1963, featured two Black Chicagoans, bassist Jerome Arnold and popular young drummer Sam Lay. Sam was a session drummer for Chess Records and played on recordings by Howlin' Wolf, Muddy Waters, and Little Walter. To boot, seasoned Black musicians helped steady the rhythm section while adding visible credibility to the experiment. Naturally, an integrated band was a positive sign. After all, integration promised Blacks and Whites could share common space on equal footing. It was possible that success of an integrated blues would make both Black and White bluesmen prosperous. Therefore, White boys audaciously marketing themselves as bluesmen was thought of as a positive sign for Black blues people. Moreover, the trend coincided with the Blues Mafia's "discovery" of Mississippi John Hurt, Skip James, and Son House, elder Delta bluesmen newly signed to contracts by young White northeastern cultural brokers and collectors. These were unsophisticated Black men, too afraid, from years of oppression, to question the motives of their White handlers who befriended them and gained their trust.

In 1964, at the Newport Folk Festival, they all convened: the Blues Mafia, White blues appropriators, folk purists, and the wide-eyed Delta bluesmen who had been collected as living primitive anthropological artifacts. Dylan sang the Tom Wilson–produced "All I Really Want to Do" at the Newport Folk Festival that year armed with only his guitar and mouth harp. The song was an existential treaty from White blues appropriators to Black blues people. "All I Really Want to Do," which opened the greatly anticipated album *Another Side of Bob Dylan*, was a clarion refrain of fellowship from the dominant class.

Bob Dylan's words echoed in the wind. The sentiment of brotherhood washed over the crowd that had come together as a utopian community to listen to their pied piper. They were Black and White, farmers and urbanites, beatniks and conservatives, Ivy League students and dropouts, Appalachians and business elites, all hanging on his every word as if he were a prophet for a new American ideal. The lyrics crystallized the folk movement's ideology. I interpret the prose of "All I Really Want to Do" as a covenant with blues people, or a kind of Ten Commandments for White blues appropriators, giving them graceful guidance for their interactions with the long maltreated Black blues people. When I hear this lyric, it is as if Dylan is singing directly to the descendants of the enslaved. He sang out—only as Bob Dylan could—that he neither wanted to usurp nor exploit blues people, all that he really wanted, was "just to be friends with you."

"All I Really Want to Do" was a resounding empathetic statement from the dominant culture to the downtrodden Negro. It was such sentiments that made Bob Dylan beloved by the White folk idealist. By 1964, Dylan was called the voice of a generation. He was a poet and a prophet. For a brief moment, while he enraptured his audience, there was bliss. But were the times really a-changing between White folkies and blues people? Was cultural colonialism a thing of the past? Could it be all the folk movement really wanted was friendship, nothing more? Indeed, the "Kumbaya" Dylan professed in "All I Really Want to Do," like nearly everything about Bob Dylan and the folk movement, was a lie.

A year later, when Bob Dylan returned to Newport in 1965 after the release of his opus "Like a Rolling Stone" (the last Dylan song produced by Tom Wilson), the air was thick with anticipation that something was about to blow. Indeed, the times were a-changing, and change was turbulent for America. The Vietnam War was expanding, and Malcolm X was assassinated; 1965 saw the horror of Bloody Sunday in Alabama and the unrest surrounding President Johnson's signing of the Voting Rights Act with Martin Luther King and other civil rights leaders in attendance at the White House, which made me, at the tender age of two, a full citizen of the United States. A change was in the air indeed. This land was my land and your land, from the smoldering ashes of the Watts riots in California to NASA's Gemini 3 space launch from Cape Canaveral, Florida. This land was, at long last, made for you and for me.

In the midst of revolution, on July 25, 1965, Bob Dylan returned to Newport, backed by members of the Paul Butterfield Blues Band. He took the stage and cranked out "I ain't gonna work on 'Maggie's Farm' no more." The electric roar of Michael Bloomfield's guitar punctuated by the thundering boom of Sam Lay's drums induced horror and confusion at the Newport Folk Festival. The ostentatious clamor of urbanized electric blues struck like a lightning bolt, shattering the very ethos of the folk movement. It was reported that folklorist Alan Lomax tried to pull the plug but was physically confronted by Dylan's burly manager Albert Grossman.

The fallout created a chasm between Dylan and his fanatics. In the liner notes of his first album for Columbia Records, Bob Dylan had been hyped as "One of the most compelling white blues singers ever recorded." Dylan had betrayed them by discarding his rustic veil and going electric. Now, he was deemed inauthentic, a trickster. He'd sold them out!

More profoundly, in the bigger picture, Dylan's electric blues performance had exposed the credulity and hypocrisy of the folk movement itself. The striking event was a precursor of things to come. White middle-class musicians quickly realized extraordinary wealth and fame awaited any White musicians who could rewrite and perform blues songs with an electric guitar and a rock and roll beat. White kids from Britain and Europe wanted in on it, too. Baby boomers across the United States began worshiping golden rock idols such as the Beatles and the Rolling Stones. Soon even Dylan himself was held up as a golden deity. The baby boomers' idolatry for expropriators, along with the expropriator's insatiable appetite for avarice, completely destroyed Dylan's covenant of brotherhood with the blues people. In fact, they would smash it up real good at the end of their concerts (see the Who) to the delight of their fanatics.

Sonny Boy Williamson was quoted saying, "Those boys in England want to play the blues so bad, and that's how they play 'em, so bad."[161] For a few years, White American blues bands featured one or two Black musicians, much like Dylan's backing band at Newport, which lent some sociological credibility. In contrast, British bands were Whiter, which gave them a marketing edge in a racist American market. These British imports set a new standard for Black music appropriation in America. They didn't possess the guilt and direct historical baggage of White American baby boomers. They didn't need to hide behind blackface nor stand on stage with Black performers for credibility. They took full advantage of the Jim Crow divide in the American music marketplace, which segregated Black blues musicians from any prosperity gained from the burgeoning White blues market that was relabeled "rock and roll."

Vicariously, through their White British blues heroes, a new generation of Anglo Americans became aware of the folk-blues, or what became known in the early '60s as Delta blues. Their parents had gotten the blues bug in the 1920s and '30s slumming in Chicago and Harlem speakeasies. In a like manner, baby boomers still preferred Black music performed by Whites. But a clear generational difference was that boomers were far less prudish. They preferred low-brow rock blues, not high-brow Victorian blues. They wanted it edgy and dirty. But most important, they wanted it *loud*.

3

MY MUSIC

EARLIEST MEMORIES

I WAS BORN ON OCTOBER 14, 1962, eighty miles upriver from New Orleans in the French-christened city Baton Rouge. My mother, Jocelyn Marie Johnson, a Creole, was born in the New Orleans Seventh Ward, the quintessential Creole section of the French Quarter and home to historically French-speaking free Creoles of color. My older brother and three older sisters were all born in New Orleans at the Charity Hospital. I was the first of my siblings to be born in Baton Rouge.

On the day my parents welcomed me into the world, frightening news broke of the Cuban Missile Crisis that threatened their very existence. A U-2 spy plane flying over Cuba discovered movement of Soviet Union nuclear missiles capable of reaching the United States. My parents, like the rest of America, feared we were on the brink of nuclear war. However, a few days later, President John F. Kennedy stared down Khrushchev and resolved the crisis.

Indeed, I grew up surrounded by chaos and social upheaval as Black Americans, during the 1960s, struggled for civil rights and integration. My parents protected us as best they could from crime and drugs—landmines imposed on our community by Jim Crow–era policies. Hopelessness, which destroyed many impoverished Black families, was not something Dad could afford with seven young children. Indeed, his music provided the glimmer of hope we desperately needed to get through some very tough times unbroken.

My earliest memories are lying on a bed sucking a bottle while staring up at the ceiling, watching a wandering fan on a great odyssey, spinning around and

183

around, but in the end, going nowhere. There are flashes of me lying between my dear mother, Jocelyn, a petite, soft-spoken woman, and my father, Ernest Joseph Thomas Sr., aka Tabby, a ruggedly built man with a deep, rich, comforting voice. Then I'm splashing around in the kitchen sink while Mother bathed me with a soapy sponge.

One night, my brother, Ernest "Tammy" Thomas Jr., five years older than I and with whom I shared a room, was spooked. Each night at bedtime our parents turned off all the lights. Tammy dreaded the dark. Mom and Dad entered our room and told us to go to sleep. They turned off the light and left the room, closing the door behind. Suddenly, out of the darkness, my brother began bellowing.

"Mama, Daddy, Mama, Daddy!" Our parents rushed in. Mom flicked on the light.

"What's going on in here?" she asked, anxiously.

"There's a man in the window!" Tammy said, his voice trembling.

Dad looked out the window. No one was there.

"Go to bed," Dad said.

Dad turned off the light and left the room. But no sooner had he disappeared.

"Daddy! Daddy!"

Dad rushed into our room again, ready for battle. This time, wielding a baseball bat. He flicked on the light. Trembling, my brother pointed at the window. Dad looked around for a culprit to no avail. This time, to reassure my brother there was nothing to fear, my father, like our guardian angel, remained in the room after switching off the light.

"Daddy, there!" Tammy clamored, pointing at the window.

There were two menacing eyes glaring in the dark, peering in the window. Dad turned on the light, calmly walked over, and removed a stuffed teddy bear from the windowsill. The teddy bear's eyes had been glowing in the dark, causing my brother's nightmare.

"Go to bed, you two." Dad sighed as he turned the light off for good, leaving us in the dark shadows of night. Darkness always frightened my brother. As for me, darkness, when the world was in slumber, became my proverbial playmate.

As early as age five, I discovered a temporary escape from my routine existence. I could amuse myself with vivid imaginary worlds. Even then, I could paint the drab canvas of my young life with innocent mischief and adventure. For hours each day I'd escape to a virtual world of my own creation. I'd imagine a secret kaleidoscope playground with valleys of purple flowers and Kool-Aid waterfalls. In my special world of make-believe, bugs could talk. Friendly talking worms and ladybugs were always ready to play with me there. There were laughing leaves on chocolate trees that tasted like cool peppermint ice cream. Grasshoppers and fireflies were modes of transportation. After playing and jumping in the imagined trampoline fields to near exhaustion, I'd flop to the ground to rest for a moment.

Mom and Dad would peep out into the backyard from behind our weather-battered screen door, anxiously checking on their bemused baby boy. Mom and Dad thought I was a most peculiar child, playing outside in the backyard, alone, for hours. I played in solitude, but I was never lonesome. I had half a dozen friends with unique personalities living in my head.

I liked to lay motionless, relaxing on my back in the tall grass. While gazing up in the clouds, my eyes would follow tiny golden raindrops as they fluttered down onto my face. I particularly loved playing in the rain. When a heavy storm would light up the skies, the old folks would say the booming thunder was the devil beating his wife because she'd burned the cornbread. The raindrops, they'd say, were her tears. As a child, I heard numerous superstitions of this sort. I guess the old folks had colorful imaginations, too.

My elders casually passed down stories of our family saga orally at family get-togethers and holidays. I have no systematic information as to where my family's lineage originated in Africa, neither whence they were stolen into American bondage nor when they first arrived in the New World from the continent of Africa or the Caribbean. Like most people of my generation whose forebears were enslaved, I felt helpless in the pursuit of such information. Birth records weren't kept. Families were sold apart; rebranded with the names of their new masters. This caused identity anxieties, unhappiness, and even self-doubt as I came of age desiring to know who am I, really? As I gradually learned to accept the things I couldn't control, I put it behind me, but those insecurities were always there in my subconscious, just waiting to be awakened.

My great-grandmother was Mary Candy. We called her Gram Mary. The ballad of my mother's side of the family begins with her. Mary Candy—maiden name unknown—was born 1870, in Sicily Island, Louisiana. Sicily Island is in Northeast Louisiana just across the river from Natchez, Mississippi, in Catahoula Parish. The United States calls its local governments *counties*, except Louisiana, which uses the anachronistic Catholic term *parish*, hence, Catahoula Parish. Louisiana's Catholic culture is distinctive. It sets us apart from the other forty-nine states.

In the aftermath of the Civil War, during Reconstruction, Gram Mary Candy, I was told, grew up farming on a plantation known by former slaves as the "Loveless Plantation," a fitting name for a vile antebellum stockade. In 1963, about a year after I was born, my parents moved from a tiny South Baton Rouge apartment at 755 South Seventeenth Street into Gram Mary Candy's narrow shotgun cottage at 1421 East Harrison Street in an area infamously known as the Bottom.

My earliest memories of Gram Mary Candy were the calming hymns and lullabies she'd sing to me as a child. Gram Mary was of dark hue. Her silvery locks illuminated the wisdom of her ninety-three years. She was self-reliant, beholden to no one. She'd farmed all her life, eventually managing several large White-owned gardens, from which she could sell a portion of the harvest for additional income.

There were fruit trees and a vegetable garden in our backyard. We also had a wooden chicken coop in which we raised a small flock of chickens, providing the family with unaffected eggs and meat. Observing the ritual of my father wringing a chicken's neck and my mother plucking the feathers set the stage for the sating feast to come. Gram Mary Candy tried to instill in my mother everything she knew about harvesting. But Mom was a Creole girl from cosmopolitan New Orleans, a young mother of the progressive 1960s. She was apathetic to Gram Mary's organic ways.

Though strong and independent her entire life, Gram Mary's health was failing. My parents were her caretakers. Eventually she needed help to stand, then help to sit, until finally she mostly stayed in bed. Mary Candy was ninety-eight years old when she finally gave up the ghost one sad morning in 1968. The week of her funeral is seared in my memory because it was a most grief-stricken week for my parents.

I was around seven years old when I began playing rhythm guitar professionally behind my father, Rockin' Tabby Thomas, "King of the Swamp Blues." By the time I was nine, I was touring as an act with my father, who, like an organ grinder, would present me as if I were his capuchin monkey sidekick. I was propped up on the bars of honky-tonks and country juke joints around South Louisiana and Mississippi, performing tricks with my guitar, gaining a reputation as a child prodigy while earning the miserly bluesman a hat full of tips. By the tender age of ten I was arrested for holding up a church and robbing a bank.

My pursuit of happiness by way of the blues has been like trying to get to Elysian Fields by taking a detour through Hades. I've been asked many times over the years, "What is the blues?" Ah, but that . . . that is the question! To answer this sphinx, one must understand how my music was conceived, as well as the inspiration that gave it life. Thus, before one can say what the betokening of my music is today, one must first understand that musical trends change like the seasons. The signification of words, along with musical expression, can take on a multitude of meanings over time. Today, for the uninitiated, it's nearly impossible to grasp the blues' true cultural relevance without the knowledge of why a people needed to invent the blues in the first place.

———

It was a rare icy winter night during the Mardi Gras season of 1972. We looked on in disbelief at the White folks gathered around a large cozy fireplace. What was supposed to be a backyard party had, due to a sudden freeze, hastily moved inside—but not us, the hired band. I was playing rhythm guitar with my dad, but I couldn't feel the strings. My fingers were numb from the cold. Dad was singing and playing lead guitar. Tammy, my older brother, was on drums. Moses "Whispering" Smith was on harp, and a White player (whose name I don't recall, so I'll refer to him as Jerry) sat in on bass. We finished an uninspired tune to no applause because no one was outside in the frigid backyard of the palatial manor to listen to us.

I stared beyond the row of tall white columns, gazing through the large French windows and doors at the moneyed social elites nestled inside the inviting chateau. It was located off Highland Road, one of Louisiana's most picturesque boulevards. They were eating, drinking, carelessly socializing. The degradation we were experiencing was plain to see, but they were oblivious to our humiliation.

"Tabby," Jerry said, "I'll sit the next one out. Be back in a few."

Jerry laid his bass guitar against his amp and went inside. I saw him welcomed. Someone handed Jerry a plate of hors d'oeuvres. He mingled and warmed up near the fireplace. I put down my guitar and started walking toward the house.

"Chris!" Dad yelled. "Boy, bring your ass back over here!"

"I'm hungry, too," I whimpered.

"Are you crazy?"

"I was just going to get a plate an' . . ."

"Those people in there talkin' 'bout money, son. And you ain't got none. If you ain't got no money, you just have to sit in the back and keep your mouth shut. You understand?"

"But Jerry went inside."

"A White man," Dad said, "can fly through the air and shit in a swinging jug!"

I was hurt, taken aback. It was the first time my dad made me painfully aware, in no uncertain terms, that I was second class. Moreover, that I was not welcome outside my caste nor my race.

By 1972, some progress had been made in the governmental sphere since the 1964 Civil Rights Act. But privately, the only way a colored man in the Deep

South could join the party was to earn enough wealth—but even then, he still wasn't White. But I was hardheaded. I'd known instinctively, even at a tender age, that I was not welcome, yet I was determined to break the rules.

I shrugged and strapped my guitar back on ready to tuff it through another song. As we got set to play another tune minus the bassist, Moses, shivering, pulled out a half pint of whiskey from his coat pocket and took a big swig.

"How much longer we got to play, Moses?" Dad said.

"Bout another two hours, Tabby," Moses said, checking his watch.

Dad glanced at the house of warm blissful faces, then turned miserably to us.

"Well," Dad insisted, "let's keep it going."

Patting his foot, Moses said, "A'one, two, three . . ."

He blew into his harp. Dad squeezed a few notes on his 335 Gibson. I strummed along on my imitation Stratocaster, and my brother kept time with a swampy backbeat. Moses sang an aching ballad by Dad's late friend Slim Harpo, "Raining in My Heart."

NOBODY EVER GAVE ME NOTHIN'

When my dad, Tabby, was a young teen in the 1940s, Baton Rouge was a pleasant place to live, but not for Blacks. The spiritedness of Creole subversion had long been suppressed and contained by Jim Crow. Tabby's generation was trapped beneath the ugly underbelly of White 1950s idealism. Purely White public swimming pools, parks, movie houses, and music venues were the norm. Newly built air-conditioned hotels and restaurant buildings along Main Street were decorated with WHITES ONLY entrance signs, welcoming newly affluent suburbanites. Harsh rationing of food and supplies due to the sacrifices of World War II were finally over. Hundreds of young servicemen had returned home to a thriving city with a new bustling downtown. The GI Bill of Rights signed into law in 1944 by Franklin D. Roosevelt lifted uneducated White veterans and their families out of squalor. The GI Bill, an extension of the New Deal, provided Whites with low-interest home and business loans and free college. In the peak year of 1947, veterans accounted for 49 percent of college admissions, effectively creating a White middle class.[1]

On the outskirts of Baton Rouge Parish, there were newly constructed subdivisions with manicured lawns in quiet, segregated neighborhoods. Modern appliances such as washing machines, vacuum cleaners, toaster ovens, and dishwashers were quintessential in subsidized suburbia. The most popular invention since the radio, the black-and-white television, a status symbol, was the centerpiece of enviable suburban homes. New pastel-colored Chevys and Fords carried White families through the streets of their new dreamland.

When Tabby came home from the service, he didn't receive the same uplift. In the segregated Jim Crow South, local White officials administered government programs like the GI Bill in the same way they administered the vote: with prejudice. Although Dad served honorably in the military, risking his life as a patriot for his country, he, like the overwhelming majority of Negro veterans around the country, was denied GI Bill benefits and guaranteed low-interest home loans. Moreover, because of governmental redlining policies, our neighborhood, like all Negro neighborhoods across America, didn't accrue equity at the rate of White neighborhoods.[2] Consequently, the chasm between White wealth and Black wealth, by the time I was born, was the corollary of Jim Crow governmental policies.

Dad often told me stories of his strict upbringing. As a child, he regularly attended Sunday school, and he sang in the church choir before getting bit by the blues bug in high school. "I used to sing at church," Dad told me. "My grandfather was a minister; he founded St. Luke"—St. Luke Baptist Church located at 240 Van Buren Street—"I used to sing in the junior choir there. My godfather's sister had a son, he was a paraplegic. He used to shine shoes up at Tick Tock record shop downtown on Third Street. He walked on crutches, but he could sing. His name was Alphonse King. Man, could he sing! I was a little young guy shining shoes, singing with him, and singing in the choir. So that's how I was able to get my voice trained."

Unlike me, Dad was quite the athlete. He boxed and played quarterback before jumping into the blues. Occasionally, I'd be with him when he bumped into one of his former teammates. They'd start reminiscing about those leather helmet days. He told me once that if he had it to do all over again, he'd be a male cheerleader on the sidelines picking up the girls, tossing them around, instead of getting sacked. Some mornings he could still feel every hit he'd ever taken.

He told me with more enthusiasm about his formal introduction to the blues and the arts. "During the time I was there, at McKinley," Dad said, "LSU brought a play over there, Shakespeare," he said blissfully. "I had never seen nothing like that. And man, I saw that, and it just inspired me. All the guys was going to their little sweet sixteen, they was talking to their girlfriend, in proper English, 'No, darling, please, let me carry this. No, darling, I will do it for you.' Man," he laughed, "everybody was gone! I just enjoyed the play. Then around 1947, they had a recording artist come to a school dance. His name was Roy Brown. He had a hot record out called 'Good Rockin' Tonight.' I had never seen no band, until he came up from New Orleans and played at McKinley with his band. There was something about what he did, I just loved it. And it stayed in the back of my mind," Dad said affectionately.

Roy Brown infected young Tabby with blues fever. Around 1947, jump blues, with its rockin' beat and gospel fervor, became the dominant form of Negro popular music. Roy Brown's 1947 rockin' blues hit "Good Rockin' Tonight" was later covered by Wynonie Harris, Elvis Presley, Ricky Nelson, Buddy Holly, and Pat Boone. It's a landmark New Orleans recording and one of the most import-ant blues songs in the development of early rock and roll. Dad, inspired by Roy Brown, vowed someday to give the rockin' blues style a try, professionally—even though he had no idea how or where to begin.

The sacred and profane joined forces in New Orleans and the blues was born again for a new generation. Blues' new euphemisms became rhythm and blues, rock and roll, and, later, soul. "Good Rockin' Tonight" "the song that made 'rockin'" hip vernacular, was recorded by Cosimo Matassa at his J&M studio located at 838 North Rampart Street. The rebirth recipe included a pinch of Jelly Roll's Spanish tinge (triplet piano fills), a big back beat, and a heavy infusion of Pentecostal fervor that both shocked and frightened suburban America.

In 1949, Fats Domino sat at Cosimo's piano and banged out "The Fat Man," the first of a string of lighthearted feel-good hits with his longtime producer and cowriter Dave Bartholomew. Fats was backed by Dave's handpicked band: the incomparable drummer Earl Palmer (credited with popularizing the rockin' back-beat), bassist Frank Fields, sax players Red Tyler and Lee Allen, Ernest McLean on guitar, and, occasionally, ivory specialists James Booker and Huey "Piano" Smith.

The wild sounds of devilment originating from J&M attracted flamboyant underground star in the making "Little" Richard Penniman. Little Richard, from Macon, Georgia, went around the chitlin circuit billing himself the new "King of the Blues," and some say, "the Queen, too." Richard was brash on stage, but during his debut recording session he was attempting to croon, subduing his flamboyance. It wasn't going well. So, Robert "Bumps" Blackwell, his cowriter and producer, paused the session. During the break, when Richard started bang-ing Cosimo's "piano, didididididididididididi . . . and starts to sing 'Awop-bop-a-loo-mop, a-good-goddamn—Tuitti Fruitti, good booty . . .' I said, 'Wow. That's what I want from you Richard. That's a hit!'"[3] Little Richard's outrageous *bleu* lyrics were cleaned up for his debut session by Dorothy LaBostrie, one of the many talented young songwriters hanging around J&M.

Roy Brown lit the fuse, Fats Domino took it to the top of the national charts, and Little Richard rocketed it out of New Orleans and into the homes of subur-ban America like Big Freedia bursting out of a 1950s debutante's cake!

To be sure, "it" was a mutation of blues fever that Tabby caught, for which there was no cure. Young Tabby was ready for some good rockin' (he later adopted the moniker Rockin' Tabby Thomas) but his pious mother and stepfather weren't having it.

Dad's mother, Mama Willie, was a preacher's daughter who conducted herself with reverence. Dad once confessed, "Mother was no angel when I was a young boy." On that frosty morning of his birth, January 5, 1929, his mother was unwed and only fifteen. She'd only known Tabby's biological father briefly. There were whispers he'd forced himself upon her.

"I was born out of wedlock. I ain't had no daddy," Dad often said. "Nobody ever gave me nothing but a hard way to go."

Tabby was in high school when Mama Willie married the deacon from her family's church, "Poppa" Gus Washington. She was reborn, giving her life to Jesus. Papa Gus, Tabby's stepfather, stood only about five foot six. Yet he loomed large over Tabby, a restless teen who yearned for something beyond his provincial milieu. As far as Papa Gus was concerned, blues practitioners were tempting agents of Satan. The two were at odds from the beginning.

Poppa Gus and Mama Willie had two sons of their own, Gus Washington Jr., born in 1945, and Donald "Ducky" Washington, the youngest, a trumpeter, born in 1947. They also took in a little girl, Woody Ann. Though Tabby was several years older, the siblings were close-knit. However, tension was building between the aspiring blues singer and his devout stepfather.

When Tabby played Mama Willie's old 78s, she would scold and punish him for listening to that "devil" music. She'd left that music behind when she got saved. By his senior year of high school, he'd bought records to study the popular styles of Big Joe Turner, Wynonie Harris, and Billy Eckstine.

After graduating, he briefly studied theology with the full encouragement—to put it mildly—of Mama Willie and Poppa Gus. Dad was urged to follow his grandfather's footsteps, to carry on the family church tradition. Indeed, my uncle Gus Jr. became a preacher in the family church. But Tabby had already caught blues fever. The time was approaching when young Tabby would have to choose between the "devil's" music and the church, like so many of his generation.

By the 1950s, the Southern Baptist Convention had so demonized the blues that singers such as Ray Charles, Sam Cooke, and Little Richard caught holy hell for mixing the profane and the sacred. By the time Ray Charles and Little Richard came to New Orleans to start their recording careers, the memory of the blues as proud Creole protest music that pushed back against WASP encroachment had largely faded. The culture was now raw mining material for gold records.

Gospel was injected into blues unapologetically by New Orleans singers. Lloyd Price hit number one on *Billboard* charts in 1952 for seven weeks with "Lawdy Miss Clawdy," a tune that follows the melody of the 1940 hit "Junkers Blues" (Junkie Blues) recorded by another New Orleanian, pianist Champion Jack Dupree. The sporting house anthem was the template for several New Orleans classics including "The Fat Man" by Fats Domino and "Tipitina's" by Professor Longhair.

Guitar Slim would top the charts in 1954 with "The Things I Used to Do," recorded at Cosimo's and arranged by a little-known blind pianist named Ray Charles, who happened to be living in New Orleans at the Dew Drop Inn in early 1953. The Dew Drop Club and Inn was where Blacks were free to let the good times roll. It had a flamboyant female impersonator emcee, the outrageous Patsy Vidalia, who would bring the entertainers on. Between the Dew Drop and Cosimo's studio, Creole blues was reborn.

Dad told me he had been offered "The Things I Used to Do" to record but turned it down, saying it wasn't in his style at the time. Ray Charles did the arrangements for Guitar Slim and accompanied him on piano. "The Things I Used to Do" sold more than a million copies. Ray Charles saw the light. He became iconic in the Black community with his hits "I Got a Woman" and "What'd I Say." From that point on blues with gospel fervor was his signature style.

The sacred and profane created dramatic tension in the new blues. It was exciting, raw material record executives had been looking for. Examining private letters from the period, it's clear the producers and musicians knew they were recording the blues. Robert "Bumps" Blackwell, Little Richard and Sam Cooke's producer, described the type of songs he was seeking for Sam Cooke's crossover from gospel to secular:

> We would like Pop tunes with a blues chord structure which lend themselves to blues backgrounds. . . . In writing the lyrics try to write "white" for the teen-age purchaser rather than "race" lyrics. It seems the white girls are buying the records these days.[4]

"It was in pursuit of that new audience that Bumps took Sam to New Orleans in December" 1956 to record his first secular recording "Wonderful" backed by Fats Domino's blues band.[5] So, let's be really clear. Commercial euphemisms *soul* or *rhythm and blues* were only marketing terms. Bumps's letter makes plain, just as King Oliver's personal letters had years before, that he was deliberately seeking blues songs to record.

The bitter generational divide in Black households didn't relent until around

1972 when Stevie Wonder, a genius songwriter able to change hearts and minds with his songs, released "Superstition." The refrain "superstition ain't the way" was ubiquitous on playgrounds, at school dances, and even at church picnics. The enlightened lyrics shamed many born-again Blacks, for fear of being seen as country and backward, into silence. Yet quietly, many continued to harbor Evangelical disdain and hatred toward blues and its practitioners.

Grounded as the city is in Voodoo spirituality, it's never been uncommon for the sacred and profane to party together in New Orleans. In Louisiana the blues was music of revelry. Tabby and his younger brother Gus, the preacher, made peace with their dissimilar callings and never looked back.

LONG ABOUT MIDNIGHT

To ease the household tension, Dad was urged by his mother to move to Detroit to stay with his aunt Laura. When Tabby moved to Detroit, like many southern Blacks before him, he believed he was heading to a promised land. Yet only a few years before Tabby left home, the city of Detroit had erupted with violence due to the growing presence of its newly exploding Black population.

In 1942, World War II production demands and the booming Ford Motor Company helped create the Great Migration. By the millions, southern Blacks and Appalachian Whites left the rural South for industrial employment opportunities in cities such as Chicago and Detroit. Rural tenant farm blues guitarists from Mississippi, such as Muddy Waters and John Lee Hooker, traded in their acoustic guitars for louder electric instruments that could be heard over the industrial noise of the city, establishing a bold, electrified brand of country fried blues.

By 1949, more than one-third of Detroit's municipal workers were Black. Recruiters would tour the South convincing Blacks, and poor Whites, to head north with promises of higher wages in newly opened factories. Negros arrived in such numbers that it was impossible to house them all because there was a shortage of "Negro Only" buildings.

Contrary to popular memory, nearly all housing projects were originally built for "White Only" families as part of Roosevelt's New Deal. Only a select few were set aside for Blacks.[6] Black families arriving to Chicago and Detroit had to double and triple up in the few project buildings set aside for them. Though many Blacks could have afforded to pay rent in segregated White buildings—they were making good money on assembly lines, in the steel mills—they were instead forced into overcrowded buildings whose conditions quickly deteriorated into slums. Northern bigotry was every bit as pervasive and malevolent as what they'd left behind in the Jim Crow South. Whites soon grew resentful working and living next to Blacks, causing many stoppages and slowdowns until cities eventually boiled over into deadly race riots.

In 1949, when Tabby arrived, Detroit was reeling. He moved in with Aunt Laura, who lived in the Brewster-Douglass Housing Projects. The tenement was also home to eventual Motown stars Smokey Robinson, Diana Ross, Mary Wilson, and Florence Ballard. Dad had trouble finding work. He didn't want to return home on a bus only carrying the tattered bags he'd left home with. He wanted to return with a sense of accomplishment, or at least in a nice Detroit automobile. He started frequenting the Brewster Center gym, working out and sparring with amateur boxers who were in an organized league for pocket change. A trainer noticed him sparring and saw some potential. The trainer asked if Tabby wanted to join the boxing team. Dad began training earnestly. There was an upcoming match arranged and they wanted Dad to go. "I enjoyed going down there and working out with the guys," Dad later told me. "But in the end, I decided I wasn't gon' mess with that."

Later, Tabby started hanging around the blues clubs and saloons on Hastings Street, the heart of Detroit's Eastside Black entertainment district. John Lee Hooker was part of an emergent blues scene on Hastings. Hooker was a popular postwar blues singer, guitarist, and songwriter from Mississippi. His stepfather, a blues guitarist from Shreveport, Louisiana, influenced him to play a unique open-tuned one-chord modal blues that didn't use the typical I, IV, V chord progression his 1948 hit "Boogie Chillun'" was based on. Dad studied Hooker but hadn't found his voice or a way into the business.

One day he noticed a billboard near the projects, JOIN THE AIR FORCE. In 1948, President Truman abolished segregation in the armed forces. Tabby decided to go down to the recruiting station to see what the air force was all about. An athletic nineteen-year-old, he had no problem passing the physical. They signed him up and sent him to basic training in San Antonio before shipping him overseas to Guam. Dad sent his mother seventy-dollar allotments each month to help out back home.

After a few years in Guam, he was honorably discharged from the air force near San Francisco. "I had a little job at a shoe store called Wrigley Shoes on Market Street. I'd go down there and wash the windows, vacuum the floor, stock the new shoes on racks," he told me. In San Francisco, he was on his own for the first time without any rigid supervision. Sometimes, he and his buddies would get together for beach parties. At the beach they'd sing, drink wine, and flirt with girls, just having an all-around fun time. The boys knew my dad had a good voice, so they egged him on to sing along with songs they heard on the portable radio. This helped them attract female admirers. It also helped Tabby gain confidence in his vocal abilities. One night at a bowling alley, a guy said, "Tabby, there's going to be a big talent show, why don't you go over there, man, and try out?"

That Sunday morning, around 10:00 AM, he went to an audition for the big talent show to be held that Monday night. Dad was there along with several contestants. He was checking everything out when he recognized the voice of the guy who was judging the tryouts. It was the popular disc jockey from KSAN AM radio station. KSAN were pioneers in broadcasting to the Black community in the Bay Area. The disc jockey was sitting at a table with the show's producer and the band director. Dad was hesitant, aloof, hanging around in the background, checking out the other contestants, measuring their abilities to his. The jockey was hostile and arrogant, cutting the contestants off before they finished their songs if he didn't like what he heard. Tabby was contemplating whether he should go through with the audition or leave and save himself the humiliation of rejection.

"Hey," the jockey asked Tabby, "what you want?"

"I just came by to see about this talent show," Dad said, nervously.

"You sing?"

"Well, uh, I try to."

"Come on over here, let me see what you can do."

His eyes followed Tabby restlessly as he walked over and stood in front of the panel. Tabby hesitated. He stared nervously.

"Well, don't just stand there boy, sing something," the jockey said.

Dad closed his eyes and sang a Roy Brown ballad, "Long About Midnight" with fervor and conviction. Dad finished the song and opened his eyes. "You're on the show tomorrow night," the jockey said, with an approving smile.

The big talent show was held at the Opera House, an aged building with balconies and red velvet seats. Lots of celebrities were there, even the comedian Red Skelton. Every seat was filled with anticipation. Etta James, an angel-voiced biracial teen, was on the show. Etta was chaperoned by her mother backstage. Each time Dad would recount this seminal event to me, he would always speak fondly of Etta. "Etta James was a beautiful young lady," Dad would often say. "She was around sixteen, seventeen, and her mom saw us talking and said, 'Etta, you come on back over here, stop talking to that boy!'" Dad said he and Etta began an admiration for each other's singing abilities that night and a friendship that lasted for years.

Another participant was Johnny Mathis, a handsomely dressed classically trained vocalist. Mathis sang with perfect diction and precise phrasing. People clapped for him so enthusiastically after he finished his song that it made Tabby feel a little nervous backstage knowing he'd have to come up behind the suave singer. The emcee called young Tabby out on stage and he sang "Long About Midnight" with the same fervor and conviction he'd shown in the audition, but there was an added depth to his singing that gave his baritone vibrato a spiritual sensibility—harkening back to the soulful voices of his family's church. He sang with just the right balance of joy and heartache to touch the audience's emotions. They clapped for him just as much as they had for Johnny Mathis.

"Looks like we got a tie!" the emcee said.

The adulation felt good to young Tabby. It inspired him. He and Johnny were invited to stand center stage with the emcee.

"I'm going to put my hand over each one of them," the emcee announced to the jubilant crowd. "And when I do, applaud for the winner!"

He put his hand over Johnny. The audience clapped and cheered loudly.

"Well, I guess he's going to win it," Dad whispered to himself.

The emcee put his hand over young Tabby. The audience stomped and clapped even louder! Dad won first prize, fifteen dollars. Tabby and his boys bought wine with the prize money and went to the beach to celebrate.

Tabby was now smitten with show business. He was ready to make a serious move as a recording artist. Johnny Mathis went on to become a major success as a crooner for Columbia Records. Etta James went on to have major success recording for Chicago's Chess Records, her most popular recording being the timeless ballad "At Last."

Dad heard about a recording studio. It happened to be right around the corner from his job near the St. Francis Drake Hotel on Geary Street. One day on his lunch hour, he went there to see if he could make a record. The studio was up a narrow flight of stairs. Tabby reached the top of the stairs and entered the office. "Can I help you?" the secretary asked. "I just come up here to look," Dad said, glancing over her shoulder into a big glass window.

The secretary allowed him to take a closer look. His eyes popped as he wandered the hall to the studio, checking out the gold records hanging on the walls along with glossy publicity photos of the artists who recorded them. He noticed a buttoned-up professional engineer behind a mixing desk in a smoky adjacent room. In the main room he marveled at instruments, microphones, cables, and wires, strategically placed to capture the musicians as they busily recorded a song. A big red light on the wall was flashing, indicating the band was in session. He walked up to the big glass window to get a closer look. The drummer, recognizing Tabby gazing in, stopped the music. He whispered something to Ollie Hunt, the producer of the session, pointing Tabby out to him. Ollie Hunt was a well-known veteran record producer in the Bay Area. Ollie approached Dad, opening the door to the recording room.

"So," Ollie said, "they tell me you sing."

"Yes, sir," Tabby said.

"Come on in here."

"Crow," Ollie said, to the piano player, "write something for him."

Crow wrote some lyrics and put them on the music stand for Tabby. The engineer set up a large ribbon microphone, perfectly adjusting it to capture Tabby's voice.

"Sing, sing these words, here," Ollie said.

"Midnight is calling, and I don't know what to do," Tabby sang, with great feeling.

"Let's cut it!" Ollie yelled, excitedly.

Tabby cut his first record on his lunch hour. "Midnight Is Calling" was released on Hollywood Records out of Los Angeles. "Man, when my record came out, it was all over 'Frisco, every jukebox had it. So that's how I got to making records," he told me.

Tabby went down to Los Angeles to promote the record. He made a stop at a popular record shop, Dolphin's of Hollywood on East Vernon Avenue near the corner of Central Avenue. Dolphin's was a gathering spot for teen hipsters, scene makers, and music fanatics. It featured a disc jockey broadcasting live inside the store over local station KRKD. The store attracted mobs of kids for record signings by their favorite artists.

On the day Tabby arrived, shining shoes in the record shop was a tough husky girl named Willie Mae Thornton. Willie Mae was an aspiring singer who eventually had a huge hit with "Hound Dog" (a song Elvis Presley famously covered) under the pseudonym "Big Mama Thornton." John Dolphin, the owner, also owned the label Hollywood Records. The label had released Dad's single, "Midnight Is Calling." Tabby did a radio promotion from the store with the disc jockey and autographed records for fans. He played a few small promotional gigs in South Central along Crenshaw Boulevard before returning to San Francisco. He had quit his shoe store job to promote his debut record. Tabby's song, however, wasn't popular enough to sustain him as a full-time singer. He was feeling a little homesick and decided to return to Louisiana. Tabby told John Dolphin he was going back to Louisiana, and John told him, "When you get to New Orleans, go by the radio station and see a DJ down there by the name of Okey Dokey."

Tabby bought a one-way train ticket on the Sunset Limited and returned to Louisiana. When Dad got off the train one morning around six o'clock in New Orleans, he taxied straight to WBOK Radio to meet Okey Dokey. People in

Baton Rouge would listen to WBOK broadcasting from New Orleans because there were no Black-oriented radio stations or Black disc jockeys in Baton Rouge. Dad said to Okey Dokey, "John Dolphin told me to come by and see you." Okey Dokey greeted him and played his record on the air. The DJ interviewed Tabby live. His voice went out over the airwaves to all South Louisiana, reaching Baton Rouge and beyond. A lady friend of Dad's mother was listening and called her, alerting Mama Willie that her boy was in New Orleans and on his way home. "Mama hadn't seen me for three or four years," Dad told me. "And man, when I rolled up in front of my house in a taxi, she comes out there hollering and screaming. Saw my mama hollering and crying, she didn't know what had happened."

Dad had his hair processed, looking just like the handsomely polished recording artists on Hollywood Records promotional photos that appeared in trade magazines. Lots of family and friends had gathered to welcome the air force veteran and recording star home. Dad had a box of records with him and he gave everyone a copy. His mom and stepfather eased their churchly ways for a night, allowing Dad's new record to be played in the house, over and over and over again.

Tabby later married and began raising a family. All the while he performed regionally between day jobs. During a regular engagement at the Dew Drop Inn Louis Armstrong happened to be in the club. Armstrong made a call, setting Dad up with Eric Shaw, a booking agent. The Eric Shaw agency started booking Tabby all over Texas and Arkansas. His biggest hit came when his neighbor, harmonica ace and popular recording artist Slim Harpo, introduced him to producer J. D. Miller, who had taken the Louisiana blues torch from Cosimo Matassa. Tabby recorded "Hoodoo Party," his biggest hit, in Miller's Crowley, Louisiana, studio in 1961. Released internationally on Excello Records, "Hoodoo Party" became his signature song. Though Tabby continued to record for various labels with mixed success, his most endearing impact would be as a live performer.

SCHOOL, CORNETS, AND GUITARS

The thought of the inferiority of the Negro is drilled into him in almost every [classroom] he enters and in almost every book he studies. If he happens to leave school after he masters the fundamentals, before he finishes high school or reaches college, he will naturally escape some of this bias and may recover in time to be of service to his people.

—Carter G. Woodson, *The Mis-education of the Negro*

GROWING UP IN A HOUSE with five sisters wasn't easy. I grew up with three older sisters, Yolanda Ann, Michelle Rose, and Joylyn Marie, along with two younger sisters, Jenean Isabelle, and Charlette Blanche. Tammy, my older brother, played the trombone in McKinley's marching band, which was funny, because Tammy had no front teeth. How he got his lips to buzz pressed against the mouthpiece without front teeth for support I couldn't tell you, but he did. Soon, I too wanted to play a horn.

Donald Washington, Dad's youngest brother, born in 1947, spent a lot of time at our house babysitting while our parents worked. Don was always enjoyable to be around. He was like a big kid himself, very playful. But when pushed, Don wouldn't hesitate to discipline us. Not physically, mind you, but in time-out. We couldn't partake in the games and fun until we learned our lesson.

The first instrument I was formally introduced to, the cornet trumpet, was the original lead instrument of the blues. In the 1890s, when all musical instruments were still acoustic—decades before the powerful electric guitar—the blaring cornet soared over the ambient noise of honky-tonk dancers and gamblers. The cornet's high notes could travel for miles in the stark quiet night of old gas-lamps, horses, and buggies. Before the advent of dense urban industrial noise, the cornet-trumpet was the tonal identifier of the band. The best cornetists, and later, the best trumpeters, had special leadership status by default.

Uncle Don played trumpet in the marching band at McKinley Senior High. He was a very talented musician. Upon graduation Don was offered a music scholarship to Florida A&M—a historically Black college with a dynamic marching band. However, Don's father, my dad's stepfather, Papa Gus, the deacon, had recently passed away. Don's mother, my grandmother, naturally wanted her baby boy to go to a nearby school. Mama Willie influenced Don to turn down the Florida scholarship and stay close to home. So, Don enrolled in nearby Southern University, also a historically Black college with a marching band on par with rival Florida A&M. However, Don was drafted into Vietnam before he could finish college. Nonetheless, he served proudly. While stationed in Japan he joined the military brass band.

Whenever I was dropped off at my grandmother's house—she would often babysit me while both my parents worked—I couldn't help but notice Mama Willie's mantel. It was adorned with pictures of Uncle Don in his military uniform posed with his trumpet. Flanked by an American flag, he looked sharp in his military attire. I wanted to follow in Don's footsteps. When he was released after serving during the Vietnam War, around 1969, I was in maybe first or second grade.

After Don returned home, he purchased a Volkswagen Beatle. A German economy car, best known in America as the "Love Bug" due to the Hollywood movie series, the Beatle was popular among college kids and hippies alike. It was an eye-catcher. It must have been a real girl magnet, too.

I was really excited the day I learned Don had brought home a present for me: a gold-colored cornet he had purchased in a pawnshop while in Osaka, Japan. I took to it right away. It made the most horrible noise, irritating everyone around me. I loved it!

Don commenced to dropping by each Saturday afternoon and picking up my brother and I for music lessons. Riding in his cool hippie love bug was a special treat. Don had moved back in with his mother upon his return. Mama Willie's health was beginning to fail, so Don looked after her. Don and his mother were very close.

Mama Willie would often make a big pot of red beans when she knew we were coming. Her secret ingredient—I didn't figure out until years later—was a pinch of brown sugar. We'd study music all evening in the back room of Mama Willie's house using Don's collection of music books and recordings he had accumulated over the years. Mama Willie's stance against the blues had softened since my dad, as a teenager, had been beaten over the head with a broom or shoe for listening to that "devil's music." Perhaps it had become more mainstream with the success of gospel-tinged melodies by Guitar Slim, Ray Charles, and Sam Cooke. Or maybe it was the late Papa Gus who had been most repulsed by the blues. My suspicion is that her youngest son, Donald "Ducky" Washington, could do no wrong in her eyes.

Uncle Don had an extensive collection of LPs. He encouraged me to go through his records and play them anytime I wished. He admired all the great trumpet players such as Roy Eldridge, Clifford Brown, Miles, and Dizzy. He taught me to appreciate the orchestrated blues of Duke Ellington, Count Basie, and Ray Charles, too. He also had old 78-rpm records—perhaps left over from Dad. I learned to play some of my first solos backed by those old phonographs. I had heard live blues in my home from the time I was born, but this was the first time I was fully aware of the artistry behind the recordings. I began to pay close attention to the subtle differences in style. Each artist had his own sound. I wondered how they did it. I was enthralled. Records seemed to be magical. I knew then that one day I, too, wanted to become a recording artist.

I would go to the old wooden gramophone, still in the back room. With its big brass horn protruding out. I'd place a needle in the sound box, wind up the gramophone spindle, then move the tone arm over some old crackling 78 to play recordings by Louis Armstrong's Hot Five, including his landmark recording, "West End Blues." Don would tell me stories about the musicians, which I found fascinating. Don could play King Oliver and Louis Armstrong's tunes on his trumpet with relative ease.

I learned that Louis Armstrong had first picked up the cornet while in a waif's home for wayward boys around my age. He had switched to the louder trumpet by the time he began recording in the early 1920s. My little cornet had a compact shape and mellow tone compared to its longer louder relative, the trumpet. Nevertheless, for a little boy just learning to play the blues, the petite cornet seemed the perfect fit for my small frame.

Uncle Don promised that once I learned my scales and got through my basic lesson books, learning treble clef, bass clef, every-good-boy-does-fine (an easy mnemonic to remember the treble staff, E, G, B, D, F), he'd teach me to play from ear. Although I was smitten with the albums, I imagined playing like Don, my first musical mentor, not the records.

The cornet, like the trumpet, is a demanding instrument. One must practice often. Not simply to develop great technique, which is important, but to keep one's upper lip muscles in shape. A trumpeter must routinely work out his embouchure by exercising the lip muscles, much like an athlete. The trumpeter's embouchure must be in top shape to hit the high notes and maintain a pleasing tone. I would practice my lessons all week trying to perfect warm tone and finger speed. Then I'd return to my uncle's house the following week, hungry for more lessons and stories about the great trumpet players.

At about eight years old, I knew I wanted to be a musician and recording artist, but not necessarily a blues artist. I knew my dad and his friends played blues, but I didn't distinguish their music by genre or style. I didn't even know music had different names like classical, jazz, and rock and funk. My parents never pushed or prodded me to learn an instrument. Instead, they hoped I would one day go to college or trade school. They hoped I would learn skills that would help me land a good-paying job. My parents knew all too well music didn't pay, especially the blues.

My musical curiosity was insatiable. Though I was taking lessons on the cornet, I wasn't settled on any one instrument. I would test myself on any instrument I could get my hands on. Lucky for me, Dad had many instruments in the house. He housed all the back-line instruments for his band: drums, guitar, bass, accordion, and amps. We had a B3 organ too, with a Leslie speaker. Dad had played the B3 to accompany his singing. I would mess around with the B3 organ, but my feet barely touched its foot pedals. B3 was not the instrument for me.

Dad was a novice on guitar when I was in my formative musical years. But when the guitar became the dominant instrument in the blues and in popular music in the late '60s, he began taking the guitar seriously. Dad would visit Earns, an elderly musician who lived on West Johnson Street in South Baton Rouge, for regular guitar lessons.

Before long, I developed an obsessive interest in Dad's guitar. Though Dad showed me some basic things, I never took formal guitar lessons. I would go to Dad's room and fool around on his rose-colored Gibson 335 when he was away at work. I became pretty good on it. As my little fingers grew stronger my ambitions grew too. I would bend his strings. I broke a few, too.

When he came home from work one day and found his strings busted, he got upset with me. He had warned me not to mess with his guitar. But that didn't stop me. I played it every chance I got whenever he was away. I discovered I could transpose the scales and songs I learned on the cornet to the guitar. Also, the guitar could play chords, which sounded full. Like a piano, it was a complete instrument. It was perfect for unaccompanied performance, whereas the cornet could only play one note at a time. Besides, if you wanted to sing while playing the horn, you had to remove it from your mouth and sing with no musical accompaniment.

Before long I was accompanying my dad on gigs here and there. I accompanied him to honky-tonks and country juke joints around South Louisiana and Mississippi, performing guitar tricks that seemed to come easy. Though I wasn't playing anything sophisticated while doing tricks, my showmanship was enough to delight audiences. I played the guitar behind my back and with my teeth or tongue. Patrons would throw money, egg me on. I happily obliged, gaining a reputation as a child wonder. I was a budding multi-instrumentalist, though my only formal musical training had been with the cornet. That year or two I spent taking lessons from my uncle Don prepared me for McKinley Junior High's marching band.

Bob Johnson, a stern disciplinarian, had been the band director at McKinley Junior High for a long time. He may have been there for over forty years before I arrived. He might even have taught at McKinley back when my dad was in school. All the kids called him "Bubblehead." Mr. Johnson sported heavy black-rimmed glasses. Always conservatively dressed, Mr. Johnson wore a white neatly pressed short sleeve shirt, thin black tie, and starchy black pants every day as though it were a uniform. Mr. Johnson kept a few sharpened pencils in his shirt pocket. He had a large bald spot on the crown of his head. I don't know why we called him Bubblehead. It may have been because veins would pop out of his head when he got upset. Sometimes, he'd get so angry with us, he'd get right in our faces and yell like an army sergeant. It wouldn't have been so bad except that spit would spray from his mouth into your face when he was angry. The class would all laugh at whomever was getting chewed out or showered in spit, but it wasn't funny whenever I was that person.

I played the first cornet in the marching band as a seventh grader, a big accomplishment. When I would play the "Star Spangled Banner," I could hit the triple C at the end—a high screeching note that takes several years to master. To hear me hit the high notes at the finale of the anthem was impressive to Mr. Johnson. But I lost interest in the cornet as my chops and reputation on the guitar grew. The guitar made a lot of noise; a lot of racket. If I'd put all my energies into the cornet, who knows, I may have become another Buddy Bolden, King Oliver, or Louis Armstrong, leading a hot Louisiana blues band with my horn. But the guitar had become the loudest and most popular instrument in modern music, capturing my imagination.

Uncle Don, after serving in the military, joined my dad's band, which also featured a short-tempered blind tenor saxophone player named Tagnough, who would drink too much on gigs and then threaten to kick everyone's ass in the car on the ride home. The drive home was always amusing. There was always one guy in the station wagon who took Tagnough's insults serious and fired verbal jabs back at him, heightening the tension. The testier the argument got, the more the others would laugh, which only further antagonized the blind saxophonist. Who would hit a blind man anyway? I must admit though, Tagnough had a dirty mouth. He possessed the quick wit of a *bleu* comic. He was hilarious, a lovable rogue. Don and Tagnough were the horn section for my dad's band. But horns were on their way out of the blues by 1969. The guitar had become the dominant solo instrument, replacing the trumpet and sax solo on blues recordings. Because of this, Don, a fine trumpeter, did not record often with my dad, even though he had been a regular in his band.

In the '50s, back when my dad was an unseasoned jump blues singer—before he picked up the guitar—the saxophone had its moment as the hot thing in popular recordings. Louis Jordan, of "Caledonia" fame, helped lead the way for the instrument in popular music, while Charlie Parker's holistic approach to the sax maximized the instrument's potential. A jump blues singer, such as Big Joe Turner, a pioneering Kansas City shouter, would perform a jump tune; the saxophone player would always play the break. The sax man would solo, even dropping to his knees in heightened passion, wailing—the crowd would eat it up. The new rock and roll audience was excited most by showmanship, not competitive technical wizardry.

Therefore, guitarists that combined musical prowess with showmanship, such as Chuck Berry in the 1950s and Jimi Hendrix in the '60s, found tremendous commercial success. The guitar became the kingmaker of solo instruments. The trumpet had reigned since the birth of the blues, but now it was relegated to the sidelines. Miles Davis, a fearless artist, attempted to transform his approach and adapt his style to compete with modern electrified guitar blues, but the trumpet, like all brass instruments, wasn't suited to wah-wah pedals and distorted amplification.

While these changes were taking place, the electric guitar helped to transform Dad's image from a jump blues singer to a swamp blues guitar man. Dad concluded, due to popular demand, he had to ask his brother to put down his trumpet and take up the bass guitar if he still wanted to play in his band. The paradigm shift in blues tastes created stress between the two brothers.

Folk purists' fixation on primitivism—believing it equaled authenticity—helped to marginalize blues to rural country aesthetics with a preference for acoustic guitars played by men wearing overalls—dressed like farmhands—thus excluding urban bluesmen like B. B. King, Bobby "Blue" Bland, and others who featured big brass horn sections. Following the folk revival era, the trumpet that was once the most expressive instrument in blues disappeared as an instrument in blues altogether.

Meanwhile, the harmonica, an instrument associated with hobos and drifters, became the only acceptable horn in a blues band. Little Walter, a harmonica great from Marksville, Louisiana, did for the harmonica what Miles Davis tried but failed to achieve with the trumpet; he electrified it. Little Walter played the harp through a microphone plugged into a guitar amplifier, added a large amount of reverberation, and created an amazing new instantly recognizable tone. Little Walter made the harmonica a lead instrument and a permanent fixture in electric blues bands.

Don was deflated by his demotion. Yet he took up the bass guitar, adapted to the changing times, and carried on. Uncle Don's heart and talent were in the trumpet, but the trumpet could not compete with the electric guitar. Dad encouraged me to put down the cornet also if I wanted to lead a band. The powerful electric guitar was the new kingmaker of the blues. I picked up the guitar and didn't look back. Besides, the guitar felt natural anyway. I soon became a professional, earning money as a sideman behind my dad and others at a tender age.

———

One day Dad returned home from one of his makeshift tours. Carrying his guitar and suitcase, he unexpectedly walked into the house. "Daddy's home!" my baby sister Charlette screamed with joy as she ran to the door to greet him. He gave her a big hug and kiss. He pulled candy from his pockets, handing it to her and me. Yolanda, my oldest sister, was sitting on the sofa talking on the phone. She wasn't excited to see him. She got up and left the room. My mom, Jocelyn, still wearing her domestic uniform, was in the kitchen making dinner. I could see from the look on her face she was indifferent to his return. Later that night, I awoke to a dreadful quarrel permeating through our thin paneled kitchen walls.

"Tabby, you've been gone for two weeks," Mom's soft voice asserted. "You said it'd be only a few days."

"Jocelyn, I told you," I heard Dad, insist, "the tour got extended."

"Otis just got hired at Ciba-Geigy," Mom said, "but he's still playing on weekends. Told me he put a word in for you."

"The plant ain't gon' let me off for road gigs," Dad said. "Now, we've been over this repeatedly," he complained. "I'm doing this for us."

"No!" Mom snapped. "It has nothing to do with us, Tabby." She'd heard it too many times before. "I live in the real world," she declared. "In the real world, it takes real money!"

I could hear every wistful word as I tossed and turned on my bed in the adjacent room.

"On the road, we met a guy," Dad said.

"I don't want to hear it."

"He's setting up a recording session for us."

"I said, I don't want to hear it!" Mom objected.

"This could be the one," Dad predicted.

Mom was often supportive, but tonight she wasn't letting up. She knew the shady music business just as well as he. She knew empty promises and hit records were fools' gold that wouldn't pay the bills.

"Look what happened to Slim Harpo," Mom argued in between thick windy swooshes from eighteen-wheelers zooming down Interstate 10 just outside my window. "He had hits, sold millions, but he drove a sugarcane truck to earn real money, because he saw no royalties. It killed him," she lamented.

"This is different," Dad bargained.

"Where's the money for the extra week, Tabby?" she chided.

I eavesdropped through the cheap thin walls dividing my bedroom from the kitchen. They seemed to argue all night. I hated hearing my mother's unhappiness. I hated hearing them argue.

"When we got to Florida," Dad whined, "the brakes went out on that damn station wagon."

Lack of money was the thing that made everyone unhappy. When Dad was unemployed, we didn't get toys for Christmas. Sometimes at Christmas he wouldn't come out of his room, not even for dinner. I guess it was like Christmas holidays, birthdays, and such that reminded him how difficult it was to raise seven children while working temporary jobs and waiting tables. For a while he'd had a steady job at Piccadilly, which was one of the better-paying jobs in Baton

Rouge—for a Black man without a college education—because waiters at Piccadilly earned good tips.

Whenever they'd argue like this, which was rare, I'd just lose myself in my
music. I had a little battery-powered AM/FM radio I kept under my pillow. I
would lay there with my ear held to it trying to keep the volume as low as possible,
listening throughout the night. I'd tune from station to station, just dialing in all
kinds of music from rock stations to R&B stations until I'd fall asleep.

Mom had a point. Never did I hear the swampy music my dad played on the
radio. She knew neither my dad nor any Black bluesman could have a hit record.
She knew Dad was more likely to bring home a unicorn than a gold record.

Tonight, listening to the radio to block out the sounds of my parents arguing
would prove futile. I could hear the argument deepen.

"I'm working two jobs," Mom lamented. "Scrubbing floors, caring for other
people's children; I don't even have the time nor the energy to tend to my own."

"Baby, this next tour, the next session, could be the one," he said,
unconvincingly.

"I'm sick of this," Mom said, her voice aching and overflowing from pain
accumulated by years of struggle and disappointment. "I don't want to hear how
the next song will be a hit and we'll buy a nice home, how about a new washing
machine?" She said, in a hushed whisper, "I was such a fool."

"I tell you what," Dad said. "If it doesn't work out, I'll give it up, if that's what
you want; come back, take that plant job, OK?" He said it with a vulnerability he
rarely displayed.

But Mom was steadfast. "We won't be here when you get back."

Mom said she was taking us back to New Orleans to live with my aunt Rose.
Then all went quiet. An eerie silence permeated our home. The silence was even
more disturbing than their quarreling.

The next day, Dad was standing in front of his station wagon, which had a
two-wheel covered trailer attached to the rear. A painted sign on the trailer said
ROCKIN' TABBY THOMAS AND HIS MIGHTY HOUSE ROCKERS. My mom and my sisters were at the window looking out. I ran out to the car.

"Daddy, take me with you," I begged.

He got out of the car. I was standing there welling up. My head hung low
staring at my bare feet on the warm prickly pavement. He leaned over, placing
one hand on my shoulder and another under my chin.

"Look at me," he said.

I raised my eyes.

"Daddy's going on a tour. This time I'll be gone a little longer, but I'll be
back."

"Can I come?" I asked.

"No," he answered. "Maybe when you get a little older."

I felt sad. I was thinking, I may not see him again. Dad glanced over to the window of the house. His weary eyes watched my mom turn and walk away from the window. Dad fixed his attention back, as if I was the most important thing in the world. Dad knelt and said, "Look, you have to be the man around the house while I'm gone, OK?" As he wiped a tear from my cheek I composed myself. He tried to prepare me for his exit. The band members waiting in the station wagon grew impatient.

"C'mon, Tabby!" they complained.

"I want you to go to school, help your mother around the house, all right?"

"We got to get going, Tabby," his House Rockers grumbled.

"In a minute, man, damn!" Dad insisted, making me feel even more special.

Then he went to the back of the wagon. Dad reached inside for a guitar case. He opened it revealing a sunburst guitar. He handed me the instrument. I nervously held the hollow body archtop.

"This guitar once belonged to Slim Harpo. I want you to have it."

I couldn't believe my eyes.

Wow! I thought, a guitar once owned by Slim. I could hardly hear what he was saying because the silent guitar was playing so loud within my psyche.

"When Slim played it, he felt free as a bird," Dad said. "Folks say they had to pry it out of his hands after he passed away."

I marveled at the guitar.

"Folks say, if you can play the right notes, the heavens will open, grant you anything you wish," Dad whispered. "Now, you take it, maybe you can find them special notes."

It didn't matter if what he said was true. Dad knew myths and legends are what captured a young boy's imagination. Like the Excalibur sword of legend, with this guitar in hand I believed I could slay the dragon—find them special notes!

I gazed proudly at the well-worn guitar, the afternoon sunlight magically reflecting from its perfectly fashioned body. The Kent guitar I'd been playing was a cheap beginner's guitar, a gift I received one Christmas because Dad was tired of me breaking his strings and such. But this, this was my first real guitar. One like all the great bluesmen played. I just stood there, holding the precious emblem, as he got into the wagon with the other musicians and drove away. I watched the dusty station wagon drive down the road until it disappeared in the glare of the afternoon sun.

That night I could not sleep. I stayed awake exploring my new guitar. I lay in bed listening to the handheld radio tucked under my pillow. I played along with every song. As I lay in bed holding the guitar, I wondered, What was it about the blues that would make my dad leave us and risk everything? The old folks said musicians turned their backs on heaven to play the devil's music. What was it about this music that made someone so insanely attracted? A lot was going through my mind. I turned off the radio. I got on my knees to say a prayer. Praying to the Lord also helped my rambling mind calm down at night. Sunday school had taught me about hell and revelations; it scared me to death imagining the horrors. Saying a prayer reduced the nightmares. From the bottom of my heart I asked the Lord, make me a great musician so I could make Mother happy. I hated seeing her sad.

THE BULLY

LEROY SCORED THE WINNING BASKET. "Pay up, niggas!" Leroy boasted, collecting change from the other team. Leroy was the best baller on the court. He was also the oldest. Leroy was about fourteen, a bully, and proud of it. He seemed to get a kick out of bullying us younger kids. Leroy, to our chagrin, would often intervene when I played basketball after school with a group of neighborhood kids, turning a careless pastime into some intimidating gangster challenge.

Lil' June gathered his school bag and left the court after suffering degrading taunts from his teammate Leroy. A female teen, a tomboy who could handle us boys at most sports, was among the few waiting to take his place as they got ready to begin another game.

"Hey, Leroy," my friend Quinton called out. "Chris ain't played yet, pick him." Quinton, a much better athlete than I, never had trouble getting on the court.

"No, Q, I got money on this 'n," Leroy said.

For a brief time, like most boys in my neighborhood, I had fantasies of being a baller. Only a select few were picked for a team sport such as basketball, which only needed a dozen players. College football teams, on the other hand, issued scholarships to hundreds of impoverished Black boys to fill out their rosters. Professional sports seemed to be one of the only ways out of poverty to an impressionable kid such as myself. Professional sports were perceived to be achievable if a boy was big, strong, and fast, but I was not endowed with such virtues. Leroy chose the girl as a replacement, leaving me, embarrassed, waiting on the sidelines.

"C'mon, man, give Chris a chance," Quinton said, sticking up for me.

"All Chris know how to do is play dat stupid guitar. He's a loser, just like his old man." Then Leroy mocked playing air guitar, "I ain't got no money, my house is falling down."

They all laughed. I moved into the space of the bully with clenched fists. Suddenly, everyone gathered around us expecting a fight. I swung at Leroy. He sidestepped, causing me to swing at air. Quinton pulled me back. Leroy placed his hand on a gun inside his sweat suit. Everyone froze. For a second, my young life flashed before me.

"Let it go, Chris!" Quinton said, stepping between us. "C'mon, man, let's go." Quinton pulled me away.

"Turn dat nigga loose! I got somethin' for his punk ass!" Leroy yelled.

Quinton and I left the court.

Quinton diffused the situation. I had accepted that I would get my ass kicked, yet I was determined to stand up to the bully. But a gun? I was not one to carry anything more than a pocketknife. I could have been killed that day on the basketball court.

"Don't let that fool get to you, man, he ain't 'bout nothin'," Quinton said, trying to lift my spirits.

The basketball game resumed. The girl joined in. I was never any good with a "real" basketball or against "real" competition. So much for being a baller.

Tabby, my road-weary dad, returned home from yet another grinding tour. He drove his beat-up station wagon up the block of run-down shotgun homes in South Baton Rouge. When you've been away from the neighborhood even for a short while, you could see it deteriorating as middle-class Blacks moved into White-flight subdivisions like Mayfair and Glen Oaks, leaving behind impoverished desperate neighbors.

Mom welcomed him home. Later, they sat at the kitchen table and talked in a whisper into the night. They looked solemn as they sat there for what seemed like hours. I couldn't hear what they were saying, but I was happy to see my dad return home. Before long Dad got hired at the Ciba-Geigy chemical plant.

Dad worked long, laborious hours. Sometimes his shift would be three or four days on, three or four days off. Because of dangerous chemicals, he wore body suits, hard hats, protective glasses, and gloves. The work took him away from his beloved music, but the money was good and steady. Christmases got more exciting; my parents added two rooms to the shotgun house we had outgrown. I never heard my dad complain about punching the clock, but I knew he didn't like being away from his music. Having a suffocating boss man standing over him all day and night didn't help either. While he toiled away, his musical dreams faded.

While Tabby was on hiatus from music, the older gentlemen would continue taking me out on gigs from time to time. "This kid needs a psychiatrist," I'd hear people say, "if he thinks he can make a living playing the blues." I played drums for a quartet of older gentlemen who sang in an old-time jubilee vocal style, like the Soul Stirrers. I got comfortable singing and playing the drums, cornet, guitar, and bass, which kept me busy with a few different bands and out of trouble. I missed days at school and got so far behind I was sure to fail the ninth grade. Although I was still underage, if I was with the older gentlemen I could get in the joints. One of the older bandleaders would vouch, "That's my boy."

But my real dad, Tabby Thomas, was busy at the plant. He grew more and more frustrated because even when he had a day or two off no one wanted to book him. Dad complained people didn't really appreciate blues from Louisiana anymore. Although he was elected union steward at Ciba-Geigy, earning a raise, he was depressed. He drove a forklift. He would come home covered in white powdery dust and soot from head to toe. Dad did whatever he had to do to feed his family, but he longed to play his music once again.

───────

One day, while I was playing touch football with kids on my block, a police car pulled up. There was nothing unusual about the police driving down our block. Except this time, the cops stopped in the middle of the street and just sat in their patrol car eerily observing me. There were no big boys around, just us young kids. I was around ten. The policemen got out of the car and approached me. "Is your name Thomas?" one of them asked. "Yes, sir," I said. "Chris Thomas." The other demanded, "Put your hands behind your back!" They squeezed handcuffs on my wrists. I was dumbfounded. Why were they putting handcuffs on me? I thought. What did I do wrong?

Many kids in the area were arrested for one minor reason or another. There had been whispers going around about cops who arrested neighborhood boys, intimidated them, fingerprinted them, dirtied up their record seemingly just to track them. I was too young at the time to comprehend what was happening and knew nothing about my rights. The cops shoved me, handcuffed, into the backseat of the police car and sped away. The cuffs were painfully tight around my wrist as they cut into my flesh. They sped through South Baton Rouge, down Highland Road toward the LSU campus.

The policemen pulled into the University Shopping Center on State Street then stopped in front of a small bank. They led me to the bank, and all the tellers stopped what they were doing and eyed my every move. I saw no customers at any of the counters. It seemed the bank was not even open for business now. I didn't recall ever being in this bank before but I knew we weren't there to make a deposit. The closest I'd ever come to this bank before today was visiting the popular McDonald's across the street a few times. My mind was aching trying to make sense of what was happening. The cops stood me in the center of the floor. One cop asked a female teller, maybe in her late twenties, if she recognized me. She was standing behind the counter looking at me. Before I could make out her name from the tag on her lapel, she coldly said, "Yes, he's the one!"

"Ma'am, are you sure?" the cop asked her. Looking me right in the eye she said, "Yes, I'm sure," with absolute certainty.

At one time in Louisiana, when a White woman identified a Black boy to the authorities as "the one," it was almost never for anything good. In fact, if only a few years earlier, I could've been lynched. Fortunately, however, this only had something to do with me robbing the bank.

We arrived at the downtown Baton Rouge police station. I still didn't really know exactly what I was accused of doing. I saw some hard-luck guys and dangerous guys in cells as they led me down the narrow corridor. The prisoners were asking, "What you in for, lil' man?" I was too intimidated to answer. I heard the guard say, "Armed robbery: a church and a bank." The prisoners were stunned by the charges. "Damn, lil' man," I heard one of the prisoners say. "You gon' be here a while, son!"

I was numbed. If found guilty of armed bank robbery along with the moral disgrace of robbing a church, I was facing juvenile detention until I turned twenty-one, then Angola State Prison possibly for the rest of my life. I was scared and dazed. When the cop was done processing me, he placed me in a holding cell alone. After a while, a plain-clothes detective moved me into a private room where we sat at a desk. He started asking me weird questions like, "What did you do with the gun?" Astonished, I managed to utter, in a tremble, "What gun?" These bizarre questions continued for a few more minutes but it seemed like hours to me. I kept repeating, "I don't know anything. I don't know what you're talking about." The detectives had little patience for my blank answers. They got hostile and told me I was in big trouble. And what's more, I would spend years behind bars if I didn't cooperate—but I had nothing for them.

They finally left the room and I began to weep. I'd never felt so alone. Whatever innocence I had before my arrest was lost forever. I was a mischievous boy; I'd done some childish and bad things like many kids around my block. I deserved discipline or punishment for bad behavior, destruction of property and such. I'd smoked marijuana and sold a few joints, but at the age of ten, I wasn't even thinking about guns and armed robbery. Kids still fought with their fists, a pock-etknife at worst. It would be nearly twenty years before crack cocaine would help turn Louisiana into the gun murder capital of America. Charges like those I was accused of were almost unheard of for a ten-year-old. I didn't know I was allowed a phone call to my parents. My parents had been at work and my brother and sisters were not outside when I was arrested. It seemed I was going to spend my life behind bars on "the Farm."

Angola Prison, also known as "the Farm," located in metro Baton Rouge, was notorious. The mere mention of Angola made even the most hardened prisoners weak in the knees. When the judge would hammer his gavel, pronouncing hard time in Angola, some big bad men were known to have fainted. There were nursery rhymes and children's songs about Angola's legendary torturous overseers, who still rode horses and snapped whips to drive prisoners like antebellum slave drivers. As a young child in my neighborhood, we knew songs and stories about prison as intimately as we knew classic childhood fables. Once the most notorious prison in America, and purveyor of convict labor, Angola was no fable. I wanted no part of the Farm.

While in limbo, in the holding cell, the hours passed slowly. I tried to rationalize what had happened. I must have done what they accused me of, why else would I have been arrested? Perhaps I had suffered a memory lapse. Maybe Angola was my destiny after all. All the while, echoing in my aching head, stirring a sense of hopelessness, was the bank teller's bone-chilling voice, "Yes, he's the one!"

After a while, a familiar voice. I moved closer to the heavy steel bars to try to hear what was being said. I heard my usually soft-spoken mother lamenting, "You have the wrong child!" Mom was terribly upset. "Not my Durwood!" I heard Mom say. My first name, Durwood, which I was not fond of, never sounded so good.

Maybe the kids I played ball with told my parents what had happened. Maybe the cops notified them about my arrest. Regardless, I was relieved to know my parents had come to my rescue. I felt God had answered my prayers. The motivation for the cops arresting me, a juvenile, without even knocking on my door to notify an adult, must have been to interrogate me, get a confession without an adult or lawyer around to protect me.

Later that night I was brought into a cramped room where cops, along with my parents, waited with another boy. I immediately recognized him. It was Leroy, the bully from the playground. A cop asked Leroy to identify me as his accomplice. Leroy looked at me with sad sunken eyes. He glanced over at my parents who were holding their breath. He looked at the cop and hesitated. They had kept Leroy and I separated the whole time trying to test our versions of the story,

I guess. Maybe Leroy had told them I was his accomplice, which caused them to arrest me. Finally, Leroy shook his head no.

The cop asked again, firmly.

"Is this the boy?"

"No, that ain't him," Leroy said. "I ain't never even seen him before."

Mom sighed in relief. Leroy had given the cops my name to cover for a friend but had then shrunk in the presence of my parents. Thankfully, he didn't follow through with his plan to implicate me.

After leaving the station, on our walk to the car I cherished the simple pleasure of breathing fresh air. With the heavy burden lifted and my mind finally cleared, I felt like my old self again. On the drive home, Mom assured me she never had any doubts about my innocence. Hovering over the jubilation of my vindication, however, was an empathy we all shared for Leroy's plight. No one was at the jailhouse to advocate for Leroy. I don't think he knew his father. Leroy was alone. He looked like a scared little kid to me, not the big bad bully from the playground.

"I really feel sorry for that boy," Dad said, driving slowly, "He didn't have anyone to speak up for him." Perhaps Dad saw a bit of himself in Leroy. He could identify with a troubled fatherless kid. Dad often said, "I ain't had no daddy. I had a hard way to go."

Looking back, the course of one's life is fragile; it can turn for the worst at any moment. Thankfully, my parents were there for me at a crucial moment. Leroy, like many of my childhood friends, spent his adult life in the state prison system. I thought, There but for the grace of God, go I.

AFROS AND BELL-BOTTOMS

AS THE SUN SET ON THE 1960s, my community was going through yet another identity crisis. Teenagers were letting their hair grow into the newly fashionable wooly Afro to express a renewed pride and symbolic connection to their African roots. An Afro was a hairstyle in which the hair is grown out naturally, without chemicals, and shaped into a halo. I'd grown used to seeing Yolanda's Afro, though I didn't know it had a name at the time. It was just the way Yolanda wore her hair. I'll never forget the first time I saw someone other than my big sister in person with a huge Afro.

I was just a little kid, maybe six or seven, walking to the store with my big sister. Yolanda, a thin teenager, wore large circular earrings and carried a large stylish handbag, perfect accessories to her average-sized brownish Afro. She looked so confident, so knowing, cool, and avant-garde in her white bell-bottomed jeans flared out wide, covering her high platform shoes as she led me down the block and around the corner to Alexander's grocery store on East Washington Street. I figured my big sister must be popular, because everyone that walked past us either spoke to her or gave warm smiles of admiration.

At home, Yolanda had a large collection of record albums, Sly and the Family Stone, Marvin Gaye, and of course anything released by Stevie Wonder. In her collection I could also find Nancy Wilson, Nina Simone, and the Carpenters. Just as she opened the door to enter the neighborhood grocery, out walked two guys. One sported a small Afro and wore smart-looking thick black-rimmed classes. He greeted Yolanda with a friendly soul shake. The other was a tall guy whom I thought had to be a brother from another planet, or at least another town. When I saw his super large Afro, it made me very nervous. His hair was so big it barely fit through the door. He immediately recognized my sister and gave her a big hug.

The brother from another planet was as loud and proud as a peacock. He made customers in the store uneasy. His clothes were fantastically stylish. His bell-bottoms made Yolanda's pants look straight. His platform shoes were higher than hers. The three of them exchanged words I didn't understand. I recall hearing in their conversation a lot of "Right on, sister" and "Power to the people." They invited my sister to an upcoming gathering. The gregarious brother from another planet, his voice rising a few decibels with each word, let go a big laugh. I said to myself, Mr., you'd better be quiet, or else the people gon' come and take you away. Before the two split, they all exchanged some funky handshake. Some years later, my sister told me the guy with the thick-rimmed glasses was H. Rap Brown, one of the leaders of the Black Panther Party. Rap Brown authored the controversial 1969 political autobiography and bestseller *Die, Nigger Die*. Rap Brown was from South Baton Rouge. He was seen regularly around the neighborhood helping to organize the Black empowerment movement.

The Afro was a rejection of fried, dyed, and laid to the side, hairstyles of many popular Black entertainers of the 1940s, '50s, and '60s. The slick look had been a boon for beauticians, necessitating the use of expensive chemicals and straighteners on the naturally kinky hair of Black men and women wanting to emulate the fashionable hairstyles of their idols.

In the 1960s, during this revolutionary period, the blues was being usurped, redefined, and outright stolen. The paradigm shift, the big swindle, was ushered in by greed. There was a demand from White baby boomers, the largest generation of teenagers in American history, for a raw and authentic "Black" sound. Greed along with the color line were the driving forces behind the swindle. Black artists were banned from FM rock radio stations. The feeling, the beat, the poetry, the guitar riffs, and the melodies of the blues were now called rock and roll or sometimes folk rock. These marketing terms were euphemisms meaning salacious Black music sanitized for White consumption.

In the 1970s in the Black community, folk-blues music was rejected outright by Yolanda's generation. Ostensibly, the blues and its unsophisticated practitioners—as they were portrayed by the burgeoning rock and folk music press—conveyed a romanticized notion of sharecropping and plantation life. The conflation of folk aesthetics and blues that White tastemakers invented and promoted had become, for Yolanda's generation, a reminder of everything the Black community wanted to leave behind. Not necessarily because they were ashamed of the past, but because the White narrative was a caricature that portrayed Blacks as submissive and inferior.

Dad used to tell me about the Roof Garden (known today as the Masonic Temple), a ballroom he would frequent back in the day to see artists such as T-Bone Walker, Guitar Slim, Ray Charles, Elmore James, and Louis Jordan. It had been opened in 1925 by the Grand United Order of Odd Fellows, a Black benevolent society who, in 1924, contracted with Conner, Bryant, and Bell, a Black-owned Baton Rouge contracting company, to erect the building at 1335 North Boulevard.

On the top floor of the four-story brick building was a large ballroom dubbed the Roof Garden. During the spring and summer months (prior to central air-conditioning) the huge windows of the Roof Garden were thrown open to let in the summer breeze. When the windows were opened, the music echoed throughout the neighborhood for all to hear and enjoy. The Masonic Temple Theater became an unofficial part of the chitlin circuit of Black theaters. Cab Calloway, Duke Ellington, Ray Charles, James Brown, B. B. King, Ella Fitzgerald, Louis Armstrong, Ike and Tina Turner, Fats Domino, and Guitar Slim are just a few of the stars who toured the chitlin circuit regularly.[7]

Chitlins (chitterlings, hog intestines) are what the enslaved were forced to eat to sustain themselves. The slaveholder would gut the hog, discard the intestines, and keep all the best parts like the loin, ham, and pork belly for his table. The slaves, on the other hand, were forced to salvage and eat the hog's intestines for sustenance. Popular subgenres of blues, such as swing and later rock and roll, created a lucrative mainstream market for White appropriators. White stars of swing and rock and roll played the best venues, stayed at the best hotels, ate at the best restaurants, and became extremely wealthy playing Black music for segregated White audiences. Conversely, the dispossessed Black theater circuit was the chitterlings; the residue left to Black artists.

Through the 1950s and '60s the Masonic Temple Theater was the centerpiece of North Boulevard, the major thoroughfare running to downtown Baton Rouge and the Mississippi River. There were more than fifty Black businesses between Twelfth and Sixteenth Streets. There were meat markets, grocers, a motor car company, furniture stores, dry cleaners, hardware stores, jewelers, tailors, drugstores, dry goods stores, barbershops, a lumber company, a coffee company, a funeral home, the Lincoln Hotel, and the Lincoln movie theater. These businesses were either Black-owned or run by Blacks.

Jewish-owned grocery and drugstore Griffon's—historically important because it subsequently became the location of my father's juke joint, Tabby's Blues Box—stood directly across the street from the Masonic Temple. George G. Griffon built the store in 1920. By the 1970s, Griffon's was operated by his son, George G. Griffon Jr.

Jewish ownership was not uncommon in my neighborhood. Businesses along North Boulevard that weren't owned by Blacks were usually Jewish owned. Black families in the neighborhood were loyal to Griffon's because the Griffon family would extend their best customers credit. Griffon's credit had nothing to do with a bank. Griffon's kept an accounting of credit transactions of each customer in a written ledger.

Many undereducated Blacks, just into the city from nearby farms and mills, found the urban transition harsh. Large families of fifteen to twenty kids had been essential during the Agrarian era. However, in the city, only low-wage employment as laborers or domestic servants awaited them. Their kids often went hungry, especially during the summer months when school meals were not an option. Indeed, families desperately needed Griffon's credit to make it through the summer, especially with tens of hungry young mouths to feed. Over time, families got smaller, but, in the meanwhile, the transition from farming life to urban living was a struggle.

During this time, a family of seven siblings, like mine, was considered average size. Some of our neighbors had around twenty children or more. One summer, there was a family of about eighteen kids living across the street. Their mother had a countryfied name that is hard to forget, Daisy Mae Fe-Fe Hatch, a typical name of someone born deep in the woods.

Daisy Mae had two young boys near my age, Curt and Burt. While at their home playing one day, Daisy Mae came home with some cute little goldfish in a tank filled with water. Curt and Burt were excited. I was excited too. It seemed all the young kids in the neighborhood were gathered around the tank to watch the fish swim. Curt and Burt were given fish feed. They were taught to sprinkle the tiny bits into the water. The fish rushed to the feed, pushing each other out of the way to swallow up all they could. The fish's feeding resembled dinnertime with our families. If you were late getting home from playing outside or the last to eat, there wasn't much left after all your brothers and sisters filled their bellies. Sometimes you had to push and shove to get a full plate.

A few days later, I went over to Curt and Burt's home to play and see the fish. But I was told they were punished and couldn't play with me. When I asked why, Lisa, their big sister, said, "Mama, punished 'em 'cause they cooked and ate the goldfish."

"What!"

I was shocked to hear such a thing. Turned out, while their mother was at work, they ate the goldfish. I couldn't believe it. I wondered, What does goldfish taste like? I thought it oddly funny. I just chalked it up to another crazy day in the 'hood.

Summers were particularly tough on parents in South Baton Rouge when kids were left alone without supervision. We'd all have to look out for each other. Usually there was an elderly woman on the block who sat on her front screened porch acting as the watchman. She'd give a report of all she'd witnessed when our parents got home.

Each summer I'd go to a center the Black Panthers ran called the Black House—a short-lived government-backed program—where young kids could play games and learn Black history. The Black House also served free breakfast. The program was designed to benefit underprivileged children in the community. The Black Panthers' doctrine held the Second Amendment in high regard. They called on Blacks to defend themselves against police brutality by forming community militias to protect against such injustices. The Panthers' platform stated Blacks should educate themselves regarding their rights to bear arms under the Constitution.

By 1972 the Christian church, which had served as the most powerful political action voice of the Black community, had to compete with more assertive movements. It became a common sight to see clean-cut young Black men from the Nation of Islam, neatly dressed in suits and bow ties, on our streets hawking the Nation's newspaper, the *Final Call*. The Black Panther Party, the more radical political movement, was also vying for the hearts and minds of the neighborhood.

On the morning of January 10, 1972, South Baton Rouge's once bustling Black business district—already struggling after desegregation due to the loss of Black professionals and their dollars—went up in smoke.

It began as a typical morning, except for a larger than usual gathering of Nation of Islam dissidents. They had been arriving in Baton Rouge from Chicago since New Year's Day. Over the past nine days, they had aggressively recruited new members. The Nation of Islam recruiters, neatly dressed in single-breasted suits and bow ties, were rallying folks as they ventured in and out of shops along the bustling thoroughfare.

The Nation of Islam leaders were well known for their fiery political rhetoric, jarringly at odds with their clean-cut, conservative demeanor. Malcolm X, the Nation's greatest spokesman, best illustrated this contradiction before separating from the Nation of Islam in 1964 because of what he deemed the moral failings of its leader, the honorable Elijah Muhammad. Malcolm X was subsequently assassinated February 21, 1965, because of such divisive polemics by members of the Nation of Islam while giving a speech in New York City at the Audubon Ballroom.

That afternoon, not satisfied with their usual tasks of recruiting and hawking *Final Call*, members began prophetically warning of an impending race riot. Before long, a crowd gathered around them, either enraptured, perplexed, or both. The members lined up, side by side, legs spread, their hands behind their backs, in a militant at-ease stance like soldiers. They blocked North Boulevard in front of Griffon's drugstore (future location of Tabby's Blues Box) and the Masonic Temple Roof Garden. Traffic came to a complete halt. Police were called, but the group stood fearlessly in a single line, stretching from one side of the street to the other. Onlookers gathered anticipating a showdown. Local news reporters arrived on the scene to cover the impending confrontation. When the police finally arrived, showing armed force, the Nation of Islam group, despite being surrounded by dozens of heavily armed police, defiantly stood their ground. *It was on!*

Shouting ensued from both sides. The police were ordered to move in. The confrontation became violent. Chaos erupted! Fistfights between Muslims and police escalated into an all-out riot involving some innocent bystanders. Amid the confusion, several shots were fired.

After the smoke had cleared (the riot was without burning and looting of local businesses) subsequent news reports stated two policemen, deputies Ralph Hancock and Dewayne Dilder, both White, had been shot to death. Two Muslim members had been shot dead too. Samuel Upton, a tall and slender outspoken member who was thought to be the leader of the group, had been killed, along with Thomas Davis, a fellow member from Chicago. Dozens more had been injured. A White reporter, Bob Johnson of WBRZ-TV, was severely beaten while covering the story. Because of his injuries, Bob Johnson became a paraplegic, subsequently losing the ability to speak. The riots led the national evening news that night. In all, five people were killed, thirty-one seriously injured.

Did the Nation of Islam members block the streets as a provocative act simply to attract media attention to their grievances? What their grievances were no one knew exactly. Did they attempt to lure the police to the scene for an ambush? That would have been out of character for the nonviolent religious group—despite their fiery rhetoric. The motive remained unclear. There seemed to be no urgent reason for the riot.

In the weeks that followed there was much speculation in the neighborhood. Everyone was trying to make sense of what became known as a "race riot." Unlike the Black Panthers, who were known to flamboyantly celebrate the virtues of the Second Amendment by openly carrying loaded guns to promote self-defense from government tyranny and police brutality, the Nation of Islam, conversely, preached that Allah, through catastrophic forces of nature, would destroy their unrepentant enemies.

Newspaper headlines across the country said Black agitators had opened fire on police. Word on the street, however, was the police had shot each other in the heat of battle. Folk artist Wayne Jones, who would later create Tabby's Blues Box's famous logo, a cool tabby cat playing a homemade guitar, was among the crowd that day.

Wayne Jones told us, when my friends and I gathered at the Black House to watch him paint images of the event, what truly happened that bloody afternoon. He said, remarkably, dozens of unarmed people were shot on that regrettable day and "police guns were solely responsible for all the killing." Wayne said, "A few brothers, in the chaos of the scuffle, wrestled guns away from a couple of pigs. They used the officers' own guns against them, in self-defense." Wayne immortalized the riot in paintings. In his illustrations, the Nation of Islam were freedom fighters and the police were depicted with pig heads and devil horns.

Our story—my community's side of the story—was seldom told in the media. So we looked to folk artist Wayne Jones, like a courtroom sketch artist, to help tell our stories. An official investigation later confirmed Wayne's account; indeed, the only bullet shells and guns found at the scene were those of the Baton Rouge police department, including the deadly bullets that killed the officers.

Although my community was poor compared to White communities, it wasn't consumed by crime and distrust. The community I'd grown up in made the transition from agricultural jobs on surrounding plantations and mills to industrial jobs in the city. The character of my community in South Baton Rouge had always been one of working and sacrificing together to survive. There had been numerous riots around the country, sparked by police violence against Blacks, either real or perceived. But the Baton Rouge riot of 1972 was unique. No prior incident of injustice was the catalyst. It seemed a senseless act by outsiders with no real connection to our community.

Sure, we had been segregated and marginalized; it made no difference if we were rich or poor, educated or illiterate, of good character or a thief, we were deemed inferior and had been discriminated against since slavery. But on that day, at that moment, we didn't want to destroy what had taken our forefathers generations to build. Although it wasn't physically set ablaze, the image of our business community had gone up in smoke in a matter of hours. Consequently, the Black businesses along North Boulevard would never recover from the after-shock of the mystifying "race riot." What's more, the stain of empty violence and lawlessness repelled progressive White citizens and emboldened our enemies, accelerating the demise of our once thriving South Baton Rouge business district.

By the summer of 1978, my older brother, Tammy, was married, living with his new family. My oldest sister, Yolanda, had since left home for college, taking her record collection with her and leaving me at home with four sisters, Michelle, Joylyn, Jenean, and Charlette. I was happy to finally have a room of my own. I was sleeping in what had been the old narrow kitchen. Everyone in the shotgun house still had to come through my room—which had no doors—to get to the bathroom, but I didn't mind.

Tammy, my older brother, lost interest in the trombone but was playing drums to supplement his income as a custodian at Louisiana State University's basketball arena. Tammy's new job was a boon for me because Tammy got me free tickets to every big-time rock concert that passed through the arena. I saw the Frampton Comes Alive Tour, Parliament Funkadelic Mothership Connection Tour, Bruce Springsteen, Marvin Gaye, Willie Nelson, Kiss, and so many others.

With money earned playing drums and guitar with various groups, I began purchasing albums of my own interest. I was mainly interested in guitar bands. I'd listen to Van Halen, Pink Floyd, and the Sex Pistols. Not much rhythm and blues, because the guitar was in the background. From time to time, I'd get into debates with my dad about the loud music I played on the home stereo. But my mother wasn't bothered by heavy rock. I remember playing Eddie Van Halen's "Eruption" over and over, trying to figure out how he created those tricky pull-offs. My mom, who was in the room with me, couldn't help but listen. "He's too gimmicky," she said. "Why bother with such drivel?"

Jocelyn, my mother, was not a person who would come to gigs or go to night-clubs. Mom had left her domestic jobs and found full-time employment at Kean's Laundry, a large dry cleaner located at the corner of Convention and North Nine-teenth Streets. She worked on the factory floor running the hot pressers. Mom would have fresh scars and burns on her arms every day when she came home.

She tried fading the scarring by covering the burns with cocoa butter cream, but it was useless because the next day she'd be tattooed again with new burns. My mother was nowhere near a soccer mom, but she was quietly supportive. When she realized music was what I wanted to do with my life, she didn't object. "You can do anything you put your mind to," she'd often say. I loved that Mom was always patient and supportive of me in her own quiet way. It's not like she'd say to me, "You better get in there and practice!" Nobody ever told me that. What I heard most was my sisters yelling, "Stop making that racket!" or, "Take that noise someplace else!"

I was also influenced by singer-songwriters of the 1970s. Although I wasn't all that interested in the acoustic guitar at the time, I could appreciate the well-written stories. One of my favorites was "Please Come to Boston" by Dave Loggins. The song told the story of a rambling musician writing to his girl back in Tennessee, asking her to join him in all these mystic cities. Of course, there were hundreds of songs by bluesmen and women with stories of rambling, but I felt a connection to the melodies I heard on FM rock radio, which started to influence my idea of songwriting. Nevertheless, heavy guitar bands were my favorite. Posters of acts like the New York Dolls and the Sex Pistols were plastered all over my walls.

One night, Dad passed through my room on his way to the bathroom. He was irked having to endure rock posters and album jackets. "You know, you should check out Jimi Hendrix," Dad said. "That's where all that shit came from." Before long I did get around to buying *Smash Hits*, a Hendrix best-of album. When I heard Jimi Hendrix playing "Red House," a slow, echo-drenched twelve-bar blues, it struck me. Wait a minute, I thought. A young flashy guy playing the blues? Same music I've heard Dad and his friends playing around the house? I didn't know it could sound like that. I ran out and bought Jimi Hendrix's *Band of Gypsys* and was blown away by his guitar opus "Machine Gun." Hendrix was a revelation. He was presenting the blues in a psychosexual way. It was a real eye-opener for me. Hendrix helped me realize the blues didn't have to be *de ol' folks* music. I could take it, like clay, and shape it and mold it until it was my own unique expression.

I began to realize, even though I was a teen, I could make my own statement with the blues. Before Hendrix, I wasn't sold on being a blues guitarist. Hell, I was just a boy; there was no such thing as a teenaged blues boy. Blues was adult music. In my formative years, I was excited to play any old riff of blues, just as a learning mechanism. But now I was attempting to write songs, to sing, seeking my own voice. Hendrix was not of my generation, but his music spoke to me.

Meanwhile, I coformed a band, Exit. Juan played keyboards, Bi-ee was on bass, "Bright" was on synth, and Greg Williams played drums. Joe Arrington III (called Junior), the son of soul star Joe Tex, was the lead vocalist. We played the top forty R&B charts because Exit's members didn't like the blues. They thought the blues was corny, except for Juan, who took an interest in blues piano. Juan Magee's home on Louisiana Avenue, when his mother was away, was the location of many smoky bedroom listening sessions. Pink Floyd was in heavy rotation.

I played guitar and arranged the songs. I began developing a good ear for transposing popular music. I could hear songs on the radio only once or twice before knowing all the arrangements to each instrument. The hit songs usually had only a few chord changes and relied on a simple 4/4 beat featuring a thumping kick drum. I wrote original songs for our band to perform instead of relying solely on cover songs.

We performed at local talent shows and won a few. Before long, we were earning positive word of mouth around town. We played at hotels, wedding receptions, fraternity parties, and banquets. We were too young for nightclubs but we played a few anyway. Joe's mother encouraged us to work up a set of original songs to showcase for Joe Tex with the hope of landing a recording deal the next time he was in town, and we did.

It wasn't long before we attracted a manager, Keith Leduff, who had made a fortune in the construction business. Keith invested in us, but he was a music business novice. Nevertheless, we were soon wearing new matching uniforms and sporting shiny new musical equipment. I purchased a double stack of Marshall amps. Having loads of expensive equipment, including stage lighting, was fantastic, except when we had to unload the damn U-Haul trailer after gigs at four in the morning.

Disco, a genre some musicians viewed as a musical plague, swept the country by the mid-'70s, putting many musicians out of work. Disco was despised because it caused clubs to abandon live dance bands like ours for disc jockeys. It was much cheaper to pay one guy instead of a band. Disco's club culture had grown out of 1960s love-ins; parties at which hippies got high and freely engaged in sexual relations with strangers they'd just met with no strings attached. By the late '70s, disco represented the sexual revolution at its most crass. Moreover, disco was a haven for guys wearing silk shirts and tight pants going clubbing every night to pick up chicks, or each other. Women and men just wanted to dance all night to mindless extended up-tempo singles like Van McCoy's "The Hustle," which topped the *Billboard* charts in 1975. Many Louisiana musicians were forced to give up music or change their style to disco to put food on the table. The hottest clubs were those that remodeled for disco, installing flashing lights, the ubiquitous crystal ball dangling from the ceiling, fog machines, and shag carpets.

Blues musicians, during the disco craze, were lucky if they could find work at dive soul food cafés. When they did find work, they were forced to play for tips because patrons refused to pay a cover for blues. Unfortunately, Louisiana's business community had no appreciation for the blues and its artistry, and no mechanism by which the larger community could embrace the musicians and their music. Even when Slim Harpo was alive—a million-selling artist—he'd rarely get any recognition in his hometown of Baton Rouge. Slim Harpo never received a high performance fee locally. As consolation, by 1970 the New Orleans Jazz and Heritage Festival arrived on the scene, filling the void once a year. But one good gig a year was not enough.

Joe Tex, Joe Arrington's dad, became the most successful local singer and songwriter to make the jump to disco. In 1965, Joe Tex made his first chart-topping southern soul record, "Hold What You've Got." The song reached number five on the *Billboard* chart. My dad and Joe Tex were close. Joe had homes in Baton Rouge and Houston, Texas. Tex's son Joe and I hung out every day, talking music, and practicing with our band.

In 1966, Joe Tex converted to the Muslim faith and changed his name to Yusuf Hazziez, but he continued to perform as Joe Tex. He didn't drink or drug—rare for a music business celebrity. Joe Tex did positive things for the community like giving away thousands of shoes each year to needy children. He lectured Angola's inmates on cleaning up their lives.

One afternoon, Joe and I drove to Ryan Airport to pick up Joe Tex from a small private plane. We drove him to one of his relatives' homes in North Baton Rouge where he would reside. During this time, Joe Tex and his wife were separated but friendly. Joe Tex learned that his son had a band and aspired to follow in his father's footsteps, like I was doing with my father. I'll never forget the conversation that ensued that night.

Joe Tex looked regal sitting in the living room after the host family had gone to bed, wearing a silk robe and silk pajamas. I was mesmerized. I had never been up close with a singer I'd seen on national television. Joe Tex was a handsome star. He sat us down that evening and told us about the perils of the music business, why we should stay in school instead. He encouraged us to play music, but only as a hobby. Of course, we weren't hearing any of that. His son assured him we were determined to pursue musical careers; I strongly concurred.

"If you really want to get into this business, you're going to do it anyway, regardless of what I say," Joe Tex said, in a raspy voice. "Y'all nice-looking boys and the little girls are gon' start running behind y'all. But you see this?" He took out a condom. "This your protection."

Joe Arrington had a girlfriend, but I wasn't comfortable around girls "my age" yet. I wasn't exactly a virgin, but I'd never seen a condom before. I wasn't one to hang out with girls and have a relationship. But Joe Tex wasn't talking about relationships; he was talking about groupies, hangers-on, gold diggers.

"Before you go to bed with her, make sure you wear one of these," he warned. "And when you're finished, take her into the bathroom with you, fill it with water, and show her it ain't broken, understand?"

We nodded, yes.

"Do you understand what I'm saying?"

"Yes, sir," we both said.

The next day our band played a showcase for Joe Tex. We'd been rehearsing for this moment for weeks. He was impressed, but not enough to set up an audition with a record label just yet. He felt we weren't ready, even though he was really impressed with my guitar playing and told me so.

In 1977, Joe Tex's star burned bright with the crossover disco hit single "Ain't Gonna Bump No More (With No Big Fat Woman)." He had performed the song on the Grammy Awards and other national television programs across the country. Disco continued to dominate the music business, but there was a backlash brewing. The disco era peaked that year with the phenomenal success of the *Saturday Night Fever* soundtrack. It wasn't long before people across the country started burning their disco records, fearing the music had become too corporate, oversexed (interracially), and gay.

By the early '80s, disco was all but banished. For many artists who had jumped on the bandwagon in the '70s, including Joe Tex, their careers were in ruins. Joe suddenly found it hard to get radio play or bookings. His regular band had become too expensive. It was during this low period that Joe Tex hired me to play lead guitar on a tour of dive bars.

Joe Tex had been a master showman, rivaling the showmanship of Jackie Wilson and James Brown during his peak years. While dancing, he would do a split, push the microphone away from his body, and then using the microphone cable he'd pull it back to him, spin around, and drop to his knees, catching the microphone just before it hit the floor. He could do these trademark moves without ever losing the groove. His performances would drive women nuts. I was becoming a good guitar soloist. Joe featured me in spots, focusing the audience's attention on me when I took solos. I'd been playing the guitar with my teeth or tongue since the age of nine. While backing Joe Tex I added new tricks like playing behind my head and back, between my legs, with beer bottles, microphone stands, or whatever an audience member handed me.

We had a good little thing going for a short time. However, by 1982 Joe was having personal and financial problems. His career had taken a sharp dive. He was playing honky-tonks in New Orleans around Claiborne Avenue and Basin

Street and on the outskirts of cities like Houston, Texas, and Jackson, Mississippi. His disco crossover had backfired, causing him to lose credibility with his core rhythm and blues audience. Young people were now into groups like Earth Wind and Fire and the Commodores. They saw Joe Tex as a novelty act. Perhaps most disappointing of all, Joe Tex was alleged to have developed an addiction to hard drugs. Joe Tex died at the age of forty-nine in Navasota, Texas, following a reported heart attack in 1982.

TABBY'S BLUES BOX

In the spring of 1979, Dad, having put his music on hold, became a supervisor and the union steward at the plant. "Well, what happened," Dad said, "I'd become the first Black union steward they had there. I ran for office and won. When many of the guys here in South Baton Rouge found out I was a union steward, they'd go out to Brown's office, the supervisor of the company, and say, 'Tabby sent me out here.' And before you knew it, half of South Baton Rouge was working down at the plant."

I rarely saw Dad because he worked odd shifts, sometimes three days on, three days off. When he was at home he was mostly sleeping. He'd been thinking about making a change and had begun regularly reading the employment section of the *Morning Advocate*.

Rose and Thomas Café (no relation) was a down-home mom-and-pop soul food café on North Boulevard. The boulevard had been an energetic bustling street in the 1940s, '50s, and '60s, but now, except for Rose and Thomas Café and the once-mighty Masonic Temple Roof Garden across the street, it was deserted. North Boulevard was a far cry from its heyday of touring chitlin circuit blues stars. The Temple Theater had been reduced to a barbershop on the ground floor and a hall for rent upstairs, in which bingo night for senior citizens was the main attraction. North Boulevard had been deteriorating steadily since the controversial "race riot" of 1972. After sunset the once-bustling Black business center was a ghost town.

One morning, as he often did a few times a week, Dad drove to Rose and Thomas Café for breakfast. He parked his car on the Temple Garden's parking lot located at the corner of Thirteenth Street and North Boulevard. While entering Rose and Thomas Café he eyed the dilapidated and boarded-up adjacent building. Rose and Thomas Café and the old Griffon store next door shared the same age-old brick building. Hanging loosely on the front door outside of Griffon's was a faded weather-beaten FOR RENT sign that looked as though it had been there since the riot seven years ago. Tabby went inside the café, sat at a table, and ordered breakfast, as usual. While sipping his coffee and browsing the want ads, he had an epiphany.

"I went in this café to eat," Tabby said. "A lady, her name was Rose, she used to go to school with my wife. They were in class together at McKinley, so I knew her well. I asked her one day, 'Hey, that building next door over there, who own that building?'"

"Mr. George Griffon owns the building," Rose answered.

"I'd like to go and talk to him," Dad said to Rose. "Where can I get a hold of him?"

"Well, he has an antique shop on Government Street. You might find him there."

After breakfast Dad drove over to Government Street and entered the antique shop. There was an office in the rear. Dad walked back there. A middle-aged Jewish man sat behind a desk.

"Mr. Griffon?" Dad asked, approaching. "I want to see Mr. Griffon," Dad said, eagerly.

"Yes?" Griffon said, curiously.

"I just came down to see you about that building you have over there," Dad said, "where Rose and Thomas at. I just didn't know if you still wanted to rent it or not?"

"Yes, I want to rent it," Griffon said, excitedly. "What you want to do there?"

"I'd like to open a little blues club."

"I'll tell you what I'm going to do," Griffon said, as he rummaged through his desk. "Here's the key." Dad was pleasantly surprised at Griffon's eagerness. "Water's on, lights are on, too," Griffon said. "You come back and see me in about three months and we'll talk about the rent."

Dad was touched by the generous offer.

"Well, I saw you have all these medicine cabinets in there and everything," Dad said.

"Do what you want to do with 'em," Griffon responded indifferently.

Dad came home that day rejuvenated. He told us excitedly of his new idea to open a blues club. He asked me and Tammy and our cousin Woodrow Vaughns to help him convert the former drugstore and grocery into a blues club. We started tearing out the rows of heavy wooden cabinets.

One day, while we were inside the building working, an older White fellow came in.

"I see you've got all these antique medicine cabinets," he said to Dad. "I want to buy them from you."

"They're not for sale," Dad said.

"You sure? I'll give you a good price," he insisted.

"No, I don't want to sell 'em."

After the old gentleman left, Tabby told us, curiously, to take an axe, take them outside, and chop them up. Tabby didn't want to go ahead and sell the cabinets? Well, Griffon had said in three months he'd come see him. Tabby thought Griffon might have sent the man by the place to test his character. "Yeah, I'm going to go there and sell the cabinets and get some money, and I ain't going to let him know that I sold them," Tabby said, introspectively. "He might have been setting me up to see what kind of man I am," Tabby said.

I worked alongside my brother, Tammy, and our cousin Woodrow every day to renovate the building. Dad also hired W. W. Woodfaulk, a carpenter by trade, who used to play drums with Lightnin' Slim. He hired Zack the Cat, a white-haired gravedigger, handyman, quirky drummer, and someone I believed to be a kind of soothsayer, to help us too. A few people in the neighborhood volunteered to help but mostly Dad relied on unpaid family labor. The buzzing noise of saws and the hyper thump of hammers echoed out of the building, drawing the attention of neighbors. Everyone stopped and peeked in to see what all the racket was about. The busy sound of progress had not been heard on the block for years.

Before integration, Black-run businesses were thriving. Mind you, I don't wish to inflate the success of pre–civil rights movement business success in the area, but North Boulevard was indeed undoubtedly a bustling thoroughfare lined with successful Negro businesses.

Over the next few weeks, we built an upstairs seating area to go along with the downstairs seating and dance area. We built a wooden stage downstairs about a foot off the floor. Woodfaulk built a guardrail around the stage. Woodfaulk's biggest contribution was an *L*-shaped wooden bar with a laminated top.

We soon discovered plumbing in the rickety building was a problem. The plumbing lines were hidden deep underneath the concrete floors. To solve the problem, we'd have to tear out the floor, practically gutting the frail building, the cost of which wasn't feasible for us nor the owner. So, we made do with the building's faulty plumbing best we could.

Over several weeks, Tammy, Woodrow, Zack the Cat, Woodfaulk, and I knocked and nailed, sawed and painted, until we turned the old building into a cool little juke joint. All the while, Dad continued working at the plant. Woodrow oversaw the project in his absence. At the time, Dad and I weren't seeing eye to eye about a lot of things—the norm, I guess, for a father and his teenaged son.

I didn't like spending long hours at the club working and hauling trash. I wasn't enjoying any of it. Woodrow, however, was a positive influence. I confided in him. He became the peacemaker between my dad and me. Woodrow told me, in a thousand different ways, my dad loved me, he only wanted the best for me. He also went on and on about how great it was that my dad was opening a club, starting his own business. Woodrow was so proud of him. Unbeknownst to me, Dad was building a sanctuary for my development as a blues artist, a makeshift music conservatory of sorts. Woodrow understood Dad's vision for me. He knew Dad envisioned himself as mentor and protector of my talents. He was convinced I could become a great blues artist with his guidance. Problem was, I wasn't interested in blues as a career. My limited view of blues was what I'd experienced so far: dead-end gigs, limited earnings and recognition. Rock or pop music stardom is what I aspired to. I saw our family juke joint as a place that would constrain my talents and aspirations. I felt I was erecting my own musical ghetto. Woodrow thought otherwise.

Meanwhile, we installed a used beer cooler, patched the faulty plumbing, and then crossed our fingers while the city inspector investigated the passibility of the patchwork building. It took a few attempts, but we eventually passed inspection. Finally, after months of knocking and nailing, the run-down building was transformed into our hopping new juke joint. My major concern was that I would be forced to work at the club day and night, missing out on a lot of parties with my friends or gigs with my band, Exit. We were starting to draw a large female following. I was definitely interested in girls at this time. I was well aware that Black teenaged females would never step a stiletto anywhere near our blues shack. Moreover, Black people my age didn't know nor care to know anything about the blues.

DEM PIG LIPS

One afternoon, our newly hired bartender, Beatrice, was hanging colored Christmas tree lights around the bar. Although it was the middle of summer, it wouldn't have been a proper juke joint without Christmas tree lights. Dad was busy stocking the beer cooler—which rarely got cold. I was unboxing whiskey for the shelves.

Two delivery men entered carrying a used jukebox. Rosemary curiously followed them in. Rosemary was a petite elderly woman—or maybe a woman aged by the harsh realities of destitution. She lived alone in the run-down shotgun house next door. You could say she was squatting; she had no electricity.

The delivery guys sat the jukebox in the corner then plugged it in. The jukebox lit up, instantly jazzing up the atmosphere. Everyone stopped what they were doing and looked on as Rosemary slowly approached the jukebox. She took the last few coins from her tattered nature sack and dropped them into the jukebox. There was thick anticipation in the room. We watched the mechanical player's arm turn, grab a 45 rpm record, and place it on the turntable. Once the needle went down on the scratchy record, it was as if lightning had struck! The jukebox lights glowed brighter, flashing to the blaring beat! Suddenly, we heard the big beat and the familiar energetic shout of Big Joe Turner singing the lustful classic, "Shake Rattle and Roll." The jump blues rocker transformed Rosemary's gaunt expression into a girlish grin. There was a twinkle in her eyes as she swayed to the beat. Perhaps the song brought back memories for Rosemary of her teen years, dancing with a young boy who certainly knew the hidden meaning behind every word Big Joe Turner sang. Despite the behest of her parents, she probably stayed out beyond curfew, cutting the rug at some house party because she couldn't resist the seductive lure of the blues.

Woodrow entered with two large jars, one of pickled pigs' feet, another of pig lips. Zack the Cat, mopping the floor, noticed the jar of pickled pigs' lips. Woodrow set the jars on the bar. Jars of salt pork scraps—a vestige of antebellum slave cuisine—were usually pickled in vinegar, salt, and water for preservation. A jar of pickled pigs' lips was a staple of juke joints, as were Christmas tree lights, off-brand whiskey, and a beat-up jukebox.

Zack strolled over to the bar.

"Hey, Tabby, gimme one of dem dere pig lips," Zack said, as he wiped the sweat from his brow with the ever-present white towel that hung across his shoulder.

"Two dollars, Zack."

My dad was never one to give his workers anything free.

Zack, dug in his pockets, searching for loose change. He was counting his coins when Beatrice offered to help.

"How much you need, Zack?" she said, digging in her purse.

"Here, Tabby." She handed Dad some change. "Give me one of 'em too."

"Thanks," Zack said, smiling. "I owe you one."

Woodrow opened the jar, stuck a fork into a few pieces of pig lips, and placed them on wax paper. He served the snack to Zack and Beatrice. That was our first sale. We were officially in business.

Tabby placed the change into a cigar box behind the bar. It seemed a cash register was a little too complex for our club. Dad took his .45 pistol out from the small of his back. He placed it right next to the cigar box. A fair warning for all to see. A cigar box happened to be an important symbol in blues culture. Many poor Black kids in the old South had made their first guitars from a cigar box. The box was used as the body, a narrow stick formed the neck, and tightly strung twine served as strings. In our joint, this primitive music box still held its useful symbolism. The name Tabby's Blues Box was a nod to a crude homemade guitar.

Finally, we were ready to hold the grand opening. Tabby's Blues Box was located at 1314 North Boulevard, near downtown, on the corner of South Thirteenth Street. Tabby vowed it would be "a sanctuary for the bluesmen and women of Baton Rouge." Now that Tabby had his own club, the next major task was to get the word out. The grand opening was set for a Wednesday night. Tabby took off from work early so he could get home and clean himself up for the occasion. The club was about twelve blocks from our house. I walked, carrying my guitar, as I would do a thousand times thereafter.

On this very special day I arrived around five that evening with my guitar slung across my back. I was ready to take part in the first night of live music in the Blues Box. There was great anticipation in the air. The brick building had an outside wall that Dad thought would be the perfect place to paint a sign. The sign would be seen clearly by cars passing by, including the Greyhound buses that passed all times of the day, on schedule, going to and from the bus station, which was just two blocks over on Florida Street.

The first thing I saw as I arrived was a little man standing high on a ladder outside the club, dressed in white painter's clothing, skillfully painting the marquee. His right hand was stretched above his head holding a paintbrush as far as his arm could reach. With the precision of a surgeon, he painted the finishing touches. I was taken aback observing the man, focused with such seriousness, as if commissioned by the blues gods. Standing there, I saw the finished sign read TABBY'S BLUES BOX, HOME OF THE BATON ROUGE BLUESMEN. I was very proud and excited for my dad.

Later that evening, musicians arrived with friends, wives, mistresses, and hangers on. Dad charged admission at the door but let all musicians in free. Seems word had only gotten around to musicians. There wasn't much of an audience except for their entourages. Everyone—the doorman, the waitress, the bartender, the musicians, and patrons—was Black. The initial word of mouth only spread as far as the surrounding neighborhood.

We were all excited to have a place to play and dance. As for Dad, it had been a long time coming. He could get on stage and play his music again. He had planned to perform the whole night with his band, which included my brother, Tammy, on drums and me on bass. But there were so many musicians who brought along their guitars and harmonicas he had to let them sit in and jam with us. Drinks flowed; the music was dynamic. The music went on all night. You'd think no one had to go to work the next morning. But these were blue-collar musicians. They all had day jobs.

Later that night, the little man was standing in front of the stage. He was waving the paintbrush around high above his head like a conductor's baton. He was right in front of us, conducting with a satisfied look on his face, as if he were conducting the Louisiana Philharmonic Orchestra. In the other hand he held a near-empty bottle of whisky in a brown paper bag. He must've brought it into the club against Dad's policy. But no one seemed to care. Everyone danced around the man, bumping into him, knocking him off balance. He was sloppy drunk. He wavered and tried his best to keep his balance as we played and dancers partied all around him.

I saw Rosemary and a young man dancing across the room. She danced gracefully with the enthusiasm of a schoolgirl. It seemed, at least for a night, there wasn't any other place in the world we would want to be. Whatever troubles we had—on the job, at home—were forgotten. Guys were dancing with one another's women and no one seemed to mind. That sort of thing usually ended up with some poor soul lying on the dance floor in his own blood, but not this night. We were lost in the moment and the moment was bliss. Over the next few weeks, word spread fast. The joint created a real buzz around town. Not everyone was thrilled. For some, the joint would become a little too spicy.

Then, one night, the police burst in! The lights came on. The music stopped abruptly. Everyone froze in place. One of the officers approached Dad, who was behind the bar.

"This your establishment?" said the cop.

"Yes, this my place. I'm Tabby Thomas. What's going on, officer?"

"Reports are, you have no liquor license." He handed Dad a citation, "When you get one, make sure its visible at all times."

"Let's move it out, the parties over," another officer commanded.

I began packing up the musical gear as we prepared for closing. Everyone moved outside. It just so happens that one of the only White people in the place was a curly haired young man who'd been sitting in on the jam, playing his harmonica. He respectfully approached Dad.

"Hey, maybe I can be of some help," he said.

"Who you?"

"John DiGiulio. I'm an attorney."

"Can't 'ford no lawyer."

"Well, you're going to need one. Besides, where else is someone going to let me on stage?"

"Yeah," Dad chuckled, "you were awful."

"I won't charge you, if you can put up with my harp playing."

Dad was slightly relieved. He looked John in the eye, sizing him up. John gave Dad his business card.

"You got a deal," Dad said. They shook on it.

Police padlocks were placed on the Blues Box's entry doors.

The next day, we went to see John at his downtown office on St. Louis Street. It turned out John DiGiulio was an excellent lawyer, a graduate of Harvard University. Good for him, because he was a terrible harp player.

Later, an embarrassing story ran in the Baton Rouge news about the raid. The story described the club in a negative light, as though it were a lawless riverside barrelhouse. We assumed the news had all but doomed the reopening of the Blues Box. John, over the next few weeks, represented Dad at downtown hearings with the alcoholic beverage control board. The first meeting didn't go well at all. Dad's application was rejected because he was located in close proximity to a playground. Too close, in fact, to be awarded a liquor license. There was nothing even a sharp lawyer like John could do to change that fact. The prospects of getting the police padlocks removed from the front doors of Tabby's looked dim.

Meanwhile, Dad worked overtime at the plant to catch up on bills derived from opening expenses. But after some time, we decided to open up again anyway, selling only sodas and snacks. We did this for a short time. But a dry club—selling only sodas and snacks—is a real buzzkill in the juke joint business. When a customer came into the bar and found out there was no alcohol, only soda pop, they turned and walked out.

John, after some brainstorming, came up with the idea to call a last-ditch meeting with the ABC board, but this time he would enlighten them regarding the history of the blues and its cultural significance. He pitched to my dad that by doing such, it would separate his club from the average hole-in-the-wall bar. John suggested Dad rename the place Tabby's Blues Box and Heritage Hall. "It's a long shot," John warned, "but it's worth a try."

We returned to the ABC board and John made a passionate presentation. After a few days we got the news. The ABC board awarded Dad a liquor license for his "Heritage Hall."

Shortly after that, the little man, who was sober and steady as an arrow during the day but drunk out of his mind at night, was back on his scaffold revising the marquee, which now read, TABBY'S BLUES BOX AND HERITAGE HALL, HOME OF THE BATON ROUGE BLUESMEN.

John had helped us get the fine reduced. He also helped Dad prepare the paperwork for an operational license, plus any additional inspection certifications needed. John became a family friend. A lasting bond grew between the two men. John was always there for us over the years, and rarely, if ever, charged us for his services. Tabby was always gracious to him. John's harp playing did become passable after a while.

We reopened with our new liquor license framed and displayed on the wall behind the bar. It turns out, the embarrassing publicity about the liquor license raid had helped create awareness among White music lovers around town. In show business they say, "Any publicity is good publicity." We were shocked when we reopened and drew a packed house! Suddenly there were more Whites in the joint than Blacks. They were spending money, too.

The first weekend, we ran out of ice and beer several times. I didn't get to play more than a song or two that week because I was running back and forth to Romano's grocery store, which was down the street across the Kansas City Southern Railroad Line tracks, to get change, ice, and beer all night long. The beer cooler's compressor went out, the beer was warm, but it didn't seem to matter as long as the music kept on swinging.

The building didn't have air-conditioning, but there was a large circular fan on the front ceiling that sucked hot air and cigarette smoke out. It hardly blew any air in. I guess that stiff humid bayou air was too thick for our rickety fan. Anyhow, it didn't take much to get sweaty on the dance floor. Folks would get soaking wet, step outside for some fresh air, return after a spell, and do it all over again.

The outdated bathroom plumbing overflowed. Zack was there with the mop bucket, trying his best to sponge up the water, but the partygoers wouldn't let the dysfunction dampen their spirits. Black men were dancing with White women, Black women were dancing with White men, this was something no one had ever experienced so openly in Baton Rouge. I'm sure there were some in the joint who were uncomfortable with this new development, but from the bandstand, I couldn't pick one out in the crowd. Everyone seemed content to "*Laissez les bon temps rouler!*"

I began to understand the powerful allure the blues had. The entertainment was risqué, the atmosphere edgy, the drinks flowed, the people danced salaciously to the intoxicating beat. Black with White, blue-collar with white-collar. It was obvious something very special was happening inside our little juke joint. It seemed Baton Rouge had been waiting for a venue like this to emerge.

Tabby's quickly gained a reputation as the cultural place to visit if one wanted an authentic musical experience in central Louisiana. Over the next weeks and months there would be sporadic French Bus Tours, which showed up without any warning. We'd have to scramble to accommodate an additional sixty or eighty people all at once. It took a while before we got a handle on group tours showing up unexpectedly. We started to demand notices of a month in advance, along with a general deposit.

Tabby's quickly became the place to be seen and heard for blues musicians all over the region, including New Orleans, a city known for music venues, but not our type of blues in particular. Word was out that European promoters would sometimes arrange bookings for musicians from the Blues Box to go on lucrative overseas tours and perform at major festivals. This new development was a big deal. In the past, we'd have to move to Chicago to attract European festival bookers.

In 1958 Muddy Waters had visited England and turned young English musicians onto electric blues for the first time. Since then, opportunities for international recognition became commonplace for Chicago musicians. On the contrary, in Louisiana all we had for years was the annual New Orleans Jazz Festival to showcase ourselves to European promoters.

But now Tabby's Blues Box was a happening six nights a week, fifty-two weeks a year. European promoters flocked to our authentic Heritage Hall when scouting in the United States. The publicity of European promoters signing up local musicians for tours and recordings gained us international recognition, as well as good paying regional gigs, for the first time. Before long, Dad was finally able to quit his day job at the plant and run his club full time.

Dad played at least one set every night. Sometimes there were more musicians in the room than paying customers, but Dad would always take the stage regardless. This was sometimes seen as ego driven, or hogging the show, but no one could really complain because it was his club. Eventually, Dad settled on headlining Friday nights. He performed consistently through the years, every Friday night, which was not easy to do in a city like Baton Rouge. But Dad had a special gift. He made people feel good.

Wednesdays developed into a weekly open jam session, the first of its kind in Louisiana. At these jam sessions, amateur musicians got a chance to play with seasoned pros. Baton Rouge, unlike New Orleans, was a working-class entertainment town. It couldn't rely on tourists throughout the week. Fridays and Saturdays, we would routinely draw standing-room-only crowds, but during the week, things slowed down.

Dad always insisted on a cover charge each night he was open. He was against free admission for live music, and for good reason. A cover charge made the customers respect the culture. He slowly taught some of the stubborn holdouts that the "old-timey" music had value. Charging at the door also served another purpose; it helped to keep petty criminals, beggars, loiterers, and troublemakers outside.

One night, Dad was working the door. Silas Hogan was advertised on posters outside. A woman came to the entrance expecting free admission.

"It's going to be two dollars," Dad said.

"I ain't gon' pay no two dollars to see Silas," she said. "I see Silas free every Tuesday night!"

"Well, that's where you'll go," Dad said. "'Cause if you come in here, it's going to be two dollars."

Some people who were used to seeing the older blues people play for free stayed away from the club at first. But after the lines got longer and the price of admission got higher, they came back because they wanted to be a part of the fun and excitement.

Several bands developed from these loose jam sessions. They inspired a new generation of musicians who got firsthand experience singing the blues to a live audience and building reputations as front men. Names like Silas Hogan and his son, Sam Hogan, Henry Gray, Guitar Kelly, Robert Milburn (brother of Amos Milburn), the Circuit Breakers, Eyewitness Blues, Blue Light Special, Michael Wolfe, Moses "Whispering" Smith, Shannon Williford, Bob Ourso, Raful Neal, Kenny Neal, Ray Neal, and the Neal Family, Kenny Acosta, George "Slim" Heard, Big Luther Kent, Cadillac, Lazy Lester, Clarence Edwards, Sammy Thornton, Larry Garner, Oscar "Harpo" Davis, Doug Brousseau, Little Jimmy Reed, John Lisi, Tab Benoit, Sonny Landreth, Troy Turner, Jimmy Dotson, Vince Hutchinson, Katie Webster, Carol Fran, J. Monque'D, Jimmy Vaughan (drummer), Smokehouse, School Boy Cleve, Chicago Al, Pine, Pie Man, and many others.

BATON ROUGE BLUES FESTIVAL 1981

IN 1981, Tabby and some of his most enthusiastic supporters formed the first blues society in Louisiana, which was also one of the first in the United States. I attended the early meetings of the multiracial group, but I was soon tossed out because of what they perceived as my naive views regarding their plans. The idea for a blues festival came out of these meetings.

It was strongly suggested that the festival should be held at Scott's Bluff on the bank of the Mississippi River on Southern University's campus. The Bluffs was a beautiful setting for an outdoor event, located high on a hill with a great view of the lazy Mississippi River below. What could be a better backdrop for a blues festival? Historically Black, Southern University was an obvious suggestion because the roots of the blues, of course, are entwined with Louisiana's Black community.

On Sunday, May 3, 1981, the first Louisiana blues festival commenced. Tabby was booked on the festival, naturally, as one of its headliners. I also performed as an accompanist, playing rhythm guitar behind all the regulars from the Blues Box, which included Silas Hogan, Arthur "Guitar" Kelly, and Moses "Whispering" Smith. I was allowed to lead a number, too.

Raful Neal and the Neal Family were featured along with Brian Lee, a talented blind guitarist who gained fame as a popular attraction on Bourbon Street. Last but not least was the colorful Ernie K-Doe of "Mother-in-Law" fame. Ernie K-Doe's performance was over the top, as expected with anything K-Doe.

Afterward, K-Doe held court backstage, charging people to touch him! Yes, to touch him, they paid a fee. This was before the advent of the CD. In the early '80s, contrary to today's record business, no bands sold albums from the stage. Albums were sold only at retail shops. Therefore, Ernie K-Doe's hustle was ahead of its time.

The turnout for the inaugural Baton Rouge Blues Festival was sparse and multiracial. The crowd was small but enthusiastic. Plans were quickly made to have annual blues festivals at Southern each year, building on the initial success.

On Sunday, April 25, 1982, the following year, we held another blues festival. The second festival was well attended. The crowd was a bit rowdy. Lots of drinking and hard partying from sunup to sundown. All the regular Blues Box artists were on the bill. We also featured some West Louisiana zydeco bands, such as John Delafose and the Eunice Playboys, Hezekiah and the House Rockers, along with Scott Dunbar and the popular blue-eyed Blues Box regulars Kenny Acosta Band.

We were astonished to learn soon after the second festival that Southern University didn't want to host our blues festival again. We received a letter informing us that, in spite of our growing success, we were no longer welcome. We were dismayed. We thought it had gone well. The festival had received good reviews, but the administration and faculty at Southern University didn't perceive our music befitting a historically Black institution of higher learning—as if college kids didn't drink beer and listen to loud, bawdy music.

They informed us the arrangement with the society was a mistake. And furthermore, we would never be welcomed on their campus again. Undoubtedly, this was seen as a major setback for the blues societies' goal of helping the local blues culture gain recognition by educating students and the public of its significance.

An emergency blues society meeting was called at Tabby's. Several new locations were suggested, but there were problems either logistically, getting permits, or they just weren't conducive to a festival atmosphere. Finally, it was suggested the festival should be held in downtown Baton Rouge. Applications for grants and permits would need to be submitted, but the chances of approval seemed slim. Unlike New Orleans, which had a long history of allowing large groups of African Americans to gather at places like Congo Square during slavery to celebrate and blow off steam to music, Baton Rouge was conservative, still anxious concerning large Black crowds and race mixing. While we awaited approval on the festival's location change, we continued to jam at the Blues Box.

SOON THIS MORN'NIN BLUES

A PROMOTIONAL FLYER wafting in the wind touched down gently on the sidewalk. A female student strolling near Louisiana State's campus along a row of trendy bars and coffeehouses picked up the flyer and read it to her friends.

Tabby had hired a few students to distribute flyers around the campus on car windshields, trees, and streetlight posts. Students at LSU's Union took note of flyers on the walls. Word got around that Tabby's Blues Box was a cool hangout. A DJ at KLSU read from a flyer on air: "It's jam night at Tabby's Blues Box," he said, while placing Dad's record, "Hoodoo Party," on the turntable. "So, bring your guitar if you want to jam. But it's not your average jam, man! Oh no! You better shed before you go. Tabby's the real deal, y'all!" Tabby's classic song "Hoodoo Party" blasted out into cars and ears all over the campus:

Well the Hoodoo King, and the Hoodoo Queen.
Gave a little party down in New Orleans . . .

The Blues Box became a hipster joint for students. They vied for seats with the adult crowd by arriving early. We didn't take reservations; it was first come first serve. The music got better each week, too, because we heard each other play and attempted to top what we heard. Friendly but intense head-cutting rivalries developed, which contributed to tighter performances. The real winners of the amiable competition, of course, was the Blues Box audience.

On any given night, Arthur "Guitar" Kelly could be found strutting his stuff on the small stage to the delight of the audience. They'd shout, "Yeah, tell it, Kelly!" Guitar Kelly would sometimes walk off the stage into the crowd, letting his guitar hang loosely by his side. While moving among the audience, Kelly gave them an exciting close-up glimpse of his callused fingers working the frets.

"Guitar" Kelly, in his sixties, didn't weigh more than 150 pounds. His ageless dark skin was smooth, his clear eyes twinkled. Kelly was not known to drink alcohol, just 7-Up. He wore thick-rimmed black eyeglasses hidden beneath the brim of his speckled trademark hat. I would often play drums behind Kelly with Sam Hogan, the son of Silas Hogan, on bass. Whenever Kelly leaped from his chair to work the crowd things got heated. To keep steady time on drums with so much adrenalin in the air was a challenge. Kelly liked the way I played behind him because I resisted the temptation to speed up the tempo—as a less experienced drummer might—when the crowd got excited.

From across the dim, smoke-filled room, you could see the perspiration stains on Kelly's brightly printed plaid shirt. Kelly pulled a guitar string with one hand while the other was behind his back. Kelly hit another note, letting it sustain out for effect *Pling!*

"All right, Kelly," a woman shouted.

Glancing at her, he pulled another string. *Pling!*

Kelly effortlessly made his guitar answer back in a flirtatious call-and-response with the woman, as if they were engaged in a lusty conversation. A perfectly timed pluck here, and two or three notes picked there, Kelly worked the Blues Box audience into euphoria! He built the music to a roaring crescendo, then ended with an extended finale. Kelly left the stage to a rousing standing ovation!

"You the man, Kelly!" they shouted as Kelly unplugged his guitar, yielding the heated bandstand to Tabby. He glanced at Dad with a cocksure smile and winked. How could Dad follow such a smoking performance? The friendly competition made us better. On a Friday or Saturday night at the Box, you had to be on top of your game if you didn't want to get embarrassed.

Nonetheless, it wasn't long before my wily dad had the crowd on their feet. Dad did his most popular song, recorded in 1961 for Excello, the "Hoodoo Party." He too, worked the joint into a frenzy. He played the guitar and sung while "Whispering" Smith played the harp. I was still on the drums, but now I ate from a smothered chicken and white bean plate from Rose and Thomas next door, which rested on the floor tom. I played with one stick in my left hand to free my right hand in an attempt to eat supper between beats. There was a disgruntled whisper among musicians that Tabby loathed his side musicians taking breaks, even to use the bathroom. It took a while before Dad grasped the understanding the crowd was not going to rush out the door just because the music paused for a fifteen-minute break. Notwithstanding, the Hoodoo Party rolled on:

Well they rocked and rolled till the break of day.
And two by two they all went away.
Everybody was wondering, where and when.
The king and the queen would boogie again.
Boogie chillun, yeah boogie chillun,
Well now boogie-woogie chillun,
 Boogie till the break of dawn . . .

Sometimes we'd continue after hours. Just before 2:00 AM, we'd have last call. The crowd would buy extra beer and liquor to tide them over. Some would just bring their own. On a magical night we kept the Hoodoo Party going until the wee hours of the morning.

After a few months had passed, we learned the blues festival would now take place in downtown Baton Rouge, on the grounds of the Old State Capitol building. This was great news for the Blues Society. It meant the city was willing to give us a larger operating budget of grants in anticipation of increased attendance.

When the blues festival moved to the once-segregated downtown, a remarkable thing happened. More than thirty-five thousand people showed up. There were a few thousand Black families, but the crowd was predominately White. They were young and old, poor and well-to-do. The festival was free, which accounted for thousands of families, including very young children running around the old state capitol grounds. They all had a joyous time!

I was booked on the show as a side musician but I performed a few songs as leader. The highlight of my set was when I sang "Hoochie Coochie Man" and "Mannish Boy," a medley of Bo Diddley and Muddy Waters tunes that I'd been singing for years, even before I understood the lusty sexual connotations in the lyrics. This medley had always inspired older women to concur, yes, I truly was a mannish boy, and they were going to tame me.

For the blues festival audience I wanted to do something extra special. So, in the middle of my performance I did all my tricks, playing the guitar between my legs, with my teeth, behind my back and head. The next morning the local papers had a large picture of me with a rave review of my performance. The older guys were starting to gain recognition, but my performance upstaged everyone that year, gaining me instant local notoriety. At the time, having a bona fide teenaged bluesman on the bill was a novelty, but it was a good omen for the future of the music.

Meanwhile, Dad left home for a tour of England. He was booked to play about thirty-five one-nighters. Whenever Dad would go away for a few weeks, he depended on me to run the Blues Box, and I did. I took the responsibility seriously. I was thrown into the fire, managing a business without any formal education to do so. Yet, he left me in charge. I kept the Blues Box running smooth. I also managed and led the house band in Dad's absence. I carried his gun, a loaded .45 caliber pistol, to protect the moneybag and myself. When managing the club, I was allowed to drive Dad's light blue Cadillac Coupe DeVille to the club. A Cadillac is something every musician of my dad's generation cherished. It was the crown jewel for a Black recording artist. He was extremely proud of his Cadillac—purchased with plant checks, not royalties. He didn't buy it new, but it was a smooth riding hog that looked really good when it was washed, and its whitewall tires were shiny. I got to drive it while running errands for the club. It was my responsibility to purchase all the beer, liquor, and cigarettes to stock the bar for the week.

Typically, I would get to the club around five o'clock in the evening, the normal time Dad would open. Beatrice, the bartender, would meet me there. She and I would stock the bar and tidy the place up from the night before. Once we'd prepared everything for the evening, we'd sit around listing to the jukebox until the customers came in. Like Dad had instructed, I'd place the gun next to the cigar box that acted as our cash register as a warning to all, letting them know I was ready for whatever.

We never opened for lunch; we didn't have a real kitchen. Besides, Rose and Thomas took care of the breakfast and lunch crowds. We only had a gas stove, a dingy vent, a small fridge, and a sink. Hell, we barely could make it through inspections to sell liquor, so there was no way we could have passed rigorous food inspections.

There was a tiny black-and-white TV behind the bar that only caught two channels. It was never on. As a diversion, until the band showed up, we played the jukebox, drank, smoked cigarettes, and engaged in the latest "street news" and gossip. Sometimes we passed the time sitting around talking for a few hours with someone from around the neighborhood. Or small talk with a truck driver or two, sitting at a table nursing a beer. The bands wouldn't start playing until around ten o'clock, so the crowd wouldn't show up until then. The early evenings were calm and relaxed before the throng of patrons arrived.

One evening I was sitting on the stoop out in front of the club having a smoke, passing the time, watching the sunset, just shooting the breeze with another guy doing the same. The heavy double entry doors to the club flung open.

"What you doing out here?" Beatrice said, scornfully eyeing me.

"Taking a break," I said.

"Well, if your daddy knew you out here, he'd be upset."

Beatrice, a short, stocky, abrasive bartender whom Dad trusted and relied on, was always riding me. She was bossy, but she was a really nice lady once you got to know her. She would even try bossing Dad around when he was there. It was just her way.

I thought to myself, I'm in charge here, I can take a break whenever I want. Nevertheless, it was clear Beatrice didn't see it that way. No sense arguing with her, I reasoned. I'd never win. So, I tossed my half-smoked cigarette on the concrete, stamped it out under my shoe, and rose up to follow her back inside the club. The guy beside me scooped my sullied cigarette butt up off the pavement, relit it, and took a long pull.

Back inside, I walked over to the jukebox and dropped a roll of quarters in the machine. I selected some of my favorite jukebox tunes, several by Johnny "Guitar" Watson, a polished urban blues guitar player who had had a string of hits recently. His tunes, along with Bobby Bland, B. B. King, Z. Z. Hill, Little Milton, Albert King, and Johnny Taylor, were jukebox staples. Beatrice was working the bar, pouring a drink of whisky for a customer. "Make me one of those," I said. Beatrice reluctantly poured me a drink. I was the only one allowed to drink without paying. This didn't sit well with Beatrice; if she had her way, she'd have charged me. But Dad didn't really pay me much, so free drinks were a concession he made to me. Though he wouldn't have if he thought for one minute I'd drink him dry. But I was a modest drinker. I only drank and smoked occasionally out of boredom.

One night while Dad was away on tour we heard a thunderous *Boom! Crash!* Alfred burst into the club. He called out from across the room, "Chr . . . Chr . . ." Alfred stuttered. "Chr . . . Chris! Some . . . Somebody just wrecked your daddy's car!"

Alfred, a lanky, muscular guy, was one of Dad's most loyal helpers. He was a bit simple yet hardened like a soldier at the same time. Alfred was the kind of guy I'd want with me in a foxhole or dark alley. Dad treated Alfred like part of the family.

We all ran outside to see what had happened. Dad's blue Cadillac, which I'd parked in front of the club, was smashed up on the driver's side—the side facing the street. Oh no, I thought, Dad's going to kill me! Some drunk had driven by and sideswiped it from back to front. The doors were jammed, windows broken.

It was a hit and run. Just then, we heard the distant screech of a loosely hanging bumper scraping against the street. We spotted the culprit zigzagging a few miles down the road. Without hesitation one of the regulars jumped into his truck. He took off in hot pursuit. He caught up to the wobbly drunkard and pulled him over. We called the police.

I anticipated Dad would blow a gasket when he returned home. I was sure the wreck would further strain our already rocky relationship. When Dad finally made it home and learned what happened from Alfred and several witnesses, he didn't blow up immediately like I'd anticipated. But why should he? After all, I wasn't the drunk driver. Regardless, he wasn't one to let such things go easily. Why let leverage, however frivolous, go to waste? Indeed, he quietly kept it over my head for months, using it as a passive-aggressive weapon he could bludgeon me with whenever I failed to follow his orders.

Some nights, lines formed early outside the door and down the block. Sometimes we made fans wait outside until a few people would leave, then more could enter. One night, the place was jumping; we were packed in tightly, elbow to elbow, dancing, smiling, having fun. Tabby was on the bandstand. Tabby had an uncanny, almost magical, ability to perceive his fans' private desires then satisfy them with just the right mix of music, poetry, and storytelling. He'd work them into a frenzy. The crowd would abandon themselves on the dance floor.

One night, Tabby, having just finished his set, headed toward the bar. I joined the band on stage, plugged in, and kept the music playing. Later, in the middle of my set, the police barged in! The bright lights came up. The party came to a confused halt. I assumed the worst—a serious crime outside, perhaps? After all, the Blues Box was in a high crime neighborhood. I figured the police were seeking perpetrators possibly hiding among us. The cops herded everyone outside. Soon we learned the cause of the problem. We were shut down for serving alcohol to a minor. Our alcohol permit was suspended immediately.

The next morning it was all over the newspapers as well as the evening news. Tabby's shut down again, this time for serving alcohol to minors. Some years ago, in direct response to public demand for stricter enforcement of laws concerning the sale and consumption of alcoholic beverages in East Baton Rouge Parish, the Metropolitan Council had created the Office of Alcoholic Beverage Control (the ABC board). The suspension was a crushing blow for us. We were already on thin ice with the ABC board dating back to the beginning, when our original liquor license had been revoked due to the board's playground-proximity ordinance.

John DiGiulio went into a phone booth, put on his cape, and came to our rescue yet again. He eventually won our license back. John even helped to pay the fines. John was my dad's "angel" attorney. If John had charged my family for his services, we couldn't have afforded him. During our lowest ebbs, thanks to John DiGiulio, we remained in business.

Later, we learned it had all been a setup. An underage girl had used a fake ID. It was well known that many LSU students in Tabby's had fake IDs. But an official investigation exposed some questionable motives. Unbeknownst to the doorman, or anyone else, her mother was parked in a car across the street, waiting, watching, as her underaged daughter entered the Box. Her mother drove away and stopped at a convenience store and dropped a dime on us, tipping off the cops.

The setup was a reminder that we had invisible enemies. There were some in Baton Rouge who didn't want to see the Blues Box succeed. Although Tabby's Blues Box was a place that brought the races together, it was still located in the Deep South. There were forces that didn't want to see Blacks and Whites socializing. The thought of miscegenation was still unbearable for some. Moreover, Baton Rouge had stringent blue laws. Although the majority of metro Baton Rouge was Catholic, Anglicized puritan values were enforced throughout the week. In contrast, New Orleans's Roman Catholics' only Sunday duty was to attend Mass—afterward, there were street parties, gaming, theater, dances, and festivals. Indeed, New Orleans had fought long and hard since the Louisiana Purchase to protect its vibrant Creole culture from Anglo puritan encroachment. Baton Rouge, only eighty miles north of the Crescent City, had long since surrendered to Americanized Anglo placidity. Baton Rouge had more in common with Protestant border states Mississippi, Arkansas, and Texas. Categorically, Tabby's Blues Box was threatening to reestablish a Creole counterculture in Baton Rouge. The Creole culture my dad was cultivating was liberating for young adults, the future of the city, but their parents and grandparents were not amused.

From that time on, we became more diligent at the door, turning away anyone who looked underage regardless of ID. Though we desperately needed their patronage—we were under scrutiny for several months—students shied away. Students had supported us on weeknights while many adults only showed up on weekends. Clearly our new policy was hurting our cash-strapped business.

Then one day Tabby came up with a promotion to attract the students back to the club. Though we'd continue our strict ID policy, we became more accommodating to students than some competitors. Paying a cover charge, plus a few dollars more for warm beer, was not alluring. Tabby came up with an idea to make beer kegs available to everyone on Thursday nights for free. They'd pay a cover and drink for free until the kegs were empty. This promotion proved magnetic. Students returned in large groups again. Thursdays became known as "Tabby's Hoodoo Party." We had a big keg of beer set up in a large tin bucket loaded down with ice. They'd just go over, get a large cup, pour their own beer. They paid a door fee, but they didn't buy the beer. We served free hot dogs, too. College kids were on tight budgets. One can stomach only so much ramen noodles. We boiled hot dogs and had a warmer for the buns, a little mustard, ketchup, and wow, those dogs went fast. They'd get out of school four or five o'clock and about eight o'clock they'd want a beer and a snack. It was happy hour geared toward students with a live band. Indeed, Tabby had a way with young people. He was charismatic and generous. They really looked up to him. There were several female students he mentored on drums. Why drums; who knows?

One young lady, originally from Texas, came from a family with a large swimming pool on the docks of the Mississippi. She used to visit with Dad regularly for lessons. Tabby taught her to play the drums. One time, Tabby went to Switzerland to play some dates. When he returned home, he told me he had run into his young friend. He was on tour with a New Orleans brass band traveling by bus. Promoters had advertised his picture and name on fliers and posters all over Zurich.

"Man, guess what?" Dad said, smiling.

"What?" I replied.

"Guess who I saw over there?"

"Who?"

"My little friend," he said, excitedly. "You know? The drummer."

He told me all about the different places he'd gone, the standing ovations he received, but he seemed most enthused about seeing his drum student.

"We got on the tour bus at our hotel," Dad said, "and went out to the place where we were going to play." He continued, "When our bus rolled up there and we were getting ready to get off, had a little blonde-haired girl, she came running. 'Hey! Tabby!' And it was the same little girl from Texas." He had the biggest grin on his face, as if it were happening as he spoke. "Man, I was so surprised to see her," Dad said. "She was going to oceanography school over there in Switzerland. She was so happy to see me, 'Hey, Tabby!'" he said, emulating her feminine voice. "She's just a friend of mine, ha ha, you know what I mean." I knew what he meant.

Tabby's relationships with the students were purely platonic. Tabby was neither a heavy drinker nor womanizer. He was madly in love with my mother. Now, I know that may sound like the naivety of a son regarding his dad's possible indiscretions, but it's true. In all the years he had the club, there were never any rumors of him dating his fans. Tabby always carried himself in a gentlemanly way. He set the tone for me. Actually, Dad was very popular with college-age female students, much more so than I. He had a large unofficial fan club. He was a natural story-teller and they loved hanging around him, listening to his stories. They wore his T-shirts. They would try, gleefully, to drag him onto the dance floor from time to time. On rare occasions, if he was in the right mood, he accepted. It brought smiles to everyone's faces to see him having a good time dancing with the young ladies.

Although I had my share of flings and one-night stands, I was in no way assertive with women who came into the Blues Box. A female would practically have to club me over the head and drag me away because I didn't respond to kind smiles and nuanced hints. A dating code was rarely spoken about between my father and I, but it was understood that I was not to date the customers. It was our family business, the way we put food on the table. Moreover, fraternizing with the patrons could also get one caught in a dangerously tangled web.

Be that as it may, occasionally I would meet women who were interested in more than my music. They were from what I perceived to be exotic places, such as Russia, France, England, Austria, and South Africa. Most of them were older professionals—teachers, professors from Southern, USL, and LSU. As my performances became ever more popular, I began attracting college girls closer to my own age. These discreet anomalous relationships, however brief, opened up a previously hidden world to me. I lived with my parents because Tabby only paid me between seven and fifteen dollars a night, regardless of how much money I brought in at the door—which sometimes was substantial. There were times when I would play a few gigs in other clubs despite Tabby's disapproval. For a time, I earned just enough to rent my own apartment. My independence didn't last because I fell behind on the rent. Tabby had the attitude that I was against him if I played at someone else's club. He'd lay a big guilt trip on me, which I always succumbed to.

On occasion, after the club would close for the night, I'd find myself whisked off to the home of a date. It was always intriguing visiting the home of an older woman and unraveling the mystery behind the facade. After hours, trying to live up to the braggadocio lyrics I sang in songs like "Hoochie Coochie Man," "Rock Me Baby," and others, I'd find myself at five in the morning, browsing her book-shelves, listening to her favorite classical, rock, and soul albums. Sometimes we would just hang out and talk. She might put on some music by Nina Simone, Joni Mitchell, Joan Armatrading, or Carole King, while we delved into the subtle nuances of each other's culture. Sometimes she'd play name that tune, testing my knowledge of recordings by Johann Sebastian Bach or Amadeus Mozart. This kind of curiosity usually only happened with older intellectual women. With those my own age, few words were ever spoken.

Regretfully, not many Black women came to the Blues Box on the regular. Black women's preference was to dress up in high heels to go someplace sophisticated, elegant—someplace I couldn't afford. On the other hand, most Whites that frequented Tabby's wanted to put on some comfortable jeans and let their hair down. For many young Blacks, Tabby's Blues Box was a backward neighborhood joint, a rustic reminder of an inglorious past. Contrarily, our White patrons came largely because of its rusticity, seeking a bygone cultural adventure.

1983

IN 1983, we were featured in a nationally shown Public Broadcasting Service documentary titled *Raining in my Heart*. It featured Raful Neal, a harp player, singer, and patriarch of the large and talented Neal family of musicians. It featured Tabby, Moses "Whispering" Smith, Henry Gray, Kenny Acosta, and former Baton Rouge guitarist Buddy Guy from his club the Checkerboard Lounge in Chicago. Over-the-air broadcast TV, in the early 1980s, was watched by millions. National TV exposure put Tabby's on the national tourism radar. In only a few short years, Tabby's had become the most famous little juke joint in the South. Tabby's Blues Box had very few rivals. There were a few blues clubs scattered from Mississippi to Florida, but they didn't have the international cultural impact and broad appeal the Blues Box was achieving.

Tabby's Blues Box was romanticized as a bygone juke joint in national magazines and newspapers. Sure, it was on the wrong side of the tracks and run by a pistol-packing bluesman in the Deep South, but that was part of its appeal. We relied on local blue-collar musicians who had day jobs, but they could sing and play with the best of them. Since the rise of folk-blues in the 1960s, White blues fans had been romanticizing a place like Tabby's. The Blues Box's humble decor and dysfunctional water closets made them feel like they were in a riverside barrelhouse and they loved it.

Meanwhile, I had to supplement the skimpy pay I received at the Box. I needed money, but I wasn't prone to do anything illegal—now that I was of age and wiser. Yet, money was never a driving force for me. I found it unattractive when a date made money too high a priority. Nonetheless, money was something I had to have. So, I found ways to supplement my income without abandoning the family business. I'd get everyone to put their beer cans in a particular trash bag, the garbage and bottles in another. I would take those cans to the dump and sell them by the pound. With money earned from recycling cans, I bought a barbecue grill and sold hot plates. There was nothing to eat in the area late night. Rose and Thomas closed around nine o'clock. The only light on around North Boulevard late was the Blues Box's marquee.

On Fridays, I'd buy my foodstuff—a few pounds of chicken, ribs, charcoal, and such—costing me, say, sixty bucks. Friday night I'd break even. Saturday night, it was all profit. It got to the point where I would sit outside on the stoop tending the grill, and then hurry in to perform while Alfred watched the grill for me. Then I'd come back out on the break to sell plates. People, when they smelled that smoky barbecue, man, I had 'em, they could not resist. What were they going to do; where else were they going to get a bite so late? I never came home with leftovers. I'd always sell everything I cooked.

I had to hustle. I was always finding a way to earn a few extra dollars. This was before bands could easily print CDs and sell them on their gigs. I always had that entrepreneur's spirit. I suppose that rubbed off on me from my old man. Being a guitar player is one thing, but there were some other things I learned from my dad, too. For example, he was his own man, had his own business. Whenever I had a bright idea or a progressive suggestion for the business, I heard, "This is my club." Dad arrogantly reminded me, "When you get your club, you can do whatever you want. But this is my club."

"Ok, Pops. Whatever, man," I'd retort dismissively.

Notwithstanding, Dad had erected the Blues Box to act as a kind of cultural temple of learning in which I was his prized pupil. He was my protector and teacher. Dad had opened the Blues Box in large part because he recognized early on the potential I possessed to become a blues master. Indeed, I learned enduring virtues in that ramshackle joint. The Blues Box helped develop my monochrome eyes to see the world in a kaleidoscope of color. It challenged my cynicism on race, allowing me to be at ease in a heterogeneous room. It taught me to treat people from all walks of life with grace. Always try to be consistent. Another thing Tabby's instilled in me was when admirers approach and praise you for your talents, benevolently accept their compliments. Never take advantage of the fans. I learned how to conduct myself in public. I was beginning to earn some celebrity, but I was still just a struggling young man. From a business standpoint, I learned, it takes money to make money. "You've got to take care of the business and the business will take care of you," Dad would say. All the same, I knew it was time for me to leave the nest and go out into the big wide world to see if I had what it took. I contemplated making a major change.

We were invited to perform at the 1983 Utrecht Blues Festival in Holland. I went along as usual to play rhythm guitar behind my dad and the Blues Box gang. Everything about my virgin voyage to Europe, from my narrow frame of reference, was extraordinary. When we landed in Amsterdam, city officials, media, and festival staff greeted us at the airport. They made such a fuss over us it was perplexing to say the least. We were feted like rock star ambassadors. At the Utrecht Festival, we performed for an arena crowd of about ten thousand paying customers. It was an eye-opener. I got a glimpse of the possibilities this "old-timey" music was capable of. I was determined to save what little money I'd earned from the tour to use toward my first recording session as a leader.

When I returned to Louisiana after the triumphant tour of Europe, I went to my band, Exit, and excitedly told them of all I'd seen and done, thinking they'd get inspired too. I thought we would go into the studio to record my new blues tunes. But that's where I lost them. They couldn't understand what had gotten into me. They had mainstream aspirations. They couldn't see beyond the teen market. They saw blues like nearly everyone of my generation had come to see it, as backward and country. They had no interest in recording the blues. They seemed genuinely ashamed of "that old-timey music" we did at the Box. Sure, I could knock it, but I took offense when others did. It was as if they were besmirching me and my family. They forced me to make a choice. I chose to record the blues on my own.

I realized I could make a cool musical statement if I could write lyrics that someone of my generation could sing and relate to within the blues genre. I got in touch with Randy McAllen, a studio owner and engineer who had a sixteen-track recording studio in his home. Randy had been recording some sessions on some of the Blues Box musicians including my dad.

I formed a new backing band with my brother, Tammy, on drums and Joe Hunter, a lanky shaggy blonde LSU student, on bass. Joe played tuba in the school band, and he had been playing electric bass at the Blues Box's jam sessions.

When we got to the studio, we learned that Randy didn't have a standard acoustic set of drums. Instead, he had the new Simmons electric drums. I'd never heard electric drums on a blues recording before. No one had. From the jump, this session was breaking the rules.

Tammy got on the electric kit and found it easy to play. The sound the kit made had a new wave tone. Joe Hunter plugged in his electric bass. I plugged my electric guitar into a Fender amp. We recorded the song I'd written, "Soon This Morn'nin Blues," in the style of Jimmy Reed, but with a fresh new vibe. There was a line in the song about getting rough with my woman, beating her, which oddly went over well with women when I sang it on live gigs.

The session went by fast; we had the track after only one take. Then we recorded a slow twelve-bar blues I'd written titled "You'll Be Sorry, Baby." I left the studio on a high, feeling I'd really captured something special. When I got home, I went into Mom and Dad's bedroom and woke them up. I wanted my dad to listen to the track, so I popped it into a cassette recorder he kept near his bed. He listened to "Soon This Morn'nin Blues" once or twice, then I cut the tape player off to hear his review.

"It sounds nice," Mom said.

She was always encouraging, but having your mom say your music sounds nice is, well, nice. Then it was Dad's turn. I could see from his body language that he was going to be highly critical of me, as he usually was.

"It sounds like shit," he swore.

I wasn't prepared to hear him say that. It was mean and hurtful.

"WXOK isn't goin' to play it," he snarled.

But this latter statement wasn't really aimed at me in particular; it was just that WXOK only played slick R&B. They had long ceased playing the blues. "That song don't have a chance in hell of being a hit," he said, decisively. Well, with that, I crawled out of their room with my tail between my legs and placed the reel-to-reel master tape of the session in my bedside drawer. I lay down in a fetal position and went to sleep.

Meanwhile, I went back to my routine of playing behind the local bluesmen and gigging around town with my brother and Joe Hunter. Sometimes I used my friends: Daniel Kinchen on drums, Kevin White on bass, and Juan Magee, formerly of Exit, on keyboards. I wanted to establish my own thing. I was playing less and less with my dad whenever he went out on the road.

After some time had passed, after I'd gotten over my dad's put-down, I printed some cassettes of "Soon This Morn'nin Blues" and took one to radio disc jockey E. Rodney Jones at WXOK-AM. Jones had a daily afternoon blues show. E. Rodney Jones, a native of Texarkana, Arkansas, had moved to Baton Rouge in 1982 from Chicago, where, since 1963, he had been a popular radio personality. When Leonard and Phil Chess of Chess Records in Chicago purchased WVON-AM in 1963, they handpicked E. Rodney Jones to be one of their featured disc jockeys. E. Rodney Jones was a respected veteran who had an ear for good blues.

WXOK began playing the tape around the clock. It was amazing, the power of radio. The station called me saying they had numerous requests to purchase the song. I had not thought it through that far. In fact, I was pleasantly surprised E. Rodney had played it at all. The reaction got Dad's attention. He decided to press five hundred 45 rpm copies on his fledgling label, Blue Beat. He personally distributed it to local stores and jukeboxes. Thanks to E. Rodney, the buzz around me grew wider. I started attracting standing-room-only crowds at the Blues Box.

THE LAST AUTHENTIC FOLK-BLUES DISCOVERY

NICK SPITZER, who was Louisiana's first state folklorist, after serving as senior folklife specialist at the Smithsonian Institute in Washington, DC, had acted as narrator for our popular 1983 PBS documentary, *Raining in My Heart*. Spitzer was instrumental in the development of Louisiana's folk music scene. He had arranged performances for Tabby, Silas Hogan, and Arthur "Guitar" Kelly at the Smithsonian Folklife Festival in DC.

In 1979, Spitzer had identified ("discovered") me as a continuum of Louisiana's musical folkways. He began encouraging me. Spitzer was always genuinely interested in what I was doing. He said it was important that I stick with the blues and continue developing my sound.

One day I gave Spitzer a cassette tape of songs I'd written to follow up "Soon This Morn'nin Blues." It had risen to be the most-played song on the jukebox in the Blues Box and a highly requested song in my shows. Spitzer liked what he heard. He offered to help me find a record label to release it nationally. He mailed the cassette tape of the songs, along with a cover letter he'd written, to Chris Strachwitz—founder of Arhoolie Records, a Berkeley, California, folk music label—raving about my potential.

Soon afterward, Chris Strachwitz wrote to me saying, "Your music is the freshest and most soulful sound I've heard in years." Chris's Arhoolie Records offered me $800 to sign a recording contract and produce a ten-song album of original material. I didn't think twice about the meager offer; I quickly signed the one-off deal.

I went back into the studio where I had first recorded "Soon This Morn'nin Blues" to write and record more songs for the album. But this time, I played all the instruments, a first for a blues album. Recording as a one-man band in the studio took me back to the backyard games of my childhood, where I alone would act out a full cast of characters in various games and fantasies. All of those imaginary playmates in my head as a child, I conjured again to create a one-man band. I applied a different personality to each instrument: one to play the drums, another bass, still another acoustic and rhythm guitar, and so on. I named the album, *It's a Cold Ass World*. I sent the master reel-to-reel tapes to Arhoolie upon completion and anxiously awaited the release. I was a bit disappointed to learn, however, the turnaround for a national release takes time to set up. The album would not be released for another year and a half.

Unbeknownst to me at the time, Arhoolie was a folk label, meaning they were a label for collectors, enthusiasts, and purists. Arhoolie was not the kind of label that expected big sales. They weren't expecting to sell hundreds of thousands of units. They would have been happy if my recordings received good reviews and subsequently had a long shelf-life. With only an $800 investment, they would be in the black in a matter of hours after the release, anyway. In time, I learned, Chris Strachwitz was more interested in the documentation of my music, similar to folklorists John and Alan Lomax, who had collected songs for the Library of Congress. I soon learned recording for Arhoolie was the ultimate endorsement of authenticity in the eyes of blues aficionados and record collectors. To have had my debut album released at the behest of a folklorist was similar to the debuts of predecessors Lead Belly, Robert Pete Williams, and Muddy Waters. Like those before me, I naively viewed my encounters with folklorists as an opportunity to become a recording star. From the folk perspective, I was a young primitive, a sociological curiosity.

THE BLUES MAFIA

LITTLE DID I KNOW, between the time of my "discovery" in 1979 by folklorist Nick Spitzer and the launch of my first album in 1986 by respected folklorist Chris Strachwitz, I would become the latest "primitive" folk-blues man to arrive on the scene—and the last.

I was immediately thrust into a weird, unrecognizable reality. Unbeknownst to me I had been introduced as a peculiarity many record collectors and researchers thought could no longer be found in the Deep South—an authentic folk-blues heir. I was not thought to be heir to my father's musical legacy necessarily, but heir to folk-blues "discoveries" such as Mance Lipscomb, Mississippi John Hurt, Bukka White, Lead Belly, Muddy Waters, and Son House: "folk" bluesmen thought to be "untainted" by modernism. All, with the exception of Lead Belly, who died in 1949, had been recast as primitive folk-blues practitioners by a consortium of shadowy record collectors and researchers known as the Blues Mafia. The Blues Mafia spearheaded the idealized folk-blues movement of the 1960s.

The term *folk-blues* was foreign to me. The Blues Mafia's criterion for folk-blues was musical traditions of an illiterate, unadulterated community passed down orally. Moreover, the more isolated from mechanization, commercialism, and professionalism the musicians were, the more authentic, according to the Blues Mafia and their followers.

The Blues Mafia had embraced me on the eve of my first album, anointing me by way of rave reviews and glowing articles. My story fit the Blues Mafia's primitivism narrative perfectly. I had had some schooling but had dropped out before finishing high school, check. I'd learned music primarily from my uncle and father and a number of functionally illiterate Louisiana bluesmen, check. Although I was just out of my teens, I'd had my share of run-ins with the law, check. My family was by no means middle class, check. Our family business was a barrelhouse, a juke joint, a honky-tonk, on the Louisiana Bayou, in a shanty of a building that seemed a throwback to a time the Blues Mafia romanticized, double check. I was a purveyor of the older guitar styles, which I'd learned firsthand, check. I had been discovered by a folklorist from the Library of Congress and signed to Chris Strachwitz's venerable folkways label, Arhoolie Records, checkmate. I met all the Blues Mafia's primitivist folk criteria.

As cultural brokers of folk-blues, the Blues Mafia held sway over the vast majority of booking agents, record executives, promoters, and festival buyers within the international blues market. I had no idea there was a narrative constructed by the Blues Mafia around my music and culture therewith, which predefined me before I could even release my first album and have a chance to define myself.

But who was this shadowy gang of record collectors and researchers? Ironically, I learned over time, the Blues Mafia were powerful cultural brokers of Black "primitivism," White self-appointed arbiters of Black musical authenticity—an absurdity stranger than fiction. They had a cartel between my culture and a new lucrative market of White rock fans interested in the musical inspirations of their rock idols.

In the late 1950s and early '60s young, middle-class White men became enamored with what they deemed primitive Negro recordings of the 1920s and '30s. They collected, journaled, and traded scratchy 78 rpm disks by Charlie Patton, Tommy Johnson, Son House, Skip James, and many others. The rarer and more primitive sounding the 78 rpm, as defined by their idiosyncratic middle-class prisms, the more valuable.

Neophytes Pete Whelan and Bill Givens launched Origin Jazz Library, a purist vanity label based in Brooklyn Heights, New York. Whelan and Givens, beginning in 1962, reissued their hiss-laden 78 collections on albums such as *The*

Immortal Charlie Patton and *Really! The Country Blues*. The latter was a polemic against blues researcher and writer Samuel Charters's 1959 landmark book and supporting LP *The Country Blues*, because it wasn't, according to the Blues Mafia, "primitive" enough.

Whelan and Givens's success as Negro cultural brokers spearheaded the rise of competing boutique labels run by fellow researchers and collectors. The most successful reissue of the period was *King of the Delta Blues Singers*, a collection of sixteen sides by Robert Johnson, issued for the first time on LP in 1961 by the powerful major record label Columbia Records. Robert Johnson was virtually unknown at the time; however, by the end of the decade, Johnson's songs were standard among British rock bands.

Around this time, two college students in Washington, DC, Tom Hoskins and Mike Stewart, upped the ante when they boldly went from collecting Depression era 78s of Black tenant farm guitarists to collecting the aging guitarists themselves.

Indeed, in 1964, during Freedom Summer, righteous White students from the Northeast were risking their lives going door to door in the Mississippi Delta to register oppressed Blacks to vote. Meanwhile, Hoskins and Stewart were "door knocking" in Black communities in the Mississippi Delta seeking to "discover" and exploit obscure bluesmen. A fierce competition to "collect" the surviving men who made those rustic Depression era recordings had commenced.

Gayle Dean Wardlow, a twenty-two-year-old White contemporary of the aforementioned blues researchers, grew up in Meridian, Mississippi. Whenever the northern researchers would venture into Mississippi, Wardlow would be their Delta liaison and guide. Wardlow would become a notable researcher and collector himself. He was one of the first researchers to find and interview Charley Patton's wife and obscure bluesman Ishman Bracey. He also interviewed legendary Delta record scout H. C. Speir. Wardlow is most noted perhaps for uncovering Robert Johnson's death certificate.

Aware of the suspicion northern researchers might attract from violent White segregationists if they were misidentified as door knocking Freedom Riders in Black neighborhoods, Wardlow insisted he drive them around the Delta because his car had a Mississippi license plate.

Hoskins and Stewart are credited with discovering Mississippi John Hurt in Avalon, Mississippi, in 1963. They immediately signed the illiterate seventy-one-year-old sharecropper to what can only be described as an indentured contract. John Hurt was whisked off, recorded, and booked by his new handlers on the northeastern coffeehouse circuit, from Cambridge, Massachusetts, to New York City's Greenwich Village. He triumphantly appeared on prestigious festival stages including the Newport Folk Festival in Newport, Rhode Island.

The rediscovery success of Mississippi John Hurt spawned a Delta gold rush by rival collectors and researchers seeking to discover their own Negro property. Although they saw themselves as benevolent preservationists of Black culture, their ulterior motives were egotism, power, and avarice. The group of collectors and researchers would soon become known as the notorious "Blues Mafia."

The Blues Mafia began to fill the deep void of anecdotal information surrounding their scavenged artifacts with primitivist fantasies, eschewing anything that didn't fit their newly constructed narrative. Before 1959, with the exception of Lead Belly, there had been a dearth of information on so-called folk-blues or country blues. However, by the time I was "discovered" in 1979, the Mafia's narrative was cannon; through the publication of books, recordings, articles, illustrations, photographs, and documentaries, it had become ubiquitous. The Blues Mafia's new narrative, complete with a fabled backstory of my music and culture therewith, was inescapable; accepted as doctrine by intellectuals and academics and patronizingly celebrated by the multibillion-dollar rock industry.

The ordeal that lay before me was a looming existential threat to my identity and humanity. Reflecting on it now, I realize there was nothing in my milieu that could have prepared me for the extreme culture shock I was about to encounter. Up to this point, before the release of "Soon This Morn'nin Blues," my identity had not been challenged. I knew who I was. The genuineness of my idiomatic talent was without question.

Existentially, I was given an ultimatum: either eschew my true identity and my culture therewith—hence, acquiesce to White primitivist fantasies of blues authenticity—or be declared inauthentic, an iconoclast, and therefore banished from opportunities to represent my own culture.

Mind you, I was not well read. My parents hadn't read bedtime stories to me. I was not interested in books about folk nor blues. I had no music conservatory training. Therefore, I had no knowledge of the revisionist history that had been carefully constructed by the Blues Mafia, sociologists, and folklorists. Nevertheless, the Blues Mafia had endorsed me. I was a "made" folk bluesman. But what did that mean?

I would come to understand the real reason they were called the Blues Mafia was that, like the mob, they had the power to make those who didn't toe the line disappear. Unlike Jimmy Hoffa, the union organizer whose body was never found, the disappearing the Blues Mafia did wasn't physical murder, but they could murder one's career.

Indeed, they could make my career disappear without a trace, erasing my name from the annals of blues history forever if I stepped out of line. They had the power to erase my entire discography from the "official" blues canon. But what disturbed me most was the power they possessed to remove me as a representative of my own culture and instead bestow my indigenous legitimacy upon certain White appropriators they favored more.

Sure, I give credit to folklorists and sociologists for documenting and preserving music and artifacts that may otherwise have been lost, but they drew flawed conclusions that were very damaging psychologically and financially to me and my community. Notwithstanding, from the beginning, I was expected to acquiesce to the Blues Mafia's narrative of my music and culture therewith.

TEXAS SOJOURN

In 1986, my debut album was released worldwide on Arhoolie Records. After the release, my debut album, *The Beginning*, garnered positive reviews. (Arhoolie retitled the album because my original title, "It's a Cold Ass World," was deemed off-color.) I was contacted for major festivals outside of Louisiana for the first time as a bandleader and recording artist. I put a band together for the road. Kevin White, my childhood friend, was on bass; Daniel Kinchen, from South Baton Rouge, became my drummer, replacing Joe Hunter and Tammy, who were bound by family and day jobs. Juan Magee was on piano. Juan had begun studying the piano-playing style of Henry Gray and brought a good versatile set of chops to the group. Juan could not make the initial dates in Texas, so Kevin, Daniel, and I went as a trio.

With festival gigs lined up in Europe later that year, I played my first festival as a leader outside of Louisiana, at an outdoor amphitheater in Houston, Texas. It was the Juneteenth Blues Festival headlined by John Lee Hooker and featuring dynamic guitarists Albert Collins and Johnny Clyde Copeland. Johnny was known as a Texas artist, but he was born in Haynesville, Louisiana. I played every song on my debut album and received a good reception.

Later that Saturday night, Albert Collins invited me to sit in with him and John Lee Hooker at Houston's premier live music club, Rockefeller's. It was a big deal for me because I really admired John Lee Hooker. I was invited on stage to play rhythm guitar behind Hooker just as the blues master went into his signature song, "Boogie Chillen." The song went on for at least twenty minutes, giving John time to work the crowd up. He looked over at me and nodded, giving me a cue to take a solo. I begin to soar. As most young performers often do when excited, I tried to fit everything I knew into that solo, trying to impress—and impress I did. After several bars of my premature jizzing, John gave me a look like, "That's nice kid, but this is my show!" Hey, I respected that. I'd grown up playing behind artists in Louisiana, I knew how to play the support role—a vamp here, a lick there—but I could hardly contain my excitement.

Sunday, the following evening, we went on to Houston's Third Ward for a performance in the projects. John Lee was not on the bill, but Albert Collins, Johnny Copeland, and my trio were scheduled to perform. The concert was attended by a largely Black audience. Appropriate because it was Juneteenth, a day of celebration commemorating the end of slavery in the United States.

I was unaware that on June 19, 1865, the Union soldiers, led by Major General Gordon Granger, landed at Galveston, Texas, with the good news that the Civil War had ended and the enslaved at long last were free. This happened two and a half years after President Lincoln's Emancipation Proclamation, which had become official two years prior, January 1, 1863. Funny thing was, I'd never heard of Juneteenth before. Louisiana, to my knowledge, had never celebrated it. Louisiana certainly didn't have a state holiday to commemorate it like Texas. Man, I shrugged, over one hundred years ago? Oh well, I guess word about such things travels slowly.

Monday morning in Houston, while having a McDonald's breakfast at the home of the festival's sponsors, I was urged to check out Antone's, a popular blues club in Austin, Texas, before returning to Baton Rouge. I spoke to Albert Collins for advice on whether or not we should sojourn to Austin to check out the music scene there. He thought it was a great idea. He told me, "Look up Clifford Antone," the owner of the club. "Let Clifford know who you are. He'll look out for you."

During our stay in Houston, we'd made a good impression. I received management offers and booking agency offers. I was told about a former college radio DJ named Mark L. who lived in Austin. A call was made to Mark by a local promoter, asking him to put us up for a night or two and Mark L. agreed. I'd gained new confidence by performing with John Lee Hooker, Albert Collins, and Johnny Copeland. They were some of the best blues musicians around. If I could hold my own with them, I thought, I could play with anyone.

Kevin, Daniel, and I drove from Houston to Austin, planning to stay for about a week. We crashed with Mark L., sleeping on the floor of his one-bedroom apartment in North Austin. Mark and I were polar opposites. He was a generation older, White, well educated, an atheist, and vegetarian. He was an audiophile geek with a large album collection, which, to my surprise, contained no blues. Remarkably, Mark and I hit it off.

At first, I was suspicious of Mark's warm kindness. I wasn't used to such acts of unselfish kindness from strangers—especially White ones. Mark would subsequently become my patron and a dear friend. He offered his apartment to us for as long as we needed. My first night in Austin was filled with expectancy. Antone's, I'd been told, was the premier blues club in America. Antone's was no bygone juke joint like Tabby's Blues Box. Antone's was a first-rate commercial showcase club, a haven for White professional blues guitar players. It had morphed from its seedy beginnings on Sixth Street in Downtown Austin to become Texas's answer to the Fillmore West—the historic music venue in San Francisco founded by the legendary concert promoter Bill Graham.

Antone's and its fans embraced and celebrated musical capitalism. Antone's did not book part-time blue-collar musicians. Like the Fillmore West, Antone's was a place where professional White blues appropriators honed and showcased their skills before graduating to lucrative major-label success and sold-out concert halls, following a trail blazed by local guitar hero Stevie Ray Vaughan.

BIG FISH, SMALL POND

The first night I drove up to Antone's on Guadeloupe Street near the University of Texas campus, it was more than I imagined. I had grown up in a juke joint but Antone's was on a larger scale. At Tabby's, everything was held together with duct tape. Antone's, by any measurement of typical juke joints, was a big-time club. For years Antone's featured rising guitarist was Stevie Ray Vaughan, who was fast becoming a rock star. He was drawing comparisons to Eric Clapton. He'd brought a lot of energy to the Austin blues scene. Now, he was being embraced by mainstream rock fans.

When I entered Antone's, accompanied by Kevin, Daniel, and Mark, a respected local guitarist and singer, W. C. Clark, an African American guitarist, was playing with his band the W. C. Clark Blues Revue. We sat at a table and listened. W. C. Clark was in fine form. It was a slow Thursday night. There were maybe fifty people scattered about, even though the club could hold three hundred or more.

In the 1960s, Clark, a middle-aged singer and songwriter, had toured as a side guitarist with Joe Tex (we had that in common). In the '70s, Clark had formed an Austin band named Triple Threat Revue, which included Stevie Ray Vaughan and Lou Ann Barton. W. C. Clark had gained notoriety recently because he co-wrote the radio hit "Cold Shot" for Stevie Ray Vaughan's album *Couldn't Stand the Weather*.

Mark L. introduced me to the manager of Antone's. The club's manager wasn't aware of my music. He was, however, familiar with Tabby's Blues Box. He sent word to W. C. Clark to invite me onto the bandstand.

Later, at the end of the night, after Clark had finished his set, he came back for an encore. By this time, there were maybe fifteen, twenty people left in the place. Clark invited me on stage to play a song with him. I did "Caledonia," a jump blues song by Louis Jordan. The sparse audience perked up. W. C. Clark was impressed. But more important, the manager of Antone's was sold on my talents. He greeted me as I came off stage.

"Where you're staying, Chris?"

"With a friend."

"How long you in town?"

"We heading home tomorrow."

"Stick around, meet Clifford," he said. "I know he'd love to hear you play."

The manager handed me a hundred-dollar bill. My jaw dropped. I could've kissed Benjamin Franklin right there.

"Clifford has big plans for the blues," he continued. "He's starting a record label."

"Well," I asked, anxiously, "will he be here tomorrow?"

"No, come back Saturday. He'll be here then."

Later, back at Mark's apartment, Mark informed me that Clifford Antone was supposedly doing time for drug trafficking. That's why he wasn't available to manage his club.

When we returned to Antone's that Saturday night, Clifford showed up to the club just as the manager promised. He came in through the back door of the kitchen. Police officers in plain clothes, whose protective movements resembled bodyguards instead of jailers, escorted him. Clifford and I were introduced. He had the aura of a 1920s gangster, a modern incarnation of a Chicago speakeasy owner, only he wasn't a bootlegger nor moonshiner. Rumor had it, he was distributing some of the finest weed in Texas. Clifford liked to present himself as the kind of guy you didn't want to screw around with. His round baby face and dark eyes resembled Al Capone. In a sense, he was that guy, though not in a vicious way. He obviously was a well-connected man. Nevertheless, what defined Clifford for me was his fervor for the blues. He loved the blues and the musicians who made it.

He took a liking to me straight away, as I to him. He remained backstage all night, hidden from the audience. While Albert Collins and Johnny Copeland ran dice games backstage between their sets, Clifford goofed around with us, fooled around on an unplugged bass guitar, and played practical jokes on us musicians.

Clifford loved to kid around. Before the last song played, his escorts slipped him out the back door, presumably back to prison.

While sojourning in Texas, I realized I would have to migrate to a bigger pond. A generation ago, Chicago would have been the destination for an aspiring blues guitarist. I was unknown in Austin except to hard-core record collectors. It would be a major challenge to establish myself in such a formidable scene. For the last few years, I'd been practically feeding my family with my talents. With the release of my debut album I became the club's main attraction. But how could I return to Tabby's after what I'd experienced in Texas? I felt the Blues Box would struggle without me, especially being that Dad couldn't underpay someone of equal drawing ability the pittance he paid me. I had become my family's bread-winner. In Baton Rouge, I was a big fish in a small pond, yet I was broke, flat busted. I needed to give Austin a chance.

I talked Daniel and Kevin into staying in Austin with me. Together, over the next few months, we tried to break into the scene. We soon learned that Austin's African American community was small and largely marginalized in East Austin. President Dwight D. Eisenhower's federally aided Highway Act of 1956 had literally divided Austin along racial lines. I-35 isolated East Austin, where Latinos and Blacks lived, from the dominant White population.

I learned that in the 1950s there had been some minor music history of note in East Austin's small, segregated Black community. There were clubs like Charlie's Playhouse, Sam's Showplace, and the cramped Victory Grill on East Eleventh Street where Black road bands and locals had their fun. By 1986, when I started going over to the east to jam with pianists Roosevelt "Grey Ghost" Williams, Erbie Bowser, and guitarist Blues Boy Hubbard, those days were but faint memories.

Stubb's, a little barbecue restaurant that had recently opened in 1986, was a new beacon of hope. It was run by Christopher B. Stubblefield. "Stubb," as he was better known, was a tall broad-shouldered Black man who wore a ten-gallon cowboy hat. I first met Stubb outside of Antone's. He would bring his grill over to Antone's and barbecue all night in the parking lot. His large powerful hands nearly crushed mine upon greeting him.

C. B. Stubblefield had recently moved to Austin from Lubbock, where for years he ran a little dive popular among musicians before it succumbed to hard times. In 1986, he had managed to open Stubb's Bar-B-Q on the edge of East Austin in a nondescript building. More restaurant than music club, it was located just off I-35.

Stubb invited me to play a regular spot at his new restaurant. Musicians were paid with barbecue, but I didn't mind. His sauce, already legendary, was finger-licking good. Stubb's restaurant was a haven for developing musicians not quite ready for the pressures of Antone's famous stage. I was ready for Antone's, but my band was deemed not ready for prime time. Austin was home to thousands of blues guitarists. Curiously, however, 99 percent of them were White, presenting yet another challenge for us.

After having stayed in Austin nearly nine weeks, sharing Mark's one-bedroom apartment, Kevin and Daniel were homesick. Besides, we couldn't find gigs as a band. Instead, I was the one getting all the attention. Antone's was stuffing hundred-dollar bills in my pocket. I shared money with my guys, but they were having a rough time. When Kevin and Daniel said they were going back home, I could understand. After all, I was regularly invited to play with Antone's house band, but my guys, not so much. I tried to support the three of us seven days a week, but it just wasn't possible. We drove home to Louisiana, but I was determined to return as soon as I could.

When I reappeared at the Blues Box, I was relieved to find Tabby's carrying on without me. I was pleased that my absence hadn't hurt my family too much. There were several new opportunistic players eagerly vying to fill the void I'd left behind. There was King Lloyd, Little Jimmy Reed, Jimmy Dotson, Kenny Neal, Larry Neal, Ray Neal Jr., Clarence Edwards, Smokehouse, Flo Lawless, and many others. Another, Tab Benoit, a White guitarist from a wealthy family in South Louisiana, would go on to forge a recording career with Tabby's mentoring. Some musicians became leaders of bands and recording artists, but there were a lot of low-key side musicians of note, too, like James Johnson and Rudy Richard, two outstanding guitarists who had recorded with the late Slim Harpo.

Larry Garner was another guitarist who got his start at the Blues Box. I remember the first time Larry Garner came to the Wednesday night jam session. He seemed unsure of himself. He asked me if it was OK if he sat in. I was like, "Yeah, sure." I didn't know him from anyone else. Larry had a pricey guitar in a pricey case. He was unassuming, except he could afford an expensive guitar, which tipped me off that he had a good day job. I thought he was just a curious novice because "real" musicians, I knew, would have pawned that guitar straight up. We couldn't afford such instruments. Our instruments were like tools; who goes to work with a golden hammer? Anyhow, at Tabby's, we gave everyone a chance.

"I'll call you up on the next song," I said.

Larry plugged into the house Fender Super Reverb amp. I got him sorted and comfortable on our bandstand. When he began playing, he surprised me. He was really good. Larry had a gospel delivery like a preacher gone bad. Larry soon became a regular. He would question me about the business, due to my recent recording success. He was eager to make an album of his own. He wanted to know how to cut a record, get it distributed. Larry had been working at the plant, making good money. In spite of that, he yearned to quit his day job and become a bluesman. As his playing and songwriting developed, Dad booked Larry on the prestigious weekend bill at the club. Over the years, Larry Garner would record dozens of records and become a respected international bluesman in his own right.

Another competing to fill the void was Troy Turner. Troy was a couple years younger than I and a guitarist with panache. He showed a lot of promise. Troy had gone from wowing the jam sessions at the Blues Box to drawing big crowds at other clubs in the area. Troy had come to the blues from a postmodern perspective. He was attracted to the blues mainly through appropriators such as Stevie Ray Vaughan. Troy had not only taken on Stevie Ray Vaughan's playing style but his mannerisms, including the way he dressed: the Texas hat, boots, everything. I thought that was odd because Troy was African American. Troy was emulating Stevie, who was emulating some of the Black guys I'd grown up around.

Troy represented a disturbing paradigm shift taking place within our culture. I began openly questioning why White musicians were starting to dominate our culture. We blues musicians had been forced to acquiesce to the rock industry. But now there was a steady encroachment on the fragile sphere of the business we relied upon. The tail was wagging the dog.

To be sure, the impact of White blues appropriators adorning the cover of blues magazines seemed to be as confusing to Troy as glamour magazines were for young Black girls. In the 1980s, the media worshiped waif-thin silky haired blonde models, which made curvy wooly-headed Black girls feel inferior. Nothing wrong with a Black child having influences from others, I certainly did, but not at the expense of my own self-worth.

Notwithstanding, Troy Turner was a talented guitarist. Troy had been featured in national commercials for the popular New Orleans restaurant chain Popeye's Chicken. It really looked like he was going places. Breakout success seemed just around the corner. Then tragically, it fell apart. It was said that Troy got caught up in the crack epidemic that had begun in Los Angeles around 1984. Sadly, like a plague, crack and the violence surrounding it was sweeping the country, devastating communities. A lot of musicians, prone to party with light drugs, got ensnarled in its addictive web. It was widely rumored Troy's drug of choice was the highly addictive crack, a cheaper form of cocaine. It was widely rumored that Stevie Ray Vaughan was addicted to cocaine. Though I won't go as far as to say Troy was emulating his hero here, it was a possibility. I had written and recorded "Cocaine (Snow White)" on my debut album warning about the problem. I was not immune. I could have easily gotten hooked. I was surrounded by users. My greatest fears, however, were getting caught in the crossfire of rival gangs and being targeted or shot by the police.

There were drive-by shootings in my neighborhood daily. Turf wars made poverty-stricken neighborhoods like mine into war zones. Nancy Reagan's Just Say No campaign did little to curtail the collateral damage of gang wars. During this dark period, there would be numerous robberies and break-ins. Criminals began breaking into the Blues Box in the wee hours of the night on the regular. We'd arrive to open; the place would be ransacked. Whiskey and cigarettes were stolen; jukebox busted for coins. Consequently, we secured the doors with chains, heavy iron bars, and locks, plus a burglar system, but to no avail. We couldn't keep them out. These were hard times indeed. Tabby's was located in the eye of a new killing floor.

There were rumors once that my own brother, Tammy, broke into the club. I doubt that to be true, nonetheless, he may have known the identity of some of those who did but decided not to snitch. Unfortunately, I learned my dear brother had also succumbed to the depraved spell of crack cocaine.

Although my family needed me at the club now more than ever, I felt I couldn't stay one day longer. I feared I'd get caught up in some hunger games. Perhaps shot and killed in some random hit. I'd vowed long ago I wouldn't resort to crime. When I was a child the neighborhood guys and I did wretched things, but as an adult the stakes were much higher. I wasn't planning to ride or die with a bunch of crack dealers and murderers. Besides, now that I'd gotten a taste of what it was like to be a national artist, I wanted more. I desperately needed out of South Baton Rouge—this time for good, while I still had a chance.

I was at a crossroad. The noise in my head became a cacophony of confusion. I needed to find that sacred passage from one parallel universe to another. I needed to cross the track, to the greener side. But high society's one-eyed Cyclops, its behemoth locomotive protector, was steaming straight ahead toward me. Could I make it across the track before the speeding demon crushed my dreams? What if I really wasn't good enough? Success in Austin was reserved for White appropriators of the blues, not someone like me. Who am I anyway, to think I could overcome what so many others couldn't? Do I really have what it takes? Why not just stay in Louisiana, where I'm popular, and build on that? I literally didn't know if I was coming or going. Regardless, whichever decision I would make, there would be no looking back. I drank a pint of whiskey seeking relief, but there was no relief to be had.

ZACK THE SOOTHSAYER

THE NEXT MORNING, I awoke hungover. The hangover was primarily from a worried mind. Restless, I took out walking, guitar slung over my shoulder. The day was hot and humid, not a rain cloud in the sky. Yet, a storm raged inside my head. After a few miles beating the streets, heat torturously rising from the pavement, I finally stepped onto the cool overgrown grass of a decaying cemetery.

I wandered down the cemetery's long and twisted path. Crumpled tombs adorned with crumbling crosses and frayed statues jutted out. This tranquil valley of the dead, once an elite antebellum shrine, was now overrun with decaying headstones of the forgotten poor. I was no fan of graveyards; I was the guy who usually power-walked when passing by one. Nevertheless, the cemetery, the deeper I journeyed inward, revealed an eerie beauty.

In the distance I spotted him, crouched under a moss-covered shady grove. The man I was seeking had come into view. Shaded from the sun's wrath, as if favored by the Sun God himself, was my white-haired friend, the gravedigger Zack the Cat. I had gone to the graveyard seeking the wisdom of the old soothsayer, caretaker of the cemetery, hoping to bend his ear for a spell. Zack was hunched over, his back to me, repairing a desecrated tomb. His shovel leaned against a nearby headstone.

"Hey, Youngblood," he said, as I approached him from behind. He neither turned nor looked up yet, miraculously, he knew it was me.

"What's up, Zack?"

Zack the Cat had been the house drummer and all-around handyman of Tabby's Blues Box since day one but had long ceased working at the club. I hadn't seen him in a while. Zack hadn't changed a bit. His ever-present white towel was neatly laid across his right shoulder.

"What brings you out here?" he asked, his back still to me, focused on the task at hand. I completed my approach. Then suddenly, I froze!

I was astonished to find Zack handling human skeletal remains. Zack rose from the bones, stood, and turned to greet me. Sensing I was uneasy, he wiped his hands on the sides of his overalls so as not to get graveyard muck on me. I reluctantly shook his hand.

"Man, ol' Zack gets lots a visitors," he said, his eyes wandering about restlessly, "but as you can see, t'aint much for conversation."

We both shyly avoided eye contact. I reached into my pocket and offered Zack a trifle in a crumpled brown paper bag. Zack looked pleased as he opened the bag and poured the contents out into his hand.

"Flower seeds," I said.

Zack bent down. Using his strong callused fingers, he dug a small hole in the soft dirt. After planting the seeds, he walked over to an above-ground tomb. Dusting it off, he offered me a seat, as if inviting me into his living room. I sat down, removed my guitar from its gig bag, began tuning it. Zack continued working.

"So," he enquired, "what's on your mind, Youngblood? You wouldn't come out here to see ol' Zack less'n something's really eatin' at you." I was apprehensive, unsure how to express the noise in my head.

"What you doing?" I asked, changing the subject.

"Robbers, in here last night."

"Grave robbers?"

"Grave robbing is ages old," Zack said. "You'd be surprised what goes on out here after dark. You see, Youngblood," Zack continued, "used to be a black market. Big shots paid 'em really good, for the right pieces." Then Zack walked over, calmly picked up a skull that had been separated from its corpse, as if carelessly picking up a coconut.

I was spooked!

"This poor sap's family," he continued, while placing the skull back into its tomb, "had to pass the hat to bury him. Wasn't buried with nothin' special. No gold teeth; no jewelry. God only knows what the hell they's lookin' for."

"Who would do such a thing?" I asked.

"Must've been damn crackheads, I reckon. Can't be Voodoo," Zack said, wiping sweat from his brow with his towel, "cause Voodoo folks, you know, they got respect."

I couldn't begin to fathom such desperate thievery.

"You remember Moses 'Whispering' Smith?"

"Of course."

"He buried, back over yonder," Zack said, pointing to the far side of the cemetery. My eyes followed to the makeshift grave where our friend rested.

"One of the best there ever was," Zack boasted.

I thought to myself, Moses "Whispering" Smith was someone I really enjoyed traveling with. I missed his jovial spirit.

"Man, he could blow that harp, couldn't he?"

I nodded in agreement.

Zack pulled a harmonica from his chest pocket. Zack, looking down at his harp, as if reminiscing thousands of gigs shared with our late friend.

"You know how some harp players got a harp for every key? Not Moses, no sir. He'd take jus' one harp to a gig. Play all night. He was one of the great ones. Taught me what little I knows." Zack sat down next to me and blew a little riff.

"Folks say he had a mojo hand. Say he buried with it." He laughed as if he thought the old superstitions pitiful. "His mama said he played the devil's music, but he knew better. Didn't pay that foolishness no mind."

I pulled out what was left of a pint of whiskey. Passed it to Zack. Picked a few soft notes on my open-tuned guitar.

"Moses couldn't 'ford no headstone," Zack continued. "Just buried like a mule in a hole in the ground. Well, that's life." Zack took a swig, a long one as if trying to drown some inner demon. We were both quiet for a moment, reflecting on Moses.

In a blood-orange sky over the bayou, the sun was setting. A cool breeze rustled leaves engulfing us. Zack passed the whiskey. I took a strong swallow, followed by another. Finally, I was ready, forthwith, to broach the reason I'd come to see the soothsayer.

"Zach, I'm thinking 'bout getting away, moving to Austin, Texas." As soon as I heard the words come out of my mouth, I gasped. They sounded foolish. I waited to hear his thoughts, but Zack was embarrassingly silent.

"Well," I shrugged, "who knows, maybe I should just bury this guitar out here, and let it be." I drank the rest of the whiskey to the last drop. "Zack," I inquired casually, "you ever wish you hadn't given up trying to make it with your music?"

"I don't know," Zack pondered. "I had a good time playing back in the day with Lightnin', and your dad, too."

"Why didn't you stick with it, then?"

"Don't know, Youngblood, too much time on the road, I reckon. Had mouths to feed. But, when Tabby hit it, man," Zack laughed and slapped his knee, "with that 'Hoodoo Party,' look'a here, man, I wished I'd a'gone."

"I don't know, Zack, I don't think I could handle working in a graveyard."

Until then, Zack and I hadn't really made eye contact. We'd been just looking out into the cemetery. But now, Zack made direct eyes with me.

"Listen, Chris, you gotta do it while you still young. Hell, you could be great. The King!" he said, confidently. "Shucks, I seen it in you, since you knee high. You jus' get one chance," Zack whispered, hoisting a finger to illustrate his point, "only one, to seize the ring!"

I looked him in the eye. Hanging on his every word. He paused for a moment, stood up, and surveyed his cemetery.

"See these folks lying around here?" he said, his eyes assessing. "Betcha they wish they had a second chance."

With that, Zack picked up his tools and went back to work humming a faint tune. With the turbulent storm in my head now calm, I pensively fingerpicked my guitar, accompanying Zack's soft melody.

———

It was dusk when Tammy drove me to the bus station. (Greyhound was but a few blocks from the Blues Box.) Tammy waited as I bought a ticket. I wished my brother could come with me, but Tammy was no longer playing drums. He was plagued by drugs, struggling to keep his young family together. He'd neither feed his family nor his habit by leaving with me and relying on music. Tammy stood there wistfully while I boarded the bus. He waited until the driver pulled away. Looking back at my pallid brother, in my gut I knew I had to leave and leave now, like Zack had said, while I still had the chance.

The bus drove past the Blues Box. The yellow portable marquee out front illuminated my name, "Chris Thomas Band Tonight." The Blues Box faded in the night as we drove onto Interstate 10 headed west across the Mississippi River bridge. I was headed back to Austin, the White blues Elysium, only this time, I was determined to prevail.

LAST DANCE

ONE OF THE YOUNG LADIES who frequented Tabby's was Karen Fernbaugh. She always had a warm smile. She was comfortable, as a White girl, in the foreboding atmosphere of the Blues Box. In the 1980s, Baton Rouge was still far behind most cities when it came to social integration. Once in a full moon, the musicians might have been out of tune or sang off-key, but inside the Blues Box, there was harmony among the races, which created an edgy optimism.

Karen came into the club many nights with different groups of people. Karen's long legs, in low-heel shoes, would attract dance partners all night long. An athletic brunette, Karen stood out. She was the kind of person who, if she had friends or relatives visiting, made sure they experienced Tabby's at least once. On many occasions, she'd come in with a male friend, but if anyone asked her to slow drag or shimmy, Black or other, she was always ready to dance.

One warm September night in 1987, Tabby was on stage when Karen walked in with a friend, LSU student Michael Sciacchetano. Michael was a regular. He'd been moonlighting as a guitarist at Tabby's Wednesday night jams. Karen greeted

Tabby with her warm smile as usual, then danced the night away with friends. Near closing time, Karen and Michael waved goodbye. When they arrived at their car parked across the street, they were alarmed to find it had been burglarized. Suddenly, they were approached by two men and a kid. One of the men pulled a gun and demanded money. Michael handed over his wallet; Karen hesitated. A struggle ensued. Michael wrestled for control of the gun, a shot rang out! A bullet struck Karen, entering her back, puncturing a lung. It lodged in her shoulder. Horrid, the doorman, yelled, "Tabby, somebody's been shot!"

Everyone rushed cautiously outside. Tabby, gun in hand, was ready to do battle. The attackers fled on foot with Michael's wallet and Karen's bloodied purse. Tabby found Michael in shock, kneeling over Karen as she lay bleeding on the sidewalk. Everyone was in disbelief. As police sirens and the ambulance approached, they were all praying that Karen would make it. Michael was by Karen's side as the paramedics rushed her to the emergency room. The ambulance sped away with sirens blaring!

I was in Austin, Texas, but I got a call about the tragedy before dawn. I felt terrible about Karen's plight. It was difficult to come to terms with the chaos. Why it had to happen to her, why at Tabby's? I sighed. This was surely the darkest of days for the Blues Box. Everyone's worst fear had been realized. North Boulevard, already a shell of its former self since integration and the riots of 1972, could now lose Tabby's, literally its last remaining light. Our detractors would claim, "Tabby's Blues Box is just another bucket of blood; a hole in the wall bar that should be shut down, this time, for good!"

Later, the *Advocate* newspaper reported that in the trauma unit at Our Lady of the Lake Regional Medical Center, Karen had received six units of blood and a chest tube had been inserted to keep her from drowning in her own blood. According to Michael, Karen, while lying on the ambulance stretcher, couldn't catch her breath. "She couldn't feel or move her legs," Michael said to the *Advocate*. "Blood was draining from her back onto the sheets of the gurney."

A medic asked Karen her age. A frightened Karen replied, "I'm nineteen," then solemnly asked, "will I make it to twenty?" Karen was certain she was dying and began to pray.

The *Advocate* went on to say Karen's parents and brother rushed to her bedside in support. According to her mother, they were crying but Karen was typically optimistic, unselfishly trying to comfort them.

In a follow-up report, the *Advocate* revealed Karen had made it through the first harrowing forty-eight hours and was transferred to a rehabilitation center. Karen survived the ordeal, but she would be paralyzed the rest of her life. Through it all, Karen remained strong and spirited, but sadly, she would dance no more.

My dad, his staff, my family, and I were devastated. We felt terrible because Karen and Michael had been part of our extended Blues Box family. Maybe if we had installed more security outside? Maybe if we had more light in the parking areas? But these were violent times, like no other in our community's history. What could one small mom-and-pop business do to change South Baton Rouge's downward trajectory into murder and mayhem? The illusory utopian mystique of Tabby's Blues Box was gone.

Condolences were conveyed to Karen's family and the doors of Tabby's were closed for several days out of respect. Before Tabby reopened, he hired an armed security guard and added better lighting for the parking areas, knowing such changes were only a hope and prayer for safety.

In time, witnesses helped identify the robbers. The three were petty young criminals who'd been casing the Blues Box for victims. Police arrested Alphonse Smith and Eugene Williams for armed robbery and two counts of attempted first-degree murder, including the juvenile, Terry Wayne St. Cyr.

A year later, the *Advocate* reported that Alphonse Smith, the nineteen-year-old who had shot and paralyzed Karen outside the club, was convicted in a ten to two vote. The judge ordered that Smith serve two consecutive ninety-nine-year armed robbery sentences and a fifty-year attempted murder sentence, consecutively. In all, Smith was sentenced to 248 years in prison. His accomplice, Eugene Williams, received fourteen years, and the third person, Terry Wayne St. Cyr, the juvenile, received ten years. Terry St. Cyr was believed to be a relative of the famous Louisiana banjoist, Johnny St. Cyr.

AUSTIN'S WHITE BLUES ELYSIUM

AUSTIN HAD BEEN a destination for national touring acts since the '70s thanks to the Armadillo World Headquarters located at the corner of Barton Springs Road and South First Street. The Armadillo booked acts of all stripes, including an upstart Bruce Springsteen; jazz greats such as Charles Mingus, Herbie Hancock, and Gil Evans; and vanguard rockers like Frank Zappa; along with regional acts Asleep at the Wheel, Austin legend Joe Ely, blues guitarist Freddie King, and a young Willie Nelson. On New Year's Eve 1980, the Armadillo closed its doors due to escalating rent and insolvency. It didn't help that the Armadillo had been sitting on valuable real estate. Its coveted land was sold as developmental property.

With the Armadillo shuttered, Austin's dope-smoking hippie cowboys were forced to get their musical fix someplace else. Austin had been a laid-back western oasis, but recent progress was transforming the city of Austin, to the dismay of starving local musicians, into a genteel unaffordable boomtown. Antone's Blues Club filled the void left by the storied Armadillo.

In 1975, at the age of twenty-five, Clifford Antone opened his first blues club at Sixth Street and Brazos. A few years earlier, Clifford had moved from Port Arthur, Texas, to attend the University of Texas in Austin. Antone's Blues Club became the lone live venue in an undesirable part of downtown Austin. Since the late '70s, Antone's had been attracting its share of weirdos to Sixth Street, a seedy area of town with all the obligatory vices and willing participants needed to incubate a lively blues scene. For White Austinites, who were first turned on by Janis Joplin's open mic sessions at Threadgill's, their blues identity hadn't truly been solidified until Clifford established Antone's Blues Club.

Clifford regularly booked his Chicago blues heroes including Muddy Waters, Eddie Taylor, Jimmy Rogers, Buddy Guy, and Hubert Sumlin. He also booked B. B. King, John Lee Hooker, and Albert Collins regularly. Albert King, the flying V maestro who was a major influence on a young Stevie Ray Vaughan, was also regularly featured. Clifford told me, "I was downtown but [city officials] didn't like my clientele or the kind of musicians I brought in." When the city of Austin decided to clean up and rezone Sixth Street as an entertainment district, Antone's, an undesirable venue, was forced to move. In 1982, after seven years on Sixth Street, Antone's relocated to the Drag (Guadeloupe Street) near the Texas University campus.

Austin was a place that prided itself on being "weird," and for me, it literally was. How was I going to fit in among these cosmic cowboys, country outlaws, and left-wing rednecks? Guys in Austin preferred vintage '50s clothes and greasy slicked-back hair. Austin dames fancied crimson lips, long cocktail dresses, '50s bobby-socks, and stilettos—a far cry from what I had been used to back home. In Louisiana, we lived and played our music in the moment. The Austin crowd, conversely, wanted to time travel, stylistically at least, to the 1950s. Instead of assimilating, I shaped my own bohemian identity. My curly hair and smooth stylings gave way to low maintenance dreadlocks (a strikingly rebellious hairstyle for the times), scruffy ripped jeans, and T-shirts. Best of all, my new grungy identity wasn't costly to maintain.

On previous sojourns to Austin I'd been itinerant, sleeping on couches, sometimes in the friendly beds of young maidens. Clifford Antone had extended an open invitation to me on my initial trip to Austin. When Clifford learned in the fall of 1987 that I was back in town for good—after several short trips to the city—he invited me to move into his high-rise penthouse until I could get settled.

Oddly, he was rarely there. Clifford maintained the penthouse in downtown Austin, overlooking Town Lake, largely, it seemed to me, as a storage place for his valuable guitar collection. While living in Clifford's plush penthouse, I was fascinated by his mint collection of more than seventy guitars. I actually counted them one day, removing each from its case, checking each guitar's tethered price tag, investigating what made one more valuable than the other. I was in high cotton. Clifford wasn't a guitarist, he just loved collecting guitars among other toys. He would buy, sell, and trade them at guitar shows, but mostly he just showed them off. He got a real kick out of giving guitars as gifts to great players he befriended. Clifford told me he'd given guitars to Hubert Sumlin and the late Muddy Waters. (Muddy died recently, in 1983.) He'd also given Stevie Ray a few. He gave two guitars to me—one of which I pawned, of course.

The Fabulous Thunderbirds, featuring Stevie's older brother, Jimmie Vaughan, were making platinum hits. Antone regulars like Mel Brown, Lou Ann Barton, Angela Strehli, Denny Freeman, and Derek O'Brien were all first-rate musicians and performed behind Buddy Guy and others who came through on tour without backing bands. I was usually the opening act. When John Lee Hooker and Albert King would come to Antone's on tour, I'd open for them too. I became part of the house band for Antone's Blues Club. While performing at Antone's I got a chance to befriend Hubert Sumlin, Buddy Guy, Albert Collins, to name but a few.

In Austin, it was clear a cultural paradigm shift was imminent. Austin's White blues guitarists were the new face of the blues. They had eclipsed the Black blues masters commercially, as personified by the Vaughan brothers. When Stevie Ray was in town, he would drop by Antone's often. Stevie Ray always looked a bit haggard to me, like he hadn't changed clothes or slept in a week. He came off like a rugged Texas cowboy. He was the baddest son-of-a-gun guitar slinger in the West. Yet Stevie was struggling, rumor had it, with addiction. His grueling tour schedule did his health no favors. Worst of all, drugs were starting to negatively affect his playing. His most recent album was *Live Alive* (1986), a collection of songs recorded live including at a reappearance at Montreux Jazz Festival where he had had a breakout performance in 1982. The album, in my opinion, was a low ebb. Stevie sounded mortal. His guitar tone was off, and Double Trouble's trademark Texas twang lacked soul. The double live album didn't possess the same passion and fire of *Texas Flood*, his debut, which had deservedly made him popular. *Texas Flood* had proved Stevie's passionate style of blues-rock could compete on FM rock radio and MTV.

Notwithstanding, people around Austin were in awe of Stevie. I wasn't in awe of Stevie Ray, like Troy Turner and so many others. I didn't imitate his playing style. I wasn't planning on wearing cowboy boots and playing the Texas shuffle although I dug the way he styled himself. Stevie was heavily influenced by Jimi Hendrix; I liked that about him. But I wasn't a Texas guy. I had to constantly remind Austinites that I represented Louisiana blues. It seemed they had never heard of the great New Orleans guitarist Lonnie Johnson, the first guitar virtuoso of blues, jazz, and rock. I knew early on who I was musically, or should I say, at least I had a clear vision of what I wanted to convey musically.

In Texas, they had a whole different thing they did, a kind of Texas swing shuffle, a kind of country twang. My groove was funkier. I was beginning to mix hip-hop rhythms with my Louisiana Voodoo. I was doing away with the swing and the shuffle feel, asking my drummers to play a tight hip-hop pocket.

While at Antone's, I could measure my talents with the heavyweights. Albert Collins was a fantastic guitar player. The talented Bonnie Raitt would come through; Carlos Santana, just about everybody. U2, when they were hitting it big with the Joshua Tree Tour, which in 1987 was one of the hottest albums in America, came into the club one night and did a late-night jam. It was cool to see them in that setting. One of their hits on the *Joshua Tree* album, "Bullet the Blue Sky" sounded like my song "Cocaine (Snow White)" released a year earlier. I dug U2. At Antone's you never knew who was going to stop by and play. It was an exciting time to be part of the scene.

One afternoon while I was on stage at Antone's rehearsing some new songs, Stevie Ray walked in. Stevie Ray and I would engage in small talk from time to time but nothing too deep. We never talked shop. What I respected most about Stevie was how he gave credit to his influences. He was the tide that was lifting all boats, including my little canoe. Stevie sat around with Clifford, watching, listening. I overheard him cavalierly ask Clifford, "What is this?" As if he thought I was playing the blues incorrect or something. I was mixing in hip-hop. I was original. That's one of the things Clifford saw in me. It's why he was grooming me to become the first artist signed to his new label, Antone's Records. I stood apart from the other two thousand guitarists who wanted to emulate Stevie Ray Vaughan.

Clifford was always bragging on me to anyone who'd listen. Clifford told me, "Stevie can kick Clapton's ass, but you can kick Stevie's." It would take a lot of money to compete with the likes of Clapton or Stevie Ray. Eric Clapton, the Fabulous Thunderbirds, and Stevie Ray Vaughan had top-notch rhythm sections, producers, and access to the best equipment and studios money could buy. They spent hundreds of thousands of dollars recording. There was a whole art and science behind capturing a great performance either live or on record. The studios I'd recorded in were primitive by Austin standards. I'd played all the instruments in a guy's living room with an $800 budget. My debut album was technically inferior to anyone signed to a major label. I was itching to get my turn at the majors. No doubt I knew my way around a live stage, but to really make it, I needed a major label to sign me.

Other blues musicians around the city were beginning to tour and be noticed nationally. Charlie Sexton had signed a contract and received extensive national promotion, becoming one of the first big MTV regulars out of Austin. Hollywood didn't suit him, and he returned to Austin to play with his brother Will Sexton, an up-and-coming musician himself. Angela Strehli and pianist and singer Marcia Ball were touring with their bands. Researcher Danny Garrett recalls,

> Scores of others were forming and reforming world-class blues bands and hoped to follow these successes; people such as Denny Freeman, George Raines, Derek O'Brien, Mark Kazanoff, Bill Campbell, Bill Carter, Johnny Nicholas, and Bobby Mack, to name only a very few. And the blues venues of Austin where these musicians played were full as well, and numerous: places such as The Rome Inn, The Aus-Tex Lounge, Alexander's, The 311 Club, and as always, The Continental Club. The blues firmament was bright in the mid-1980s, but no star in it shone as bright as Antone's, Austin's Home of the Blues. Clifford decided to take it all on the road. And thus was conceived Antone's West: '88 Blues Cruise Tour, a mission to bring Austin's red-hot blues scene to the clubs and the music fans of the West Coast.[8]

In January 1988, Clifford booked me on his biggest investment to date. He put me on a tour bus in a caravan of buses filled with guitars and musicians. The tour featured Kim Wilson, Albert Collins, Buddy Guy, Luther Tucker, Jimmy Rogers, Pinetop Perkins, James Cotton, Angela Strehli, Mel Brown, Chris Thomas (as I was known then), the Muddy Water's Rhythm Section with Calvin Jones, Willie "Big Eyes" Smith, and the Antone's Band.

We played every major city on the West Coast from Santa Cruz, where Buddy Miles, former Hendrix sideman, sat in, to Portland. In San Francisco, where legendary promoter Bill Graham presented us, Carlos Santana came out and sat in there. At each stop, I was featured. I would do about thirty to forty minutes of original material. We played the Paramount in Seattle, Washington, and we played Vancouver, Canada. In all, we must have played twenty or more sold-out shows, yet Clifford lost money on the venture.

Afterward, back in Austin, Clifford received calls from A&R representatives of major labels inquiring about my availability. I signed a publishing deal with Clifford's new publishing company, and I was one of the first acts signed to his boutique label, Antone's Records. News spread that Bonnie Raitt had signed a big record deal with Capitol Records and was looking for new songs. Clifford sent her a song I'd written called "Last Real Man." She considered changing it to "Last Real Woman." But in the end, she didn't use it.

Clifford continued to invest in me, but others weren't sold on the fact that I could sell records for a major label. My Arhoolie record had only sold a few thousand copies. Regardless, Clifford was resolute. He set me up in a professional studio for the first time. Demos from the sessions were sent around to producers on the West Coast.

Meanwhile, HighTone, out of Oakland, California, the independent record company that had produced Robert Cray's breakthrough, *Strong Persuader*, approached Clifford about buying my contract. Robert Cray, a West Coast singer and guitarist whom I admired, had become very successful. If the deal went through, I would record for HighTone exclusively. Clifford and HighTone, after some back and forth, reached an agreement. HighTone's contract purchased from Clifford settled his investment in me, and then some. I don't know what the final price was—nothing came my way—but now I answered to HighTone. I recorded a new session under the direction of HighTone co-owner and producer Bruce Bromberg. Bromberg sent those fresh new recordings to major labels in Los Angeles and New York.

In between sessions, when I was idle, I'd stumble into legal trouble. I was no longer under the watchful protection of the well-connected Clifford Antone. I was on my own, renting a house off of South Congress. I drove an old Buick. It must have been fifty feet long. The thing was built like an army tank. It was almost unbearable driving around all summer in the scorching Texas heat with a busted air conditioner. I never had the proper stickers, insurance, or registration. I would steal somebody else's sticker off their car, stick it on mine, petty stuff, nothing too serious. I'd get pulled over and the cops would run a check, no tags, no insurance, I'd end up in jail for a couple of nights until Bruce Bromberg, who lived in Pacific Palisades, California, would arrange my bail. Alcohol and nonstop partying helped me pass the time between all the ups and downs. Onstage, I was in control and confident, but offstage, I was a mess.

A kind woman who nurtured me through some ups and downs was Diane Scott. Diane and I were not lovers or business associates. Like my friend Mark, who had originally welcomed me to Austin, she became a patron, helping me get through difficult moments unconditionally. Diane urged management at the Chicago House, located at San Jacinto Boulevard and Sixth Street, where she was an employee, to hire me to play as a solo acoustic performer. The Chicago House, one of Austin's few pure folk coffeehouse clubs, had acted as a cool workshop for aspiring songwriters.

In the interim, an A&R man from Columbia Records in New York, Joe Mc-Ewen, liked what he heard on the new HighTone tapes. When Columbia Records asked HighTone to set up a showcase, Diane helped to arrange my showcase for Columbia at the Chicago House. Joe McEwen flew down to Austin to hear me perform in person. The day of the showcase I was on edge. I was determined to stay sober so that I could be at my best later that night. I performed music by Robert Johnson, Son House, Muddy Waters, and Jimi Hendrix, along with several songs I'd written in the past year. My ace song was "Help Us, Somebody," about gun violence and desperation. A radio-friendly original was "Wanna Die with a Smile on My Face," a love song and the highlight of my set. I also performed a song by Bob Marley, "Redemption Song," and Bob Dylan's "It Ain't Me Babe."

Immediately following my performance, Joe McEwen told me he wanted to sign me to a long-term contract with Columbia Records. After he left, I rushed to a pay phone and called my mom and dad. "Guess what," I said, "I'm going to record for Columbia Records!" I told them I was sticking around Austin a little while longer. They were happy to hear things were finally starting to break.

After the initial weeks of excitement, negotiations with Columbia began to stall. While HighTone was negotiating the Columbia contract, Joe McEwen got an offer to move from Columbia Records to Warner Brothers. This caused another frustrating delay for my long-delayed sophomore album. Months passed while Joe negotiated his transition and mine. After a year of turmoil, Joe McEwen finally moved over to Warner Brothers as head of A&R and brought me with him. I was told there were a few minor details to be negotiated before I could officially sign my new contract with Warner. My contract had gone from Clifford's Antone Records to HighTone Records, to Columbia Records, to Warner Brothers. Through it all, I was still broke.

FROM MINOR TO MAJOR

JOE MCEWEN INVITED ME to New York City for a big benefit performance at the Roadhouse in Manhattan to do a guest performance with Willie Dixon, the legendary Chess Records songwriter, upright bassist, and producer. It was my first time to the Big Apple. I was excited and looked forward to the experience of meeting the great Willie Dixon. Headlining the show, in a rare club appearance, was ZZ Top. Muddy Waters had passed away before I had the chance to see him perform or get to know him personally, but Willie Dixon, even more so than anyone, was the personification of Chicago blues for me.

I saw Willie Dixon as one of America's great songwriters, on par with George Gershwin or Cole Porter. A few of his most popular compositions included "Little Red Rooster," "Hoochie Coochie Man," "Spoonful"—one of the best lyrics of all time—"Back Door Man," "I Just Want to Make Love to You," "I Ain't Superstitious," "My Babe," "Wang Dang Doodle," "I Can't Quit You, Baby," and so many others. They were all written for Chess recording artists during its peak years, the 1950s and early '60s. His songs helped make the careers of Muddy Waters, Howlin' Wolf, Otis Rush, Little Walter, and Koko Taylor, to only name a few. Willie Dixon had been instrumental in the development of rock and roll, too. He had produced Chuck Berry and played bass on his Chess recordings. He also produced Bo Diddley in the late 50s. His songs were covered by Bob Dylan, Cream, Led Zeppelin, the Yardbirds, the Rolling Stones, Queen, the Doors, the Allman Brothers Band, the Grateful Dead, and so many more.

I rehearsed with Willie in New York City a few days before the concert. The backing band consisted of New York session musicians. I was awestruck in his presence. Willie looked just as he did in photographs. He stood about six feet four and weighed about three hundred muscular pounds. He walked with a cane, which was as much a stylish accessory as it was a necessary walking stick. He wore a classic white derby and a dignified tailor-made suit. Born in 1915, Willie looked very athletic for an aged man.

After Willie ran over some songs with the backing band, it was my turn to join them. I was to sing two of his songs and one of my own, which was intimidating with such a master in the room. One of the songs was "Hoochie Coochie Man," a Dixon song I'd been singing since I was nine years old. As we got midway through the song, Willie, who was playing upright bass, smiled at me. He seemed to like the way I handled his songs.

The next day I sat next to Willie at a press conference in an art museum in the Village. I observed the way Willie handled the press. He had such a way with words. He was a poet; a gentle giant. One of the things he said that day, I'll never forget: "A blues artist spends most of his time trying to create something beautiful, trying to bring beauty into the world."

That night we performed together for a packed room of celebrities, music executives, and enthusiastic New Yorkers. The gig was the most high-profile event I'd ever performed. When it was time to do Willie Dixon's songs, with Willie on upright bass accompanying me, I tried to channel the spirit of the Blues Box. I thought to myself, You can do this. You've played these songs a thousand times.

I sang "Hoochie Coochie Man" and played a guitar solo in the middle section. By the end of the solo, the audience was on their feet, they were hanging on every note we played. I glanced over at Willie, then I backed off. I felt I was upstaging Willie Dixon; that wasn't my intention. I thought of the time I was on stage with John Lee Hooker back in Houston, Texas. Hooker had let it be known that he was the star, not me. But Willie waved his large hand at me to go back to the microphone and let it rip. He yelled, "Go 'head! Sing the blues!" And sing the blues I did!

We received a standing ovation at the end of the set, took a bow, and waved goodbye to the celebrity audience. The New York media, the major record companies, and the master of the blues, Willie Dixon, had all embraced me. My moment with Willie overshadowed the hard times going on around me. It was a remarkable night!

The next morning, Willie's manager said Willie wanted to meet me for lunch at a nearby New York deli. This sounded good because the performance only paid my expenses. I was practically starving. I would get to talk with my hero and have a good meal. I walked from the hotel I was staying at to the nearby deli. Willie was sitting with his manager when I arrived. Willie bought me lunch and told me about a song of his he wanted me to record. I couldn't believe my ears. I asked him about the sessions for some of my favorite songs from his songbook. He told me stories about recording sessions and how some of his lyrics came to him. I was taking mental notes.

He told me of a song he'd written for Otis Rush, a Chicago blues singer and guitarist whose Dixon song "I Can't Quit You, Baby" in 1956 reached number six on *Billboard*'s R&B chart. But the song Willie had in mind for me was one he tried to record with Otis, but Otis couldn't get the phasing to Willie's satisfaction. So it was shelved. He was interested in writing several songs for me and invited me, if I ever came out to California, to visit his home in Los Angeles. Willie had won lawsuits regarding the copyrights of his songs such as Led Zeppelin's "Whole Lotta Love" and was a millionaire. He was his own man, which I admired. Like W. C. Handy before him, he had been burned early in his career by crooked publishers, but then he learned how to protect himself from the ruthless thieves. Willie set up his own company and earned millions from his copyrights. I told him after lunch I'd truly look forward to visiting with him again, soon.

I returned to Austin feeling that I was on the cusp of something big. There were articles in national music magazines about me. Word on the streets was I was about to sign one of the richest record deals any blues musician had ever signed. I was invited to exclusive parties at the homes of some well-to-do Austinites. I was beginning to be recognized around Austin when I went down to Sixth Street's live music venues.

Antone's attracted a mature audience. However, at the age of twenty-five I was interested in socializing with those my own age for a change, testing my new blues sound on them. If my own generation could relate to my original music, it didn't matter what an older audience thought about it, as far as I was concerned.

In addition to solo gigs at Chicago House, I played regularly with a band at a rowdy dive bar, The Black Cat, a real funky club that was a cross between CBGB and a biker bar. My long dreadlocks, rock-edged guitar playing, and rap sensibilities were beginning to fit in with a younger alternative crowd, more so than the conservative blues patrons at Antone's.

University of Texas females on the scene were not at all shy when it came to vying for my attention. They sometimes even got into catfights over me, which amused and turned me on at the same time. I tried to assure them not to worry; there was enough of me to go around. Gossip spread around town about my exploits and how much money I had. The romantic gossip and bad behavior, although exaggerated, created a mystique for me, which was cool. Thanks to small advances from HighTone, I was able to dump the Buick and buy a motorcycle. My bad boy reputation was kicked up a notch when I started making the scene on my new Harley.

I happened to be in jail the day I got the call from Bruce Bromberg saying the Warner Brothers deal was finalized. They had negotiated a contract for me worth more than three million dollars. Warner even guaranteed half a million for the first two of a seven-album deal. Multi-album guarantees were nearly unheard of for a new artist. It sounded like my troubles were over at long last. Mercifully, after nearly two years—from the time Columbia first offered me a deal at the Chicago House—I finally signed the doggone contract.

Next thing I know, I was whisked out to Los Angeles and began recording feverishly, finishing all the music I'd started recording for Antone's two years earlier, plus some new songs. I was in Los Angeles for several months working at the Village Recorders, the famous studio in Santa Monica where Fleetwood Mac recorded *Rumours*. I finished the recordings in the summer of 1989. The album, *Cry the Prophets*, my major-label debut, was in the can.

ROBERT JOHNSON AND THE DEVIL'S ADVOCATE

Back in Austin, I shot a music video for the first single, "Wanna Die with a Smile on My Face," at the grungy Black Cat Lounge. The video was edited and ready for release. It was exciting. I was about to launch my career as a major artist. But suddenly everything was put on hold. The release of the single, album, and video were halted. I was alerted by Warner Brothers that a poster in the background that featured the mythical blues legend Robert Johnson, one of my major influences, was unauthorized. Warner's was forced to put the long-planned promotional launch for my new album on hold. I was floored. After all the excitement, all the anticipation, I was in limbo, again.

Only two photos of the mysterious bluesman were known to exist, and Stephen LaVere, a notorious record collector and researcher, owned them both. LaVere, a leading Blues Mafioso, also owned the rights to all twenty-nine of Robert Johnson's recordings. He was threatening to sue Warner and I if I didn't meet his price for using Johnson's image.

The music video had cost me more than $125,000 in advances to make. I was told by my video's producers that we needed to either reshoot the scene without the image—which would cost tens of thousands more—or pay LaVere a substantial amount of money. Either way, it was going to be a hard pill for me to swallow because the additional charges, I was informed, would be recouped out of my future royalties. I had no problem with blues collectors making money from intellectual property. But how the property came into their possession was worthy of scrutiny, especially given America's torturous history of buying and selling Africans as property and owning the fruits of their labor.

Robert Johnson was an exceptional blues singer, guitarist, and composer born in Mississippi around 1911. In two short years, between 1936 and '37, Johnson recorded twenty-nine songs, including, "I Believe I'll Dust My Broom," "Love in Vain," and the standard "Sweet Home Chicago." Johnson's recordings sold poorly during his lifetime. He was not popular even among his peers. He died penniless in 1938 at the age of twenty-seven. It was said that Johnson became morbidly ill following a performance. The cause of his sudden illness was murky. There was much speculation over the years that he was poisoned. Whatever the cause, he died a few days later. Johnson was buried in an unmarked grave and left no will.

I wondered how this person, Stephen LaVere, had come to possess Robert Johnson's legacy and catalog. I had known this kind of thing was out there, a loose consortium of White interlopers, record collectors who outdueled one another to gain control of valuable artifacts and intellectual property rights of obscure bluesmen. I had often wondered what motivated such enthusiasm, such fanatical devotion. In LaVere, I found my answer—greed.

In 1973, after learning a rival record collector and researcher, Mack McCormick, of Houston, Texas, had uncovered the first known photo of Robert Johnson from a surviving sibling, Stephen LaVere, in hopes of making a deal of his own, aggressively tracked down a previously unknown sibling, Carrie Harris Thompson, Robert's half sister, near Baltimore, Maryland. Mrs. Thompson, thought to be Johnson's lone heir, knew as much about the ruthless music business as she did about astronomical aviation. Robert Johnson's music and legacy, thirty-five years after his death, had become a multimillion-dollar treasure. Thanks to covers of his songs by the likes of Jimmy Page, Mick Jagger, Keith Richards, Bob Dylan, and Eric Clapton—names no Black senior citizen would have known in 1973—Robert Johnson's copyrights had become a tomb raider's dream.

Carrie Harris Thompson was not aware of her half brother's fame and accumulated fortune. But savvy Hollywood veteran Stephen LaVere was. LaVere persuaded the elderly woman to assign all her rights over to him. In return, he would pay her 50 percent of any royalties he collected—after his expenses, of course. Moreover, Thompson gave LaVere exclusive rights to the only known photo of Robert Johnson, heirlooms she had kept for years in her Bible. Subsequently, Carrie Harris Thompson passed away in 1983, leaving Stephen LaVere in full control.

Mack McCormick, who had "discovered" Mance Lipscomb in 1960 working as a foreman of a highway mowing crew in Grimes County, Texas, had ambitions of his own. He was a veteran producer of rare album compilations, liner notes, and articles. McCormick had coproduced, with Chris Strachwitz, the album that launched Arhoolie Records, Mance Lipscomb's *Texas Songster* in 1960. McCormick had planned to write the first Robert Johnson biography, in which he would unveil for the first time the photo he had copied—but neither licensed nor purchased—from Thompson. McCormick also planned to produce a companion anthology of Robert Johnson's music for Columbia Records.

However, Stephen LaVere one-upped his rival tomb raider by way of the old double-cross. LaVere, a more ruthless grave robber, having acquired control of Johnson's estate from the unwitting Thompson, threatened Columbia Records and McCormick with legal action, forcing McCormick to abandon his projects.

Finally, in 1990, after fifteen years of protracted litigation, LaVere was about to release his own greatly anticipated Robert Johnson anthology, *The Complete Robert Johnson Sessions*, for Columbia Records. I had unwittingly gotten tangled up in the protracted litigation. After some hasty negotiations, Warner Brothers settled with Stephen LaVere on my behalf, allowing my major label debut album, *Cry of the Prophets*, to finally be released. My album and LaVere's *The Complete Robert Johnson Sessions* were released only weeks apart in the spring and summer of 1990.

CRY OF THE PROPHETS PROFITS

Saturday, May 5, 1990, there was a big homecoming party planned for me by Warner Brothers back at the Blues Box to celebrate my new release. Warner flew in writers from *Rolling Stone* magazine and major newspapers from across the country to cover the event. They invited Peter Guralnick, the highly respected music writer—Peter had been instrumental in turning Columbia Records on to me originally—to fly down and cover it. My mom labored for two days making jambalaya and gumbo for the party. It was going to be a big deal for Baton Rouge. Warner would pick up the tab for the lavish party.

I had returned to the Blues Box on a huge private rock star tour bus, to the dismay of many of the blues purists and Mafia types covering the event, who would've preferred I arrive on the back of a pickup truck. The bus was almost bigger than the club. My opening act was Chicago Al and the Back Burners. Chicago Al later told me he was not allowed to visit with me because my security team had kept everyone at bay. I must admit, I did have a rather large protective entourage. My new five-piece band included childhood friends Juan on keyboards and Kevin, now a budding blues guitarist, on rhythm guitar. My band was rounded out by expensive hired guns.

Our well-rehearsed performance was barely contained in the tiny club. It didn't go over well, because we were too loud for the room and lacked dynamics. The bombastic performance was like a fly in the gumbo. It left me indifferent despite the magical night in my honor.

I was launched as a major talent. I would no longer be able to play at the Blues Box for fifteen dollars. I had a guitar tech, roadies, a driver, a road manager, lawyers, business managers, a personal manager, a salaried band, and publicists, all on my payroll. I rented a new bachelor pad near downtown Austin off South Congress Boulevard. If Dad wanted to book me now, he'd have to pay at least thirty dollars. Things were going to be different for me from now on, I thought. I had filled a pretty big void at the Blues Box over the years. I played the guitar, I played the bass, and I played the drums, I mopped the floors and ran the bar. I left a large void for my family to fill. Despite losing me, Dad was very proud that night. The positive national publicity only solidified the club's reputation.

Following the big send-off, everyone around the Blues Box wondered, "What are we going to do now that Chris is gone, for good?" Well, there were always lots of players waiting to step in. My triumph attracted a whole new crop of eager musicians looking to duplicate my success.

Cry of the Prophets was released internationally on Sire/Reprise/Warner Brothers in the summer of 1990. In the *Village Voice* respected rock critic Greil Marcus wrote:

> He's the son of '50s Louisiana bluesman Tabby Thomas, and if this LP had been released in the mid-60s, in the heyday of deep feeling deep South R&B, it would have seemed like a curio: too eclectic. Today it's a shock, because deep soul has hardly been heard in public since Al Green's *The Belle Album*, and because nobody's heard deep soul guitar or deep soul crying applied to crack and Uzis. Up against the likes of N.W.A, Thomas sounds pathetic—but also real.

Greil Marcus's view that I sounded "pathetic—but also real" was really saying I was "pathetic—but also [authentic]." The backward compliment from the celebrated rock critic illustrated my dichotomy. I wrote "Help Us, Somebody" to give voice to the disillusion I often felt on my bumpy journey. "Help Us, Somebody" was a ballad in the folk protest tradition, an anguished plea for atonement, a flare illuminating in the dark, a warning of a looming apocalypse. It was a folk ballad that may have flowered in the late '50s if sung by Harry Belafonte or Odetta. But in the '90s, the vibes of inner cities were too dark, too gritty, and too violent for such a genteel melody, and I knew it. As a musician from the hip-hop generation, I could relate more to protest songs like "Fuck Tha Police," a rap song by N.W.A, than I could any blues recording that was being released by the successful Chicago label Alligator Records. Blues recordings were generally out of touch with poor Blacks left behind in the hood. A quote from novelist and essayist James Baldwin regarding this type of faux Negro entertainment sums it up best. The so-called blues of the early '90s "assuages [suburban] guilt about Negroes and it attacks none of their fantasies."

The blues of generations ago had been reduced, basically, to emotionally empty beer commercials. The national image, which the Blues Mafia's narrative had shaped in the public's conscious, was an elderly Black man in an ill-fitting suit sitting, playing the guitar, for the behest of some patronizing rock musician. My natural embrace of hip-hop and rap was the most direct way, at the time, I could have my music reflect my worldview. I genuinely was a part of the hip-hop generation. I knew it was important for my blues to reflect that. It was blues with an attitude. By rapping, sampling, using drum loops and effects, I would be no more trying to gain approval from rap or rock gatekeepers than Pink Floyd or the Rolling Stones were trying to reach the Black audience by covering Slim Harpo.

Embracing hip-hop would, for the most part, allow me to take agency of my own "authenticity."

I signed on with a major booking agency in California, Monterey Peninsula, and embarked on a headlining national tour. One stop on the tour was Tipitina's in New Orleans, where the local press proudly claimed me as one of their own. In New York City on June 26 I returned to Tramps, where I had shared the stage with Willie Dixon. This time I was the headliner. Up-and-coming guitarist Smokin' Joe Bonamassa was my opening act. The highlight of the tour was my major television network debut. I appeared on *The Late Show with David Letterman*.

On August 27, 1990, while between tours back in Austin, news broke that Stevie Ray Vaughan had been killed in a helicopter crash. It was a very sad night. At the time of his death, Stevie, who had often struggled with addiction, was reportedly clean and sober. His popularity was at an all-time high. I attended a spontaneous candlelight vigil that night at Auditorium Shores near Town Lake to commemorate his passing.

Later, during a break from the Village Studios in Santa Monica, I returned to Austin to put demos together on my own terms in a makeshift home studio. I purchased a Proteus rack-mounted synthesizer that emulated a wide variety of sounds by using a new technology called MIDI, which universally allowed different instruments to communicate with one another. For example, a MIDI-enabled keyboard could play back numerous orchestral sounds and percussions.

The Proteus was the cutting edge of synthesizers. It integrated perfectly with another new application called Pro Tools. The Proteus offered features such as full sixteen-part MIDI multi-timbrality and thirty-two-voice polyphony. These terms are common in studios today, but in the late '80s and early '90s almost no one I worked with in folk-blues spoke this language. Though it was still in its infancy, I recognized the revolutionary potential of the new technology. I envisioned the day I could produce major-label-quality albums in my bedroom. A digital music revolution was about to take place and I was on the vanguard.

Following weeks of writing and recording a mesh of hip-hop blues and blues-rock originals, I returned to Los Angeles and presented my demos to Warner Brothers executives. After listening to my demos, they were confused.

BLUES MAFIA DISCIPLES

PURISTS, THAT IS, the Blues Mafia and their disciples (many of whom, by the 1990s were record executives, lawyers, managers, and agents; major decision-makers throughout the music food chain), thought it blasphemous to record the blues digitally with Pro Tools using a Macintosh computer. Moreover, the way I had sampled and meshed hip-hop aesthetics with the blues seemed to frighten them. The way in which I chose to represent my culture jarred their worldview, or at least their view of a Negro folk bluesman.

I was an iconoclast, the most dangerous type of blues artist. I aspired to create great dissident art of revelation. But my vision wasn't shared by my handlers. In their minds, it was unimaginable. A folk bluesman wasn't capable of creating high art such as *Sgt. Pepper's Lonely Hearts Club Band* by the Beatles or *Pet Sounds* by the Beach Boys. That's why rock critics preferred the term "bluesman." A blues *artist*, in the truest sense of the word, in their myopic minds, was an oxymoron.

After having vouched for me, trumpeting to the world that I was categorically authentic, the Blues Mafia was afraid that I, with the backing of one of the most powerful music companies in the world, would blow up their primitivist narrative of my culture.

They were afraid I just might pull it off similarly to Bob Dylan, in whom they had invested heavily in the 1960s, only later to be mocked by their idol. Though Bob Dylan hadn't returned to the Newport Folk Festival since he went electric in 1965, he was still essentially a folk artist decades later. Dylan nearly had a nervous breakdown after being demonized for turning his back on the purists. Still, he prevailed. But Bob Dylan was White—different rules. I would be risking everything to redefine the authenticity of my music and its culture therewith.

On the night of March 2, 1991, news broke of a videotaped beating by Los Angeles police officers of a Black motorist named Rodney King. The disturbing video was shown on the national news over and over again, heightening tensions between the races. Blacks saw it as a modern lynching; police cruelly acting as judge, jury, and executioner. Whereas Whites saw it, for the most part, as the police subduing a savage Black male, just doing their job. The contrasting views divided the nation. The beating also crystallized the generational gap between older Blacks and my generation. Older Blacks had been lured into believing African Americans had made great progress since the civil rights movement. My generation, those left behind and trapped in desperate cities, saw it differently.

The watered-down blues of the '90s, packaged and sold to the suburbs, was devoid of any real social conscious. It lacked the spirited discordance necessary to reach hardened Black youth left behind and caught in the crossfire of police and drug violence. I wanted to address such issues in my hip-hop blues songs.

In Los Angeles on April 29, 1992, a verdict in the Rodney King trial was announced. The cops that were videotaped beating Rodney King were acquitted. The verdict touched off a firestorm. The riots in L.A. nearly tore that city apart. Widespread looting, assault, and arson immediately followed. Property damages topped roughly one billion dollars.

A lot of the pain my generation was expressing leading up to the riots had largely been ignored. African Americans who had made it into the middle class had been sedated by *The Cosby Show*. Indeed, Dr. Huxtable's elite upper-middle-class family lived in a different world from average Black families. In spite of this, Bill Cosby's show was one of the highest rated TV shows ever. It even had a popular spin-off, titled, ironically, *A Different World*. The Rodney King riots along with the emergence of gangster rap interrupted the spell *The Cosby Show* had on Black America. Its ratings were cut in half following the unrest. *The Cosby Show* retired into syndication later that year.

Even though I was born into the blues, my generation wanted our own representative expression in music. Young White suburbia embraced the rebelliousness of gangster rap. However, when it came to blues, record buyers in the suburbs did not want to hear an antagonizing blues album that would assuage none of their guilt and attack all of their fantasies. Corporate America controlled the airwaves prior to high-speed internet and social media. In an attempt to suppress the rise of discontent, they hastily pushed onto the airways—to tranquilize our pain—government-approved opioid hip-hop from nonthreatening groups such as P.M. Dawn and Arrested Development. The latter, in their video for "Tennessee," depicted themselves as happy slaves or sharecroppers, singing and dancing while praying to the Lord to take them "to that special place," somewhere. Meanwhile, the music that really moved the people was sold from the trunks of cars and on street corners, bypassing major label gatekeepers and consequently enriching enterprising young Black hip-hop entrepreneurs.

With tensions at an all-time high in 1992, my label mates Ice-T and Body Count released their album *Cop Killer*. Critics had been saying that rap music was not real music because it's done with machines. But when Body Count and I attempted to bring live musicianship to it, which was innovative for rap, we were met with resistance. Ice-T's record sparked a huge controversy with shareholders of Time Warner (Warner Brothers Records' parent company). Unfortunately for me, after all my battles with Warner, *Cop Killer* killed any chance of my rap blues album being released by the label.

My album, when finished, wouldn't have been much different aesthetically. I had written songs like "Kill Somebody Tonight," a suicide note that could easily have been mistaken for a murder anthem. The song "21st-Century Blues" was essentially about shooting a bad cop. Songs like "Fuck Tha Police," "21st-Century Blues," and "Cop Killer" helped trigger national protests against rap music. The FBI investigated N.W.A.

Perversely, however, one of Eric Clapton's biggest hits for Warner had been Bob Marley's song "I Shot the Sheriff." But when we wrote about the same subject, we were deemed obscene and banned by the powers that be. Back in 1920, Mamie Smith's recording of "Crazy Blues," celebrated as the first ever blues recording sung by a Negro, contained the inaugural cop killer blues lyric, "I'm gonna do like a Chinaman, go and get some hop. / Get myself a gun, and shoot myself a cop. / I ain't had nothin' but bad news, now I've got the crazy blues."

Freedom of expression can seem extreme when tensions run high. Still, I wouldn't back down. I was resolute. I was more determined than ever to record my new album regardless of censorship. Besides, I'd written more than enough songs for two albums. Instead of putting only one or two rap songs on the record, I vowed I'd record an entire rap blues statement, even though it was becoming clear such an album would never be released by Warner Brothers. The *Cop Killer* gangsta rap brouhaha at Time Warner caused my album to be shelved. The controversy taught me a valuable lesson about the dichotomy between art and commerce.

My contract with Warner Brothers was frozen while they decided what to do with me. I returned to Louisiana to perform at one of the only festivals in America that would have me, the New Orleans Jazz and Heritage Festival. Afterward, I decided to take a much-needed reprieve at the Blues Box, supporting my dad, until things got sorted out in Los Angeles. My experience with Warner Brothers was strained, to say the least. The entire episode had been detrimental to my psyche. I was moping around the house and performing uninspired sets at the club.

In Baton Rouge, on June 2, 1992, a meeting was called among the leading bluesmen to discuss, among other grievances, our discontent with the performance fees paid to us by the Baton Rouge Blues Festival organizers. The festival had become, since relocating downtown from Southern University in the early '80s, more White and more profitable, a good thing for any African American festival, for the most part. Granted, we were only about 12 percent of the national population. However, Whites began dominating the music on stage, too. The roles of African American musicians, administrators, and volunteers had greatly diminished. Some in the Black community saw this conundrum as a major setback. There was disappointment the festival had abandoned its original mission.

Before the general public had high-speed internet, elaborate video games, and streaming music, the blues, though marginalized into a small sphere, was a healthy market. The festival attracted a variety of sponsors and vendors who made substantial profits from crowds that now exceeded fifty thousand annually. With increased budgets—funded by taxpayer dollars and grants—the festival had become a roaring financial success. The problem was, they were paying tens of thousands of dollars to White blues appropriators while Blacks were paid in the hundreds of dollars. The Blues Festival had become a major success for everyone except the Black blues musicians for whom the festival, founded by my dad and his blues society, was missioned to promote. Dad's blues society had lost control of the festival shortly after it moved downtown near the Mississippi River and gained major sponsors and popularity. The new organizers seemed to have a different mission altogether. There were rumblings among us that the festival had been hijacked.

I attended the meeting along with Tabby, Raful Neal, Larry Garner, Rudy Richard, Henry Gray, and Big Bo Melvin. We were considering a boycott of the upcoming festival and looking at alternatives. Johnny Palazzotto, a veteran local promoter, wanted to create a for-profit festival by putting up fences and charging admission. Johnny was sure he could sell thousands of tickets that would allow him and his backers, he insisted, the means to offer us higher fees. Johnny told a local reporter from the *Advocate*, whom we had invited to cover the meeting, "All I know is I see blues artists in this town not being treated like they should be, and this is a way to make a statement in a nonconfrontational way."

I saw Johnny and his backers essentially as carpetbaggers seeking to seize what had become a great cultural happening for the community. Johnny's motives may have been sincere, but I didn't believe he truly understood our discontent. As a free festival, families came out to soak up the music and atmosphere. Babies in diapers along with aging grandparents of all races could learn, become inspired, and as a result, support our music and its culture year-round. To trade that in for an exclusive event would mean only adults who were already inclined to attend such an event would buy pricey tickets. What's more, it would only incentivize promotors to book bigger name White blues appropriators or hard rock acts in order to sell more tickets to turn bigger profits for its investors. We Black blues musicians would once more, as happened with rock and roll, be left behind and marginalized. I said to the reporter from the *Advocate*, "Protest options with less potential to do serious harm to the Blues Festival should be explored." Palazzotto's solution would not solve our main problem. It would only push us further into the background of our own event. Our grievance wasn't solely about money, which seemed to be his major concern. It was troublesome to us that our music and culture were being distorted and Whitened. The lower fees only added to our injury.

None of us belonged to a musician's union. We had no one to speak for us. My dad, the former union steward from Ciba-Geigy, became spokesman by default. He expressed his doubts about Palazzotto's plan. Tabby knew the festival helped create new converts who would visit the Blues Box from time to time throughout the year. Dad also expressed how the recognition of the festival helped to raise the profile of us all, increasing our performance fees throughout the year.

The usurpation that was taking place wasn't restricted to Louisiana alone. We weren't the only ones experiencing this troubling trend. White misappropriation of the blues was a phenomenon that had swept the country as a whole. It wasn't enough that rock and roll (blues for Whites by Whites) had dominated music for decades, which prompted Dad to initially open his juke joint and heritage hall, form a blues society, and help found a nonprofit festival based on grants and fundraisers to keep our music and culture alive. Now, after some success, they wanted to commandeer it.

Each year the representatives and cultivators of the blues grew paler, which in part, caused African Americans to participate less and less in its cultivation and presentation. This was a disturbing trend I was fighting on a corporate level to no avail. What could we bluesmen and women do alone? Without help from the intelligentsia and business leaders in the Black community, a group of poorly educated blues people were powerless to quell the trend of Whites taking ownership and stewardship of what had been unquestionably African American music and culture.

We all had doubts about Johnny Palazzotto's proposition, but he was determined to win us over. Before he made his final pitch to us, before the meeting went any further, he demanded the reporter we'd invited leave the building. In the end, Palazzotto did create a ticketed blues festival, with mixed results and significantly lower attendance. The original free festival my dad helped to found floundered separately another year or two before fading away, in part because dueling festivals created public confusion.

One night, a guy came into the Blues Box with a group of friends. He was dressed like Jake from *The Blues Brothers* movie: dark glasses, black hat, black suit and tie. He was loud, obnoxious, and privileged, making crude advances to the waitresses, touching and feeling them just because he thought he could, then trying to stuff money in their bras to buy their tolerance. One of the women in his group was impatient with his behavior—I assumed she was his girlfriend—but she couldn't get him to conduct himself accordingly. He was treating the waitresses and bartender as if he were in an old Western bordello. Granted, the blues in Louisiana is no stranger to brothels and sporting houses, but even there a code of decorum is expected or you're tossed out, roughed up, and banished from returning.

"Play 'Brown Eyed Girl,'" he said, dropping large bills in the band's tip jar.

"Sorry, we don't know that one," I said. "Maybe you'll like this next one; it's one of mine."

Of course I knew Van Morrison's song (though maybe not every note or lyric). I was of a mind, however, that if you came to the Blues Box, you came to hear me do what I do. You came to hear me carry on a long tradition. Although the Blues Box's audience had gone from 95 percent Black when it opened in 1979 to about 90 percent White over the years, I still believed the blues was rooted in my culture.

In the middle of my set, he started heckling me, showing off in front of his friends. "Play some real blues!" he yelled, as if he were an authority on "real" blues, or worse, as if I weren't already playing them. It was offensive. I tried to ignore him. Later, he came up to the stage and tried to take my microphone off the stand. He wanted to sing, do a mocking Jake Blues, of the *Blues Brothers*. It wasn't jam night. On Saturdays there's no room for amateurs, and even on jam night we never allow mocking or karaoke. I took the microphone back from him.

"Go and sit down," I said.

He retook his seat but heckled even louder, with his buddies egging him on.

"Play some real blues, play Stevie Ray!"

We hadn't opened Tabby's Blues Box and Heritage Hall, "Home of the Baton Rouge Bluesmen," so we could pay tribute to the music of the Paul Butterfield Blues Band, Stevie Ray Vaughan, or the Blues Brothers. I wasn't going to perform some shuffling act for those drunken fools. Rather than the Blues Box's culture continuing to be the force it had been, it was threatening to become not only a common tourist trap but a place where I had to emulate White musicians emulating Black musicians for the amusement of an indifferent audience whose ignorance was so impenetrable it was offensive.

The customers couldn't ignore the louts. They were spoiling everyone's evening. The doorman went over and asked them to keep it down. I could see that Dad, stationed behind the bar, was uneasy. Yet he resisted throwing the bums out, not wanting to bite the hand that fed.

My frustrations grew. White folks' blatant appropriation, once veiled as "rock and roll," was now devouring the blues in a gluttonous orgy. They were becoming the face of blues as such. The annexation of my music and culture therewith threatened to make me a dutiful hack, not an artist. I tried to convince myself the crowd still came to the Blues Box to hear me perform my art and experience my culture. After all, had they not paid to see me? Was not my name on the marquee?

"Fake Jake Blues" came over; this time he stood in front of us singing into a beer bottle, doing a drunken sideshow for his friends. Then he crashed, falling onto the bandstand, spilling beer on stage and my amplifier. His girlfriend helped him up. I could no longer play through the commotion. I brought the band to a halt.

"This is the worst music I have ever heard!" he shouted at me, as his girlfriend helped pick him up off the stage.

"Come on," his embarrassed girlfriend pleaded, "let's go." She pulled him by the arm.

"Here," I said, handing him the tip jar. "We don't want your money."

He slapped the tip jar out of my hand. Money spilled to the floor. The bassist gathered up the cash.

"You want the blues? You want the 'real' blues?" I said, bitterly.

I counted off the band and rapped my most defiant rap over the band's bemused funky beat:

This the blues of the 21st century,
and I don't give a damn if you can't get with me!
The KKK took off the white sheets,
changed with the time became the police
Now don't be caught on a dead end street,
in the middle of the night or you're gonna get beat
I can see it so clearly,
I seen it before because I know my history
This is the blues of the 21st century,
and I don't give a damn if you can't get with me!

The band struggled to meet my energy. Guitar cranked, I simultaneously rapped and played with a defiant drive I'd not shown in the Blues Box before.

The missionary man he may mean well,
but what he calls heaven that's my hell
You see, I got to tell the truth,
I'm a blues singing brother from the land of Duke

Now don't be confused,
although I may be rapping this is hard core blues
This is the blues of the 21st century,
this is the blues of the 21st century.
This the blues of the 21st century,
And I don't give a damn if you can't get with me!

No one in the joint had ever heard anything like it. "Jake" stood there trying to say something, but the roar of my guitar drowned him out. I rapped the motif at him again and again. It felt exhilarating!

This is the blues of the 21st century,
and I don't give a damn if you can't get with me!

When the song ended, there was sparse confused applause. However, my most ardent fans sitting at one table stood up and applauded enthusiastically. The condescending louts, led by Fake Jake, hastily stormed out of the club. The band took a break. Dozens of patrons, uncomfortable with my music, hastily made their way out the door. Ironically, my music seemed more offensive to some patrons than the antics of the fake Blues Brother.

Standing behind the bar, Dad peered at me with a perplexed look on his face. Then it hit me. I'd crossed the line. I'd nearly cleared the house. Dad waved angrily for me to meet him in the small storage room behind the bar.

"What the hell was that!" Dad yelled.

"I don't know, man," I said. "It just came out."

He went on and on about how he'd trained me better than that.

"This is a business, understand? This is a blues club. We do nothin' but the blues here."

I knew the Jake Blues impersonator and his ignorant group could be found on Bourbon Street or Beale Street, or at any college frat party, and they would blend in perfectly. But I'd bought into Dad's credo, as if he'd been Socrates high on a hill in Ancient Greece, lecturing me about our great Creole blues culture and heritage. I wanted that philosophy to continue to mean something, something more than what it was threatening to become.

"This my club!" Dad shouted, right into my face, "I'm not going to let you ruin my business." We stood face to face in the tightly cramped storage room.

"You don't care, do you? You don't give a damn about nothing but yourself."

"You're right," I remarked, "this ain't for me." I bumped past him to leave. Immediately, he grabbed me and slammed me against the wall. I violently shrugged him off. Suddenly, we froze, realizing we were about to jump over the ledge; descend into a hate-filled abyss from which we may never return. We stared at each other for a moment in shame and shock. Then I left him standing there, packed my guitar, and left the club, leaving him to play the last set of the night without me.

For days afterward I was numb. I was experiencing serious delusion, an artistic madness, if you will, where I questioned everything around me. They only saw me from their right side up point of view—a point of view that had been carefully constructed by my existential nemesis, the Blues Mafia. I longed to play music I was passionate about, true to who I thought I was. But every step of the way it seemed my humanity was being challenged.

If I had just gone along in the role of the primitive as expected, perhaps everything would've been OK. If I could revert back to the kid guitar prodigy I once was, my music would have been a lot more satisfying for the audience, and thus, good for business. More beer would have been sold, helping the family business. But that's not who I'd grown to be. I couldn't express myself that way anymore. Besides, I'd seen where that road leads—it was a dead end.

I concluded that my new brand of "blues with an attitude" was going to repel the customers. It wasn't going to put food on my mother's table. What's more, the Blues Mafia was in the process of erasing me from their blues narrative. My career as an authentic folk bluesman was practically over. Unable to earn a living and blacklisted from clubs and festivals, I needed a fresh start. With the walls closing in on me, I rounded up just enough money to buy a one-way ticket out of America.

EXILED IN EUROPE

MOM AND DAD DROVE me to Ryan Airport. They came to the gate to see me off. Dad told me to contact a promoter he had toured with, Briton Julian Piper, who was also a guitarist and music journalist, as a possible host, someone to help with my transition. Julian Piper lived in the town of Exeter a few hours south of London. Julian had visited the Blues Box over the years and developed a friendship with Tabby. Julian's band had booked and backed Dad on a few European tours. Dad suggested maybe Julian could arrange some gigs for me while I was in the UK. Other than Julian, I knew no one in England. Regardless of this, I was moving to London hoping that people there would be a little more open-minded to the style of blues I wanted to play and record.

It was an emotional farewell for me, more so than for my parents, because I didn't let on I was leaving America permanently. I had about eighty dollars to my name. Mom might have given me another forty or so. With less than two hundred dollars and a one-way ticket, I entered the plane carrying my guitar in a gig bag. I put it in the overhead luggage compartment and sat in a window seat. As we sped down the runway, I was looking out the window. I saw Mom and Dad waving through the huge terminal windows. Then the loud roar of the plane ascended into the sky. Gazing out the window, into the horizon, chemical pollution from the plants hovered over the levee. Ships on the Mississippi River looked like toys I once played with in my muddy backyard. I pulled my headphones over my ears, clicked on my CD Walkman, sunk back, closed my eyes, and daydreamed with an uneasy apprehension what would become of me.

> This is a song for the genius child.
> Sing it softly, for the song is wild.
> Sing it softly as ever you can—
> Lest the song get out of hand.
> *Nobody loves a genius child.*[9]

The great bird finally touched down on Heathrow Airport's crowded runway. After arriving with almost no cash and no return ticket, it took the longest time to get through customs. Luckily Julian Piper, my only UK contact, vouched for me. I had no idea which way to go as I departed the subway station at Piccadilly Circus. There was a light snow. I turned my collar to the cold icy wind. I wandered about, looking for a cheap room. I rented one at a youth hostel and set out to find a place to play to earn a few quid.

I had to hustle like never before just to stay dry and warm. During the day, in order to save enough money for fish and chips, I slept in the park near Piccadilly Circus and congregated all night in Soho, around Bar Italia, an after-hours café across the street from Ronny Scott's jazz club. Eventually I rounded up a pickup band and managed to play a few gigs in Soho, including a couple nights at the once famous Marquee Club.

In the 1960s, Soho had been a grimy beatnik neighborhood, awash in cheap alcohol, live music, and free love. It crawled with schoolboys who, if they couldn't get into sold-out shows at the Marquee Club to see the Rolling Stones or the Jimi Hendrix Experience, slipped into strip clubs instead. Soho had once thumbed its nose at convention, partied its way through the punk '70s and new wave '80s. However, by the time I arrived on the scene, in the early '90s, it had seen its best days. Like the stench of regret sex after waking up with a hangover, middle-aged

Londoners had washed away those rebellious days, cut their hair, and got on with becoming their parents. Indeed, "Whatever happened to the revolution?" I lamented in a recent song I'd written and recorded. The revolution had gone corporate.

It was obvious there could never be another Jimi Hendrix rocketing to fame in England because over the years, London's music business had become Americanized, importing the same misconceptions and misunderstandings as back home.

Julian Piper was connected with blues societies across the UK. It was a small but enthusiastic network. With Julian's backing as promotor, and also providing a rhythm section, I was able to play the circuit, earning enough to support myself and stay warm. My new blues music didn't earn standing applause, but it wasn't rejected either. I won over new converts with each performance. Problem was, no record companies were willing to buy me out of my expensive Warner Brothers contract.

OKeh/Sony Records was a 1920s imprint I'd pushed Sony to reactivate for me after leaving Warner, to no avail. They subsequently reactivated it just as I'd proposed, but ironically, they didn't sign me. Instead they signed others emulating my style and vision for a reactivated OKeh label.

I soon learned that in London, if one didn't have a gimmick, you didn't get signed to a major label. The Brits preferred their musicians to have a shtick. It didn't matter how talented you were, even Elton John wore funny glasses. One needed to behave badly for the music press, set your guitar on fire (seen that already), or wear conspicuous makeup. I had no such gimmick. After a few months, I was delighted to get reacquainted with a Danish girlfriend who I first met while in Austin. Mariann traveled to London from Denmark to spend a few days with me. We had a great time.

A few months later, she invited me to Denmark to visit her there. The first day we went out for a stroll in Copenhagen the queen of Denmark miraculously walked right past us with her large entourage. Mariann was blown away. She'd never seen her queen in person. Mariann confided in me later that she believed nearly bumping into the queen was a sign we were meant to be together. I had planned to spend only a few days in Copenhagen. However, a few days turned into a few years.

Playing house with Mariann and our baby girl, Maha, who was born in Denmark, was wonderful, but my creative spirit was stir-crazy. One day, while visiting Mariann's family in Hørning, a small pastoral town near Aarhus, I was in the workshop out back assisting Torben, Mariann's brother. Torben, an architectural major, was crafting wooden toy penguins for him and Mariann to sell in the town square. I confided in him my artistic quandary. Torben, who had been a drummer in a high school band himself, presumed that now that I had a family, I would toss music aside and get serious about a day job, possibly in a nearby warehouse or factory. I made it clear to Torben, even though I had no connections in the Copenhagen music scene and my prospects wear bleak, I had no plans to seek a day job while in Denmark.

Later, I got the cold shoulder from Mariann's parents. I assumed Torben had shared our conversation, but they couldn't understand. Mariann's father spoke no English, her mother only a few words. They spoke a dialect of Jutland. Thus, having a meaningful conversation directly with her parents was out of the question.

Torben introduced me to a friend of his, Thomas Walbum, a talented pianist. Finally, someone to talk music with. Thomas and I clicked immediately. Thomas's younger brother, Jakob, was a drummer. They had both trained at a music conservatory and were well versed in American jazz. I found it interesting to pick the brains of Danish musicians. In turn, I learned about great Danish artists that Americans knew nothing about. I realized there were Italian artists who sold out theaters all over Europe but America knew nothing of them. America never played Italian, Danish, or French language music on popular radio stations. But in Europe, I heard all styles, in all languages.

In Copenhagen, where I shared an apartment with Mariann and our daughter, I finally got into a comfortable musical zone. Thomas, Jakob, and I joined with Lars, a bassist who happened to have a makeshift recording studio. Refreshingly, the Blues Mafia's demagoguery had not penetrated Denmark. When I said, "Hey, man, this is the way I like to play the blues, mixed with hip-hop and rap," they were like, "OK, let's try it. What key you do that in?"

"What?" I couldn't believe it. No argument? No debate?

For the first time I felt free. I was no longer bound by a stereotypical image. I learned most of those tropes had not been fully imported into Scandinavia. For the first time, I was free to paint with a clean canvas. There were no preconceived notions of who I should be or could be. Over time, it became clear I wasn't moving back to London. I was content to live the life of an expatriate in Copenhagen, Denmark, with my new family. We began recording what would become *21st Century Blues . . . from da 'Hood.*

Our apartment was located near the center of Copenhagen, at Ægirsgade 22, 4.TV, 2200 N, and I settled into my life as an immigrant Dane. I took care of my daughter while Mariann attended nursing school. I changed diapers, took Maha to the playground; I even wore an apron while cleaning the apartment and cooking dinner, which I always had ready by the time Mariann returned home. In between chores, I feverishly wrote new songs to record with Thomas, Jakob, and Lars.

I found the day-to-day life of an average Dane strikingly comfortable. Because of universal health care, free college education, and high living wages, Denmark was practically free of extreme poverty. Gun violence was unheard of. I was astonished once when, in the middle of the night, we called a pediatrician for the baby. She was running a fever. Within minutes the doctor was at the door with his medical bag. After treating Maha, who was now about two years old, he didn't bill us. We didn't even have to tip him. Moreover, a tip would have been an insult. In contrast, the only folks in America making house calls were pizza deliverers. Furthermore, without insurance, I was more likely to die in an emergency room while waiting for a doctor back in America. If lucky enough to see a doctor, I might have a heart attack when I got the bill.

Before I knew it, another year had passed. I'd even learned a little Danish. I had to, it was my daughter's first language. Adjusting to the cold, however, was another matter altogether. Maneuvering through knee-high snow during the holidays was overwhelming for this Louisiana boy. During the winters, which seemed to last for eight months, it got dark in the early afternoons. It was crazy. There were only about six weeks a year to enjoy the beaches. Nevertheless, it was the open-mindedness of the Danes, the warmth of friendship, their sincerity, that won me over and made me feel at home.

MY PAIN, YOUR PLEASURE

ONE DAY, while collecting the daily mail, I noticed an official proposal from Warner Brothers Records. My signature was required to finalize my release from Warner's exclusive seven-album recording contract. In order to settle, I had agreed that whatever money owed me would go to HighTone, my former production company, as some kind of recoupable payment. I didn't contest the exploitative terms. It seemed my only way out of major label purgatory. I promptly signed the release and mailed it back to Los Angeles. Finally, I could earn a living for my young family. After years in exile, I had agency to get on with producing my hip-hop blues opus. Ultimately, with my newfound freedom I could pursue a new record deal.

Reinvigorated, Thomas, Jakob, Lars, and I hit the studio. During breaks, I performed across Europe, traveling between England, France, and Spain picking up gigs where I could. Thomas, Jakob, and Lars rarely left Denmark to perform with me. It wasn't feasible. Besides, Europe was full of fine musicians, even though my groundbreaking hip-hop blues style presented challenges.

One day, while on tour in Spain, I was out strolling the picturesque streets of Barcelona. The quaint wrought-iron balconies, the cathedrals and cabildos, made me sentimental for New Orleans. The architecture and bright color palettes were similar. After all, Spain rebuilt the French Quarter in the late eighteenth century. In the town center, at sidewalk cafés, Spaniards casually conversed over wine and coffee. Surprisingly, Spain had a peculiar custom. Shops closed for lunch. Shopkeepers were encouraged to go home, take a nap, have some wine, relax. They'd return at various times in the evening to reopen shop. By contrast, Americans were driven like worker bees.

I wandered into the Picasso Museum. Picasso's childhood paintings were depicted in a time line along museum walls. Admiring his formative paintings, I recognized motifs in his artistic development. Drawn to the voice of a guide in an adjacent room, I followed it into a gallery: ". . . A child prodigy, Picasso's father, Jose Ruiz, was a painter and art teacher."

I learned that Picasso, at the foot of his father, mastered the traditional portrait. But later he rejected his father's conventional aesthetics in favor of Cubism. Similarly, I had learned traditional blues from my dad. And like Picasso, I'd broken with tradition, straining my relationship with my father. My interest in young Pablo's artistic growth intensified as I began to see analogies in our artistic journeys. The guide quoted Picasso as having said, "In art, one has to kill one's father." Picasso's words echoed in my subconscious.

"Chris!" a familiar voice yelled. There was a commotion near the entrance. "C'mon, man." It was Steven Coldrige, my bassist and tour manager. In an instant I realized I was late for pickup. Decorous museum tourists glared at me and the rambunctious, unkempt Englishman with the posh accent. We were shoved outside by security. Steven looked back at the guards, spit on the ground, gave the finger. We rushed down the street to our beat-up dusty tour van.

"You're always wandering off," Steven said, bitingly. "Now we're late for Madrid."

"It's only a few hours away," I said.

"Not in this van," Andrea remarked, sitting shotgun.

Andrea was a featured singer and rhythm guitarist for our tour. Andrea was also Steve's girlfriend. Steven got behind the wheel on the right—English side. Our drummer, Alejandro, sat in the cramped backseat with me and the gear.

"Man," I groaned, "been gigging all over Europe, ain't seen nothing. Just clubs, hotels, and this stinky ass van."

Steven shot back, "See it on your own time," as we sped through the town center and onto the freeway.

After dark, we pulled up to the venue in Madrid. Large posters were plastered outside. CHRIS THOMAS BAND, EN VIVO EN PERSONA. I thought to myself, my name, Chris Thomas, didn't have enough pizzazz. In fact, it was rather plain. In Scandinavia, Chris and Thomas were first names that always sounded unfinished. I made a mental note to work on a better moniker.

The promoter stood out front. Waiting. "*Llegas tarde!*" he shouted, pointing at his watch. We rushed to set up our instruments. A restless audience awaited. The lights went down. The crowd applauded. I wailed on guitar while rapping a blues. Even though my raps were likely lost in translation, the audience grooved along.

The next day, we sat for lunch at a café in Madrid. We were booked later that evening on a national TV talk show to plug our tour of Spain.

"I'll meet you guys at the van," I said. Andrea looked scathingly over to Steve.

"Chris, man," Steve said, anxiously, "don't go wandering off again."

"I need strings, batteries for my Walkman. No worries. Be right back," I promised.

Later that afternoon, strolling along the Grand Via, an upscale boulevard of shops in the center of Madrid, while placing batteries into my Walkman, I was suddenly disturbed.

"*Alto, no te muevas!*" a bellicose policeman threatened me in Spanish.

Is he talking to me, I thought.

"*Levanta tus manos!*"

"I don't speak Spanish."

The officer aimed his gun, heightening the threat.

"*Ponte en el suelo!*" Get on the ground.

Pedestrians in the crossfire began to flee. I feared for my life. It seemed his nervous finger would pull the trigger at any moment. In what seemed like an instant, a swarm of *policía* jumped out of cars and wrestled me violently to the ground. Knowing I'd done nothing wrong, my natural reflex was to resist. More guns were pointed. Obscenities were hurled at me. On the ground, stunned and confused, I was forced to absorb painful kicks and punches. Handcuffed. Shoved into the back of a *policía* car. I was sped away. Sirens blaring.

When we arrived at the jail, they searched me and found my passport. When they realized I was American, in the country legally, they argued among themselves, often turning to look in my direction. I knew they were arguing about my status. I couldn't understand what they were saying. But from their agitated body language, it seemed someone had made a big mistake. After some time, an officer escorted me to a solitary cell and slammed the heavy iron bars shut. I was bloodied and pained; my nose broken, face swollen. I sat on the concrete bed head in hands. I sighed. Thinking, Thank God they didn't shoot.

The cold cell had no windows. I lost all track of time. I took what seemed like short naps. I wasn't sure. I couldn't see the sun. In dark isolation, I was forced to confront my demons and worst fears. I wasn't given food or water. I dreamed of my childhood. I relived the time I could have spent my life in juvenile detention before being shipped to Angola. I ached for innocent Black men and women rotting in human storage dungeons back in America. It was brutally clear hatred of Blacks like me had no borders.

"Thomas!" a jailer called out.

"In here!" I sprung up.

"*Eres libre de irte.*" You're free to go, he said, opening the gate.

The jailer walked me down the long corridor to the checkout room. Gathering my personals, I realized my passport was missing. A clerk held it up. "This stays," he said in English.

I emerged from jail into the warm sunlight. Steven and Andrea were waiting in our rusty van across the street. With three-day-old dry blood covering my swollen face and clothes, I hopped in, relieved. The dingy van seemed like a golden chariot that had swung down to rescue me. We sped away.

"At first," Steven remarked, "we thought you were just fucking off again."

"We looked all over," Andrea said. "When you missed the show, we knew something was wrong."

Steven passed me the newspaper. "This morning the *El País* said 'Negro American attack Police.'"

"They tried to kill me."

"Fascist fucks," Andrea grumbled. "That's why I hate playing Spain."

"Why didn't you call?" Steven sighed. "Anyway, it's over now."

"Bullshit, they took my passport."

Broken, bloodied, and pained, I was driven to the American embassy. The stars and stripes flying over the building was a sight for swollen eyes. The officials already knew from news reports what had happened. I was expecting my embassy to feel my pain, defend me against the unjustified brutality of the Spanish police department. But they were dispassionate about my ordeal. An embassy official coolly told me he could return my passport and allow travel privileges out of the country only. Nothing he could do about the police. After a heated back-and-forth, I was allowed to denounce the Madrid police, at least, in a written statement. We left the embassy and drove back to the hotel.

An attorney offered to represent me in court. Turns out, because I was *Negro* with long dreadlocks, the police mistook me for an illegal resident from Africa. I soon learned there had been a recent spike in police brutalities against African immigrants. Being that I was an American citizen visiting Spain, and a notable music artist with a legitimate work permit, my case would be a good one to expose police fascism and Spain's xenophobic policies toward Africans. The attorney explained that he represented a group fighting on behalf of Africans subjected to similar abuses—sometimes deadly. To be sure, I wanted to stay to see to it the police were punished. However, I couldn't afford to stay in Spain for months to fight the case, even though the lawyer offered to work pro bono. In the end, when my passport was returned, I quietly retreated back to Denmark. Afterward, I wrote a blues rap, "Homesick Blues," inspired by my harrowing ordeal with the Spanish police. The song added a gritty realism to the *21st Century Blues* album.

One day, back in Copenhagen, I received a letter from Dad. We corresponded regularly. He always kept me abreast of the latest Blues Box news. My dad took great pleasure in letter writing. Writing was one pleasure he and I didn't share. I'd occasionally write back. Most often, however, I'd send postcards. Sitting in our fourth-floor apartment, at the small kitchen table, I opened the letter. Dad's letters stood out. He always wrote to me on his business stationery, "Rockin' Tabby Thomas, 'King of the Swamp Blues.'" I thought his letters should be on regular paper. Closer to what I thought a "normal" father-son correspondence should be. Nevertheless, I always admired Dad's handwriting. His penmanship had an artistic flair, especially for a bluesman of his generation. It was obvious he enjoyed letter writing. His letters brought out a sentimentality in me that I wished to suppress. He often wrote how proud he was that I was out on my own, taking advantage of opportunities he never had, making a name for myself across Europe. I was always relieved to learn that no one back home was gravely ill, and everyone in the family seemed to be doing as well as always. I would learn one of my sisters had a new baby. My brother, Tammy, would make a brief recovery, then fall prey again to his vices. But for the most part, Dad's letters were positive and encouraging. As I sat in my kitchen reading his latest handwritten letter, I could hear my dad's voice speak to me as if he were across the table. "We had 'em tonight but I don't know how much longer I can keep the club open. I hear there's a plan to tear down the Blues Box. If I don't come up with money to buy the building, we could lose the club."

In a previous letter, he spoke of a company that offered to move the Blues Box into a new casino on the river. The deal, I presumed, would surely provide enough money to save the club. But upon further reading, I learned Dad's deepest concern. "What the casino have in mind is nothing like what we've got here. I think we'll all have to find someplace else to play if they move the club down there into the Casino. Everybody I came up with, Lightning Slim, Slim Harpo, Moses

'Whispering' Smith, Silas Hogan, they all got their hats. I'm one of the last ones still out here. All I can do is try to keep it going as long as I can."

A clipping from a local business magazine quoted Tabby saying, "Freedom is worth more than money." Although hard times had been persistent on North Boulevard, Dad was resisting a takeover by casino operators Jazz Enterprises Inc., of Catfish Town, a proposed riverboat gambling development in downtown Baton Rouge on the Mississippi River. A lucrative offer was on the table, but Tabby was hesitant. "Right now, I'm free, I do what I want to do," he told a reporter.

Jazz Enterprises wanted to relocate the Blues Box to the downtown levee property known as Catfish Town, to act as a major attraction for their proposed floating riverboat casino. The issuance of gambling licenses along the Baton Rouge Louisiana levee was controversial, morally and politically, in part because of suspected bribery. Prominent Louisiana prosecutors convened a grand jury to investigate bribes and corruption between Jazz Enterprises and Louisiana's colorful governor, Edwin Edwards, who had recently defeated Klansman David Duke for reelection.

There were articles and news reports daily, updating the public on the ongoing negotiations between potential casino operators and Baton Rouge officials. Many in the community thought Tabby should cash in. He's paid his dues, they said. Indeed, at the age of sixty-five, Tabby had earned a pristine reputation as a cultural ambassador and a genuine folk icon. Many LSU students he'd touched with his positive spirit were now professionals, shaping the future of the city and state. Tabby was someone they greatly admired. An endorsement from Tabby would be a huge get for any potential casino operator.

However, pressure was mounting on Jazz Enterprises. Moral outrage by concerned citizens sparked religious and civic leaders to carefully scrutinize the granting of casino licenses. The community feared gambling addiction could ruin the lives of those most vulnerable in nearby communities. Jazz Enterprises Inc. was forced to make concessions to win over political advisories, and, most important, the public, who would eventually vote on their license bid. In a public relation move, Jazz Inc. proposed money for gambling addiction counseling, school renovations, and downtown upgrades. Tabby's Blues Box would have been a feather in their PR cap, helping to win over an apathetic public.

However, Tabby was a street scholar. He'd come up the hard way. He'd seen every hustle and huckster over the years. He sensed that an alignment with the casino would tarnish his good name. Jazz Inc. increased their offer, which seriously tempted my father. He expounded, in subsequent letters, on the pros and cons of the casino deal. What's more, the landlord of the Blues Box was always threatening to sell the building for one reason or other, and Tabby couldn't come up with the money to buy the building. I felt a little culpable myself, because I wasn't home to help.

Sometimes I questioned, during my exile, had I turned my back on my family, my cultural calling? I wasn't sure. Emotionally, I felt Dad was using his letters to pull me back home. At times, I felt if only I could change genre, do straight pop, R&B, or hip-hop, my music would have a better chance of commercial success. Maybe I could, then, earn the riches of popular stars and send money home. Except the blues, my culture, was all-consuming to me, and my father knew it. Subliminally, his every letter reminded me, don't turn your back on your culture.

Later, in 1994, Dad's omen was confirmed. His instincts about the casino move were on point. Although he would have earned a huge payday from Jazz Enterprises, in the end, he walked away from the money and kept his reputation untarnished. His folk legend only grew in the community as someone championing the arts and Black culture who was incorruptible.

Other prominent leaders didn't fare so well. The federal investigation of Governor Edwin Edwards and his associates landed Edwards behind bars. It even brought down an NFL owner, the San Francisco 49ers owner, Edward J. DeBartolo Jr., who admitted to paying the governor some $400,000 under the table for the governor's guarantee in securing a casino license.

In contrast, it was estimated, in a local business report, the Blues Box only netted Dad around $25,000 annually after expenses. He supplemented that with occasional touring, local gigs, T-shirts, and a few record sales. He and my mother lived in poverty. But poverty was all my family and I had ever known. We'd learned how to smile and celebrate life without knowing how we were going to make ends meet. Poverty had become like a comfortable old pair of jeans, well-worn and full of holes. Of course we longed to be wealthy, carefree, but at what price? When Dad said "Freedom is worth more than money," he meant it.

While in Copenhagen, I established my own production company, 21st Century Blues. During our Copenhagen recording sessions, I had a premonition that the sessions could yield a landmark recording. I was the first artist to merge rap and blues. When we completed enough songs for an album, I decided against sending the tapes to myopic blues labels because they were likely to meddle with my vision or reject it. Besides, they wouldn't have had the means to promote such an iconoclastic artistic statement.

What I really desired, in due time, was to start my own label. I figured I could do just as well as those small independent blues labels on my own. But that idea would have to wait until I had more leverage. For now, a well-funded, well-staffed label, with major distribution, is what I wanted and needed, because the record was like no other in the market.

I mailed some tapes around to major A&R types. The tapes floated around different executives in England and Los Angeles. After a few months, interest began heating up. Two respected producers, John Wooler and John Porter, contacted me by phone at my apartment in Copenhagen with serious interest in the tapes. They happened to be two of the most successful executives in the business for producing blues. John Wooler, based in London, was senior vice president at Virgin Records UK and president of Point Blank Records, a label he launched and ran as a subsidiary of Virgin. He was responsible for John Lee Hooker's recent crossover success. Wooler had recently signed Hooker, Van Morrison, John Hammond, Pops Staples, and many others. John Porter was based in London and Los Angeles. His recent projects included producing Buddy Guy's signature album *Damn Right I Got the Blues*. Moreover, John Porter was married to Linda Keith, a former British *Vogue* model, who in 1966, at twenty years of age, lent a then-unknown Jimi Hendrix a white Fender Stratocaster belonging to her then-boyfriend Keith Richards of the Rolling Stones. Linda dragged all her music business friends down to see Jimi showcase at Cafe Au Go Go in New York's Greenwich Village and the rest was history. John Porter and his wife, Linda Keith-Porter, loved my tapes and the short documentary video I had sent along with them.

John Porter persuaded House of Blues to offer me a long-term recording agreement. I had never heard of House of Blues. I'd lost touch with American popular culture. There was no widespread internet yet. Long-distance calls were extremely expensive. Word from the States only came by letter. I was told by John Porter that Isaac Tigrett, the owner of House of Blues, had said he wanted to get involved with me because I sounded like the future.

Isaac Tigrett, the founder of the Hard Rock Cafe, had sold his interest in that franchise. He was launching a new venture, the House of Blues, a first-rate blues-themed live music and restaurant chain. The franchise also included a record label, House of Blues Records. Isaac was out there, a real forward thinker and very spiritual. John Porter and House of Blues offered me a fresh start back in Los Angeles. The company was flush with cash. They were building a franchise of blues clubs, and they wanted to invest in me. Tigrett had big ideas for the blues, including national TV and radio shows. They were going big, and they wanted to do it with the blues. It was unprecedented.

We reached a tentative agreement and House of Blues flew me back to Los Angeles to finish the record. I left Mariann and my baby girl, Maha, in Copenhagen, but promised to send for them when I got settled. Thomas, Jakob, and Lars were hopeful that we would be signed as a band, but the House of Blues was only interested in me as a solo artist. This caused some friction between us, but it was resolved with small payments to each musician and the promise of a future tour together. Later, we did a brief tour of American clubs, including a stop in Chicago.

House of Blues bought rights to my album and made a few vital concessions: they gave me creative control, including control of my image and presentation—a first for a blues artist. Bertelsmann Music Group (BMG), one of the world's largest distributors, was the distributor for the House of Blues.

MY RETURN FROM EUROPEAN EXILE

RAISING A YOUNG FAMILY in Copenhagen, Denmark, over the last few years had broadened my worldview. Prior to living in Europe, I identified people, for the most part, in Black and White—a common mistake of someone born and raised in the South. Thankfully, while living abroad my understanding of race classifications was enlightened. I returned to America with new eyes.

While living in London, I had Black friends with whom I had little in common except melanin. I established relationships throughout Europe with folks who naturally identified by their birth country. My daughter had been born neither African Danish nor Black nor Negro Danish, she was simply Danish. Conversely, in the United States of America, I was born a Negro, grew up Colored, became Black, and subsequently, in the last decade or so, was labeled African American. Now, at long last, I was returning home, in mind and spirit, as an American, nothing else.

My views on America had been transformed, too. I was ready to embrace my country wholeheartedly, notwithstanding its history of slavery and Jim Crow. In Madrid, Spain, I had been a victim of racial profiling and police brutality, affirming that prejudice had no borders. The question was, What could I do to effect change? If I were to chop down a tree in Paris, would anyone back home hear it? I had considered settling down in Paris, writing poetry, recording music, debating the meaning of life over French wine at sidewalk cafés with fellow artists, but I chose to return to America instead. The fact that I had the volition to choose was liberating. I had been a fugitive from my own culture. Nevertheless, I was returning freely, as an American man.

———

Upon my return to America, I decided to stop briefly in Louisiana to see my parents. After a quick visit with Mom, I went directly down to the Blues Box because

I knew Dad would be there. It was a Saturday night. I wanted to surprise him. I was longing to see old acquaintances, folks I hadn't seen in a while. I entered Tabby's Blues Box without drawing attention to myself.

The musky scent of stale beer and cigarette fumes mixed with the sweaty scent of desire immediately reminded me of happy times, old friends, and good vibes. The bittersweet funk of decadence in the cramped river city juke joint—which felt spacious because of its two-story high ceiling—was dulled by air circulating from two large ceiling fans. The narrow rectangular shape of Tabby's Blues Box meant that in order to get to the bar on the opposite end, I had to weave my way through the crowd of partiers. I was pleasantly surprised the place was packed.

I made my way from one end to the other, bumping and squeezing past a throng of unfamiliar White faces. I stood near the bar, which bustled with action, savoring the moment, engrossed by the atmosphere. The lighting was dim except around the bar and stage. The decor was pleasantly unchanged. The bar's tall antique wooden shelves—which housed half-emptied bottles of off-brand whiskey, cartons of cigarettes, and jars of pickled pigs' lips—were decorated with Christmas tree lights, just as I remembered. The old jukebox against the far wall brought back fond memories, too. Gazing at pictures on the plastered walls that I had taped up as a teen was like thumbing through an old tattered family scrapbook. Posters of local blues legends, such as Silas Hogan, Guitar Kelly, Lightnin' Slim, Lonesome Sundown, Lazy Lester, and of course my dad, Rockin' Tabby, all posed with their trademark guitars, made me feel right at home.

There were, however, a few changes. The elevated stage, which had been high above the bar, was back on the floor. The elevated stage was never embraced by the fans, because they liked to be closer to the musicians. Besides, some of the old guys used to complain; it wasn't easy climbing up that rickety staircase to get backstage. I was happy to see the stage had been moved back down near the dance floor.

What I found most unsettling, however, was the music. It was louder than I recalled. But the volume was not the main problem. It sounded homogenized. A group of White musicians were onstage playing in the Chicago style. They sounded well enough, but their repertoire was the sort one could find at any generic blues bar from Cambridge, Massachusetts, to Des Moines, Iowa. It wasn't what I had grown up with in my family's juke joint. The loud volume only exacerbated the mendacity.

"Chris!" someone yelled over the blaring music.

I looked down the bar. It was my old friend Henry Gray, a sight for sore ears. The piano man was dressed in a powder blue two-piece suit, white button shirt, collar casually open, no tie. Henry, who was born January 19, 1925, in Kenner, Louisiana, didn't have one wrinkle of age on his smooth dark skin. He was of slight build; he sported a brown felt derby hat. He was sitting at the bar nursing a drink. One look at the mischievous grin beneath his well-groomed mustache and I knew what was on his mind: whiskey and women, but not in that order.

As a young boy Henry played piano in church. By the time he was sixteen, he was playing in blues clubs. Henry's father initially threatened his wayward son for choosing the blues over gospel, but, after seeing the money his boy was making, his father said to young Henry, "Carry on."

"Hey, Chris!" a friendly waitress said as she hurried past me, carrying a tray of drinks. Henry's wandering eyes followed her until she disappeared into the crowd. Though Henry was nearly twice my age, it was as if we were brothers. His vitality was infectious. I pushed closer to greet my friend.

"I hear you's a big star overseas," Henry said. "I toured over there, many times; Germany, Switzerland, all over. They treat musicians like they's 'posed to be treated. Not like over here."

In 1943, Henry had joined the army but was subsequently discharged early for medical reasons. He then migrated to Chicago in 1946 and soon became a sought-after pianist. Over the years, Henry had recorded and performed with Jimmy Rogers, Sonny Boy Williamson, Muddy Waters, Homesick James, Buddy Guy, Robert Lockwood Jr., Johnny Shines, Little Walter, Otis Rush, James Cotton, Jimmy Reed, and Koko Taylor, among others. In 1956, he landed a coveted gig as Howlin' Wolf's piano man. He played with Wolf for twelve years. In 1968, he quit Wolf and the Windy City and returned to the bayou. Henry had seen and heard it all. He was even playing piano on Elmore James's last gig, before James's heart attack in 1963. Henry had been with us, like family, since we first opened the Blues Box in 1979.

"Why you ain't on stage, Henry?"

"Ask your dad, he do the booking."

"What about this band?" I asked. "Been playin' here long?"

"'Bout a year or two," Henry yelled over the loud music. "They're a whole lot better now than when they first came in here, that's for sure," Henry said, then coughed deep and hard.

"You OK?"

"I'm fine," Henry assured me as he attempted to gather himself. Doctors had warned Henry about his legendary boozing and kinetic lifestyle. "They sound OK," Henry continued, "but I been playing the blues all my life. I got my own sound. You see, that's what these folks don't understand. Everybody wants to sound like Muddy Waters. Hell, I played with Muddy, Howlin' Wolf, Lil' Walter, but you got to have your own sound. That's the only way you can make it."

In all the years Henry and I had played together, he never tried to jazz up his tunes, no major ninths or augmented fourths, just straight twelve- and eight-bar blues, no more, no less. Henry could play with anybody, no matter how terrible. His timing was steady as a rock, his voice as convincing as any. Willie Dixon's wife once confided to me, "Henry's the best blues pianist still out there."

Regrettably, however, the usurpation of Tabby's stage was something Henry and I were going to have to come to terms with. So many of Henry's contemporaries were long gone. There were only a handful of Black musicians of my generation in all of America who cared to play the blues anymore. What I had known the blues to be, a bohemian, subversive, Creole form of music that proudly celebrated secularism, freedom of expression, and the pursuit of happiness, on the dance floor and off, regardless of race or class, had been subverted.

Blacks of my generation, whose school libraries were now filled with the Blues Mafia's dogma, wanted no part of it. Trouble was, they had been miseducated about their own culture. My burden was that I knew better, and what I knew was like a cross I had to bear alone. Nevertheless, I could do little to change the ostensible misconceptions. I knew blues didn't represent a romanticization of Black poverty and suffering, which Blacks were led to believe. I had come to understand it had nothing to do with slavery.

My experiences in Europe had helped me realize the widespread influence our culture was having from London to Copenhagen. Still, it was exasperating to return home to America, to my own family's juke joint, and walk in on an all-White generic band headlining.

The conundrum for Henry and I was that the audience's interpretation of the blues would change when we performed it. When the band on stage went into Gregg Allman's "Tied to the Whipping Post," the White audience, from my observation, imagined the "whipping post" as a metaphor for the wrath of an evil woman. They cheered blissfully; the warm beer seemed cold; they danced and they partied. For the White patrons, songs with such lyrics were merely bawdy fun when sung by a White man or woman.

On the other hand, if a Black man stood on stage, such as Henry or me, and sang the same song, "Feel like I'm tied to the whipping post," the same White audience would imagine a physical antebellum "whipping post." It would conjure images of slaves stripped of their clothes, lashed and whipped until their skin swelled and ripped and blood oozed from their mangled backs.

My goodness, what a total buzzkill that would conjure.

Indeed, if I sang that same song to Tabby's White patrons, suddenly, the warm beer would taste flat, they wouldn't feel like dancing anymore, and what's worst, they would feel pity and guilt. The festive atmosphere in the Blues Box would be over. Truly, that's no way to spend a Saturday night.

I was going to have to accept that as long as the blues remained erroneously tethered to slavery in the psyche of the public, and the eschewing of its true bohemian history continued unabated, it was better business, sadly, for my own family's juke joint to headline White "guilt free" blues bands instead of me or my good friend Henry Gray.

FROM NEW ORLEANS TO PARIS

A WEEK LATER, for the first time in years, I landed at LAX in Los Angeles, California. I was introduced to Greg Lewerke, a manager at Vault Management, by my new producer, John Porter. I signed on with Greg's firm, which had offices just up the hill from the legendary Rainbow Club, one of my favorite Sunset Boulevard hangouts. House of Blues and management immediately began putting together a team of international booking agents, publicists, and pluggers. In addition to the tens of thousands in living advances I received via House of Blues/Private/BMG, we also received an $80,000 recording advance. Studio time was booked at Red Zone Studios, Burbank, and Devonshire Studios in North Hollywood, to add some final touches to the Copenhagen sessions. I insisted to John Porter that I didn't want to rerecord the whole thing entirely. An over-polished Hollywood production is not what I envisioned. I wanted to maintain the raw edge and fearless spirit captured in the original tapes.

Back in 1990, when I'd recorded the first demos for what would eventually become *21st Century Blues . . . from Da 'Hood*, there was no blues guitar hip-hop. Run DMC and Aerosmith had created the landmark rap-rock track "Walk This Way" in 1986, on Run DMC's album *Raising Hell*, but neither act was committed beyond novelty. There were a few groups using jazz samples, such as Digable Planets, who successfully melded hip-hop with jazz loops in the song "Rebirth of Slick (Cool Like Dat)." Guru's *Jazzmatazz* was another notable album, which included performances from Branford Marsalis and Donald Byrd. But during the time I was writing and recording in Copenhagen I wasn't aware of these records, so they hadn't influenced my creative choices. It's interesting to me that one of the last recordings by jazz giant Miles Davis was "Doo-Bop," a little-known hip-hop endeavor that predated the Euro jazz lounge genre. Like Miles, my musical spirit would always be in motion. I was adopting hip-hop today, but who knows what tomorrow.

John Porter brought in some of L.A.'s top musicians to complete the original tapes. The new sessions went quickly. Tony Braunagel added drums and percus-

sion; Lester Butler, harmonica; Reggie McBride, bass; and Mick Weaver, organ.
Joe McGrath was the engineer, Jeff Robinson his assistant, with John Porter producing and adding rhythm guitar. When finished, what I had created was the first
truly contemporary blues recording of the decade. No other blues band or artist
filled that void. I stood at the vanguard, alone. The night we finished the final
mixes, I went out to celebrate. I partied, got wasted, and ended up in a tattoo parlor to brand myself with a new tattoo. I had my trademark "21st Century Blues"
tattooed on my right arm, under a dragon wrapped around an Egyptian cross.

As part of my generous deal with House of Blues, I would reside in Los Angeles until the album was released. The label covered all living expenses, including
the purchase of a new car. They put me up in a furnished corporate condo in
Burbank. I drove off a nearby car lot in a candy-apple red sports car after paying
cash. To celebrate my new success, I went clubbing on the Sunset Strip. I eagerly
partook in some good old-fashioned rock star excess.

Being that I had been in a kind of Nordic hibernation the past two years,
living in Denmark's dark, frigid, and dreary climate, I justified going a little crazy
in the California sun. Meanwhile, I lost touch with Mariann back in Copenhagen. I had promised her as soon as I got settled, I'd send for her. But weeks passed
without any communication. Hollywood had seduced me.

As preparation for my album's release got underway, I was summoned to
attend marketing meetings at the label's offices in Beverly Hills. We fought over
the first single to introduce the album. I wanted to release "My Pain, Your Pleasure" as the first single and video. Ron Goldstein, the president, wanted to release
"Kickin' True Blue." Ron got his way. We knew that neither BET nor MTV
would play a blues video unless it reached the top of the charts—but it wasn't
going to reach the top of the US charts without radio or video play, the old catch-
22. Because of that, Europe would be our initial focus. House of Blues had spent
lavishly on me, thanks to Isaac Tigrett, since the day I'd landed in Los Angeles.
In fact, my personal advances were far more generous than what blues artists
normally received. Only the top 1 percent of blues artists had six-figure budgets.
Although House of Blues had no way of knowing whether or not the album
would be a hit, it was already a financial success in my book. I hit the road as the
embodiment of Tigrett's vision for House of Blues.

An article appeared in *Billboard* on March 4, 1995, written by Chris Morris. It
was one of the first of numerous articles that would appear in national magazines
about the album. He wrote, "Chris Thomas' desire to make a truly contemporary
blues recording resulted in a three-year odyssey through continental Europe and
Scandinavia. That journey will culminate with the April 11 release of his label debut
for Private Music [House of Blues], '21st Century Blues . . . From da 'Hood.'"

Soon after the album's release, I began a two-week residency in Paris, France, at the Continental Café, a small club located a block off the Champs-Élysées. It was a challenge to bring the album to life with only a trio of guitar, bass, and drums. I instructed my road manager and sound engineer, David Arias, to feed sampled loops from his position at the soundboard to the stage monitors. He mixed that, along with the live instruments, into the house PA. To reproduce organ sounds, I installed a Roland MIDI connector on my Stratocaster that triggered a Roland guitar synth playing B3 sound pads underneath my guitar chords. Even though we were a three-piece band, we sounded much bigger.

We began to attract the French music press, who raved about my new music. I landed on the front page of the *Libération* national newspaper. The *Libération* praised my music as a striking new paradigm. People in France got me. The French proclaimed me as an exceptional paradigm-shifting artist, making me the latest member of a select Black American creative fraternity of writers, poets, and musicians. The French validated my artistic vision for the rest of Europe. The sacrifices I had made for my art were finally paying off.

I was booked into French theaters and on national TV shows. I was added to some of the best festivals France had to offer. On the streets of Paris, fans and autographs seekers began following me around.

I returned to America briefly for a press tour before returning to Paris to build on my success with an expanded European tour.

On August 1, 1995, a glowing review appeared in New Orleans from veteran music journalist Geraldine Wyckoff in *Offbeat* magazine. It was very important to me at the time to have New Orleans get my artistic vision for the blues. Wyckoff wrote:

> I always did like rap for its poetry, its edge, its rhythm, its groove. But as a lover of the sound of real live instruments—a horn section versus synthesizer, a trap set versus a drum machine—it was difficult to derive full satisfaction from music that was devoid of these musical elements. I also sometimes had trouble with some blues that got so rocked, especially rhythmically, that it lost its backbeat and soulful core.
>
> Baton Rouge bluesman Chris Thomas, son of bluesman Tabby Thomas (of Tabby's Blues Box fame), has solved both these problems, rappin' the blues and playin' his guitar on his latest CD, *21st Century Blues . . . From Da 'Hood*. Here we have the low-down funkiness of blues and the low-down funkiness of rap from a musician with deep roots in the traditions, but who, at 29, is young enough to be of the hip-hop generation. Make no mistake—this is a rap album, not just a little rappin' goin' down over music. Thomas makes that altogether

clear in the intro: "You want the blues, you can't have the goddamn blues," he says, before going on to the funky "21 CB," on which he raps, "This is the blues of the 21st century, and I don't give a damn if you can't get with me." Meanwhile, his guitar is spiking his lyrics, giving them a solid kick. Mick Weaver's organ fills the tune, giving it a warm base. Thomas makes lots of references to his blues roots—he grew up in the genre and as a young man played with Buddy Guy and other legends. I'd bet money that there's no rap out there that includes names like Lightnin' Slim, Whispering Smith, and Slim Harpo in the lyrics as does his tune "Blues from Da 'Hood," a little history lesson of sorts. There are some fairly hard edged raps as well, but on "Kill Somebody" Thomas doesn't say he is going to do the deed, but feels like it—a different thing entirely. For the most part Thomas' raps are sometimes angry, but they also contain a positive element. And then again, a real band led by Thomas' excellent guitar gives the songs a sense of humanity. "I was inspired by [filmmakers] Spike Lee and John Singleton, who decided to take more control of the images they would put out," says Thomas of his new work. He succeeds in this. He has remained true to his roots and himself on *21st Century Blues . . . From Da 'Hood*, sacrificing neither the essence of rap nor the blues, and taking the music to a new and appropriate place.

Joseph V. Tirellla wrote in *Vibe* magazine:

Chris Thomas takes his music seriously. The Baton Rouge, La, bluesman quotes the lessons learned from such masters as Muddy Waters, Jimmy Reed, and Aretha Franklin the way a philosophy professor quotes Plato, Aristotle, and Nietzsche. "When Aretha sang 'Respect,' that sounded an alarm." Which is exactly what Thomas hopes to do with his third album, *21st Century Blues . . . From da 'Hood*.

In *Time* magazine pop culture journalist Christopher John Farley, in an article titled "Painting the Town Blue," compared my new release with two other CDs released by artists Chris Whitley and PJ Harvey. They weren't blues artist but used blues as an influence. Farley wrote:

A new crop of young rockers is discovering that for angst and existential misery, there's nothing quite like the blues. One of the last songs Kurt Cobain recorded before he committed suicide was Lead Belly's "Where Did You Sleep Last Night?" Now several other young performers are adding a blue tint to their sound. Last month British-born art screecher PJ Harvey released a blues-shaded album, *To Bring You My Love*; Houston-born rocker Chris Whitley has just come out with the bluesy CD *Din of Ecstasy*; and this week Chris Thomas of Baton Rouge, Louisiana, releases his blues rap album, *21st Century Blues . . . from da Hood.*

Farley had harsh criticism for Harvey and Whitley. Farley continued: "Authenticity is an essential element of the blues, and the problem with Polly Jean Harvey's CD is that there is not a single honest emotion in it. In contrast to Harvey, Chris Whitley on *Din of Ecstasy* is painfully, almost uncomfortably honest; he comes at the listener like a drunk friend at an office party, trapping you in the corner and telling you how terrific your wife is in bed." Of my new album Farley was less critical:

> Thomas' *21st Century Blues . . . from da 'Hood*, with its unusual but mostly successful attempt to combine blues and rap, is the most ambitious of the three new CDs. His songs boast a crunching blues beat, brash guitars and howling harmonica solos. Thomas, 29, tries to bring the blues into the present. As he sings on the title track, "whoever says the blues was dead/ Needs to come where I'm from where the streets are red." It's a gutsy album that works best when Thomas stops rapping and lets his music do the talking.

Time magazine, though a respected news journal, was light years removed from music journals like *Rolling Stone*, *NME*, or *Vibe*. Therefore, Farley's stuffy take on my music was a reflection of *Time*'s readers' sensibilities. I took the *Time* magazine review as a win. Indeed, just to be mentioned in the magazine meant I was affecting popular culture. I was well aware of Bob Dylan's disdain for *Time* magazine reporters via his '60s film documentary, *Don't Look Back*. But I didn't take myself so seriously as to do much more than smile or shrug when reading something someone wrote about my art. I knew there were few major articles of praise written in real time, by any mainstream journal, when it came to blues artistic innovations. It's only after a decade or two has passed that its significance and influence could be measured. I knew that chart positions and radio ads were no real measure either. No one had ever heard Tommy Johnson and Robert Johnson on popular radio when their records were originally released. But I also knew that it was significant to be deemed noteworthy by the *Time* magazines of the world. There were reviews and articles in *Rolling Stone* and dozens of European magazines.

In early October 1995, I returned to Paris. Because of the Parisians' embrace, I had graduated from the French club circuit to prestigious French theaters. The tour would also include TV appearances.

European Fall Tour 1995

October 10	U.K: London Spash Club,
October 12	France: Nancy Terminal Export
October 13	France: Strasbourg Lalaiterie
October 14	France: Salaise Sur Sanne City Hall
October 16	France: Paris Erotika
October 18	France: Rennes
October 19	France: Montpellier Victoire 2
October 21	Holland: Hengelo Metropol
October 22	Holland: Media + TV
October 24	Belgium: Antwerp Pacific
October 25	Holland: Alkmaar Atlantis
October 26	France: Stquentin Festival
October 28	Austria: Vienna Metropol
October 30	Germany: Berlin Quasimodo
November 1	Sweden: Stockholm Studion
November 2	Denmark: Copenhagen Cafe Rust
November 4	Germany: Franfurt Nachtleben
November 6	Germany: Munich Tilt
November 8	Switzerland: Geneva Vernler Sur Rock
November 9	Switzerland: Luzern Leschuur
November 12	Italy: Milan Rainbow
November 14	Spain: Barcelona Festival
November 15	Spain: Madrid Revolver

On November 2, we arrived in Copenhagen to play a date at a packed Café Rust. It was a chance for me to see my girlfriend and daughter for the first time in nearly a year. I realized, after seeing Mariann again, that my love for her was strong enough to make a lifetime commitment. It's a cliché—absence makes the heart grow fonder—but it had. She was still living in the apartment we had shared, struggling to finish nursing school. Though she forgave me, I felt small for not having kept promises I had made to her. I didn't know how to fit her and my daughter into my hectic lifestyle, but after seeing them again, I knew that if I didn't try, I would regret it for the rest of my life. She was the only one who could tame my impetuous nature and force me to mature. The morning after our gig, as I climbed into the bus in front of our hotel in downtown Copenhagen, I promised Mariann and my daughter, again, that I would send for them, as soon as I got back to Los Angeles—and I did.

THE FALL OF HOUSE OF BLUES

ISAAC TIGRETT's House of Blues company owned syndicated radio shows and state-of-the-art live music venues throughout America. They were broadcasting a concert series live each weekend on national television from their Hollywood venue on Sunset. They had everything one needed to launch my album and support it until it found an audience. Tigrett was a deeply spiritual man who said he was in India studying Buddhism when the idea for the House of Blues came to him. He insisted he was being advised by his spiritual master to uplift the blues. He spent lavishly to upgrade the blues' perception. His slogan, borrowed from Dan Aykroyd and John Belushi's *Blues Brothers* movie, was "I'm on a mission from God." Dan Aykroyd was also an investor in the company.

Tigrett insisted money was not his ruler, it was just a means to an end. But he soon found himself in a cultural war with the powerful Blues Mafia for ownership of the blues. Because of HOB's success, Tigrett was a threat to the Mafia's cartel as cultural brokers of "Black primitivism." What began in the 1960s as a cottage industry by the '90s had become a worldwide phenomenon. The Blues Mafia, and their devotees, wanted to destroy Isaac Tigrett and his plans for blues modernity.

I may have been powerless against my archenemies the Blues Mafia in the past, but Tigrett was a powerful ally. I was happy to finally have someone share my understanding and vision for the future of the blues. Nevertheless, the House of Blues brand was being tarnished in the press by the Blues Mafia. I had been busy touring Europe and promoting my album for House of Blues/Private Music/ BMG. As a consequence, I had no knowledge of the bitter cultural clash of the titans taking place back in America. Indeed, the Blues Mafia and Isaac Tigrett were involved in a high-stakes turf war over ownership of the blues and its culture therewith. Tigrett and Disney were being excoriated for "stealing" and modernizing my culture. The eugenic primitivist mythology—which had shackled me since my "folk discovery" in 1979—was being debunked and replaced with twenty-first-century modernity. Granted, I was but a pawn in their battle; Tigrett's ivory towers were far above my pay grade. Nevertheless, the winner of this pivotal cultural war, which my album had come to symbolize, would control not only my future but the future and popular narrative of African American blues culture.

In November 1995, a vilifying article "Who Owns the Blues?" appeared in the *New York Times* written by journalist Phil Patton. It accused Isaac Tigrett, Disney, and House of Blues of usurping the blues. Patton wrote:

> Two different visions compete for the soul of the blues. One defines them as a folk art, a collective expression of black American culture and a record of oppression. The other sees the blues as a modernist art of individual genius melding tradition and innovation with technology and commerce, one whose influence pervades all of pop music today. Nowhere is the conflict more sharply drawn than in the House of Blues. To some, it is the last best chance to keep the form vital; to others, it reduces one of the most profound forms of American music to a Disney cartoon.

In the *Times* article, the Blues Mafia's demonization of Isaac Tigrett tarnished the House of Blues brand, making the Disney corporation—its major investor—nervous. Tigrett tried to defend himself. Echoing my sentiments, Tigrett said:

> I've been on the Blues Foundation board for years in Memphis. We have fights internally just about what the blues is. It's brutal. It is a cultish thing, I don't think musicians are even part of the cult, it's basically a bunch of record [collectors] and some critics and writers [collectively known at the Blues Mafia] . . . They don't want to see it change or be opened to the masses. [The Blues Mafia gets] pissed off and say, "Oh, you're ruining the blues clubs. What are you doing?" Tigrett continued, "I'll tell you what I'm doing. I'm creating a clean place where musicians don't have to change in the car. I'm paying them more money. You don't want them to get as much money? Is that what you want? You want them to get less? I'm putting them on the radio, I'm doing things that no one else can do for them. What are you mad about? Because it's getting out of your control? I've had some strong people in the blues community, who have known me all my life, say, 'You can't do that.' I ask, Do what? Turn young people on; turn the masses on to the blues? Why? [Isaac said, to the Blues Mafia,] You want to keep it to yourself, keep it in a little cult thing? No way."

Tigrett insisted he wasn't trying to own my music and culture; all he wanted to do was promote it. Tigrett said: "This music has to make it through the millennium. It's got to become part of the next century. It's just as important as pop music. . . . I don't mind the criticism. It's really only going to be a handful of very vocal cultists who don't approve of what I'm doing. The people will speak. If people don't like it, the places will close."

The controversy led to hostile disagreements with investors, board members, and executives of the House of Blues entertainment company. In addition to Disney, its investors included billionaire Paul Allen along with Isaac's friend Dan Aykroyd. A conflict regarding Tigrett's vision, compounded by the Blues Mafia's hit on the brand, led to several members of the board suggesting that Tigrett, its visionary founder, be removed. Consequently, in 1995, just months after the release of *21st Century Blues . . . from da 'Hood*, and only weeks after my last tour date in Europe, the company's board of directors ousted Isaac Tigrett, my biggest supporter.

It was the beginning of the end for my creative vision being promoted by House of Blues. As for the House of Blues venues, their mission was no longer to promote the blues and its practitioners. My old nemesis the Blues Mafia proved to be even more powerful than I had previously imagined. They had prevailed yet again. In the end, the notorious Blues Mafia did a Jimmy Hoffa on Isaac Tigrett. They made him disappear. He was erased from the annals of blues never to be heard from again.

IN THE NAME OF PROGRESS

With the writing on the wall—though not yet official—Mariann and I would need to make some alternative living arrangements. I knew it was just a matter of time before I'd be without a label and patron. I had been in this position before. It wasn't a place a recording artist wanted to be, especially now with a young family to support in America.

I sorted out my tangled affairs in Los Angeles and flew down to Baton Rouge for a visit to introduce my daughter for the first time to my family. Mariann's blonde hair and blue eyes were no surprise, but until one welcomes someone from a different culture into their family, no one really knows how the family will react. They just adored Maha. Everyone was at ease. It was obvious to my family Mariann was head over heels for me.

To introduced Mariann to my Creole culture we attended Mardi Gras. We caught beads, stumbled over drunks along Bourbon Street, drank wine, and danced until we were too exhausted to sleep. I can only imagine what was going through her mind. Mariann is liberal minded but shy and prudish, not accustomed to spontaneous dancing and public affection. Perhaps she was wondering what she was getting into. As for me, she exceeded all my desires and assuaged all my insecurities. It was during Mardi Gras we decided to make it official. With zero planning we were married at the justice of the peace with Maha as our witness on February 13.

In the spring of 1996, Mariann and I settled into New Orleans East in Frenchmen's Warf apartments located in the upper Ninth Ward on a service road just off of Interstate 610. The East, as it was known, was a suburb east of the Industrial Canal and north of the Intracoastal Waterway. Developed in the 1960s, the East was the northern portion of the downtrodden Lower Ninth Ward. The East was devoid of good jobs, healthy restaurants, and many other conveniences those who lived near the streetcars of Uptown could take for granted. Public transport for the East residents into the heart of the city for work and back home was unbearably slow. To work a nine-to-five, one had to leave home hours before clock-in, then return home hours after clocking out, creating a terrible parental void for children. It was as if there was an embargo on the Upper and Lower Ninth Wards.

As we settled in, the few remaining businesses were poorly stocked and on the brink of closing. A half-vacant mall, a movie theater, and a few retail chain stores were surviving, but just barely. Redlined Black communities historically were poverty stricken due to vestiges of free labor, prejudice, Black Codes, and disenfranchisement. Due to its underfunded schools and high unemployment, the crime rate in New Orleans East was high. It was not a safe area to raise a family, but it was affordable. And there were great musicians all over the place. One of Jay-Z's favorite rappers, Jay Electronica, lived next door to me. His mother and sister became a friendly extended family. New Orleans East was also home to a small number of Black professionals and wealthy entrepreneurs, including a few musical celebrities, such as Fats Domino in the Lower Ninth Ward. Settled into an affluent gated community nearby was Aaron Neville and Cash Money Records brothers Bryan "Birdman" Williams and Ronald "Slim" Williams, along with their budding rap superstar protégé Lil Wayne. I would perform regularly at Tipitina's Uptown, Maple Leaf, Margaritaville, and House of Blues with local musicians. On occasion I performed at Tabby's Blues Box in Baton Rouge for my dad.

On June 23, 1998, in Baton Rouge, *Business Report* magazine published an article headlined "Path to Progress" about the demise of Tabby's Blues Box. Under a process called eminent domain, the city government, according to the article, planned to seize and demolish Tabby's "in the name of progress." The threat to raze Tabby's Blues Box was seen as a controversial act of gentrification. Tabby's demise was editorialized in regional newspapers and discussed at watercoolers throughout Louisiana. Mariann and I discussed the problem and decided that maybe the best way to stop it would be to buy the Griffon building ourselves.

But could we afford to buy it? I was of the mind that if I owned the building, the city would have to fight with me directly. In addition, I was assured inexpensive legal representation from sympathetic supporters. It was a noble cause the community was ready to rally around.

I went to visit Dad to share the good news. But to my dismay, he was less than thrilled. He said he'd decided he would secure his own loan and buy the building himself. I thought I could rescue the family jewel. I thought it was my duty, as a loyal son, to do what I could to save the family business. After all, I had poured my blood, sweat, and tears into Tabby's. But Dad, ironically, saw my offer as some type of hostile takeover. It seemed he'd rather have the Griffons as landlords than have his son own the building. I tried to reason with him that I would continue to rent to Rose & Thomas Café at the same rate—which I had calculated in my payment formula—and pay the mortgage myself. I assured him he would no longer pay rent. The conversations with my dad went nowhere. Dad was often too proud and too stubborn for his own good. I was sorely disappointed. It seemed to me he'd rather the place go up in flames than have me lord over his club. I didn't see it that way at all.

I began to realize there were things about my dad—about the older folks from his generation—that I would never understand. There had been so many people over the years who had approached Tabby, offered to become his business partners and spend the money necessary to modernize his business. I knew of some successful businessmen of good character who over the years had made legitimate offers, but Tabby always found a chink in their armor.

Regrettably, to make matters worse, the blues and its culture had been recast, at least ostensibly, as the sorrowful lament of lowly ignorant heretics whose bad luck and troubled lot in life were caused by their own shortcomings and unchristianly behavior. I knew deep down this was not the case. I believed such backward superstitions were vestiges of the Dark Ages. For many, the Blues Box was a relic; an antediluvian reminder of a time they would rather forget. Yet, I remained hopeful the ostensible inglorious notion of my music and its culture therewith would one day give way to a more honest reflection. I believed deeply that I had an obligation to do what I could to deconstruct such fallacious notions because real damage had been done. The culture of blues was no more imperfect than any other, but it was less hypocritical than most. It was a culture of tolerance cultivated in seedy Louisiana juke joints. It was one of the few public stages where Black men and women could think freely, express their innermost desires, fears, and emotions without fear of persecution. If the Blues Box were to disappear, I felt an essential part of me would vanish with it. Indeed, it had been the cornerstone of my identity. I was sure I would be lost without it. I was shaken. I decided

I had better take a step back, not intrude, find a new way forward. My journey with the Blues Box had reached an end.

The following Sunday, June 28, 1998, we celebrated Mariann's thirty-first birthday. After a celebratory dinner, she and I strolled the French Quarter. We window-shopped on Royal Street, taking in the Vieux Carré's frayed beauty. Earlier in the year we had contemplated moving back to Europe. Mariann had a Green Card but would not renounce her Danish citizenship. I had seriously entertained the idea of resettling in Europe, but the longer we stayed in New Orleans, the more she fell in love with the old city. The sight of kids playing their horns for tips on street corners; the sounds of street musicians on every block; painters and poets selling their art along Jackson Square set a romantic atmosphere. She was home. The Crescent City, always intellectually stimulating, would forever be my muse.

O BROTHER, WHERE ART THOU?

ONE DAY, at home in New Orleans, I got a visit from my new manager, Jim Bateman. He was excited to have received a new movie script. The producers of the film wanted me to read for a mythical blues character. "Take a look at it," Jim said, "see what you think." I was skeptical. I'd been invited to audition for commercials around New Orleans in the past, but I always felt awkward in those auditions. I either tried too hard or maybe the casting directors were put off because I had dreadlocks down to my waist. Besides, I was uncomfortable with auditions of any kind. So, I never put much stock in them. "It's not an open audition," Jim assured me. "They're interested in you for a major role!" He left me the script to read over.

The first thing I noticed was the eccentric title, *O Brother, Where Art Thou?* It seemed a very odd title for a movie. The recent trend had been one-word titles, *Titanic, Magnolia, Armageddon.* Usually, movies had two-word titles such as *American Beauty, The Hurricane, Girl, Interrupted,* or *Deep Impact.* I assumed *O Brother, Where Art Thou?* was only a working title to be changed later. Of course, no film studio would ever go for such an oddly named movie.

The script had a sticky note attached to it directing me to study the character Tommy Johnson, a Depression-era itinerant blues guitarist. I quickly thumbed through the first few pages. Hollywood rarely produced movies starring blues characters. Besides, whenever they had, those films embarrassed us blues musicians. *Crossroads* (another one-word title) starring Ralph Macchio came to mind.

I read only a quarter through the 120-page script before growing impatient. I wanted to see in what scene Tommy was killed. The one Black character in major studio films always met his maker before the end of the plot. So, I peeked at the ending. To my surprise, Tommy was alive.

At second glance, the *O Brother* script was refreshing—not that I'd read many movie scripts, mind you. I continued reading, anticipating the scene where I'd be embarrassed by pompous Hollywood writers who hadn't done enough research on the subject. But the more I read, the more convinced I became that I was reading something very special. To be sure, Tommy Johnson didn't have many pages of dialogue, but he was a major character with lots of scenes. He sang too!

In a campfire scene, they wanted me to sing "Hard Time Killing Floor Blues" in character. Initially I thought they meant the Howlin' Wolf song by the same name, which had been in my repertoire for years. I soon learned they meant the obscure Skip James song.

I realized the Tommy Johnson character was a big role, a real acting opportunity. When I read the line about Tommy's Faustian pact with the devil—"Well, I wasn't using it"—I laughed out loud. That did it. I had to play Tommy Johnson. Besides, I felt I was uniquely suited for the role. Although more polished actors were being considered, I was confident I could deliver the music better than anyone.

On the phone the next day, I enthused to Jim, "The script's great!" He shared my enthusiasm. "What's the chance I get it?" I asked, knowing a cold audition could be disastrous. Jim was anticipating a conference call later that day with the producers. Afterward, he called me back.

"They want you to send in a video right away," Jim said.

The directors, Joel and Ethan Coen, known for writing and directing uniquely stylish films such as *Blood Simple*, *Barton Fink*, and *Fargo*, wanted to see me on film as soon as possible. I had made two highly produced music videos, "Kickin' True Blue" and "Impatiently." In the former, I rapped; in the latter, I serenaded a love interest on the Brooklyn Bridge dressed in rock star regalia. In addition to my striking dreadlocks, I sported a suede vest and dark sunglasses. To be sure, I didn't look like the archetypical bluesman. I thought my video image would be too distracting for audition purposes. Nonetheless, Jim shipped the video package off and we hoped for the best. After a few days, we heard back from the producers. They asked that I do a screen test. That was big! I had crossed the first threshold.

———

Tommy Johnson was an obscure bluesman. There were no videos of Tommy and only one known photograph, a Paramount Records publicity shot. Few people knew his music, even fewer knew his story. I was vaguely aware of Tommy's story, but I was well aware of one of his songs, "Canned Heat," which was adopted by a rock band as their name in the '60s. One of the founding members of Canned Heat was guitarist and harmonica player Al Wilson (1943–1970). While a music major at Boston University, Al Wilson played the Cambridge, Massachusetts, folk-blues coffeehouse circuit.

Wilson first gained attention during Son House's "rediscovery" in 1964, when Son House was brought up to Cambridge to perform on its folk circuit. It was evident that House had forgotten his songs due to his long absence from music. Wilson retaught House to play the songs just as House had recorded them in 1930 and 1942. Wilson demonstrated them on guitar to revive House's memory.[10] The irony that in 1964, the seminal year of the so-called folk-blues revival, a White Cambridge student taught Son House "the proper way" to play his music must not be brushed over.

Imagine a young Black student sitting with a seventy-year-old Bob Dylan and teaching him the proper way to play and sing his classic hits. It would be utterly absurd. Albeit, we would all enjoy it if Dylan performed recognizable versions of his early classics, however, it's understood an artist has creative agency. However, such creative agency was not afforded Black folk-revival blues artists. Blacks were taught to perform their music aesthetically to please a new White audience.

Son House's manager, Dick Waterman, remarked in *Jazz Journal* in 1965 that Al Wilson, who was backing Son House on his folk-blues revival debut for Columbia Records, *Father of the Delta Blues*, "is good, and the record will prove it." Indeed, Al Wilson, a folk-blues purist, had a remarkable feel for country blues. Canned Heat went on to have chart success with "Going Up the Country" and "On the Road Again," the latter a 1953 cover of Arkansas bluesman Floyd Jones's song of the same name, which resembled Tommy Johnson's "Big Road Blues," recorded in 1928. Al Wilson allegedly suffered from depression and died of a drug overdose at age twenty-seven.

I went down to Louisiana Music Factory and browsed around until I stumbled upon a poorly designed Tommy Johnson CD on the Document label. The record would've been better packaged if it had been in a brown paper bag. It featured the best of Tommy's songs, "Big Road Blues," "Canned Heat," and "Cool Drink of Water Blues."

Tommy Johnson was not born in the Delta. In 1896 he was the sixth of thirteen children born on George Miller's plantation on the border of Hinds and Copiah Counties, about twenty miles south of Jackson. According to folk-blues historian David Evans, his father, Idell Johnson, was related to the first great blues guitarist, Lonnie Johnson of New Orleans.[11]

Indeed, Lonnie Johnson was the hero of every early Delta blues guitarist from Charlie Patton to Robert Johnson. For example, Mississippi guitarist Johnny Shines, who traveled and performed with Robert Johnson in the early 1930s, said Robert Johnson would promote himself as Lonnie Johnson to get gigs. Similarly, I wouldn't be surprised if Tommy Johnson's claim to be related to Lonnie Johnson was only a boastful claim. However, it is possible Tommy Johnson was actually a relative of the great Lonnie Johnson.

I listened over and over to Tommy's scratchy CD, hoping to find a speaking voice for my character. As a consequence, Tommy Johnson, who made his first recordings in Memphis, Tennessee, in 1928, left an indelible impression on me. His baritone vocal was emotionally alluring. He sang several octaves and had a delightful falsetto. However, when he yodeled, you knew you were listing to a special talent. Tommy's guitar playing was unconventional. On guitar, he was neither as polished nor inventive as his hero Lonnie Johnson. Yet he had an unmistakable style all his own. Be that as it may, I had no desire to learn Tommy Johnson's riffs too perfectly. Rather, my interest lay in his essence. This approach served me well. Besides, none of his songs were in the script. The Coen brothers were neither making a biography nor telling a true story. They were having fun with southern myths, legends, and backwoods superstitions.

A week went by and I still had no voice for the character. My screen test was fast approaching. Finally, I reached deep into my past to find an alternative. I decided on "Guitar" Kelly, one of my mentors from the Blues Box. Kelly was soft-spoken. I had played drums, bass, and guitar with him for years. I knew his body language. He was a young man during the Depression era, maybe just a few years behind Tommy. I tried Kelly's voice on for size, reading a few lines from the script and wham. That was it!

With Mariann and the kids—my son, Dylan, had been born in 1998—visiting her parents in Denmark, I fell into a daily routine. Every evening I'd go down to the Quarter, sit on a bench on the Mississippi levee near Tower Records, to practice my lines and play guitar in character. I was seeking the essence of Skip James's "Hard Time Killing Floor Blues." I arranged the tune for slide guitar in open Dm. I worked at it for the next few nights. I decided I would try looking the part, too. Jim and I visited thrift stores on Decatur Street and searched uptown on Magazine Street, looking for a period suit and tie. We found a brown suit that fit the period. I borrowed a grey Stetson hat from my brother, Tammy. I rehearsed my lines with Marilyn Bateman, Jim's wife, who had acted in community plays. Jim and Marilyn arranged to film my screen test with a home video camera in

Audubon Park. By tying my dreadlocks back as tight as I could, along with the vintage thrift store suit and borrowed grey Stetson with a black band and feather, I transformed into a 1930s film character. We headed to Audubon Park to shoot my screen test.

Marilyn fed me George Clooney's lines. I answered them comfortably in character. However, I decided not to perform "Hard Time Killing Floor Blues." Instead, I performed Robert Johnson's "Come on in My Kitchen" and my own "Soon This Morn'nin Blues." We sent the screen test video to Hollywood for the Coens to review—and waited.

While awaiting a call from the casting directors, I went on the road for previously planned tour dates, about four shows opening solo acoustic for Son Volt, a critically acclaimed Minnesota-based outfit. The first show was at a club near the University of Southern Mississippi in Hattiesburg. Backstage, before the gig, we all engaged in small talk about our frustrations with the music business. It seemed Son Volt was starved for commercial success. However, I was resigned to the relatively meager commercial prospects of a Black bluesman. They expressed their frustrations with their management and label, Warner Brothers. I had been there but was done with that. Actually, because of recent developments, I was feeling rather optimistic. I was hopeful my days hustling from bar gig to bar gig, especially as an opening act, were numbered.

The next stop of the tour was Rick's Café in Starkville, Mississippi. Again, I was backstage with Son Volt waiting for the lights to go down when I got a phone call from Jim Bateman saying the Coens, along with T-Bone Burnett, the music supervisor, wanted to fly me to Nashville the next morning to audition for them in person.

Although not official, I felt there was no way I could lose out on an in-person reading because I was fully prepared. I wanted to share the big news with someone, anyone, so I told Son Volt, sharing my excitement backstage. They begrudgingly congratulated me. I got the impression they were on the verge of splitting up because their label didn't really get their music. I sympathized with them on that count, because corporations can suck the spirit out of your music if you're not careful. I really don't remember if I played my set or if I hopped in my car straight away and got the hell out of Rick's and back to New Orleans. If I did perform, it was probably a very short set. To be sure, it was standard in my contracts that I could pull out of a tour on short notice if I was booked in a motion picture or on a major network television show. However, it was a clause I had never optioned because those opportunities never happened. My agency helped Son Volt find a replacement for their tour.

The following day, Jim and I arrived at a Nashville recording studio. I changed into the same vintage suit I had worn for the screen test. I went into a meeting room in the studio, sat across the table from the directors Ethan and Joel Coen. The casting director, Ellen Chenoweth, was also in the room. Later I learned she may have heard me for the first time on NPR while promoting my album *Red Mud*. Chenoweth fed me the lines and I went into character. When we got to the lines where I was asked why I sold my soul to the devil, I responded, "Well, I wasn't using it." The Coens laughed long and hard at my deadpan delivery.

When I left the room, they were smiling brightly. The Coens thanked me for my time but didn't say I had the part. There was yet another threshold awaiting me. I was asked to go into the studio and perform "Hard Time Killing Floor Blues" for T-Bone Burnett. I walked into the control room to meet T-Bone for the first time and heard playback of my playing on the control room speakers. I was surprised. While I was sitting around waiting for the live reading with the Coens, I had been playing my guitar just warming up, but it turned out the tape was rolling. It wasn't an ambush, it's something that any good producer does. The tape is always rolling during a recording session because you never know when inspiration will strike.

T-Bone Burnett was someone I had heard of, but I didn't really know his body of work, except that he'd been the musical director for previous Coen movies and had produced some successful rock records. Burnett was a tall fellow with a somewhat odd personality—if someone is meeting him for the first time. He exuded confidence that one could interpret as cocky, which can put some people off. However, anyone who loved honest music and respected its history could relate to Burnett straight away.

The Coens wanted my character, Tommy, to perform his own music live on the set of the film, which would be revolutionary for Hollywood. It was standard to have the music prerecorded. The actors usually lip-synced to playback on the film set. Everyone from Frank Sinatra, Elvis, even Barbra Streisand, lip-synced on film. That's just the way things were done in Hollywood. But my role was going to be different. I was expected to be in character while singing and playing live to the cameras to bring an authentic field recording quality to the film.

My character's musical performance would be critical to the success of the film. Granted, just one day of filming could easily cost hundreds of thousands of dollars. Therefore, the producers were really demanding a lot of me. I felt the pressure to deliver. There were a few musicians lounging about the studio, perhaps auditioning for other roles. The musicians cleared the music room while I set up to record "Hard Time Killing Floor Blues" for T-Bone and the film's producers.

I performed the song with a slide like I'd rehearsed it, in open Dm. It was one thing to play the unique arrangement; it was another to sing while playing it.

I think the rapping and singing I'd been doing over the years helped greatly with my coordination. After I finished a take, T-Bone came in. "Can you do it again without the slide?" he asked. "I want it as close to the original as possible." I tried it again without the slide, but it wasn't as good as the first take because I hadn't rehearsed it in a fingerpicking style. After the session, I changed back into my street clothes and waited in the lobby for Jim to come out of a meeting with the producers. He came into the hallway where I was waiting and delivered the good news. I had the part! I was really pleased and relieved to officially join the cast of *O Brother, Where Art Thou?* Within days I signed a contract with Working Title Pictures to play Tommy Johnson. The movie was set to begin shooting near Jackson, Mississippi, the last week of June 1999. I was contracted to film all summer with only a brief Fourth of July break.

The Coen brothers invited me back to Nashville to work with Colin Linden, a Nashville-based fingerstyle guitarist from Toronto, Canada. I put away my slide arrangement of Skip James's song and learned to play it exactly as Skip had played it, note for note, with the help of Colin Linden. As an artist, I always strove to make a cover song my own. But in this case, contemporary touches would have spoiled the illusion. In the 1930s, my character wouldn't have been familiar with Chuck Berry, rockabilly, electric blues, or hip-hop. Colin Linden helped me improve my fingerstyle technique and we struck up a friendship in the process.

O Brother had been filming for about a week before my arrival. The day before I was to begin shooting, on July 2, 1999, I sat in makeup peering into the mirror as the hairstylist cut off my precious dreadlocks. There was no way to hide dreads from the camera. Dreadlocks in 1930s America was unimaginable. Even so, I insisted on waiting until the first day of shooting before letting them cut my precious locks.

Early the following morning, a driver chauffeured me about an hour north of Jackson to the set where we were to shoot the mythical crossroad scene. I arrived around six o'clock in the morning and went to the refreshment area to get a cup of coffee when some greasy-haired guy wearing overalls said, "Allow me," then proceeded to pour me a cup of coffee. "Hi, Chris, I'm George." It was George Clooney, the star of the film, making me, a rookie, coffee? "Nice to meet you," I said.

George's unselfish demeanor allowed me to feel at ease amid the expansive, bustling Hollywood set. George and I shook hands. We continued a light conversation about the heat, how pleased we both were to be a part of the film and working—which I would soon learn was never taken for granted by actors—along with a few jokes from George about his three-legged pig and recent practical jokes he had played on the cast and crew.

George was called away to makeup just as the smiling Coen brothers, Joel and Ethan, approached. They welcomed me and introduced me to the assistant director and camera crew. They gave me a walkthrough for the first scene of the day. I thought it funny how the Coens finished each other's sentences.

George Clooney and the Coens had skillfully made me comfortable. I settled into my trailer with my lines and waited to be called for the first shoot. By noon, the scorching July heat was unbearable. Fortunately, I had a stand-in during those long hours between scenes. I even had my own production chair with my name on it, sitting right next to George and Joel. During the lunch break, I had a chance to meet the rest of the actors and crew. We shot most of the exterior day-time scenes in Mississippi that summer. We wrapped for about a month before relocating in the fall to the Warner Brothers Studio lot in Burbank, California, for nighttime exterior shooting. We filmed the great flood scene at Universal Studios.

While in Los Angeles, T-Bone Burnett took me into Sunset Sound Studio to record the campfire song prior to shooting. The session went well, but T-Bone assured me it was only a safety recording. He, Joel, and Ethan were determined to film me in character live on set, performing the piece similar to a John Lomax field recording. "Your performance is the pivotal musical piece of the movie," T-Bone said. In his own way, T-Bone let me know he was confident I could deliver. "You're going to add essential credibility to the Soggy Bottom Boys," he said.

The Soggy Bottom Boys was the fictional group my character was a part of, along with George Clooney, John Turturro, and Tim Blake Nelson. In my mind I saw the campfire scene as an opportunity to conjure the spirit of the Blues Box, immortalizing it on film. It was a bonus to expose moviegoers to the legend of Tommy Johnson. Legend was, according to his older brother LeDell (1892–1972), Tommy was the person who actually went around the Delta bragging to anyone who'd listen that he'd sold his soul to the devil. Granted, this wasn't to be taken literally. It was only a folktale. Tommy's legend was associated with Robert Johnson, who was erroneously attached to the crossroad tale by promoters, in part because of the Voodoo imagery of "Cross Road Blues," his most popular song. Who knows, maybe some folks would think I made a Faustian bargain, too. *Sigh*.

We recorded the campfire scene on location, not in a movie studio, just as T-Bone had promised. It was basically a field recording by a real campfire on a Los Angeles area ranch in the wee hours of the night. George Clooney, John Turturro, Tim Blake Nelson, and I sat around a campfire dreaming out loud about what we were going to do with all that dough supposedly robbed from the Piggly Wiggly. Right on cue, I began playing and singing "Hard Time Killing Floor Blues."

I performed the song once but was asked to stop halfway through because of a technical issue. The next take, I missed some lyrics. The script editor briefly refreshed me. This caused some uneasiness among the producers. I thought I overheard T-Bone, who was gathered with the producers while we reset the scene, reassure them he had a safety recording from our earlier session at Sunset Sound if needed. I tried to un-hear what I'd just heard. I convinced myself I was going to nail the performance on the next take. We started again. There was another premature stop for technical reasons. Finally, I knew exactly how I should act and perform the scene.

"Action," Joel said, again. The set went quiet.

I began the spellbinding acoustic guitar motif. My voice echoed in the cool autumn air as naturally as the crickets chirped in tune in the distance. Shadowed by the dusky night sky, the warm campfire illuminated my face and hands. Over the crackle, and the glowing fire, I sang:

> Hard times yearn, everywhere you go
> Has it harder, than ever been before
> People are drifting, from door to door
> Can't find no heaven, I don't care where they go

From there I was in a zone. I was able to block out the cameras, the large crew, the pressures, and just perform as if sitting in the graveyard with old Zack the Cat. Or maybe at the Blues Box on a slow Monday night, playing music from my heart to a few patrons sitting, listening, nursing a beer, connecting every word I sang to their own personal experiences. I fingerpicked the vintage, small-bodied Gibson acoustic. Gently massaging a note here, a note there, for a vibrato effect. My musically callused fingers fell perfectly in time, as if time itself hinged on my every stroke. For a brief moment, the world revolved around my disembodied voice. I played a soft finale as my whimper trailed off, followed by a long decaying note that slowly resolved from aural bliss to silence intermittent by nature.

"Check the gate!" the assistant director shouted. Meaning, we had our scene.

Finally, I broke character and exhaled. I was relieved. Strangely, the crew seemed to look at me differently. Nearly everyone on the set began to walk over and shake my hand, congratulating me on a job well done. I too began to sense something extraordinary was captured. Something words could not convey. Everyone, including the producers, T-Bone, Clooney, Joel, and Ethan had a new kind of reverence toward me that I hadn't experienced before.

It seemed during the pivotal campfire scene, I'd truly conjured some mystical Voodoo, which Roger Deakins, the cinematographer, had masterfully captured. I hadn't swiveled my hips on Ed Sullivan, set my guitar on fire at Monterey Pop, nor moonwalked on Motown's twenty-fifth anniversary stage. Yet, somehow, it was understood we'd caught lighting in a bottle.

Later that night, I was alone in my candle-lit trailer. I began to think about my dad. I felt I'd done him proud. I could envision my campfire scene playing in a dark movie house, transporting everyone in the room to a virtual Tabby's Blues Box. After a few more weeks of filming, *O Brother, Where Art Thou?* was finally in the can. Joel and Ethan's gamble on me had paid off:

> Come on in my kitchen,
> for it's going to be raining outdoors
> —Robert Johnson

On stage at the King Biscuit Festival in Little Rock, the rain poured down, but I didn't mind. I sang "Dark Clouds" from the *Red Mud* album and dedicated it to the weeping sky. The rain felt like tears of joy, not depressing gloom.

Later that month, I was booked on a six-week international tour. I joined a blues caravan in Ankara, Turkey, headlined by veteran blue-soul man Bobby Rush. I was a featured guest along with a flashy Chicago guitarist, Eddy "the Chief" Clearwater. The tour took us to Bucharest, Romania, Istanbul, Turkey, Moscow, Russia, and dozens of other cities in Eastern Europe. The tour lasted six weeks. After the long tour, I returned home to the Upper Ninth Ward, exhausted, just in time for Thanksgiving dinner.

On January 1, 2000, I awoke to the familiar smell of black-eyed peas and cabbage cooking in the kitchen of our New Orleans East apartment. I was slightly hungover from carousing in the French Quarter after a lively New Year's Eve gig. Maha and my son, Dylan, were in the living room watching the parades with their mother.

The dreaded Y2K had finally arrived. Planes had not fallen from the sky; civilization hadn't collapsed. The people who displayed paranoia on CNN by stockpiling food and ammunition in underground bunkers I'm sure felt foolish when the sun came up that morning.

Seemingly overnight, I'd become a respected movie actor and a bourgeoning film composer. During the first few weeks of the New Year, I attended the Sundance Film Festival in snowy Park City, Utah. I hobnobbed and networked with fellow actors. The experience was eye-opening and refreshing. Suddenly, I was a hot commodity. My name was mentioned in Hollywood trades like *Variety* and *Hollywood Reporter*. I quickly learned the film business was entirely different from the music business. For example, in the record business, a criminal could get released from prison one day and sign a naive minor to a long-term contract the next. In contrast, as an actor, I was protected by the Screen Actors Guild, a powerful union that didn't tolerate the types of contracts drawn up by the hucksters, liars, and thieves of the music business.

Change was swift in the new millennium. Old-school music executives were suddenly dinosaurs. They felt threatened by digital distribution's democratizing innovations. Indeed, digital technology had taken a quantum leap forward. Napster, the peer-to-peer file-sharing network introduced by Shawn Fanning and Sean Parker, was driving the corporate record industry out of business. Digital recording aesthetics, which I'd pioneered in blues, was suddenly a threat to the entire major studio ecosystem. I had coined, trademarked, and promoted the phrase "21st Century Blues." Now I was living in it.

But change was tempestuous. Digital start-ups were not immune to twenty-first-century volatility. Dot-com companies spent millions of dollars on Super Bowl television ads only to go out of business a few weeks later. New digital technologies were arriving and going obsolete within months. In January, America Online—whom any savvy Internet user tried to avoid because of their slow and inadequate dial-up Internet access portal—made news following their purchase of Time Warner, America's largest media company. I saw this as confirmation the old media gatekeepers were dumber than a bag of nails when it came to 1s and 0s. Indeed, the dot-com bubble, like a digital cloud, burst open and rained down on Wall Street. However, the sun rose and lit a new path forward for artists and creative types of my generation.

What is more, due to my role in a greatly anticipated feature film, labels began bidding on my new unfinished album. I licensed *Me, My Guitar and the Blues* to Blind Pig Records, retaining ownership of the master. The album was rush released on March 16. My career seemed to be pregnant with new possibilities for success. However, the foundation on which it was built was about to crumble.

———

I was at home in New Orleans when word came from my family in Baton Rouge that Dad's eviction was near. He was planning a farewell jam and wanted me to attend. On the day of Tabby's last jam, I packed my guitar and went to visit him at the Blues Box to pay my respects. I wanted to catch up with my father during the calm hours before the throng of musicians and supporters arrived, knowing it would be our final chance to talk before eviction. I found Dad sitting alone at a table near the bar and joined him. We talked about the situation and reminisced.

Later that night, we held an unspoken jazz funeral for the Blues Box. With everyone on their feet he sang one of his most requested songs, "I Love Big Fat

Women." The upbeat refrain was a tongue-in-cheek anthem serenading voluptuous women. It never failed to pack the dance floor. I even grabbed someone and danced—a rare gesture for me—knowing it would be my last opportunity.

Just before sunrise, in Tabby's Blues Box and Heritage Hall, just before the last melodious echoes of an era faded from memory, before I unplugged my guitar for the last time, scant cries for an encore echoed from the remaining patrons. But there would be no encore for the Blues Box. It was the end. The music fell silent.

The Creolized Hoodoo blues project was over. Our guitars and amplifiers were packed away for the final time. The glowing rainbow of Christmas tree lights decorating the bar went dark, closing the curtain on the most crucial era of my life. As I drove away, Tabby's Blues Box and Heritage Hall disappeared in my rearview mirror.

THE DREAM

SOMETIME LATER, I dreamed I was in my pajamas. Upriver in Baton Rouge, while everyone was in slumber, bulldozers like thieves in the night tore into the hallowed walls of the Blues Box. In New Orleans, I tossed and turned restlessly. In my dream, the demolition felt like part of my spirit was being ripped away. I was pulled by a magnetic force, not walking but gliding without moving my bare feet toward the desolate building. Hoping it was still standing. However, when I arrived, it was torn into pieces. The broken boulevard was eerily quiet and lifeless, as if I were the only inhabitant in the world. Solemnly, I searched through the ruins for some sign of life. The dream seemed real to the touch. A few feet away, I recognized the old tip bucket. In another corner, I recognized Dad's smashed and crumpled cigar box. Scattered around were bits and pieces of crushed Christmas lights. Strewed about the debris were pieces of vinyl records that had been ripped from the jukebox. I sifted through the former Blues Box relics, trying to understand what had happened. I was looking for some kind of deeper meaning. I came across ripped ghostly photos of bluesmen and women holding silent guitars.

Then I heard out in the distance what sounded like the cry of an eerie guitar. The familiar notes jarred my memory. I remembered a clandestine invitation from my childhood. I was no longer the imaginative child of wonder playing hide-and-seek in the rain with ghostly whisperers in my backyard. My long, winding journey had transformed me. I was my own man. I remembered darkness had always been my proverbial playmate. Suddenly, I awoke from the exhausting dream.

JOHN LAW

THE COEN BROTHERS invited me to perform at a special benefit concert at the historic Ryman Auditorium in Nashville on May 24. Billed as "Down from the Mountain," it would take place at the legendary Grand Ole Opry. I was thrilled for the rare opportunity. The revered Opry stage helped make legends of country music artists such as Earl Scruggs, Bill Monroe, Uncle Dave Macon, Ernest Tubb, Patsy Cline, Hank Williams, the Carter Family, Johnny Cash, and Elvis Presley. The history of the Opry could be intimidating for even a seasoned veteran. It's been said, if you could make it on to the Opry stage, you could make it anywhere. I hadn't planned on becoming a country music star. But if I went over well, I thought, an opportunity to win over a few country fans might present itself.

Granted, very few Black performers had ever stood at the center of the Opry stage and sang to a sold-out Opry audience. The first recurring Black performer on the original Grand Ole Opry show was DeFord Bailey, a harmonica player with few peers. One of his best-known harmonica arrangements created the aural illusion of a freight train leaving the station. DeFord Bailey was a regular on the Opry radio show from 1927 through 1941.

Down from the Mountain would be the partnering concert documentary by the legendary filmmaker—who practically invented the genre of concert film documentary—D. A. Pennebaker. He was known for documenting the 1967 Monterey Pop Festival, which famously captured Jimi Hendrix's fiery sacrifice of his beloved guitar. Pennebaker also directed the controversial *Don't Look Back* film in 1965, a behind-the-scenes look at the chaos of Bob Dylan's controversial UK tour.

D. A. Pennebaker and I met briefly over lunch to talk about the filming. I found him unassuming for a filmmaker so accomplished. Having Pennebaker behind the camera meant *Down from the Mountain* was somehow extraordinary. It seemed he was always there, with his camera ready, whenever an exciting new development in music shook the earth. What we were going to perform, however, was old-timey stuff. There would be no destroying of instruments here. We weren't even using amplifiers. My innovative hip-hop blues was out of the question.

I had written a new song for the concert, "John Law Burned Down the Liquor Sto'." The lyrics were inspired by the recent razing of our juke joint. I was always attracted to song lyrics with double meanings. The lyrics to "John Law" could be interpreted literally or allegorically. The song could be an ode to a secret whiskey still where moonshiners congregated, drinking white lightning and rum and racing their souped-up cars through the backwoods to stay one step ahead of John Law. Historically, John Law was the Scottish banker whose company in the eighteenth century established and monopolized the Atlantic slave trade business in Louisiana.

During rehearsals inside the Ryman, I found an empty hallway where I could practice my new song. I was a bit nervous because I hadn't sung it in public before. Colin Linden, the Canadian blues guitarist who earlier taught me the fingerpicking style of Skip James's "Hard Time Killing Floor Blues" for my role in *O Brother*, joined me to perform the song on stage. We performed "John Law" as a dobro guitar duo accompanied by upright bass and mandolin.

> Moonshine whiskey ought to be a crime
> When I start to drinking, I'm bound to lose my mind
> Oh, brother, a dime would get through hard times
> Now, what's that smoking, yonder cross the fields?
> Looks like our secret hideaway we had so many years
> Now John Law done come and run us way from here
>
> He burned down the liquor sto'
> He burned down the liquor sto'
> John Law burned down the liquor sto'
> He burned down the liquor sto'
> For that bootleg whiskey, where we gonna' go?

Our performance went over well with the discerning Ryman audience. T-Bone Burnett recorded *Down from the Mountain* for a live album release. You couldn't put your finger on it, but something electrifying was taking place around the folk music of *O Brother, Where Art Thou?*

TABBY'S BENEFIT CONCERT

DAD SEEMED genuinely excited to move to a new location in downtown Baton Rouge, in spite of the financial setback. I had only a faint interest in it. Putting my feelings aside, however, Tabby was still my dad, so of course, I wished him well. The eviction along with the remodel of the new venue created a financial dilemma for Mom and Dad. Irrespective of my stance about the new Tabby's Blues Box, I wanted to do anything I could to ease the burden for my mother and father.

I decided to use my newly earned recognition to arrange a benefit concert that would help offset my parents' expenses. I arranged and hosted a benefit concert at the House of Blues in the French Quarter. I invited Kenny Neal and his dad, Raful Neal, along with Gatemouth Brown and several other New Orleans performers, including Coco Robicheaux, Joe Krown, Rockie Charles, and J. Monque'D, to share the bill. The benefit concert was set for June 4 at 8:00 PM with advance tickets priced at twelve dollars.

Mom and Dad attended the concert and sat in the upper balcony as honored guests. My dad didn't perform but I paid tribute to him by performing his classics, including "Hoodoo Party." It was a remarkable night. I have an indelible memory of looking up and seeing my mother's beaming smile. I performed with guests throughout the night. In addition, I joined the headliner, Gatemouth Brown, for a few numbers. We raised around $15,000 and I turned the proceeds over to my parents the next day. It didn't cover all of their loses, but I'm certain it helped ease Mom and Dad's financial burden following their costly eviction and relocation.

By the summer of 2000, Baton Rouge, that French-christened city upriver, once a thriving metropolis with a bustling downtown that proudly advertised WHITES ONLY entrance signs to its restaurants and hotels, had become a desolate, deserted, abandoned district. It was a mere shell of its former self. White flight, which began in the '60s, had left the area barren after dark. Baton Rouge had long moved away from the downtown area to the suburbs, having abandoned meaningful integration during the '70s and '80s. There were a few governmental buildings still operational during the day, but at night Tabby's Blues Box and Heritage Hall, like a lighthouse flickering in a distant fog, provided the only glimmer in the darkness of a brighter future.

The new Tabby's, with its long rectangular shape, occupied the bottom floor of a three-story brick building at the corner of Florida and Lafayette Streets. Florida Street sloped down a steep hill to the levee, which was only about three hundred yards from the new club. The Mississippi River was seen easily from the club's front door.

Dad had envisioned a grand opening-day parade with a second-line brass band, perhaps a homecoming of regional acts that included his friend and former Baton Rouge blues guitarist Buddy Guy. However, downtown was no place for a parade or celebration of any kind after dark. It was a ghost town. Besides, not enough time had passed between venues for the public to properly grieve over the loss of the original Blues Box. The community, like myself, was still mournful of the raze.

The opening happened with little notice or fanfare. Unshaken, however, Dad, now seventy-two, forged ahead. Except for an expensive build-out including a new bar and stage and various repairs of the long-abandoned building, his monthly rent was virtually free. Free rent was perhaps the most attractive thing about the new location. At long last, Baton Rouge had serious plans to redevelop its abandoned downtown. Giving Tabby a sweet deal looked attractive on the surface, yet, upon closer inspection, not so much. Seemingly no one else was willing to pay rent or risk opening an entertainment business in such an abandoned and blighted part of town.

Nevertheless, I finally set aside my cynicism long enough to visit our new Blues Box and Heritage Hall. He should have purchased a building near LSU in the University Shopping Center just off the campus, I thought, as I drove up to the new club. Students, in recent years, had become his most loyal patrons. As I got out of my car and made my way toward the entrance carrying my guitar, I thought about the time I'd casually mentioned my thoughts on relocation to Tabby just before he signed the new lease. I knew what he was going to say before he said it. "When you get your club, you can move wherever you want, but this is my club." I could hear his husky voice echoing the crude sentiment again in my mind. Standing outside, I hesitated briefly before entering.

When I finally stepped inside the new Blues Box, it was immediately clear the building was fully functional. My sisters Yolanda and Joylyn both worked at the club part-time in addition to their day jobs. Yolanda greeted me warmly at the door on my arrival. She sold tickets, T-shirts, and CDs from a well-designed sales booth near the door. Hanging from the walls inside of her welcoming booth were Blues Box T-shirts and other memorabilia sporting sales tags. Arthur, the security man and the assistant manager, was busy cordially greeting everyone who entered while checking their IDs. He gave me a friendly bear hug.

I then walked through a long frilly curtain of foil hanging from the ceiling to camouflage the line of sight to the main room. Once beyond the foil curtain, I could step down onto the main floor of the club. The walls were plastered with mementos from the old Blues Box, including photos of favorite local bluesmen and women who were once obscure but had become legends during the life of the club. It threw me for a loop to see myself immortalized in several posters and pictures along the walls. I, too, had gone from obscurity to legend, thus becoming part of the immortal Blues Box fraternity. Of course, there were also pictures of Dad posed with some of his most impassioned fans.

I went to the long bar extending lengthwise along the right side of the room. The bar was positioned across from the spacious and colorfully lit raised bandstand. Jason, one of the young bartenders, a pre-law student and LSU's student body vice president, served me a cold beer. I sat on the red vinyl barstool and took in the atmosphere. Slim, the janitor and handyman, who was simple with a friendly demeanor, came over and welcomed me. I was glad to see Slim, who like Arthur and Jason, were holdovers from the original Blues Box.

Unlike the former building, the new club was more spacious and had modern comforts. It had a good plumbing infrastructure. The bathrooms worked properly, which was a major upgrade from the old club's rustic water closets. Its central air-conditioner kept the place cool. Dad also installed a brand-new beer box that actually kept the beer cold. The new space also allowed for a private office, from which Dad ruled over the club from a comfortable reclining leather throne stationed behind a large worn wooden desk. As I sat at the bar nursing a beer, I thought, It's amazing how much a new location could change the feel and the clientele of a blues club. I found new faces, new sounds, and new patrons forming a new identity at Tabby's.

A heavily tattooed White guitarist, John Lisi, was playing to a few dozen people. Lisi, a New Jersey native, had visited the original Blues Box only a few years earlier and, like many before him, was inspired to relocate to Baton Rouge in order to hone his guitar chops under the watchful eye of Rockin' Tabby Thomas. Lisi was now one of the mainstays at the new downtown location. Lisi and others wished to rekindle the spirit of the original Blues Box, but the circumstances surrounding the blues and its culture therewith had changed.

The social and cultural climate that incubated the original Blues Box couldn't be resuscitated. First, the neighborhood Blacks who had given the original club a genuine community vibe were nowhere to be found. Neither were buses of tourists showing up with flashing cameras and tourists' dollars. The European festival promoters were no longer visiting regularly on scouting sojourns, bidding against each other for the right to bring the best Blues Box artists overseas. The New Orleans Jazz and Heritage Festival had become the biggest pop music festival in the United States. In the process, Jazz Fest relegated blues music to a small tent on the fringe of the main festival grounds. We used to be dispersed throughout the main stages. Moreover, European promoters no longer frequented Jazz Fest seeking new talent, either. They had become content with their own French, German, or Scandinavian blues musicians. The new Blues Box seemed slightly off-key when compared to the Creole Hoodoo spirit of the original. But for those discovering Tabby's for the first time, it was still an intriguing cultural hangout.

In August, I moved my wife and kids out of our cramped Upper Ninth Ward apartment and into an Uptown bungalow at 5527 Willow Street, just blocks from the student union of Tulane University. The leafy area was only a few short blocks from St. Charles Avenue. Our new neighborhood was a far cry from our isolated lifestyle across the canal. Suddenly, the whole city seemed to be within walking distance or a bike ride or a ride on the nearby St. Charles streetcar. I spent most mornings jogging in Audubon Park and lounging in coffeehouses along Magazine Street. Our daughter, Maha, attended Lusher Primary School on Freret Street, one of the most desirable public schools in the state of Louisiana. Life was good, thanks to heavy national and international touring along with CD sales and royalties from my growing catalog of music. My touring calendar was filled with good-paying concert dates for the next two years. For the first time, I could provide a sense of financial stability for my young family.

UP TO THE MOUNTAINTOP

ON DECEMBER 5 the *O Brother, Where Art Thou?* soundtrack was released. On December 22, just before Christmas, the movie hit theaters nationwide. By January 2001, *O Brother, Where Art Thou?* had become Joel and Ethan's highest grossing film to date. But what was more surprising was the unexpected phenomenal success of the soundtrack. It became an instant classic. The soundtrack climbed into the *Billboard* top twenty albums chart to eventually become the number one album in the United States, surpassing a staggering six million in sales with no sign of slowing down. (The soundtrack went on to sell more than ten million copies in the United States alone.)

On June 13, 2001, I was invited to coheadline a historic concert at Carnegie Hall celebrating the phenomenal success of *O Brother, Where Art Thou?* The concert was to be one of the most important nights of folk music held at Carnegie Hall since the From Spirituals to Swing series was held there in 1938 and '39. That first legendary concert was the one in which curator and talent scout John Hammond Sr. attempted to book an obscure Delta guitarist named Robert Johnson—who was unknown at the time except to fellow tenant farm musicians in the Delta and a few hundred record buyers—but instead, learned of Robert Johnson's premature death at age twenty-seven.

The coheadlining sold-out concert, billed as "Down from the Mountain," was the highpoint of my touring career to that point. I was on a roll no other folk-blues singer could have ever imagined. I was now flying high beyond the reach of myopic blues gatekeepers. I no longer had to acquiesce to the dogma of the Blues Mafia and their neophytes who had alienated me from my own culture. In fact, my career transcended the blues. I had even found acceptance among bluegrass fans and was recognized in country music circles. Indeed, I was beginning to influence mainstream popular culture.

The live *Down from the Mountain* album recorded earlier in Nashville became the follow-up to the *O Brother* soundtrack. *Down from the Mountain* was released on July 24 and immediately went gold, selling over five hundred thousand copies. It eventually sold over one million copies and won Grammy awards. My composition, "John Law Burned Down the Liquor Sto,'" from *Down from the Mountain* subsequently became a standard in the repertoires of bluegrass, country, and roots music groups. The Blues Mafia and their acolytes built an existential gate that frustrated and anguished me over the years—but it hadn't been erected high enough. They couldn't have imagined the heights I would soar without their stamp of approval.

SITTING ON TOP OF THE WORLD

THE SUN WAS SETTING over Sunset Boulevard. I sat at the Hyatt Hotel bar in West Hollywood sipping a cocktail while a fresh out of college screenwriter, awkwardly trying to project more experience and more success than he had, pitched me a movie script. He was offering me the lead role. He wished to have me, a hot new actor from an Oscar-winning movie, officially attached. He could then shop his script to studios.

It was February 2002. Such scenes had become the norm on recent visits to Hollywood. People handing me scripts, pitching stories they were trying to get made. I was half-listening to the budding writer, watching the moon rise over the Sunset Strip, thinking where I might go to party later that night. Pre-Grammy parties were happening all over town. Hollywood was abuzz with *O Brother* fever. The *O Brother, Where Art Thou?* soundtrack was up for numerous awards including the biggest of them all, Album of the Year. I was competing with folk-rock legend Bob Dylan, stadium rock stars U2, southern alternative rap duo Outkast, and newcomer India Arie.

It was a little scary being recognized by complete strangers on the strip who thought I was actually the character I had played in the movie. Having random people rudely approach me as if they knew me was strange. I always had the feeling I was being watched. Not watched in the normal way for a Black man in America, where a person is giving you that look, trying to figure out if you're a threat in some way. That was a look I'd unfortunately grown used to, though never comfortable with. This new look had that same sense of slight fear in the stranger's eyes except for a controlled excitement, such as, I know this guy from somewhere, or pointing, that's the guy from the movie!

My newfound celebrity was striking yet disquieting. Oddly, I was finally comfortable in my own skin. I was where I thought I always belonged. Unexpectedly, however, people had new expectations for me, socially and professionally. I needed to be a mind reader, though, to figure out what those new expectations were. If I failed to live up to the notions of strangers, they were disappointed. Ah, the pressures of fame.

I was a shooting star. I was experiencing that rare golden Hollywood moment. It was exhilarating for me and intoxicating for everyone around me. Only once could you be a rising star. Then Hollywood could shape and mold me to be a permanent fixture among its galaxy, one that burns brightly for a lifetime. On the other hand, I might be a flickering star, burning out in a flash like a cheap firework on the Fourth of July.

Along with new fame came greater social responsibility. Which, as a musician, I didn't have to deal with, necessarily. Musicians were allowed to sleep with dozens of women, drink gallons of Jack Daniel's, do a variety of drugs. In spite of such bad behavior—or maybe because of it—they were celebrated. In contrast, a movie star attracted women of a higher class and drank from the personal wine cellars of wealthy admirers. Most important, however, an actor's partying and excesses must always remain inconspicuous. As an actor, my personal life mustn't ever seem out of control. Movies were far too expensive to make. No studio wanted to risk millions of dollars on an out-of-control actor. As an actor, I was expected to be in the gym in the wee hours before dawn. In contrast, a rock star kept vampire hours. We often went to bed at dawn. As an actor, one must be on set, in the makeup chair by 5:00 AM, not 5:05 AM. Just how much partying could I do, then look my best for the cameras at such a bewitching hour, anyway? I was caught in between. I was best known as an actor, perhaps, but I was still a blues guitarist, a musician, which made my social and professional rise all the more unwieldly.

Universal Music Group, the largest record company in the world, was the label behind the *O Brother* album via one of its subsidiaries in Nashville, Lost Highway Records. Although *O Brother* was on its way to going diamond, selling over ten million copies and grossing over $100 million for Universal, you would think Universal would have at least offered to pay for my hotel suite while I was in town to attend the Grammy Awards promoting their hottest product. But no, they didn't offer to fly me out to L.A., nor had they sent a limo to chauffeur me to the red carpet. In fact, they didn't offer to buy me a drink nor a meal. I was forced to spend my own dime for my flight, hotel suite, limo, entertainment, and publicists. Moreover, I didn't expect anything from Universal. I didn't ask for any advances. Therefore, I owed Universal Music Group nothing. Not a penny. As a consequence, there would be nothing for Universal to recoup from my royalties. I was not signed to one of their labels. I was exclusively recording for my own nationally distributed label, 21st Century Blues Records. My own label paid all of my expenses. There was nothing to deduct for recording expenses because the movie budget of Universal Pictures had paid for everything. Neither was there anything to deduct for music videos, which cost most artists hundreds of thousands of dollars, if not millions. Worse still, popular bands were expected to shoot several MTV videos for a charting album, owing their labels millions more, which would all be recouped in the end.

I always thought big budget music videos were foolish, anyway. A good movie could be made for the cost of some promotional videos. After pricey recording expenses, videos, radio promotions, plus touring advances, manufacturing deductions, publicity campaigns, and the like, a popular band could easily sell one million records then receive a royalty statement from their label showing they were still deeply in the red. Well, this scenario was not going to happen to me, not this time. Besides, I was an artist who didn't have expensive handlers or an entourage. The major record companies had long ago written me off. I was *damaged goods*, a lawyer once told me. But now I was on the cover of magazines, including *Entertainment Weekly*, as one of the Entertainers of the Year. Star of stage and screen. No doubt these were exciting times and I was planning on enjoying every minute.

A few days later, while lounging around the hotel, I had time to reflect on my relationship with Mariann. I'd spent most of the past year on the road. I'd grown lonesome without her. We had had an argument back in New Orleans before I left that changed her mind about accompanying me to the Grammys. *My Dearest Mariann*, as I often addressed her in letters from the road, almost never came to my gigs. We were social opposites. She didn't drink. Rarely could I get her to drink a glass of champagne on New Year's Eve. She felt awkward and uncomfortable in the limelight. She was most comfortable at home with the kids. Now, I couldn't even remember what we'd argued about. I couldn't remember if I was wrong or what I should apologize for. Maybe she'd pulled a stunt simply to exempt herself from the stress of having to find a proper dress and fly out to Los Angeles for the week to walk the red carpet with me. In spite of that possibility, I had no desire to experience the week without her. We'd been through so much together. I yearned to have her share the moment. We had experienced many disappointments, yet she always believed in me. I wanted to be there for her, too. Together, I thought, we should share the gratification of our finally rising above all of the detractors, doubters, haters, and thieves. I had to find a way to apologize for whatever, and then persuade her to fly out to Hollywood immediately. For if she didn't, I thought, I wouldn't enjoy the experience. During a long phone conversation, I apologized and convinced Mariann to fly in the following day.

After shopping in Beverly Hills and visiting tailors, Mariann and I attended the Grammy telecast at the Staples Center in Los Angeles on February 27, 2002. *O Brother, Where Art Thou?* won numerous Grammy Awards, as did the live album *Down from the Mountain*, on which I'd written "John Law Burned Down the Liquor Sto'." Backstage, after accepting my awards, I posed for pictures holding an armful of golden statues. I spoke to the gathered press about my influences and thanked my dad by dedicating my success to him.

Our chauffeur drove us to an exclusive *O Brother* afterparty where we socialized with a host of A-list celebrities including George Clooney, Joel and Ethan Coen, and T-Bone Burnett, along with dozens of their Hollywood friends and well-wishers. I found myself sitting alone at a small table sipping a drink, eating sushi, when Bono of U2 came over to say hello to me. He sat down on my right and started up a conversation. Then, the Edge, the innovative guitarist of U2, came over to join us. He sat on my left. The Edge said he was starving, so I offered him the remainder of my sushi, which he dug into right away. Bono teased the Edge, warning me Edge was going to talk my ear off about the new mansion he was building in Santa Monica. Over the next twenty minutes or so while we sat there joking and making small talk, we noticed the room closing in around us.

A crowd stood around our small table vying for Bono's attention. It was incredible how, in a room full of stars, Bono was the brightest. While Bono sat next to me, doing an impromptu meet and greet to his dismay, the Edge and I began talking shop. Edge expressed his admiration for my fingerpicking and open tuning in the *O Brother* movie and on its soundtrack. He congratulated me on beating his band out for Album of the Year honors. I shared my admiration for his guitar arrangements—unlike most major rock stars, such as Clapton, the Stones, or Led Zeppelin, his style was refreshing to my ear because it was original, not built on blues riffs, except for his signature Bo Diddley–inspired rhythmic delay effects.

U2's success was not based on ripping off obscure American blues. A few obvious tunes in their catalog sounded like blues covers—they had even recorded and toured with B. B. King—but they seemed to have done so as a way to authenticate themselves into the roots of American music. I said to Edge that I admired they weren't heavy on blues riffs. I didn't mention my song "Cocaine (Snow

White)," which I believed was the foundation for U2's "Bullet the Blue Sky" from the *Joshua Tree* album. Edge humbly replied he would've stolen more riffs if only he had the chops to pull it off. I laughed at his self-deprecating humor and felt we were bonding a little as fellow guitarists. Then, out of nowhere, Elvis Costello, an eclectic rock star who looked more like a bespectacled journalist than Elvis, forced his way through the circle of admirers surrounding our table and sat his big butt right in my lap, conspicuously, to draw attention to himself. So, now I'm sandwiched between Bono and Edge with Elvis sitting in my lap. All eyes and cameras flashed brightly upon us. Elvis was sitting on my lap, but I was sitting, as the old song says, "On Top of the World," with a hit movie, the number one album in America, and an upcoming sold-out coheadlining arena tour on my summer schedule. I didn't bother to pinch. My wildest dreams had been realized.

Before Mariann and I left the party, a representative of Universal Records whispered she'd seen our new eye-popping royalty checks due to be mailed in the coming weeks. I felt tipsy in the limo on the drive back to the Hyatt. Mariann was sober and relieved. We both realized our lives had changed. I had seized the ring! Become king. Just like Old Zack said I would. I was the hottest blues artist in the world. Yet, I wasn't overwhelmed because when you're a shooting star you're flying too high, too fast, to stop and smell the roses. Besides, there was no time to dwell on success. Mariann and I were quietly reflective about the triumphant night as we cruised down an eerily quiet Sunset Boulevard back to the Hyatt.

The next day, Mariann flew home to New Orleans. I remained in Los Angeles attending meetings with my new television agents from the William Morris Agency. Dozens of movie studio heads and TV producers had requested meetings with me. I left Hollywood some days later with several movie scripts in hand and offers for celebrity appearances. Unfortunately, my busy touring schedule would not allow me to take advantage of those new opportunities immediately. Unlike most actors, I was a musician with a full touring schedule. I had to leave Hollywood and hit the road for dozens of previously scheduled concert dates and festivals with my band.

Back in New Orleans, prior to the summer tour, the governor of Louisiana, Mike Foster Jr., invited me to a series of special events to launch a commemorative Louisiana quarter. Mingling with politicians was something I was uncomfortable with. I attended a black-tie gala in the French Quarter with some of the most powerful people in Louisiana. During the reception, I attracted a lot of attention, but I had no idea how to converse with elite political types. I was a fish out of water. I was cornered by the governor's wife and her wealthy friends. I hadn't developed any cause or personal charity to advocate for. Now that I had influence, it was time to think about such things.

On May 30, at one of the events held outside the Mint Building in the French Quarter, I invited Dad to perform a duet of "The Thrill Is Gone (From Here)" with me—a song we recorded together for my recent album, *Dirty South Hip-Hop Blues*. I rapped and played guitar while Dad sang the blues verses. The governor and other dignitaries sat behind us, perhaps cringing, hoping I wouldn't go too far with my ghetto poetry.

That summer I was booked on a major coheadlining arena tour with fellow *O Brother* soundtrack artists Alison Krauss and Union Station, veteran bluegrass legend Ralph Stanley, the Fairfield Four, Emmylou Harris, and more. The tour was a complete sell-out, a remarkable feat for a purely acoustic and a cappella folk tour:

June 25: Louisville, KY	Freedom Hall
June 26: Detroit, MI	DTE Energy Music Theatre
June 28: Buffalo, NY	Darien Lake Performing Arts Center
June 29: Philadelphia, PA	Mann Center for the Performing Arts
June 30: Lowell, MA (Boston)	Paul E. Tsongas Center
July 2: Uncasville, CN (Hartford)	Mohegan Sun Arena
July 3: Toronto	Molson Amphitheater
July 5: Ottawa	Cisco Systems Bluesfest
July 6: Washington, DC	Bull Run Reg. Park Special Events Center
July 7: Cuyahoga Falls, OH (Cleveland)	Blossom Music Center
July 9: Cincinnati, OH	Firstar Center
July 10: Columbus, OH	Schottenstein Center
July 12: Portsmouth, VA	NTELOS Pavilion at the Harbor Center
July 13: Charlotte, NC	Cricket Arena
July 14: Raleigh, NC	Entertainment & Sports Arena
July 16: Knoxville, TN	Smokies Stadium
July 17: Atlanta, GA	Chastain Park
July 19: Austin, TX	Frank Erwin Center
July 20: Dallas, TX	Smirnoff Music Centre
July 22: Chicago, IL	United Center
July 23: St. Paul, MN	Theatre Bowl at Xcel Energy Center
July 25: Boise, ID	Idaho Center Amphitheater
July 26: Salem, OR	L.B. Day Amphitheater
July 27–28: Seattle, WA	Chateau St. Michelle Winery
July 30: San Jose, CA	Compaq Center @ San Jose
July 31: San Diego, CA	Coors Amphitheater
August 1: Los Angeles, CA	Greek Theatre
August 2: Santa Barbara, CA	Santa Barbara Bowl
August 4: Denver, CO	Red Rocks

On July 19, I pulled my spanking new lemon-yellow luxurious Prevost tour bus up to the Frank Erwin Center in Austin, Texas. It was a victorious return to the city where I'd gotten my first big break at the now-defunct little folk club the Chicago House on Sixth Street. Folk-blues had never gotten as big as *O Brother* before, especially for a Black performer. I had seen Stevie Ray Vaughan and Double Trouble at the Erwin Center. I'd seen B. B. King in a half-filled Erwin Center. But neither concert compared to the phenomenal success of our *Down from the Mountain* tour. A folk bluesman wasn't supposed to show up for concerts in their own million-dollar private tour coach. I had come a long way since the days of my precursors Lead Belly, Jelly Roll Morton, Skip James, Bukka White, Lonnie Johnson, Son House, and Mississippi John Hurt.

I took the opportunity to connect with some old friends while in Austin, many of whom never doubted I would make it. I pulled up to Antone's new club for a short visit after the concert. Antone's had moved back downtown but was now just one of many live music clubs on either side of Congress Boulevard. I spoke briefly with Susan Antone, Clifford's sister and partner, but Clifford was away. When I got back on my bus that night to head to Dallas for our next show, it was clear I was the new face of folk-blues, replacing the ghosts of Robert Johnson, Tommy Johnson, Skip James, and Lead Belly. I was redefining what it meant to be a folk bluesman for a new generation. I was flying too high to hear the cacophony of resentment directed at me by my existential nemesis, the Blues Mafia and their neophytes. The tour was a major success both artistically and financially. It grossed over $20 million according to *Variety* magazine. *O Brother* changed the course of popular music. Banjos and mandolins were suddenly mainstream instruments.

On October 15, I released *Dirty South Hip-Hop Blues*. It wasn't the album the industry expected. I had returned to my controversial rap blues impulses instead of building on the acoustic folk aesthetic of *O Brother*. I was taking a major career risk. The album was received as a revolutionary recording in both folk-blues and hip-hop circles. *Dirty South* was my label's most influential album to date. In November, although critics praised the album as an important work, *Rolling Stone* magazine only gave *Dirty South* an unenlightened three-star review. Perhaps the biggest triumph of *Dirty South* was that it was praised in conservative blues and folk magazines such as *Living Blues*, *Blues Revue*, and *Sing Out*. I was astonished to see the editors of such magazines embrace my vision. The influential in-store magazine *Tower Records* called it "a masterpiece" and gave it five stars.

After riding nonstop on the freight train of success for the past three years, I decided to take a much-needed pause to catch my breath. Of course, there were the obligatory "local boy does good" stories in Louisiana. There were dozens of nice perks too. I regularly received free meals at the most exclusive restaurants in New Orleans. There were guitar endorsements with Gibson and dozens of other brands. It was funny, I thought. Now that I can afford all these expensive instruments, they want to give them to me for free. There were spending sprees, cash payments for new cars, and expensive vacations including a family sojourn to Shanghai, China. I purchased all manner of thing that caught my fancy. Yet, I was never conspicuously materialistic. Diamonds, jewels, and gold-plated rims for my cars didn't interest me. If I were to splurge, it would be on a $10,000 microphone or preamplifier; a piece of vintage gear for my expanding personal recording workspace, 21st Century Blues Studios. Mariann was modest, unselfish, but she would spoil the kids.

One day, during the restoration and expansion of our Uptown bungalow, Mariann and I went into a high-end Royal Street antique shop in the French Quarter to buy bedroom furniture. I was carrying about $25,000 cash. I had planned to spend it all in the store for bedroom accessories. To my dismay, the store manager met us with rudeness. She refused to show us her most valued pieces. I left her store without spending a dime.

Another time, I was in Manhattan shopping for clothes and came across a silk paisley shirt with a price tag of $4,500. I brought it to the counter for purchase along with other items and my subconscious whispered to me, Are you crazy? Who spends that amount of money on a shirt—off the rack? Well, it's easy to get into a frivolous mode when you've been poor all of your life, I thought to myself. After a long pause, I told the clerk I'd changed my mind. I left the items on the counter and walked out of the store.

I soon came to realize spending money as a form of entertainment was foolish. Even though I had everything I thought I needed, I had an urge to spend anyway because it was exhilarating. Collecting boutique studio gear was my weakness. I had to learn financial self-control. Having new money meant I had to learn about investing, stocks, bonds, and such. I did my best to follow the advice of my accountants to seek tax shelters and donate to charities.

In 2003, the Baton Rouge Area Foundation, charged with the revitalization of downtown Baton Rouge, entered a new phase of their master plan. The dilapidated Capitol House Hotel across from the new Tabby's received $70 million for its restoration project. Also, a $55 million construction project was happening a few blocks away at 100 Lafayette Street. In addition, the new state-of-the-art 125,500-square-foot Shaw Center for the Arts had broken ground. Indeed, property values along Lafayette Street were about to skyrocket. This was good news for downtown Baton Rouge, but bad news for the new family juke joint.

On March 3, 2003, I received a letter from John DiGiulio, Dad's longtime angel attorney and friend, making me aware of my parents' newly precarious situation. The letter from John was regarding Bob Dean Properties, Tabby's landlord and owner of half the properties downtown. Bob Dean was applying pressure on Tabby, I presumed because he planned to charge top dollar for his building. Rent downtown could now run from $8,000 to $15,000 or more per month. There was no way Tabby could stay in business with that kind of monthly rent plus overhead and payroll. Pressure on my family was mounting once again. Bob Dean Properties said Tabby needed to up his insurance immediately or he'd be promptly evicted. This was only the latest in a long list of ultimatums. I wrote to John DiGiulio asking that he make some arrangements and I'd cover all costs.

On March 13, 2003, I received a letter from Bob Dean, via Mr. DiGiulio, stating that now that Tabby has a million-dollar insurance policy, his lease would be extended—but only until November 8, 2003. This back-and-forth drew me back into the family business. It helped rekindle the loyalties I always had to my family and our juke joint's survival. I started playing shows at the new Blues Box for free when I wasn't touring or shooting a movie. Moreover, I was earning enough to send money home to help Mom and Dad find comfort, now that they were approaching their twilight years. It wasn't that I'd reconciled and accepted the new place or its location, totally, but family is family.

RAY

In March 2003, I began filming the movie *Ray*. I also contributed to the score with Ray Charles himself on piano as I sang and played guitar. My first week of the film production was spent in Los Angeles with the star, Ray Charles Robinson, at his private studio recording songs and background music for the score. Director Taylor Hackford had cast me to play Lowell Fulsom, an influential blues guitarist, singer, and songwriter, who had given Ray Charles his first big break in the music business by hiring him to play piano behind him on a national tour.

In the studio, Ray Charles accompanied me on the piano as if he were once again playing behind Lowell Fulson. We recorded three songs together, including one of the best renditions ever, in my opinion, of "Everyday I Have the Blues." I found that playing with Ray Charles was a lot like playing with my friend and piano master Henry Gray. We were playing twelve-bar blues just as if we were back in one of those funky smoke-filled honky-tonks in the 1940s or '50s. And Ray, I imagine, recalled his younger days on the chitlin circuit with Lowell Fulson, or maybe at the Dew Drop Inn in New Orleans for inspiration. Ironically, I'd toured with Lowell Fulson myself around 1980 as a teenager. I was his rhythm guitarist on tours he did in the Southeast. Lowell had a larger-than-life stage presence. When you were around Lowell Fulson you knew you were in the presence of blues royalty.

One day during the sessions we had some problems because Ray and the studio musicians weren't on the same page. Among the musicians in the room was rock guitar hero Slash, formerly of Guns N' Roses. Slash was someone I'd met a few times and had played on the same bill with when he was fronting his own side band. There were several songs we needed to record for the film in the styles of country, big band, blues, and swing. Although Slash was an ace rock guitarist, he struggled noticeably with the arrangements. Seeing Slash struggle with the blues was not a surprise to Ray nor me. The music we were scoring from the 1940s and '50s was played mostly on acoustic instruments in dives no bigger than the dressing rooms Slash was accustomed to.

After a few false starts to adjust the tempo and feel of a tune to suit Taylor Hackford's vision, Ray and I locked into a groove like we'd been jamming together for a long time. I came to the studio every day with great anticipation. It was a learning experience that could not be duplicated in a classroom.

Jamie Foxx, who starred in the movie as Ray, didn't attend the recording sessions. Although Jamie was a talented musician in his own right, there's no way he could've played the piano blues and sang like Ray Charles. Therefore, Ray played and sang every note of the score. I was delighted to have worked with the great man. The experience gave me a major confidence boost.

On my last day working with Ray Charles, as I said goodbye, he asked for my phone number. He told me he'd like to keep in touch. I was delighted! I wrote my number down and gave it to Ray Jr., one of the film's producers, who was standing next to his dad. This upset Ray. Ray scolded me, "I asked you for the number, man, that means you hand it to me, see." Embarrassed, I took my information away from his son and put it in his hand. At that moment, I got a small glimpse into what he had to overcome to become the great man he became. Even I, someone who was in awe of him, was ignorantly condescending when I had no intention to be.

MY 21ST CENTURY BLUES INFLUENCE IS FELT

IN THE FOLLOWING WEEKS, during filming, Jamie Foxx would lip-sync and silently finger the piano just like Ray had done in the studio. Jamie's performance was truly believable on film. Much like George Clooney, Jamie had a real talent for making you believe every note he synced in the film was real. Similarly to *O Brother*, in *Ray*, I was the only major actor to sing and play the music of his character live for the movie.

During the months of filming *Ray* in and around New Orleans and Algiers, Jamie asked me to get together with him to record some music. I thought it could be interesting to invite Jamie to my studio to do some rap blues tracks. We talked about it while hanging around the set, but our schedules never allowed us to get together. Later, however, when I heard he and Kanye West's "Gold Digger," a blues rap very much in line with my sound, I felt like, damn, that should've been me.

Indeed, by this time my influence was everywhere. Not only did I have some influence on Jamie Foxx and Kanye West—Kanye West had also covered "I'll Fly Away" from *O Brother, Where Art Thou?* on his debut album *The College Dropout*—the gifted rapper Nas and his father, trumpeter Olu Dara, recorded a hip-hop blues album influenced by the recordings I'd made with my dad such as "Da Thrill Is Gone (From Here)." Nas and Olu Dara's album was appropriately titled *Bridging the Gap*. The skillful hip-hop producer Timbaland used my sound and image to produce a White southern rapper named Bubba Sparxxx. I found it hilarious to see Timbaland play me in a video for his popular song "Deliverance." I smiled every time I saw the video on MTV. In addition, two rappers I admired, Chuck D of Public Enemy and Chicago rapper Common, got in on my flavor as well, recording rap blues in Chicago for a documentary film using my style—although they didn't mention me as usual, but that's how things traditionally went for blues innovators.

I was the hip-hop generation's blues artist. The hip-hop generation didn't know Muddy Waters or Willie Dixon or Jelly Roll Morton, yet I was recognized on the streets of Harlem. Influential producers and rappers were finding new inspiration from my recordings. My influence wasn't only with Black youth. It crossed generations and genres. I was starting to influence country music, too. Young Nashville producers and songwriters, who loved *O Brother* and attended our sold-out concerts, would later duplicate my sampling and hip-hop programming techniques. I was one of the first to do hip-hop and prominently feature and play banjos, dobros, and steel guitars, as illustrated on *Dirty South Hip-Hop Blues*. A decade later, I would hear my sounds and ideas creeping into modern country songs until it began dominating Nashville and country radio.

Even some of the older blues musicians followed in my footsteps, blending new hip-hop and rap sounds into their music. Fat Possum Records, a Mississippi label, enticed R. L. Burnside from Hill Country, Mississippi, to copy my twenty-first-century hip-hop blues sound. R. L. Burnside released a version of my Grammy-winning "Hard Time Killing Floor Blues" on his album *Wish I Was in Heaven Sitting Down*.

Fellow Louisianan and electric blues guitar hero Buddy Guy picked up an acoustic guitar—an instrument he almost never plays in public—and covered my version of "Hard Time Killing Floor Blues" on his 2003 album, *Blues Singer*. For the fiery Buddy Guy, it was a huge departure. Buddy Guy remade himself as an acoustic folk-bluesman on the album to appeal to the millions of fans who had recently discovered acoustic folk-blues through me. In addition, a new band I hadn't heard of before, until a lawyer brought them to my attention for possibly infringing on my trademark, the White Stripes, went much further than those who were simply influenced by my records. Indeed, they used my musical ideas, but they crossed the line when they named their biography *21st Century Blues* after my trademark.[12] I considered a lawsuit against them and their publisher but instead sent the White Stripes' publisher a cease-and-desist letter. I struggled to tone down the avalanche on my sound and brand.

I had no desire to take legal action against the White Stripes, nor anyone else. My biggest disappointment was that none of these people acknowledged my influence on their work, and journalists and reviewers let them get away with it. But this was not new. The exploitation of originators and innovators of the blues goes all the way back to the beginning. The great pianist and composer Jelly Roll Morton couldn't patent his style either. Neither could Bo Diddley. If I had been a corporate artist signed to a major management company and a major label, I could have more easily exploited the niche I'd created. But I was small and independent. I didn't have the resources nor access to the most powerful lawyers and executives in the business who could fully exploit and protect my brand.

It was a new century, I thought, but there was not much I could do. Nevertheless, when I step back and look at my legacy from a bird's-eye view, my success and growing international influence was a clear victory over my existential nemesis.

My success was somewhat ironic because my gold and platinum records happened to be acoustic folk-blues records. I even won Country Music Association and bluegrass awards, of which I am extremely proud. My success was not embraced by the blues community, entirely. I was continually shunned by various blues awards. But the Blues Mafia were no longer the arbiters of my authenticity. Indeed, to continue denying my bona fides would only have called into question their own credibility. Though I hadn't necessarily redefined the ostensible notion of my culture, broadly speaking, I had indeed achieved the artistic agency needed to define my own individual authenticity.

TABBY'S STROKE

I RUSHED OUT THE DOOR and into the cold night air. I drove to Baton Rouge as fast as I could. It was January 2004. I was at home in New Orleans when I got an urgent call that Dad had been rushed by ambulance to the hospital. I arrived at the emergency room less than an hour later. My family was all gathered, Mom, Joylyn, Missy, Yolanda, Charlette, and Jenean. Dad's brothers, Don the trumpeter and Reverend Gus Washington Jr., were also there. The grandkids and spouses filled the hospital halls.

"Daddy had a stroke," Charlette said.

I quietly walked into the hospital room where Dad was hooked up to an IV. Dad, my big strong guardian angel, seemed a shell of himself. He was partially paralyzed on one side of his body. Joylyn, at Dad's bedside, told me what had happened.

The first thing she heard coming from out of his office was "Somebody, call an ambulance!" said Joylyn. "So, I rushed over to see what had happened." The call had come from Tammy. Joylyn recalled that Dad was nearly drowned out by the boisterous patrons and loud music of the house band in the densely packed club.

"He was sitting in his office waiting to go on stage," Joylyn said. "The band was introducing him. He got up from behind his desk and lost his balance, falling hard to the floor. They tried to help him up. 'Daddy! You OK?' Tammy asked. But he just lay there, motionless, panic in his eyes." Joylyn fought back tears. "He could only manage mumbled utterances no one could understand."

She went on to tell me how Slim, Art, and Tammy struggled to lift him off the floor. But Yolanda, my oldest sister, a registered nurse, urged them not to move him. She called 911 from the office phone. Yolanda, I was told, didn't panic. She had calmly directed the action around my dad.

"Most of the customers in the club never knew what was going on," Joylyn said.

They decided not to worry the patrons with the emergency. They chose to be discreet and let the music continue. The band continued to play even as the paramedics rolled Dad out of the club and into an ambulance, I was told.

After a while, a doctor briefed us. The doctor said Tabby was fortunate because my family acted immediately to get him emergency medical attention. He said there was a fair chance he could recover some of his motor skills in due time with therapy. As a family, we embraced each other and gave thanks. Uncle Junior said a prayer as we gathered and held hands.

In the months that followed, we all became caretakers of my dad. The great bluesman was now seventy-five years old and hampered by a severe stroke that nearly paralyzed the entire left side of his body. He could no longer play guitar. He couldn't control the movements of his left arm, hand, or fingers. When eating, my mother had to place a bib on him as if he were an infant child. Walking without assistance was also difficult. His equilibrium was out of balance. He relied on the assistance of a walking cane to get around. It was around this time that I proposed to my mother that I buy her a new home. My mother had been ailing too, due to advanced diabetes and heart complications.

I was in a financial position to make my parents' daily lives somewhat comfortable. I decided I wanted to give a gift to my mother—one that every young man who rises out of poverty dreams of. I set out to purchase a condo for Mom, getting my parents out of a decaying home in South Baton Rouge and into an easy, comfortable retirement lifestyle. So, I asked my sister Joylyn to find a condo for them in a building that was conducive for the handicapped. I wanted to set them up in a place where there was no yard or garden to maintain. A place where there were no stairs to climb. For most Black boys born into poverty this was the greatest dream: to take care of your mother, to set her up in comfort. I spent hours at a time on the phone talking to my mother about the kind of place she would be comfortable in. She seemed excited, but there was always a hesitance in her voice; sometimes there were long pauses and short yes and no answers. Then at other times, I would call and she would talk my ear off about it.

Joylyn found a place she thought would be ideal. Mom eventually accompanied Joylyn and my wife, Mariann, to tour the new condo we had decided on. Then Dad shot down any notion I had of him moving with Mom. He said she could go but he was staying put. He went on to say, in so many words, he didn't need anything from me and was happy in his longtime home.

The former shotgun home was in desperate need of repairs and a total kitchen update. I explained to Dad I could have those repairs done when he and Mom were out of the house. He was not hearing any of it. I further explained he would have two homes. Following the renovations, they could move back in and rent the condo if they chose to or stay in the condo and rent their updated home. I wanted to hear from him one good reason why he wouldn't go along with the plan. I pleaded that Mom didn't even have a proper dishwasher. Her kitchen was badly outdated. The cleaning and upkeep of an old house can be a burden for any woman. And now my mother was also expected to be his caretaker. After about forty-five minutes of weak excuses, each one I was able to resolve, he finally ended the conversation. "The only way I leave this house," Dad proclaimed, "is with my toes tied, on my way to see King Dusty."

My sister Joylyn had become the matriarch of the family. She took it upon her-self to look after our parents' daily needs. Joylyn later said, "You know how Daddy is. He's stubborn and you can't change him." She was right, yet it hurt me deeply. I ached for my mother and resented what I perceived was my dad's selfish attitude.

I reasoned there had to be something deeper. Maybe Black men of his genera-tion both admired and resented the success of the post–civil rights generation. Some parents are elated for their child's success and will demand the child lavish them with gifts. And some parents are too prideful to accept charity. Having grown up with Jim Crow and marginal opportunities, Dad must have thought if only he had been a young ambitious man in the twenty-first century, there'd be no limit to what he could have achieved. America had dealt his generation a bad hand. Yet in spite of that losing hand, he managed to win in his own way. Maybe not financially, but he was greatly admired and had become a cultural icon and beloved. He was a man of great character who had enriched the lives of many with his many gifts. In the end, I had the maturity to love my complicated father unconditionally.

Meanwhile, my schedule was full of movie offers and concert appearances. There were interview requests almost daily. On September 29, 2004, the movie *Ray* was released in theaters across the country and reached number one at the box office. Sadly, Ray Charles passed away months before the release of his film. That same weekend I was booked at the Apollo Theater in Harlem along with several other artists to perform for a benefit concert. After sound check, I walked outside and down the street for a drink in a nearby lounge and heard my music blaring out of a nearby restaurant. On my way back to the Apollo a car slowed down. The driver rolled down the window and said, "You're Chris Thomas King, right? From the movie?" I smiled and nodded, "Yes." This series of events was one of my greatest moments of recognition. I was not in Europe or Spain or Denmark or France, I was in my country, America. I was gratified to have finally penetrated the consciousness of Black youth with my brand of 21st Century Blues—at last.

When I returned home to New Orleans, I learned that Bob Dean Properties,

Dad's landlord, would not renew his lease. Downtown Baton Rouge was being redeveloped. Our blues club couldn't afford to compete with deep-pocketed businesses. Tabby announced publicly that he would retire and not seek another venue for the Blues Box.

Finally, on November 20, 2004, I arrived at the downtown Blues Box around 6:00 PM. There were party decorations hanging around the room. A large farewell cake sat on a table beside party finger foods. Joylyn and Yolanda were the main coordinators of the farewell party. Mom and Dad, who was getting around better and even got on stage to sing, were the honored guests. I played guitar and sang. We had one last jam to say goodbye to beloved Rockin' Tabby Thomas and his Tabby's Blues Box and Heritage Hall (number two) before the curtains closed on an era. The sounds of Tabby's: the Creole Hoodoo Parties, the rowdy musicians, the ringing guitars, the hand clapping, ambient chatter, glasses clattering, and the happy shuffling of dancing feet, made a lasting impression that is forever recorded in my memory. It's a sound of great joy. "Good night, everybody, good night," Dad and I sang, as we bid farewell to our most enthusiastic supporters.

MY WEST AFRICAN PILGRIMAGE

A YEAR LATER, still wounded by the loss of Tabby's, I experienced the tragedy of Hurricane Katrina striking New Orleans. "Baptized in Dirty Water," I was flooded out of my home. While displaced during Katrina's catastrophic aftermath, I became painfully aware that fragile remnants of my music and culture could be lost forever. Over the next ten years I spent every waking hour uncovering and piecing together little-known facts. While on tour I planned out extra days necessary to seek informants and journal as much as I could. I embarked on a personal pilgrimage: a serial road trip retracing the migration history of the blues, exploring its transformative impact on cities, cultures, and people across America and the world.

In February 2009, I landed at the Abuja Airport of Nigeria, full of wonderment. I was so excited to have been invited to perform concerts with my band and host a few workshops in West Africa. I didn't have a permanent lineup at the time, so David Arias, my trusted road manager and confidant, scouted around. David invited a rhythm section that worked the French Quarter circuit to accompany us: my longtime friend Darryl White and his bassist Johnathan "Cuju" Limjuco.

I saw the trip as an opportunity to fill in some blanks regarding my musical roots because, after all, I had been told ad nauseam that the origins of the blues could be found in West Africa. I had a desire to test the primitivism hypothesis of sociologists by visiting some of the more remote towns out in the countryside to break bread with musicians in an attempt to seek a connection perhaps to a forgotten music. I was not persuaded by the notion of an African origin of the blues, but to be fair in my research, I wanted tangible evidence to disprove such a widespread thesis. By going into the field with my portable recorder, I thought maybe I would stumble upon an old-time musician that might remember a bygone age.

Unfortunately, without armed escorts, there was no safe way I could go out to such isolated areas. Besides, I've always believed such sociological methods that purposely bypass advanced metropolises when seeking the origins of the blues were misguided. Folklorists believed the blues to be a primitive expression from an imagined savage people. Therefore, they would go digging in the jungles of Africa seeking clues. Conversely, if one believes the blues is an enlightened expression, from a civilized people, one wouldn't look in a jungle for clues—a place where you'd go to find wild animals—one would look for clues where civilization and high art is cultivated.

While hosting a workshop at the University of Abuja for local musicians and educators, I was asked to perform some folk-blues songs and share stories about Delta blues. Afterward, we had a question and answer session that proved to be quite revealing. I received the most intelligent questions from the gathering. They didn't simply ask me about the vintage of my guitar or did I play with this or that bluesman like America fans. They were more interested in blues thought. The philosophy behind the music. For the first time, I heard and saw my music through an African prism.

I had been sharing my personal story; demonstrating my hip-hop blues music with the audience. But when I began the Delta blues segment and told the story of how it is said to originate in West Africa, one university student in the audience stood up and said dismissively, "You'd starve to death in this country, performing THAT music." Instantly, I knew the gentleman was onto the Delta blues trope. He was right: neither he, nor I, nor any of his Nigerian contemporaries, could sell Delta blues and its Western Anglicized narrative to Nigerians as an art form with origins in West Africa—especially not to Nigerians educated on the subject.

I had always doubted the Anglo narrative. It was reaffirming in that setting to have its absurdity illuminated. I was asked a few leading questions, and out of habit, or convenience, I had given stock answers. Afterward, I felt irresponsible for doing so. I should have been better prepared. It was a learning experience. My knowledge of African culture, at succeeding workshop exchanges, was enhanced greatly as I became the student.

The following week we flew to Lagos, Nigeria, home to more than twenty million people on the coast of the Atlantic Ocean. At first glance, the skyline of Lagos rivaled that of Chicago, with numerous skyscrapers and bustling highways. But after settling into my hotel, I found it tropical, more like Miami, with white sandy beaches stretching as far as the eye could see.

On our first night in Lagos, we were escorted to several nightclubs outside the urban center to experience some rural music and culture. Some of the clubs we visited were country shacks filled with friendly people enjoying good music and food. The atmosphere reminded me of some tattered honky-tonk or juke joint back home. Bands I heard that night played mostly Americanized R&B, with Nigerian sensibilities. American songs were sung in English, others in regional languages.

Another night I managed to go club hopping in downtown Lagos to experience the local Saturday night popular music. One of the clubs I visited was hosting a CD release party for Danosaur, a flashy Nigerian rapper. Danosaur's music would have been categorized in America as gangster rap.

It was obvious to me that hip-hop wasn't indigenous to Africa. However, rap had become the expressive genre of choice for the post-independence generation. Hip-hop did not emerge out of any traditions on African soil but rather began as a direct imitation and appropriation of imported American rap.[13]

As we approached another club, people stood roped-off in a long line outside, waiting to get in. When I entered, the place was bumping. Laser lights flickered across the dance floor where a throng of attractive dark-skinned women and stylish swarthy men partied like they were in a blinged-out rap video. The party was sponsored by MTV Nigeria. In the VIP areas of the club a select few were practically bathing in high-dollar champagne. The whole vibe—the music, the atmosphere—was ultra-aspirational. American rap and hip-hop had become the modern-day high-life music of Nigeria.

Even though I couldn't understand the lyrics because they rapped for the most part in native tongues, I could understand the sentiment. Although the music was creative and moved me on a personal level, it had not yet, in my opinion, become Africanized. I left the club believing the challenge for Nigerian rappers going forward would be to maintain their popularity among fans infatuated with American music yet find their own voice within it.

Later in the week, while performing a concert at a theater in Lagos, I invited a talented singer, actress, and politician, Onyeka Onwenu, on stage to sing with me. She was soulful. Her spirit filled the room with a joyful familiarity only a hometown favorite could inspire.

West African musical culture—at least the music I'd encountered—had not been what I expected. Hip-hop poetry echoed in my ears. Rhymes about blood diamonds and getting paid, though very commercial, provided me an authentic African experience. We were told the blues began in West Africa, yet as a visiting blues musician, I found no real genealogy to my music.

After observing Nigeria's musical culture for myself, I returned to America more convinced than ever that the "truism" that blues origins are West African was a fallacy. But by no means did I come to this conclusion solely on my sojourn to Nigeria. Africa is a vast continent of more than fifty countries and hundreds of languages, cultures, and musical traditions. For a deeper understanding, I relied most heavily on Africans themselves. The historical knowledge gleaned from Nigerians whom I encountered at university workshops was enlightening. To balance my firsthand observations, I consulted the works of noted musicologists and historians.

Sam Charters, an acclaimed musicologist, traveled to Senegal, Gambia, Sierra Leone, and Mali in the 1970s seeking to prove his hypothesis that the blues began in West Africa, and moreover, that its antecedents were imported by those enslaved during the Atlantic slave trade. "I went to Africa to find the roots of the blues," wrote Charters in *The Roots of the Blues: An African Search* published in 1981. "It was clear," according to Charters, "that the two styles of music (West African and American blues) were different from each other."[14]

Charters had attempted to connect his primitive country blues thesis, first put forth in his 1959 book, *The Country Blues* (generally regarded as the first scholarly book on folk-blues), to a romanticized primitive jungle in Africa but failed. Charters ultimately concluded: "As a style, the blues represented something else. It was essentially a new kind of song that had begun with the new life in the American South."[15]

No one, not Sam Charters nor anyone else, has presented indisputable facts to support the claim that blues origins began in West Africa. Even so, the fallacy persists. The only way to destroy a myth is to deconstruct it, brick by brick, with reliable facts.

Ghanaian ethnomusicologist and composer J. H. Kwabena Nketia, born in 1921, drew a clear distinction between the musical folkways of traditional European and African societies. Nketia said, in his acclaimed 1974 book, *The Music of Africa*, "North Africa is inhabited by societies whose languages and cultures are very closely related to those of the Arab world of the Middle East, while the southern portion is dominated by settler populations from Europe. By extension, the music practiced by these societies belongs to stylistic families outside of Africa."[16]

In other words, Nketia, who attended the University of London on scholarship at age twenty-three, stated unequivocally that North Africa (including

Ancient Kemet) had an indigenous Black African culture prior to the Arab invasion.

Second, "Although the music of these cultures appears to have developed some characteristics of its own on the African continent," Nketia explained, "it belongs to the Oriental family of modal music. Its classical, folk and popular idioms are so distinct from those of the rest of Africa that it cannot, on stylistic grounds, be included in the family of indigenous African music."[17] It's important to understand, "The partition of Africa by Europe grouped indigenous cultures and tribes into disparate colonial borders, remaking Africa as it had been known to indigenous Africans for thousands of years," Nketia wrote. "The suppression of traditional African music and drumming by European Christian occupiers, had a tremendous effect on the indigenous music community's continuum."

J. H. Kwabena Nketia became a professor of African studies at UCLA in 1963, where he helped establish the Institute of Ethnomusicology and never argued that indigenous African music was the origin of the blues. And why would he? His focus was on the beautiful indigenous music of his homeland; what it was, what it wasn't, how, and why it was expressed in various community gatherings, including worship and celebrations.

Ultimately, what I found most fascinating, however, was the similarities of my high school's music program and that of the Ghanaians under colonial rule. Ghanaians were taught to play European music so they could entertain those who lived in the European forts and castles.[18] Indeed, "Traditional African music was forbidden in the classroom, the Church, and any respectable governmental institutions," Nketia said. "The suppression splintered those who held onto indigenous rituals and wholeheartedly rejected Western values, and those who eagerly assimilated." Similarly, the institution of slavery in the Americas splintered the African musical continuum further.

One of the strongest proponents of the African origin myth was Gerhard Kubik. As a longtime professor of cultural anthropology at the University of Vienna, Kubik published numerous articles, essays, and books on the subject. Kubik was a student of the clarinet as a teen. In the 1940s, he idolized Benny Goodman. Following the end of World War II, at around age eleven, he was introduced to Glenn Miller and American swing by way of US Air Force radio in Europe.

As a young man inspired by Britain's "discovery" and interest in African American blues guitar in the 1950s and '60s—which on closer examination was really only the infatuation of the roots of his British rock idols' inspirations, not the roots of Black American blues as such—Kubik is said to have grown so infatuated with the idea that the origins of the blues could be found in Africa that he hitchhiked as a young man in 1959 from his home in Vienna all the way to Africa.

Kubik returned home annually, convinced he would eventually find the grail of American blues in West Africa. Gerhard Kubik, Sam Charters, Alan Lomax, and numerous others spent the next forty years searching unsuccessfully in West Africa for the origins of American blues.

By the 1990s, the culmination of their published works led to the public's interest in a supposed West African blues genealogy. There was a demand in the roots music marketplace for an African artist to emerge as the embodiment of American blues roots. Guitarist Ry Cooder helped fill the void when, in 1994, he recorded *Talking Timbuktu* with a distinctive Malian farmer and guitarist named Ali Farka Touré, who, before the release of the album, was a little-known recording artist outside of Mali.

Ry Cooder, a multi-instrumentalist and accomplished slide guitarist from Los Angeles, at the age of seventeen recorded with the Rising Sons. The leader of the Rising Sons happened to be an ascending young African American blues star, Taj Mahal. The talented but short-lived band recorded their only album for Columbia Records in 1966.

By the 1970s and '80s, Ry Cooder had become an in-demand session guitarist. In 1984 Cooder was celebrated for his slide guitar work on a recording of Blind Willie Johnson's "Dark Was the Night, Cold Was the Ground," which appeared on the soundtrack of Wim Wenders's film *Paris, Texas*. He also provided slide guitar for the movie score of *Crossroads*, a 1986 movie based on Robert Johnson's Mississippi crossroads legend. Ry Cooder's world music interests and his slide guitar accomplishments made him the perfect producer to bring the West African roots of the blues hypothesis into fruition.

Back in 1995, as I recall, a lot of hype surrounded the release of *Talking Timbuktu*, especially in folkloric circles. I, like many Black Americans, had longed to have a meaningful connection with the motherland. So, I bought and listened to the recording upon its release. Hand percussions drove the modal acoustic guitar work that accompanied Ali Farka's rich vocals. I enjoyed the trancelike arrangements and the masterful acoustic tonality of the record.

However, I didn't hear the roots of my music. Instead, I thought Ali Farka Touré had been influenced by acoustic guitarists Robert Pete Williams and John Lee Hooker. Similarly, West African musicians would later absorb rap and hip-hop. But we wouldn't say hip-hop came from Africa.

In the 1990s, I took no strong position on the genealogy question one way or the other. Moreover, at the time, I had not visited West Africa. Therefore, I wasn't sure what to make of the hype culturally. Besides, I was busy writing and recording hip-hop blues and dealing with corporate record companies who were suppressing my own expression of the blues.

Nevertheless, as a consequence of Ry Cooder and Ali Farka Touré's international success, there was a flurry of collaborations. Louisiana-born blues guitar veteran Clarence "Gatemouth" Brown was a featured guest on the *Talking Timbuktu* album. Also, Taj Mahal, Ry Cooder's former bandmate, who had been featured on Ali Farka's previous album, *The Source*, released in 1992, continued his guest appearances with Ali Farka Touré. Gatemouth and Mahal were but a few of the many Black American artists to collaborate with Ali Farka Touré during the spike in interest.

TAJ MAHAL

EVER SINCE HE WAS a young college student in Boston, Taj Mahal had promoted the idea that the origins of the blues were West African. "As a kid," Mahal said, "I always felt connected to Africa, it was something I was very proud of. I was always looking for evidence of these common musical roots . . . but I was too young to know that what I was doing was called ethnomusicology."[19]

Taj Mahal, born Henry Saint Clair Fredericks, in 1942, grew up in Springfield, Massachusetts. He attended the University of Massachusetts with the idea of getting into agriculture or veterinary medicine, but instead he got involved in the burgeoning Cambridge folk scene at the legendary 47 Club in the early 1960s.[20] While a college student, Mahal eagerly pursued what had recently become known as country blues, a style of music that was scarce where he had grown up.

One day, Mahal was invited to join the Pioneer Valley Folksong Society on the campus of UMass. Even though he vaguely knew what folk music was, he jumped at the chance to join when he was told, erroneously, that blues was folk music. Taj said, "You didn't have to say any more after that."[21]

In the early 1960s, in Cambridge coffeehouses such as Club 47 where Taj Mahal got his start, the flawed conflation of a rustic folk-blues origin was beginning to blossom. To be clear, *folk* was defined as rural music orally passed from generation to generation by an illiterate people—in the case of Blacks, that meant it began with those enslaved. Yet the illiteracy of enslaved Africans in America was largely created by law. On the other hand, Appalachian folk music, that of preliterate "lower class" settlers from England, Scotland, and Ireland, despairingly referred to as "poor white trash," were not illiterate by force of law. Therefore, I would argue, illiteracy was a deeply flawed and condescending measurement for African American folk purity.

Mahal learned about the blues in an academic environment during the epoch of the folk-blues revival. He was indoctrinated by a loose-knit group of aspiring White blues musicians and researchers who fancied themselves blues aficionados. When Taj Mahal began performing, he was quickly embraced by the Harvard Square coffeehouse scene—a scene that was first incubated in Harvard classrooms back at the turn of the century. The American Folklore Society, founded in Cambridge in 1888, was the inspiration in 1907 for Harvard student John Lomax to form the Texas Folklore Society. The work of John Lomax and his Texas Folklore Society, led for a time by Dorothy "the Song-catcher" Scarborough, negatively infected scholars' and musicians' ideas of blues origins because it totally ignored its original Creole music philosophy. Jim Crow–era folklorists gave no consideration to blues thought. Indeed, Scarborough concluded "the colored mind is not essentially logical."[22] Yet their romanticized idea of blues as a savage expression of innate Negro primitivism was, subsequently, taught to many Black musicians in Massachusetts. The false equivalency made it into curriculums at historically Black colleges and subsequently miseducated Black students nationally.

White folk revivalists cajoled Black musicians of Taj Mahal's generation to perform the music in the Anglicized colonialist aesthetic. These Black musicians went on to influence younger generations of Black musicians who were not rooted in the authentic culture. I was keenly aware that participating in a market does not mean one has to fully embrace the ideology of that market. I mean, we all have to make a living. Nevertheless, the result was the establishment of an Anglicized blues origin fairy tale rooted in the belief of Negro inferiority.

Taj Mahal went on to become a multiple Grammy winner and an international success. His body of work has been eclectic but always rooted in folk-blues. Taj Mahal said, "It always amazed me that Black people never made the connection to the Newport Folk Festival with all the roots Black musicians there." He went on to say, "The direction I took was a pretty adventurous direction because there weren't that many young Black cats into the music. Now a lot more have started . . . maybe I helped open it up."[23] Taj Mahal was indeed a great influence on subsequent generations of Black musicians, including Grammy winner Keb' Mo'. Another Taj Mahal–influenced acoustic blues guitarist was Corey Harris, who went to Mali to record with Ali Farka Touré for "Feel Like Going Home," a documentary episode produced by Martin Scorsese.

FEEL LIKE GOING TO MALI

Corey Harris, born and raised in Denver, Colorado, earned a bachelor's degree in 1991 and moved to Napoleonville, Louisiana, to take a teaching job at a local school. While living in Louisiana he worked for a time in New Orleans at Tower Records, a vast record store in the French Quarter. While working at Tower Records, Corey Harris gained access to the history of recorded music. Prior to digital streaming, a record collector had to purchase a record in order to listen to it. However, because record stores received free promotional copies, store clerks such as Corey Harris could open nearly any album and play it in the store, then write it off as a promotional copy. In 1995, after a few years of study, Harris released his critically acclaimed debut album, *Between Midnight and Day*.

Like Taj Mahal, Corey Harris's early understanding of blues, ostensibly at least, was academic. Don't get it twisted, I'm a strong advocate for education. However, because cultural colonialism dominated the curriculum, I feared my music and its culture therewith was in danger of losing its very soul in academic circles.

The main problem, as I saw it, was the primitivist folk aesthetic applied to blues. By using such misguided eugenic assumptions as criteria, folklorists and sociologists were taught to avoid advanced urban cities in Africa. They didn't think to search through thousands of historical books in Timbuktu for clues. Neither did they consult with respected African museum curators nor university historians because illiteracy was one of their main criteria for authenticity. This strange behavior was consistent with how they eschewed New Orleans from the origin's narrative of the blues because of its urbane cosmopolitanism and instead looked to the twentieth-century cotton plantations of the Mississippi Delta for informants.

The West African to American blues origin hypothesis reached its zenith in Martin Scorsese's PBS documentary series *The Blues*. Of which, I played a small part. I portrayed "Blind Willie Johnson" in Wim Wenders's film *The Soul of a Man*. I performed my hip-hop blues with DJ Spin in the concert episode, but my hip-hop blues performance was edited out of the final film.

The seven-part series was supposed to be a companion series to Ken Burns's series *Jazz*, which, although it had its narrative problems, was a better blues documentary overall, especially regarding its origins, than Martin Scorsese's bloated and disjointed series. Scorsese hired six directors to direct seven episodes. But neither film captured the true essence of the blues. The bloated and confusing series was a lost opportunity for the culture.

In "Feel Like Going Home," the episode directed by Scorsese himself, Corey Harris performed with Ali Farka Touré and Habib Koité. In 2003, after the release of the series, Harris made a record titled *Mississippi to Mali*, which further explored the West African genealogy theory. As Harris lived for a time in New Orleans, the birthplace of the blues, I thought it ironic he looked to Africa for its origins.

In 2007, during a reflective radio interview broadcast by Afropop Worldwide, when asked about Ali Farka Touré, Gerhard Kubik said, "Popular formulations such as 'From Mali to Mississippi' are anathema to historical studies."

Such disdain coming from Kubik was surprising considering he had spent most of his life trying to prove the West African roots of the blues. Kubik said, "Marketing people came, and they tried to promote Ali Farka [sic] on the basis that he represented history. He represented connections to the blues . . . Ali Farka Touré was just one of many young men in Africa who" Kubik said, "during the last fifty, sixty years, have become interested in one or another form of African American music." Another scholar, Eric Charry, said plainly, blues was "unknown in Africa until imported from the United States."[24] It's refreshing that today a few academics are slowly starting to admit there never was any genealogy of blues origins in Africa.

Ali Farka Touré, like the Nigerian hip-hop musicians I encountered on my 2009 sojourn to Africa, near the end of his career was attempting to Africanize his American musical influences. By embracing the blues—he sung in dozens of languages—he was able to touch international audiences that wouldn't have related to his music otherwise. Afterward, Corey Harris said, "Ali would never call himself a bluesman. He's aware of the blues, but his own tradition is so strong in itself."[25] I commend Corey Harris. He may have exploited the brief market demand for a Mali connection, but didn't go full "Mali is the origin of blues" after all.

Gerhard Kubik said in retrospect, "All the talk about roots of the blues in Mali [was] just enough to satisfy the public's need for wild imagination." In his book *Africa and the Blues*, in the final chapter Kubik wearily confessed, "Blues is an African-American tradition that developed under certain social conditions on U.S. American soil in the Deep South. It did not develop as such in Africa."[26]

Too often in Western history, the African American story begins with slavery. In his book *They Came Before Columbus* professor Ivan Van Sertima of Rutgers University put forth evidence that challenged the narrative that the first Black Africans to sail to the Americas arrived on slave ships. There are many archeological facts to support his thesis that Black Africans had a presence in the Americas, in Mexico, prior to 1492.[27]

Van Sertima uncovered in his extensive research that ancient navigation, shipbuilding, and cultural analogies exist between Native Americans and Africans. Van Sertima studied the Mali master ships that had sailed in 1310 along with the sea expeditions of the Mandingo king in 1311, among others.[28]

West Africa, a center for international trade, easily had the wealth from gold and salt, along with the knowledge—Timbuktu was a great center of book knowledge—to build a fleet of ships and sail the seas. After all, the richest person in all history, richer than Bill Gates, the Rothschild family, and the Rockefellers, was Mansa Musa I who ruled West Africa's Malian Empire in the early 1300s. His wealth exceeded $400 billion when adjusted for today.[29]

Mansa Musa's predecessor reportedly built a fleet of ships, including supply boats, capable of sailing the ferocious torrents of the Atlantic. Musa had accumulated his vast wealth by exploiting his country's natural resources of books, salt, and gold. He bequeathed his fortune to his heirs following his death in 1331. However, his wealth and West Africa's wealth were depleted by civil wars and subsequently stolen by foreign invaders. The natural resources of West Africa were colonized by Europeans; its people were taken as prisoners of war and enslaved.

Technically speaking, the state of Mississippi didn't certify the Thirteenth Amendment, abolishing slavery, until February 7, 2013, 148 years after it was ratified. Technically, until then, Delta blues was slave music. By that measure, my authentic narrative could be considered a neo-slave narrative. But let's not get too technical. Why must the authentic narrative of my music and culture include Mansa Musa I, you might ask? Because it is important to provide some historical pretext to West Africa and the Atlantic slave trade. Moreover, such information helps to dispel the eugenic primitivist trope that for too long has been tethered to the blues and West Africa. The point is, medieval Anglo-Saxon Europe was in darkness and themselves overwhelmingly preliterate, while, prior to being conquered, colonized, and pillaged of its natural and human resources, the medieval kingdom of Mali possessed enormous wealth in gold and was a literate seafaring civilization. West African inferiority is a myth.

My sojourn to West Africa helped affirm for me that the African origin blues story that many Americans believe to be true, including most Blacks even today, is at best an outmoded Anglo-Saxon fairytale rooted in the White nationalist folklore of the Grimm Brothers—especially when you throw in the Mississippi crossroads myth. At its worst and most dangerous, it was a deliberate deception rooted in eugenics and racial science because blues expression was anathema to White Christian American supremacy.

The authentic narrative of my music and culture began in Old New Orleans where musicians made a conscious decision not to acquiesce. It was a break from conventionally held wisdom that European art and culture were superior. They smartly shrugged off harsh criticisms from both White and Black critics. The blues was neither a particular beat, chord sequence, nor pattern. It was a Creole musical philosophy. An enlightened idea that boldly questioned the tyranny of Western composition. Blues expression was anathema to White Christian American supremacy. "We build our temples for tomorrow, strong as we know how, and we stand on top of the mountain, free within ourselves." All in all, the blues was tailor-made to celebrate, unapologetically, the genius and resilience of the Black diaspora.

UNTITLED - A POEM

I have the anatomy of a human; arms, legs, hands, feet and a head with two eyes to see. But my damned eyes lie to me, disfiguring my perception. No, I am not blind. My vision is just fine. It's my vantage point, my lowly point of view if you will, which obstructs my vision. I see the world through an alien lens. I've come to the realization that my cognitive reality is not the accepted reality. I go through life as though I'm some sort of strange creature trapped in an alternate pragmatism, desperately seeking, but unable to find the exit door.

Indeed, red blood runs through my veins, yet I am not a man.

I have an overwhelming desire to be a man, of great talent and intellect with a full range of emotions, and yet, the only emotions I can convey, no matter how hard I try, are sadness and melancholy. For if I were fully human, I could experience happiness genuinely.

O' how I long to be truly happy!

The problem is I experience life downside up. I'm cursed you see? Doomed to move through life not as a human being, but as something other, without the sentience of man. I've been forced to put aside my own truth and adapt the mendacities of others, regardless of my own incredulity.

Imagine if you will, a flying bat, which not only roosts upside down but flys upside down as well, and you'll begin to see the picture. Though I'm known to be nocturnal, I am not a bat, nor do I have fangs or wings. My dilemma is that society sees me, and I see it, 180 degrees apart. The alienation I've experienced living life downside up has been vexing to say the least.

As an innocent child I thought I was human just like every other child. I trusted my eyes, my touch, my taste, smell and heart, unconditionally. In Sunday school I was taught every one of God's children was born upright with their minds closest to heaven, so that God's satellite transmission is unencumbered. Then, one day in my youth I came to realize my virtue had been cruelly interrupted on the way to becoming a buoyant young man. I suddenly realized a horrid downside up affliction had been cast upon me. Society had infected me, incident by dehumanizing incident, as if preparing me for some depraved shadowy mission.

The change was gradual. It came forth serendipitously, I thought. I was not yet in grade school when a beguiling whisperer first began to visit me. I can recall it vividly as if it were yesterday.

I was alone playing childish games in my backyard. I enjoyed pretending I was someone heroic. I found solace playing alone more so than with my childhood friends. I found it easy to entertain myself with the wonders of nature. While engaged in the frolics of my own little world, I faintly heard a luring call. It was an airy whisper blowing ever so gently, lightly rustling the trees in the yard. I thought I heard my name. But I wasn't sure. I looked up curiously with the naïve instincts of a doe eyed fawn whose little ears were aroused by a slight foreign noise, did someone just call my name, I wondered?

Quickly, I turned around to see who was there. Then suddenly it called from the opposite side of the yard. Again, I turned swiftly to see, but saw nothing. It was as if I stood playing hide-and-seek with a ghostly whisperer. Then, when I stilled myself, and fixed my ears to hear my name once more, the whisperer suddenly vanished, wafting away in the humid wind, but leaving behind what sounded like an eerie pentatonic chime of a guitar. The strum of which seemed a clandestine invitation. To what, I could only imagine.

This happened time and again as if the unseen whisperer was a lonely child seeking a playmate. But over time, as I grew and became aware of my affliction, I learned this was no friendless child, it had been a ghostly Machiavellian messenger.

I was an enigma. As I matured, I began asking questions about my origins. No one could say for sure. Such vagueness grew frustrating creating more questions. My inquisitiveness made those I questioned uncomfortable. So, I looked inward. I began to grapple with my downside upness. My lack of humanity.

If I am not human, I thought, then what am I?

I soon came to know one thing with great certainty, and that was, music was in my DNA. Therefore, I concluded, I am music. Soon after this enlightening self-discovery I learned that music, at its apex, has transformative powers.

It was this epiphany that rekindled my hope of transformation, of one day becoming fully human.

Nevertheless, I assure you my arrival was no immaculate conception. According to society it was just the opposite. Yes, I am music, but more specifically, I am the blues. Although I've been told my beginnings was a real phenomenon, I'm no musical God, such as Bacchus or Apollo. I've been described by society as grotesque, bestial and evil, closely resembling the characteristics affixed to Bes, the Egyptian God of music. In spite of that analogy, I am not a deity, at least not yet.

It seemed that before I could become fully human, and furthermore, achieve celestial status, I first needed to suffer. It seemed my fate was to somehow absolve the sins of man. I had to absolve; the alienated and the broken hearted, the sick and the poor, the murderers and the thieves, the adulteresses and the adulterers. I had to absolve life's winners, too; be they merciless or greedy, slaveholders or slave merchants, false prophets or non-believers. I also had to absolve the good and true among us. And lastly, I absolved those who deceived the whole world by hiding my true identity. I absolved you all.

For, I am the blues.

My blueness came as a shock. While getting dressed one morning I glanced my reflection in the mirror. I looked happy. I felt happiness. Yet the mirror deceived me. For as soon as I stepped outside, I was quickly reminded by the outside world, that I couldn't have been genuinely happy. Society convinced me I was really sad and depressed. I'd been cast into an absurd downside up alternate reality for which there seemed no escape. In turn, when I'd get depressed, society said I was really happy, but I was really sad. At times I felt like a circus clown whose painted frown masked his joy from audiences. The delirium this quandary caused was enough to make me wish I were faceless. It was then I realized I'd been robbed of my once fully human potential.

I suffered further. Whenever I experienced and exhibited great pain, audiences derived great pleasure from my wailing. What's more, the pleasures they experienced were deemed innocent and clean. But, on the contrary, whenever I experienced great pleasure, society convinced me that my pleasure was wickedly immoral. I was critically reminded that my joy was not joyful after all. Society declared my ecstasy absolute wretchedness. At times the confusion caused me to be so dizzyingly mixed-up I didn't know if I was downside up or upside down. To move through life this way has been a most strange dichotomy. But now, at long last, it's a nightmare from whence I am finally awakening.

After decades of suffering, I am gaining a renewed consciousness. My milieu, which seemed a cross too heavy to bear in my youth, has become the source of my fortitude and self-discovery. In my quest to complete my ascendancy out of darkness, I was compelled to record my story. From its perceived primitive beginnings, to its cultured eminence, it has been a most weird and wondrous journey.

Sure, you may think you already know the story of the blues. You may feel you've heard it all before. But it's all been from the Machiavellian right side up viewpoint. By sharing with you for the first time my authentic story, it is my great hope that in the end, you will finally decipher my smile, and see me, hear me, and speak of me, as I truly am.

CODA

It was New Year's Eve, December 31, 2013. As the sun was setting over Baton Rouge, I walked into the nursing room carrying my acoustic Gibson J45 just as I had on many occasions, to ease his pain with a song and conversation. He was alone. It had been a few years now since Mom transitioned. On his good days, he'd remember me; on bad days, he only pretended to, out of kindness. I sat in a chair next to his bed. He was on an IV, unresponsive. But I knew in there somewhere was my old man.

I pulled out my guitar and told him about my family, how Dylan was growing up fast. I shared a funny story about a recent gig. Told him several fans had asked about him and wished him well. I told him I'd been working up a new arrangement of a tune, Billie Holiday's "Good Morning Heartache," based on Diana Ross's *Lady Sings the Blues Live* featuring Ron Carter, and I wanted him to be the first to hear it. I played the opening chord and sang:

Good morning heartache
You old gloomy sight
Good morning heartache
Thought we said goodbye last night
I tossed and turned til it seemed you had gone
But here you are with the dawn

Dad just lay there. Tube in nose, breathing, but nearly lifeless. Tears ran down my cheeks. I didn't wipe them away. I knew he could hear me. I mean, I needed to believe Dad could hear me. I sang deeper:

Stop haunting me now
Can't shake you nohow

In the small window above his bed, light flashed. The faint sounds of early evening fireworks burst, popped, and crackled in the background.

The next forty-eight hours were a blur. I was onstage with my band—drummer Jeff Mills and bassist Danny Infante—sweating under the lights, playing my Stratocaster and singing at Blues Alley in Georgetown, Washington, DC. It was the first of eight shows. It had become an annual tradition, me booked at Blues Alley for the week to kick off the New Year. On January 1, before leaving home, I learned Dad had passed away soon in the morning after I played for him, those few special notes, for the last time.

NOTES

Author's Note
1 Abbe Niles, "Ballads, Songs and Snatches: Jazz, 1928, An Index Expurgatorius," 1928.

Prologue
1 George Goodman, "Miles Davis: 'I Just Pick Up My Horn and Play,'" *New York Times*, June 28, 1981, www.nytimes.com/1981/06/28/arts/miles-davis-i-just-pick -up-my-horn-and-play.html.
2 Chris Smith, *The Whole Okra: A Seed to Stem Celebration* (White River Junction, VT: Chelsea Green, 2019), 53.
3 Robin J. DeAngelo, *White Fragility: Why It's So Hard for White People to Talk About Racism* (Boston: Beacon Press, 2018), 15.
4 Bob Dylan said guitarist Bruce Langhorne was one of his inspirations. Allen Ginsberg and many Dylanologists say Dylan began writing the song after hanging out at the Mardi Gras celebration in New Orleans in 1964. *See* A. Scaduto, "Bob Dylan: An Intimate Biography, Part Two," *Rolling Stone*, June 25, 2018. Retrieved July 13, 2020, from https://www.rollingstone.com/music/music-news /bob-dylan-an-intimate-biography-part-two-237760; Richard Clayton, *The Life of a Song: 'Mr Tambourine Man.'* July 25, 2016, www.ft.com/content/f8ec51da -501a-11e6-8172-e39ecd3b86fc.

1. My Culture
1 Mark Twain, *The Adventures of Huckleberry Finn* (New York: Signet Classic, 2013).
2 Twain, *Huckleberry Finn*.
3 Janelle Collins, ed., *Defining the Delta* (Fayetteville: University of Arkansas Press, 2015), 11.
4 Mark Twain, *Life on the Mississippi* (New York: Signet Classics, 2009) 2.
5 Collins, *Defining the Delta*, 12.
6 Joe Trotter, Earl Lewis, and Tera Hunter, eds. *The African American Urban Experience: Perspectives from the Colonial Period* (New York: Palgrave Macmillan, 2004), 60.

7   Alan Lomax, *Mister Jelly Roll: The Fortunes of Jelly Roll Morton, New Orleans Creole and "Inventor of Jazz"* (Berkeley: University of California Press, 2001), 137.

8   "A River Steamer Burned; A Great Calamity Narrowly Averted," *New York Times*, November 19, 1883.

9   "A River Steamer Burned."

10   Rosalie David, *Religion and Magic in Ancient Egypt* (New York: Penguin Books, 2002), 7.

11   David Brion Davis, *Inhuman Bondage: The Rise and Fall of Slavery in the New World* (New York: Oxford University Press, 2006), 102.

12   The Australian Museum, "Funerals in ancient Egypt," November 21, 2018, https://australianmuseum.net.au/learn/cultures/international-collection/ancient-egyptian/funerals-in-ancient-egypt.

13   Cheikh Anta Diop, *The African Origin of Civilization: Myth or Reality* (Chicago: Lawrence Hill Books, 1974), 1.

14   Herodotus, G. C. Macaulay, trans., *An Account of Egypt* (Harvard Classics), 16.

15   Diop, *African Origin*, 1.

16   Ibram X. Kendi, *Stamped from the Beginning: The Definitive History of Racist Ideas in America* (Ne), 6.

17   Craig Steven Wilder, *Ebony and Ivy: Race, Slavery, and the Troubled History of America's Universities* (New York: Bloomsbury, 2013), 84.

18   Wilder, *Ebony and Ivy*, 75.

19   Wilder, *Ebony and Ivy*, 122.

20   Wilder, *Ebony and Ivy*, 230.

21   Edward Gibbon, *The History of the Decline and Fall of the Roman Empire* (London, 1776–1788).

22   Tacitus, Thomas Gordon, trans., *Germany* (Harvard Classics), 118.

23   Simson R. Najovits, *Egypt, Trunk of the Tree: A Modern Survey of an Ancient Land* (New York: Algora, 2004), 55.

24   Gibbon, *Decline and Fall*, 134.

25   Gibbon, *Decline and Fall*, 134.

26   https://en.wikipedia.org/wiki/Single-reed_instrument, citing A. R. Rice, *The Baroque Clarinet* (New York: Oxford University Press,1992).

27   Rice, *Baroque Clarinet*.

28   Jane Landers, *Black Society in Spanish Florida* (Urbana: University of Illinois Press, 1999),11.

29   Gerald Horne, *The Counter-Revolution of 1776: Slave Resistance and the Origins of the United States of America* (New York: New York University Press, 2016), 88; Landers, *Black Society*, 46.

30   Freddi Williams Evans, *Congo Square: African Roots in New Orleans* (Lafayette: University of Louisiana at Lafayette Press, 2011), 70.

31   Benjamin Henry Boneval Latrobe, *Impressions Respecting New Orleans, Diary and Sketches, 1818–1820* (New York: Columbia University Press, 1951), 49–50.

32   French and Spanish rulers of Louisiana kept detailed records of the enslaved. Details historians thought were lost to history, such as names, their birthplaces in Africa, their skills, their health, and in many cases a description of their

personality and degree of rebelliousness. New Orleans historian Gwendolyn Midlo Hall spent decades searching through decaying colonial courthouse records from Spanish Louisiana, as well as in archives in Spain, France, and Texas aided by several research assistants. Hall translated and computerized the largest collection of individual slave information ever assembled. *See also*, David Firestone, "Identity Restored to 100,000 Louisiana Slaves," *New York Times*, July 30, 2000.

33 Gary Hartman, "Música Tejana: Mexican American Music in the Southwest," in *The History of Texas Music* (College Station: Texas A&M University Press, 2008), 21.

34 Reynold Alleyne Nicholson, *A Literary History of the Arabs* (Alpha Editions: 2019), 418.

35 Salma Khadra Jayyusi, ed., *The Legacy of Muslim Spain* (New York: E. J. Brill, 2010), 117.

36 Ivan Van Sertima, *The Golden Age of the Moor* (New Brunswick: Transaction Publishers, 1992), 267.

37 Jayyusi, *Legacy of Muslim Spain*, 117.

38 Robert W. Lebling Jr., "Ziryab, Poet of Cordoba," Cities of Light, http://www.islamicspain.tv/Arts-and-Science/flight_of_the_blackbird.htm.

39 Farah Halime, "The Martha Stewart of A.D. 800 Was an Arabic Dude," OZY, August 31, 2015, accessed April 28, 2018, https://www.ozy.com/flashback/the-martha-stewart-of-ad-800-was-an-arabic-dude/62166.

40 "The Louisiana Slave Database," Whitney Plantation, accessed 2015, https://www.whitneyplantation.org/the-louisiana-slave-database. Note: Authored work of Gwendolyn Midlo Hall on 107,000 Louisiana slaves whose African origins were clearly identified between 1719 and 1820.

41 Maurice J. Summerfield, *The Classical Guitar: Its Evolution, Players and Personalities Since 1800* (UK: Ashley Mark, 2002).

42 Hartman, "Música Tejana."

43 Tim Brookes, *Guitar: An American Life* (New York: Grove Press, 2005),18.

44 Jane Landers, *Atlantic Creoles in the Age of Revolutions* (Boston: University of Harvard Press, 2010), 34.

45 Landers, *Black Society*, 8.

46 Landers, *Black Society*, 15.

47 Landers, *Black Society*, 139–140.

48 Wilder, *Ebony and Ivy*, 46.

49 Horne, *Counter-Revolution of 1776*, 88.

50 Horne, *Counter-Revolution of 1776*, 89.

51 Gwendolyn Midlo Hall, "The Formation of Afro-Creole Culture," in *Creole New Orleans: Race and Americanization*, ed. Arnold R. Hirsch and Joseph Logsdon (Baton Rouge: Louisiana State University Press, 1992), 79.

52 Hall, "The Formation of Afro-Creole Culture," 79.

53 Hartman, "Música Tejana," 21.

54 Nancy Isenberg, *White Trash: The 400-Year Untold History of Class in America* (New York: Viking, 2016), 13.

55 I Isenberg, *White Trash*, 13.

56 Declaration of the Rights of Man and of the Citizen (Article 11).

57 Ethan Malveaux, *The Color Line: A History: The Story of Europe and the African, from the Old World to the New* (Xlibris, 2015), 399.

58 Judith P. Zinsser, *Emilie Du Chatelet: Daring Genius of the Enlightenment* (New York: Penguin, 2007), 130.

59 Davis, *Inhuman Bondage*, 108.

60 Davis, *Inhuman Bondage*, 107.

61 Davis, *Inhuman Bondage*, 103.

62 Davis, *Inhuman Bondage*, 123.

63 Hall, "Formation of Afro-Creole Culture," 69.

64 Hall, "Formation of Afro-Creole Culture," 63.

65 Emily Berquist, "Early Anti-Slavery Sentiment in the Spanish Atlantic World, 1765–1817" *Slavery & Abolition* 31, no. 2 (2010): 181–205, https://doi.org/10.1080/01440391003711073.

66 Joseph G. Tregle Jr., "Creoles and Americans," in *Creole New Orleans: Race and Americanization* (Baton Rouge: Louisiana State University Press, 1992), 134.

67 Angel S., Storyville New Orleans, http://www.storyvilledistrictnola.com/theatres.html.

68 W. E. B. Du Bois, *Black Reconstruction in America, 1860–1880* (New York: Simon and Schuster, 1998), 154.

69 Eileen Southern, *The Music of Black Americans: A History* (New York: W. W. Norton, 1971).

70 "Pierre Bélain, sieur d'Esnambuc," Encyclopædia Britannica, https://www.britannica.com/biography/Pierre-Belain-sieur-dEsnambuc.

71 Edward E. Baptist, *The Half Has Never Been Told: Slavery and the Making of American Capitalism* (New York: Basic Books, 2014), 43.

72 Alain Guédé, *Monsieur De Saint-George: Virtuoso, Swordsman, Revolutionary: A Legendary Life Rediscovered*, trans. Gilda M. Roberts (New York: Picador, 2003).

73 Guédé, *Monsieur De Saint-George*, 149.

74 Guédé, *Monsieur De Saint-George*, 141.

75 Guédé, *Monsieur De Saint-George*, 140.

76 Guédé, *Monsieur De Saint-George*, 132.

77 Guédé, *Monsieur De Saint-George*, 132.

78 Gabriel Banat, *The Chevalier de Saint-Georges: Virtuoso of the Sword and the Bow* (Sheffield, MA: Pendragon Press, 2006), 162; Guédé, *Monsieur De Saint-George*, 111.

79 Guédé, *Monsieur De Saint-George*, 120–121.

80 Guédé, *Monsieur De Saint-George*, 133.

81 Guédé, *Monsieur De Saint-George*, 121.

82 Stanley Sadie, *Mozart: The Early Years, 1756–1781* (New York: Norton, 2006) 452–453.

83 Guédé, *Monsieur De Saint-George*, 98.

84 Sadie, *Mozart*, 454–455.

85 Sadie, *Mozart*, 455.

86 Sadie, *Mozart*, 459.

87 Banat, *Chevalier de Saint-Georges*, 171

88 Banat, *Chevalier de Saint-Georges*.

89 Banat, *Chevalier de Saint-Georges*, 174.

90 Banat, *Chevalier de Saint-Georges*, 174.

91 Sadie, *Mozart*.

92 Philip Kennicott, "A Challenge for the Arts: Stop Sanitizing and Show the Great Works as They Were Created," *Washington Post*, October 4, 2014.

93 Banat, *Chevalier de Saint-Georges*, 166.

94 David B. Gaspar and David P. Geggus, eds., *A Turbulent Ttime: The French Revolution and the Greater Caribbean* (Bloomington: Indiana University Press, 1997), 60.

95 The Jacobins were members of an influential political club during the French Revolution. They were radical revolutionaries who plotted the downfall of the king and the rise of the French Republic.

96 Gwendolyn Midlo Hall, *Africans in Colonial Louisiana: The Development of Afro-Creole Culture in the Eighteenth Century* (Baton Rouge: Louisiana State University Press, 1992), 373.

97 Hall, *Africans in Colonial Louisiana*, 344.

98 Hall, *Africans in Colonial Louisiana*, 357.

99 Encyclopedia of World Biography, "Chevalier de Saint-George Joseph Boulogne Biography," https://www.notablebiographies.com/supp/Supplement-Mi-So /Chevalier-de-Saint-George-Joseph-Boulogne.html.

100 Encyclopedia of World Biography, "Chevalier de Saint-George."

101 C. L. R. James, *The Black Jacobins: Toussaint L'Ouverture and the San Domingo Revolution* (New York: Vintage, 1989).

102 Du Bois, *Black Reconstruction*, 451.

103 Hall, "The Formation of Afro-Creole Culture," 86.

104 Le Page du Pratz, *The History of Louisiana*, Joseph G. Tregle Jr., ed. (Baton Rouge: Louisiana State University Press, 1975).

105 Hall, "The Formation of Afro-Creole Culture," 86.

106 Tregle, "Creoles and Americans."

107 Arnold Hirsch and Joseph Logsdon, eds., *Creole New Orleans: Race and Americanization* (Baton Rouge: Louisiana State University Press, 1992).

108 Sally McKee, *The Exile's Song: Edmond Dédé and the Unfinished Revolutions of the Atlantic World* (New Haven, CT: Yale University Press, 2017), 58.

109 McKee, *Exile's Song*, 13.

110 Du Bois, *Black Reconstruction*, 471.

111 Tregle, "Creoles and Americans," 149.

112 Tregle, "Creoles and Americans," 149.

113 Du Bois, *Black Reconstruction*, 35.

114 Nick Douglas, "Know Your Black History: Deconstructing The Quadroon Ball," AFROPUNK, October 27, 2016, https://afropunk.com/2016/10/know-your -black-history-deconstructing-the-quadroon-ball.

115 Tregle, "Creoles and Americans," 134.

116 In the eighteenth century French Acadians were expelled from parts of Canada and Nova Scotia by the British. They resettled in the bayous and prairies of southwest Louisiana. Cajuns developed their own blues made popular throughout the United States by accordionist Clifton Chenier (1925–1987), the "King of Zydeco." A pioneering giant of Acadian zydeco named Amédé Ardoin established the Cajun connection to New Orleans blues. In "Blues de Basile" and "Les Blues de voyage," Amédé is heard transposing New Orleans blues guitar and piano for the French accordion. While Cajuns eagerly assimilated into White Anglo culture during the Jim Crow era, more recently they've begun to embrace the term Creole, intermingling many of their traditions with that of African Creoles. John Broven, *South to Louisiana: The Music of the Cajun Bayous* (Gretna, LA: Pelican, 1987), 103.

117 Du Bois, *Black Reconstruction*, 468.

118 Du Bois, *Black Reconstruction*, 471

119 Du Bois, *Black Reconstruction*, 469.

120 Du Bois, *Black Reconstruction*, 469.

2. The Authentic Narrative

1 Alan Lomax, *Mister Jelly Roll: The Fortunes of Jelly Roll Morton, New Orleans Creole and "Inventor of Jazz"* (New York: Duell, Sloan and Pearce, 1950), 20.

2 Lomax, *Mister Jelly Roll*, 21.

3 Dan Vernhettes and Peter Hanley, "The Desdunes Family," *Jazz Archivist* XXVII (2014).

4 Vernhettes and Hanley, "The Desdunes Family."

5 Vernhettes and Hanley, "The Desdunes Family."

6 Vernhettes and Hanley, "The Desdunes Family."

7 Rodolphe Lucien Desdunes, *Our People and Our History: Fifty Creole Portraits*, Dorothea Olga McCants, trans. (Baton Rouge: Louisiana State University Press, 2001).

8 Vernhettes and Hanley, "The Desdunes Family."

9 Joseph Longsdon and Caryn Cossé Bell, "The Americanization of Black New Orleans, 1850–1900," in *Creole New Orleans: Race and Americanization*, ed. Arnold R. Hirsch and Joseph Logsdon (Baton Rouge: Louisiana State University Press, 1992), 203.

10 Vernhettes and Hanley, "The Desdunes Family."

11 William Dukes Lewis, *Marching to the Beat of a Different Drum: Performance Traditions of Historically Black College and University Marching Bands* (Chapel Hill: University of North Carolina, 2003).

12 Donald M. Marquis, *In Search of Buddy Bolden: First Man of Jazz* (Baton Rouge: Louisiana State University Press, 1978), 92.

13 Gary Krist, *Empire of Sin* (New York: Crown, 2015).

14 Marquis, *In Search of Buddy Bolden*, 99.

15 Marquis, *In Search of Buddy Bolden*, 57.

16 John McCusker, *Creole Trombone. Kid Ory and the Early Years of Jazz* (Jackson: University of Mississippi Press, 2012).

17 Nat Shapiro and Nat Hentoff, *Hear Me Talkin' to Ya: The Story of Jazz as Told by the Men Who Made It* (New York: Dover Publications, 1966).

18 Marquis, *In Search of Buddy Bolden*, 57–58.

19 Marquis, *In Search of Buddy Bolden*, 100.

20 Charlie Love, "Buddy Bolden," on *Music of New Orleans, Vol. 4: The Birth of Jazz* (Folkways Records FW02464 / FA 2464, 1959), https://folkways.si.edu/music-of-new-orleans-vol-4-the-birth-of-jazz/ragtime/album/smithsonian.

21 Marquis, *In Search of Buddy Bolden*, 131.

22 John Adams and Abigail Adams, *My Dearest Friend: Letters of Abigail and John Adams*, ed. Margaret A. Hogan and C. James Taylor (Cambridge, MA: Belknap, 2007).

23 Gerald Horne, *The Counter-Revolution of 1776: Slave Resistance and the Origins of the United States of America* (New York: NYU Press, 2016).

24 Adams and Adams, *My Dearest Friend*, 124–125.

25 Harlow Giles Unger, *John Quincy Adams* (Boston: Da Capo, 2012).

26 John Quincy Adams wasn't an abolitionist, but he defended the *Amistad* rebellion case. Adams had formally retired from public life in 1840 when he decided to take on a Supreme Court case in order to represent a group of fifty-three Africans who were bound to be sold into slavery.

27 Longsdon and Bell, "The Americanization of Black New Orleans, 1850–1900."

28 Longsdon and Bell, "The Americanization of Black New Orleans, 1850–1900," 204.

29 Longsdon and Bell, "The Americanization of Black New Orleans, 1850–1900," 207.

30 Longsdon and Bell, "The Americanization of Black New Orleans, 1850–1900," 211.

31 Marcus Christian, "The First African Baptist Church of New Orleans, 1817–1842" (Typescript in Marcus Christian Papers, University of New Orleans), 6–8. The quotation is from R. W. Coleman, "Church Anniversary of the First African Baptist Church," quoted in Marcus Christian, "The Negro Church in Louisiana" (Chapter in MS WPA History of the Negro in Louisiana, in Christian Papers). Quoted Longsdon and Bell, "The Americanization of Black New Orleans, 1850–1900," 211–212.

32 Some sources say Jelly Roll Morton was born 1890. His death certificate stated his birth as 1889. His half sister and he himself said the year of his birth was 1885.

33 Lomax, *Mister Jelly Roll*.

34 The quote was in Jelly Roll's handwriting from a fragment of an unfinished manuscript written by Jelly Roll Morton in 1938 at Roy J. Carew's suggestion.

35 St. Sukie de la Croix, *Chicago Whispers: A History of LGBT Chicago before Stonewall* (Madison: University of Wisconsin Press, 2012), 104.

36 Lomax, *Mister Jelly Roll*, 43.

37 Lomax, *Mister Jelly Roll*, 43–45.

38 David Ehrenstein, "Gay New Orleans 101," *Advocate*, October 11, 2005, 50.

39 The original blue, risqué lyrics to Little Richard's 1950s hit "Tutti Frutti," recorded at Cosimo Matassa's J & M Studio in New Orleans in September 1955, before the lyrics were cleaned up for the session, is what comes to my mind.

40 Lomax, *Mister Jelly Roll*, 104.

41 Lomax, *Mister Jelly Roll*.

42 Philip Pastras, *Dead Man Blues: Jelly Roll Morton Way Out West* (Berkeley: University of California Press, 2001), 19.

43 Lomax, *Mister Jelly Roll*, 113.

44 Lomax, *Mister Jelly Roll*, 41.

45 Howard Reich and William Gaines, *Jelly's Blues: The Life, Music, and Redemption of Jelly Roll Morton* (Cambridge, MA: Da Capo, 2003), 41

46 Stephen Kinzer, "From Oblivion to Ovation: An Opera Right Out of the Harlem Renaissance," *New York Times* Archive, December 28 2002, www.nytimes.com/2002/12/28/arts/from-oblivion-to-ovation-an-opera-right-out-of-the-harlem-renaissance.html.

47 Howard Reich and William Gaines, "A Jazz Man's Revival," *Chicago Tribune*, December 14, 1999, https://www.chicagotribune.com/news/ct-xpm-1999-12-14-9912170023-story.html.

48 Lomax, *Mister Jelly Roll*, 260.

49 Frederic Ramsey and Charles Edward Smith, *Jazzmen* (New York: Harcourt, Brace, 1939), 25. *See also* Bunk Johnson's *Billboard* magazine obituary July 16, 1949: "A legendary jazz figure, he began his career in New Orleans. He first played with Adam Oliver's band, but, unable to read, he switched to Buddy Bolden's band, which improvised. Johnson was soon recognized as the originator of the New Orleans style of jazz trumpet playing.
"During the Spanish-American and the First World wars he directed Army bands overseas. In 1931 Johnson lost his teeth and dropped out of music until he was rediscovered about eight years later by William Russell, who arranged to get him false teeth."

50 Louis Armstrong, *Louis Armstrong, In His Own Words: Selected Writings,* ed. Thomas Brothers (Oxford: Oxford University Press, 1999), 40–41.

51 Charles Suhor, "Jazz in New Orleans in the 1960s," *Jazz Archivist* X, (May–December 1995): 1–2.

52 Michael White, "Dr. Michael White: The Doc Paulin Years," *Jazz Archivist* XXIII (2010).

53 Ramsey and Smith, *Jazzmen*, 84.

54 Ramsey and Smith, *Jazzmen*, 78.

55 White, "Dr. Michael White."

56 Garry Boulard, *The Big Lie: Hale Boggs, Lucille May Grace, and Leander Perez in 1951* (Gretna, LA: Pelican, 2001).

57 David Van Holtby, *Forty-Seventh Star: New Mexico's Struggle for Statehood* (Norman: University of Oklahoma Press, 2016).

58 Larry Birnbaum, *Before Elvis: The Prehistory of Rock 'n' Roll* (Lanham, MD: Scarecrow, 2013).

59 McCusker, *Creole Trombone*.

60 Al Jolson was a blackface-performing star who starred in the first talking picture in 1927, *The Jazz Singer*. The movie's success helped to cement *jazz* as the marketing term for the evolving blues of the 1920s and '30s.

61 Marc Myers, *Why Jazz Happened* (Berkeley: University of California Press, 2013).

62 Katherine M. Maskell, "Who Wrote Those 'Livery Stable Blues'?: Musical Ownership in Hart et al. v. Graham." (Edward F. Hayes Graduate Research Forum 26, 2012).

63 Karl Koenig, *Jazz in Print (1856–1929): An Anthology of Early Source Readings in Jazz History* (Sheffield, MA: Pendragon, 2002), 120–21.

64 "Blues Are Blues, Court Decrees, and No One Wins," *Chicago Daily Tribune*, Saturday, October 13, 1917, 13

65 "Court Findings," Series 8, Folder 2, Item 4, 2–3, The Dominic "Nick" LaRocca Collection, Hogan Jazz Archive, Tulane University, New Orleans, LA.

66 Michael J. West, "Trumpeting Alternative Facts," *Slate*, February 23, 2017, Retrieved March 05, 2021, https://slate.com/culture/2017/02/nick-larocca-and-the-first-jazz-record-at-100.html.

67 The *New York Clipper* reviewing the vaudeville act of Freddie Keppard and the Creole Band, December 11, 1915: "THAT CREOLE BAND of six pieces, cornet guitar, clarinet fiddle, and bass violin played a rather ragged selection for a starter, the clarinet being particularly strong for comedy effect. The old darky whom they were serenading responded by singing 'Old Black Joe' and the band chimed in with fine harmony both instrumentally and vocally. The playing of some ragtime melodies worked the old darkey to dancing pitch, and he did pound those boards until the kinks in his knees reminded him of his age. Lots of bows, an encore, more bows, and another encore stamped this offering O. K."

68 Sam Charters, *A Trumpet around the Corner: The Story of New Orleans Jazz* (Jackson: University Press of Mississippi, 2008), 109.

69 Ramsey and Smith, *Jazzmen*, 112.

70 Henry Louis Gates and Evelyn Brooks Higginbotham, eds., *Harlem Renaissance Lives* (New York: Oxford University Press, 2009), 259.

71 McCusker, *Creole Trombone*, 146.

72 In the original article the word *jazz* was used here, not *blues*. Anglo New Orleans officials adopted the name *jazz*—when referring to the blues—from outraged northern newspaper editors and music critics. The original Creole term for the music was *blues*, therefore, for clarity, I inserted the proper historical term the original creators used in their own words—the blues. After all, they were the authorities on their music. It must be understood that in 1918, King Oliver, Jelly Roll Morton, and Louis Armstrong called the music they played blues. Nevertheless, around this time the word *jazz* became interchangeable with the word *blues* in Chicago and New York City. Consequently, the Creole vernacular and Creole etymology of the word *blues* was lost in translation outside of New Orleans. *Blues* also became a pejorative term the music publishing industry couldn't sell to mainstream respectable audiences. Therefore, jazz, swing, and other synonyms were used instead of blues.

73 "Wish I Can Shimmy Like My Sister Kate" was a popular blues song written by Clarence Williams and his publishing partner, Armand J. Piron. It was published in 1919.

74 Perry Bradford, *Born with the Blues: Perry Bradford's Own Story: True Story of the Pioneering Blues Singers and Musicians in the Early Days of Jazz* (New York: Oak Publications, 1965), 95.

75   Barry Mazor, *Ralph Peer and the Making of Popular Roots Music* (Chicago: Chicago Review Press, 2014), 115.

76   Philip R. Ratcliffe, *Mississippi John Hurt: His Life, His Times, His Blues* (Jackson: University Press of Mississippi, 2018), 50.

77   James Sallis, *The Guitar Players: One Instrument and Its Masters in American Music* (Lincoln: University of Nebraska Press, 1994), 37.

78   Bill Malone and David Stricklin, *Southern Music, American Music* (Lexington: University of Kentucky Press, 2003).

79   Elijah Wald, *Escaping the Delta: Robert Johnson and the Invention of the Blues* (New York: HarperCollins, 2004), 86.

80   W. E. B. Du Bois, *Black Reconstruction in America 1860–1880* (New York: The Free Press, 1998), 431.

81   John W. Work III, Lewis Wade Jones, Samuel C. Adams Jr., *Lost Delta Found: Rediscovering the Fisk University-Library of Congress Coahoma County Study, 1941–1942* (Nashville: Vanderbilt University Press, 2005), 304.

82   John C. Willis, *Forgotten Time: The Yazoo-Mississippi Delta after the Civil War* (Charlottesville: University of Virginia Press, 2000).

83   Work, Jones, and Adams, *Lost Delta Found,* 305.

84   John C. Hudson, "The Yazoo-Mississippi Delta as Plantation," Fire Ecology Conference Proceedings 16, (1979), 70, https://talltimbers.org/wp-content/uploads/2018/09/66-Hudson1979_op.pdf.

85   *The Century Illustrated Monthly Magazine* 79: 379.

86   Clyde Woods and Ruth Wilson Gilmore, *Development Arrested: The Blues and Plantation Power in the Mississippi Delta* (London: Verso, 2017).

87   Woods and Gilmore, *Development Arrested.*

88   Paul Lewinson, *Race, Class, and Party: A History of Negro Suffrage and White Politics in the South* (New York: Grosset and Dunlap, 1965).

89   New York Public Library, *The New York Public Library African American Desk Reference* (New York: John Wiley and Sons, 1999).

90   Hiram Tong, "The Pioneers of Mound Bayou," *The Century Magazine* 79 (1910): 396, https://www.google.com/books/edition/The_Century_Illustrated_Monthly_Magazine/o4_d+monthly+magazine+Mound+bayou&pg=PA390&printsec=frontcover.

91   Minor Ferris Buchanan, *Holt Collier: His Life, His Roosevelt Hunts, and the Origin of the Teddy Bear* (Jackson, MS: Centennial Press, 2002).

92   Buchanan, *Holt Collier.*

93   Lottie Armistead, "Holt Collier Materials," in George P. Rawick, ed., *The American Slave: A Composite Autobiography* (Westport, CT: Greenwood Press, 1979), 447–448.

94   Buchanan, *Holt Collier.*

95   History.com Editors, "Eugenics," History.com, November 15, 2017, Retrieved December 10, 2020, https://www.history.com/topics/germany/eugenics.

96   History.com Editors, "Eugenics."

97   David Evans, *Big Road Blues: Tradition and Creativity in Folk Blues* (New York: Da Capo Press, 1987).

98 Marybeth Hamilton, *In Search of the Blues* (New York: Basic Books, 2008), 51.

99 Howard W. Odum, *Social and Mental Traits of the Negro: Research into the Conditions of the Negro Race in Southern Towns; A Study in Race Traits, Tendencies and Prospects* (New York: Columbia University, 1910).

100 Christopher N. Breiseth, "Black Minds Matter: Review of a Book on a Major Black Scholar," *Who.What.Why.*, August 4, 2016, https://whowhatwhy.org/2016/08/04/black-minds-matter-review-book-major-black-scholar.

101 Ralph Ellison, *Invisible Man* (New York: Random House, 1952).

102 Ralph Ellison, *Living with Music: Ralph Ellison's Jazz Writings*, ed. Robert O'Meally (New York: Modern Library, 2002).

103 Albert Murray, *Stomping the Blues* (New York: Da Capo, 1976).

104 LeRoi Jones, *Blues People: Negro Music in White America* (New York: Morrow, 1963).

105 Dennis McNally, *On Highway 61: Music, Race, and the Evolution of Cultural Freedom* (Berkeley: Counterpoint, 2014), 111.

106 Ted Gioia, *Delta Blues: The Life and Times of the Mississippi Masters Who Revolutionized American Music* (New York: W. W. Norton, 2008), 4.

107 Wald, *Escaping the Delta*, 5.

108 Dave Marsh, "Out on Highway 61," *New York Times*, February 24, 2008.

109 Hamilton, *In Search of the Blues*.

110 Greil Marcus, *The Old, Weird America: The World of Bob Dylan's Basement Tapes* (New York: Picador, 2011) 86.

111 Marcus, *The Old, Weird America*, 86.

112 Oliver Paul, *Barrelhouse Blues: Location Recording and the Early Traditions of the Blues* (New York: Basic Books, 2009)

113 According to researcher Paul Oliver in his book *Barrelhouse Blues*, a musician by the name of T. C. Johnson recorded during the Memphis sessions. We don't know, however, if it was he or someone else John Hurt was referring to.

114 Robert Gordon, *Can't Be Satisfied: The Life and Times of Muddy Waters* (New York: Little, Brown, 2002).

115 Robert L. Doerschuk, ed., *Playing from the Heart: Great Musicians Talk about Their Craft* (San Francisco: Backbeat, 2002), 24.

116 Bob Dylan, *Chronicles: Volume One* (New York: Simon and Schuster, 2005), 157.

117 John Avery Lomax, *Adventures of a Ballad Hunter* (New York: Macmillan, 1947).

118 Hamilton, *In Search of the Blues*.

119 Guy B. Johnson, "Recent Contributions to the Study of American Negro Songs," *Social Forces* 4, no. 4 (June 1926): 788–792, https://doi.org/10.2307/3004464, Accessed December 10, 2020.

120 Hamilton, *In Search of the Blues*.

121 Handy's article, circa 1919, titled "The Significance of the Blues" was published in two Black newspapers, the *Chicago Defender* and the *Indianapolis Freeman*.

122 Jennifer Schuessler, "Crossing the Lines Dividing the Races," *New York Times*, September 3, 2013, www.nytimes.com/2013/09/04/books/uncovering-strangers-in-a-strange-land.html.

123 Valerie Boyd, *Wrapped in Rainbows: The Life of Zora Neale Hurston* (New York: Scribner, 2004), 57.

124 Boyd, *Wrapped in Rainbows.*

125 Yuval Taylor, *Zora and Langston: A Story of Friendship and Betrayal* (New York: W. W. Norton, 2020).

126 Claudia Roth Pierpont, "A Society of One: Zora Neale Hurston, American Contrarian," *New Yorker*, February 10, 1997, https://www.newyorker.com/magazine/1997/02/17/a-society-of-one, Accessed December 11, 2020.

127 Monica L. Miller, "Jumpin' at the Sun: Reassessing the Life and Work of Zora Neale Hurston," *S & F Online* 3, no. 2 (Winter 2005), http://sfonline.barnard.edu/hurston/archives_01.htm.

128 Pierpont, "A Society of One."

129 Pierpont, "A Society of One."

130 Rebecca Panovka, "A Different Backstory for Zora Neale Hurston's 'Barracoon,'" *Los Angeles Review of Books*, July 7, 2018, https://lareviewofbooks.org/article/different-backstory-for-zora-neale-hurstons-barracoon/?.

131 Panovka, "A Different Backstory."

132 New World Encyclopedia contributors, "Lead Belly," *New World Encyclopedia*, June 22, 2018, http://www.newworldencyclopedia.org/entry/Lead_Belly.

133 Moses Asch and Alan Lomax, eds., *The Leadbelly Songbook* (New York: Oak Publications, 1962), 14.

134 New World Encyclopedia contributors, "Lead Belly."

135 New World Encyclopedia contributors, "Lead Belly."

136 Benjamin Filene, *Romancing the Folk: Public Memory & American Roots Music* (Chapel Hill: University of North Carolina Press, 2000), 63.

137 Filene, *Romancing the Folk*, 63.

138 Filene, *Romancing the Folk*, 63.

139 Editors of Encyclopaedia Britannica, "Lead Belly." *Encyclopedia Britannica*, December 2, 2020, https://www.britannica.com/biography/Leadbelly.

140 David Brion Davis, *Inhuman Bondage: The Rise and Fall of Slavery in the New World* (New York: Oxford University Press, 2006), 80.

141 Rick Beyer, *The Greatest Music Stories Never Told: 100 Tales from Music History to Astonish, Bewilder, and Stupefy* (New York: Harper, 2011), 10.

142 Barry Ulanov, *A History of Jazz in America* (New York: Viking Press, 1952), 11–12.

143 Solomon Northup, *Twelve Years a Slave*, Sue L. Eakin and Joseph Logsdon, eds. (Baton Rouge: Louisiana State University Press, 1968), 184.

144 Northup, *Twelve Years a Slave.*

145 Ian Carr, Digby Fairweather, and Brian Priestley, *The Rough Guide to Jazz 3* (New York: Rough Guides, 2004), 868.

146 Ellen Noonan, *The Strange Career of Porgy and Bess: Race, Culture, and America's Most Famous Opera* (Chapel Hill: University of North Carolina Press, 2012).

147 W. C. Handy, *Father of the Blues: An Autobiography* (New York: Da Capo, 1969).

148 Adam Gussow, "Racial Violence, 'Primitive' Music, and the Blues Entrepreneur: W. C. Handy's Mississippi Problem," *Southern Cultures* 8, no. 3 (Fall 2002): 56–77. doi:10.1353/scu.2002.0029.

149 Booker T. Washington, "Preface," *Twenty-Four Negro Melodies Transcribed for the Piano by S. Coleridge-Taylor Op.59* (Boston: Oliver Ditson, 1904).

150 Leonard G. Feather, *The Book of Jazz from Then Till Now; a Guide to the Entire Field* (New York: Dell Books, 1976), 23.

151 W. C. Handy Historical Memphis Marker.

152 Lynn Abbott and Doug Seroff, *The Original Blues: The Emergence of the Blues in African American Vaudeville* (Jackson: University Press of Mississippi, 2017), 172.

153 Mississippi Blues Trail Marker: The Enlightenment of W. C. Handy. Cleveland, MS. Handy scholar Elliott Hurwitz shared his research on the Handy manuscripts that identified Prince McCoy. Other research assistance: David Evans, Cheryl Line, Nancy Kossman, Yale University Library, and the W. C. Handy Museum in Florence, Alabama.

154 Mississippi Blues Trail Marker: The Enlightenment of W. C. Handy. Cleveland, MS.

155 Peter Hanley, "Ferd Joseph Morton," http://www.doctorjazz.co.uk/draftcards1. html, November 2005, Retrieved December 11, 2020; Peter Hanley, "Jelly Roll Morton: An Essay in Genealogy," http://www.doctorjazz.co.uk/genealogy.html, 2002, Retrieved December 11, 2020.

156 Ferdinand, "'Jelly Roll' Morton, 'I created jazz in 1902, not W.C. Handy,'" *DownBeat*, August, 1938: 3, 31; September, 1938: 4, in Ralph de Toledano, *Frontiers of Jazz!* 19621: 104–8. Morton's quote was redacted in subsequent publications by *DownBeat* magazine following Handy and his lawyer's threats of legal action against the magazine for publishing Morton's polemic to the editor in 1938.

157 Washington, *Twenty-Four Negro Melodies.*

158 lupine22, "Robert Pete Williams – Scrap Iron Blues," YouTube, posted July 3, 2007, https://www.youtube.com/watch?v=3AdhY7XQn9Q&feature=emb_logo.

159 Michael Hall, "The Greatest Music Producer You've Never Heard of Is . . ." *TexasMonthly*, January 6, 2014, Retrieved December 11, 2020, https://www .texasmonthly.com/the-culture/the-greatest-music-producer-youve-never-heard -of-is.

160 Andrea Svedburg, "I Am My Words," *Newsweek*, November 4, 1963, https://www .newsweek.com/bob-dylans-75th-birthday-revisit-our-infamous-1963-profile -462801.

161 Charles Shaar Murray, *Crosstown Traffic: Jimi Hendrix and the Post-War Rock 'n' Roll Revolution* (New York: St Martin's Griffin, 1991), 81.

My Music

1 Jeff Nilsson, "How the G.I. Bill Changed America," *Saturday Evening Post*, June 22, 2019.

2 Richard Rothstein, *The Color of Law: A Forgotten History of How Our Government Segregated America* (New York: Liveright, 2017).

3 Jim Cogan and William Clark, *Temples of Sound: Inside the Great Recording Studios* (San Francisco: Chronicle Books, 2003), 105.

4 Peter Guralnick, *Dream Boogie: The Triumph of Sam Cooke* (New York: Little Brown, 2005), 153.

5 Guralnick, *Dream Boogie*, 153.

6 Rothstein, *Color of Law*, 20.

7   The chitlin circuit of theaters included the Apollo Theater in Harlem, New York City; Club DeLisa and the Regal Theatre in Chicago; the Howard Theatre in Washington, DC; the Uptown Theatre in Philadelphia; the Royal Theatre in Baltimore; the Fox Theatre in Detroit; the Victory Grill in Austin, Texas; the Hippodrome Theatre in Richmond, Virginia; the Ritz Theatre in Jacksonville, Florida; and the Masonic Temple Theater in Baton Rouge, Louisiana.

8   Danny Garrett, https://dannygarrett.com/MusicArt/Antones/ AnBluesCruiseJan88.php.

9   Langston Hughes, "Genius Child," *Selected Poems of Langston Hughes* (New York: Vintage, 1990).

10 Ted Gioia, *Delta Blues: The Life and Times of the Mississippi Masters Who Revolutionized American Music*, 2nd ed. (New York: W. W. Norton, 2008), 372.

11 David Evans, *Tommy Johnson* (Lancashire, UK: November Books, 1971).

12 Dick Porter, *The White Stripes: Twenty First Century Blues* (Medford, NJ: Plexus, 200), 4.

13 Eric Charry, ed., *Hip Hop Africa: New African Music in a Globalizing World* (Bloomington: Indiana University Press, 2012).

14 Samuel Charters, *The Roots of the Blues: An African Search* (Boston: M. Boyars, 1981), 123.

15 Charters, *Roots of the Blues*, 127.

16 J. H. Kwabena Nketia, *The Music of Africa* (New York: W. W. Norton, 1974), 3.

17 Nketia, *Music of Africa*, 3.

18 Nketia, *Music of Africa*, 15.

19 Christopher Blagg, "Melodic Links between Mali and Mississippi," *Christian Science Monitor*, March 12, 2004.

20 Eric Von Schmidt and Jim Rooney, *Baby, Let Me Follow You Down: The Illustrated Story of the Cambridge Folk Years*, 2nd ed. (Garden City, NY: Anchor, 1979), 215.

21 Schmidt and Rooney, *Baby, Let Me Follow*, 216.

22 Dorothy Scarborough and Ola Lee Gulledge, *On the Trail of Negro Folk-Songs* (Cambridge, MA: Harvard University Press, 1925).

23 Schmidt and Rooney, *Baby, Let Me Follow*, 218.

24 Charry, *Hip Hop Africa*, 4.

25 Blagg, "Melodic Links."

26 Gerhard Kubik, *Africa and the Blues* (Jackson: University Press of Mississippi, 1999), 197.

27 Ivan Van Sertima, *They Came Before Columbus: The African Presence in Ancient America* (New York: Random House, 2003), 26.

28 Van Sertima, *They Came Before Columbus*, 74.

29 Naima Mohamud, "Is Mansa Musa the Richest Man Who Ever Lived?," BBC News, March 10, 2019, https://www.bbc.com/news/world-africa-47379458.

INDEX